THE

DEPTHS OF THE SEA.

THE
DEPTHS OF THE SEA.

AN ACCOUNT OF THE GENERAL RESULTS
OF THE
DREDGING CRUISES OF H.M.SS. 'PORCUPINE' AND 'LIGHTNING
DURING THE SUMMERS OF 1868, 1869, AND 1870,
UNDER THE SCIENTIFIC DIRECTION OF
DR. CARPENTER, F.R.S., J. GWYN JEFFREYS, F.R.S.,
AND DR. WYVILLE THOMSON, F.R.S.

BY
C. WYVILLE THOMSON,
LL.D., D.Sc., F.R.SS. L. & E., F.L.S., F.G.S., Etc.
Regius Professor of Natural History in the University of Edinburgh,
And Director of the Civilian Scientific Staff of the 'Challenger' Exploring Expedition.

WITH NUMEROUS ILLUSTRATIONS AND MAPS.

New York and London:
MACMILLAN AND CO.
1873.

LONDON:
R. CLAY, SONS, AND TAYLOR, PRINTERS,
BREAD STREET HILL.

TO

MADAME HOLTEN

This Volume is dedicated,

IN

GRATEFUL REMEMBRANCE OF THE PLEASANT TIMES

SPENT BY HIMSELF AND HIS COMRADES

AT THE

GOVERNOR'S HOUSE IN THORSHAVN,

BY

THE AUTHOR.

PREFACE.

At the close of the Deep-sea Dredging Expeditions which had been undertaken by the Admiralty at the instance of the Council of the Royal Society during the years 1868, 1869, and 1870, it was thought right that those who had been entrusted with their scientific direction should, in addition to their official reports, lay before the general public some account of their proceedings with the objects;—first, of showing, if possible, that the value of the additions which had been made to human knowledge justified the liberality of Government in acceding to the request of the Council of the Royal Society, and placing means at their disposal to carry out the desired researches; and, secondly, of giving such a popular outline of the remarkable results of our work as might stimulate general interest, and induce those who have the proclivities and the opportunity, to penetrate farther into the new and strange region on whose borders we have had the good fortune to have been among the first to encroach.

It was originally intended that the general account should have been a joint production, each of us contributing his part. There were difficulties, however, in the way of this arrangement. We were all fully occupied with other matters, and the amount of communication and correspondence between us, required to carry out the plan of joint authorship, seemed likely to prove a cumbrous complication.

It was therefore decided that *quoad* the popular exposition I should take upon myself the office of 'reporter,' and thus it comes about that I am individually and solely responsible for the opinions and statements contained in this book, save where they are included within quotation marks, or their sources otherwise acknowledged.

Since we began these deep-sea investigations, inquiries have come in from all quarters, both at home and abroad, as to the implements and methods which we employ. To supply the desired information, I have described, in detail, the processes both of sounding and dredging; and I hope that the special chapters on these matters—the result of considerable experience—may be found useful to beginners.

I pretend to no special knowledge of physics, and I should have greatly preferred confining myself to the domain of Biology, my own proper province; but certain physical questions raised during our late explorations have so great importance in relation to the distribution of living beings, and have of late been brought into so great prominence by Dr. Carpenter, that it has been impossible for me to avoid giving my earnest consideration to their general bearings on Physical Geography, and forming decided opinions, which, I regret to say, do not altogether coincide with those of Dr. Carpenter. The chief points on which my friend and I 'agree to differ' are discussed in the chapter on the Gulf-stream.

It was at first my intention that appendices should be added to the different chapters, containing lists and scientific descriptions of the animal forms which were observed. This it was found impossible to accomplish, chiefly on account of the large number of undescribed species which were placed in the hands of the experts who undertook the examination of the several groups. I am not sure that, even if it had been possible to furnish them in time, such lists would have been altogether an appropriate addition to what is intended merely as a popular preliminary sketch.

The metrical system of measurement, and the centigrade thermometer scale, have been adopted throughout the volume. The metrical system is probably familiar to most of my readers. In case the centigrade notation, which comes in very frequently owing to the frequent discussion of questions of the distribution of temperature, should not be equally familiar, a comparative scale, embodying those of

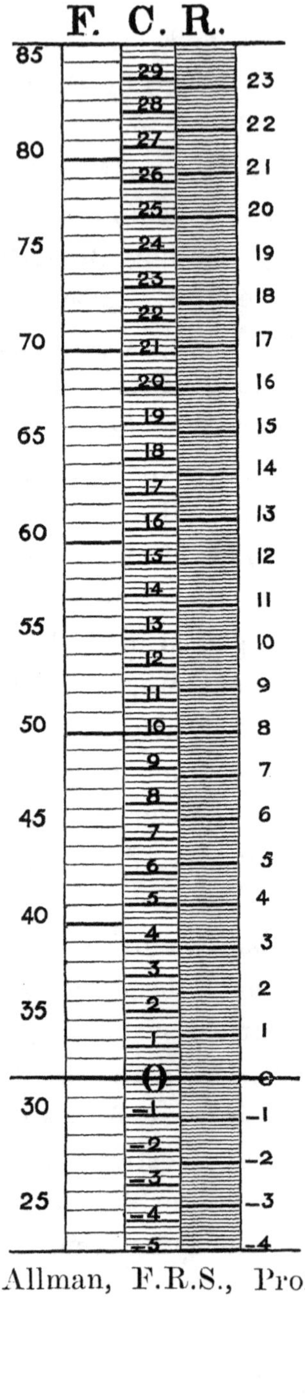

Fahrenheit, Celsius, and Réaumur, is introduced for comparison.

My various sources of information, and the friendly assistance I have received on all hands during the progress of our work, are acknowledged, so far as possible, in the text. I need here only renew my thanks to Staff-Commander May and the officers of the 'Lightning,' and Captain Calver and the officers of the 'Porcupine,' without whose hearty sympathy and co-operation our task could never have been satisfactorily accomplished; to my colleagues, Dr. Carpenter, F.R.S., and Mr. Gwyn Jeffreys, F.R.S., who have cordially assisted me in every way in their power; and to the naturalists into whose hands the animals of various classes were placed for description and study,—the Rev. A. Merle Norman, Professor Kölliker, Dr. Carter, F.R.S., Dr. Allman, F.R.S., Professor Martin Duncan, F.R.S., and Dr. M'Intosh, for information courteously supplied.

The whole of the illustrations in the book—with the exception of the vignettes of Færoe scenery for which I am indebted to the accomplished pencil of Madame Holten—are by my friend Mr. J. J. Wild. I need scarcely thank him for the admirable way in which he has accomplished his task, for every figure was with him a labour of love, and I almost envy him the gratification he must feel in the result. To Mr. J. D. Cooper I owe my sincere thanks for the singularly faithful and artistic rendering of Mr. Wild's beautiful drawings on the wood-blocks.

On the return of the 'Porcupine' from her last cruise, so much interest was felt in the bearings of the new discoveries upon important biological geological and physical problems, that a representation was made to Government by the Council of the Royal Society, urging the despatch of an expedition to traverse the great ocean basins, and take an outline survey of the vast new field of research—the bottom of the sea.

Rear-Admiral Richards, C.B., F.R.S., the Hydrographer to the Navy, warmly supported the proposal, and while I am writing a noble ship is lying at Sheerness equipped for scientific research under his wise and liberal directions, as no ship of any nation was ever equipped before.

The scientific staff of the 'Challenger' are well aware that for some time to come their *rôle* is to work and not to talk; but now, on the eve of departure, I think it is only right to take this opportunity of saying that nothing has been left undone by the Government to ensure the success of the undertaking, and that dire misfortune only ought to prevent our furnishing a valuable return.

C. WYVILLE THOMSON.

EDINBURGH,
December 2*nd*, 1872.

CONTENTS.

CHAPTER I.

INTRODUCTION.

The Question of a Bathymetrical Limit to Life.—The general Laws which regulate the Geographical Distribution of Living Beings.—Professor Edward Forbes' Investigations and Views.—Specific Centres.—Representative Species.—Zoological Provinces.—Bearings of a Doctrine of Evolution upon the Idea of a 'Species,' and of the Laws of Distribution. —The Circumstances most likely to affect Life at great Depths : Pressure, Temperature, and Absence of Light ... ... *Page* 1

CHAPTER II.

THE CRUISE OF THE 'LIGHTNING.'

Proposal to investigate the Conditions of the Bottom of the Sea.—Suggestions and Anticipations.—Correspondence between the Council of the Royal Society and the Admiralty.—Departure from Stornoway.—The Færoe Islands.—Singular Temperature Results in the Færoe Channel.—Life abundant at all Depths.—*Brisinga coronata.*—*Holtenia carpenteri.* —General Results of the Expedition ... ... *Page* 49

APPENDIX A.—Particulars of Depth, Temperature, and Position at the various Dredging Stations of H.M.S. 'Lightning,' in the Summer of 1868 ; the Temperatures corrected for Pressure ... ... *Page* 81

CHAPTER III.

THE CRUISES OF THE 'PORCUPINE.'

The Equipment of the Vessel.—The first Cruise, under the direction of Mr. Gwyn Jeffreys, off the West Coast of Ireland and in the Channel between Scotland and Rockall.—Dredging carried down to 1,470 fathoms.

—Change of Arrangements.—Second Cruise; to the Bay of Biscay.—Dredging successful at 2,435 fathoms.—Third Cruise; in the Channel between Færoe and Shetland.—The Fauna of the 'Cold Area.' *Page* 82

Appendix A.—Official Documents and Official Accounts of preliminary Proceedings in connection with the Explorations in H.M. Surveying-vessel 'Porcupine,' during the Summer of 1869 ... ... *Page* 133

Appendix B.—Particulars of Depth, Temperature, and Position at the various Dredging Stations of H.M.S. 'Porcupine,' in the Summer of 1869 ... ... *Page* 142

CHAPTER IV.

THE CRUISES OF THE 'PORCUPINE' (*continued*).

From Shetland to Stornoway.—Phosphorescence.—The *Echinothuridæ.*—The Fauna of the 'Warm Area.'—End of the Cruise of 1869.—Arrangements for the Expedition of 1870.—From England to Gibraltar.—Peculiar Conditions of the Mediterranean.—Return to Cowes. *Page* 145

Appendix A.—Extracts from the Minutes of Council of the Royal Society, and other official Documents referring to the Cruise of H.M.S. 'Porcupine' during the Summer of 1870 ... ... *Page* 197

Appendix B.—Particulars of Depth, Temperature, and Position at the various Dredging-stations of H.M.S. 'Porcupine' in the Summer of 1870 ... ... *Page* 202

CHAPTER V.

DEEP-SEA SOUNDING.

The ordinary Sounding-lead for moderate Depths.—Liable to Error when employed in Deep Water.—Early Deep Soundings unreliable.—Improved Methods of Sounding.—The Cup-lead.—Brooke's Sounding Instrument.—The 'Bull-dog;' Fitzgerald's; the 'Hydra.'—Sounding from the 'Porcupine.'—The Contour of the Bed of the North Atlantic ... *Page* 205

CHAPTER VI.

DEEP-SEA DREDGING.

The Naturalist's Dredge.—O. F. Müller.—Ball's Dredge.—Dredging at moderate Depths.—The Dredge-rope.—Dredging in Deep Water.—The 'Hempen tangles.'—Dredging on board the 'Porcupine.'—The Sieves.—

The Dredger's Note-book.—The Dredging Committee of the British Association.—Dredging on the Coast of Britain.—Dredging abroad.—History of the Progress of Knowledge of the Abyssal Fauna. *Page* 236

APPENDIX A.—One of the Dredging Papers issued by the British Association Committee, filled up by Mr. MacAndrew ... ... *Page* 281

CHAPTER VII.

DEEP-SEA TEMPERATURES.

Ocean Currents and their general Effects on Climate.—Determination of Surface Temperatures.—Deep-sea Thermometers.—The ordinary Self-registering Thermometer on Six's principle.—The Miller-Casella modification.—The Temperature Observations taken during the Three Cruises of H.M.S. 'Porcupine' in the year 1869, etc. ... ... *Page* 284

APPENDIX A.—Surface Temperatures observed on board H.M.S. 'Porcupine' during the Summers of 1869 and 1870 ... ... *Page* 329

APPENDIX B.—Temperature of the Sea at different Depths near the Eastern Margin of the North Atlantic Basin, as ascertained by Serial and by Bottom Soundings ... ... *Page* 352

APPENDIX C.—Comparative Rates of Reduction of Temperature with Increase of Depth at Three Stations in different Latitudes, all of them on the Eastern Margin of the Atlantic Basin ... ... *Page* 353

APPENDIX D.—Temperature of the Sea at different Depths in the Warm and Cold Areas lying between the North of Scotland, the Shetland Islands, and the Færoe Islands; as ascertained by Serial and by Bottom Soundings ... ... *Page* 354

APPENDIX E.—Intermediate Bottom Temperatures showing the Intermixture of Warm and Cold Currents on the Borders of the Warm and Cold Areas ... ... *Page* 355

CHAPTER VIII.

THE GULF-STREAM.

The Range of the 'Porcupine' Temperature Observations.—Low Temperatures universal at great Depths.—The Difficulty of investigating Ocean Currents.—The Doctrine of a general Oceanic Circulation advocated by Captain Maury and by Dr. Carpenter.—Opinion expressed by Sir John Herschel.—The Origin and Extension of the Gulf-stream.—The Views of Captain Maury; of Professor Buff; of Dr. Carpenter.—The Gulf-stream off the Coast of North America.—Professor Bache's 'Sections.'—The Gulf-stream traced by the Surface Temperatures of the North Atlantic.—Mr. Findlay's Views.—Dr. Petermann's Temperature Charts.—Sources of the underlying Cold Water.—The Arctic Return Currents.—Antarctic Indraught.—Vertical Distribution of Temperature in the North Atlantic Basin ... ... *Page* 356

CHAPTER IX.

THE DEEP-SEA FAUNA.

The Protozoa of the Deep Sea.—*Bathybius.*—'Coccoliths,' and 'Coccospheres.'—The Foraminifera of the Warm and Cold Areas.—Deep-sea Sponges. — The Hexactinellidæ. — *Rossella.* — *Hyalonema.* — Deep-sea Corals. — The Stalked Crinoids. — *Pentacrinus.*—*Rhizocrinus.*—*Bathycrinus.*—The Star-fishes of the Deep Sea.—The general Distribution and Relations of Deep-sea Urchins.—The Crustacea, the Mollusca, and the Fishes of the 'Porcupine' Expeditions ... ... *Page* 407

CHAPTER X.

THE CONTINUITY OF THE CHALK.

Points of Resemblance between the Atlantic Ooze and the White Chalk.—Differences between them.—Composition of Chalk.—The Doctrine of the Continuity of the Chalk.—Objections.—Arguments in favour of the View from Physical Geology and Geography.—Former Distribution of Sea and Land.—Palæontological Evidence. — Chalk-flints. — Modern Sponges and Ventriculites—Corals.—Echinoderms.—Mollusca.—Opinions of Professor Huxley and Mr. Prestwich.—The Composition of Sea-water. —Presence of Organic Matter.—Analysis of the contained Gases.—Differences of Specific Gravity.—Conclusion ... ... *Page* 467

APPENDIX A.—Summary of the Results of the Examination of Samples of Sea-water taken at the Surface and at various Depths. By William Lant Carpenter, B.A., B.Sc. ... ... *Page* 502

APPENDIX B.—Results of the Analyses of Eight Samples of Sea-water collected during the Third Cruise of the 'Porcupine.' By Dr. Frankland, F.R.S. ... ... *Page* 511

APPENDIX C.—Notes on Specimens of the Bottom collected during the First Cruise of the 'Porcupine' in 1869. By David Forbes, F.R.S. *Page* 514

APPENDIX D.—Note on the Carbonic Acid contained in Sea-water. By John Young Buchanan, M.A., Chemist to the 'Challenger' Expedition. *Page* 518

INDEX ... ... *Page* 523

LIST OF ILLUSTRATIONS.

WOODCUTS.

FIG.		PAGE
1.	ASTEROPHYTON LINCKII, Müller and Troschel. A young specimen slightly enlarged (No. 75)	19
2.	GLOBIGERINA BULLOIDES, D'Orbigny. Highly magnified	22
3.	ORBULINA UNIVERSA, D'Orbigny. Highly magnified	23
4.	CARYOPHYLLIA BOREALIS, Fleming. Twice the natural size. (No. 45)	27
5.	BRISINGA CORONATA, G. O. Sars. Natural size. (No. 7)	67
6.	HOLTENIA CARPENTERI (sp. n.). Half the natural size. (No. 12)	71
7.	TISIPHONIA AGARICIFORMIS (sp. n.). Natural size. (No. 12) ...	74
8.	GONOPLAX RHOMBOIDES, Fabricius. Young. Twice the natural size. (No. 3)	87
9.	GERYON TRIDENS, Kroyer. Young. Twice the natural size. (No. 7)	88
10.	ORBITOLITES TENUISSIMUS, Carpenter MSS. Magnified. (No. 28)	91
11.	POROCIDARIS PURPURATA (sp. n.). Natural size. (No. 47) ...	102
12.	POURTALESIA JEFFREYSI (sp. n.). Slightly enlarged. (No. 64)	108
13.	STYLOCORDYLA BOREALIS, Loven (sp.). Natural size. (No. 64)	114
14.	SOLASTER FURCIFER, Von Duben and Koren. Natural size. (No. 55)	119
15.	KORETHRASTER HISPIDUS (sp. n.). Dorsal aspect. Twice the natural size. (No. 57)	119
16.	HYMENASTER PELLUCIDUS (sp. n.). Ventral aspect. Natural size. (No. 59)	120
17.	ARCHASTER BIFRONS (sp. n.). Dorsal aspect. Three-fourths of the natural size. (No. 57)...	122
18.	EUSIRUS CUSPIDATUS, Kroyer. (No. 55)	125
19.	CAPRELLA SPINOSISSIMA, Norman. Twice the natural size. (No. 59)	126

FIG. PAGE
20. ÆGA NASUTA, Norman. Slightly enlarged. (No. 55) 127
21. ARCTURUS BAFFINI, Sabine. About the natural size. (No. 59) 128
22. NYMPHON ABYSSORUM, Norman. Slightly enlarged. (No. 56) 129
23. THECOPHORA SEMISUBERITES, Oscar Schmidt. Twice the natural size. (No. 76) 147
24. THECOPHORA IBLA (sp. n.). Twice the natural size. (No. 76) 148
25. ARCHASTER VEXILLIFER (sp. n.). One-third the natural size. (No. 76) 150
26. ZOROASTER FULGENS (sp. n.). One-third the natural size. (No. 78) 153
27. CALVERIA HYSTRIX (sp. n.). Two-thirds the natural size. (No. 86) 156
28. CALVERIA HYSTRIX (sp. n.). Inner surface of a portion of the test showing the structure of the ambulacral and interambulacral areas 157
29. CALVERIA FENESTRATA (sp. n.). One of the four-valved pedicellariæ 159
30. LOPHOHELIA PROLIFERA, Pallas (sp.). Three-fourths the natural size. (No. 26) 169
31. ALLOPORA OCULINA, Ehrenberg 170
32. OPHIOMUSIUM LYMANI (sp. n.). Dorsal surface. Natural size. (No. 45) 172
33. OPHIOMUSIUM LYMANI (sp. n.). Oral surface 173
34. DORYNCHUS THOMSONI, Norman. Once and a half the natural size; everywhere in deep water 174
35. AMATHIA CARPENTERI, Norman. Once and a half the natural size. (No. 47) 175
36. CHRONDROCLADIA VIRGATA (sp. n.). One-half the natural size. (No. 33, Pl. V.) 187
37. THE 'CUP-LEAD' 210
38. } BROOKE'S DEEP-SEA SOUNDING APPARATUS ... ... { 211
39. } { 213
40. THE 'BULL-DOG' SOUNDING MACHINE 215
41. THE 'FITZGERALD' SOUNDING MACHINE 217
42. THE 'HYDRA' SOUNDING MACHINE 218
43. 'MASSEY'S' SOUNDING MACHINE 225
44. OTHO FREDERICK MÜLLER'S DREDGE. A.D. 1750 239
45. 'BALL'S DREDGE' 240
46. THE STERN DERRICK OF THE 'PORCUPINE,' SHOWING THE 'ACCUMULATOR,' THE DREDGE, AND THE MODE OF STOWING THE ROPE 248
THE END OF THE DREDGE-FRAME 250

FIG. PAGE

48. DREDGE-FRAME, SHOWING THE MODE OF ATTACHMENT OF THE BAG 251
49. THE END OF THE DREDGE-FRAME, SHOWING THE MODE OF ATTACHMENT OF THE BAG 252
50. DIAGRAM OF THE RELATIVE POSITION OF THE VESSEL, THE WEIGHTS, AND THE DREDGE, IN DREDGING IN DEEP WATER 253
51. DREDGE WITH 'HEMPEN TANGLES' 257
52. SET OF DREDGING SIEVES 260
53. THE MILLER-CASELLA MODIFICATION OF SIX'S SELF-REGISTERING THERMOMETER 291
54. COPPER CASE FOR PROTECTING THE MILLER-CASELLA THERMOMETER 292
55. SERIAL SOUNDING, Station 64 312
56. SERIAL SOUNDING, Station 87 312
57. CURVES CONSTRUCTED FROM SERIAL SOUNDINGS IN THE 'WARM'- AND 'COLD-AREAS' IN THE CHANNEL BETWEEN SCOTLAND AND FÆROE 315
58. CURVES CONSTRUCTED FROM SERIAL AND BOTTOM SOUNDINGS IN THE CHANNEL BETWEEN SCOTLAND AND ROCKALL 319
59. DIAGRAM REPRESENTING THE RELATION BETWEEN DEPTH AND TEMPERATURE OFF ROCKALL 322
60. DIAGRAM REPRESENTING THE RELATION BETWEEN DEPTH AND TEMPERATURE IN THE ATLANTIC BASIN 322
61. CURVES CONSTRUCTED FROM SERIAL AND BOTTOM TEMPERATURE SOUNDINGS IN THE ATLANTIC BASIN 324
62. DIAGRAM REPRESENTING THE RELATION BETWEEN DEPTH AND TEMPERATURE, FROM THE TEMPERATURE OBSERVATIONS TAKEN BETWEEN CAPE FINISTERRE AND CAPE ST. VINCENT, AUGUST 1870 327
63. "EINE GRÖSSERE CYTODE VON BATHYBIUS MIT EINGEBETTETEN COCCOLITHEN" (x. 700) 412
64. 'COCCOSPHERE' (x. 1000) 414
65. ROSSELLA VELATA (sp. n.). Natural size. (No. 32, 1870) ... 419
66. HYALONEMA LUSITANICUM, Barboza du Bocage. Half the natural size. (No. 90, 1869) 421
67. ASKONEMA SETUBALENSE, Kent. One-eighth the natural size. (No. 25, 1870) 429
68. FLABELLUM DISTINCTUM. Twice the natural size. (No. 28, 1870) 432
69. THECOPSAMMIA SOCIALIS, Pourtales. Once and a half the natural size. (No. 57, 1869) 433
70. PENTACRINUS ASTERIA, Linnæus. One-fourth the natural size ... 436
71. PENTACRINUS WYVILLE-THOMSONI, Jeffreys. Natural size. (No. 17, 1870) 443

FIG. PAGE

72. RHIZOCRINUS LOFFOTENSIS, M. Sars. Once and a half the natural size. (No. 43, 1869) 451
73. BATHYCRINUS GRACILIS (sp. n.). Twice the natural size. (No. 37, 1869) 453
74. ARCHASTER BIFRONS (sp. n.). Oral aspect. Three-fourths the natural size. (No. 57, 1869) 455
75. SOLASTER FURCIFER, Von Duben and Koren. Oral aspect. Natural size. (No. 55, 1869) 456
76. BUCCINOPSIS STRIATA, Jeffreys. Færoe Channel 464
77. LATIRUS ALBUS, Jeffreys. Twice the natural size. Færoe Channel 464
78. PLEURONECTIA LUCIDA, Jeffreys. Twice the natural size. *a*, from the Eastern Atlantic; *b*, from the Gulf of Mexico ... 465
79. PECTEN HOSKYNSI, Forbes. Twice the natural size 465
80. VENTRICULITES SIMPLEX, Toulmin Smith. Once and a half the natural size 483
81. VENTRICULITES SIMPLEX, Toulmin Smith. Outer surface; four times the natural size 484
82. VENTRICULITES SIMPLEX, Toulmin Smith. Section of the outer wall, showing the structure of the silicious network (x. 50) 485
83. CŒLOSPHÆRA TUBIFEX (sp. n.). Slightly enlarged. Off the Coast of Portugal 485
84. 'CHOANITES.' In a flint from the white chalk 486

VIGNETTES.

THE FÆROE ISLANDS xii
TINDHOLM 48
THORSHAVN 80
THE GOVERNOR'S HOUSE, THORSHAVN 132
LILLE DIMON 196
NOLSÖ, FROM THE HILLS ABOVE THORSHAVN 235
FUGLÖ, FROM THE EASTERN SHORE OF VIDERÖ 280
VAAŸ CHURCH IN SUDERÖ 328
THE GIANT AND THE HAG 406
BORDÖ, KUNÖ, AND KALSÖ, FROM THE HAMLET OF VIDERÖ 466
KUNÖ, FROM VAAŸ IN BORDÖ 501

MAPS AND PLATES.

PLATE		To face page
I.	—Track of H.M.S. 'Lightning'—1868	59
II.	—First Cruise of H.M.S. 'Porcupine'—1869	87
III.	—Second Cruise of H.M.S. 'Porcupine'—1869	95
IV.	—Third Cruise of H.M.S. 'Porcupine'—1869	106
V.	—Track of H.M.S. 'Porcupine'—1870	180
VI.	—Diagram of the 'Porcupine' Soundings in the Atlantic and in the Færoe Channel, showing the Relation between Temperature and Depth,—the Serial Soundings reduced to Curves. The Numbers refer to the Stations on the Charts, Plates II., III., and IV. ...	323
VII.	—Physical Chart of the North Atlantic: showing the Depth, and the General Distribution of Temperatures for the Month of July	363
VIII.	—Map showing the General Distribution of the Tertiary, the Cretaceous, and the Jurassic Systems in the North-West of Europe with reference to Contour	474

THE

DEPTHS OF THE SEA.

THE DEPTHS OF THE SEA.

CHAPTER I.

INTRODUCTION.

The Question of a Bathymetrical Limit to Life.—The general Laws which regulate the Geographical Distribution of Living Beings.—Professor Edward Forbes' Investigations and Views.—Specific Centres.—Representative Species.—Zoological Provinces.—Bearings of a Doctrine of Evolution upon the Idea of a 'Species,' and of the Laws of Distribution.—The Circumstances most likely to affect Life at great Depths: Pressure, Temperature, and Absence of Light.

THE sea covers nearly three-fourths of the surface of the earth, and, until within the last few years, very little was known with anything like certainty about its depths, whether in their physical or their biological relations. The popular notion was, that after arriving at a certain depth the conditions became so peculiar, so entirely different from those of any portion of the earth to which we have access, as to preclude any other idea than that of a waste of utter darkness, subjected to such stupendous pressure as to make life of any kind impossible, and to throw insuperable difficulties in the way of any attempt at investigation. Even men of science seemed to share this idea, for they gave little heed to the apparently well-authenticated instances of animals, comparatively high in the scale of life, having been brought up on sounding lines from great depths, and welcomed any suggestion of the animals having got entangled when swimming on the surface, or of carelessness on the part of the observers. And this was strange, for every other question in Physical Geography had been investigated by scientific men with consummate patience and energy. Every gap in the noble little army of martyrs striving to extend the boundaries of knowledge in the wilds of Australia, on the Zambesi, or towards the North or South Pole, was struggled for by earnest volunteers, and still the great ocean slumbering beneath the moon covered a region apparently as inaccessible to man as the 'mare serenitatis.'

A few years ago the bottom of the sea was required for the purpose of telegraphic communication, and practical men mapped out the bed of the North Atlantic, and devised ingenious methods of ascertaining the nature of the material covering the bottom. They laid a telegraphic cable across it, and the cable got broken and they went back to the spot and fished up the end of it easily, from a depth of nearly two miles.

It had long been a question with naturalists whether it might not be possible to dredge the bottom of the sea in the ordinary way, and to send down water-bottles and registering instruments to settle finally the question of a 'zero of animal life,' and to determine with precision the composition and temperature of sea-water at great depths. An investigation of this kind is beyond the ordinary limits of private enterprise. It requires more power and sea skill than naturalists can usually command. When, however, in the year 1868, at the instance of my colleague Dr. Carpenter and myself, with the effective support of the present Hydrographer to the Navy, who is deeply interested in the scientific aspects of his profession, we had placed at our disposal by the Admiralty sufficient power and skill to make the experiment, we found that we could work, not with so much ease, but with as much certainty, at a depth of 600 fathoms as at 100; and in 1869 we carried the operations down to 2,435 fathoms, 14,610 feet, nearly three statute miles, with perfect success.

Dredging in such deep water was doubtless very trying. Each haul occupied seven or eight hours; and during the whole of that time it demanded and received the most anxious care on the part of our commander, who stood with his hand on the pulse of the accumulator ready at any moment, by a turn of the paddles, to ease any undue strain. The men, stimulated and encouraged by the cordial interest taken by their officers in our operations, worked willingly and well; but the labour of taking upwards of three miles of rope coming up with a heavy strain, from the surging drum of the engine, was very severe. The rope itself, 'hawser-laid,' of the best Italian hemp, $2\frac{1}{2}$ inches in circumference, with a breaking strain of $2\frac{1}{4}$ tons, looked frayed out and worn, as if it could not have been trusted to stand this extraordinary ordeal much longer.

Still the thing is possible, and it must be done again and again, as the years pass on, by naturalists of all nations, working with improving machinery, and with ever-increasing knowledge. For the bed of the deep sea, the 140,000,000 of square miles which we have now added to the legitimate field of Natural History research, is not a barren waste. It is inhabited by a fauna more rich and varied on account of the enormous extent of the area, and with the organisms in many cases apparently even more elaborately and delicately formed, and more exquisitely beautiful in their soft shades of colouring and in the rainbow-tints of their wonderful phosphorescence, than the fauna of the well-known belt of shallow water teeming with innumerable invertebrate forms which fringes the land. And the forms of these hitherto unknown living beings, and their mode of life, and their relations to other organisms whether living or extinct, and the phenomena and laws of their geographical distribution, must be worked out.

The late Professor Edward Forbes appears to have been the first who undertook the systematic study of Marine Zoology with special reference to the distribution of marine animals in space and in time. After making himself well acquainted with the fauna of the British seas to the depth of about 200 fathoms by dredging, and by enlisting the active co-operation of his friends—among whom we find MacAndrew, Barlee, Gwyn Jeffreys, William Thompson, Robert Ball, and many others, entering enthusiastically into the new field of Natural History inquiry—in the year 1841 Forbes joined Capt. Graves, who was at that time in command of the Mediterranean Survey, as naturalist.

During about eighteen months he studied with the utmost care the conditions of the Ægean and its shores, and conducted upwards of one hundred dredging operations at depths varying from 1 to 130 fathoms. In 1843 he communicated to the Cork meeting of the British Association an elaborate report on the Mollusca and Radiata of the Ægean Sea, and on their distribution considered as bearing on Geology.[1] Three years later, in 1846, he published in the first volume of the 'Memoirs of the Geological Survey of Great Britain,' a most valuable memoir upon the Connection between the existing Fauna and Flora of the British Isles, and the geological Changes which have affected their Area, especially during the Epoch of the Northern Drift.[2] In the year 1859 appeared the Natural History of the European Seas by the late Professor Edward Forbes, edited and continued by Robert Godwin Austen.[3] In the first hundred pages of this little book, Forbes gives a general outline of some of the more important of his views with regard

[1] Report on the Mollusca and Radiata of the Ægean Sea, and on their Distribution, considered as bearing on Geology. By Edward Forbes, F.L.S., M.W.S., Professor of Botany in King's College, London. (Report of the Thirteenth Meeting of the British Association for the Advancement of Science; held at Cork in August 1843. London, 1844.)

[2] On the Connection between the Distribution of the existing Fauna and Flora of the British Isles and the geological Changes which have affected their Area, especially during the Epoch of the Northern Drift. By Edward Forbes, F.R.S., L.S., G.S., Professor of Botany at King's College, London; Palæontologist to the Geological Survey of the United Kingdom. (Memoirs of the Geological Survey of Great Britain, vol. i. London, 1846.)

[3] The Natural History of the European Seas, by the late Professor Edward Forbes, F.R.S., &c. Edited and continued by Robert Godwin Austen, F.R.S. London, 1859.

to the distribution of marine forms. The remainder of the book is a continuation by his friend Mr. Godwin Austen, for before it was finished an early death had cut short the career of the most accomplished and original naturalist of his time.

I will give a brief sketch of the general results to which Forbes was led by his labours, and I shall have to point out hereafter, that although we are now inclined to look somewhat differently on certain very fundamental points, and although recent investigations with better appliances and more extended experience have invalidated many of his conclusions, to Forbes is due the credit of having been the first to treat these questions in a broad philosophical sense, and to point out that the only means of acquiring a true knowledge of the *rationale* of the distribution of our present fauna, is to make ourselves acquainted with its history, to connect the present with the past. This is the direction which must be taken by future inquiry. Forbes, as a pioneer in this line of research, was scarcely in a position to appreciate the full value of his work. Every year adds enormously to our stock of data, and every new fact indicates more clearly the brilliant results which are to be obtained by following his methods, and by emulating his enthusiasm and his indefatigable industry.

Forbes believed implicitly, along with nearly all the leading naturalists of his time, in the immutability of species. He says (Natural History of the British Seas, p. 8), "Every true species presents in its individuals, certain features, *specific characters*, which distinguish it from every other species; as if the Creator had set an exclusive mark or seal on each type." He likewise believed in specific centres of distribution. He held that all the individuals composing a species had descended from a single progenitor, or from two, according as the sexes might be united or distinct, and that consequently the idea of a species involved the idea of the relationship in all the individuals of common descent; and the converse, that there could by no possibility be community of descent except in living beings which possessed the same specific characters. He supposed that the original individual or pair was created at a particular spot where the conditions were suitable for its existence and propagation, and that the species extended and migrated from that spot on all sides over an area of greater or less extent, until it met with some natural barrier in the shape of unsuitable conditions. No specific form could have more than a single centre of distribution. If its area appeared to be broken up, a patch not in connection with the original centre of distribution occurring in some distant locality, it was accounted for by the formation, through some geological change after the first spread of the species, of a barrier which cut off a part of its area; or to some accidental transport to a place where the conditions were sufficiently similar to those of its natural original habitat to enable it to become naturalized. No species once exterminated was ever recreated, so that in those few cases in which we find a species abundant at one period over an area, absent over the same area for a time, and recurring at a later period, it must be accounted for by a change in the conditions of the area which forced the emigration of the species, and a subsequent further change which permitted its return.

Forbes defined and advocated what he called the law of representation. He found that in all parts of the world, however far removed, and however completely separated by natural barriers, where the conditions of life are similar, species and groups of species occur which, although not identical, resemble one another very closely; and he found that this similarity existed likewise between groups of fossil remains, and between groups of fossils and groups of recent forms. Admitting the constancy of specific characters, these resemblances could not be accounted for by community of descent, and he thus arrived at the generalization, that in localities placed under similar circumstances, similar though specifically distinct specific forms were created. These he regarded as mutually representative species.

Our acceptance of the doctrines of specific centres and of representation, or, at all events, the form in which we may be inclined to accept these, depends greatly upon the acceptance or rejection of the fundamental dogma of the immutability of species; and on this point there has been a very great change of opinion within the last ten or twelve years, a change certainly due to the remarkable ability and candour with which the question has been discussed by Mr. Darwin[1] and Mr. Wallace,[2] and to the genius of Pro-

[1] The Origin of Species by means of Natural Selection; or, the Preservation of Favoured Races in the Struggle for Life. By Charles Darwin, M.A., F.R.S., L.S., G.S., &c. &c. London, 1859, and subsequent editions.

[2] Contributions to the Theory of Natural Selection. A Series of Essays by Alfred Russel Wallace. London, 1870.

fessor Ernst Haeckel,[1] Dr. Fritz Müller,[2] and others of their enthusiastic disciples and commentators. I do not think that I am speaking too strongly when I say that there is now scarcely a single competent general naturalist who is not prepared to accept some form of the doctrine of evolution.

There is, no doubt, very great difficulty in the minds of many of us in conceiving that, commencing from the simplest living being, the present state of things in the organic world has been produced solely by the combined action of 'atavism,' the tendency of offspring to resemble their parents closely; and 'variation,' the tendency of offspring to differ individually from their parents within very narrow limits: and many are inclined to believe that some other law than the 'survival of the fittest' must regulate the existing marvellous system of extreme and yet harmonious modification. Still it must be admitted that variation is a *vera causa*, capable, within a limited period, under favourable circumstances, of converting one species into what, according to our present ideas, we should be forced to recognize as a different species. And such being the case, it is, perhaps, conceivable that during the lapse of a period of time—still infinitely shorter than eternity—variation may have produced the entire result.

[1] Generelle Morphologie der Organismen. Allgemeine Grundzüge der organischen Formen-Wissenschaft mechanisch begründet durch die von Charles Darwin reformirte Descendenz-Theorie. Von Ernst Haeckel. Berlin, 1866.—Natürliche Schöpfungsgeschichte. Von Dr. Ernst Haeckel, Professor an der Universität Jena. Berlin, 1870.

[2] Für Darwin. Von Dr. Fritz Müller. Leipzig, 1864. Translated from the German by W. S. Dallas, F.L.S. London, 1869.

The individuals comprising a species have a definite range of variation strictly limited by the circumstances under which the group of individuals is placed. Except in man, and in domesticated animals in which it is artificially increased, this individual variation is usually so slight as to be unappreciable except to a practised eye; but any extreme variation which passes the natural limit in any direction clashes in some way with surrounding circumstances, and is dangerous to the life of the individual. The normal or graphic line, or 'line of safety,' of the species, lies midway between the extremes of variation.

If at any period in the history of a species the conditions of life of a group of individuals of the species be gradually altered, with the gradual change of circumstances the limit of variation is contracted in one direction and relaxed in another; it becomes more dangerous to diverge towards one side and more desirable to diverge towards the other, and the position of the lines limiting variation is altered. The normal line, the line along which the specific characters are most strongly marked, is consequently slightly deflected, some characters being more strongly expressed at the expense of others. This deflection, carried on for ages in the same direction, must eventually carry the divergence of the varying race far beyond any limit within which we are in the habit of admitting identity of species.

But the process must be infinitely slow. It is difficult to form any idea of ten, fifty, or a hundred millions of years; or of the relation which such periods bear to changes taking place in the organic world.

We must remember, however, that the rocks of the Silurian system, overlaid by ten miles' thickness of sediment entombing a hundred successive faunæ, each as rich and varied as the fauna of the present day, themselves teem with fossils fully representing all the existing classes of animals, except perhaps the highest.

If it be possible to imagine that this marvellous manifestation of Eternal Power and Wisdom involved in living nature can have been worked out through the law of 'descent with modification' alone, we shall certainly require from the Physicists the longest row of cyphers which they can afford.

Now, although the admission of a doctrine of evolution must affect greatly our conception of the origin and *rationale* of so-called specific centres, it does not practically affect the question of their existence, or of the laws regulating the distribution of species from their centres by migration, by transport, by ocean currents, by elevations or depressions of the land, or by any other causes at work under existing circumstances. So far as practical naturalists are concerned, species are permanent within their narrow limits of variation, and it would introduce an element of infinite confusion and error if we were to regard them in any other light. The origin of species by descent with modification is as yet only a hypothesis. During the whole period of recorded human observation not one single instance of the change of one species into another has been detected; and, singular to say, in successive geological formations, although new species are constantly appearing and there is abundant evidence of progressive change, no single case has yet been observed of one species passing through a series of inappreciable modifications into another. Every species appears to have an area of maximum development, and this has been called the metropolis of the species; and practically we must employ the same methods in investigating the laws of its distribution as if we still regarded it as having been specially created in its metropolis.

It is the same in dealing with the law of representation. Accepting an evolution doctrine, we should certainly regard closely allied or 'representative' species as having descended comparatively recently from a common ancestry, and as having diverged from one another under somewhat different conditions of life. It is possible that as our knowledge increases we may be able to trace the pedigree of our modern species, and some attempts have already been made to sketch out the main branches of the universal genealogical tree;[1] but practically we must continue to accord a specific rank to forms which exhibit characters to which we have been in the habit of assigning specific value.

"Every species has three maxima of development,—in depth, in geographic space, in time. In depth, we find a species at first represented by few individuals, which become more and more numerous until they reach a certain point, after which they again gradually diminish, and at length altogether disappear. So also in the geographic and geologic distribution of animals. Sometimes the genus to which the species belongs ceases with its disappearance, but not unfrequently a succession of similar

[1] Ernst Haeckel, op. cit.

species are kept up, representative as it were of each other. When there is such a representation, the minimum of one species usually commences before that of which it is representative has attained its correspondent minimum. Forms of representative species are similar, often only to be distinguished by critical examination."[1]

As an illustration of what is meant by the law of 'representation,' I may cite a very curious case mentioned by Mr. Verril and Mr. Alexander Agassiz. On either side of the Isthmus of Panama the Echinoderm order *Echinidea*, the sea-urchins, are abundant; but the species found on the two sides of the Isthmus are distinct, although they belong almost universally to the same genera, and in most cases each genus is represented by species on each side which resemble one another so closely in habit and appearance as to be at first sight hardly distinguishable. I arrange a few of the most marked of these from the Caribbean and Panamic sides of the Isthmus in parallel columns.

EASTERN FAUNA.	WESTERN FAUNA.
Cidaris annulata, GRAY.	*Cidaris thouarsii*, VAL.
Diadema antillarum, PHIL.	*Diadema mexicanum*, A. AG.
Echinocidaris punctulata, DESML.	*Echinocidaris stellata*, AG.
Echinometra michelini, DES.	*Echinometra van brunti*, A. AG.
,, *viridis*, A. AG.	,, *rupicola*, A. AG.
Lytechinus variegatus, A. AG.	*Lytechinus semituberculatus*, A. AG.
Tripneustes ventricosus, AG.	*Tripneustes depressus*, A. AG.
Stolonoclypus ravenellii, A. AG.	*Stolonoclypus rotundus*, A. AG.
Mellita testudinata, KL.	*Mellita longifissa*, MICH.

---

[1] Edward Forbes, Report on Ægean Invertebrata, op. cit. p. 173.

EASTERN FAUNA.	WESTERN FAUNA.
Mellita hexapora, A. AG.	*Mellita pacifica*, VER.
Encope michelini, AG.	*Encope grandis*, AG.
,, *emarginata*, AG.	,, *micropora*, AG.
Rhyncholampas caribbœarum, A. AG.	*Rhyncholampas pacificus*, A. AG.
Brissus columbaris, AG.	*Brissus obesus*, VER.
Meoma ventricosa, LÜTK.	*Meoma grandis*, GRAY.
Plagionotus pectoralis, AG.	*Plagionotus nobilis*, A. AG.
Agassizia excentrica, A. AG.	*Agassizia scrobiculata*, VAL.
Mœra atropos, MICH.	*Mœra clotho*, MICH.

Supposing species to be constant, this singular chain of resemblances would indicate simply the special creation on the two sides of the Isthmus of two groups of species closely resembling one another, because the circumstances under which they were placed were so very similar; but admitting 'descent with modification,' while gladly availing ourselves of the convenient term 'representation,' we at once come to the conclusion that these nearly allied 'representative species' must have descended from a common stock, and we look for the cause of their divergence. Now on examining the Isthmus of Panama we find that a portion of it consists of cretaceous beds containing fossils undistinguishable from fossils from the cretaceous beds of Europe; the Isthmus must therefore have been raised into dry land in tertiary or post-tertiary times. It is difficult to doubt that the rising of this natural barrier isolated two portions of a shallow-water fauna which have since slightly diverged under slightly different conditions. I quote Alexander Agassiz:—"The question naturally arises, have we not in the different Faunæ on both sides of the Isthmus a standard by which to measure the changes which these species have undergone since the raising of the Isthmus of Panama and the isolation of the two Faunæ?"[1]

Edward Forbes distinguished round all seaboards four very marked zones of depth, each characterized by a distinct group of organisms. The first of these is the littoral zone, the space between tide-marks, distinguished by the abundance of sea-weeds, on the European shores of the genera *Lichina*, *Fucus*, *Enteromorpha*, *Polysiphonia*, and *Laurencia*, which severally predominate at different heights in the zone, and subdivide it into subordinate belts like a softly-coloured riband border. This band is under very special circumstances, for its inhabitants are periodically exposed to the air, to the direct rays of the sun, and to all the extremes of the climate of the land. Animal species are not very numerous in the littoral zone, but individuals are abundant. The distribution of many of the littoral species is very wide, and some of them are nearly cosmopolitan. Many are vegetable feeders. Some characteristic genera on the coast of Europe are *Gammarus*, *Talitrus*, and *Balanus* among Crustacea, and *Littorina*, *Patella*, *Purpura*, and *Mytilus* among Mollusca, with, under stones and in rock-pools, many stragglers from the next zone.

The Laminarian zone extends from low-water mark to a depth of about fifteen fathoms. This is specially

[1] Preliminary Report on the Echini and Starfishes dredged in Deep Water between Cuba and the Florida Reef, by L. F. de Pourtales, Assistant U.S. Coast Survey; prepared by Alexander Agassiz. Communicated by Professor B. Peirce, Superintendent U.S. Coast Survey, to the Bulletin of the Museum of Comparative Zoology, Cambridge, Mass., 1869.

the zone of 'tangles' for the first few fathoms, and in deeper water of the beautiful scarlet sea-weeds (*florideæ*). It is always under water except at the very lowest ebb of spring tides, when we get a glimpse of its upper border. The laminarian zone produces abundance of vegetable food, and, like the littoral zone, may be divided into subordinate bands distinguished by differently tinted algæ. Animals swarm in this zone, both as to species and individuals, and are usually remarkable for the brightness of their colouring. The molluscan genera *Trochus*, *Lacuna*, and *Lottia* are characteristic of this belt in the British seas.

The Laminarian zone is succeeded by the Coralline zone, which extends to a depth of about fifty fathoms. In this belt vegetation is chiefly represented by coral-like millipores, and plant-like hydroid zoophytes and bryozoa abound. All of the higher orders of marine invertebrates are fully represented, principally by animal feeders. The larger crustaceans and echinoderms are abundant; and the great fishing-banks frequented by the cod, haddock, halibut, turbot, and sole, belong properly to this zone, although they sometimes extend into water more than fifty fathoms deep. Characteristic molluscan genera are *Buccinum*, *Fusus*, *Ostrea*, and *Pecten;* and among echinoderms in the European seas we find *Antedon sarsii* and *celticus*, *Asteracanthion glaciale* and *rubens*, *Ophiothrix fragilis*, and on sand, *Ophioglypha lacertosa* and *albida*.

The last belt defined by Forbes as extending from about fifty fathoms to an unknown lower limit is the zone of deep-sea corals. "In its depths the number of peculiar creatures are few, yet sufficient to give a marked character to it, whilst the other portions of its population are derived from the higher zones, and must be regarded as colonists. As we descend deeper and deeper in this region, its inhabitants become more and more modified, and fewer and fewer, indicating our approach towards an abyss where life is either extinguished, or exhibits but a few sparks to mark its lingering presence."[1]

Forbes pointed out that the groups of animals having their maximum development in these several zones are thoroughly characteristic, and that groups of representative forms occupy the same zones all over the world, so that on examining an assemblage of marine animals from any locality, it is easy to tell from what zone of depth they have been procured. At all periods of the earth's history, there has been the same clear definition of zones of depth, and fossil animals from any particular zone are in some sense representative of the fauna of the corresponding zone at the present day. We can, therefore, usually tell with tolerable certainty to which zone of depth a particular assemblage of fossils is to be referred.

Although we must now greatly modify our views with regard to the extent and fauna of the zone of deep-sea corals, and give up all idea of a zero of animal life, still we must regard Forbes' investigation into the bathymetrical distribution of animals as marking a great advance on previous knowledge. His experience was much wider than that of any other naturalist of his time; the practical difficulties in the way of testing his conclusions were great, and

[1] Edward Forbes, Natural History of the European Seas, p. 26.

they were accepted by naturalists generally without question.

The history of discovery bearing upon the extent and distribution of the deep-sea fauna will be discussed in a future chapter. It will suffice at present to mention in order the few data which gradually prepared the minds of naturalists to distrust the hypothesis of a zero of animal life at a limited depth, and led to the recent special investigations. In the year 1819 Sir John Ross published the official account of his voyage of discovery during the year 1818 in Baffin's Bay.[1] At page 178 he says, "In the meantime I was employed on board in sounding and in trying the current, and the temperature of the water. It being perfectly calm and smooth, I had an excellent opportunity of detecting these important objects. Soundings were obtained correctly in 1,000 fathoms, consisting of soft mud, in which there were worms, and, entangled on the sounding line, at the depth of 800 fathoms, was found a beautiful *Caput Medusæ* (Fig. 1). These were carefully preserved, and will be found described in the appendix." This was in lat. 73° 37′ N., long. 77° 25′ W., on the 1st of September, 1818, and it is, so far as I am aware, the first recorded instance of living animals having been brought up from any depth approaching 1,000 fathoms. General Sir Edward Sabine, who was a member of Sir John Ross's expedition, has kindly furnished Dr.

[1] A Voyage of Discovery made under the Orders of the Admiralty in His Majesty's ships 'Isabella' and 'Alexander,' for the purpose of exploring Baffin's Bay, and inquiring into the Possibility of a North-west Passage. By John Ross, K.G., Captain Royal Navy. London, 1819.

Carpenter with some more ample particulars of this

FIG. 1.—*Asterophyton linckii*, MÜLLER and TROSCHEL. A young specimen slightly enlarged. No. 75.

occurrence:[1]—"'The ship sounded in 1,000 fathoms, mud, between one and two miles off shore (lat.

[1] Preliminary Report, by Dr. William B. Carpenter, V.P.R.S., of Dredging Operations in the Seas to the North of the British Islands, carried on in Her Majesty's steam-vessel 'Lightning,' by Dr. Carpenter and Dr. Wyville Thomson. (Proceedings of the Royal Society, 1868, p. 177.)

73° 37′ N., long. 77° 25′ W.); a magnificent Asterias (*Caput Medusæ*) was entangled by the line, and brought up with very little damage. The mud was soft and greenish, and contained specimens of *Lumbricus tubicola.*' So far my written journal; but I can add, from a very distinct recollection, that the heavy deep-sea weight had sunk, drawing the line with it, several feet into the soft greenish mud, which still adhered to the line when brought to the surface of the water. The star-fish had been entangled in the line so little above the mud that fragments of its arms, which had been broken off in the ascent of the line, were picked up from amongst the mud."

Sir James Clark Ross, R.N., dredging in 270 fathoms, lat. 73° 3′ S., long. 176° 6′ E., reports:[1] "*Corallines, Flustræ*, and a variety of invertebrate animals, came up in the net, showing an abundance and great variety of animal life. Amongst these I detected two species of *Pycnogonum; Idotea baffini*, hitherto considered peculiar to the Arctic seas; a *Chiton*, seven or eight bivalves and univalves, an unknown species of *Gammarus*, and two kinds of *Serpula* adhering to the pebbles and shells . . . It was interesting amongst these creatures to recognize several that I had been in the habit of taking in equally high northern latitudes; and although, contrary to the general belief of naturalists, I have no doubt that, from however great a depth we may be enabled to bring up the mud and stones of the bed of the ocean,

[1] A Voyage of Discovery and Research in the Southern and Antarctic Regions during the Years 1839-43. By Captain Sir James Clark Ross, R.N. London, 1847.

we shall find them teeming with animal life; the extreme pressure at the greatest depth does not appear to affect these creatures; hitherto we have not been able to determine this point beyond a thousand fathoms, but from that depth several shell-fish have been brought up with the mud."

On the 28th of June 1845, Mr. Henry Goodsir, who was a member of Sir John Franklin's ill-fated expedition, obtained in Davis' Strait from a depth of 300 fathoms, "a capital haul,—mollusca, crustacea, asterida, spatangi, corallines, &c."[1] The bottom was composed of fine green mud like that mentioned by Sir Edward Sabine.

About the year 1854 Passed-midshipman Brooke, U.S.N., invented his ingenious sounding instrument for bringing up samples from the bottom. It only brought up a small quantity in a quill. These trophies from any depth over 1,000 fathoms were eagerly sought for by naturalists and submitted to searching microscopic examination; and the result was very surprising. All over the Atlantic basin the sediment brought up was nearly uniform in character, and consisted almost entirely of the calcareous shells, whole or in fragments, of one species of foraminifer, *Globigerina bulloides* (Fig. 2). Mixed with these were the shells of some other foraminifera, and particularly a little perforated sphere, *Orbulina universa* (Fig. 3), which in some localities entirely replaces *Globigerina;* with a few shields of diatoms, and spines and trellised skeletons of Radiolaria. Some soundings from the Pacific were of the same character, so

[1] Natural History of the British Seas. By Professor Edward Forbes and R. Godwin-Austen. P. 51.

that it seemed probable that this gradual deposition of a fine uniform organic sediment was almost universal.

Then the question arose whether the animals which secreted these shells lived at the bottom, or whether they floated in myriads on the surface and in the upper zones of the sea, their empty shells falling after death through the water in an incessant shower. Specimens of the soundings were sent to the eminent

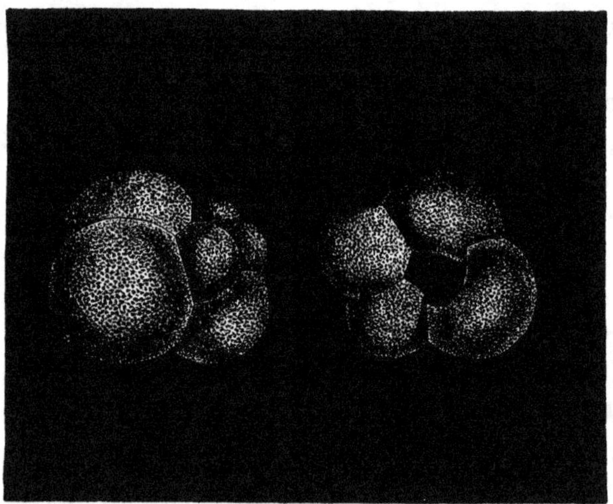

FIG. 2.—*Globigerina bulloides*, D'ORBIGNY. Highly magnified.

microscopists Professor Ehrenberg of Berlin and the late Professor Baily of West Point. On the moot question these two naturalists gave opposite opinions. Ehrenberg contended that the weight of evidence was in favour of their having lived at the bottom, while Baily thought it was not probable that the animals live at the depths where the shells are found, but that they inhabit the water near the surface, and when they die their shells settle to the bottom.[1]

The next high authority who expressed an opinion was Professor Huxley, and he was very guarded. The samples procured by Capt. Dayman in the 'Cyclops,'

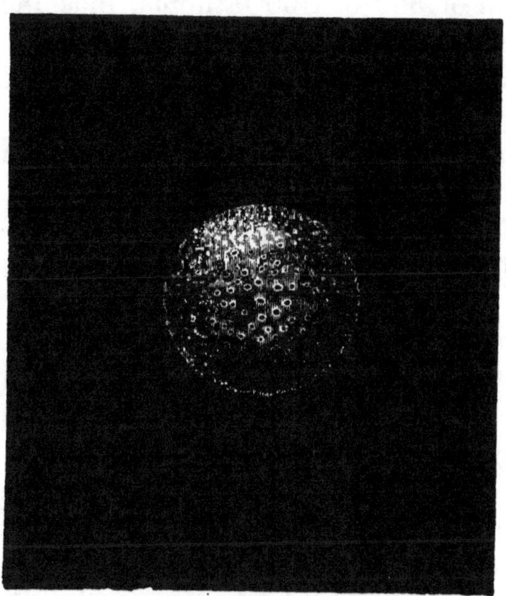

FIG. 3.—*Orbulina universa*, D'ORBIGNY. Highly magnified.

in 1857, were submitted to him for examination, and in his report to the Admiralty[2] in 1858 he says :—

[1] Explanations and Sailing Directions to accompany the Wind and Currents Charts. By M. F. Maury, LL.D., Lieut. U.S.N., Superintendent of the National Observatory. 6th Edition. Philadelphia, 1864. P. 299.

[2] Appendix A to Deep Sea Soundings in the North Atlantic Ocean between Ireland and Newfoundland, made in H.M.S. 'Cyclops,' Lieut.-Commander Joseph Dayman, in June and July 1857. Published by order of the Lords Commissioners of the Admiralty. London, 1858.

"How can animal life be conceived to exist under such conditions of light, temperature, pressure, and aëration as must obtain at these vast depths? To this one can only reply that we know for a certainty that even very highly-organized animals do contrive to live at a depth of 300 or 400 fathoms, inasmuch as they have been brought up thence, and that the difference in the amount of light and heat at 400 and at 2,000 fathoms is probably, so to speak, very far less than the difference in complexity of organization between these animals and the humble Protozoa and Protophyta of the deep-sea soundings. I confess, though, as yet, far from regarding it proved that the *Globigerinæ* live at these depths, the balance of probabilities seems to me to incline in that direction."

In 1860 Dr. Wallich accompanied Captain Sir Leopold McClintock in H.M.S. 'Bulldog' on her sounding expedition to Iceland, Greenland, and Newfoundland, as naturalist. During the cruise soundings were taken, and specimens of the bottom were brought up from depths from 600 to 2,000 fathoms; many of these were the now well-known grey 'Globigerina ooze,' while others were volcanic detritus from Iceland, and clay and gravel the product of the disintegration of the metamorphic rocks of Greenland and Labrador. On the return voyage, about midway between Cape Farewell and Rockall, thirteen star-fishes came up from a sounding of 1,260 fathoms, "convulsively embracing a portion of the sounding-line which had been payed out in excess of the already ascertained depth, and rested for a sufficient period at the bottom to permit of their attaching themselves to it." On his return Dr. Wallich published in 1862, an extremely valuable work which will be frequently referred to hereafter, upon 'The Atlantic Sea-bed.'[1] He warmly advocated the view that the conditions of the bottom of the sea were not such as to preclude the possibility of the existence of even the higher forms of animal life, and discussed fully and with great ability the arguments which had been advanced on the other side. The first part only of Dr. Wallich's book appeared, in a somewhat costly and cumbrous form, and it scarcely came into the hands of working naturalists, or received the attention which it deserved. At the time, however, it was merely an expression of individual opinion, for no new facts had been elicited. Star-fishes had come up on several previous occasions adhering to sounding-lines, but the absolute proof was still wanting that they had lived upon the ground at the depth of the sounding. Dr. Wallich referred the star-fishes procured to a well-known littoral species, and complicated their history somewhat irrelevantly with the disappearance of the 'Land of Buss.' Fortunately the artistic if not very satisfactory figure which he gives of a star-fish clinging to the line does not bear out his determination either in appearance or attitude, but suggests one or other of two species which we now know to be excessively abundant in deep water in the North Atlantic, *Ophiopholis aculeata*, O. F. MÜLLER, or *Ophiacantha spinulosa*, MÜLLER and TROSCHEL.

[1] The North Atlantic Sea-bed: comprising a Diary of the Voyage on board H.M.S. 'Bulldog,' in 1860; and Observations on the presence of Animal Life, and the Formation and Nature of Organic Deposits at great Depths in the Ocean. By G. C. Wallich, M.D., F.L.S., F.G.S., &c. Published with the sanction of the Lords Commissioners of the Admiralty. London, 1862.

Dr. Wallich's is the only book which discusses fully and systematically the various questions bearing upon the biological relations of the sea-bed, and his conclusions are in the main correct.

In the autumn of the year 1860 Mr. Fleeming Jenkin, C.E., now Professor of Engineering in the University of Edinburgh, was employed by the Mediterranean Telegraph Company to repair their cable between Sardinia and Bona on the coast of Africa, and on January 15, 1861, he gave an interesting account of his proceedings at a meeting of the Institution of Civil Engineers.[1]

This cable was laid in the year 1857. In 1858 it became necessary to repair it, and a length of about 30 miles was picked up and successfully replaced. In the summer of 1860 the cable completely failed. On taking it up in comparatively shallow water on the African shore, the cable was found covered with marine animals, greatly corroded, and injured apparently by the trawling operations in an extensive coral fishery through which it unfortunately passed. It was broken through in 70 fathoms water a few miles from Bona. The sea-end was however recovered, and it was found that the cable which thence traversed a wide valley nearly 2,000 fathoms in maximum depth, was perfect to within about 40 miles of Sardinia. It was then picked up from the Sardinian end, and the first 39 miles were as sound as when it was first laid down. At this distance from the shore there was a change in the nature of the bottom, evidenced by the different colour of the mud, and the wires were

[1] Minutes of Proceedings of the Institution of Civil Engineers, with Abstracts of the Discussions. Vol. xx. p. 81. London, 1861.

much corroded. Shortly afterwards the cable gave way in a depth of 1,200 fathoms, at a distance of one mile from the spot where the electrical tests showed that the cable had been previously broken.

With these 40 miles of cable much coral and many marine animals were brought up, but it did not appear that their presence had injured the cable, for they were attached to the sound as well as to the corroded portions. On his return, Mr. Fleeming Jenkin sent specimens of the animals which he had himself taken from the cable, noting the respective depths, to Professor Allman, F.R.S. for determination. Dr. Allman gives a list of fifteen animal forms, including the ova of a cephalopod, found at depths of from 70 to 1,200

FIG. 4.—*Caryophyllia borealis*, FLEMING. Twice the natural size. No. 45.

fathoms. On other portions of the cable species of *Grantia*, *Plumularia*, *Gorgonia*, *Caryophyllia*, *Alcyonium*, *Cellepora*, *Retepora*, *Eschara*, *Salicornaria*, *Ascidia*, *Lima*, and *Serpula*. I observe from Professor

Fleeming Jenkin's private journal, which he has kindly placed in my hands for reference, that an example of *Caryophyllia*, a true coral (Fig. 4), was found naturally attached to the cable at the point where it gave way; that is to say, at the bottom in 1,200 fathoms water.

Some portions of this cable subsequently came into the custody of M. Mangon, Professor at the Ecole des Ponts et Chaussées in Paris, and were examined by M. Alphonse Milne-Edwards, who read a paper upon the organisms attached to them, at the Academy of Sciences, on the 15th of July, 1861.[1] After some introductory remarks which show that he is thoroughly aware of the value of this observation as a final solution of the vexed question of the existence of animal life at depths in the sea greatly beyond the supposed 'zero' of Edward Forbes, M. Milne-Edwards gives a list of the animals which he found on the cable from the depth of 1,100 fathoms. The list includes *Murex lamellosus*, CRISTOFORI and JAN, and *Craspedotus limbatus*, PHILIPPI, two univalve shells allied to the whelk; *Ostrea cochlear*, POLI, a small oyster common below 40 fathoms throughout the Mediterranean; *Pecten testæ*, BIVONA, a rare little clam; *Caryophyllia borealis*, FLEMING, or a nearly allied species, one of the true corals; and an undescribed coral referred to a new genus and species under the name of *Thalassiotrochus telegraphicus*, A. MILNE-EDWARDS.

[1] Observations sur l'Existence de divers Mollusques et Zoophytes à de très grandes profondeurs dans la Mer Méditerranée: Annales des Sciences Naturelles; quatrième série—Zoologie. Tome xv. p. 149. Paris, 1861.

It is right, however, to state that Prof. Fleeming Jenkin's notes refer to only one or two species, and especially to *Caryophyllia borealis*, as attached to the cable at a depth of upwards of 1,000 fathoms. From this depth he took examples of *Caryophyllia* with his own hands, but he suspects that specimens from the shallower water may have got mixed with those from the deeper in the series in the possession of M. Mangon, and that therefore M. Milne-Edwards' list is not entirely trustworthy.

Up till this time all observations with reference to the existence of living animals at extreme depths had been liable to error, or at all events to doubt, from two sources. The appliances and methods of deep-sea sounding were imperfect, and there was always a possibility, from the action of deep currents upon the sounding line or from other causes, of a greater depth being indicated than really existed; and again, although there was a strong probability, there was no absolute certainty that the animals adhering to the line or entangled on the sounding instrument had actually come up from the bottom. They might have been caught on the way.

Before laying a submarine telegraphic cable its course is carefully surveyed, and no margin of doubt is left as to the real depth. Fishing the cable up is a delicate and difficult operation, and during its progress the depth is checked again and again. The cable lies on the ground throughout its whole length. The animal forms upon which our conclusions are based are not sticking loosely to the cable, under circumstances which might be accounted for by their having been entangled upon it during its passage through the water, but they are moulded upon its outer surface or cemented to it by calcareous or horny excretions, and some of them, such as the corals and bryozoa, from what we know of their history and mode of life, must have become attached to it as minute germs, and have grown to maturity in the position in which they were found. I must therefore regard this observation of Mr. Fleeming Jenkin as having afforded the first absolute proof of the existence of highly-organized animals living at depths of upwards of 1,000 fathoms.

During the several cruises of H.M. ships 'Lightning' and 'Porcupine' in the years 1868, 1869, and 1870,[1] fifty-seven hauls of the dredge were taken in the Atlantic at depths beyond 500 fathoms, and sixteen at depths beyond 1,000 fathoms, and in all cases life was abundant. In 1869 we took two casts in depths greater than 2,000 fathoms. In both of these life was abundant; and with the deepest cast, 2,435 fathoms, off the mouth of the Bay of Biscay, we took living, well-marked and characteristic examples of all of the five invertebrate sub-kingdoms. And thus the question of

[1] Preliminary Report, by Dr. William Carpenter, V.P.R.S., of Dredging Operations in the Seas to the north of the British Islands, carried on in Her Majesty's steam-vessel 'Lightning' by Dr. Carpenter and Dr. Wyville Thomson, Professor of Natural History in Queen's College, Belfast. (Proceedings of the Royal Society of London, 1868.)

Preliminary Report of the Scientific Exploration of the Deep Sea in H.M. surveying-vessel 'Porcupine,' during the Summer of 1869. Conducted by Dr. Carpenter, V.P.R.S., J. Gwyn Jeffreys, F.R.S., and Professor Wyville Thomson, LL.D., F.R.S. (Proceedings of the Royal Society of London, 1870.)

Report of Deep Sea Researches carried on during the months of July, August, and September 1870, in H.M. surveying-ship 'Porcupine,' by W. B. Carpenter, M.D., F.R.S., and J. Gwyn Jeffreys, F.R.S. (Proceedings of the Royal Society of London, 1870.)

the existence of abundant animal life at the bottom of the sea has been finally settled and for all depths, for there is no reason to suppose that the depth anywhere exceeds between three and four thousand fathoms; and if there be nothing in the conditions of a depth of 2,500 fathoms to prevent the full development of a varied fauna, it is impossible to suppose that even an additional thousand fathoms would make any great difference.

The conditions which might be expected principally to affect animal life at great depths of the sea are pressure, temperature, and the absence of light which apparently involves the absence of vegetable food.

After passing a zone surrounding the land, which is everywhere narrow compared with the extent of the ocean, through which the bottom more or less abruptly shelves downwards and the water deepens; speaking very generally, the average depth of the sea is 2,000 fathoms, or about two miles; as far below the surface as the average height of the Swiss Alps. In some places the depth seems to be considerably greater, possibly here and there nearly double that amount; but these abysses are certainly very local, and their existence is even uncertain, and a vast portion of the area does not reach a depth of 1,500 fathoms.

The enormous pressure at these great depths seemed at first sight alone sufficient to put any idea of life out of the question. There was a curious popular notion, in which I well remember sharing when a boy, that, in going down, the sea-water became gradually under the pressure heavier and heavier, and that all the loose things in the sea floated at different levels.

according to their specific weight: skeletons of men, anchors and shot and cannon, and last of all the broad gold pieces wrecked in the loss of many a galleon on the Spanish Main; the whole forming a kind of 'false bottom' to the ocean, beneath which there lay all the depth of clear still water, which was heavier than molten gold.

The conditions of pressure are certainly very extraordinary. At 2,000 fathoms a man would bear upon his body a weight equal to twenty locomotive engines, each with a long goods train loaded with pig iron. We are apt to forget, however, that water is almost incompressible, and that therefore the density of sea-water at a depth of 2,000 fathoms is scarcely appreciably increased. At the depth of a mile, under a pressure of about 159 atmospheres, sea-water, according to the formula given by Jamin, is compressed by the $\frac{1}{144}$ of its volume; and at twenty miles, supposing the law of the compressibility to continue the same, by only $\frac{1}{7}$ of its volume—that is to say, the volume at that depth would be $\frac{6}{7}$ of the volume of the same weight of water at the surface. Any free air suspended in the water, or contained in any compressible tissue of an animal at 2,000 fathoms, would be reduced to a mere fraction of its bulk, but an organism supported through all its tissues on all sides, within and without, by incompressible fluids at the same pressure, would not necessarily be incommoded by it. We sometimes find when we get up in the morning, by a rise of an inch in the barometer, that nearly half a ton has been quietly piled upon us during the night, but we experience no inconvenience, rather a feeling of exhilaration and buoyancy, since it requires a little less exertion to move our bodies in the denser medium. We are already familiar, chiefly through the researches of the late Professor Sars, with a long list of animals of all the invertebrate groups living at a depth of 300 to 400 fathoms, and consequently subject to a pressure of 1,120 lbs. on the square inch; and off the coast of Portugal there is a great fishery of sharks (*Centroscymnus cœlolepis*, Boc. and Cap.), carried on beyond that depth.

If an animal so high in the scale of organization as a shark can bear without inconvenience the pressure of half a ton on the square inch, it is a sufficient proof that the pressure is applied under circumstances which prevent its affecting it to its prejudice, and there seems to be no reason why it should not tolerate equally well a pressure of one or two tons. At all events it is a fact that the animals of all the invertebrate classes which abound at a depth of 2,000 fathoms do bear that extreme pressure, and that they do not seem to be affected by it in any way. We dredged at 2,435 fathoms *Scrobicularia nitida*, Müller, a species which is abundant in six fathoms and at all intermediate depths, and at 2,090 fathoms a large *Fusus*, with species of many genera which are familiar at moderate depths. Although highly organized animals may live when permanently subjected to these high pressures, it is by no means certain that they could survive the change of condition involved in the pressure being suddenly removed. Most of the mollusca and annelids brought up in the dredge from beyond 1,000 fathoms were either dead or in a very sluggish state. Some of the star-fishes moved for some time feebly, and the spines and pedicellariæ moved on the shells of the urchins, but all the animals had evidently received from some cause their death-shock. Dr. Perceval Wright mentions[1] that all the sharks brought up by the long lines from 500 fathoms in Setubal Bay are dead when they reach the surface.

Various methods have been proposed to test the actual pressure at great depths, but as all the elements in the calculation are well known, it is easier to work out the question in the study than in the field. A neat instrument was constructed for the American Coast Survey. A brass piston or plunger was fitted accurately into a cylindrical hole in the wall of a brass water-tight chamber. The chamber was completely filled with water, and a clasping index on the plunger marked to what extent the plunger had been driven into the water contained in the chamber by the extreme pressure. The required indication is no doubt given, but such an instrument is at the same time an extremely delicate thermoscope, and until lately there has been no perfect means of correcting for temperature. A more important application of the pressure gauge is to check the accuracy of deep soundings. Probably the best arrangement which has been proposed for the purpose is a long capillary glass tube, calibrated and graduated to millimetres, open at one end, and provided with a moveable index to show to what amount the air contained in the tube has been compressed by the entrance of the water. The principal objection to this device is the

[1] Notes on Deep Sea Dredging, by Edward Perceval Wright, M.D., F.L.S., Professor of Zoology, Trinity College, Dublin. (Annals and Magazine of Natural History, December 1868.)

great difficulty in arranging an index which will measure with accuracy the extremely small space into which even a long column of air is compressed when the pressure becomes very great. It can scarcely be made available beyond 1,000 fathoms (200 atmospheres).

We have in Sir John Herschel's 'Physical Geography,'[1] and in Dr. Wallich's 'Atlantic Sea-bed,'[2] where it is given in the fullest detail, the doctrine of the distribution of deep-sea temperature as it seems to have been almost universally adopted up till the time of the cruise of the 'Lightning.' It was generally understood that while the surface temperature, which depended upon direct solar radiation, the direction of currents, the temperature of winds, and other temporary causes, might vary to any amount; at a certain depth the temperature was permanent at 4° C., the temperature of the greatest density of fresh water. It is singular that this belief should have met with so general acceptance, for so early as the year 1833 M. Depretz[3] determined that the temperature of the maximum density of sea-water, which contracts steadily till just above its freezing-point, is $-3°·67$ C.; and even before that time observations of sea-temperatures at great depths, which were certainly trustworthy within a few degrees, had indicated several degrees below the freezing-point of fresh water.

The question of the distribution of heat in the sea,

[1] Physical Geography; from the "Encyclopædia Britannica." By Sir John F. W. Herschel, Bart. K.H. &c. &c., p. 45. Edinburgh, 1861.

[2] Atlantic Sea-bed, p. 98.

[3] Recherches sur le Maximum de Densité des Dissolutions aqueuses. (Annales de Chimie, tome lxx. 1833, p. 54.)

which is one of the greatest interest in connection with the distribution of marine animals, will be fully discussed in a future chapter. The broad conclusions to which we have been led by late investigations are, that instead of there being a permanent deep layer of water at 4° C. the average temperature of the bottom of the deep sea in temperate and tropical regions is about 0° C., the freezing-point of fresh water; and that there is a general surface movement of warm water, produced probably by a combination of various causes, from the equatorial regions towards the poles, and a slow under-current, or rather indraught, of cold water from the poles towards the equator. From cases which are recorded, chiefly by the earlier American sounding expeditions, of the sounding-line having been run out into long loops in soundings where, from the nature of the sea-bed, the bottom water appeared to be still, it would seem that there are also in some places intermediate currents; but with reference to their limits and distribution we have as yet no data. That a cold flow from the polar seas passes over the bottom seems to be proved by the fact that in all parts of the world wherever deep temperature soundings have been taken, from the arctic circle to the equator, the temperature sinks with increasing depth, and is lower at the bottom than the normal temperature of the crust of the earth; an evidence that a constantly renewed supply of cold water is cooling down the surface of the crust, which, being a bad conductor, does not transmit heat with sufficient rapidity to affect perceptibly the temperature of the cold indraught. It is probable that in winter, in those parts of the arctic sea which are not directly influenced by the northern extension of the gulf stream, the whole column of water from the surface to the bottom is reduced to the lowest temperature which it will bear without freezing, and is thus an ample source of the coldest water of the highest specific gravity.

The proof that the flow of the cold indraught is almost secular in its slowness, is that over a large portion of the ocean where the low bottom temperature is known to prevail, the sea-bed is covered with a light fleecy deposit of microscopic organisms of great delicacy, into which the sounding-lead has in some instances sunk several feet, and which must inevitably be drifted away by a current of appreciable velocity. In all places where any perceptible current exists, the bottom consists of sand or mud or gravel and rolled pebbles. In some cases also, sounding in the deep water of the mid-Atlantic, the line, after running out greatly in excess of the depth, has been found to have coiled itself in a tangled mass right over the lead—a proof of almost absolute stillness.

In some places, owing to the conformation of the neighbouring land or of the sea-bottom, warm and cold currents are circumscribed and localized, and this sometimes gives us the singular phenomenon of a patch or stripe of warm and a patch of cold sea meeting in an invisible but very definite line. There is a curious instance of this in the 'cold wall' which defines the western border of the gulf stream along the coast of Massachusetts, and another scarcely less marked which we discovered during the trial cruise of the 'Lightning' has been fully described by Dr. Carpenter in his report of that cruise, and will be referred to hereafter.

In moderate depths sometimes the whole mass of water from the surface to the bottom is abnormally warm, owing to the movement in a certain direction of a great body of warm water, as in the 'warm area' to the north-west of the Hebrides; and sometimes the whole body of water is abnormally cold, as in the 'cold area' between Scotland and Færoe, and in the northern part of the German Ocean. In deep water however, after the first few hundred fathoms, the thermometer usually sinks gradually and very slowly till it reaches its minimum at the bottom, a little above or below the zero of the centigrade scale.

The temperature of the sea apparently never sinks at any depth below $-3^{\circ}\cdot5$ C., a degree of cold which, singularly enough, is not inconsistent with abundant and vigorous animal life, so that in the ocean, except perhaps within the eternal ice-barrier of the antarctic pole, life seems nowhere to be limited by cold. But although certain sea-animals—many of them, such as the siphonophora, the salpæ, and the ctenophorous medusæ, of the most delicate and complicated organization—are tolerant of such severe cold, it would appear to be temperature almost entirely which regulates the distribution of species. The nature of the ground can have little to say to it, for on every line of coast of any extent almost every condition and every kind of sediment is usually represented. From their inhabiting a medium which differs but little in weight from the substance of their bodies, and from the great majority of them producing free-moving larvæ or fry in vast numbers which are floated along from place to place by currents, marine animals would seem to have every possible chance of extending their area, and yet the geographical distribution of most of the shallow-water species is well defined, and frequently somewhat restricted. Unfortunately we know as yet very little about the general distribution of marine animals. Except along the coasts of Britain and Scandinavia, a part of the North American coast, and a part of the Mediterranean, we know absolutely nothing beyond the shore zone, or at all events beyond 10 or 15 fathoms. What little we do know is confined almost entirely to the mollusca, and is due, not so much to scientific research as to the commercial value which the acquisitive zeal of conchologists has placed upon rare shells. It may be supposed, however, that the same laws which regulate the distribution of littoral and sub-littoral mollusca, affect in like manner that of shallow-water annulosa, echinoderms, and cœlenterates; indeed, from the scattered observations which have been made on the distribution of these latter groups, it seems certain that such is the case.

Woodward[1] regarded the marine mollusca as occupying eighteen well-defined 'provinces,' fulfilling more or less completely the condition of having at least one-half of the species peculiar to the province. Edward Forbes defined twenty-five such 'regions;' but it must be remembered that in both cases at least three-fourths of the number of areas defined were based upon the most imperfect knowledge of the larger and more conspicuous shore shells only. It has been constantly observed in the few cases confined entirely to the shores of the North Atlantic and the Mediterranean,

[1] A Manual of the Mollusca. By S. P. Woodward. London, 1851. P. 354.

in which dredging has been attempted at any considerable depth, say 30 or 40 fathoms, that the number of species common to the province dredged and to the province to the north of it, is greatly increased by the investigation being carried into a deeper zone.[1] Thus in the lusitanian province Mr. McAndrew dredged off the coast of Galicia and Asturias, 212 species, 50 per cent. of which were common to the coast of Norway; and off the south of Spain 335 species were obtained, of which 28 per cent. were common to Norway (boreal province), and 51 per cent. to Britain (chiefly celtic province). The shells common to the two or three provinces were chiefly those dredged from considerable depths. The littoral forms had a much more distinct aspect. The mollusca of the 'Porcupine' expedition have not yet been thoroughly worked out. They are in the hands of Mr. Gwyn Jeffreys, and his preliminary reports give a most interesting forecast of what we may expect when his labour is completed. He announces something like 250 new species. Some of the more interesting of these, and the general phenomena of their distribution, will be referred to in a future chapter.

The echinoderms of the expedition are more limited in number, and have already been examined by the writer with some care. The general distribution of the Echinodermata is not so well known as that of the Mollusca. There are many littoral and sub-littoral species. Many of these are local, but many have a wide geographical distribution, usually along what Edward Forbes calls a 'homoiozoic belt,' a belt of nearly similar circumstances of climate extending

[1] Woodward, loc. cit. p. 362.

through many degrees of longitude, but few of latitude. As a class, however, they prefer a depth rather beyond 20 fathoms,[1] beyond the reach of very violent climatic vicissitudes. They are conspicuous things, showing usually sufficiently bold specific characters, and thus they are less liable to confusion than most other groups. They involve in their history and economy several of the principal questions discussed in this volume; while giving, therefore, such a brief sketch as the space at my disposal and the amount of my present information may permit, of the additions which have been made during our dredging cruises to the knowledge of the other invertebrate classes, I will use the echinoderms and the protozoa principally for the purpose of general illustration.

Littoral and shallow-water species of animals must be much more liable to have their migrations interrupted by 'natural barriers,' such as deep water through which they cannot pass, or currents of warmer or of colder water; they must likewise be much more affected by local circumstances, such as extreme differences between summer and winter temperature; so that they might be expected to be more circumscribed and local in their distribution than the denizens of greater depths—and they certainly are so. The conditions of the bottom in the zone from 20 to 50 fathoms are much more equable than near the surface. Direct solar radiation in temperate regions affects this zone very slightly, so that it probably

[1] Distribution of Marine Life. By Professor Edward Forbes, F.R.S., President of the Geological Society. (From the Physical Atlas of Natural Phenomena, by Alexander Keith Johnston, F.R.G.S., &c. Edinburgh, 1854.)

maintains nearly the same conditions of temperature through many degrees of latitude; and when as it passes southwards it does become gradually affected by increasing warmth, it may be supposed merely to sink a few fathoms deeper, carrying its conditions and its fauna along with it. For example, animal forms which abound in the celtic province at 25 fathoms with a mean temperature of 10° C., may be expected in greatest number in perhaps 40 or 50 fathoms, with the same temperature, in the lusitanian province. Such a zone may thus be continuous for a great distance, while the surface climate has been altering greatly, and the migrations of littoral forms have been again and again interrupted. But the deeper zone also sometimes meets with a 'natural barrier,' as at the line of junction between the warm and cold areas already mentioned; which causes a curious sifting out of those species which are intolerant of a change of temperature. Thus the fauna of the temperate northward flow of water off the west coast of Scotland is materially different from that of the cold indraught along the east coast.

If there be this overlapping between the lusitanian and celtic provinces, the same relation may be anticipated between our own and the boreal province; and it is well known that this is the case, for the great majority of the mollusca which have been dredged by McAndrew, Barlee, and especially by Gwyn Jeffreys, from depths below 50 fathoms, are identical with those found in shallower water on the Scandinavian coast. Our recent work, while it has brought out more fully the overlapping, has gone much farther towards the indication of a general law.

It seems probable that the distribution of marine animals is determined by the extremes of temperature rather than by the means. The mean winter temperature of the surface and of moderate depths off the north coast of Norway is about 2° C., and the extreme about 0° C.; and on the coast of Greenland the mean sinks to −1° C., and the extreme to −3° C.

The temperature of the trough between Scotland and Færoe at the depth of 500 fathoms is from 0° to −1° C., and we find in that trough, along with many undescribed forms which are special to very deep water, every one of the echinoderms hitherto found on the coast of Scandinavia and Greenland, with the single exception, I believe, of *Ophioglypha stüwitzii*, a shallow-water Greenland form among the ophiurids, and of one or two holothurids which have as yet evaded us.

The temperature of the telegraphic plateau at 1,000 to 2,000 fathoms is apparently usually from 3° to 2° C., and at 2,500 fathoms in the Bay of Biscay it is 2° C. From 800 to 2,000 fathoms all along the west coasts of Scotland, Ireland, and France, we have dredged Scandinavian echinoderms in abundance, and from the deep water as far south as the coast of Portugal I have received examples of some of the best marked northern forms, such as *Echinus elegans*, D. and K.; *Toxopneustes drobachiensis*, O. F. MÜLLER; *Brissopsis lyrifera*, FORBES; *Tripylus fragilis*, D. and K.; the magnificent *Brisinga coronata*, G. O. SARS (Fig. 7), and *B. endecacnemos*, ABSJÖRNSEN; *Pteraster militaris*, M. and T.; *Ophiacantha spinulosa*, M. and T.; *Ophiocten sericeum*, FORBES; *Ophioglypha sarsii*, LÜTK.; *Asteronyx lovéni*, M. and T.; and *Astero-*

phyton linckii, M. and T, from Mr. Gwyn Jeffreys' dredgings in 1870. Deep-sea forms dredged round our coast identical with northern species have been usually regarded as 'boreal outliers' (Forbes), or at all events as species which have extended their distribution from northern centres. This idea probably arose in a great measure from their having been discovered and first described in Scandinavia. We actually know nothing about their centres of distribution; all we know of them is that they are the inhabitants of an enormously extended zone of special thermal conditions, which 'crops out,' as it were, or rather comes within range of the ordinary means of observation, off the coasts of Scandinavia.

Edward Forbes pointed out long ago the kind of inverted analogy which exists between the distribution of land animals and plants and that of the fauna and flora of the sea. In the case of the land, while at the level of the sea there is, in temperate and tropical regions, a luxuriant vegetation with a correspondingly numerous fauna, as we ascend the slope of a mountain range the conditions gradually become more severe; species after species belonging to the more fortunate plains beneath disappear, and are replaced by others whose representatives are only to be found on other mountain ridges, or on the shores of an arctic sea. In the ocean, on the other hand, there is along the shore line and within the first few fathoms, a rich and varied flora and fauna, which participates and sympathises in all the circumstances of climate which affect the inhabitants of the land. As we descend, the conditions gradually become more rigorous, the temperature falls, and alterations of temperature are less felt.

The fauna becomes more uniform over a larger area, and is manifestly one of which the shallower water fauna of some colder region is to a great extent a lateral extension. Going still deeper, the severity of the cold increases until we reach the vast undulating plains and valleys at the bottom of the sea, with their fauna partly peculiar and partly polar—a region the extension of whose extreme thermal conditions only approaches the surface within the arctic and antarctic circles.

We have as yet very little exact knowledge as to the distance to which the sun's light penetrates into the water of the sea. According to some recent experiments which will be referred to in a future chapter, it would appear that the rays capable of affecting a delicate photographic film are very rapidly cut off, their effect being imperceptible at the depth of only a few fathoms. It is probable that some portions of the sun's light possessing certain properties may penetrate to a much greater distance, but it must be remembered that even the clearest sea-water is more or less tinted by suspended opaque particles and floating organisms, so that the light has more than a pure saline solution to contend with. At all events it is certain that beyond the first 50 fathoms plants are barely represented, and after 200 fathoms they are entirely absent. The question of the mode of nutrition of animals at great depths becomes, therefore, a very singular one. The practical distinction between plants and animals is, that plants prepare the food of animals by decomposing certain inorganic substances which animals cannot use as food, and recombining their elements into organic compounds upon which animals can feed. This process is, however, so far as we are at present aware, constantly effected under the influence of light. There seems to be little or no light at the bottom of the sea, and there are certainly no plants except such as may sink from the surface, but the bottom of the sea is a mass of animal life. At first sight it certainly seems difficult to account for the maintenance of this vast animal population living without any visible means of support. Two explanations have been suggested. It is conceivable that certain animal forms may have the power of decomposing water, carbon dioxide, and ammonia, and re-combining their elements into organic compounds without the agency of light. Dr. Wallich supports this view, and in doing so he states that "No exceptional law is invoked, but, on the contrary, that the proof of these organisms being endowed with the power to convert inorganic elements for their own nutrition rests on the undisputed power which they possess of separating carbonate of lime or silica from waters holding these substances in solution."[1] This, however, seems scarcely satisfactory. All the substances employed in the nutrition of animals are offered to them finally in solution in water, and the abstraction of these from their watery solutions cannot be regarded as a 'chemical separation.' The broad distinction still remains, that when carbon dioxide in solution is presented to a green plant in the sunshine it can decompose it, while an animal cannot.

I believe we have a simpler explanation. All sea-water contains a certain quantity of organic

[1] North Atlantic Sea-bed, p. 131.

matter, in solution and in suspension. Its sources are obvious. All rivers contain a considerable quantity. Every shore is surrounded by a fringe which averages a mile in width, of olive and red sea-weed. In the middle of the Atlantic there is a marine prairie, the 'Sargasso sea,' extending over three millions of square miles. The sea is full of animals, which are constantly dying and decaying. The amount of organic matter derived from these and other sources by the water of the ocean is very appreciable. Careful analyses of the water were made during the several cruises of the 'Porcupine' to detect it and to determine its amount, and the quantity everywhere was capable of being rendered manifest and estimated, and the proportion was found to be very uniform in all localities and at all depths. Nearly all the animals at extreme depths—practically all the animals, for the small number of higher forms feed upon these—belong to one sub-kingdom, the Protozoa; whose distinctive character is that they have no special organs of nutrition, but absorb nourishment through the whole surface of their jelly-like bodies. Most of these animals secrete exquisitely formed skeletons, some of silica, some of carbonate of lime. There is no doubt that they extract both these substances from the sea-water; and it seems more than probable that the organic matter which forms their soft parts is derived from the same source. It is thus quite intelligible that a world of animals may live in these dark abysses, but it is a necessary condition that they must chiefly belong to a class capable of being supported by absorption through the surface of their bodies of matter in solution, developing but little heat, and incurring a very small amount of waste by any manifestation of vital activity. According to this view it seems probable that at all periods of the earth's history some form of the Protozoa—rhizopods, sponges, or both—predominated greatly over all other forms of animal life in the depths of the warmer regions of the sea. The rhizopods, like the corals of a shallower zone, form huge accumulations of carbonate of lime, and it is probably to their agency that we must refer most of those great bands of limestone which have resisted time and change, and come in here and there with their rich imbedded lettering to mark like milestones the progress of the passing ages.

TINDHOLM.

CHAPTER II.

THE CRUISE OF THE 'LIGHTNING.'

Proposal to investigate the Conditions of the Bottom of the Sea.—Suggestions and Anticipations.—Correspondence between the Council of the Royal Society and the Admiralty.—Departure from Stornoway.—The Fǽroe Islands.—Singular Temperature Results in the Fǽroe Channel.—Life abundant at all Depths.—*Brisinga coronata.*—*Holtenia carpenteri.*—General Results of the Expedition.

Appendix A.—Particulars of Depth, Temperature, and Position at the various Dredging Stations of H.M.S. 'Lightning,' in the Summer of 1868; the Temperatures corrected for Pressure.

*** *The bracketed numbers to the woodcuts in this chapter refer to the dredging stations on Plate I.*

In the spring of the year 1868, my friend Dr. W. B. Carpenter, at that time one of the Vice-Presidents of the Royal Society, was with me in Ireland, where we were working out together the structure and development of the Crinoids. I had long previously had a profound conviction that the land of promise for the naturalist, the only remaining region where there were endless novelties of extraordinary interest ready to the hand which had the means of gathering them, was the bottom of the deep sea. I had even had a glimpse of some of these treasures, for I had seen the year before, with Professor Sars, the forms which I have already mentioned dredged by his son at a depth of 300 to 400 fathoms off the Loffoten islands. I propounded my views to my fellow-labourer, and we discussed the subject many times over our microscopes. I strongly urged Dr. Carpenter to use his influence at head-quarters to induce the Admiralty, probably through the Council of the Royal Society, to give us the use of a vessel properly fitted with dredging gear and all necessary scientific apparatus, that many heavy questions as to the state of things in the depths of the ocean which were still in a state of uncertainty, might be definitely settled. After full consideration, Dr. Carpenter promised his hearty co-operation, and we agreed that I should write to him on his return to London, indicating generally the results which I anticipated, and sketching out what I conceived to be a promising line of inquiry. The Council of the Royal Society warmly supported the proposal; and I give here in chronological order the short and eminently satisfactory correspondence which led to the Admiralty placing at the disposal of Dr. Carpenter and myself the gunboat 'Lightning' under the command of Staff-Commander May, R.N., in the summer of 1868, for a trial cruise to the north of Scotland, and afterwards to the much wider surveys in H.M.S. 'Porcupine,' Captain Calver, R.N., which were made with the additional association of Mr. Gwyn Jeffreys in the summers of the years 1869 and 1870.

From Prof. Wyville Thomson, Belfast, to Dr. Carpenter, V.P.R.S.

May 30, 1868.

MY DEAR CARPENTER,—When I last saw you, I suggested how very important it would be to the advancement of science to determine with accuracy the conditions and distribution of Animal Life at great depths in the ocean; I now resume the facts and considerations which lead me to believe that researches in this direction promise valuable results.

All recent observations tend to negative Edward Forbes's opinion that a *zero* of animal life was to be reached at a depth of a few hundred fathoms. Two years ago, M. Sars, Swedish Government Inspector of Fisheries, had an opportunity in his official capacity of dredging off the Loffoten Islands at a depth of 300 fathoms. I visited Norway shortly after his return, and had an opportunity of studying with his father, Prof. Sars, some of his results. Animal forms were *abundant;* many of them were new to science; and among them was one of surpassing interest, the small Crinoid of which you have a specimen, and which we at once recognized as a degraded type of the APIOCRINIDÆ, an order hitherto regarded as extinct, which attained its maximum in the Pear-encrinites of the Jurassic period, and whose latest representative hitherto known was the *Bourguetticrinus* of the Chalk. Some years previously, M. Absjörnsen, dredging in 200 fathoms in the Hardangerfjord, procured several examples of a Starfish (*Brisinga*) which seems to find its nearest ally in the fossil genus *Protaster.* These observations place it beyond a doubt that animal life is abundant in the ocean at depths varying from 200 to 300 fathoms, that the forms at these great depths differ greatly from those met with in ordinary dredgings, and that, at all events in some cases, these animals are closely allied to, and would seem to be directly descended from, the fauna of the early Tertiaries.

I think the latter result might almost have been anticipated; and probably further investigation will add largely to this class of data, and will give us an opportunity of testing our determination of the zoological position of some fossil types by an examination of the soft parts of their recent representatives. The main cause of the destruction, the migration, and the extreme modification of Animal types, appears to be change of climate, chiefly depending upon oscillations of the earth's crust. These oscillations do not appear to have ranged, in the northern portion of the Northern Hemisphere, much beyond 1,000 feet since the commencement of the Tertiary epoch. The temperature of deep water seems to be constant for all latitudes at 39°; so that an immense area of the North Atlantic must have had its conditions unaffected by Tertiary or Post-tertiary oscillations.

One or two other questions of the highest scientific interest are to be solved by the proposed investigations:—

1st. The effect of pressure upon animal life at great depths. There is great misapprehension on this point. Probably a perfectly equal pressure to any amount would have little or no effect. Air being highly compressible, and water compressible only to a very slight degree, it is probable that under a pressure of 200 atmospheres, water may be even more aërated, and in that respect more capable of supporting life, than at the surface.

2nd. The effect of the great diminution of the stimulus of Light. From the condition of the Cave Fauna, this latter agent probably affects only the development of colour and of the organs of sight.

I have little doubt that it is quite practicable, with a small heavy dredge, and a couple of miles of stout Manilla rope, to dredge at a depth of 1,000 fathoms. Such an undertaking would, however, owing to the distance and the labour involved, be quite beyond the reach of private enterprise. What I am therefore anxious for is, that the Admiralty may be induced, perhaps at the instance of the Council of the Royal Society, to send a vessel (such as one of those which accompanied the Cable Expedition to take soundings) to carry out the research. I should be ready to go any time after July; and if you would take part in the investigation, I cannot but believe that it would give good results.

I would propose to start from Aberdeen, and to go first to the Rockall fishing-banks, where the depth is moderate, and thence north-westward, towards the coast of Greenland, rather to the north of Cape Farewell. We should thus keep pretty nearly along the isotherm of 39°, shortly reaching 1,000 fathoms depth, where, allowing 1,000 feet for oscillations in level, and 1,000 feet for influence of surface-currents, summer heat, &c., we should still have 4,000 feet of water whose conditions have probably not varied greatly since the commencement of the Eocene epoch.

Yours most truly,

WYVILLE THOMSON.

From Dr. Carpenter, V.P.R.S., to the President of the Royal Society.

UNIVERSITY OF LONDON, BURLINGTON HOUSE, W.
June 18th, 1868.

DEAR GENERAL SABINE,—During a recent visit to Belfast, I had the opportunity of examining some of the specimens (transmitted by Prof. Sars of Christiania to Prof. Wyville Thomson) which have been obtained by M. Sars, jun., Inspector of Fisheries to the Swedish Government, by *deep-sea* dredgings off the coast of Norway. These specimens, for reasons stated in the enclosed letter from Prof. Wyville Thomson, are of singular interest alike to the zoologist and to the palæontologist; and the discovery of them can scarcely fail to excite, both among naturalists and among geologists, a very strong desire that the zoology of the *deep sea*, especially in the Northern Atlantic region, should be more thoroughly and systematically explored than it has ever yet been. From what I know of your own early labours in this field, I cannot entertain a doubt of your full concurrence in this desire.

Such an exploration cannot be undertaken by private individuals, even when aided by grants from Scientific Societies. For dredging at great depths, a vessel of considerable size is requisite, with a trained crew, such as is only to be found in the Government service. It was by the aid of such an equipment, furnished by the Swedish Government, that the researches of M. Sars were carried on.

Now, as there are understood to be at the present time an unusual number of gun-boats and other cruisers on our northern and western coasts, which will probably remain on their stations until the end of the season, it has occurred to Prof. Wyville Thomson and myself, that the Admiralty, if moved thereto by the Council of the Royal Society, might be induced to place one of these vessels at the disposal of ourselves and of any other naturalists who might be willing to accompany us, for the purpose of carrying on a systematic course of deep-sea dredging for a month or six weeks of the present summer, commencing early in August.

Though we desire that this inquiry should be extended both in geographical range and in depth as far as is proposed in Prof. Wyville Thomson's letter, we think it preferable to limit ourselves on the present occasion to a request which will not, we believe, involve the extra expense of sending out a coaling-vessel. We should propose to make Kirkwall or Lerwick our port of departure, to explore the sea-bottom between the Shetland and the Færoe Islands, dredging around the shores and in the fiords of the latter (which have not yet, we believe, been scientifically examined), and then to proceed as far north-west into the deep water between the Færoe Islands and Iceland as may be found practicable.

It would be desirable that the vessel provided for such a service should be one capable of making way under canvas as well as by steam-power; but as our operations must necessarily be slow, *speed* would not be required. Considerable labour would be spared to the crew if the vessel be provided with a 'donkey-engine' that could be used for pulling up the dredge.

If the Council of the Royal Society should deem it expedient to prefer this request to the Admiralty, I trust that they may further be willing to place at the disposal of Prof. Wyville Thomson and myself, either from the Donation Fund or the Government-Grant Fund, a sum of £100 for the expenses we must incur in providing an ample supply of spirit and of jars for the preservation of specimens, with other scientific appliances. We would undertake that the choicest of such specimens should be deposited in the British Museum.

I shall be obliged by your bringing this subject before the Council of the Royal Society, and remain,

Dear General Sabine, yours faithfully,

WILLIAM B. CARPENTER.

The President of the Royal Society.

From the Minutes of the Council of the Royal Society, June 18, 1868.

These letters having been considered, it was resolved,—"That the proposal of Drs. Carpenter and Wyville Thomson be approved, and recommended to the favourable consideration of the authorities of the Admiralty; and that a sum, of not exceeding £100, be advanced from the Donation Fund to meet the expenses referred to in Dr. Carpenter's letter."

The following draft of a letter to be written by the Secretary, to the Secretary of the Admiralty, was approved :—

MY LORD,—I am directed to acquaint you, for the information of the Lords Commissioners of the Admiralty, that the President and Council of the Royal Society have had under their consideration a proposal by Dr. Carpenter, Vice-President of the Royal Society, and Dr. Wyville Thomson, Professor of Natural History in Queen's College, Belfast, for conducting dredging operations at greater depths than have heretofore been attempted in the localities which they desire to explore—the main purpose of such researches being to obtain information as to the existence, mode of life, and zoological relations of marine animals living at great depths, with a view to the solution of various questions relating to Animal Life, and having an important bearing on Geology and Palæontology. The objects of the operations which they wish to undertake, and the course which they would propose to follow, as well as the aid they desire to obtain from the Admiralty, are more fully set forth in the letter of Dr. Carpenter to the President, and that of Professor Thomson, copies of which I herewith enclose.

The President and Council are of opinion that important advantages may be expected to accrue to science from the proposed undertaking; accordingly they strongly recommend it to the favourable consideration of her Majesty's Government, and earnestly hope that the Lords Commissioners of the Admiralty may be disposed to grant the aid requested. In such case the scientific appliances required would be provided for from funds at the disposal of the Royal Society.

I am, &c.,

W. SHARPEY, Sec. R.S.

Lord H. Lennox, M.P., Secretary of the Admiralty.

From the Minutes of the Council of the Royal Society for Oct. 20, 1868.

ADMIRALTY, 14*th July*, 1868.

SIR,—In reply to your letter of the 22nd ultimo, submitting a proposition from Dr. Carpenter and Professor Thomson to investigate, by means of dredging, the bottom of the sea in certain localities, with a view to ascertain the existence and zoological relations of marine animals at great depths,—a research which you and the Council of the Royal Society strongly recommend in the interests of science to the favourable consideration of her Majesty's Government, for aid in furtherance of the undertaking,—I am commanded by my Lords Commissioners of the Admiralty to acquaint you that they are pleased to meet your wishes so far as the Service will admit, and have given orders for her Majesty's steam-vessel 'Lightning' to be prepared immediately, at Pembroke, for the purpose of carrying out such dredging operations.

I am, Sir,

Your obedient Servant,

W. G. ROMAINE.

To the President of the Royal Society.

It will be seen by the letters from my colleague and myself what our ideas were at that time, and what our anticipations as to the result of our labours. We both more than doubted the 'anti-biotic' view which was then very generally received, and we expected to be able to trace a relationship between the living inhabitants of the deep sea and the fossils of some of the later geological formations which we looked upon as their direct and not very remote ancestors. We had adopted the current strange misconception with regard to the distribution of ocean temperature; and it is perhaps scarcely a valid excuse that the fallacy of a universal and constant temperature of 4° C. below a certain depth varying according to latitude, was at the time accepted and taught by nearly all the leading authorities in Physical Geography.

From the time that the Admiralty gave their sanction to the use of a Government vessel for the investigation, Dr. Carpenter's labours in working out all the necessary arrangements and preparations were unceasing, and to his influence in the Council of the Royal Society, and to the confidence placed in his judgment by members of the Government and men in official positions, the success of the undertaking is unquestionably due.

The surveying ship 'Lightning' was assigned for the service—a cranky little vessel enough, one which had the somewhat doubtful title to respect of being perhaps the very oldest paddle-steamer in her Majesty's navy. We had not good times in the 'Lightning.' She kept out the water imperfectly, and as we had deplorable weather during nearly the whole of the six weeks we were afloat, we were in considerable discomfort. The vessel, in fact, was scarcely seaworthy, the iron hook and screw-jack fastenings of the rigging were worn with age, and many of them were carried away, and on two occasions the ship ran some risk. Still the voyage was on the whole almost pleasant. Staff-Commander May had lately returned from Annesley Bay, where he had been harbour-master during the Abyssinian war; and his intelligence and vivacity, and the cordial good-fellowship of his officers, who heartily seconded my colleague and myself in our work and sympathised with us in our keen interest in the curious results of the few trials at great depths which we had it in our power to make, made the experience, a very novel one to us, certainly as tolerable as possible.

The 'Lightning' left Pembroke on the 4th of August, 1868, and arrived at Oban on the evening of the 6th. At Oban Dr. Carpenter, his son Herbert, and I joined, and, after having taken observations for the chronometers, completed coals and water, and being otherwise ready, we left Oban on the 8th of August, anchored on that evening in Tobermory Bay, and after a gusty passage through the Minch we reached Stornoway on the evening of the 9th. At Stornoway we were received by Sir James and Lady Matheson with a courteous hospitality which on many subsequent occasions has made us leave their island kingdom with regret and return to it with pleasure. We took in as much coal as we could carry, stowing as much as was safe in bags on the deck, set up a dredging derrick over the stern, took final observations, and departed to the northward on the morning of the 11th. We took a haul or two the same afternoon in from 60 to 100 fathoms, about 15 miles to the north of the Butt of the Lews, to try our dredging-tackle and donkey-engine and to trace the limits of the shallow-water species. All the appliances worked well, but the dredge brought up few animal forms, and all of them well-known inhabitants of the seas of the Hebrides. The next day we were met by a breeze from the N.E., which continued for three days with such force that we were compelled to lie-to under canvas, drifting to the northward towards the edge of the Færoe Banks, any attempt to dredge being out of the question. On the 13th, during a lull, we sounded and found no bottom at 450 fathoms (Station 1, Pl. I.), with a minimum temperature of 9°·5 C., the temperature of the surface water being 12°·5 C. This was so high a temperature for so considerable a depth that we suspected some error in the indications of the thermometers, three of Six's registering instruments of the Hydrographic Office pattern. Subsequent observations however in the same locality showed us that the temperature to the depth of 600 to 700 fathoms in that region is the moderate temperature of the northward current of the gulf stream.

The Færoe Banks are greatly frequented in the fishing season by English and foreign fishing-smacks. Of course the principal object is to prepare cured or hard-fish, but many of the English vessels are welled for the supply of fresh cod for the London market.

A large square tank occupies the middle of the vessel, and holes in the sides allow the water to pass freely through it. The water in the tank is thus kept perfectly fresh; the best of the cod are put into it, and they stand the voyage perfectly. It is curious to see the great creatures moving gracefully about in the tank like gold-fish in a glass globe. They are no doubt 'quite unaccustomed to man,' and consequently they are tame; and with their long smooth mottled faces, their huge mouths, and lidless unspeculative eyes, they are about as unfamiliar objects as one can well see. They seem rather to like to be scratched, as they are greatly infested by *caligi* and all kinds of suctorial copepods. One of them will take a crab or a large fusus or buccinum quietly out of one's hand, and with a slight movement transfer it down its capacious throat into its stomach, where it is very soon attacked and disintegrated by the powerful gastric secretions. In one welled smack I visited on one occasion, one of the fish had met with some slight injury which spoiled its market, and it made several trips in the well between London and Færoe and became quite a pet. The sailors said it knew them. It was mixed up with a number of others in the tank when I was on board, and certainly it was always the first to come to the top for the chance of a crab or a bit of biscuit, and it rubbed its 'head and shoulders' against my hand quite lovingly.

On the 15th and 16th we dredged over the Færoe Banks at a depth of from 200 to 50 fathoms, the bottom gravel and nullipore, and the temperature from 8° to 10° C. The banks swarm with the common brittle star *Ophiothrix fragilis*, with the Norway lobster *Nephrops norvegicus*, large spider crabs, several species of the genus *Galathea*, and many of the genus *Crangon*. So ample a supply of their favourite food readily accounts for the abundance and excellence of the cod and ling on the banks.

There is some rough rocky ground on the Færoe Banks, and notwithstanding all possible care and the use of Hodge's 'accumulators' to ease the strain on the dredge ropes, we lost two of our best dredges and some hundreds of fathoms of rope. On the morning of the 17th we sighted Færoe, as usual only getting now and then a glimpse of the islands of this remote little archipelago by the lifting of the curtain of mist which almost constantly envelopes them. Towards mid-day the weather improved a little, and as we threaded among the islands towards the little harbour of Thorshavn we greatly enjoyed our first view of their fantastic outlines, partly shrouded in their veil of mist; their soft green and brown colouring rendered still softer by the subdued sub-arctic light, and the streams and cascades embroidering the gentle slopes of the hills and falling over the cliffs like silver threads and tassels.

The Færoe Islands are basaltic; terrace over terrace of soft easily decomposed anamesite probably of Miocene tertiary age. This uniform structure, and the absence of trees or any prominent form of vegetation, gives a singular sameness of effect. The scattered habitations are usually sad-coloured and roofed with growing turf, so that they are actually invisible at a little distance. We were greatly struck sometimes by the difficulty of estimating distance and height; from the total want of familiar objects for comparison it was sometimes difficult to tell, passing among the islands and looking at them through the moist transparent air, whether the ridge was 500 feet high, or double or four times that height. The intermediate height is usually nearest the truth.

Thorshavn, the capital of Færoe, is a strange little place. The land shelves down rather abruptly to a little bay, round the head of which the town is built; and the habitations are perched among the rocks on such flat spaces as may be found for their reception. The result is irregular and picturesque; and very peculiar, for something like a scramble is necessary to get along some of the principal 'streets.' Above the town a little clearing forms a miniature lawn and garden gay with bright flowers in front of the Governor's house, a pretty wooden cottage residence like a villa in a suburb of one of the Scandinavian towns.

Færoe, with its wet sunless climate and precarious crops of barley; its turf-thatched cottages and quiet little churches; its glorious cliffs and headlands and picturesque islets, the haunt of the eider-duck and the puffin; and its hardy, friendly islanders, with their quaint, simple, semi-Icelandic semi-Danish customs, has been described again and again. Færoe only came to us as a pleasant haven of rest in the middle of our northern work. We paid it two visits of a week each in successive years, and one of the most pleasant memories in the minds of all of us connected with these expeditions will always be the cordial sympathy which we received from our friend M. Holten the Danish Governor, and his accomplished wife. M. Holten received us with the most friendly hospitality, and did everything in his power at all times to render us assistance and to further our views. He introduced us to the leading inhabitants of his dominion, and during the many pleasant evenings which we spent at his residence we heard all that we could of the economy of this simple little community, perhaps the most primitive and the most isolated in Europe. To Governor Holten I have already had the pleasure of dedicating a singularly beautiful sponge-form which we discovered during our return voyage; and to Madame Holten, to whose graceful pencil I am indebted for the vignettes of Færoe scenery which so appropriately close these chapters, I now dedicate this volume, in remembrance of the great kindness which we invariably experienced from her and from her excellent husband.

We lay in Thorshavn harbour till the 26th of August, the weather being so bad as to make all idea of pursuing our work outside hopeless. Whenever it was possible we dredged in the fiords with Færoese boats and native boatmen, and we made the acquaintance of Sysselman Müller, the representative of Færoe in the Danish Parliament, who had made himself thoroughly conversant with the mollusca of Færoe, and had contributed his information to a list published in 1867 by Dr. O. A. L. Mörch. The shallow-water fauna seems to be scanty, as we find frequently to be the case on a bed of decomposing trap. It is of a character intermediate between that of Shetland and the Scandinavian coast. The forms which perhaps interested us most were *Fusus despectus*, L.—a handsome shell which may possibly be only a very marked variety of *Fusus antiquus*, L.; but if so, it is one with very definite limit of distribution, as it occurs only rarely in very deep water in the British seas. In water of moderate depth among the Færoes it is abundant, apparently replacing *F. antiquus*. Another common Færoe shell is *Tellina calcarea*, CHEMNITZ,—a very abundant British glacial clay fossil, but not hitherto found recent in the British area. In the glacial clays near Rothesay it is in regular beds associated with *Mya truncata*, L., var. *uddevallensis*, FORBES; *Saxicava norvegica*, SPRENGLER; *Pecten islandicus*, O. F. MÜLLER, and other northern forms, and frequently so fresh that the two valves are still in position and held together by their connecting ligament. A somewhat peculiar variety of *Echinus sphæra*, O. F. MÜLLER, was met with in one of the Fjords associated with a large form of *E. flemingii*, BALL; and what appears to be a small form of *Cucumaria frondosa*, GUNNER, was very common in shallow water on the tangles.

While we were lying in Thorshavn harbour the Danish gunboat 'Fylla' and the French steam transport 'L'Orient' came in on their way from Iceland. Both of the vessels from the north had come through bad weather, and were glad to run into shelter. During the stay of the three war-ships the little capital was quite gay, and the Governor had abundant opportunity of exercising his genial hospitality. On the 26th of August, as the barometer rose a little and there seemed to be some slight sign of improvement, we left Thorshavn and steamed southward to dredge if possible in the deep channel between Færoe and Shetland; but the same evening wild weather set in again with a strong gale of wind from the north-westward, and the barometer down to 29·08. The hook and screw-jack fastenings of the main rigging went one after another, and we narrowly escaped losing the mast. The gale lasted till the 29th, when there was rather better weather; and after lying-to and drifting to the north-east for nearly three days, we took a sounding in lat. 60° 45′ N., long. 4° 49′ W. (Station 6). This gave a depth of 510 fathoms and a bottom temperature of 0° C. On the evening of the 29th and on the 30th the weather was sufficiently moderate to allow us to work our dredging gear, and the first trials were of great interest, as it was our first opportunity of making the attempt in so great a depth of water. The operation seemed however to present no special difficulty, and nearly every haul was successful. The bottom was sand and gravel, mostly derived from the disintegration of the old rocks of the Scottish plateau. Animal life was not abundant, but several groups were fairly represented. Sandy rhizopods of a large size were numerous, and there were several conspicuous crustaceans and echinoderms, among the latter an example of *Astropecten tenuispinus*, of a brilliant scarlet colour, which came up entangled on the line.

On the 31st bad weather set in again, and we could neither sound nor dredge. On the 1st of September we got one temperature sounding in 550 fathoms with $-1^{\circ}\cdot 2$ C., but could do no work.

The next day, September 2, was more moderate, and we dredged all day at a depth of only 170 fathoms over a very restricted shoal, which, singularly enough, we could not find when we sought for it the year after in the 'Porcupine.' Here we found animal life abundant and varied—a mixture of celtic and scandinavian forms. The bottom was chiefly small rounded pebbles of the dark anamesite of the Færoes, and sticking to them, singly or in little groups like plums on their stems, were many large specimens of the rare brachiopod *Terebratula cranium*, O. F. MÜLLER, along with abundance of the commoner form *Terebratulina caput-serpentis*, L.

The following day, September 3, we were again in deep water, about 500 fathoms, with a bottom temperature a little below the freezing-point, the thermometer at the surface giving $10^{\circ}\cdot 5$ C. Here we took representatives of many invertebrate groups—rhizopods, sponges, echinoderms, crustaceans, and molluscs;

among them a magnificent specimen of a new star-fish which has been since described by M. G. O. Sars under the name of *Brisinga coronata* (Fig. 5). The genus *Brisinga* was discovered in 1853 by M. P. Chr. Absjörnsen, who then dredged several specimens of another species, *B. endecacnemos*, ABSJ., at a depth of 100 to 200 fathoms in the Hardangerfjord on the Norway coast a little to the south of Bergen.* These are certainly very wonderful creatures. At first sight they look intermediate between ophiurids and star-fishes, the arms too thick and soft for the former, but much more long and delicate than we usually find them in the latter group.

The disk is small, about 20 to 25 mm. in diameter; in *B. endecacnemos* nearly smooth, in *B. coronata* covered with spines. The madreporiform tubercle is on the dorsal surface close to the edge of the disk. A firm ring of calcareous ossicles forms and supports the edge of the disk, and gives attachment to the arms. The arms are ten or eleven in number: the latter number is probably abnormal. They are sometimes as much as 30 centimetres in length; narrow at the base, where they are inserted into the ring; enlarging considerably towards the middle, where the ovaries are developed; and tapering again to the end. Rows of long spines border the ambulacral grooves; the spines are covered with a soft skin, which, when the animal is quite fresh, forms a little transparent, sack-like expansion full of fluid at the end of each spine. The soft covering of the spines is full of small pedicellariæ, and pedicellariæ are likewise scattered in groups over the surface of the arms and disk.

The arms in *B. endecacnemos* are nearly smooth,

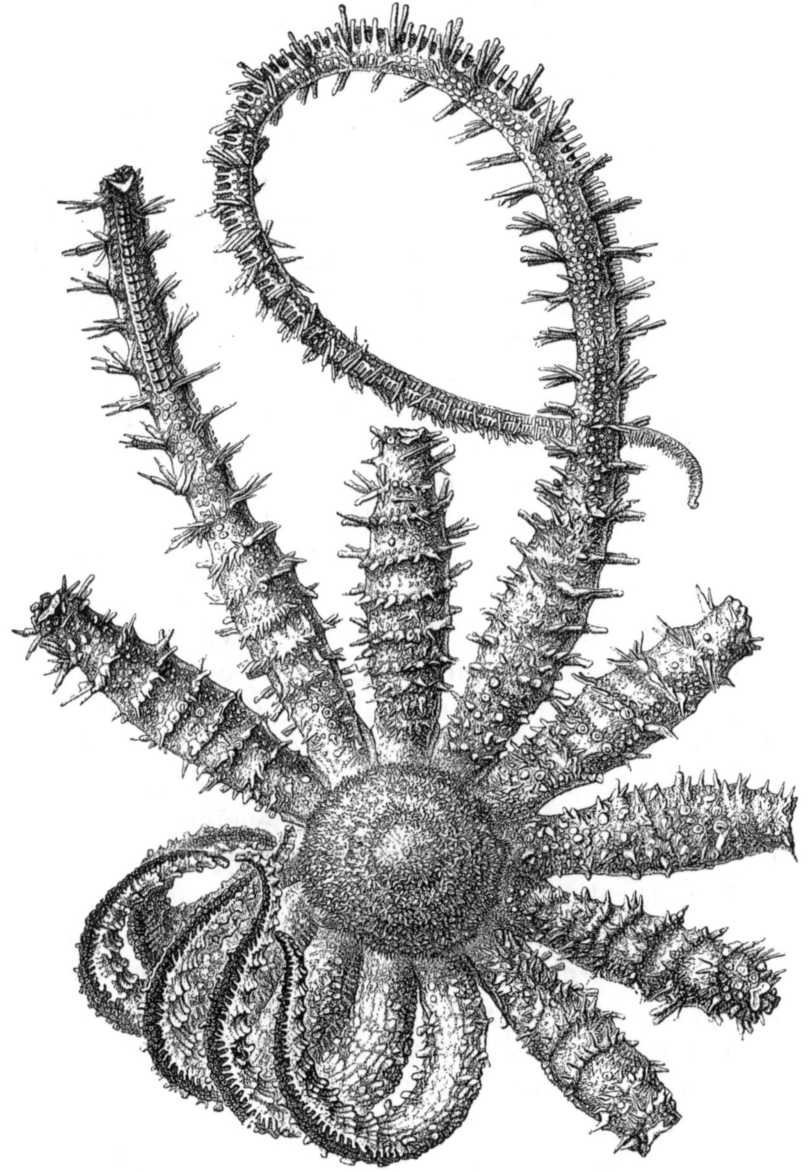

FIG. 5.—*Brisinga coronata*, G. O. SARS. Natural size. (No. 7.)

ribbed transversely here and there by slightly raised calcareous bands passing irregularly partly or wholly across them. In *B. coronata* these ridges are surmounted by crests of spines. Both species are of a rich crimson colour, passing into orange-scarlet. The arms are easily detached from the disk. We never got one of either species nearly entire, but even coming up in pieces they were certainly the most striking objects we met with. One was sufficient to give a glorious dash of colour to a whole dredgeful. "Le nom Brisinga est dérivé d'un bijou brillant (Brising) de la déesse Freya," which brings a pleasant flavour of Scandinavian heathendom about it. "J'ai trouvé cette Astérie brillante à Hardangerfjord à l'aide du dredge à la fin du mois d'août 1853, à la profondeur de 100 à 200 brasses, où elle était placée sur le plan latéral et perpendiculaire d'une montagne, qui semblait descendre de 80 à 90 brasses jusqu'à 200 brasses et même de plus. Elle se trouve bien rarement; en draguant plus de huit jours avec beaucoup d'assiduité dans la même localité et dans les environs je trouvais seulement quelques bras, et quelques individus plus ou moins grands, dont le plus petit entre les pointes des bras opposés avait une grandeur de 6 pouces, le plus grand environ 2 pieds de diamètre. Aucun d'eux n'était sans être endommagé; l'animal est extrêmement fragile et semble, comme les comatules et quelques espèces d'Ophiolepis et d'Ophiotrix, à cause de la pression diminuante de l'eau, tiré vers la surface, par un effort vigoureux, se défaire de ces bras, qui toujours se détachent à l'endroit où ils sont unis avec l'anneau du disque. Le surpois du bras en comparaison du disque très petit, et la grandeur considérable de l'animal, augmente aussi les difficultés à le faire sortir du dredge sans être déchiré. Quoique je fusse assez heureux pour le saisir avant qu'il sortait de l'eau, et malgré toute la précaution possible, je réussis seulement à conserver deux disques d'une paire de bras fermes, mais à ceux-ci même le peau était rompue. Quand l'animal est complet et cohérent, ainsi que je l'ai vu une ou deux fois sous l'eau dans le dredge, il est véritablement un exemplaire de luxe, une 'gloria maris.' "[1]

The bad weather was unrelenting, and again interrupted us for a couple of days: we got a sounding however on the 5th of September, in lat. 60° 30′ N. and long. 7° 16′ W., with no bottom at 450 fathoms and a minimum temperature about the freezing-point. It will be seen by the chart that the last five stations, Nos. 7 to 11, form an oblique line from south-east to north-west between the northern part of Orkney and the Færoe Bank. The bottom is throughout a mixture of gravel and sand, with patches of mud; Nos. 7 and 8 principally the débris of the metamorphic rocks of the north of Scotland; Nos. 9, 10, and 11 chiefly volcanic, the detritus of the Færoe traps. This line of soundings is entirely within what we afterwards learned to call the 'cold area,' the thermometer for depths below 300 fathoms indicating a temperature slightly above or below 0° C.

As we were now again approaching the Færoe fishing-banks, we shaped our course southwards, and on the morning of September 6th we sounded and

[1] Description d'un Nouveau Genre des Astéries, par P. Chr. Absjörnsen, in "Fauna littoralis Norvegiæ," by Dr. M. Sars, J. Koren, and D. C. Danielssen. Seconde Livraison. Bergen, 1856, p. 96.

dredged in lat. 59° 36′, long. 7° 20′ (Station 12), with a depth of 530 fathoms and a 'warm area' temperature of 6°·4 C. The dredging here was most interesting. The bottom was for the first time 'Atlantic ooze,' a fine bluish-grey tenacious calcareous mud, with some sand and a considerable admixture of *Globigerinæ.* Imbedded in this mud there came up an extraordinary number of silicious sponges of most remarkable and novel forms. Most of these belonged to an order which had been described by the writer a couple of years before as 'Porifera vitrea,' a tribe at that time but little known, but which have since become very familiar to us as denizens of the abyssal zone. Working from more extended data, Professor Oscar Schmidt afterwards defined the group more exactly as a family, under the name of *Hexactinellidæ*—the term which I shall here adopt.

The relations and peculiarities of this singular group will be fully discussed in a future chapter. The most characteristic forms which we met with on this occasion were the beautiful sea-nests of the Setubal shark-fishers, *Holtenia carpenteri,* Wy. T. (Fig. 6), and the even more strange *Hyalonema lusitanicum,* Barboza de Bocage, closely related to the glass-rope sponges of Japan which have so long perplexed naturalists to determine their position in the animal series, and their relation to their constant companion the parasitic *Palythoa.*

Holtenia carpenteri is an oval or sphere 90 to 100 mm. in height, with one large oscular opening at the top about 30 mm. in diameter, whence a simple cylindrical cavity cupped at the bottom passes down vertically into the substance of the sponge to the depth of 55 mm. The outer wall of the sponge

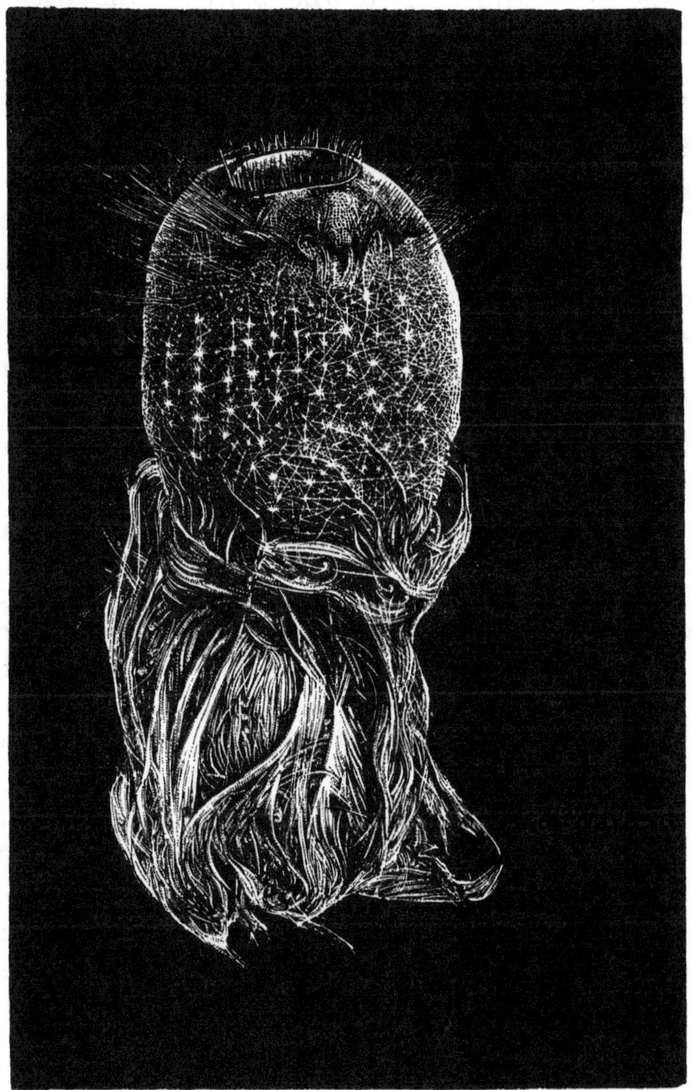

FIG. 6.—*Holtenia carpenteri*, WYVILLE THOMSON. Half the natural size. (No. 12.)

consists of a complicated network of the cross-like

heads of five-rayed spicules. One ray of each spicule dips directly into the body of the sponge, and the other four, which are at right angles to it, form a cross on the surface, giving it a beautiful stellate appearance. The silicious rays of one star curve towards and meet the rays of the neighbouring stars, and run parallel with them. All the rays of all the spicules are thickly invested with consistent semi-transparent gelatinous matter, which binds their concurrent branches together by an elastic union, and fills up the angles of the meshes with softly curved viscous masses. This arrangement of the spicules, free and yet adhering together by long elastic connections, produces a strong, flexible, and very extensible tissue. The cylindrical oscular cavity within the sponge is lined with nearly the same kind of network.

When the sponge is living, the interstices of the silicious network are filled up both outside and in with a delicate fenestrated membrane formed of a glairy substance like white of egg, which is constantly moving, extending or contracting the fenestræ, and gliding over the surface of the spicules. This 'sarcode,' which is the living flesh of the sponge, contains distributed through it an infinite number of very minute spicules, presenting the most singular and elegant forms very characteristic of each species of sponge. A constant current of water carried along by the action of cilia passes in by apertures in the outer wall, courses through the passages in the loose texture of the intermediate sponge-substance carrying organic matter in solution and particles of nourishment into all its interstices, and finally passes out by the large 'osculum' at the top. Over the upper third of the sponge a multitude of radiating rigid silicious spicules form a kind of ornamental frill, and from the lower third a perfect maze of delicate glassy filaments, like fine white hair, spread out in all directions, penetrating the semi-fluid mud, and supporting the sponge in its precarious bed by increasing its surface indefinitely while adding but little to its weight.

This is only one of the ways by which sponges anchor themselves in the ooze of the deep sea. *Hyalonema* sends right down through the soft mud a coiled whisp of strong spicules, each as thick as a knitting needle, which open out into a brush as the bed gets firmer, and fix the sponge in its place somewhat on the principle of a screw pile. A very singular sponge from deep water off the Loffoten Islands spreads into a thin circular cake, and adds to its surface by sending out a flat border of silky spicules, like a fringe of white floss-silk round a little yellow mat; and the lovely *Euplectella*, whose beauty is imbedded up to its fretted lid in the grey mud of the seas of the Philippines, is supported by a frill of spicules standing up round it like Queen Elizabeth's ruff.

The sponges of the deep-water ooze are by no means confined to one group. The *Hexactinellidæ* are perhaps the most abundant, but corticate sponges even, closely allied to those which look so rigid when fixed to stones in shallow water, send out long anchoring spicules and balance themselves in the soft mud (Fig. 7); and off the coast of Portugal Mr. Gwyn Jeffreys dredged in 1870 several small forms of the *Halichondridæ*, with long supporting fibrous beards.

From its appearance when brought up *Holtenia* evidently lives buried in the mud to its upper fringe of spicules. When freshly dredged, it is loaded with

FIG. 7.—*Tisiphonia agariciformis*, WYVILLE THOMSON. Natural size. (No. 12.)

pale grey semi-fluid sarcode, full of *Globigerinæ*, *Triloculinæ*, and other rhizopods, and covered in our northern localities with the little ophiurid *Amphiura abyssicola*, SARS, and the exquisitely delicate transparent clam, *Pecten vitreus*, CHEMNITZ. *Holtenia* extends from the Butt of the Lews to Gibraltar, in from 500 to 1,000 fathoms. Mr. Saville Kent, dredging in Mr. Marshall Hall's yacht 'Norna,' found a singular variety off the coast of Portugal, which from its flatter, more hemispherical form, and more rigid anchoring spicules, probably inhabits a firmer medium.[1]

As might be expected, the Atlantic ooze of this station, rich in rhizopods giving an ample supply of food, and with a comparatively mild climate, yielded many living forms belonging to various orders. Along with *Globigerinæ* and other small forms there were many large rhizopods, among them *Rhabdammina abyssorum*, SARS, a singularly regular triradiate sandy form of a bright orange colour, and very hard; from analyses made by Dr. Williamson at the request of Dr. Carpenter, its hardness is apparently owing to the cement employed by the animal in the construction of its case containing phosphate of iron, the only instance of the use of this substance for such a purpose of which we are yet aware: *Astrorhiza limicola*, SANDAHL, a large irregularly-formed rhizopod with a soft test of mud and sand: many large *Cornuspiræ* and *Textulariæ*, and large *Bi-* and *Triloculinæ* and other miliolines: a few zoophytes, and especially common the curious sea-pen *Kophobelemmon mülleri*, SARS, and the fine branching coral,

[1] On the Hexactinellidæ, or Hexradiate Spiculed Silicious Sponges, taken in the 'Norna' Expedition off the coast of Portugal; with Description of New Species and Revision of the Order. By W. Saville Kent, F.L.S., F.R.M.S., of the Geological Department, British Museum. (Monthly Microscopic Journal, November 1st, 1870.)

Lophohelia prolifera, PALLAS: among Echinoderms some beautiful varieties of *Echinus norvegicus*, D. and K., *E. elegans*, D. and K., *Ophiocten sericeum*, FORBES, and *Ophiacantha spinulosa*, M. and T., which seems to be universal in deep water, and the curious little crinoid *Rhizocrinus loffotensis*, SARS, which will be described hereafter: some remarkable crustaceans, including as one of the most prominent a scarlet *Munida* with remarkably large brilliant eyes, of the colour and lustre of burnished copper.

We now proceeded towards Stornoway, which we reached on the 9th of September, dredging on our way in shallowing water, and still meeting with interesting things such as *Antedon celticus*, BARRETT, collected previously by Mr. Gwyn Jeffreys on the coast of Ross-shire; abundance of 'the piper,' *Cidaris papillata*, LESKE, until lately one of the prizes of the British collector, now known to be perhaps the most abundant of the larger living forms at depths from 250 to 500 fathoms in the British seas.

The weather now looked more promising. I was unfortunately obliged to return to my duties in Dublin; but as the results already obtained led Dr. Carpenter strongly to desire an opportunity of examining both the temperature and the animal life of still deeper waters, it was thought by him and Captain May that, notwithstanding the lateness of the season, it would be worth while to venture another short cruise in a westerly direction, where it was known from previous soundings that the depth was beyond 1,000 fathoms. Accordingly, after re-fitting, an operation which in some respects was sorely needed, and restoring as far as possible the lost dredging gear, the 'Lightning' once more steamed out of Stornoway Harbour on the 14th of September.

After a fine run of 140 miles in a north-westerly direction from the Butt of the Lews, a sounding was taken on the morning of September 15th, in lat. 59° 59′, long. 9° 15′, with a bottom of Atlantic ooze, at a depth of 650 fathoms (Station 14). Still running north-westward sixty miles further, another sounding was taken on the 18th, at 570 fathoms, when the scoop of the sounding instrument brought up scarcely anything but entire *Globigerinæ*, like the finest sago. Fifty miles further, in the same direction, bottom was found at 650 fathoms; but on this occasion the sounding-lead and three thermometers were unfortunately lost in hauling up, so that the temperature was not ascertained. A haul of the dredge was taken, however, at this great depth, 120 fathoms deeper than at any of the previous stations, perfectly successfully, the dredge bringing up 2½ cwt. of very viscid greyish white mud. The mud was everywhere traversed by the long glassy root-fibres of anchoring sponges, and about 50 fathoms from the dredge there were two white tufts of such fibres sticking to the rope, no doubt pulled off the ground, as they entangled in their meshes some ophiurids, some small crustaceans, and one or two tube-forming annelids. In the mud was a remarkable sea-pen, which Professor Kölliker, who has undertaken the description of such things procured in our several expeditions, refers to a new genus under the name of *Bathyptilum carpenteri*, and some large foraminifera. Dr. Carpenter now stood due north, wishing to get into the deep trough between the Hebrides and

Rockall, and on the morning of September 17th sounded at a depth of 620 fathoms, in lat. 59° 49′, long. 12° 36′, with a 'warm area' temperature.

The weather now again broke, became too unfavourable for work, and grew worse until the forenoon of the 20th, when St. Kilda was in sight and it was blowing a strong gale with a heavy sea. At daylight on Monday the 21st off Barra Head the south point of the Hebrides, a fresh easterly wind blowing the barometer low and appearances suspicious, Capt. May did not deem it advisable to stand to sea again. He therefore, after consultation with Dr. Carpenter, determined to conclude the work, proceeded down the Sound of Mull, and anchored at Oban on the same afternoon.

At Oban Dr. Carpenter and his young son, who had manfully borne no little hardship and helped to lighten the evil times to his seniors, went on shore and proceeded southwards by land.

Her fate pursued the 'Lightning.' After lying a couple of days at Oban, Captain May started for Pembroke on the 24th September. On the 25th off the Calf of Man, the barometer having suddenly fallen and the wind and sea fast rising, he determined to run for Holyhead, when suddenly, without increase of wind and in a roll not heavier than usual, the whole of the weather fore-rigging went by the straightening or breaking of the iron hooks which held it. Luckily the mast did not fall, and after an hour spent in temporarily repairing it the 'Lightning' proceeded on her course and anchored in the new harbour of Holyhead about 6 P.M.

The general results of the 'Lightning' expedition

were upon the whole as satisfactory as we had ventured to anticipate. The vessel was certainly not well suited for the purpose, and the weather throughout the cruise was very severe. During the six weeks which elapsed between our departure from Oban and our return only ten days were available for dredging in the open sea, and on four of these only we were in water over 500 fathoms deep. On our return Dr. Carpenter submitted to the Royal Society a preliminary report on the general results of the cruise, and these were regarded by the Council of the Society as sufficiently new and valuable to justify a strong representation to the Admiralty urging the importance of continuing an investigation which had already, even under unfavourable circumstances, achieved a fair measure of success.

It had been shown beyond question that animal life is varied and abundant, represented by all the invertebrate groups, at depths in the ocean down to 650 fathoms at least, notwithstanding the extraordinary conditions to which animals are there exposed.

It had been determined that, instead of the water of the sea beyond a certain depth varying according to latitude having a uniform temperature of 4° C., an indraught of Arctic water may have at any depth beyond the influence of the direct rays of the sun a temperature so low as − 2° C.; or on the other hand, a warm current may have at any moderate depth a temperature of 6°·5 C.: and it had been shown that great masses of water at different temperatures are moving about, each in its particular course; maintaining a remarkable system of oceanic circulation, and yet keeping so distinct from one another that an hour's sail may be sufficient to pass from the extreme of heat to the extreme of cold.

Finally, it had been shown that a large proportion of the forms living at great depths in the sea belong to species hitherto unknown, and that thus a new field of boundless extent and great interest is open to the naturalist. It had been further shown that many of these deep-sea animals are specifically identical with tertiary fossils hitherto believed to be extinct, while others associate themselves with and illustrate extinct groups of the fauna of more remote periods; as, for example, the vitreous sponges illustrate and unriddle the ventriculites of the chalk.

THORSHAVN.

APPENDIX A.

Particulars of Depth, Temperature, and Position at the various Dredging Stations of H.M.S. 'Lightning,' in the Summer of 1868; the Temperatures corrected for pressure.

Number of Station.	Depth in Fathoms.	Bottom Temperature.	Surface Temperature.	Position.	
6	510	0°·5 C.	11°·1 C.	60° 45′ N.	4° 49′ W.
7	500	1·1	10·5	60 7	5 21
8	550	−1·2	11·7	60 10	5 59
10	500	0·3	10·5	60 28	6 55
11	450	−0·5	10·0	60 30	7 16
12	530	6·4	11·3	59 36	7 20
14	650	5·8	11·7	59 59	9 15
15	570	6·4	11·1	60 38	11 7
17	620	6·4	11·1	59 49	12 36

CHAPTER III.

THE CRUISES OF THE 'PORCUPINE.'

The Equipment of the Vessel.—The first Cruise, under the direction of Mr. Gwyn Jeffreys, off the West Coast of Ireland and in the Channel between Scotland and Rockall.—Dredging carried down to 1,470 fathoms.—Change of Arrangements.—Second Cruise; to the Bay of Biscay.—Dredging successful at 2,435 fathoms.—Third Cruise; in the Channel between Færoe and Shetland.—The Fauna of the 'Cold Area.'

APPENDIX A.—Official Documents and Official Accounts of preliminary Proceedings in connection with the Explorations in H.M. Surveying-vessel 'Porcupine,' during the Summer of 1869.

APPENDIX B.—Particulars of Depth, Temperature, and Position at the various Dredging Stations of H.M.S. 'Porcupine,' in the Summer of 1869.

*** *The bracketed numbers to the woodcuts in this chapter refer to the dredging stations on Plates II., III., and IV.*

ON the 18th of March, 1869, an oral communication was made by the Hydrographer to the Navy that the Lords Commissioners of the Admiralty had acceded to the wish of the Council of the Royal Society, and that H.M. Surveying-vessel 'Porcupine' had been assigned for the service.

The equipment of the 'Porcupine' progressed rapidly under the direction of her commander, Captain Calver, with the careful superintendence in all matters bearing upon the efficiency of the scientific appliances, of Dr. Carpenter assisted by a committee composed of the officers and a few of the members of the Royal Society. The 'Porcupine,' though a small vessel, was well suited for the work; thoroughly seaworthy, very steady, and fitted up for surveying purposes. Captain Calver and his officers had long been engaged in the arduous and responsible duty of conducting the survey of the east coast of Britain, and were trained to minute accuracy and thoroughly versed in the use of instruments and in the bearings of scientific investigation. The crew were chiefly known and tried men, Shetlanders who had spent many successive summers in the 'Porcupine' under Captain Calver's command; returning to their homes in Shetland for the winter, while the vessel was laid up and the officers employed in bringing up their office work at their head-quarters in Sunderland.

The working of the dredge was superintended throughout by Captain Calver, whose trained ability very early gave him so complete a mastery over the operation that he found no difficulty in carrying it down to depths at which this kind of exploration would have been previously deemed out of the question. It is impossible to speak too highly of the skill he displayed, or too warmly of the sympathy he showed in our work. It is a pleasure to add that the other officers of the 'Porcupine,' Staff-Commander Inskip, Mr. Davidson, and Lieutenant Browning, most heartily and zealously seconded their commander in promoting alike the scientific objects of the expedition and the welfare and comfort of all who were engaged in carrying them out.

As it was intended that the exploration in the 'Porcupine' in the summer of 1869 should occupy much more time, and if possible be much more thorough than that in the 'Lightning' the year before, the preparations for the 'Porcupine' expedition were much more elaborate and comprehensive. The Committee of the Royal Society were desirous that various important questions as to the physical condition and chemical composition of the water at great depths should be investigated; and the singular temperature results of the former cruise ably discussed by Dr. Carpenter in his preliminary report had excited so much curiosity and interest that their further elucidation was regarded as vieing in importance with that of the distribution and conditions of animal life. It was consequently decided that the naturalists directing the expedition should be accompanied by assistants trained in chemical and physical work, and the chart-room of the vessel was fitted up as a temporary laboratory, with physical and chemical apparatus and microscopes.

The vessel was available from the beginning of May to the middle of September, and as it was impossible for those who had conducted the previous expedition to be absent so long from their public duties, it was resolved to have three separate cruises; and Mr. Gwyn Jeffreys, F.R.S., whose co-operation was specially valuable from his thorough knowledge of the species and distribution of recent and fossil mollusca, was associated with Dr. Carpenter and myself, and undertook the scientific charge of the first cruise.

Mr. Gwyn Jeffreys was accompanied by Mr. W.

Lant Carpenter, B.Sc., as chemist and physicist; and during the first cruise they explored the west coast of Ireland, the Porcupine Bank, and the channel between Rockall and the coast of Scotland. It was originally arranged that the second expedition, under the charge of the writer with the assistance of Mr. Hunter, M.A., F.C.S., assistant in the Chemical Laboratory in Belfast, in the physical department, should take up the ground to the north of Rockall, leading northwards to the point where we had left off the year before; but subsequently, for reasons which will be explained hereafter, we altered our plan and took the second cruise in the Bay of Biscay. Dr. Carpenter took the direction of the last cruise, in which we carefully worked over the 'Lightning channel,' and checked our previous observations; Mr. P. Herbert Carpenter, our former companion in the 'Lightning,' doing the analyses of water, and determining the amount and composition of its contained air; while I went as supernumerary and made myself generally useful.

The special appliances and apparatus which were prepared under Dr. Carpenter's superintendence, after much consultation among experts in different departments, for carrying out the various investigations, will be described, each in its place, when describing the several methods of investigation and their general results.

For the management of the dredging operations two assistants were appointed on the recommendation of Mr. Gwyn Jeffreys,—Mr. Laughrin, of Polperro, an old coast-guard man and an associate of the Linnæan Society, for dredging and sifting; and Mr. B. S. Dodd, for picking out, cleaning, and storing the specimens procured. Both remained with us the whole summer.

The first cruise of the 'Porcupine' under the scientific charge of Mr. Gwyn Jeffreys commenced on the 18th of May and ended on the 13th of July. It extended for a distance of about 450 miles along the Atlantic coasts of Ireland and Scotland, from Cape Clear to Rockall; and included Lough Swilly and Lough Foyle and the North Channel to Belfast.

The first dredgings were made about 40 miles off Valentia, in 110 fathoms water with a bottom of mud and sand. The result of this dredging gives a fair idea of the fauna of the 100-fathom line on the west coast of Ireland. The mollusca are mostly northern species, such as *Neæra rostrata*, SPRENGLER; *Verticordia abyssicola*, JEFFREYS; *Dentalium abyssorum*, SARS; *Buccinum humphreysianum*, BENNETT; and *Pleurotoma carinatum*, BIVONA. Some however, as *Ostrea cochlear*, POLI; *Aporrhaïs serresianus*, MICHAUD; *Murex lamellosus*, CRISTOFORI and JAN; and *Trochus granulatus*, BORN,—are Mediterranean forms, and impart somewhat of a southern character to the assemblage. *Cidaris papillata*, LESKE; *Echinus rarispina*, G. O. SARS; *E. elegans*, D. and K.; *Spatangus raschi*, LOVÉN; and several varieties of *Caryophyllia borealis*, FLEMING, were abundant: but these species seem to abound at a depth of from 100 to 200 fathoms from the Mediterranean to the North Cape.

After coaling at Galway they proceeded southwards, and as the weather was very rough and unpromising they dredged in shallow water, from 20 to 40 fathoms, in Dingle Bay: and the next week, with improving weather, off Valentia and between Valentia and Galway, at depths varying from 80 to 808 fathoms (Station 2), with a temperature at the latter depth of 5°·2 C. The general character of the fauna was that which we have hitherto been in the habit of regarding as Northern. Several interesting things were met with—*Nucula tumidula*, MALM.; *Leda frigida*, TORELL; *Verticordia abyssicola*, JEFFREYS; and *Siphonodentalium quinquangulare*, FORBES. Among the echinoderms a multitude of the large form of *Echinus norvegicus*, D. and K., which I am now inclined to regard, along with several of its allies, as a mere variety of *E. flemingii*, BALL; and the fine asterid already mentioned, *Brisinga coronata*, G. O. SARS. Some interesting crustaceans, including *Gonoplax rhomboides*, FAB. (Fig. 8), a well-known Mediterranean species, and a young specimen of *Geryon tridens*, KROYER (Fig. 9), a rare Scandinavian form, and the only known North European brachyurous crustacean

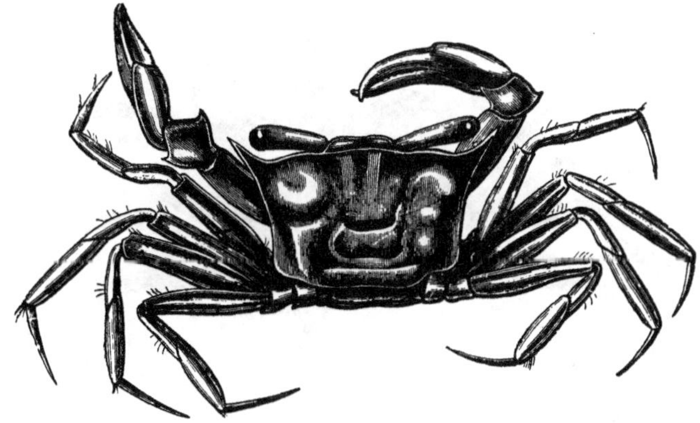

FIG. 8.—*Gonoplax rhomboides*, FABRICIUS. Young. Twice the natural size. (No. 3.)

which had not previously been taken in the British seas.

Here the Miller-Casella thermometers were tried for the first time and compared with those of the ordinary construction. The minimum recorded by one of the former was 5°·2 C., while that recorded by one of the best ordinary instruments of the Hydrographic Office pattern was 7°·3 C. As this difference of 2° C. was almost exactly what the results of the experiment previously made had indicated as the effect

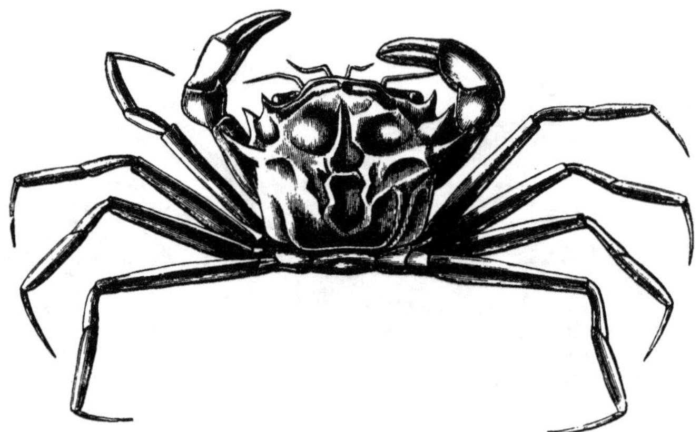

FIG. 9.—*Geryon tridens*, KROYER. Young. Twice the natural size. (No. 7.)

of a pressure of 1 ton on the square inch, which is about equal to the pressure of a column of sea-water of 800 fathoms, this close coincidence gave great confidence in the practical working of the protected instrument, a confidence which all subsequent experience has fully justified.

Mr. Gwyn Jeffreys and his companions next proceeded to examine the sea-bed between Galway and Porcupine Bank, a shoal discovered during one of the previous cruises of our little vessel under the command of Lieut. Hoskyn, R.N. The deepest dredging of this excursion was 1,230 fathoms, with a minimum temperature of 3°·2 C., and a bottom of fine grey mud with a considerable admixture of sand. Animals were abundant even at this great depth: among the mollusca several new forms allied to *Arca; Trochus minutissimus*, MIGHEL, a North American species; and several others; several crustaceans, and many interesting foraminifera. As in previous dredgings in deep water, the miliolines were of very large size, and the large cristellarians showed every gradation in their axis of growth from the rectilineal to the spiral. In the shallower dredgings of this cruise the general character of the fauna was much the same as before. It had what we have been in the habit of considering a northern 'facies,' but probably, as already explained, because the largely extended deep-water fauna at a temperature of 0° to + 3° C., of which it forms a part, has hitherto only been investigated off the coast of Scandinavia, where it crops up within reach of observation.

Limopsis aurita, BROCCHI; *Arca glacialis*, GRAY; *Verticordia abyssicola*, JEFFREYS; *Dentalium abyssorum*, SARS; *Trochus cinereus*, DA COSTA; *Fusus despectus*, L.; *F. islandicus*, CHEM.; *F. fenestratus*, TURT; *Columbella haliæeti*, JEFFREYS; *Cidaris papillata*, LESKE; *Echinus norvegicus*, D. and K.; and *Lophohelia prolifera*, PALLAS, were found in these dredgings.

The 'Porcupine' next put into Killibegs Bay, on the north coast of Co. Donegal, and coaled there for her trip to Rockall. As it was anticipated that this trip would require a clear fortnight, as much coal was stacked on deck as was considered prudent.

This cruise was entirely successful. The weather was remarkably fine, and Mr. Gwyn Jeffreys' party found it possible to work the dredge during seven days at depths exceeding 1,200 fathoms, and on four days at less depths. The greatest depth achieved was 1,476 fathoms (Station 21), and this dredging yielded mollusca, a stalked-eyed crustacean with unusually large eyes, and a fine specimen of *Holothuria tremula*.

The deep dredgings in this trip yielded an abundance of novel and most interesting results in every sub-kingdom of the invertebrates. Among the mollusca were valves of an imperforate brachiopod, with a septum in the lower valve, which Mr. Jeffreys proposes to name *Atretia gnomon*. Among the crustacea were new species of the *Diastylidæ*, and many forms of *Isopoda*, *Amphipoda*, and *Ostracoda*, several of them new to science.

Two or three specimens were obtained at a depth of 1,215 fathoms (Station 28) of a very remarkable echinoderm belonging to the genus *Pourtalesia*, A. AG. All these specimens were apparently immature, judging by the condition of the ovaries. I have named this species provisionally *Pourtalesia phiale*. After careful consideration I have come to the conclusion that it is not the young of a form of which we afterwards took a mature example in the cold area between Færoe and Shetland (Station 64), which will be described hereafter. Fine corals were constantly dredged in the more moderate depths, particularly great living masses of *Lophohelia prolifera* (Fig. 30), with smaller tufts of *Amphihelia ramea*, and everywhere the several varieties of *Caryophyllia borealis.*

The foraminifera, as before, were remarkable for their size, and the same types were predominant; but species were here obtained for the first time of a

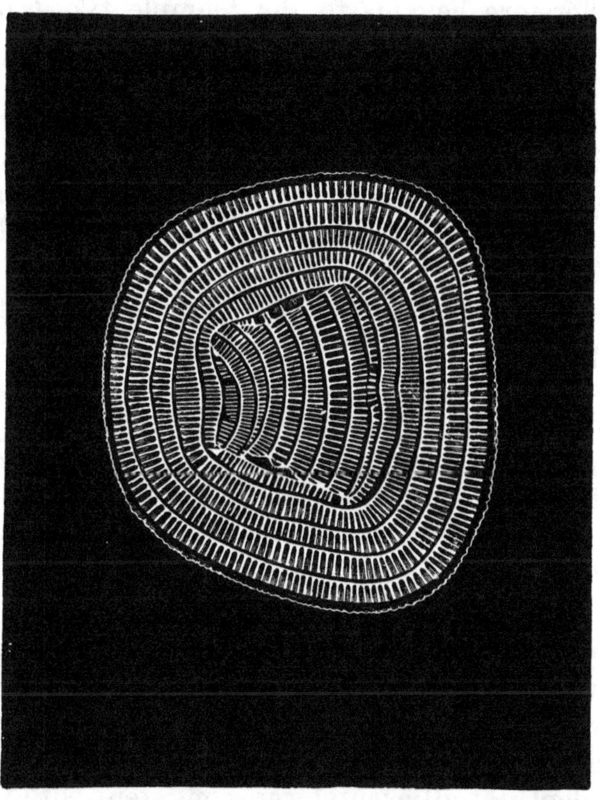

FIG. 10.—*Orbitolites tenuissimus*, CARPENTER MSS. Magnified. (No. 28.)

peculiarly interesting Orbitolite, a type not hitherto discovered farther north than the Mediterranean, and there attaining a comparatively small size. *Orbitolites tenuissimus*, CARPENTER MSS. (Fig. 10), is when complete about the size of a sixpence, and as thin as paper. From its extreme tenuity and the ease with which the rings of chamberlets of which it is composed separate from one another, all our large specimens were more or less injured. All the chamberlets are on the same plane; this species therefore belongs to the 'simple type' of the genus, though the form of the chamberlets corresponds, as Dr. Carpenter has pointed out, with those of the superficial layer in the complex type. Another peculiarity which Dr. Carpenter regards as of special importance in its general bearings, is that, instead of commencing with a 'central' and 'circumambient' chamber like the ordinary *Orbitolites*, this form commences with a spine of several turns like that of a young *Cornuspira*, thus showing the fundamental conformity of this cyclical type to the spiral plan of growth.[1]

As I have already mentioned, it was the original intention to devote the second cruise to the exploration of an area to the west of the outer Hebrides, between Rockall and the south-western limit of last year's work in the 'Lightning.' During the first cruise however dredging had been carried down successfully to a depth of nearly 1,500 fathoms; and the result so far realized our anticipations, and confirmed the experience of last year. The conditions (to that great depth at all events) were consistent with the life

[1] Researches on the Foraminifera. Part I. In the Philosophical Transactions of the Royal Society of London for the year 1855. P. 193 *et seq.*

Introduction to the Study of the Foraminifera. By William B. Carpenter, M.D., F.R.S., F.L.S., F.G.S., &c. Published for the Ray Society, 1862. P. 106 *et seq.*

of all the types of marine invertebrata; though undoubtedly in very deep water the number of species procured of the higher groups was greatly reduced, and in many cases the individuals appeared to be dwarfed. From these observations (which thoroughly corroborated those of Dr. Wallich and others, about which there had been some difference of opinion on account of the imperfection of the appliances at the command of the observers), we concluded that probably in no part of the ocean were the conditions so altered by depth as to preclude the existence of animal life,—that life had no bathymetrical limit. Still we could not consider the question thoroughly settled; and when upon consultation with Captain Calver we found him perfectly ready to attempt any depth, and from his previous experience sanguine of success, we determined to apply to the Hydrographer to sanction an attempt to dredge in the deepest soundings within our reach, viz. 2,500 fathoms indicated on the chart 250 miles west of Ushant. The deepest reliable soundings do not go much beyond 3,000 fathoms; and we felt that if we could establish the existence of life, and if we could determine the conditions with accuracy down to 2,500 fathoms, the general question would be virtually solved for all depths of the ocean, and any further investigation of its deeper abysses would be mere matter of curiosity and of detail. The Hydrographer cordially acquiesced in this change of plan; and on the 17th of July the 'Porcupine' left Belfast under the scientific direction of the writer; Mr. Hunter, F.C.S., Chemical Assistant in Queen's College, Belfast, taking charge of the examination and analysis of the sea-water.

The weather was very settled. On the Sunday, as we steamed down the Irish Channel there was nearly a dead calm, a slight mist hanging over the water and giving some very beautiful effects of coast scenery. On the evening of Sunday the 18th we anchored for the night off Ballycottin, a pretty little port about fifteen miles from Queenstown, and dropped round to Queenstown on Monday morning, where we anchored off Haulbowline Island at 7 A.M. At Queenstown Mr. P. Herbert Carpenter joined Mr. Hunter in the laboratory, to practise under his direction the gas-analysis, which it had been arranged that he should undertake during the third cruise. Monday the 18th was employed in coaling and procuring in Cork some things which were required for the chemical department; and at 7 P.M. we cast off from the wharf at Haulbowline and proceeded on our voyage.

During Monday night we steamed in a south-westerly direction across the mouth of the Channel. On Tuesday we dredged in 74 and 75 fathoms on the plateau which extends between Cape Clear and Ushant, on a bottom of mud and gravel with dead shells and a few living examples of the generally diffused species of moderate depths. The weather was remarkably fine, the barometer 30·25 in., and the temperature of the air 22°·5 C.

On Wednesday, July 21, we continued our south-westerly course, the chart indicating during the earlier part of the day that we were still in the shallow water of the plateau of the Channel. At 4.30 A.M. we dredged gravel and dead shells in 95 fathoms, but towards mid-day the lead gave a much greater depth;

and in the afternoon, rapidly passing over the edge of the plateau, we dredged in 725 fathoms with a bottom of muddy sand (Station 36). This is about the bathymetrical horizon at which we find the vitreous Sponges in the northern area; and although the bottom is here very different, much more sandy with but a slight admixture of globigerina ooze, we dredged a specimen, tolerably perfect though dead, of *Aphrocallistes bocagei*, WRIGHT, a vitreous sponge lately described by Dr. E. Perceval Wright from a specimen procured by Professor Barboza de Bocage from the Cape-Verde Islands, and one or two small specimens of *Holtenia carpenteri*, WY. T. The muddy sand contained a considerable proportion of gravel and dead shells.

On Thursday, July 22, the weather was still remarkably fine. The sea was moderate, with a slight swell from the north-west. We sounded in lat. 47° 38′ N., long. 12° 08′ W., in a depth of 2,435 fathoms (Station 37), when the average of the Miller-Casella thermometers gave a minimum temperature of 2°·5 C.

As this was about the greatest depth which we had reason to expect in this neighbourhood, we prepared to take a cast of the dredge. This operation, rather a serious one in such deep water, will be described in detail in another chapter. It was perfectly successful. The dredge-bag which was safely hauled on deck at 1 o'clock on the morning of the 23rd, after an absence of 7¼ hours and a journey of upwards of eight statute miles, contained 1½ cwt. of very characteristic grey chalk-mud. The dredge appeared to have dipped rather deeply into the soft mud, as it contained amorphous paste with but a small proportion of fresh shells of *Globigerina* and *Orbulina*. There was an appreciable quantity of diffused amorphous organic matter, which we were inclined to regard as connected, whether as processes, or 'mycelium,' or germs, with the various shelled and shell-less Protozoa, mixed very likely with the apparently universally distributed moner of deep water, *Bathybius*.

On careful sifting, the ooze was found to contain fresh examples of each of the Invertebrate sub-kingdoms. When examined at daylight on the morning of the 23rd none of these were actually living, but their soft parts were perfectly fresh, and there was ample evidence of their having been living when they entered the dredge. The most remarkable species were :—

MOLLUSCA.—*Dentalium*, sp. n., of large size.

Pecten fenestratus, FORBES, a Mediterranean species.

Dacrydium vitreum, TORELL ; Arctic, Norwegian, and Mediterranean.

Scrobicularia nitida, MÜLLER ; Norwegian, British, and Mediterranean.

Neæra obesa, LOVÉN ; Arctic and Norwegian.

CRUSTACEA.—*Anonyx hölbollii*, KROYER (=*A. denticulatus*, BATE), with the secondary appendage of the upper antennæ longer and more slender than in shallow-water specimens.

Ampelisca æquicornis, BRUZELIUS.

Munna, sp. n.

One or two ANNELIDES and GEPHYREA, which have not yet been determined.

ECHINODERMATA.—*Ophiocten sericeum*, FORBES; several well-grown specimens.

Echinocucumis typica, SARS. This seems to be a very widely distributed species; we got it in almost all our deep dredgings, both in the warm and in the cold areas.

A remarkable stalked crinoid allied to *Rhizocrinus*, but presenting some very marked differences.

POLYZOA.—*Salicornaria*, sp. n.

CŒLENTERATA. — Two fragments of a hydroid zoophyte.

PROTOZOA.—Numerous foraminifera belonging to the groups already indicated as specially characteristic of these abyssal waters; together with a branching flexible rhizopod, having a chitinous cortex studded with globigerinæ, which encloses a sarcodic medulla of olive-green hue. This singular organism, of which fragments had been detected in other dredgings, here presented itself in great abundance.

One or two small SPONGES, which seem to be referable to a new group.

On Friday, July 23, we tried another haul at the same depth; but when the dredge came up at 1.30 P.M. it was found that the rope had fouled and lapped right round the dredge-bag, and that there was nothing in the dredge. The dredge was sent down again at 3 P.M., and was brought up at 11 P.M., with upwards of 2 cwt. of ooze.—We got from this haul a new species of *Pleurotoma* and one of *Dentalium; Scrobicularia nitida*, MÜLLER; *Dacrydium vitreum*, TORELL; *Ophiacantha spinulosa*, M. and T.; and *Ophiocten kröyeri*, LÜTKEN; with a few crustaceans and many foraminifera.

In both of these last deep dredgings the dredge brought up a large number of extremely beautiful *Polycystina*, and some forms apparently intermediate between *Polycystina* and Sponges, which will be described shortly. These organisms did not seem to be brought from the bottom, but appeared to be sifted into the dredge on its way up. They were as numerous adhering to the outside of the dredging-bag as within it. During the soundings taken near this locality quite a shower of several beautiful species of the *Polycystina* and *Acanthometrina* fell upon the chart-room skylight from the whole length of the sounding-line while it was being hauled in.

We were now steaming slowly back towards the coast of Ireland; and on Monday, July 26, we dredged in depths varying from 557 to 584 fathoms (Stations 39–41) in ooze, with a mixture of sand and dead shells. In these dredgings we got one or two very interesting alcyonarian zoophytes, and several ophiurideans, including *Ophiothrix fragilis*, *Amphiura ballii*, and *Ophiacantha spinulosa*. Many of the animals were most brilliantly phosphorescent, and we were afterwards even more struck by this phenomenon in our northern cruise. In some places nearly everything brought up seemed to emit light, and the mud itself was perfectly full of luminous specks. The alcyonarians, the brittle-stars, and some annelids were the most brilliant. The *Pennatulæ*, the *Virgulariæ*, and the *Gorgoniæ* shone with a lambent white light, so bright that it showed quite distinctly the hour on a watch; while the light from *Ophiacantha spinulosa* was of a brilliant green, coruscating from the centre of the disk, now along one arm, now along another, and sometimes vividly illuminating the whole outline of the star-fish.

On the 27th we dredged in 862 fathoms (Station 42), the weather being still very fine, and the sea quite smooth. The bottom was ooze, with sand and dead shells. Among the Mollusca procured were a new species of *Pleuronectia*, *Leda abyssicola* (Arctic), *Leda messinensis* (a Sicilian tertiary fossil), *Dentalium gigas* (sp. n.), *Siphonodentalium* (sp. n.), *Cerithium metula*, *Amaura* (sp. n.), *Columbella haliæeti*, *Cylichna pyramidata* (Norwegian and Mediterranean), and many dead shells of *Cavolina trispinosa*. These latter were very common in all the northern dredgings, though we never saw a living specimen on the surface.

During the afternoon we took a series of intermediate temperatures, at intervals of 50 fathoms, from the bottom at 862 fathoms to the surface.

On the 28th we dredged in 1207 fathoms (Station 43), with a bottom of ooze. A large *Fusus* of a new species (*F. attenuatus*, Jeffreys) was brought up alive, with two or three *Gephyrea*, and an example each of *Ophiocten sericeum* and *Echinocucumis typica*. We again dredged on the 29th and 30th, gradually drawing in towards the coast of Ireland in 865, 458, 180, and 113 fathoms successively (Stations 44, 45). In 458 fathoms (Station 45) we procured a broken example of *Brisinga endecacnemos*, previously taken by Mr. Jeffreys off Valentia, and a number of interesting Mollusca; and in 458 and 180 fathoms (Stations 45 and 45*a*) an extraordinary abundance of animal life, including many very interesting forms—*Dentalium abyssorum*, *Aporrhaïs serresianus*, *Solarium* *fallaciosum*, *Fusus fenestratus*, with abundance of *Caryophyllia borealis*, and all the ordinary deep-water forms of the region.

The last station, 45*a*, gave us a most singular assemblage of *Ophiurideans*. *Ophioglypha lacertosa* was in large numbers and of extraordinary size, and associated with it were two most conspicuous species, new to science; one a large species of *Ophiothrix*, coming near *O. fragilis*, but of much larger size; the disk in the larger specimens 25 mm. in diameter, and the span from tip to tip of the rays 275 mm. The colours of the disk are very vivid, purple and rose; and all the plates of the disk, and the dorsal plates of the arms, are studded with delicate spines. Notwithstanding its totally different aspect, I had a misgiving that this might yet prove only an extreme variety of *O. fragilis*. My friend Dr. LÜTKEN, however, protests that it is totally distinct. On such a question I bow to his authority, and dedicate it to him, doubts and all, under the name of *Ophiothrix lütkeni*. The second novelty was a fine species of *Ophiomusium*.

About mid-day on Saturday, the 31st of July, we steamed into Queenstown. Having coaled at Haulbowline on Monday, the 2nd of August, we were moored in the Abercorn Basin, Belfast, after a pleasant return passage up the channel, on the evening of Wednesday, the 4th.

As it was necessary that her boilers should be thoroughly cleared out after having been so long at sea, the 'Porcupine' did not leave Belfast till Wednesday, the 11th of August; when she proceeded to Stornoway, her final port of departure.

The scientific staff consisted of Dr. Carpenter, Mr. P. Herbert Carpenter (who had gone through his apprenticeship in making analyses under unfavourable circumstances in the former cruise with Mr. Hunter, and was now prepared to undertake this task on his own account), and myself; and our intention was, in accordance with our original programme, to go carefully over again the region which we had examined in the 'Lightning,' to test with better appliances and more trustworthy instruments the singular distribution of temperatures in the 'warm' and 'cold' areas, to map out as accurately as we could the paths of the warm and cold currents, and to determine the influences of these currents upon the character and distribution of animal life.

We left Stornoway on the afternoon of Sunday the 15th of August, and made straight for the scene of our most successful 'warm area' dredging of the year before. We were equally successful on this occasion, and procured several good specimens of *Holtenia*, and a beautiful series of *Hyalonema*, ranging from 2 mm. in length up to 30 and 40 centimetres, and thus giving all the stages in the development of the wonderful 'glass rope,' and proving to demonstration its relation to the body of the sponge—Dr. J. E. Gray's so-called *Carteria*.

The most interesting novelty however which rewarded us was a very fine Echinid belonging to the Cidaridæ to which I had given the name *Porocidaris purpurata* (Fig. 11). I believe I am justified in referring this handsome species to the genus *Porocidaris*, although in it the special character is absent on which that genus was founded by Desor. Some

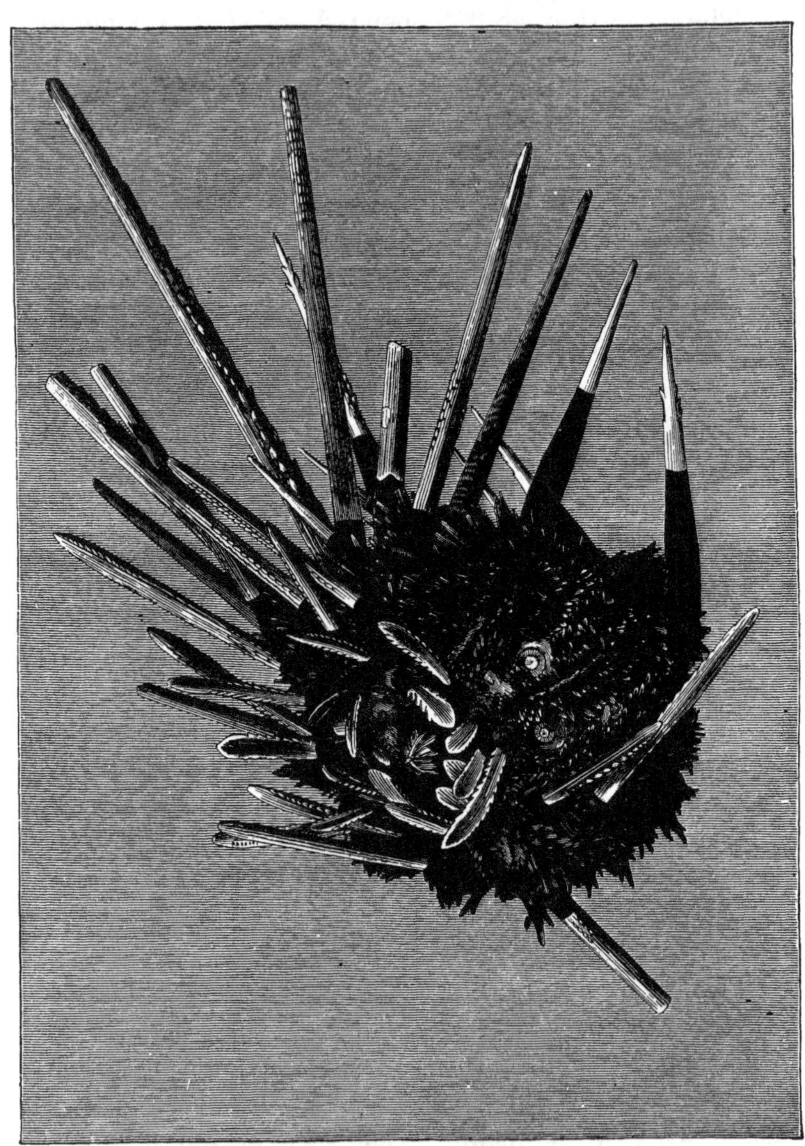

FIG. 11.—*Porocidaris purpurata*, WYVILLE THOMSON. Natural size. (No. 47.)

'radioles,' as the fossil spines of Cidarites are usually called, presenting a very marked character, had been found in various formations from the lower oolite upwards. These spines are paddle-shaped, compressed, longitudinally grooved, flattened almost into plates, and strongly serrated on the edges. In the nummulitic beds of Val-Dominico near Verona such spines were found associated with plates much resembling those of *Cidaris*, but with the unique peculiarity of a row of holes penetrating the test in the areolar space round the primary tubercle. This character our new Urchin does not possess, but the radioles have the flatness, the longitudinal striæ, and the serrated edges of those of *Porocidaris*.

I do not attach much importance to the perforations in the plates. From Desor's figures they are not round and defined in outline, but lengthened and somewhat irregular, and they radiate from the insertion of the spine. Our species has a set of depressions occupying the position of these perforated grooves which are undoubtedly for the insertion of the muscles moving the large long spines, and as the test is thin these grooves might readily penetrate the plate, or so nearly penetrate it as to be worn into holes by very little drifting or wear.

Our recent species and the eocene form have another character in common; the areolar circles are not well defined, and the areolæ tend to become confluent.

Scattered plates only of this genus have been found fossil, and the ovarial plates were till now unknown. They present a very singular character, which is certainly of generic value. The ovarial aperture does not penetrate the plate, but perforates a membrane which fills up a diamond-shaped space, one-half of which is cut out of the outer edge of the ovarial plate in the form of a large triangular notch, while the other half is formed by a separation into a like notch of the two upper interradial plates, in the middle line of the interradial space. The characteristic paddle-shaped spines are ranged in several rows round the mouth. The large spines round the equator of the corona are diverse in form, some of them cylindrical, only slightly tapering towards the tip, and others bulging out and thick near the neck and coming somewhat rapidly to a sharp point. The colouring of the animal is very remarkable. The short spines covering the test are of a rich purple, and a purple of even a deeper and richer hue dyes about one-third of the length of the spine, from the head of the spine outwards, ending abruptly in a sharply defined line. The spine beyond this purple portion is of a beautiful pale rose colour. Two mature examples of this fine species were found, and two young ones, one nearly half-grown and the other much smaller.

We now moved slowly to the northward towards the Færoe Bank, and soundings were taken to fix as closely as possible the point of passage from the warm water into the cold: a temperature sounding taken in lat. 59° 37′, long. 7° 40′, gave a depth slightly less than that of the '*Holtenia* ground,'—475 fathoms,—with a slightly higher bottom temperature, 7°·4 C.; and at Station 50, lat. 59° 54′, long. 7° 52′, with a depth of 335 fathoms, the minimum temperature had risen to 7°·9 C. A sounding at Station 51, lat. 60° 6′, long.

8° 14′, gave 440 fathoms, and a bottom temperature of 5°·5 C., showing that we were passing into another set of conditions; and at Station 52, lat. 60° 25′, long. 8° 10′, only a few miles further on, with a depth of 384 fathoms, nearly the same as that of Station 20, the thermometers recorded a minimum of −0°·8 C. We now altered our course towards the east-south-east, and, after a run of about 25 miles, sounded in 490 fathoms, with a bottom temperature of −1°·1 C. The following six stations, Nos. 54 to 59, were all in the cold area with a temperature below the freezing-point of fresh water. At the last station, No. 59, lat. 60° 21′, long. 5° 41′, at a depth of 580 fathoms, the guarded thermometer recorded the lowest temperature which was met with −1°·3 C. While we were passing through the cold area and making these observations, the weather was extremely settled and fine, and under the careful management of Captain Calver all our appliances worked admirably. The temperatures were noted in every case by the same pair of Miller-Casella thermometers, which were sometimes compared with other instruments and found to give perfectly accurate indications, even after being so frequently subjected to prodigious pressure. The sounding instruments and the dredges never failed, and an ingenious device, for which we are indebted to our Captain, enabled us sometimes to multiply our prizes a hundred-fold. A number of tangles of teazed-out hemp, like the 'swabs' for cleaning the deck, were hung in a way which will be explained hereafter at the bottom of the dredge. These hempen tangles swept by the sides of the dredge, pulling along and picking up everything which was moveable and rough. As echinoderms, crustaceans, and sponges were very numerous in the cold area, the tangles often came up absolutely loaded, while there was but little within the dredge-bag.

In the course of the last series of dredgings we crossed the position of the bank on which we got large specimens of *Terebratula cranium* in so great abundance the year before, but we could not find it. The bank appears to be of very limited area, and both on this occasion and on the previous one the sky was so overcast for several days together, just when we were in this neighbourhood, that it was impossible to fix the position either of the 'Lightning' or of the 'Porcupine' by observation. A dead-reckoning is of course kept under great disadvantages when the vessel is drifting for the greater part of the time half anchored by a dredge.

From Station 59 we proceeded northward to Thorshavn, where we were warmly received by our kind friend Governor Holten, who had been forewarned of our visit, and at once came off in his barge to welcome us. Governor Holten was uncommonly proud of this barge, and he had some reason. She was a very handsome trim boat; and, manned by a dozen stout Færoese boatmen in their neat uniform, and with the Danish ensign flying at the stern, and our handsome friend muffled in his military cloak, and with a thick hood to keep out the somewhat palpable and intrusive 'climate' of Færoe, she looked all that could be desired. When the Governor came on board, he proposed to Captain Calver to try a race with him for the honour of old England and the white ensign. Some of us were going ashore, and when the Governor came up from the cabin our whale-boat was lying alongside with twelve blue-jacketed Shetlanders sitting like statues, their white oars glittering in the sun. The Governor looked with the critical eye of a sailor at the two boats,—he still spoke lovingly of the 'Maid of Færoe,' but I suppose he saw that, as Tennyson says, 'we were all of us Danes;' and the question of a trial of strength lapsed by mutual consent!

We were obliged to remain a few days at Thorshavn replenishing in various ways, and while there we were very anxious to have had an opportunity of seeing Myling Head—a magnificent cliff at the north-western point of Stromöe, which falls perpendicularly, even slightly overhanging its base, from a height of upwards of 2,000 feet into the sea. The tide runs among and round these islands like a mill-race, and the Governor told us that if we started with the morning flood, and our vessel kept pace with the tide, we might make the circuit of the island, passing under Myling, and returning to Thorshavn in six hours. If we did not carry the tide with us, it became a matter of difficulty only to be achieved at considerable expense both of fuel and time.

We found that high water would occur on the following Monday, Aug. 23, at 4 o'clock in the morning; and as the weather was brilliant up to the evening of Sunday—unusually brilliant for those regions—we made all our arrangements in high hope of a pleasant trip, as we had persuaded our kind host and hostess to accompany us. With the first dawn of Monday morning it was blowing and pouring, and we were obliged to defer our visit to the celebrated headland to some possible future opportunity.

The next morning was fine again, and we left

Thorshavn about noon, steaming east by south, so as to cross the deep channel between Færoe and Shetland. Our first two stations were on the Færoe plateau, at depths a little over a hundred fathoms, but the third sounding, taken in the evening of the 24th at a depth of 317 fathoms, gave a bottom temperature of −0°·9 C.; we were therefore once more in the cold current. Having kept the same course under easy steam during the night, we took a sounding next morning, lat. 61° 21′ N., long. 3° 44′ W., at a depth of 640 fathoms, with a bottom temperature of − 1°·1 C. A haul of the dredge brought up rolled pebbles and

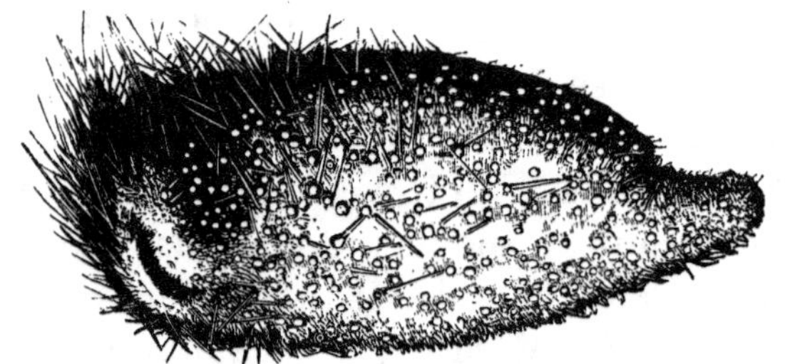

FIG. 12.—*Pourtalesia jeffreysi*, WYVILLE THOMSON. Slightly enlarged.[1] (No. 64.)

fine gravel with few animal forms, but among them one of extraordinary interest, a large specimen of a fine species of the genus *Pourtalesia*, a heart-urchin, one of whose congeners had been discovered by M. de Pourtales in the gulf-stream explorations off the American coast, and a second by Mr. Gwyn Jeffreys near Rockall. The present example (Fig. 12) was much larger than either of those previously dredged, and it appeared to be specifically distinct.

[1] I have the pleasure of dedicating this interesting species to our accomplished colleague, J. Gwyn Jeffreys, F.R.S.

The shell is singularly unlike that of any other known living echinoderm. It is about two inches in length, almost cylindrical, ending posteriorly in a blunt rostrum, and the anterior extremity is truncated. The surface of the shell is covered with short spatulate spines, and near the anterior end there is a kind of fringe of long thin cylindrical spines, especially congregated on the upper surface. The mouth is at the bottom of a deep anterior and inferior groove, and the excretory opening is at the bottom of a pit on the dorsal surface, above the terminal rostrum. The arrangement of the ambulacra is most peculiar. The four ovarial openings and the madreporic tubercle are on the dorsal surface, just above the truncated anterior end at the base of which the mouth lies, and the three ambulacral vessels of the 'trivium' take a short course from the oral vascular ring, one along the centre of the anterior face, and the other two round its edges to meet in a ring surrounding the ovarial openings. The two vessels of the 'bivium' have a very singular course. They run back into the great posterior prolongation of the shell, on the sides of which they form long loops, sending conical water-feet through single pores in long double lines of somewhat irregularly-formed ambulacral plates, which finally converge in a point a considerable distance behind the point of convergence of the three ambulacra of the bivium. Between these two points of convergence, which are both on the middle line of the back, several plates are intercalated. We have thus the three anterior ambulacra ending in their ocular plates, meeting at one point, where there are likewise four genital plates, and the madreporic tubercle; and the two posterior ambulacra, with their ocular plates, meeting at another point and forming a kind of secondary apex. The fifth genital plate is obsolete. The specially interesting point is that, while we had so far as we were aware no living representative of this peculiar arrangement of what is called 'disjunct' ambulacra; we have long been well acquainted with a fossil family, the *Dysasteridæ*, possessing this character. Many species of the genera *Dysaster*, AGASSIZ, *Collyrites*, DESMOULINS, *Metaporhinus*, MICHELIN, and *Grasia*, MICHELIN, are found from the lower oolite to the white chalk, but there the family had previously been supposed to have become extinct.

The next attempt was one of our very few entirely unsuccessful hauls, the dredge coming up empty. This we attributed to an increase of wind and swell, and consequent drift on the vessel, which seemed to have prevented the dredge from reaching the ground.

We devoted the morning to a series of temperature soundings at intervals of 50 fathoms from the surface to the bottom, and this we accomplished in a very satisfactory manner, with results which will be fully discussed hereafter. After a rapid descent for the first 50 fathoms the next 150 fathoms maintained a high and a tolerably equable temperature, and there was then a rapid fall between 200 and 300 fathoms, the thermometer at the greater depth indicating 0° C. From 300 fathoms to the bottom the temperature fell little more than a degree. "Thus the entire mass of water in this channel is nearly equally divided into an upper and lower stratum, the *lower* being *an Arctic stream* of nearly 2,000 feet deep, flowing in a south-westerly direction, beneath an *upper* stratum of comparatively warm water moving slowly towards the north-east; the lower half of the latter, however, having its temperature considerably modified by intermixture with the stratum over which it lies." [1]

Our next few dredgings were on the Shetland plateau, in depths under 100 fathoms, and over ground already carefully worked by our colleague Mr. Gwyn Jeffreys. We got few novelties, but owing to our very effective dredging appliances we took some of the 'Haaf' rarities, such as *Fusus norvegicus*, CHEMN.; *Fusus berniciensis*, KING; *Pleurotoma carinatum*, BIVONA; in considerable numbers. The hempen tangles stood us in good stead with the echinoderms. On one occasion the dredge brought up at a single haul, in the bag and on the tangles, certainly not less than 20,000 examples of the pretty little urchin, *Echinus norvegicus*, D. and K.

On the 28th of August we anchored in Lerwick Harbour. We remained at Lerwick several days taking in necessary supplies, looking at the geology and the many remarkable antiquities of the neighbourhood, and ransacking the haberdashers' shops for those delicate fleecy fabrics of wool which imitate in a scarcely grosser material, and with almost equal delicacy of design, the fretted skeletons of *Holtenia*, *Euplectella*, and *Aphrocallistes*.

In this earlier part of the cruise nearly all the dredgings had been confined to the cold area, and

[1] Dr. Carpenter, in "Preliminary Report on the Scientific Exploration of the Deep Sea, 1869." (Proceedings of the Royal Society, vol. xvii. p. 441.)

over that region we had found a great uniformity of conditions. As already mentioned, the average bottom temperature throughout was a little below the freezing-point of fresh water, and it sometimes fell to nearly 2° C. below the zero of the centigrade scale. The bottom was uniformly gravel and clay, the gravel on the Scottish side of the channel consisting chiefly of the *débris* of the laurentian gneiss and the other metamorphic rocks of the North of Scotland, and the devonian beds of Caithness and Orkney. On the Færoe side of the channel, on the other hand, the pebbles were chiefly basaltic. This difference shows itself very markedly in the colour and composition of the tubes of annelids, and the tests of sundry foraminifera. The pebbles are all rounded, and the varying size of the pebbles and roughness of the gravel in different places give evidence of a certain amount of movement of material along the bottom.

There seems to be but little doubt, from the direction of the series of depressions in the isothermal lines of the region (Pl. 7), that there is a direct movement of cold water from the Spitzbergen Sea into the North Sea, and that a branch of this cold indraught passes into the Færoe Channel. The fauna of the cold area is certainly characteristic, although many of its most marked species are common to the deep water of the warm area whenever the temperature sinks below 2° or 3° C.

Over a considerable district in the Færoe Channel there is a large quantity of a sponge which is probably identical with *Cladorhiza abyssicola*, SARS, dredged by G. O. SARS in deep water off the Loffoten Islands. This sponge forms a kind of bush or shrub, which appears to clothe the bottom in some places over a large area like heather on a moor. There are at least three species. In one the branches are strict and rigid; while in another the arrangement is more lax, side branches coming off from a flexible central rachis like the barbs from the shaft of an ostrich feather. The branches seem in some cases to be from 50 to 80 centimetres in height, and the stems near the base are 2 to 3 centimetres in diameter. The stem and branches consist of a firm central axis, semi-transparent and of a peculiar yellowish green colour; composed of a continuous horny substance filled with masses of needle-shaped spicules arranged longitudinally in dense sheaves. This axis is overlaid by a soft bark of sponge substance supported by needle-shaped spicules, and full of the bihamate 'spicules of the sarcode' so characteristic of the genus *Esperia* and its allies. The crust is covered with pores, and rises here and there into papillæ perforated by large oscula. This sponge appears to belong to a group allied to the Esperiadæ, and perhaps even more closely allied to some of the fossil branching forms whose remains are so abundant in some beds of the cretaceous period. A still finer species of the same group was dredged by Mr. Gwyn Jeffreys in the first cruise of the following year.

Another peculiar sponge (Fig. 13) is very abundant and of a large size. This form was admirably described by Professor Lovén—unaccountably under the name of *Hyalonema boreale*. It is certainly very far from *Hyalonema*. It is more nearly allied to *Tethya*, for the body of the sponge must certainly be referred to the corticate type, though it differs from all the other known members of the order in being supported on a long symmetrical stalk formed, as Professor Lovén has shown, of sheaves of short spicules bound together

FIG. 13.—*Stylocordyla borealis*, LOVÉN (Sp.). Natural size. (No. 64.)

by horny cement. A tuft of delicate fibres fixes the base of the stem in its position. Professor Oscar Schmidt, in his "Outline of the Sponge Fauna of the Atlantic," refers this form to his genus *Cometella*, and this he associates with *Suberites*, *Tethya* greatly restricted, and one or two other generic groups, to form a family the Suberitidinæ, a part of the old order Corticatæ, which order he now proposes to dismember. I doubt if this arrangement will hold good, for the silicious sponges whose skeleton consists mainly of radiating sheaves of long spicules, form a conspicuous and natural assemblage. *Stylocordyla* is evidently nearly related in habit and general character to the Mediterranean stalked sponge figured by Schmidt under the name of *Tetilla euplocamos.*[1]

Foraminifera are not very abundant in the cold area, though here and there in isolated patches large numbers of large and remarkable forms came up on the 'hempen tangles.' These were principally of the Arenaceus type. On one occasion, at Station 51, one of the intermediate dredgings between the warm area and the cold, the tangles brought up a multitude of tubes three-quarters of an inch to an inch long, composed of sand-grains cemented together, and with a slight appearance externally of beading, as if they were divided into segments. During the 'Lightning' excursion the year before, on the middle bank along with the specimens of *Terebratula cranium*, we had found in abundance a sandy *Lituola* with very much the same appearance, except that at one end the *Lituolæ* had a prominent mouth, and on breaking them open this mouth was repeated, definitely moulded of peculiarly

[1] Die Spongien der Küste von Algier. Von Dr. Oscar Schmidt Professor der Zoologie und vergleichenden Anatomie, Director des Landschaftlichen zoologischen Museums zu Gratz. Leipzig, 1868.

coloured sand grains, for every chamber of the series into which the test was divided. The new form, however, was found not to be divided into chambers, but to have its cavity continuous throughout, "though traversed in every part of its length by irregular processes, built up partly of sand-grains and partly of sponge-spicules," resembling those described by Dr. Carpenter in the gigantic fossil form *Parkeria*.[1] One extremity of this chamber is arched over, spaces being left between the agglutinated sand-grains, through which it appears that the gelatinous being within communicates with the outer world by protruding its sarcode processes. The other end was so constantly broken off, leaving a rough fracture, that Dr. Carpenter was inclined to believe that this form to which he gave the generic name of *Botellina*, grew attached to the bottom or to some foreign body.

The cold area teems with echinoderms. In the channel north and west of Shetland, we added to the fauna of the British area besides a large number of species new to science, nearly every one of the forms described by the Scandinavian naturalists as inhabiting the seas of Norway and Greenland.

In comparatively shallow water *Cidaris hystrix* was most abundant, and of large size. The large form of *Echinus flemingii*, BALL, was rare; but every haul at all depths brought up some variety or other which was referred with doubt to *E. elegans*, D. and K., to one or other form of *E. norvegicus*, D. and K., or to *E. rarituberculatus*, G. O. SARS; and although it may, perhaps, be necessary still to describe all these which certainly in their extreme forms present very

[1] Philosophical Transactions, 1869, p. 806.

marked differences as distinct species, after having gone over some thousands of them—some brought up in nearly every haul of the dredge from Færoe to Gibraltar—I am inclined to suspect that they may be all varieties of *Echinus flemingii.* I have already alluded to the countless myriads in which the small form of *E. norvegicus*, D. and K., 15 mm. in diameter, swarms on the 'Haaf' fishing banks. These little urchins are mature so far as the development of their generative products is concerned; and I suspect from the abundance of three sizes, that they attain their full size in two years and a half or three years; but in colouring, in sculpture, and in the form of the pedicellariæ, I do not see any character to distinguish them from a form four times the size, common in deep water off the coast of Ireland; nor, again, can I distinguish these last by any definite character which one would regard as of specific value from the shallow water form of *Echinus flemingii*, as large as the ordinary varieties of *E. sphæra.*

The Shetland variety of *Equus caballus* is certainly not more than one-fourth the size of an ordinary London dray-horse, and I do not know that there is any good reason why there should not be a pony form of an urchin as well as of a horse.

Professor Alexander Agassiz[1] has discovered that the Florida species of *Echinocyamus* is nothing more than the young of a common Florida clypeastroid, *Stolonoclypus prostratus*, AG., and he suggests the possibility of our *Echnocyamus angulosus*, LESKE, being one of these stunted 'pony' varieties, or undeveloped young, either of the American *Stolo-*

[1] Bulletin of the Museum of Comparative Zoology, No. 9, p. 291.

noclypus, the pluteus 'pseudembryo' having been carried along and distributed by the gulf-stream, or of some European deep-water clypeastroid hitherto unknown.

The three so-called species of the genus *Toxopneustes* of the cold area must, I fear, submit to fusion. *T. pictus*, NORMAN, and *T. pallidus*, G. O. SARS, are certainly varieties of *T. drobachiensis*, O. F. MÜLLER.

The young of *Brissopsis lyrifera*, FORBES, were abundant at all depths, but mature examples did not occur beyond 200 fathoms, and were larger and more abundant from 50 to 100 fathoms. *Tripylus fragilis*, D. and K., a rather scarce Scandinavian form, was added to the British fauna; several specimens having been taken, unfortunately usually crushed on account of its great delicacy, in the deeper and colder hauls. Magnificent specimens of the handsome heart-urchin, *Spatangus raschi*, were very abundant, associated in the same zone of depth with *Cidaris*.

Star-fishes were very numerous, rare and new species sometimes actually crowding the hempen tangles. The two species of Brisinga, *B. endecacnemos*, ABSJ., and *B. coronata*, G. O. SARS, came up occasionally and were always regarded as prizes, although it was a matter of some difficulty to extricate their spiny arms one after the other from the tangles; they were scarcely ever within the dredge. *Salaster papposus*, FORBES, apparently their nearest of kin though far removed, was represented abundantly by a very pretty deep-water variety, with ten arms about forty millimetres across from tip to tip, of a bright orange-scarlet even at Station 64, at a depth of 640 fathoms; and we dredged abundantly *S. furcifer*, D. and K. (Fig. 14), previously known

FIG. 14.—*Solaster urcifer*, VON DUBEN and KOREN. Natural size. (No. 55.)

only in the Scandinavian seas. *Pedicellaster typicus*, SARS, occurred but sparingly, and more frequently the

FIG. 15.—*Korethraster hispidus*, WYVILLE THOMSON. Dorsal aspect. Twice the natural size. (No. 57.)

pretty biscuit-like *Astrogonium granulare*, MÜLLER and TROSCHEL. *A. phrygianum*, O. F. MÜLLER, and

Asteropsis pulvillus, O. F. Müller, were not met with beyond the 100-fathom line. A curious little group of cushion stars, hitherto supposed to be confined to high latitudes, were represented by *Pteraster militaris*, M. and T., and *P. pulvillus*, Sars, and by two forms new to science,—one, *Korethraster hispidus*, sp. n., with the whole of the upper surface covered with long free paxillæ like sable brushes (Fig. 15). Ranges of delicate spatulate spines border the

Fig. 16.—*Hymenaster pellucidus*, Wyville Thomson. Ventral aspect. Natural size. (No. 59)

ambulacral grooves. As in *Pteraster*, there is a double row of conical water feet. The other genus (Fig. 16) is perhaps even more remarkable. The star-fish is very flat, the dorsal surface covered with short paxillæ which support a membrane as in *Pteraster*. A row of spines fringing the ambulacral grooves is greatly lengthened and webbed, and the web running along the side of one arm meets and unites with the web of the adjacent arm, so that the angles between the arms are entirely filled up by a delicate membrane stretched on and supported by spines, and the body thus becomes regularly pentagonal. There is no trace on the ventral surface of the arms of the transverse ranges of membranous comb-like plates which are so characteristic in *Pteraster*.

By far the most abundant and conspicuous forms among the star-fishes in deep water were the genera *Astropecten* and *Archaster*, and their allies. At one to two hundred fathoms the small form of *Astropecten irregularis, A. acicularis* of NORMAN, literally swarmed in some places, usually in company with the small form of *Luidia savignii,* M. and T., *L. sarsii,* D. and K. I feel no doubt that these two forms, *A. acicularis* and *L. sarsii,* are mere deep-water varieties of the forms which attain so much larger proportions in shallow water. Mr. Edward Waller took charge of Mr. Gwyn Jeffreys' yacht during the summer of 1869, on a dredging cruise off the south coast of Ireland. He worked principally about the 100-fathom line and a little within it, and procured a magnificent series both of *Astropecten* and *Luidia* showing a gradual transition through all intermediate stages between the large and the small varieties.

The cold area gave us *Astropecten tenuispinus* in great abundance and beauty. The tangles sometimes came up scarlet with them, and associated with this species a handsome new form of a peculiar leaden grey colour, and with paxillæ arranged on the dorsal surface of the disk in the form of a rosette, or the petaloid ambulacra of a *Clypeaster*. *Astropecten arcticus*, SARS, was met with sparingly in some of the deeper dredgings. The known northern species of *Archaster* were abundant and of large size; *A. parellii*, D. and K., passing into comparatively shallow water; and *A. andromeda* abundant at greater depths.

FIG. 17.—*Archaster bifrons*, WYVILLE THOMSON. Dorsal aspect. Three-fourths of the natural size. (No. 57.)

At Stations 57 and 58, and at various others in the cold area we took many specimens of a fine *Archaster* (Fig. 17) with a double row of large square marginal plates giving the edges a thickened square-cut appearance like those of *Ctenodiscus;*

each marginal plate covered with miliary grains, and with a prominent rigid central spine. This is a large form, one of our most striking additions to the tale of known species. It measures 120 mm. from tip to tip of the arms across the disk. The colour is a rich cream, or various shades of light rose.

Ctenodiscus crispatus occurred rarely and of rather small size, not more than 25 mm. across. Nearly every haul brought up small specimens of *Asteracanthion mülleri*, M. SARS, and specimens of all sizes of *Cribrella sanguinolenta*, O. F. MÜLLER.

The distribution of Ophiuoridea was altogether new to a British dredger. By far the most abundant form in moderate depths was *Amphiura abyssicola*, M. SARS, a species hitherto unknown in the British seas; and at greater depths this species was associated in about equal numbers with *Ophiocten sericeum*, FORBES.

Everywhere *Ophiacantha spinulosa*, M. and T., abounds, and the common *Ophioglypha lacertosa* of shallow water is replaced by *O. sarsii*, LÜTKEN, while *Ophiopholis aculeata*, O. F. MÜLLER, loves to nestle among the branches of corals and stony polyzoa. In such characteristic cold area dredgings as Stations 54, 55, 57, and 64, we find the two species of *Ophioscolex*, *O. purpurea*, D. and K., and *O. glacialis*, M. and T.; the former in some places in great abundance, and the latter much more scarce. Both species are new to the British area, and two very remarkable forms which accompany them are new to science. One of these is a very large ophiurid with thick arms, upwards of three decimetres long, and a large soft disk resembling that of *Ophiomyxa*, to which genus it seems to be allied. The specimens which have been hitherto procured are scarcely sufficiently perfect to allow of its being thoroughly worked out. The other is a large handsome species of Ljungmans genus *Ophiopus*. The plates covering the disk are small and obscure, and partly masked by a netted membrane. In moderate depths *Amphiura balli*, THOMPSON, was common, and we now and then dredged a stray example of the beautiful little *Ophiopeltis securigera*, D. and K., lately added to the Shetland fauna by the Rev. A. Merle Norman.

It was a matter of some surprise to us as well as of great pleasure to bring up in many of our cold area hauls considerable numbers of the handsomest of the northern free crinoids, *Antedon escrichtii.* So far as I am aware, this species has not hitherto been met with in the Scandinavian or Spitzbergen seas; all our museum specimens come from Greenland or Labrador. This is also the case with *Ctenodiscus crispatus.* In neither instance do the specimens from the north of Scotland appear to be quite so large as those from Greenland. One or two hauls in moderate water gave us abundant examples of *Antedon celticus*, BARRETT, a form still more common however in the Minch; and almost every haul we found a broken specimen or some fragments of *Antedon sarsii.*

Once or twice we found a fragment of the stem of *Rhizocrinus*, but singularly enough no living specimen of this interesting little crinoid rewarded us from the cold water, although our conclusion seemed to be just, that the Arctic indraught sets into the Færoe

Channel directly from the seas of the Loffotens where it abounds.

We dredged many Holothuriæ; notably everywhere below 200 or 300 fathoms the delicate little *Echinocucumis typica*, M. SARS; and *Psolus squamatus*, KOREN, which does not seem however to be common, through we dredged it in great profusion on one occasion in the 'Lightning,' its white scaly disks showing out against the smooth black pebbles of Færoe basalt to which they were attached. *Holothuria ecalcarea*, SARS, was met with occasionally, and formed another

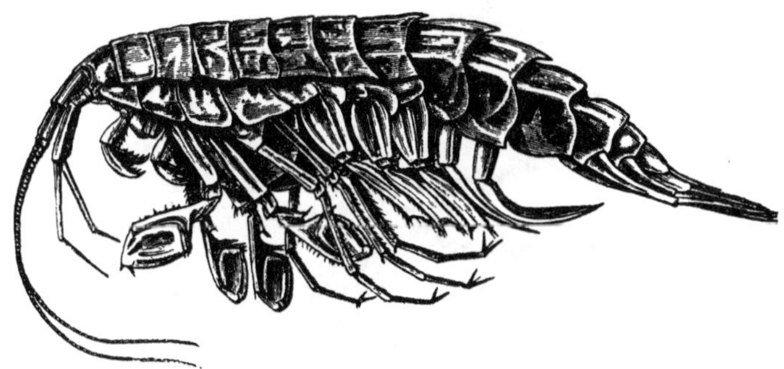

FIG. 18.—*Eusirus cuspidatus*, KROYER. (No. 55.)

interesting addition to the British fauna. It always had a peculiar effect coming up among a number of much smaller and more delicate things, like a massive German sausage twenty or thirty centimetres long.

In the characteristic hauls in the cold area we met with some very interesting crustaceans, one or two of which I figure as they are highly suggestive of the source of the cold water. They are some of the gigantic forms of amphipoda and isopoda of the Arctic sea.

Eusirus cuspidatus, KROYER (Fig. 18), had previously been known only in the Greenland sea, and

FIG. 19.—*Caprella spinosissima*, NORMAN. Twice the natural size. (No. 59.)

the genus was represented for the seas of Britain by an imperfect example of another species.

Fig. 19 is a large and hitherto unknown species of

the genus *Caprella*, the odd-looking group of skeleton shrimps which fix themselves by their hind claspers, usually in this locality to branching sponges, and wave their gaunt grotesque bodies about in the water.

Æga nasuta, NORMAN (Fig. 20), is another new species, one of the 'normal' isopods. Much larger specimens of this curious genus are however known on the British coasts, usually semi-parasitical on large fishes.

Arcturus baffini, SABINE (Fig. 21), is another of the 'isopoda normalia'—normal to a certain extent in its structure, but very peculiar in its appearance and

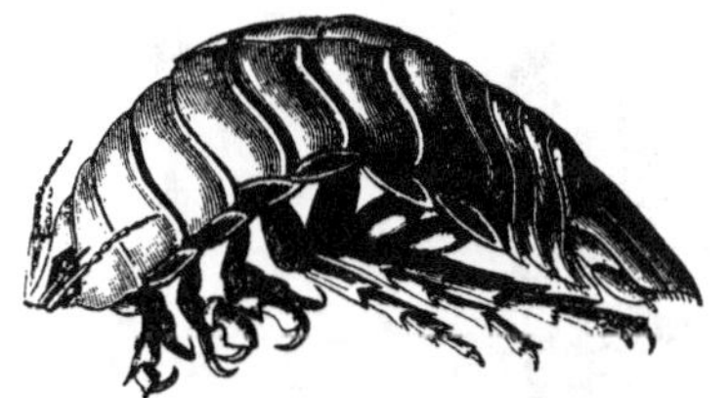

FIG. 20.—*Æga nasuta*, NORMAN. Slightly enlarged. (No. 55.

habits. *Arcturus* has, like *Caprella*, the habit of clinging to some foreign body by its claspers, and rearing up the anterior part of its body in a queer manner; but it has in addition a pair of enormously developed antennæ, and to these the young cling by their claspers, and range themselves along like a couple of living fringes. *Idotea* (*Arcturus*) *baffini* was first described in the Appendix to Captain Parry's fourth voyage. This, or a nearly allied species, seems to occur also in the Antarctic seas. Sir James Clark Ross remarks,[1] that in dredging at a depth

[1] A Voyage of Discovery and Research, vol. i. p. 202.

of 270 fathoms, lat. 72 31 S., long. 173° 39 E., "corallines, flustræ, and a variety of marine invertebrate animals came up in the net, showing an abundance and great variety of animal life. Amongst them I detected two species of *Pycnogonum*, *Idotea baffini*, hitherto considered peculiar to the Arctic

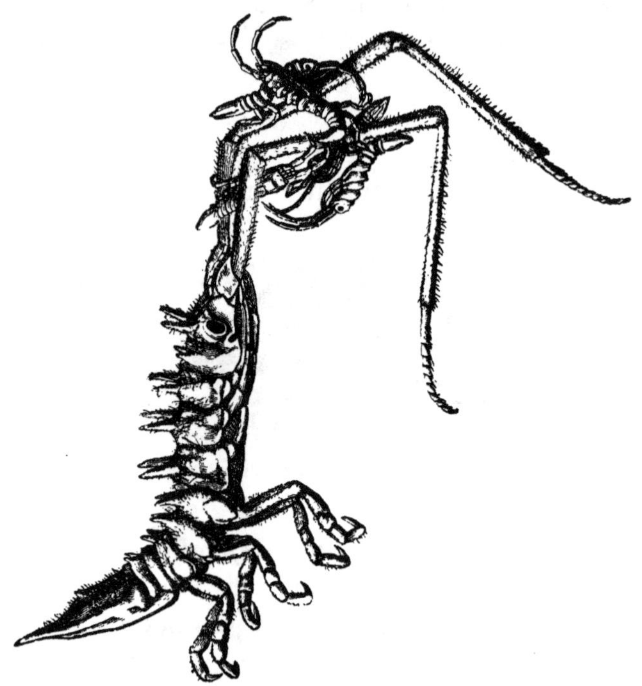

FIG. 21.—*Arcturus baffini*, SABINE. About the natural size. (No. 59.)

seas"—and some other forms. The figure represents *Arcturus baffini* and a few of its progeny, which however have got somewhat into disorder. The nursery arrangements are usually much more regular.

One or two species of the singular marine arachnida of the genus *Nymphon*, of a very large size, were frequently entangled in large numbers on the loose hemp. This group seems to be specially characteristic of the sea at an arctic temperature. They are reported of almost incredible size, thirty centimetres or so across, from the late German and Swedish polar expeditions, and they have also been found enor-

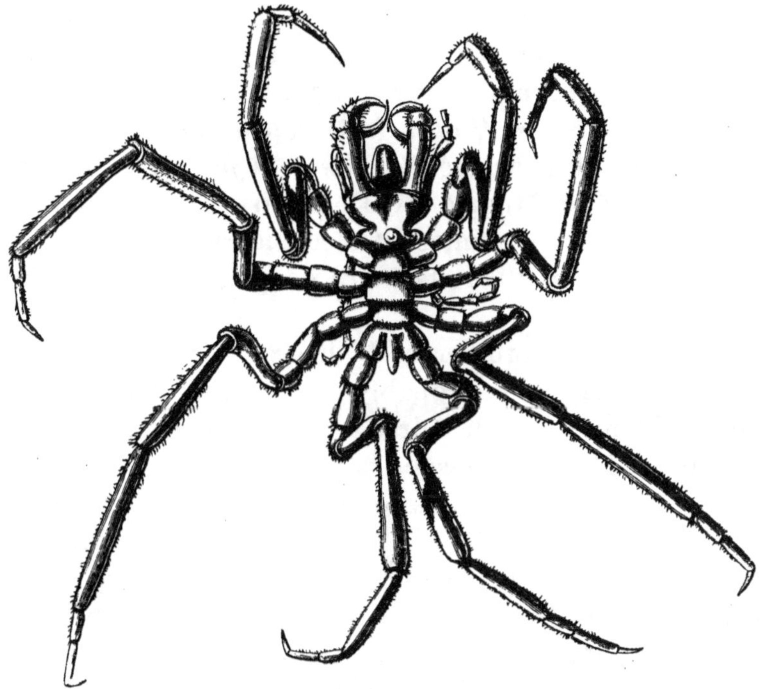

FIG. 22.—*Nymphon abyssorum*, NORMAN. Slightly enlarged (No. 56.)

mously large in deep water in the antarctic regions. They often come up clinging to the sounding line.

The Mollusca, which in the preceding cruises usually constituted the principal results of the dredging, were here quite subordinate as regards both number and variety to the groups already mentioned; and the difference between the molluscan fauna of the cold and that of the warm area was not by any means so great as that shown in other groups. One of the most interesting types which we met with was *Terebratula septata*, PHILIPPI = *T. septigera*, LOVÉN, a brachiopod found living at Station 65 in the Shetland Channel, at a depth of 345 fathoms, and a bottom-temperature of $-1^{\circ}\cdot 1$C. A variety of this species, from the Pliocene beds of Messina, has been described and figured by Professor Seguenza under the name of *Waldheimia peloritana;* and it is clearly the same as the *Waldheimia floridana*, found in the Gulf of Mexico by De Pourtales, which our own numerous specimens so considerably exceed in size as to show that its more congenial home is in frigid water.

Only a small number of Fishes were procured, but their scarcity may probably have been due to the unsuitableness of the dredge as a means for their capture. The few species taken were placed in the hands of Mr. Couch of Polperro by Mr. Loughrin, and were examined by him after our return. The list includes a new generic form intermediate between *Chimæra* and *Macrourus*, which was brought up from a depth of 540 fathoms in the cold area; a new species of a genus allied to *Zeus;* a new *Gadus* approaching the common Whiting; a new species of *Ophidion;* a species of a new genus near *Cyclopterus; Blennius fasciatus*, BLOCH, new to Britain; *Ammodytes siculus;* a fine new *Serranus;* and a new *Syngnathus*.

Death put an end to the labours of the veteran Cornish naturalist while he was preparing descriptions and figures of our new species. He died full of years and work, and this last task, on which he had entered with keen interest, must be finished by other hands.

It will be seen that the bottom temperature of the cold area, at 500 fathoms, does not differ by more than two or three degrees from that of the warm area, at depths beyond 1,500 fathoms. It seems, in fact, as Dr. Carpenter has well pointed out, as if all the extreme climatal conditions which, in the deep water of the Atlantic are extended over a vertical distance of two or three miles, are here compressed, without greatly altering their proportions, into the compass of half a mile. We have the same surface super-heating and rapid fall for the first short distance; the same hump on the curves, indicating the presence of a layer of water heated by some other cause than direct solar radiation; the same rapid fall through a 'stratum of intermixture;' and, finally, the same long excessively slow depression through a deep bottom bed of cold water nearly at a uniform temperature.

As might be anticipated, if the view be correct that arctic conditions are in a broad sense continuous throughout the abyssal regions of the sea, a large number of the inhabitants of the 'cold area' are common to the deep water off Rockall and as far south as the coast of Portugal; but the fauna of the Færoe channel includes besides these generally distributed forms, an assemblage of species—for example the large crustaceans and arachnida and some of the starfishes—which are not only generally characteristic of frigid conditions, but specially of that part of the arctic province represented by the seas of Spitzbergen,

Greenland, and Loffoten. There can be little doubt that this especially arctic character of the fauna is maintained by the continual migration of arctic species along with the arctic current indicated by the depressions in the lines of equal temperature. Many species characteristic of the 'cold area' were not met with beyond its limits, owing doubtless to the entire banking in and disappearance of the cold water, and the obliteration of the arctic current as such at the western opening of the channel between the Færoe banks and the Hebrides.

THE GOVERNOR'S HOUSE, THORSHAVN.

APPENDIX A.

Official Documents and Official Accounts of Preliminary Proceedings in connection with the Explorations in H.M. Surveying-vessel 'Porcupine,' during the Summer of 1869.—*Extracts from the Minutes of the Council of the Royal Society, setting forth the origin of the 'Porcupine' Expedition, and the objects which it was designed to carry out:*—

January 21, 1869.

The Preliminary Report of the Dredging Operations conducted by Drs. Carpenter and Wyville Thomson (in the 'Lightning') having been considered, it was

Resolved,—That, looking to the valuable results obtained from these Marine Researches, restricted in scope as they have been in a first trial, the President and Council consider it most desirable, with a view to the advancement of Zoology and other branches of science, that the exploration should be renewed in the course of the ensuing summer, and carried over a wider area; and that the aid of Her Majesty's Government, so liberally afforded last year, be again requested in furtherance of the undertaking.

Resolved,—That a Committee be appointed to report to the Council on the measures it will be advisable to take in order to carry the foregoing resolution most advantageously into effect. The Committee to consist of the President and Officers, with Dr. Carpenter, Mr. Gwyn Jeffreys, and Captain Richards.

February 18, 1869.

Read the following Report of the Committee on Marine Researches:—

"The Committee appointed by the Council on the 21st of January, to consider the measures advisable for the further prosecution of Researches into the Physical and Biological Conditions of the Deep Sea in the neighbourhood of the British Coast, beg leave to Report as follows:—

"The results obtained by the Dredgings and Temperature-Soundings carried on during the brief Cruise of H.M.S. 'Lightning' in August and September, 1868, taken in connection with those of the Dredgings recently prosecuted under the direction of the Governments of Sweden and of the United States, and with the remarkable Temperature-Soundings of Captain Shortland in the Arabian Gulf, have conclusively shown—

"1. That the Ocean-bottom, at depths of 500 fathoms or more, presents a vast field for research, of which the systematic exploration can scarcely fail to yield results of the highest interest and importance, in regard alike to Physical, Biological, and Geological Science.

"2. That the prosecution of such a systematic exploration is altogether beyond the reach of private enterprise, requiring means and appliances which can only be furnished by Government.

"It may be hoped that Her Majesty's Government may be induced at some future time to consider this work as one of the special duties of the British Navy; which possesses, in the world-wide distribution of its Ships, far greater opportunities for such researches than the Navy of any other country.

"At present, however, the Committee consider it desirable that the Royal Society should represent to Her Majesty's Government the importance of at once following up the suggestions appended to Dr. Carpenter's 'Preliminary Report' of the Cruise of the 'Lightning,' by instituting, during the coming season, a detailed survey of the deeper part of the Ocean-bottom between the North of Scotland and the Færoe Islands, and by extending that survey in both a N.E. and a S.W. direction, so as thoroughly to investigate the Physical and the Biological conditions of the two Submarine Provinces included in that area, which are characterized by a strongly marked contrast in Climate, with a corresponding dissimilarity in Animal Life, and to trace this climatic dissimilarity to its source; as well as to carry down the like survey to depths much greater than have been yet explored by the Dredge.

"This, it is believed, can be accomplished without difficulty (unless the weather should prove extraordinarily unpropitious) by the employment of a suitable vessel, provided with the requisite appliances, between the middle of May and the middle of September. The Ship should be of sufficient size to furnish a Crew of which each 'watch' could carry on the work continuously without undue fatigue, so as to take the fullest advantage of calm weather and long summer days; and should also provide adequate accommodation for the study of the specimens when freshly obtained, which should be one of the primary objects of the Expedition. As there would be no occasion to extend the Survey to a greater distance than (at the most) 400 miles from land, no difficulty would be experienced in obtaining the supplies necessary for such a four months' cruise, by running from time to time to the port that might be nearest. Thus, supposing that the Ship took its departure from Cork or Galway, and proceeded first to the channel between the British Isles and Rockall Bank, where depths of from 1,000 to 1,300 fathoms are known to exist, the Dredgings and Temperature-Soundings could be proceeded with in a northerly direction, until it would be convenient to make Stornoway. Taking a fresh departure from that port, the exploration might then be carried on over the area to the N.W. of the Hebrides, in which the more moderate depths (from 500 to 600 fathoms) would afford greater facility for the detailed survey of that part of the Ocean-bottom on which a Cretaceous deposit is in progress—the Fauna of this area having been shown by the 'Lightning' researches to present features of most especial interest, while the careful study of the deposit may be expected to elucidate many phenomena as yet unexplained which are presented by the ancient Chalk Formation. A month or six weeks would probably be required for this part of the Survey, at the end of which time the vessel might again run to Stornoway for supplies. The area to the N. and N.E. of

Lewis should then be worked in the like careful manner; and as the 'cold area' would here be encountered, special attention should be given to the determination of its boundaries, and of the sources of its climatic peculiarity. These would probably require the extension of the survey for some distance in a N.E. direction, which would carry the vessel into the neighbourhood of the Shetland Isles; and Lerwick would then be a suitable port for supplies. Whatever time might then remain would be advantageously employed in dredging at such a distance round the Shetlands as would give depths of from 250 to 400 fathoms, Mr. Gwyn Jeffreys' dredgings in that locality having been limited to 200 fathoms.

"The Natural-History work of such an Expedition should be prosecuted under the direction of a Chief (who need not, however, be the same throughout), aided by two competent Assistants (to be provided by the Royal Society), who should be engaged for the whole Cruise. Mr. Gwyn Jeffreys is ready to take charge of it during the first five or six weeks, say, to the end of June, when Professor Wyville Thomson would be prepared to take his place; and Dr. Carpenter would be able to join the Expedition early in August, remaining with it to the end. It would be a great advantage if the Surgeon appointed to the Ship should have sufficient knowledge of Natural History, and sufficient interest in the inquiry, to participate in the work.

"The experience of the previous Expedition will furnish adequate guidance as to the appliances which it would be necessary to ask the Government to provide, in case they accede to the present application.

"With reference to the Scientific instruments and apparatus to be provided by the Royal Society, the Committee recommend that the detailed consideration of them be referred to a Special Committee, consisting of gentlemen practically conversant with the construction and working of such instruments."

Resolved,—That the Report now read be received and adopted, and that application be made to Her Majesty's Government accordingly.

The following Draft of a Letter to be transmitted by the Secretary to the Secretary of the Admiralty was approved :—

"THE ROYAL SOCIETY, BURLINGTON HOUSE,
"*February* 18, 1869.

"SIR,—Referring to the 'Preliminary Report' by Dr. Carpenter of the Results of the Deep-Sea Exploration carried on during the brief Cruise of Her Majesty's Steam-vessel 'Lightning' in August and September last, which has already been transmitted for the consideration of the Lords Commissioners of the Admiralty—I am directed by the President and Council of the Royal Society to state that, looking to the valuable information obtained from these Marine Researches, although comparatively restricted in duration and extent, they deem it most desirable, in the interests of Biological and Physical Science, and in no small degree also for the advancement of Hydrographical knowledge, that a fresh exploration should be entered upon in the ensuing summer, and extended over a wider area ; and they now desire earnestly to recommend the matter to the favourable consideration of My Lords, in the hope that the aid of Her Majesty's Government, which was so readily and liberally bestowed last year, may be afforded to the undertaking now contemplated, for which such support would be indispensable.

"In favour of the practicability and probable success of the proposed fresh exploration, I am directed to explain that the objects to be aimed at, as well as the course to be followed and the measures to be employed for their attainment, have mainly been suggested by the observations made and the experience gained in the last Expedition.

"Further information as to the proposed exploration will be found in the Report, herewith transmitted, of a Committee to whose consideration the subject was referred by the Council.

"It is understood that the requisite Scientific Apparatus and the remuneration of the Assistants to be employed would be provided by the Royal Society. With regard to the appliances which Her Majesty's Government may be asked to provide, the experience of the previous Expedition will furnish adequate guidance, whenever the general scheme may be approved. It has appeared to the President and Council, that if the ship required for the proposed service could be provided by the temporary employment of one of Her Majesty's Surveying Vessels now in commission, anything beyond a trifling outlay on the part of the Government would be rendered unnecessary.

"I remain,

"Your obedient Servant,

"W. SHARPEY, M.D.,

"*The Secretary to the Admiralty.*" "*Sec. R.S.*"

Resolved,—That a Committee be appointed to consider the Scientific Apparatus it will be desirable to provide for the proposed Expedition. The Committee to consist of the President and Officers, with Dr. Carpenter, Captain Richards, Mr. Siemens, Dr. Tyndall, and Sir Charles Wheatstone, with power to add to their number.

That a sum of £200 from the Government grant be assigned to Dr. Carpenter for the further prosecution of Researches into the Temperature and Zoology of the Deep Sea.

March 18, 1869.

An oral communication was made by the Hydrographer to the effect that the Lords Commissioners of the Admiralty had acceded to the request conveyed in Dr. Sharpey's letter of February 18; that Her Majesty's Surveying-vessel 'Porcupine' had been assigned for the service; and that the special equipment needed for its efficient performance was proceeding under the direction of her Commander, Captain Calver.

April 15, 1869.

Read the following letter from the Admiralty:—

"ADMIRALTY, *March* 19, 1869.

"SIR,—With reference to previous correspondence, I am commanded by My Lords Commissioners of the Admiralty to acquaint you that Dr. Carpenter and his Assistants, who have been deputed by the Royal Society to accompany the Expedition about to be dispatched to the neighbourhood of the Færoe Isles for the purpose of investigating the bottom of the Ocean by means of deep-sea soundings, will be entertained whilst embarked on board the 'Porcupine' at the Government expense.

"I am, Sir,
"Your obedient servant,
"W. G. ROMAINE."

"*The President of the Royal Society.*"

June 17, 1869.

Read the following Report:—

"The Committee appointed Feb. 18, 1869, to consider the Scientific Apparatus it will be desirable to provide for the proposed Expedition for Marine Researches, beg leave to lay before the Council the following Report:—

"The chief subjects of Physical Enquiry which presented themselves as interesting on their own account, or in relation to the existence of Life at great depths, were as follows:—

"(1) The temperature both at the bottom and at various depths between that and the surface.

"(2) The nature and amount of the dissolved Gases.

"(3) The amount of Organic matter contained in the water, and the nature and amount of the Inorganic salts.

"(4) The amount of Light to be found at great depths.

"Among these subjects the Committee thought it desirable to confine themselves in the first instance to such as had previously to some extent been taken in hand, or could pretty certainly be carried out.

"The determination of Temperatures has hitherto rested chiefly upon the registration of *minimum* Thermometers. It is obvious that the temperature registered by minimum thermometers sunk to the bottom of the sea, even if their registration were unaffected by the pressure, would only give the lowest temperature reached *somewhere* between top and bottom, not *necessarily* at the bottom itself. The temperatures at various depths might indeed, provided they nowhere increased on going deeper, be determined by a series of minimum thermometers placed at different distances along the line, though this would involve considerable difficulties. Still, the liability of the index to slip, and the probability that the indication of the thermometers would be affected by the great pressure to which they were exposed, rendered it very desirable to control their indications by an independent method.

"Two plans were proposed for this purpose, one by Sir Charles Wheatstone, and one by Mr. Siemens. Both plans involved the employment of a voltaic current, excited by a battery on deck; and required a cable for the conveyance of insulated wires. The former plan depended upon the action of an immersed Breguet's thermometer, which, by an electro-mechanical arrangement, was read by an indicating instrument placed on deck. The latter plan made the indication of temperature depend on the existence of a thermal variation in the electric resistance of a conducting wire. It rested on the equalization of the derived currents in two perfectly similar partial circuits, containing each a copper wire running the whole length of the cable, the sea, and a resistance-coil of fine platinum wire; the coil in the one circuit being immersed in the sea at the end of the cable, and that in the other being immersed in a vessel on deck, containing water the temperature of which could be regulated by the addition of hot or cold water, and determined by an ordinary thermometer.

"The instruments required in Sir Charles Wheatstone's plan were more expensive, and would take longer to construct; and, besides, the Committee were unwilling to risk the loss of a somewhat costly instrument in case the cable were to break. On these accounts they thought it best to adopt the simpler plan proposed by Mr. Siemens; and the apparatus required for carrying the plan into execution is now completed, and in use in the expedition.

"Meanwhile a plan had been devised by Dr. Miller for obviating the effect of pressure on a minimum thermometer, without preventing access to the stem for the purpose of setting the index. It consists in enclosing the bulb in an outer bulb rivetted on a little way up the stem, the interval between the bulbs being partly filled with liquid, for the sake of quicker conduction. The Committee have had a few minimum thermometers constructed on this principle, which have been found to answer perfectly. The method is described in a short paper which will be read to the Society to-morrow.

"For obtaining specimens of water from any depth to which the dredging extends, the Committee have procured an instrument constructed as to its leading features on the plan of that described by Dr. Marcet in the Philosophical Transactions for 1819, and used successfully in the earlier northern expeditions.

"Mr. Gwyn Jeffreys is now out on the first Cruise of the 'Porcupine,' the vessel which the Admiralty have sent out for the purpose, and is accompanied by Mr. W. L. Carpenter, B.Sc. (son of Dr. Carpenter), who undertakes the general execution of the physical and chemical part of the inquiry. A letter has been received by the President from Mr. Jeffreys, who speaks highly of the zeal and efficiency of Mr. Carpenter. The thermometers protected according to Dr. Miller's plan, and the instrument for obtaining specimens of water from great depths, have been found to work satisfactorily in actual practice. Mr. Siemens' instrument was not quite ready when the vessel started on her first Cruise, and was not on board when the above letter was written. The gas-analyses have been successfully carried on, notwithstanding the motion of the vessel. From a letter subsequently received from Mr. Carpenter, it appears that Mr. Siemens' apparatus, so far as it has yet been tried, works in perfect harmony with the thermometers protected according to Dr. Miller's plan."

"*June* 16, 1869."

Resolved,—That the Report now read be received and entered on the Minutes.

APPENDIX B.

Particulars of Depth, Temperature, and Position at the various Dredging-stations of H.M.S. 'Porcupine' in the Summer of 1869 :—

Number of Station.	Depth in Fathoms.	Bottom Temperature.	Surface Temperature.	Position.	
1	370	9°·4 C.	12°·3 C.	51° 51′ N.	11° 50′ W.
2	808	5·2	12·3	51 22	12 25
3	722	6·1	12·5	51 38	12 50
4	251	9·7	12·0	51 56	13 39
5	364	9·3	12·2	52 7	12 52
6	90	10·0	12·2	52 25	11 40
7	159	10·2	11·8	52 14	11 48
8	106	10·7	12·3	53 15	11 51
9	165	9·8	12·0	53 16	12 42
10	85	9·7	12·5	53 23	13 29
11	1630	—	—	53 24	15 24
12	670	5·9	11·2	53 41	14 17
13	208	9·8	12·0	53 42	13 55
14	173	9·8	11·8	53 49	13 15
15	422	8·3	11·2	54 5	12 17
16	816	4·2	11·7	54 19	11 50
17	1230	3·2	11·8	54 28	11 44
18	183	9·7	11·8	54 15	11 9
19	1360	3·0	12·6	54 53	10 56
20	1443	2·8	13·0	55 11	11 31
21	1476	2·7	13·4	55 40	12 46
22	1263	2·9	13·8	56 8	13 34
23	630	6·4	14·0	56 7	14 19
23*a*	420	8·0	13·7	56 13	14 18
24	109	8·0	14·3	56 26	14 28
25	164	8·1	13·7	56 41	13 39

Number of Station.	Depth in Fathoms.	Bottom Temperature.	Surface. Temperature.	Position.	
26	345	8°·2 C.	14°·1 C.	56° 58′ N.	13° 17′ W.
27	54	9·1	13·1	Rockall Bank.	Rockall Bank.
28	1215	2·8	14·2	56 44	12 52
29	1264	2·7	13·8	56 34	12 22
30	1380	2·8	13·3	56 24	11 49
31	1360	2·9	13·8	56 15	11 25
32	1320	3·0	13·3	56 5	10 23
33	74	9·8	18·4	50 38	9 27
34	75	9·8	18·9	49 51	10 12
35	96	10·7	17·4	49 7	10 57
36	725	6·1	17·7	48 50	11 9
37	2435	2·5	18·6	47 38	12 8
38	2090	2·4	17·9	47 39	11 33
39	557	8·3	17·2	49 1	11 56
40	517	8·7	17·4	49 1	12 5
41	584	8·1	17·4	49 4	12 22
42	862	4·3	17·0	49 12	12 52
43	1207	3·2	16·5	50 1	12 26
44	865	4·1	16·2	50 20	11 34
45	458	8·9	15·9	51 1	11 21
46	374	7·7	12·1	59 23	7 4
47	542	6·5	12·2	59 34	7 18
48	540	—	—	59 32	6 59
49	475	7·4	12·0	59 43	7 40
50	355	7·9	11·4	59 54	7 52
51	440	5·5	10·9	60 6	8 14
52	384	−0·8	11·2	60 25	8 10
53	490	−1·1	11·2	60 25	7 26
54	363	−0·3	11·4	59 56	6 27
55	605	−1·2	11·4	60 4	6 19
56	480	−0·7	11·4	60 2	6 11
57	632	−0·8	11·1	60 14	6 17
58	540	−0·6	10·6	60 21	6 51
59	580	−1·3	11·5	60 21	5 41
60	167	6·9	9·7	61 3	5 58
61	114	7·2	10·2	62 1	5 19
62	125	7·0	9·8	61 59	4 38
63	317	−0·9	9·4	61 57	4 2

Number of Station.	Depth in Fathoms.	Bottom Temperature.	Surface Temperature.	Position.	
64	640	– 1°· 1 C.	9° 3 C.	61° 21′ N.	3° 44′ W.
65	345	– 1 · 1	11 · 1	61 10	2 21
66	267	7 · 6	11 · 3	61 15	1 44
67	64	9 · 5	11 · 0	60 32	0 29
68	75	6 · 7	11 · 4	60 23	0 33 E.
69	67	6 · 5	12 · 0	60 1	0 18 E.
70	66	7 · 3	11 · 9	60 4	0 21
71	103	9 · 2	11 · 6	60 17	2 53
72	76	9 · 4	11 · 3	60 20	3 5
73	84	9 · 4	11 · 5	60 29	3 6
74	203	8 · 7	11 · 4	60 39	3 9
75	250	5 · 5	10 · 8	60 45	3 6
76	344	– 1 · 1	10 · 1	60 36	3 58
77	560	– 1 · 2	10 · 5	60 34	4 40
78	290	5 · 3	11 · 2	60 14	4 30
79	76	9 · 4	11 · 2	59 44	4 44
80	92	9 · 6	11 · 8	59 49	4 42
81	142	9 · 5	11 · 8	59 54	5 1
82	312	5 · 2	11 · 2	60 0	5 13
83	362	3 · 0	11 · 7	60 6	5 8
84	155	9 · 5	11 · 4	59 34	6 34
85	190	9 · 3	12 · 1	59 40	6 34
86	445	– 1 · 0	12 · 0	59 48	6 31
87	767	5 · 2	11 · 4	59 35	9 11
88	705	5 · 9	12 · 0	59 26	8 23
89	445	7 · 5	11 · 7	59 38	7 46
90	458	7 · 3	11 · 7	59 41	7 34

CHAPTER IV.

THE CRUISES OF THE 'PORCUPINE' (*continued*).

From Shetland to Stornoway.—Phosphorescence.—The *Echinothuridæ*. —The Fauna of the 'Warm Area.'—End of the Cruise of 1869. Arrangements for the Expedition of 1870.—From England to Gibraltar.—Peculiar Conditions of the Mediterranean.—Return to Cowes.

APPENDIX A.—Extracts from the Minutes of Council of the Royal Society, and other official documents referring to the Cruise of H.M.S. 'Porcupine' during the Summer of 1870.

APPENDIX B.—Particulars of Depth, Temperature, and Position at the various Dredging-stations of H.M.S. 'Porcupine' in the Summer of 1870.

⁂ *The bracketed numbers to the woodcuts in this chapter refer to the dredging-stations on Plates IV. and V.*

WE left Lerwick on the 31st of August, and ran south- and westward, passing close to Sumburgh Head; Fair Isle, of evil repute among mariners, lying on the southern horizon like a little grey cloud. The weather was still very fine, and we had a good tossing with scarcely a breath of wind in the famous Roost of Sumburgh. Past Norna's eyrie on the 'Fitful Head;' past in the falling shadows of the autumn night the rocky Island of Foula, still the haunt of one or two pairs of the great skua gull, *Lestris cataractes*, a species fast hastening to join the dodo and the gair-fowl among the creatures of bygone times.

We now steered somewhat to the north of west, and early on the 1st of September sounded in lat. 60° 17′, long. 2° 53′, at a depth of 103 fathoms, and a bottom temperature of 9°·2 C. We were still in the shallow water, and had not touched the arctic stream. All day we slipped over the edge of the plateau, dredging chiefly well-known Shetland forms, and the temperature falling slightly, reaching in the afternoon at a depth of 203 fathoms, 8°·7 C. (Station 74). The next sounding, about ten miles farther north, gave us the stratum of intermixture, a temperature of 5°·5 C. at a depth of 250 fathoms. We ran about thirty miles in the night, and early next morning dredged in the frigid water again in lat. 60° 36′ N., long. 3° 58′ N., at a depth of 344 fathoms, with a bottom temperature of −1°·1 C., the temperature at the surface being 10°·1 C. Five-and-twenty miles to the westward, we sounded again at noon of the same day at 560 fathoms, with −1°·2 C.

In these two or three last cold dredgings the character of the bottom was much the same—gravel of the older rocks, and clay. The preponderance of echinoderms and sponges was again remarkable, and the paucity of mollusca, though in this region we took a single specimen of a mollusk which seemed to be greatly out of its latitude. This was a pretty little brachiopod, *Platydia an omioides*, SACCHI (*Morrisia*, DAVIDSON), hitherto found only in the Mediterranean. The size of this specimen greatly exceeded that of Mediterranean examples of the same species a singular circumstance which leads our friend Mr. Gwyn Jeffreys to the somewhat hazardous presumption that "its original home is in the boreal, perhaps even in the arctic region."

Two very peculiar little sponges were met with here rather frequently sticking to stones. A short smooth column, about 20 mm. in height, is surmounted in one species, which must I think be identified with *Thecophora semisuberites*, OSCAR SCHMIDT, by a soft

FIG. 23.—*Thecophora semisuberites*, OSCAR SCHMIDT. Twice the natural size. (No 76.)

pad of spongy matter, with one or two projecting tubes with oscula in the centre. The other, which I shall call *Thecophora ibla* (Fig. 24), from its resemblance to the cirripede of that name, ends in a scaly cone with a single osculum in the middle. The outer wall of the column in both forms is firm and glossy, under the microscope composed of closely-packed sheaves of needle-shaped spicules with their termination blunt and slightly bulbous. The sheaves are arranged vertically, and this peculiar tissue forms a complete sheath surrounding a pulpy mass of granular horny and sarcodic matter which fills the interior. In this inner spongy substance sheaves of similarly-shaped spicules are likewise arranged vertically, but much more loosely; and the projecting scales forming the head of *Thecophora ibla* are formed by the projecting ends of such sheaves. Among echinoderms, *Ophiacantha spinulosa* was one of the

FIG. 24.—*Thecophora ibla*, WYVILLE THOMSON. Twice the natural size. (No. 76.)

prevailing forms, and we were greatly struck with the brilliancy of its phosphorescence. Some of these hauls were taken late in the evening, and the tangles were sprinkled over with stars of the most brilliant uranium green; little stars, for the phosphorescent light was much more vivid in the younger and smaller individuals. The light was not constant, nor continuous all over the star, but sometimes it struck out a line of fire all round the disk, flashing, or one might rather say glowing, up to the centre; then that would fade, and a defined patch, a centimetre or so long, break out in the middle of an arm and travel slowly out to the point, or the whole five rays would light up at the ends and spread the fire inwards. Very young *Ophiacanthæ*, only lately rid of their 'plutei,' shone very brightly. It is difficult to doubt that in a sea swarming with predaceous crustaceans, such as active species of *Dorynchus* and *Munida* with great bright eyes, phosphorescence must be a fatal gift. We had another gorgeous display of luminosity during this cruise. Coming down the Sound of Skye from Loch Torridon, on our return, we dredged in about 100 fathoms, and the dredge came up tangled with the long pink stems of the singular sea-pen *Pavonaria quadrangularis*. Every one of these was embraced and strangled by the twining arms of *Asteronyx lovéni*, and the round soft bodies of the star-fishes hung from them like plump ripe fruit. The *Pavonariæ* were resplendent with a pale lilac phosphorescence like the flame of cyanogen gas; not scintillating like the green light of *Ophiacantha*, but almost constant, sometimes flashing out at one point more brightly and then dying gradually into comparative dimness, but always sufficiently bright to make every portion of a stem caught in the tangles or sticking to the ropes distinctly visible. From the number of specimens of *Pavonaria* brought up at one haul we had evidently passed over a forest of them. The stems were a metre long, fringed with hundreds of polyps.

Ophiocten sericeum, FORBES, and *Ophioscolex purpurea*, D. and K., were likewise very common, and in sand patches, *Ophioglypha sarsii*, LÜTKEN. The most abundant asterid was *Asteropecten tenuispinus*, always a marked object from its bright red colour—with here and there an example of *Archaster andromeda* and *Pteraster militaris*. Every haul brought up several specimens of the so-called large

FIG. 25.—*Archaster vexillifer*, WYVILLE THOMSON. One-third the natural size. (No. 76.)

form of *Echinus norvegicus*, here of a pale colour, somewhat conical, and looking suspiciously like small forms of *E. flemingii*.

Along with one or two specimens of *Archaster andromeda*, we took at Station 76 an exceedingly beautiful *Archaster* (Fig. 25), certainly by far the finest species yet dredged in the Northern Seas.

The arms are flattened, somewhat square in section

owing to the position and size of the marginal plates, which run up nearly vertically from the side of the unusually wide ambulacral groove till they meet the edge of the perisom of the dorsal surface. The marginal plates are thickly covered with rounded scales and bear three rows of spines—one at the upper edge (and this series in combination form a fringe round the dorsal surface of the star-fish), one near the centre, and one a little farther down towards the ventral edge. The ambulacral groove is bordered by obliquely placed combs of spines, short towards the apex and centre of the arm, but becoming longer towards its base, and forming at the re-entering angles between the ambulacral grooves large singularly beautiful pads; each plate bearing a double row of spines, and each spine having a second short spine or scale on the end, an arrangement which adds greatly to the richness of the bordering. The inner spine of each comb on the side of the ambulacral groove is longer than the others, and bears on the end a little oblong calcareous plate usually hanging from it somewhat obliquely like a flag, with sometimes a rudiment of a second attached to it in a gelatinous sheath, which makes it probable that it is an abortive pedicellaria. From this character, which is one which cannot escape observation, I have called the species '*vexillifer*.' I know no star-fish in which the ambulacral grooves are so wide and the ambulacral tubes so large in proportion to the size of the animal as in this species. The dorsal perisom is closely covered with rosette-like paxillæ. The colour is a pale rose, with a tinge of buff. The ambulacral tubes, which when the animal is living present a very marked feature from their great size, are semi-transparent and of a pale pink colour.

We now took a run once more to the southward, recrossing the boundary of the cold stream, and sounding successively in 290 fathoms, with a bottom temperature of 5°·3 C., and in 76 fathoms, with a temperature of 9°·4, practically the same result as in the former case; and in the next four Stations, 80, 81, 82, and 83, we repeated the operation inversely, sounding in 92 fathoms, with a temperature of 9°·7 C.; in 142, with 9°·5; in 312, with 5°·2; and in 362, with 3°·0.

After a run of about sixty miles in a south-easterly direction nearly parallel with the 100-fathom line, on the morning of Saturday the 4th of September we sounded in lat. 59° 34′ N., long. 6° 34′ W., with a depth of 155 fathoms and a temperature of 9°·5 C. Two other Stations after running distances of six and eight miles only took us once more over the edge of the bank and into the cold river, the first giving a depth of 190 fathoms, with a temperature of 9°·3, and the second 445 fathoms, and - 1°·0.

As we were satisfied for the present with our work in the cold area, and as the next day was the day of rest, we steamed quietly westwards for about 100 miles, past the Butt of the Lews and beyond the entrance of the channel to Station 87, lat. 59°·35′ N., long. 2° 11′ W., a point nearly in the middle line of the deep water of the channel, and consequently in the axis of the cold stream, the line in which the peculiarities of the cold area are most pronounced. Here a sounding gave us a depth of 767 fathoms and a bottom temperature of 5°·2 C. We were thus in the warm area, and the dead-cold water of the cold area lying fifty or sixty miles off, with the bottom at a higher level, was completely banked in. The bottom temperature here corresponded so closely with that of the same depth in the Rockall Channel that apparently scarcely a drop of the Arctic in-

FIG. 26.—*Zoroaster fulgens*, WYVILLE THOMSON. One-third the natural size. (No. 78.)

draught makes its escape in this direction. The dredge here brought up half a ton of Atlantic 'globigerina ooze,' a load which tested its tackle and the donkey-engine to the utmost. The weight of the dredge itself with the weight attached was 8 cwt., so that altogether the burden reached not far short of a ton, and the distance it had to be dragged through the water was not much less than a mile. As was frequently the case when these great loads came up, there were few of the higher animal forms in the dredge. The tangles brought up, however, two or three specimens of a very handsome star-fish, the type of a new genus.

Zoroaster fulgens (Fig. 26) is a five-rayed star-fish, 250 mm. from tip to tip of the arms, which run close up to the centre leaving a small disk not more than 20 mm. in diameter. There are four rows of sucking feet in the ambulacral grooves, a character which places the genus in the first division of the Asterida, along with *Asteracanthion.* The arms are compressed laterally, and run up to a central longitudinal ridge, which bears a row of large pointed spines articulated to a row of projecting knob-like ossicles. From this ridge bands of ossicles curve downwards to the edge of the ambulacral groove so close together and so thick and solid that the arms are continuously and strongly mailed over. The disk is paved with large calcareous tubercles with articulated spines; the tubercles and spines becoming larger towards the centre of the disk. The whole surface of the body is covered with long fine spines, with here and there a group of pedicellariæ on short soft stalks attached to the tops of special spines, while a row of such spines bearing large groups of pedicellariæ runs along the edges of the ambulacral grooves. When living, the whole surface of the animal is covered with a quantity of glairy mucus. The colour of the perisom is a magnificent yellow scarlet, but it is very evanescent, fading immediately in spirit. This is a distinct, as well as a very striking form. We only met with it on this occasion. The skeleton of this star-fish at first sight closely resembles that of some species of *Ophidiaster*, for instance *O. asperulus*, LÜTKEN. It is at once distinguished, however, by the fundamental character of the quadruple row of ambulacral suckers; and the texture of the surface of the star-fish is utterly different. The arrangement of the ossicles of the frame-work is perhaps nearest to that in *Arthraster dixoni*, FORBES, from the lower chalk of Balcombe pit near Amberley, Sussex; but the only specimen of that species, now in the British Museum, unfortunately does not show the arrangement of the plates in the ambulacral grooves.

As our coals were beginning to run short, and what remained were blowing off fast—steaming against rather a strong head wind—we thought it prudent to retrace our steps slowly towards Stornoway, dredging on our way. Accordingly, in the afternoon, we took a haul in lat. 59° 26′, N., long. 8° 23′ W., with a depth of 705 fathoms, and a temperature of 5°·9 C. Continuing our easterly course during the night, but heading slightly northwards so as to come upon the ground where we had been previously so successful in dredging the singular anchoring sponges, we dredged in the morning in lat. 59° 38′ N., long. 7° 46′ W., with a depth of 445 fathoms and a temperature of 7°· 5 C. This haul was not very rich, but it yielded one specimen of extraordinary beauty and interest. As the dredge was coming in we got a glimpse from time to time of a large scarlet urchin in the bag. We thought it was one of the highly-coloured forms of *Echinus flemingii* of unusual size, and as it was blowing fresh and there was some little difficulty in getting the dredge capsized, we gave little heed to what seemed to be an inevitable necessity—that it should be crushed to pieces. We were somewhat surprised, therefore, when it rolled out of the bag uninjured; and our surprise increased, and was cer-

FIG. 27.—*Calveria hystrix*, WYVILLE THOMSON. Two-thirds the natural size. (No. 86.)

tainly in my case mingled with a certain amount of nervousness, when it settled down quietly in the form of a round red cake, and began to pant—a line of conduct, to say the least of it very unusual in its rigid undemonstrative order. Yet there it was with all the ordinary characters of a sea-urchin, its inter-ambulacral areas, and its ambulacral areas with their rows of tube feet, its spines, and five sharp blue teeth; and curious undulations were passing through its perfectly flexible leather-like test. I had to summon up some resolution before taking the weird little monster in my hand, and congratulating myself on the most interesting addition to my favourite family which had been made for many a day.

Calveria hystrix—for I have named this genus and species after our excellent Commander and his tidy

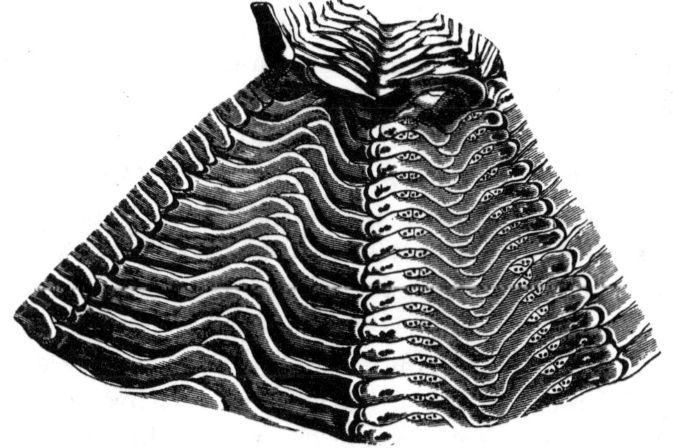

FIG. 28.—*Calveria hystrix*, WYVILLE THOMSON. Inner surface of a portion of the test showing the structure of the ambulacral and interambulacral areas.

little vessel, in grateful commemoration of the pleasant times we had together—is circular and depressed, rather more than 120 mm. in diameter, and about 25 mm. high (Fig. 28). Both interambulacral and ambulacral areas are wide. The peristome and the periproct are unusually large; the former covered with calcareous scale-like plates, perforated up to the rim of the mouth for the passage of ambulacral tube-feet, as in *Cidaris;* the latter with a large madreporic tubercle and five large round openings in the ovarial plates in the centre of which open the wide ducts from the ovaries. The jaw pyramid, 'Aristotle's lantern,' is large and strong, and formed on the plan of the Diadematidæ, and the teeth are large and simply channelled. The point of structure, however, in which *Calveria* differs from all previously described recent urchins is the arrangement of the ambulacral and interambulacral plates. These, instead of meeting edge to edge and abutting against one another so as to form a continuous rigid shell as in most other echinids, overlap one another; the plates of the interambulacral areæ from the apical pole towards the mouth, those of the ambulacral areæ from the mouth towards the apical disk (Fig. 28). In *Calveria*, the outer portions of the interambulacral plates leave spaces between them which are filled up with membrane, and the inner ends of the plates form large wide expansions, which overlap greatly. The ambulacral pairs of pores are singularly arranged: they are in arcs of three, but two of the pairs of each arc penetrate small special accessory plates, while the third pair penetrates the ambulacral plate near the end. The outer ends of the interambulacral plates overlap the outer ends of the ambulacral plates, so that the ambulacral areæ are essentially within the interambulacral. The interambulacral plates bear each close to the outer end where they overlap the ambulacral plates, a large primary tubercle; and two imperfect rows of primary tubercles bearing long spines are ranged in the middle of the ambulacral areæ; the remainder of the surface of the plates is thickly studded with secondary tubercles and miliary grains.

The spines are very delicate and hollow, with projecting processes arranged in an imperfect spiral; and resemble somewhat the small spines of the Diadematidæ. The colour of the test is a rich crimson with a dash of purple, and it is very permanent; the only perfect specimen procured which is preserved in spirit has not lost colour greatly to the present time.

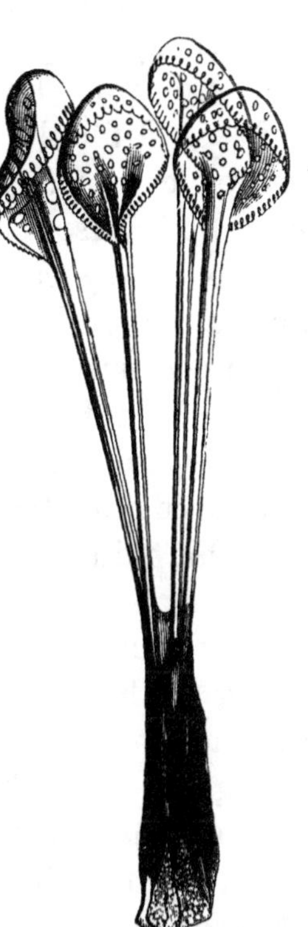

FIG. 29.—*Calveria fenestrata*, WYVILLE THOMSON. One of the four-valved pedicellariæ.

In the summer of 1870, Mr. Gwyn Jeffreys, dredging on the coast of Portugal, took two nearly perfect specimens and several fragments of another species of the genus *Calveria*; and subsequent careful examination of fragments and *débris* has shown that this second species, *C. fenestrata*, occurs likewise in the deep water off the coast of Scotland and Ireland. The interambulacral plates are narrower, and leave larger membranous spaces between them, and the great key-like overlapping expansions in the middle line are much larger. The spines have the same form and are arranged nearly in the same way; but parallel to the outer row of large spines on each interambulacral space there is a row of four or five or more pedicellariæ, of quite a peculiar type. The head of the pedicellaria which is supported on a long stalk, consists of four valves (Fig. 29), the wide terminal portion of each forming a beautiful double fenestrated frame, with a peculiar twist in it reminding one of a *Campylodiscus*, and a very elegant crenated border. These disks are raised on delicate hollow pedicels, which expand beneath, at their point of attachment to the common stalk. A large mass of muscle envelopes the lower part of the group of pedicels, and doubtless determines the movement of the valves in reference to one another.

It is difficult to see what relation in position the valves can occupy when the instrument, whatever may be its use, is closed.

We now steamed onwards to the south-east for about ten miles, and put down our dredge, fully equipped with 'hempen tangles' and every accessory device for entrapping the denizens of the deep, exactly, as our Commander assured us, over the spot where we had dredged the *Holteniæ* early in the cruise. We got there in the evening, and adopted a plan which we had tried successfully once or twice before; we allowed the dredge to remain down all night, moving along with the drift of the vessel, and hauled it up in the early morning. I do not believe human dredger ever got such a haul. The special inhabitants of that particular region—vitreous sponges and echinoderms—had taken quite kindly to the tangles, warping themselves into them and sticking through them and over them, till the mass was such that we could scarcely get it on board. Dozens of great *Holteniæ*, like

"Wrinkled heads and aged,
With silver beard and hair,"

a dozen of the best of them breaking off just at that critical point where everything doubles its weight by being lifted out of the water, and sinking slowly away back again to our inexpressible anguish; glossy whisps of *Hyalonema* spicules; a bushel of the pretty little mushroom-like *Tisiphonia;* a fiery constellation of the scarlet *Astropecten tenuispinus;* while a whole tangle was ensanguined by the 'disjecta membra' of a splendid *Brisinga*.

There was not much in the dredge-bag that was new. Some large *Munidæ*, with their 'sphëery eyne;' some fine specimens of *Kophobelemnon mülleri;* an example of the Euryalid, *Asteronyx loveni*, nearly the only Scandinavian echinoderm which we had not previously taken; and an injured specimen of a flexible urchin, which we supposed to be of the same species as that procured the day before, although it differed greatly in colour, being of a uniform pale grey. Upon further examination, however, it proved to be the type of a totally different generic group of the same family.

Phormosoma placenta resembles *Calveria* in having the perisom flexible, the plates overlapping in the same way and in the same directions; but the plates overlap one another only slightly, and they leave no membranous spaces between, so that they form a continuous shell. The great peculiarity of this form is that the upper surface is quite different from the lower. Above, the ambulacral and interambulacral areæ are well defined and in ordinary proportion, the interambulacral areæ being just twice as wide as the ambulacral, and the spines are much like those of *Calveria*, and are arranged nearly in the same manner. At the periphery the shell comes to a kind of ridge, and alters entirely; from the edge to the mouth the distinction between ambulacral and interambulacral areæ is apparently lost, and the sutures between the plates can scarcely be made out; the pore areæ are reduced to mere lines of double pores, and the whole of the surface of the shell is studded over uniformly with the very large areolæ of primary tubercles, bearing spines which are small and delicate and apparently quite out of proportion to the mass of muscle connected with them which fills the areolæ. As in *Calveria*, the tubercles are perforated.

We have thus become acquainted with three members of a family of urchins which, while differing in a most marked way from all other known living groups, bear a certain relation to some of these, and easily fall into their place in urchin classification. They are 'regular echinids,' and have the normal number and arrangement of the principal parts. They resemble the Cidaridæ in the continuation of the lines of ambulacral pores over the scaly membrane of the peristome to the mouth, and they approach the Diadematidæ in their hollow spines, in the form of their small pedicellariæ, and in the general structure of the jaw pyramid. From both of these families they differ in the imbricated arrangement of the plates and in the structure of the pore areæ, to the widest extent compatible with belonging to the same sub-order.

Many years ago Mr. Wickham Flower of Park Hill, Croydon, procured a very curious fossil from the upper chalk of Higham near Rochester. It consisted of a number of series of imbricated plates radiating from a centre, and while certain sets of these plates were perforated with the characteristic double pores of the urchins, these were absent in alternate series. Some points about this fossil, particularly the imbricated arrangement of the plates over portions indicating a circle at least four inches in diameter, caused great difficulty in referring it to its place. Edward Forbes examined it, but would not hazard an opinion. The general impression was that it must be the scaly peristome of some large urchin, possibly of a large *Cyphosoma*, a genus abundant in the same bed. Some years after the discovery of the first specimen, a second was obtained by the Rev. Norman Glass, from Charlton in Kent. This specimen appeared at first to solve the difficulty, for it contained in the centre a well-developed 'lantern of Aristotle;' there then was the peristome of the urchin, of which Mr. Flower's specimen was the periproct. The late Dr. S. P. Woodward examined the two specimens carefully, and found that the question was not so easily settled. He detected the curious reversal of the imbrication of the plates in the ambulacral and interambulacral areæ which I have described in *Calveria*, and at one point he traced the plates over the edge of the specimen, and found that they were repeated inverted on the other side. With great patience and great sagacity he worked the thing out, and came to the conclusion that he was dealing with the representative of a lost family of regular echinids.

Woodward names his new genus *Echinothuria*, and describes the chalk species, *E. floris*, almost as fully and accurately as we could describe it now with a full knowledge of its relations — for *Echinothuria* is closely related to *Calveria* and *Phormosoma*. In all essential family characters they agree. The plates imbricate in the same directions and on the same plan, and the structure of the ambulacral areæ, which is so special and characteristic, is the same. *Echinothuria* differs from *Calveria* in the wider inter-ambulacral and ambulacral plates, in the smaller amount of overlapping, and in the absence of membranous intervals; and from *Phormosoma* it differs in having the structure and ornament of the apical and oral surfaces of the test the same.

As the genus *Echinothuria* was the first described, I have felt justified in naming the family the Echinothuridæ. I have done this with the greater pleasure, as it brings into prominence a term suggested by my late friend Dr. Woodward, whose early death was a serious loss to science. In Dr. Woodward's memoir, the following curious paragraph occurs:—

"After this apparently conclusive demonstration, it appears desirable to give a name to this fossil and to attempt a short description, although its rank and affinities are still a matter of conjecture. At present it is one of those anomalous organisms which Milne Edwards compares to solitary stars belonging to no constellation in particular. The disciples of Von Baer may regard it as a 'generalized form' of echinoderm, coming, however, rather late in the geological day. The publication of it should be acceptable to those who base their hopes on the 'imperfection of the geological record,' as it seems to indicate the former existence of a family or tribe, whose full history must ever remain unknown." The special bearings of the discovery of this group, and of several other animal forms allied to chalk fossils living among the recent chalk-mud of the Atlantic sea-bed, will be discussed in a future chapter.

While we were examining our wonderful dredge-load the little 'Porcupine' was steaming slowly southwards—past the island of Rona, and Cape Wrath looking out into the north cold and blue, with the waves now curled up asleep at its feet, as if they never did any harm; past the welcome Butt of the Lews, and into the little harbour of Stornoway. Here we remained some days; not sorry—even although our cruise had been thoroughly pleasant—to exchange the somewhat cramped routine of life in a gun-boat for the genial hospitalities of Stornoway Castle.

The fauna of the 'warm area' is under circumstances altogether special and peculiar, which must be discussed in full hereafter. While the cold area is sharply restricted, the warm area extends continuously from the Færoes to the Strait of Gibraltar. At all events the same conditions are continuous; but as will be explained more fully hereafter, the whole 600 or 700 fathoms of water down to the bottom at the mouth of the Færoe Channel, corresponds with the surface layer only to a like depth in the Rockall Channel or in the Atlantic basin. The first 700 to 800 fathoms in all cases are actually warm, but where the depth greatly exceeds 800 fathoms, there is a mass of cold water beneath sinking slowly to nearly the freezing-point. The bottom therefore, the habitation of the fauna, is only warm where the depth is not greater than 800 fathoms, and in such a case only can the term 'warm area' be correctly applied. Such are the conditions off Færoe, and it is this which makes the contrast between the warm and cold areas so marked in that region. The warm area, however, even as thus restricted, is continuous southwards so far as we know indefinitely for the North Atlantic, occupying the zone of depth along the coast from say 300 to 800 fathoms. At great depths everywhere the climatal conditions approach those of the cold area, and the actual character of a fauna—an assemblage of animals at any one spot—must depend not merely upon temperature but upon the laws regulating the distribution of deep-sea animals; a subject on which we know as yet very little.

The bottom in the cold area in the Færoe Channel is rough gravel. That in the warm is everywhere nearly homogeneous 'globigerina ooze.' This circumstance alone is sufficient to determine a marked difference in the habits of the animals and their mode of life.

Referring then to the foraminifera, the dredge came up throughout the warm area full of *Globigerina* and *Orbulina*, and fine calcareous mud, the product of their disintegration. Among these were multitudes of other forms, most of them of large size. I quote from Dr. Carpenter. Speaking of the *Holtenia* ground, he says:—"The *Foraminifera* obtained on this and the neighbouring parts of the warm area presented many features of great interest. As already stated, several arenaceous forms (some of them new) were extremely abundant; but in addition to these we found a great abundance of *Miliolines* of various types, many of them attaining a very unusual and some even an unprecedented size. As last year, we found *Cornuspiræ* resembling in general aspect the large

Operculinæ of tropical seas, and *Biloculinæ* and *Triloculinæ* far exceeding in dimensions the littoral forms of British shores; and with these were assocated *Cristellariæ* of no less remarkable size, presenting every gradation from an almost rectilineal to the nautiloid form, and having the animal body in so perfect a state as to enable it to be completely isolated by the solution of the shell in dilute acid."

Sponges were extremely abundant, but they were restricted to only a small number of species; all of them with one form or another of the curious anchoring habit. Among the Hexactinellidæ *Holtenia* was the most striking and the most abundant form. *Hyalonema* was also common; but we got few perfect specimens with the sponge and glass-rope in connection. The conical sponge heads were very numerous; they seemed to have been torn off by the edge of the dredge, the rope remaining in the mud, and the ropes were frequently brought up without the sponge. Almost all the ropes were encrusted with the constant 'commensal' of *Hyalonema*, *Palythoa fatua*. Very young examples of *Hyalonema*, with the whisp from 5 mm. to 20 mm. long, had usually no *Palythoa* on them; but when they had attained above the latter dimensions in almost every case one could see the first polyp of the *Palythoa* making its appearance as a small bud, and its pink-encrusting cœnosarc spreading round it. By far the most common sponge in the chalk-mud is the pretty little hemispherical corticate form *Tisiphonia agariciformis*. This species, though differing from it greatly in appearance and habit, seems to be closely allied to a strong, heavy encrusting sponge which we met with frequently sticking to stones in the 'cold area.' The form of the spicules was nearly though not quite the same, and their arrangement was very similar. It appeared as if the two forms placed in intermediate circumstances might have approached one another very closely.

In the warm area, as in the cold at these great depths, there is a singular absence of Hydrozoa. A few species of *Sertularia* and *Plumularia*, and one or two allied forms occurred, and they are now in the skilful hands of Dr. Allman for determination; but their small number and insignificance is remarkable.

Neither are the true corals represented by numerous species, although in some places individuals are enormously abundant. During the 'Porcupine' cruises of 1869 twelve species of Madreporaria were procured which have been determined by Professor Martin Duncan. None of these belong to 'reef-building' genera, but to a group which are recognized as deep-sea corals, a group which appears to have had numerous representatives during all the later geological periods. In a band somewhat restricted in depth, extending downwards from the 100-fathom line, we met in some places with very large numbers of many varieties of *Caryophyllia borealis*, FLEMING (Fig. 4); and at depths of 300 to 600 fathoms the handsome branching *Lophohelia prolifera*, PALLAS (Fig 30), forms stony copses covering the bottom for many miles, the clefts of its branches affording fully appreciated shelter to multitudes of *Arca nodulosa*, *Psolus squamatus*, *Ophiopholis aculeata*, and other indolent 'commensals.'

Five species of *Amphihelia* are cited by Professor Martin Duncan from the 'Porcupine' expedition:—*A. profunda*, POURTALES; *A. oculata*, L. sp.; *A. miocenica*, SEGUENZA; *A. atlantica*, n. sp.; and *A. ornata*,

FIG. 30.—*Lophohelia prolifera*, PALLAS (sp.). Three-fourths the natural size. (No. 26.)

n. sp.; and on one or two occasions, chiefly on the verge of the cold area, the hempen tangles involved some elegant fragments of the stony coral *Allopora oculina*, EHRENBERG (Fig. 31).

Although many of the echinoderms of the cold area are common to the warm, the general facies of the echinoderm fauna is different, and there are a number of additional and very striking forms.

Cidaris papillata, LESKE, is abundant at moderate

FIG. 31.—*Allopora oculina*, EHRENBERG.

depths. On our second visit to the *Holtenia* ground we dredged one small specimen of the handsome urchin already described, *Porocidaris purpurata*. A fine brilliantly-coloured urchin of the *Echinus flemingii* group, but distinguished from *E. flemingii* by characters which I must regard as of specific value, *Echinus microstoma*, WYVILLE THOMSON, was common and of large size; and along with it many very beautiful brightly-coloured examples of the smallest form of *E. norvegicus*.

The three species of the Echinothuridæ, *Calveria hystrix*, *C. fenestrata*, and *Phormosoma placenta* have as yet been met with in this region only, and they seem to have a wide distribution, stretching at about the same depth and temperature from the Færoe Islands to the south of Spain. I hear from Professor Alexander Agassiz that Count Pourtales has dredged fragments of one of the species under nearly similar circumstances in the Strait of Florida. *Cribrella sanguinolenta* was in thousands, of all colours—scarlet, bright orange, and chocolate brown. Several examples were found of a fine *Scytaster*, probably identical with the *Asterias canariensis* of D'Orbigny, and if so having a southern distribution. The curious little *Pedicellaster typicus* of Sars was not unfrequent; a form which looks very much like the young of something else. One small specimen of *Pteraster militaris* came up from the Holtenia ground, but with the exception of *Astropecten tenuispinus*, which seemed to be more abundant than ever, the characteristic arctic echinoderms were absent. We took no examples here of *Toxopneustes drobachiensis*, *Tripylus fragilis*, *Archaster andromeda*, *Ctenodiscus crispatus*, *Astropecten arcticus*, *Euryale linkii*, *Ophioscolex glacialis*, or *Antedon escrichtii*. It is very likely that there may be colonies in the 'warm area' of some or of all of these—for the region in which they are common under very different climatal conditions is within a few miles, and there is no intervening barrier—but

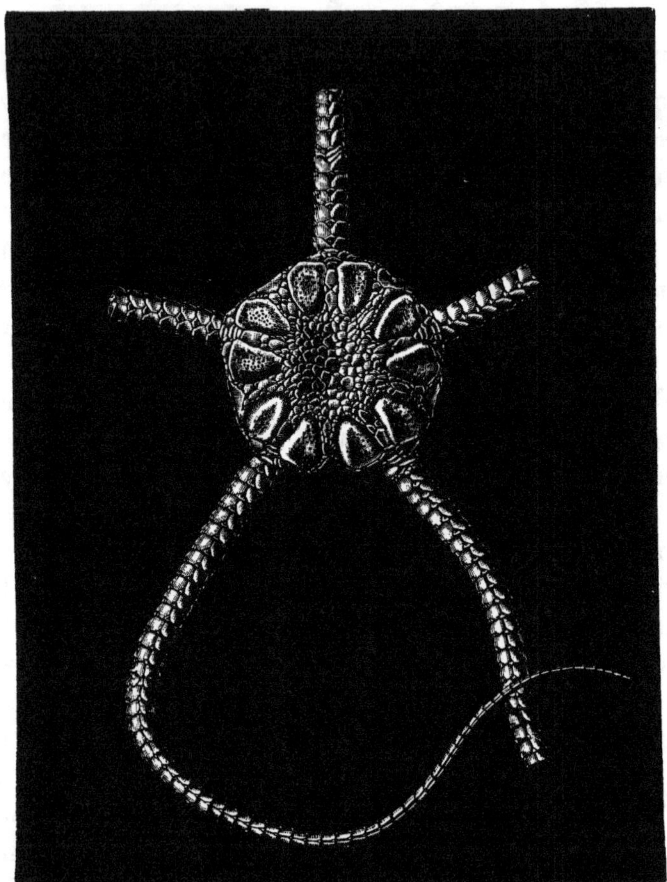

FIG. 32.—*Ophiomusium lymani*, WYVILLE THOMSON. Dorsal surface ; natural size. (No. 45.

they certainly are not abundant. *Amphiura abyssicola*, SARS, was in great numbers sticking to the sponges, and *Ophiacantha spinulosa* was nearly as common as in the cold area.

We took one or two small examples of a very fine ophiurid, of which larger specimens had been previously found at about the same depth and temperature during the second cruise of the same season off the coast of Ireland. This form probably ought to be referred to Lyman's genus *Ophiomusium*,

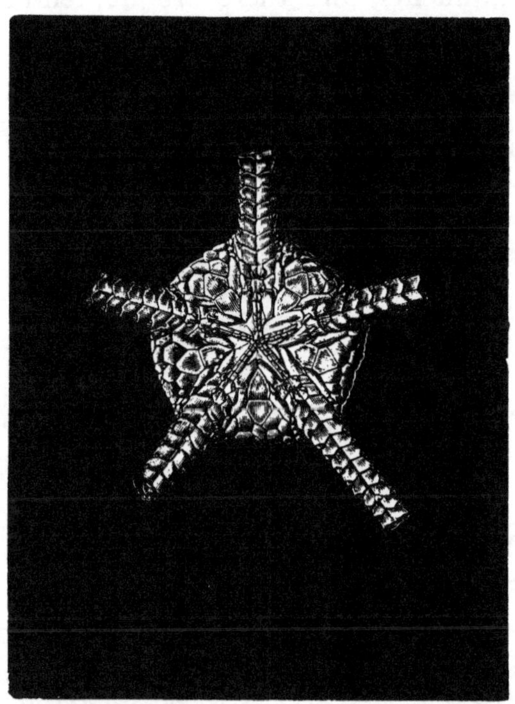

FIG. 33.—*Ophiomusium lymani*, WYVILLE THOMSON. Oral surface.

though the characters of the genus must be somewhat altered to admit it. *Ophiomusium eburneum*, LYMAN, of which several specimens were taken by Count Pourtales at depths of from 270 to 335 fathoms, off Sandy Key, is distinguished by the great solidity and complete calcification of the perisom. The plates of the disk are soldered together, so as to form a close mosaic (μυσεῖον). The mouth-papillæ are fused into two lines, their number being only indicated by grooves. The lateral arm-plates are united together above and below, the upper and lower arm-plates are reduced to mere rudiments, and there are no tentacle pores beyond the first arm-joints.

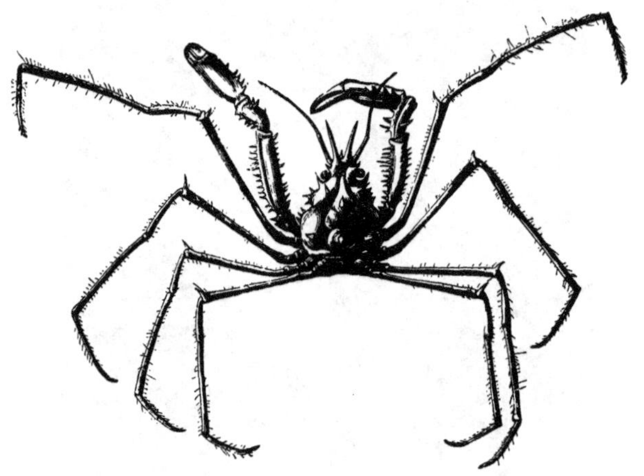

FIG. 34.—*Dorynchus thomsoni*, NORMAN. Once and a half the natural size ; everywhere in deep water.

In our new species, which I name provisionally *Ophiomusium lymani*, the diameter of the disk is 28 mm., and the length of each arm 100 mm. in large specimens. The two lateral arm-plates, fused together above and below, form complete rings, their distal edge notched on each side for the insertion of seven arm spines, of which the lowest is much longer than the rest. The dorsal arm-plates are small and diamond-shaped, let in between the lateral arm-plates at the distal end of their upper line of junction. The ventral arm-plates are entirely absent. This is a large handsome star-fish. I am not aware of any fossil form which can be referred to the same genus; but it looks like a thing which might be expected to have congeners in the upper chalk. Holothurids were not frequent, but the singular little *Echinocucumis typica* of Sars, covered with spiny plates, turned up in every sifting.

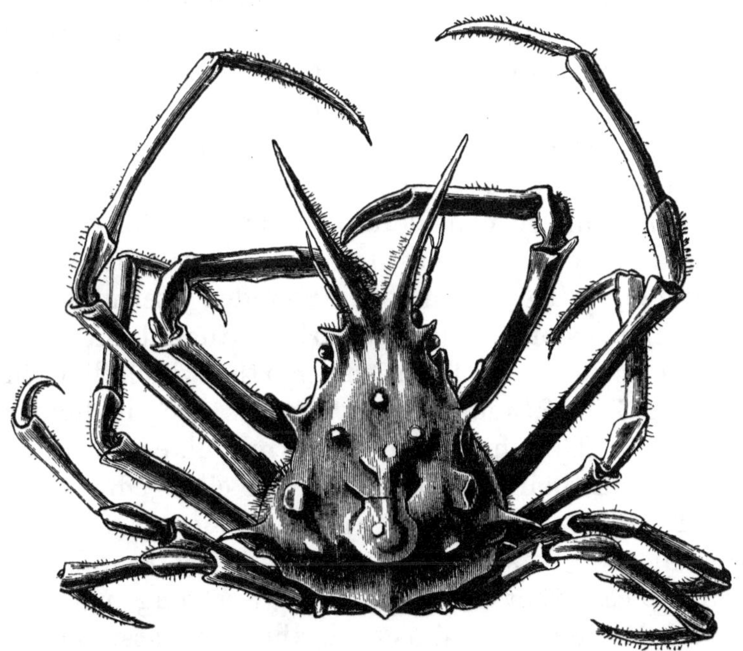

FIG. 35.—*Amathia carpenteri*, NORMAN. Once and a half the natural size. (No. 47.)

Crustacea are numerous; but we have here entirely lost the gigantic Arctic amphipods and isopods of the 'cold area.' A pretty little stalk-eyed form *Dorynchus thomsoni*, NORMAN (Fig. 34), small and delicate, and very distinct from all previously described species of the genus, is very widely diffused.

This crab, from its long spiny legs and light body, very often comes up entangled on the part of the rope which had been passing over the ground. Another handsome new species, *Amathia carpenteri*, NORMAN (Fig. 35), was common in the sandy chalk-mud of the 'Holtenia ground.' The genus had previously been familiar as a Mediterranean form.

I quote from a preliminary notice of the Crustacea by the Rev. A. Merle Norman: "*Ethusa granulata* (sp. n.), the same species as that found off Valentia, but exhibiting a most extraordinary modification of structure. The examples taken at 110—370 fathoms in the more southern habitat have the carapace furnished in front with a spinose rostrum of considerable length. The animal is apparently blind, but has two remarkable spiny eye-stalks, with a smooth rounded termination where the eye itself is ordinarily situated. In the specimens however from the north, which live in 542 and 705 fathoms, the eye-stalks are no longer moveable. They have become firmly fixed in their sockets, and their character is quite changed. They are of much larger size, approach nearer to each other at their base, and instead of being rounded at their apices they terminate in a strong rostrate point. No longer used as eyes, they now assume the functions of a rostrum; while the true rostrum so conspicuous in the southern specimens has, marvellous to state, become absorbed. Had there been only a single example of this form procured, we should at once have concluded that we had found a monstrosity, but there is no room for such an hypothesis by which to escape from this most strange instance of modification of structure under altered conditions of life. Three specimens were procured on two different occasions, and they are in all respects similar."

Mollusca are much more abundant and varied in the warm area than in the cold. Mr. Gwyn Jeffreys remarks, however, that there is not such a decided difference in the Molluscan fauna of the two regions as might have been expected from the difference in their conditions; very many species being common to both. At 500 fathoms the sponges are full of *Pecten vitreus*, CHEM., and *Columbella haliœti*, JEFFREYS; and throughout the area species occur of many Molluscan genera, including *Lima, Dacridium, Nucula, Leda, Montacuta, Axinus, Astarte, Tellina, Neœra, Dentalium, Cadulus, Siphonodentalium, Rissoa, Aclis, Odostomia, Aporrhais, Pleurotoma, Fusus*, and *Buccinum.*

Taken as a whole the fauna of the warm area off the north of Scotland seems to be an extension of a fauna with which we are as yet very imperfectly acquainted, occupying what we must now call moderate depths, say from 300 to 800 fathoms, along coasts which are bathed by currents of equatorial water. The fauna of this zone is evidently extremely rich; and as it is beyond the reach of ordinary dredging from an open boat, and yet not at a sufficient depth to present any very great difficulty from a yacht of average size, its exploration seems to present just the combination of adventure and novelty to stimulate amateurs; so we may hope shortly to have its conditions and distribution cleared up. A most successful step in this direction has been made already by Mr. Marshall Hall, who, with his yacht 'Norna,' and with the aid of Mr. Saville Kent, has thrown a good deal of additional light upon the zoology of the 'warm area' off the coast of Portugal.

We left Stornoway on the 13th of September, and in the afternoon dredged for a few hours in Loch Torridon without much result. Late in the evening, steaming down Raasay Sound, we came upon the luminous forest of *Pavonaria* to which I have already referred. At noon, on the 14th, we were abreast of the Island of Mull, and on the 15th we were once more moored in the Abercorn Basin, Belfast, where we took leave of the 'Porcupine' and our highly-valued friends her captain and officers; in the hope of meeting them again shortly, and thoroughly satisfied with the success of our summer's work.

On the 24th of March, 1870, a letter was read at the council meeting of the Royal Society from Dr. Carpenter, addressed to the President, suggesting that an exploration of the deep sea, such as was carried out during 1868 and 1869 in the regions to the north and west of the British Islands, should now be extended to the south of Europe and the Mediterranean, and that the council of the Royal Society should recommend such an undertaking to the favourable consideration of the Admiralty, with a view to obtain the assistance of Her Majesty's Government, as on the previous occasions. The official correspondence, with reference to the expedition of the summer of 1870, is given in Appendix A to the present chapter.

It was intended, as on the previous occasion, to divide this year's expedition into cruises; and again Mr. Gwyn Jeffreys undertook the scientific direction of the first cruise, at a time when both Dr. Carpenter and I were occupied with our official work. A young Swedish naturalist, Mr. Joshua Lindahl of the University of Lund, accompanied him as zoological assistant, and Mr. W. L. Carpenter took charge of the chemical department. It was arranged that Mr. Jeffreys' cruise should extend from Falmouth to Gibraltar. Dr. Carpenter and I were to have relieved him at Gibraltar, meeting the vessel there, and to have worked together as we did the year before; but I was unfortunately laid up with an attack of fever, and the whole charge of the last cruise in the Mediterranean rested with Dr. Carpenter. Owing to this untoward circumstance, I must give at second-hand the brief account of the first part of the work of the year 1870 which is necessary to complete the sketch of what has been done towards the illustration of the condition and fauna of the North Atlantic. In the Mediterranean Dr. Carpenter found the conditions of temperature and of the distribution of animal life entirely exceptional, as might have been to a certain extent anticipated from the exceptional circumstances of that land-locked sea. The investigation of 1870 can only be said to have broken ground towards the solution of a series of very special and peculiar problems; and I am not in a position to go farther at present than to indicate the general results at which my colleague has arrived.

The 'Porcupine' left Falmouth on the 4th of July, but was detained in the Channel for several days by fogs and contrary winds. On the 7th of July, they reached the slope from the plateau of the Channel to the deep water of the Atlantic, and took a first haul in 567 fathoms. Mr. Jeffreys reports the contents of the dredge as small but very interesting. Among the mollusca he notes *Terebratula septata*, *Limopsis borealis*, *Hela tenella*, *Verticordia abyssicola*, *Turbo filosus*, and *Ringicula ventricosa*. *Turbo filosus* and its variety *T. glabratus* had previously been known only as fossils in the tertiaries of Calabria and Messina. *Terebratula septata*, *Limopsis borealis*, and *Hela tenella* are likewise fossil in the Pliocene beds of southern Italy, and are found living in the Scandinavian seas. Mr. Norman notes among the crustaceans new species of *Ampelisca* and of six other genera; and the beautiful scarlet *Echinus microstoma* was the most conspicuous echinoderm.

The wind, as the vessel passed over the slope of the Channel, was rather too light for successful dredging; the drift-way was scarcely sufficient to carry the dredge along. The tangles were most valuable, coming in as highly effective aids, particularly in securing all things provided with anything in the form of spines or other asperities.

On the 8th the first haul was nearly a failure. Other hauls later in the day, at 690 and 500 fathoms, gave important results. *Rhynchonella sicula*, SEGUENZA; *Pleuronectia*, sp. n.; and *Actæon*, sp. n., occurred: besides the usual northern species. Mr. Norman reports as to No. 3: "A most important dredging, the results among the crustacea being more valuable than all the rest put together—at any rate of the first cruise. It contains almost all of the choicest of the new species in last year's expedition, and four stalk-eyed crustaceans of great interest, three of which are new, and the fourth,

Geryon tridens, is a fine Norwegian species. With these are associated two forms of a more southern character, *Inachus dorsettensis* and *Ebalia cranchii*, which I should not have expected at so great a depth." The echinoderms were a very northern group. They included *Cidaris papillata*, *Echinus norvegicus* and *E. microstoma*, the young of *Brissopsis lyrifera*, *Astropecten arcticus*, *Archaster andromeda*, and *A. parellii*, with a small specimen of *Ophiomusium lymani*, several examples of *Ophiacantha spinulosa*, and as usual one or two of the universally distributed *Echinocucumis typica*. Dr. McIntosh, to whom the annelids were referred, notices as a species supposed to be specially northern, *Thelepus coronatus*, FAB.; and *Holtenia carpenteri*, our familiar anchoring sponge, of all sizes and ages and in considerable numbers, was entangled in the hempen 'swabs.'

July 9th.—The wind still too light for effective work. Dredged in 717 and 358 fathoms, the assemblage of mollusca having the usual character of being to a great extent common to the recent fauna of the seas of Norway and to the pliocene fauna of Sicily and the Mediterranean. It included on this occasion *Terebratella spitzbergensis*, an arctic and Japanese form, *Pecten vitreus*, and *P. aratus*, *Leda pernula*, *Trochus suturalis*, *Odostomia nitens*, and *Pleurotoma hispidulum*. Among the echinoderms was a fine specimen of *Brisinga endecacnemos*, ABSJÖRNSEN, very markedly different from *B. coronata*, which was the form commonly met with in the north. The corals were represented by *Amphihelia oculata* and *Desmophyllum crista-galli*. Among the annelids were *Pista cristata*, O. F. MÜLLER, and *Trophonia glauca*,

MALMGREN, both of them Arctic species. The 10th was Sunday, and the vessel lay-to, and on the 11th they dredged, still on the slope of the channel plateau, with nearly the same result as before, the fauna maintaining the same character.

Mr. Gwyn Jeffreys was now anxious to get a haul or two in the very deep water off the mouth of the Bay of Biscay, which we had explored successfully in 1869. They therefore steamed southwards, going a considerable distance without dredging, as they were afraid of coming in contact with the cable between Brest and North America. When they got to their ground unfortunately bad weather set in, and they were obliged to make for Vigo. On Thursday, July 14th, they passed Cape Finisterre, and dredged in 81 fathoms about 9 miles from the Spanish coast. Along with a number of familiar forms, some of them with a wide northern extension, they here took on the tangles two specimens, one young and one apparently mature, both considerably injured, of the singular Echinidean already mentioned, *Calveria fenestrata*. This is evidently not a rare form nor is it confined to very deep water; it is rather remarkable that it should have escaped notice so long. On the 15th, they sounded in from 100 to 200 fathoms, about 40 miles from Vigo, and on the 16th took one or two hauls in Vigo Bay at a depth of 20 fathoms. This locality had already been well-nigh exhausted by Mr. McAndrew in 1849, and only a few additions were made to his list.

They left Vigo on the 18th. I quote from Mr. Gwyn Jeffreys:—

"*Wednesday, July 20th.*—Dredged all day with

considerable success at depths from 380 to 994 fathoms (Stations 14-16): the wind and sea had now gone down; and we took with the scoop-net a few living specimens of *Clio cuspidata*. The dredgings in 380 and 469 fathoms yielded among the mollusca *Leda lucida* (Norwegian and a Sicilian fossil), *Axinus eumyarius* (also Norwegian), *Neæra obesa* (Spitzbergen to the West of Ireland), *Odostomia*, n. sp., *O. minuta* (Mediterranean), and *Cerithium*, n. sp.; and among the echinoderms were *Brisinga endecacnemos* and *Asteronyx loveni*. But the results of the dredging in 994 fathoms were so extraordinary as to excite our utmost astonishment. It being late in the evening, the contents of the dredge could not be sifted and examined until daylight the next morning. We then saw a marvellous assemblage of shells, mostly dead, but comprising certain species which we had always considered as exclusively northern, and others which Mr. Jeffreys recognized as Sicilian tertiary fossils, while nearly 40 per cent. of the entire number of species were undescribed, and some of them represented new genera. The following is an analysis of the mollusca perfect and fragmentary taken in this one haul:—

Orders.	Total number of Species.	Recent.	Fossil.	Undescribed.
Brachiopoda	1	1	—	—
Conchifera	50	32	1	17
Solenoconchia . . .	7	3	—	4
Gasteropoda	113	42	23	48
Heteropoda	1	1	—	—
Pteropoda	14	12	—	2
	186	91	24	71

The northern species above referred to are 34 in number, and include *Dacridium vitreum, Nucula pumila, Leda lucida, L. frigida, Verticordia abyssicola, Neæra jugosa, N. obesa, Tectura fulva, Fissurisepta papillosa, Torellia vestita, Pleurotoma turricula, Admete viridula, Cylichna alba, Cylichna ovata,* JEFFREYS n. sp., *Bulla conulus,* S. WOOD not DESHAYES (Coralline Crag), and *Scaphander librarius. Leda lucida, Neæra jugosa, Tectura fulva, Fissurisepta papillosa, Torellia vestita,* as well as several other known species in this dredging, are also fossil in Sicily. Nearly all these shells, as well as a few small echinoderms, corals, and other organisms, had evidently been transported by some current to the spot where they were found; and they must have formed a thick deposit similar to those of which many tertiary fossiliferous strata are composed. It seemed probable also that the deposit was partly caused by tidal action, because a fragment of *Melampus myosotis* (a littoral pulmonibranch) was mixed with deep-water and oceanic Pectinibranchiates and Lamellibranchiates. None of the shells were Miocene or of an older period.

"This remarkable collection, of which not much more than one-half is known to conchologists, notwithstanding their assiduous labours, teaches us how much remains to be done before we can assume that the record of Marine Zoology is complete. Let us compare the vast expanse of the sea-bed in the North Atlantic with that small fringe of the coast on both sides of it which has yet been partially explored, and consider with reference to the dredging last mentioned what are the prospects of our ever becoming acquainted with all the inhabitants of the deep throughout the globe! We believe, however, that a thorough examination of the newer Tertiaries would materially assist us in the inquiry; and such examination is feasible and comparatively easy. Much good work has been done in this line; but although the researches of Brocchi, Bivona, Cantraine, Philippi, Calcara, Costa, Aradas, Brugnone, Seguenza, and other able palæontologists in the south of Italy have extended over more than half a century, and are still energetically prosecuted, many species of molluscous shells are continually being discovered there, and have never been published. Besides the Mollusca in this dredging from 994 fathoms, Professor Duncan informs us that there are two new genera of corals, and *Flabellum distinctum*, which last he regards as identical with one from North Japan. It coincides with the discovery on the Lusitanian coasts of two Japanese species of a curious genus of Mollusca, *Verticordia*, both of which are fossil in Sicily and one of them in the Coralline Crag of Suffolk."

In the same dredging there are a number of very singular undescribed sponges, many of them recalling some of the most marked characters of one of the sections of Ventriculates. These will be referred to in a future chapter.

On Thursday, the 21st of July, dredging was carried on all day at depths from 600 to 1095 fathoms, lat. 39° 42′ N., long. 9° 43′ W., with a bottom temperature at 1095 fathoms of 4°·3 C. and at 740 fathoms of 9°·4 C. The dredging was most successful; many of the new and peculiar mollusca of the last dredging were taken here alive, with several additional forms.

Several undescribed crustaceans were added;—a new species of the genus *Cœnocyathus* among the corals, and a species of an unknown genus allied to *Bathycyathus*. *Brisinga endecacnemos* and some new ophiurids were part of the treasures, but the greatest prize was a splendid *Pentacrinus* about a foot long, of which several specimens came up attached to the tangles. This northern Sea-lily, on which my friend Mr. Gwyn Jeffreys has bestowed the name *Pentacrinus wyville-thomsoni*, will be described hereafter with some other equally interesting members of the same group.

Cape Espichel was reached on the 25th. The weather was now, however, so rough that Captain Calver was obliged to take shelter in Setubal Bay. Professor Barboza de Bocage of Lisbon had given Mr. Gwyn Jeffreys a letter of introduction to the coastguard officer at Setubal, who knew the place where the deep-sea shark and the *Hyalonema* are taken by the fishermen, but the state of the weather prevented his taking advantage of it.

Off Cape Espichel in 740 and 718 fathoms, with a temperature of 10°·2 C., the mollusca were much the same as those from Station 16, but included *Leda pusio*, *Limopsis pygmæa* (Sicilian fossils), and *Verticordia acuticostata*. The last-named species is interesting in a geological as well as a geographical point of view. It is fossil in the Coralline Crag and the Sicilian Pliocene beds, and it now lives in the Japanese archipelago. Mr. Jeffreys suggests a mode of accounting for the community of so many species to the eastern borders of the Atlantic basin and the Mediterranean, in which several Japanese brachiopods and crustaceans are found, and the seas of

Northern Asia, by supposing a migration through

FIG. 36.—*Chondrocladia virgata*, WYVILLE THOMSON. One-half the natural size. (No. 33, Pl. V.)

the Arctic Sea. We must know, however, much

more than we yet do of the extension both in time and space of the fauna of deep water before we can come to any certain conclusion on these questions.

Dredging across the entrance of the Strait of Gibraltar in 477, 651, and 554 fathoms, Stations 31, 32, and 33, with a bottom temperature of 10°·3, 10°·1, and 10°·0 respectively, many remarkable forms were dredged, including a very elegant sponge, apparently allied to, if not identical with, Oscar Schmidt's, *Caminus vulcani,* and some beautiful forms of the Corallio-spongiæ, which will be noticed in a future chapter. Station No. 31 yielded a sponge form which recalled the branching heather-like *Cladorhiza* of the cold area off Færoe. *Chondrocladia virgata* (Fig. 36) is a graceful branching organism from twenty to forty centimetres in height. A branching root of a cartilaginous consistence, formed of densely packed sheaves of needle-shaped spicules bound together by a structureless organic cement, attaches the sponge to some foreign body, and supports it in an upright position; and the same structure is continued as a solid axis into the main stem and the branches. The axis is made up of a set of very definite strands like the strands of a rope, arranged spirally, so as to present at first sight a strong resemblance to the whisp of *Hyalonema* ; but the strands are opaque, and break up under the point of a knife; and under the microscope they are found to consist of minute needle-like spicules closely felted together. The soft sponge substance spreads over the surface of the axis and rises into long curving conical processes, towards the end of which there is a dark greenish oval mass of granular sponge matter, and the outline of the cone is continued beyond this by a number of groups of needle-shaped spicules which surround a narrow oscular opening. All parts of the sponge are loaded with triple-toothed 'bihamate' spicules of the sarcode.

On the 5th of August the 'Porcupine' steamed into Tangier Bay, after ineffectually trying to dredge in 190 fathoms off Cape Spartel. In Tangier Bay two casts were taken at a depth of 35 fathoms. The fauna was chiefly British, with a few more southern forms.

On the 6th of August Mr. Jeffreys went to Gibraltar, and there yielded up the reins to Dr. Carpenter, going on to Sicily *viâ* Malta, for the purpose of examining the newer tertiary formations in the south of Italy, and the collections of fossil shells at Catania, Messina, Palermo, and Naples, in connection with the results of his cruise.

On Monday, the 15th of August, Captain Calver, with Dr. Carpenter, who fortunately retained the services of Mr. Lindahl as assistant, in charge of the science department, steamed out into the middle of the Strait for the purpose of commencing a series of observations on the currents of the Strait of Gibraltar.

These experiments, which at the time were not considered very satisfactory, were repeated and extended in the summer of 1871 by Captain Nares, R.N., and Dr. Carpenter, in H.M.S. 'Shearwater.' Their curious results have been given in great detail by Dr. Carpenter in the Proceedings of the Royal Society of London, and by Captain Nares in a special report to the Admiralty. As it is my purpose to confine myself at present almost exclusively to the description of the phenomena of the deep water in the Atlantic so far as these have been worked out, I will not here repeat the narrative of the experiments in the Strait. I will, however, give a brief sketch of Dr. Carpenter's cruise in the Mediterranean, as the remarkable phenomena connected with the distribution of temperature and of animal life which he observed, illustrate while they contrast with the singularly different conditions which have been already described in the outer ocean.

The first sounding in the basin of the Mediterranean was taken on the 16th of August, lat. 36° 0′ N., long. 4° 40′ W., at a depth of 586 fathoms, with a bottom of dark grey mud. The surface temperature was 23°·6 C., and the bottom temperature 12°·8 C., about three degrees higher than at the same depth in the ocean outside. A serial sounding was taken to determine the rate of the diminution of temperature, with the following curious result:—

Surface	23°·6 C.
10 fathoms	20·9
20 ,,	18·6
30 ,,	17·5
40 ,,	16·7
50 ,,	15·6
100 ,,	12·8
586 ,,	12·8

Thus the temperature fell rapidly for the first 30 fathoms, more slowly for the next 20, from 50 to 100 lost only 3° C., and before reaching the depth of a hundred fathoms had attained its minimum temperature, there being no further diminution to the bottom. This serial sounding and all the subsequent temperature observations taken during the Mediterranean cruise showed that the trough of the Mediterranean from the depth of 100 fathoms downwards is filled with a mass of water at almost exactly the same temperature throughout, a temperature a little above or below 12°·75 C.

The following instances have been cited by Dr. Carpenter from the earlier observations in the Mediterranean basin, to show the great uniformity of the bottom temperature for all depths :—

Number of Station.	Depth in Fathoms.	Bottom Temperature.	Surface Temperature.	Position.	
41	730	13°·4C.	23°·6C.	Lat. 35° 57′ N.	Long. 4° 12′ W.
42	790	13·2	23·2	35 45	3 57
43	162	13·4	23·8	35 24	3 [illegible] 30″
44	455	13·0	21·0	35 42 20″	3 00 30″
45	207	12·4	22·6	35 36 10″	2 29 30″
46	493	13·0	23·0	35 29	1 56
47	845	12·6	21·0	37 25 30″	1 10 30″

At this last Station (No. 47) a serial sounding was taken, which entirely confirmed the results of the first (No. 40) :—

Surface	20°·9 C.
10 fathoms	15·2
20 "	14·4
30 "	13·8
40 "	13·3
50 "	13·1
100 "	12·6
845 "	12·6

—again a mass of water lying at the bottom, 745 fathoms—not far from a mile—in depth, at the uniform temperature of 12°·6 C. (54°·7 F.)

The dredge was sent down at each successive station, but with very poor result; and Dr. Carpenter was driven to the conclusion that the bottom of the Mediterranean at depths beyond a few hundred fathoms is nearly azoic. The conditions are not actually inconsistent with the existence of animal life, for at most of the stations some few living forms were met with, but they are certainly singularly unfavourable. Thus at Station 49, at a depth of 1412 fathoms, and a temperature of 12°·7 C., the following species of mollusca were obtained: *Nucula quadrata*, n. sp.; *N. pumila*, ABSJÖRNSEN; *Leda*, n. sp.; *Verticordia granulata*, SEG.; *Hela tenella*, JEFFREYS; *Trochus gemmulatus*, PH.; *Rissoa subsoluta*, ARADAS; *Natica affinis*, GMELIN; *Trophon multilamellosus*, PH.; *Nassa prismatica*, BR.; *Columbella haliæti*, JEFF.; *Buccinium acuticostatum*, PH.; *Pleurotoma carinatum*, CRISTOFORI and JAN; *P. torquatum*, PH.; *P. decussatum*, PH.

Near the African coast the fauna was more abundant, but the bottom was so rough that it was unsafe to use the dredge, and the tangles were usually sent down alone. Many polyzoa, echinoderms, corals, and sponges were taken in this way, but they were mostly well-known Mediterranean species. After remaining for a few days at Tunis and visiting the ruins of Carthage, dredging was resumed on the 6th of September on the 'Adventure' Bank, so called from its having been discovered by Admiral Smyth when surveying in H.M.S. 'Adventure.' Here, at depths from 30 to 250 fathoms, animal life was tolerably abundant. With other mollusca the following were found:—*Trochus suturalis*, PH. (Sicilian fossil); *Xenophora crispa*, KÖNIG (Sic. fossil); *Cylichna striatula*, FORBES (Sic. fossil); *C. ovulata*, BROCCHI (Sic. fossil); *Gadinia excentrica*, TIBERI; *Scalaria frondosa*, J. SOWERBY (Sicilian and Coralline Crag fossil); *Pyramidella plicosa*, BRONN (Sic. and Cor. Crag fossil); *Actæon pusillus*, FORBES (Sic. fossil). The Echinodermata were abundant so far as individuals went, but the number of species was small, and they were nearly all well-known Mediterranean forms. *Cidaris papillata*, LESKE, showing many varieties, but differing in no specific character from the many forms of the same species which range from North Cape to Cape Spartel in the ocean outside. The Mediterranean varieties of this species are certainly *Cidaris hystrix*, of Lamarck. I feel a degree of uncertainty about the pretty little *Cidaris*, described by Philippi under the name of *C. affinis*. Characteristic examples of it, which are abundant on the 'Adventure' Bank and along the African coast, look very distinct. They are of a beautiful deep rose red, the spines are banded with red and brownish-yellow, and come to a fine point, while those of *C. papillata* are usually blunt at the point, and frequently even a little expanded or cupped; and the portion of the interambulacral plates covered with miliary granules is wider, and two defined rows of body spines nearly of equal size lie up against the bases of the primary spines, over the alveolæ. These would appear to be characters of specific value, but then again there are a mass of intermediate forms; and although after careful consideration I have described the two species as distinct, I find it a matter of great difficulty to draw the line between them. Several specimens of a handsome *Astrogonium* allied to *A. granulare* were taken on the 'Adventure' Bank. Professor Duncan reports some interesting corals, and Professor Allman two new species of *Aglaophenia;* and Dr. Carpenter detected once more the delicate *Orbitolites tenuissimus,* and the large nautiloid *Lituola,* with which he was familiar in the dredgings in the Atlantic.

After a short stay at Malta, on September 20th the 'Porcupine' steamed out of Valetta Harbour, and steered in a north-easterly direction, towards a point seventy miles distant, at which a depth of 1700 fathoms was marked on the chart. This was reached early the next morning, and the line ran out 1743 fathoms, lat. 36° 31′ 30″ N., long. 15° 46′ 30″ (No. 60), with a temperature of 13°·4 C., more than half a degree higher than the temperature of the deepest sounding in the western basin. The tube of the sounding apparatus brought up a sample of yellow clay, so like the bottom at some of the most unproductive spots in the western Mediterranean, that it was not considered advisable to delay the time necessary for even a single cast of the dredge, which at that depth would have occupied nearly a day. Having thus satisfied themselves as far as they could by a few observations that the physical conditions of the eastern basin of the Mediterranean were similar to those of the western, they steered for the coast of Sicily. Quietly along the Sicilian coast during the night, in early morning through the narrowest part of the Strait between Messina and Reggio, past Charybdis and the castled rock of Scylla, and so out of the 'Faro' into the open sea to the north of Sicily, studded with the Lipari Islands. A temperature sounding taken near Stromboli, lat. 38° 26′ 30″ N., long. 15° 32′ E., gave a depth of 730 fathoms, and a bottom temperature of 13°·1 C., while the temperature of the surface was 22°·5 C.

Under the rugged cone of Stromboli the dredgers took another set of temperatures, with the result common to the whole volcanic neighbourhood of Sicily, of a temperature slightly higher than that of the deep water in the western basin of the Mediterranean, a phenomenon of which it would take long and careful observation to determine the cause ; and while doing so they pondered on the cloud of smoke hanging over the peak, so suggestive of the theatre of subterranean change beneath, and admired the industry and enterprise of those who, rendered contemptuous by the familiarity of ages, carried their vineyards "all over the cone, save on two sides, looking north-west and south-east, over one or other of which there is a continual discharge of dust and ashes."

Their course was now laid straight for Cape de Gat, which they passed on the 27th of September, arriving at Gibraltar on the 28th. At Gibraltar, Dr. Carpenter resumed his observations and experiments on the currents of the Strait. These observations were continued until the 2nd of October, when it became necessary for Captain Calver to return homewards. The coast of Portugal was repassed in fine weather, the time at their disposal not allowing any further use of the dredge in the deep water, and after encountering a fresh breeze in the chops of the Channel, on the evening of October the 8th, the 'Porcupine' anchored at Cowes.

LILLE DIMON.

APPENDIX A.

Extracts from the Minutes of Council of the Royal Society, and other Official Documents referring to the Cruise of H.M.S. 'Porcupine' during the Summer of 1870 :—

March 24, 1870.

A Letter was read from Dr. Carpenter, addressed to the President, suggesting that an Exploration of the Deep Sea, such as was carried out during 1868 and 1869 in the regions to the North of the British Islands, should now be extended to the South of Europe and the Mediterranean, and that the Council of the Royal Society should recommend such an undertaking to the favourable consideration of the Admiralty, with a view to obtain the assistance of Her Majesty's Government as on the previous occasions.

Resolved,—That a Committee, consisting of the President and Officers, with the Hydrographer, Mr. Gwyn Jeffreys, Mr. Siemens, Professor Tyndall, and Dr. Carpenter, with power to add to their number, be appointed, to consider the expediency of adopting the proposal of Dr. Carpenter, and the plan to be followed in carrying it out, as well as the instruments and other appliances that would be required, and to report their opinion thereon to the Council; but with power previously to communicate to the Admiralty a draft of such report as they may agree upon, if it shall appear to them expedient to do so in order to save time.

April 28, 1870.

Read the following Report :—

" The Committee appointed on the 24th of March to consider a proposal for a further Exploration of the Deep Sea during the ensuing summer, as well as the scientific preparations which would be required for a new expedition, beg leave to report as follows :—

"The general course proposed to be followed, and the chief objects expected to be attained in a new expedition, are pointed out in the following extract from the letter of Dr. Carpenter, read to the Council on the 24th ult., which was referred to the Committee :—

"'The plan which has been marked out between my colleagues in last year's work and myself is as follows :—

"'Having reason to hope that the "Porcupine" may be spared towards the end of June, we propose that she should start early in July, and proceed in a S.W. direction towards the furthest point to which our survey was carried last year; carefully exploring the bottom in depths of 400 to 800 fathoms, on which, as experience has shown us, the most interesting collections are to be made; but also obtaining a few casts of the Dredge with Temperature-soundings at greater depths, as opportunities may occur.

"'The course should then be nearly due South, in a direction of general parallelism with the coast of France, Spain, and Portugal, keeping generally within the depths just mentioned, but occasionally stretching westwards into yet deeper waters. From what has been already done in about 400 fathoms' water off the coast of Portugal, there is no doubt that the ground is there exceedingly rich. When approaching the Straits of Gibraltar, the survey, both Physical and Zoological, should be carried out with great care and minuteness; in order that the important problem as to the currents between the Mediterranean and Atlantic Seas, and the relation of the Mediterranean Fauna to that of the Atlantic (on which Mr. Gwyn Jeffreys is of opinion that the results of our last year's work throw an entirely new light), may be cleared up.

"'Mr. Gwyn Jeffreys is prepared to undertake the scientific charge of this part of the expedition; and if Professor Wyville Thomson should not be able to accompany him, it will not be difficult to find him a suitable assistant.

"'The ship would probably reach Gibraltar early in August,

and there I should be myself prepared to join her, in place of Mr. Jeffreys, with one of my sons as an assistant. We should propose first to complete the survey of the Straits of Gibraltar, if that should not have been fully accomplished previously; and then to proceed eastwards along the Mediterranean, making stretches between the coasts of Europe and Africa, so as to carry out as complete a survey, Physical and Zoological, of that part of the Mediterranean basin as time may permit. Malta would probably be our extreme point; and this we should reckon to reach about the middle of September.

"'It is well known that there are questions of great Geological interest connected with the present distribution of Animal life in this area; and we have great reason to believe that we shall here find at considerable depths a large number of Tertiary species which have been supposed to be extinct. And in regard to the Physics of the Mediterranean, it appears, from all that we have been able to learn, that very little is certainly known. The Temperature and Density of the water, at different depths, in a basin so remarkably cut off from the great ocean, and having a continual influx from it, form a most interesting subject of inquiry, to which we shall be glad to give our best attention, if the means are placed within our reach.'

"Considering the success of the two previous Expeditions, and especially that of the 'Porcupine' last year, the Committee are persuaded that no less important acquisitions for the furtherance of scientific knowledge would be gained by the renewed exploration as now proposed; and they accordingly recommend that a representation to that effect be made to the Admiralty, with a view to obtain the aid of Her Majesty's Government as on the previous occasions.

"The Committee approve of a proposal made by Mr. Gwyn Jeffreys to accept the services of Mr. Lindahl, of Lund, in the expedition as unpaid Assistant Naturalist.

"As regards scientific instruments, the Committee have to report that those employed in last year's voyage will be again available for use; and Mr. Siemens hopes to render his electro-thermal indicator of more easy employment on ship-board.

"The Committee, having learned that Dr. Frankland has contrived an apparatus for bringing up the deep-sea water charged with its gaseous contents, have resolved to add his name to their number; and they request leave to meet again in order to complete the arrangements and make a final report to the Council."

Resolved,—That the Report now read be received and adopted, and that the Committee be requested to continue their meetings and report again on the arrangements when finally decided on.

Resolved,—That the following draft of a Letter to be addressed to the Secretary of the Admiralty be approved, viz.:—

"SIR,—I am directed by the President and Council of the Royal Society to acquaint you, for the information of the Lords Commissioners of the Admiralty, that, considering the important scientific results of the Physical and Zoological Exploration of the Deep Sea carried on in 1868 and 1869 through the aid of Her Majesty's Government, they deem it highly desirable that the investigation should be renewed during the ensuing summer, and extended over a new area.

"The course which it would be proposed to follow in a new Expedition, the principal objects to be attained, and the general plan of operations, are sketched out in the enclosed extract from a Letter addressed to the President by Dr. Carpenter, and have in all points been approved by the Council.

"The President and Council would therefore earnestly recommend such an undertaking to the favourable consideration of My Lords, with the view of obtaining the assistance of Her Majesty's Government so liberally accorded and effectively rendered on the previous occasions.

"The scientific conduct of the expedition would, as in the last year, be shared by Dr. Carpenter, Professor Wyville Thomson, provided that gentleman is able to undertake the duty, and Mr. Gwyn Jeffreys. It is also proposed that Mr. Lindahl, a young Swedish gentleman accustomed to marine researches, should accompany the expedition as Assistant Naturalist.

"I have to add that whatever appertains to the strictly Scientific equipment of the Expedition will, as formerly, be at the charge of the Royal Society.

"W. SHARPEY, *Secretary*."

A sum of £100 from the Government Grant was assigned for the Scientific purposes of the Expedition.

May 19, 1870.

Read the following Letter from the Admiralty:—

"ADMIRALTY, 10*th May*, 1870.

"SIR,—Having laid before My Lords Commissioners of the Admiralty your letter of the 2nd inst., requesting that further researches may be made of the deep sea, I am commanded by their Lordships to acquaint you that they will spare Her Majesty's Steam-vessel 'Porcupine' for this service, and that the Treasury have been requested, as on the former occasion, to defray the expense of the messing of the scientific gentlemen composing the Expedition.

"I am, Sir,
"Your obedient Servant,
"VERNON LUSHINGTON."

"To W. Sharpey, Esq., M.D.,
"Secretary of the Royal Society, Burlington House."

APPENDIX B.

Particulars of Depths, Temperature, and Position at the various Dredging-stations of H.M.S. 'Porcupine,' in the Summer of 1870:—

Number of Station.	Depth in Fathoms.	Bottom Temperature.	Surface Temperature.	Position.	
1	567	—	—	48° 38′ N.	10° 15′ W.
2	305	14°· 8 C.	16°· 2 C.	48 37	10 9
3	690	—	—	48 31	10 3
4	717	7 · 5	16 · 3	48 32	9 59
5	100	10 · 7	16 · 8	48 29	9 45
6	358	10 · 0	16 · 9	48 26	9 44
7	93	10 · 6	16 · 2	48 18	9 11
8	257	9 · 9	15 · 9	48 13	9 11
9	539	8 · 9	17 · 8	48 6	9 18
10	81	11 · 9	16 · 4	42 44	9 23
11	332	10 · 2	16 · 1	42 32	9 24
12	128	11 · 3	16 · 3	42 20	9 17
13	220	11 · 0	18 · 1	40 16	9 37
14	469	10 · 8	18 · 4	40 6	9 44
15	722	9 · 8	20 · 0	40 2	9 49
16	994	4 · 5	21 · 0	39 55	9 56
17	1095	4 · 3	19 · 8	39 42	9 43
18	1065	4 · 5	18 · 2	39 29	9 44
19	248	11 · 0	18 · 1	39 27	9 39
20	965	—	—	39 25	9 45
21	620	10 · 2	19 · 5	38 19	9 30
22	718	10 · 7	19 · 1	38 15	9 33
23	802	9 · 0	19 · 0	37 20	9 30
24	292	11 · 5	19 · 6	37 19	9 13

Number of Station.	Depth in Fathoms.	Bottom Temperature.	Surface Temperature.	Position.	
25	374	11°· 9 C.	20°· 9 C.	37° 11′ N.	9° 7′ W.
26	364	11 · 5	22 · 0	36 44	8 8
27	322	10 · 6	22 · 7	36 37	7 33
28	304	11 · 7	21 · 8	36 29	7 16
28*a*	286	—	—	36 27	6 54
29	227	12 · 9	22 · 8	36 20	6 47
30	386	11 · 7	22 · 6	36 15	6 52
31	477	10 · 3	21 · 7	35 56	7 6
32	651	10 · 1	21 · 8	35 41	7 8
33	554	10 · 0	22 · 4	35 32	6 54
34	414	10 · 1	21 · 8	35 44	6 53
35	335	10 · 9	23 · 2	35 39	6 38
36	128	12 · 9	23 · 8	35 35	6 26
37	190	11 · 8	22 · 0	35 50	6 0
38	503	11 · 8	22 · 0	35 58	5 26
39	517	13 · 3	21 · 0	35 59	5 27
40	586	13 · 4	23 · 6	36 0	4 40
41	730	13 · 4	23 · 6	35 57	4 12
42	790	13 · 2	23 · 2	35 45	3 57
43	162	13 · 4	23 · 8	35 24	3 54
44	455	13 · 0	21 · 0	35 42	3 0
45	207	12 · 4	22 · 6	35 36	2 29
46	493	13 · 0	23 · 0	35 39	1 56
47	845	12 · 6	21 · 0	37 25	1 10
48	1328	12 · 8	23 · 0	37 10	0 31
49	1412	12 · 7	22 · 0	36 29	0 31
50	51	—	—	36 14	0 17 E.
50*a*	152	—	—	36 18	0 24
51	1415	12 · 7	24 · 0	36 55	1 10
52	660	—	—	36 38	1 38
52*a*	590	—	—	36 36	1 38
53	112	13 · 0	25 · 0	36 53	5 55
54	1508	13 · 0	24 · 4	37 41	6 27
55	1456	12 · 8	24 · 8	37 29	6 31
56	390	13 · 6	25 · 6	37 3	11 37
57	224	—	—	37 6	13 10
58	266	13 · 6	24 · 1	36 43	13 36
59	445	13 · 6	24 · 6	36 32	14 12
60	1743	13 · 4	23 · 3	36 31	15 46

Number of Station.	Depth in Fathoms.	Bottom Temperature.	Surface Temperature.	Position.	
61	392	13°·1 C.	22°·5 C.	38° 26′ N.	15° 32′ E.
62	730	13·0	22·5	38 38	15 21
63	181	12·4	20·2	36 1	5 26 W.
64	460	12·4	18·8	35 58	5 28
65	198	12·1	17·3	35 50	5 57
66	147	—	—	35 56	5 57
67	188	12·8	22·9	35 49	6 21

CHAPTER V.

DEEP-SEA SOUNDING.

The ordinary Sounding-lead for moderate Depths.—Liable to Error when employed in Deep Water.—Early Deep Soundings unreliable.—Improved Methods of Sounding.—The Cup-lead.—Brooke's Sounding Instrument.—The 'Bull-dog'; Fitzgerald's; the 'Hydra.'—Sounding from the 'Porcupine.'—The Contour of the Bed of the North Atlantic.

In all deep-sea investigations it is of course of the first importance to have a means of determining the depth to the last degree of accuracy, and this is not so easy a matter as might be at first supposed. Depth is almost invariably ascertained by some modification of the process of sounding. A weight is attached to the end of a line graduated by attached slips of different coloured buntine (the woollen material of which flags are made, in which the colours are particularly bright and fast) into fathoms, tens of fathoms, and hundreds of fathoms; or, for deep-sea work, with white buntine at every 50, black leather at every 100, and red buntine at every 1,000 fathoms. The weight is run down as rapidly as possible, and the number of fathoms out when the lead touches the bottom gives a more or less close approximation to the depth.

The ordinary deep-sea lead is a prismatic leaden block about two feet in length and 80 to 120 lbs. in weight, narrowing somewhat towards the upper end, where it is furnished with a stout iron ring. Before heaving, the lead is 'armed,' that is to say the lower end, which is slightly cupped, is covered with a thick coating of soft tallow. If the lead reach the bottom it brings up evidence of its having done so in a sample sticking to the tallow. Usually there is enough to indicate roughly the nature of the ground, and it is on the evidence of samples thus brought up on the 'arming' of the lead that our charts note 'mud,' 'shells,' 'gravel,' 'ooze,' or 'sand,' or a combination of these, as the kind of bottom at the particular sounding; thus we have $\overset{2,000}{\text{m. sh. s.}}$, mud, shells, and sand at 2,000 fathoms; $\overset{2,050}{\text{oz. st.}}$, ooze and stones at 2,050 fathoms; $\overset{2,200}{\text{m. s. sh. sc.}}$, mud, sand, shells, and scoriæ at 2,200 fathoms, and so on.

When no bottom is found, that is to say, when there is no arrest to the running out of the line and nothing on the 'arming' of the lead, the sounding is entered on the chart thus, $\frac{\cdot}{3,200}$, no bottom at 3,200 fathoms. Such soundings are not to be depended upon in deep water, but they are usually quite reliable for moderate depths, so far as they go. They give us no help in the exploration of the bottom of the sea, but they are of great practical value, and indeed they give all the information which is directly required for the purposes of navigation; for if there be 'no bottom' at 200 fathoms, there is probably no dangerous shoal in the immediate neighbourhood.

Soundings are usually taken from the vessel, and while there is some way on. Where great accuracy is required, as in coast-surveying, it is necessary to sound from a boat, which can be kept in position by the oars and reference to some fixed objects on shore.

This ordinary system of sounding answers perfectly well for comparatively shallow water, but it breaks down for depths much over 1,000 fathoms. The weight is not sufficient to carry the line rapidly and vertically to the bottom; and if a heavier weight be used, ordinary sounding line is unable to draw up its own weight along with that of the lead from great depths, and gives way. No impulse is felt when the lead reaches the bottom, and the line goes on running out, and if any attempt be made to stop it it breaks. In some cases bights of the line seem to be carried along by submarine currents, and in others it is found that the line has been running out by its own weight only, and coiling itself in a tangled mass directly over the lead. All these sources of error vitiate very deep soundings. In many of the older observations made by officers of our own navy and of that of the United States, the depth returned for many points in the Atlantic we now know to have been greatly exaggerated; thus Lieutenant Walsh, of the U.S. schooner 'Taney,' reported a cast with the deep-sea lead at 34,000 feet without bottom;[1] Lieutenant Berryman, of the U.S. brig 'Dolphin,' attempted unsuccessfully to sound mid-ocean with a line 39,000 feet long;[2] Captain Denham, of H.M.S. 'Herald,' reported bottom in the

[1] Maury's Sailing Directions, 5th edition, p. 165, and 6th edition (1854), p. 213.

[2] Maury, Physical Geography of the Sea. Eleventh edition, p. 309.

South Atlantic at a depth of 46,000 feet;[1] and Lieutenant Parker, of the U.S. frigate 'Congress,' ran out a line 50,000 feet without reaching the bottom.[2] In these cases, however, the chances of error were too numerous; and in the last chart of the North Atlantic, published on the authority of Rear-Admiral Richards in Nov. 1870, no soundings are entered beyond 4,000 fathoms, and very few beyond 3,000.

A great improvement in deep-sea sounding, first introduced in the United States navy, was the use of a heavy weight and a fine line. The weight, a 32 or 68 lb. shot, is rapidly run down from a boat; and when it is supposed to have reached the bottom, which is usually indicated with tolerable certainty by a sudden change in the rate of running out of the line, the line is cut at the surface, and the depth calculated by the length of line left on the reel.

As the great problems of physical geography, the strength and direction of currents, and the general conditions of the bottom of the sea began to acquire more general interest, the particles brought up on the 'arming' of the lead from great depths were eagerly sought for and scrutinized; it thus became important that a greater quantity should be procured, enough at all events for the purposes of chemical and microscopical examination. Many instruments have been contrived from time to time for this purpose, and a vast amount of information has been gained by their use. It has now been shown that dredging on a large scale is possible at all depths, but dredging can only be performed under specially favourable circumstances, and requires a vessel specially fitted at con-

[1] Loc. cit. [2] Loc. cit.

siderable expense. We must still, therefore, depend mainly upon some form of sounding apparatus for the gradual accumulation of observations which will give us in time a consistent idea of the nature of the bottom of the sea throughout. A simple instrument which will bring up a surface sample of a pound or so, from a depth of 2,000 fathoms, without much trouble and with some certainty, is still a desideratum.

In the year 1818, Sir John Ross, in command of H.M.S. 'Isabella,' on a voyage of discovery for the purpose of exploring Baffin's Bay, invented a machine "for taking up soundings from the bottom of any fathomable depth," which he called a 'deep-sea clamm.' A large pair of forceps were kept asunder by a bolt, and the instrument was so contrived that on the bolt striking the ground, a heavy iron weight slipped down a spindle and closed the forceps, which retained within them a considerable quantity of the bottom, whether sand, mud, or small stones.[1] On the 1st of September, 1818, Sir John Ross sounded in 1,000 fathoms, lat. 73° 37′ N., long. 75° 25′ W. The soundings consisted of "soft mud, in which there were worms, and, entangled on the sounding-line, at the depth of 800 fathoms, was found a beautiful *Caput Medusæ.*" On the 6th of September Sir John Ross sounded in 1,050 fathoms, lat. 72° 23′ N., long. 73° 075′ W., and the clamms brought up 6 lbs. of very

[1] A Voyage of Discovery made under the Orders of the Admiralty in His Majesty's Ships 'Isabella' and 'Alexander,' for the purpose of exploring Baffin's Bay, and inquiring into the Possibility of a North-west Passage. By John Ross, K.S., Captain Royal Navy. London: 1819; p. 178.

soft mud. I mention these soundings thus particularly because they are the first authentic instances of any quantity of the bottom having been brought up from such depths. The clamms were used with strong whale line made of the best hemp, 2½ inches in circumference. The weight recommended by Sir John Ross for the sounding in the North Sea is fifty pounds.

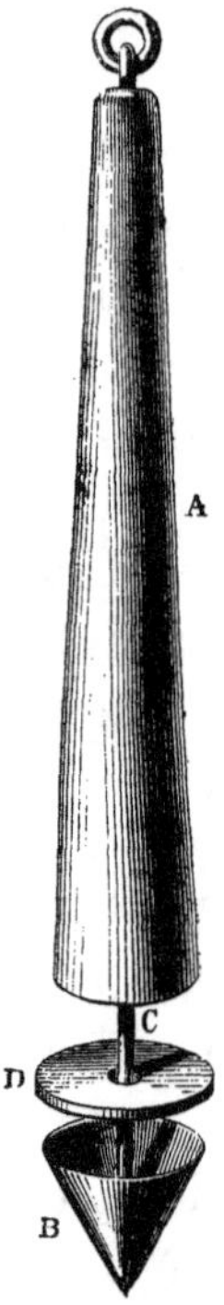

One of the earliest and certainly not the worst of these miniature dredges is a simple modification of the common deep-sea lead, the 'cup-lead' (Fig. 37). A rod of iron passes through the lead, and ends a few inches beneath it in a conical iron cup. A thick bend-leather washer slides freely on the rod between the end of the lead and the cup. The theory of this instrument is, that as the lead runs down, the current of water keeps up the washer, leaving the mouth of the cup free. On reaching the ground, the weight of the lead drives the cup into the mud or sand, and the lead falls to one side. When the lead is hauled up, a sample of the bottom goes into the cup, and is retained there by the washer, which is pressed down upon the top of the cup during its upward journey by the reversal of the current. The 'cup-lead' is very useful for moderate depths. Twice out of three times it brings up a sample, but the cup is too open and the means of closing it are too crude, and the third time everything is washed out and the cup comes up perfectly clean. Deep soundings take too

FIG. 37.—The 'Cup lead.'

much time and are too valuable to admit so large an average of losses.

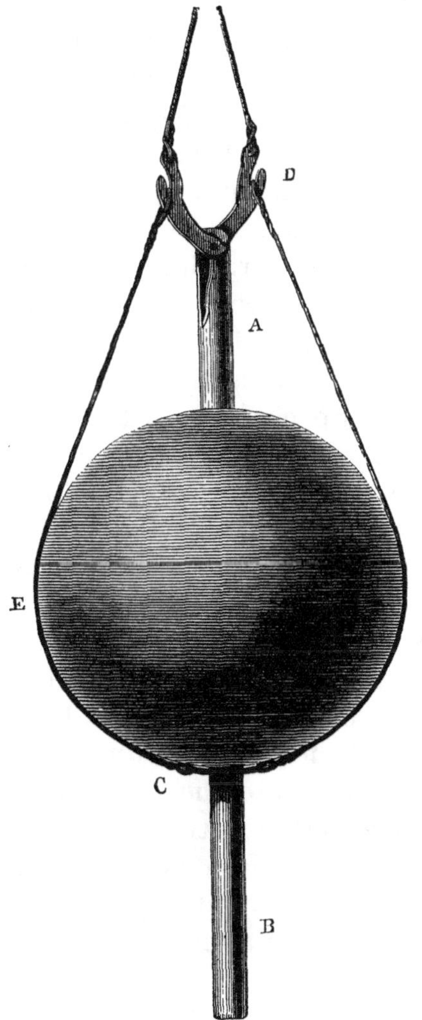

FIG. 38.—Brooke's Deep-Sea Sounding Apparatus.

About the year 1854, J. M. Brooke, passed-midshipman in the U.S. navy, a clever young officer who was at the time doing duty in the Observatory, proposed to Captain Maury a contrivance by which the shot might be detached as soon as it reached the bottom, and specimens brought up in its stead. The result of this suggestion was Brooke's deep-sea sounding apparatus (Figs. 38 and 39), of which all the more recent contrivances have been to a great extent modifications and improvements, retaining its fundamental principle, the detaching of the weight. The instrument as devised by Mr. Brooke is very simple. A 64 lb. shot E is cast with a hole through it. An iron rod A has a chamber B at the lower end, and two moveable arms hinged to the upper end with eyes to fasten two cords by which the rod is suspended; so that when the instrument is hanging free the arms are nearly vertical (Fig. 38). Each arm bears a projecting notched tooth, and before sounding the shot is suspended, with the rod passing through it, in a canvas or leather sling C attached by cords whose loops pass over the teeth. The cup at the lower end of the rod is filled with tallow 'arming,' in which a chamber has been made by pushing in a wooden plug. When the instrument strikes, the end of the rod is driven into the material of the bottom, which fills the chamber in the arming, the two jointed arms fall down, the loops of the sling are relieved from the teeth, and the rod slips through the hole in the shot and comes up alone with its enclosed sample of sediment.

In this simplest and earliest form Brooke's sounding apparatus had some of the defects of the cup-lead. The sample of the bottom was too small, and ran a risk of being washed out in hauling up. Modifications were soon made. Commander Dayman made

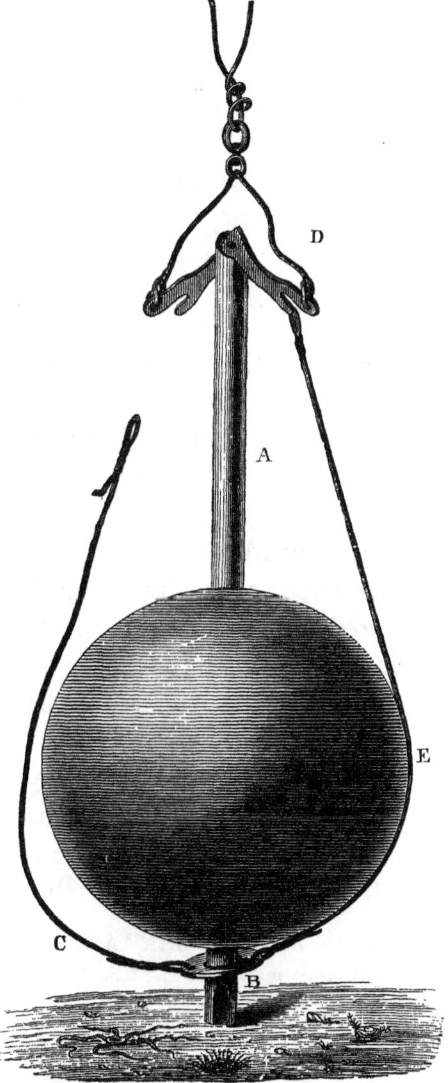

FIG. 39.—Brooke's Deep-Sea Sounding Apparatus.

several improvements for the sounding voyage of

H.M.S. 'Cyclops' in 1857.[1] He used iron wire braces to support the sinker, as these detach more freely than slings of rope; he replaced Brooke's round-shot by a leaden cylinder to diminish the resistance and thus increase the velocity in descending; and he adapted a valve opening inwards, to the terminal chamber in the rod, to prevent the washing out of the sample. Commander Dayman seems to have found the apparatus thus improved to answer well. He used it throughout his important survey of the 'telegraph plateau.'

The 'Bull-dog' sounding machine (Fig. 40) is now probably the most generally known of these dredging-leads. This instrument is an adaptation of Sir John Ross' deep-sea clamms, with the addition of Brooke's principle of the disengaging weight. It was invented during the famous sounding voyage of H.M.S. 'Bull-dog' in the year 1860, and Sir Leopold M'Clintock gives the chief credit of its invention to the assistant-engineer on board, Mr. Steil.[2] A pair of scoops A close upon one another scissorwise on a hinge, and have two pairs of appendages B, which stand to the opening and closing of the scoops in the relation of scissor handles. This apparatus is permanently attached to the sounding-line by the rope F, which in the figure is represented hanging loose, and which is fixed to

[1] Deep-Sea Soundings in the North Atlantic Ocean, between Ireland and Newfoundland, made in H.M.S. 'Cyclops,' Lieut.-Commander Joseph Dayman, in June and July 1857. Published by order of the Lords Commissioners of the Admiralty. London: 1858.

[2] Remarks illustrative of the Sounding Voyage of H.M.S. 'Bull-dog' in 1860; Captain Sir Leopold M'Clintock commanding. Published by order of the Lords Commissioners of the Admiralty. London: 1861.

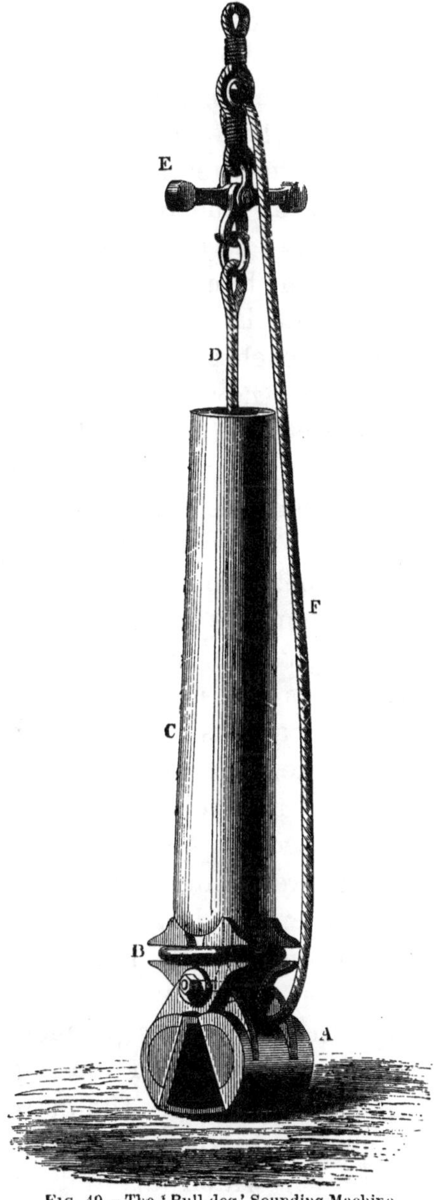

FIG. 40.—The 'Bull-dog' Sounding Machine.

the spindle on which the cups turn. Attached to the same spindle is the rope D, which ends above in an iron ring. E represents a pair of tumbler hooks, fastened likewise to the end of the sounding-line; C a heavy leaden or iron weight, with a hole through it wide enough to allow the rope D with its loop and ring to pass freely; and B, a strong india-rubber band which passes round the handles of the scoops. In the figure the instrument is represented as it is sent down and before it reaches the bottom. The weight C and the scoops A are now suspended by the rope D, whose ring is caught by the tumbler hooks E. The elastic ring B is in a state of tension, ready to draw together the scoop handles and close the scoops, but it is antagonized by the weight C, which, pressing down into a space between the handles, keeps them asunder. The moment the scoops are driven into the ground by the weight, the tension on the rope D is relaxed, the tumblers fall and release the ring, and the weight falls and allows the elastic band to close the scoops and to keep them closed upon whatever they may contain; the rope D slips through the weight, and the closed scoops are drawn up by the rope F. This is a pretty idea, and an ingenious and elegant apparatus, but it is rather complicated. I have never seen it in use, but I should fear that the observer might often be thwarted by the scoops falling in a wrong direction, or by pebbles getting into the hinges and preventing their closing thoroughly. The simpler all these things are the better.

We used in our trip in the 'Lightning' in 1868 an instrument (Fig. 41) which at first sight scarcely looks promising from its apparent want of compactness, but I will say this for the 'Fitzgerald' sounding apparatus that I never knew it fail; and we were obliged, unfortunately for ourselves, to try it frequently in very bad weather and under most unfavourable circumstances. The sounding-line ends in a loop passing through an eye in the centre of a bar of iron F. The bar terminates at one end in a claw and at the other in a second eye, to which a chain is attached. A scoop A, with a sharp, spade-like lip, is fixed to a long and rather heavy iron rod D, with an expanded rudder-shaped end to steady it in passing quickly through the water, and beneath this an eye, which fits the claw of the bar F. A door B fits the scoop to which it is hinged, and it is also hinged to the arm C, which, when held in a vertical position, keeps it open. The arm C is attached by the chain to the eye in the bar F, and the arm and chain correspond in length to the rod D. Two teeth E E project from D, and on these are hung a heavy weight. The

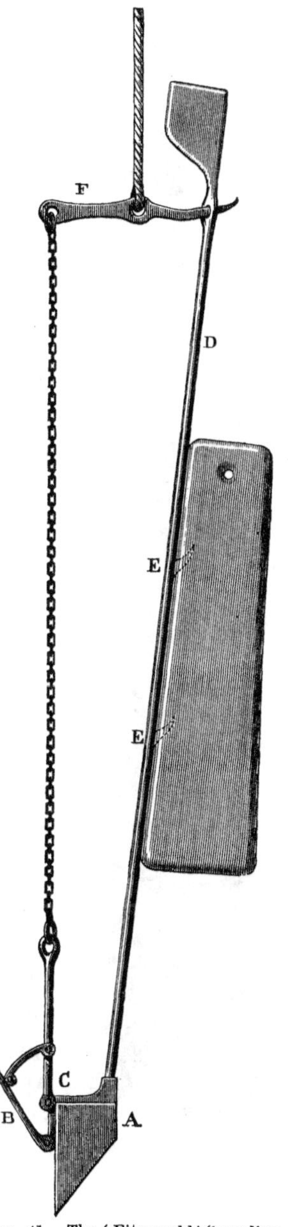

FIG. 41.—The 'Fitzgerald' Sounding Machine.

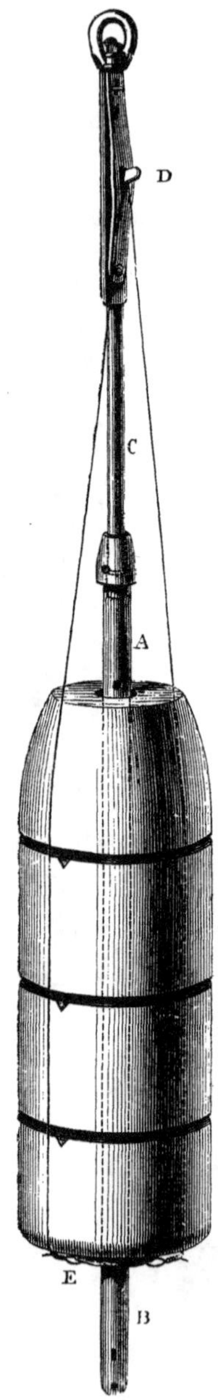

FIG. 42.—The 'Hydra' Sounding Machine.

apparatus is so adjusted, that when the weight is attached and the instrument hanging ready for use, as represented in the figure, the rod F maintains a horizontal position. When the instrument strikes the ground, the tension on the bar F is relieved, the weight draws the rod D off the claw and slips off, at the same time filling the scoop. When hauling up, all the instrument falls into a nearly vertical line, and the scoop comes up full in the middle, the weight of D keeping its mouth closed up against its lid.

The apparatus used during the cruise of the 'Porcupine," where sounding was carried on to the utmost attainable accuracy and at great depths, was a somewhat elaborate modification of Brooke's sounding machine which had been previously employed by Captain Shortland in the voyage of H.M.S. 'Hydra,' sounding across the Arabian Gulf preparatory to laying the Indian Cable.

This special modification, which certainly answered remarkably well, appears to have been due entirely to Mr. Gibbs, the blacksmith on board the vessel.[1] We christened it the

[1] Sounding Voyage of H.M.S. 'Hydra,' Captain P. F. Shortland, 1868. Published by order of the Lords Commiss. of the Admiralty. London: 1869.

'Hydra,' in recognition of its inventor and of the vessel in which it was first used.

The axis of the 'Hydra' (Fig. 42) is a strong brass tube, which unscrews into four chambers. The three lowest of these are closed above by conical valves opening upwards, but not fitting absolutely tightly, so as to allow a little water to pass; and the lowest chamber B is closed by a butterfly valve also opening upwards. The upper (fourth) chamber A contains a piston, and the piston-rod C is continued upwards into a rod which ends in the ring to which the sounding-line is attached. The upper chamber in which the piston works has a large hole on either side about the middle of its length, and a small hole passes through the piston itself. Projecting from the upper part of the rod there is a notched tooth D, and over the tooth passes an arched steel spring, with a slit which allows the tooth to pass through its centre, and its two ends fastened moveably to the rod. When the spring is forcibly pushed back, it allows the tooth with its notch to protrude through the central slit. The weight consists of three or four cylinders of iron F, toothed and notched so as to fit into one another and make one mass. The weight used in the 'Porcupine' was from two to three hundredweight, according to the depth. The weight is suspended by an iron wire sling which passes over the notched tooth, the spring having been pressed back. The weight is amply sufficient to retain the spring in that position.

The figure represents the instrument prepared to let go, the whole weight suspended from the ring at the top of the piston-rod, which is thus fully drawn out of its cylinder. As the instrument runs down the water passes freely through the tube and valves, and pours out by the holes in the wall of the cylinder. When it touches the ground the piston is pulled down by the weight, but its progress is somewhat arrested by the water in the lower part of the cylinder, which can only escape slowly, thus giving the weight time to force the terminal chamber with the butterfly valves into the ground. The weights then rest upon the bottom and relieve the spring which throws the sling off the tooth. The tube comes up free with all the valves closed, and the last chamber filled with the substance of the bottom, and the other chamber with bottom water.

In the skilful hands of Captain Calver the 'Hydra' never once failed, and from the great weight used it is admirably suited for accurate soundings in deep water; but it is somewhat complicated, and it brings up very small samples of the bottom. In the case of the cruise of the 'Porcupine,' where the large dredge was sent down at almost every sounding-station, this was of little consequence; but where dredging is impracticable, and all information as to the condition of the bottom must be got from soundings, some simple adaptation of the 'Bull-dog' scoops or the Fitzgerald apparatus would certainly have a great advantage.

During the cruise of the 'Porcupine' in 1869 soundings were taken with the utmost care at ninety stations, and in 1870 at sixty-seven stations, and on every occasion the operation was conducted by Capt. Calver himself, whose great experience on the surveying service was in itself a guarantee of the greatest possible accuracy. Captain Calver told me that on every occasion, even at the greatest depths, he felt distinctly the shock of the arrest of the weight upon the bottom communicated to his hand. A careful sounding was always taken immediately before letting go the dredge. I will take as an example the sounding which determined the depth of the deepest haul of the dredge yet made, in 2,435 fathoms in the Bay of Biscay on the 22nd of July, 1869, and describe the *modus operandi.*

The 'Porcupine' was provided at Woolwich with an admirable double cylinder donkey-engine of 12-horse power (nominal), placed on the deck amidships, with a couple of surging drums. This little engine was the comfort of our lives; nothing could exceed the steadiness of its working and the ease with which its speed could be regulated. During the whole expedition it brought in with the ordinary drum, the line, whether sounding-line or dredge-rope, with almost any weight, at a uniform rate of a foot per second. Once or twice it was over-strained, and then we pitied the willing little thing panting like an over-taxed horse; and sometimes we put on a small drum for very hard work, gaining thereby additional power at some expense of speed.

Two powerful derricks were rigged for sounding and dredging operations, one over the stern and one over the port bow. The bow derrick was the stronger, and we usually found it the more convenient to dredge from. Sounding was most frequently carried on from the stern. Both derricks were provided with accumulators, accessory pieces of apparatus which we found of great value. The block through which the sounding-line or dredging-rope passed was not attached directly to the derrick, but to a rope which passed through an eye at the end of the spar, and was fixed to a 'bitt' on the deck. On a bight of this rope between the block and the 'bitt' the accumulator was lashed. This consists of thirty or forty or more of Hodge's vulcanized india-rubber springs fastened together at the two extremities, and kept free from one another by being passed through holes in two round wooden ends like the heads of churn-staves. The loop of the rope is made long enough to permit the accumulator to stretch to double or treble its length, but it is arrested far within its breaking point. The accumulator is valuable in the first place as indicating roughly the amount of strain upon the line; and in order that it may do so with some decree of accuracy it is so arranged as to play along the derrick, which is graduated from trial to the number of cwts. of strain indicated by the greater or less extension of the accumulator; but its more important function is to take off the suddenness of the strain on the line when the vessel is pitching. The friction of one or two miles of cord in the water is so great as to prevent its yielding freely to a sudden jerk such as that given to the attached end when the vessel rises to a sea, and the line is apt to snap. A letting-go frame like that used on board the 'Hydra,' a board with a slit through which the free end of the sounding machine passed, and which supported the weights while the instrument was being prepared, was fitted under the stern derrick. The sounding instrument was the 'Hydra,' weighted with 336 lbs. The sounding-line was wound amidships just abaft the donkey-engine on a large strong reel, its revolution commanded by a brake. The reel held about 4,000 fathoms of medium No. 2 line of the best Italian hemp, the No. of threads 18, the weight per 100 fathoms 12 lbs. 8 ozs., the circumference 0·8 inch, and the breaking strain, dry, 1,402 lbs., soaked a day 1,211 lbs., marked for 50, 100, and 1,000 fathoms.

The weather was remarkably clear and fine; the wind from the north-west, force = 4; the sea moderate, with a slight swell from the north-west. We were in lat. 47° 38′ N., long. 12° 08′ W., at the mouth of the Bay of Biscay, about 200 miles to the west of Ushant. The sounding instrument, with two Miller-Casella thermometers and a water bottle attached a fathom or two above it, was cast off the letting-go frame at 2h. 44m. 20s. p.m. The line was run off by hand from the reel and given to the weight as fast as it would take it, so that there might not be the slightest check or strain. The following table gives the absolute rate of descent:—

Fathoms.	Time.	Interval.	Fathoms.	Time.	Interval.
	h. m. s.	m. s.		h. m. s.	m. s.
0	2 44 20	—	1300	2 58 5	1 23
100	2 45 5	0 45	1400	2 59 37	1 32
200	2 45 45	0 40	1500	3 1 9	1 32
300	2 46 30	0 45	1600	3 2 42	1 33
400	2 47 25	0 55	1700	3 4 19	1 37
500	2 48 15	0 50	1800	3 6 6	1 47
600	2 49 15	1 0	1900	3 7 53	1 47
700	2 50 24	1 9	2000	3 9 40	1 47
800	2 51 23	0 59	2100	3 11 29	1 49
900	2 52 45	1 22	2200	3 13 24	1 55
1000	2 54 0	1 15	2300	3 15 23	1 59
1100	2 55 21	1 21	2400	3 17 15	1 52
1200	2 56 42	1 21	2435	3 17 55	0 40

In this case the timing was only valuable as corroborating other evidence of the accuracy of the sounding, for even at this great depth, nearly three miles, the shock of the arrest of the weight at the bottom was distinctly perceptible to the commander, who passed the line through his hand during the descent. This was probably the deepest sounding which had been taken up to that time which was perfectly reliable. It was taken under unusually favourable conditions of weather, with the most perfect appliances, and with consummate skill. The whole time occupied in descent was 33 minutes 35 seconds; and in heaving up, 2 hours 2 minutes. The cylinder of the sounding apparatus came up filled with fine grey Atlantic ooze, containing a considerable proportion of fresh shells of *Globigerina*. The two Miller-Casella thermometers registered a minimum temperature of 2°·5 C.

Various attempts have been made to devise an instrument which should determine accurately the amount of vertical descent of the lead by self-registering machinery. The most successful apparatus for this purpose, and the one most in use is 'Massey's sounding-machine.' This instrument, in its latest and most improved form, to be used with the common lead, is shown in Fig. 43. Two thimbles F F pass through the two ends of the heavy oval brass shield A A; to the upper of these the sounding-line is attached, and to the lower the weight at about half a fathom from the machine. A set of four brass vanes or wings B are soldered obliquely to an axis in such a position that as the machine descends the axis revolves by the pressure of the water against the vanes. The revolving axis communicates its motion to the indices on the dial-plate C, which are so adjusted that the index on the right-hand dial passes through a division for every fathom of

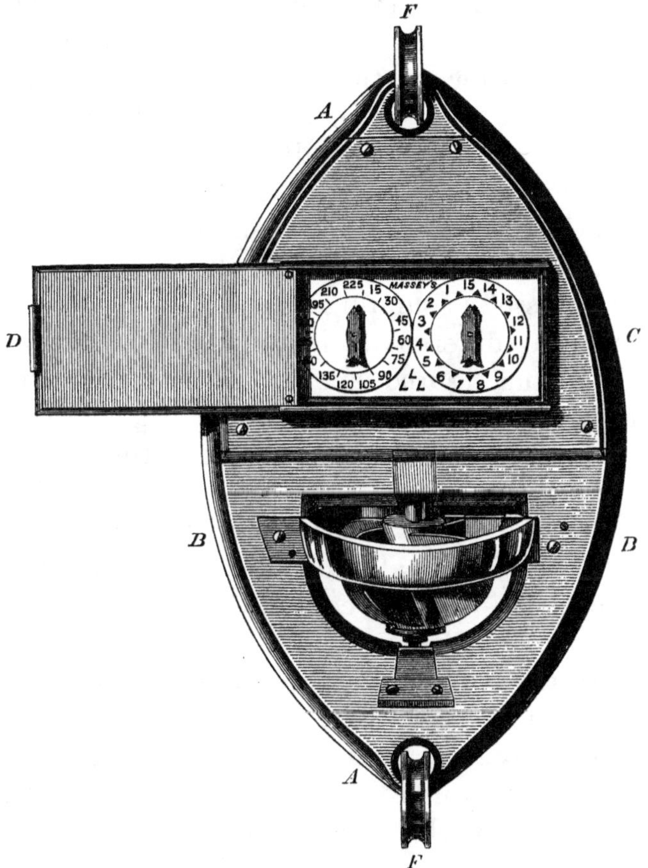

FIG. 43.—'Massey's' Sounding Machine.

vertical descent, whether quick or slow, and makes an entire revolution for 15 fathoms, while the left-hand index passes through a division on the circle for 15 fathoms, and makes an entire revolution during a descent of 225 fathoms. Where greater depths are required it is only necessary to add another dial and index. This sounding instrument answers very well in moderately deep water, and is extremely valuable for checking soundings by the ordinary method, where deep currents are suspected, as it *ought* to register vertical descent only. It is not satisfactory in very deep water, and its uncertainty is shared apparently by all instruments involving metal wheel-work. It is difficult to tell the reason. The machinery seems to get jammed in some way under the enormous pressure of the water.

The 'Massey's sounding-machine' in common use is somewhat different from the 'shield' instrument described and figured above. It is constructed on precisely the same principle, but it is bolted to a special form of sounding lead, and is thus somewhat more cumbrous.

Besides the increasing attention which has been paid of late years to all subjects of scientific interest, and especially to those connected with physical geography, the conditions of the depths of the sea, the nature of the bottom, the force and direction of deep currents, the temperature at great depths, and, in fact, all the conditions affecting the sea bottom, have lately acquired great practical importance in connection with telegraphic communication by ocean cables.

The Atlantic Ocean, with the accessible portions of the Arctic Sea, has naturally, from the relation in which it stands to the first maritime and commercial nations of the present period, been the most carefully surveyed; and as it appears to contain depths nearly if not quite as great as any to be found in the other ocean basins, it may probably be taken as a fair example of ordinary conditions. It is open from pole to pole, and thus participates in all conditions of climate, and it communicates freely with the other seas. We have still but scanty information about the beds of the Indian, the Antarctic, and the Pacific oceans, but the few observations which have hitherto reached us seem to indicate that neither is the depth extreme in these seas, nor does the nature of the bottom differ greatly from what we find nearer home. The Mediterranean—a closed *cul-de-sac* almost cut off from the general ocean—is under most peculiar circumstances, which will be discussed hereafter. The general result to which we are led by the careful and systematic deep-sea soundings which have been undertaken of late years by our own Admiralty and by the American and Swedish Governments, is that the depth of the sea is not so great as was at one time supposed. I have already mentioned that in some of the earlier sounding expeditions enormous depths were registered from various parts of the Atlantic, and I have also mentioned the reasons, depending chiefly upon defective appliances, why many of these soundings are now considered untrustworthy. Lieutenant Berryman, of the U.S. brig 'Dolphin,' reported 4,580 fathoms (27,480 feet), equal to the height of Dwalagiri, in lat. 41° 7′ N., long. 49° 23′ W., half-way between New York and the Açores; 'no bottom' at 4,920 fathoms (29,520 feet), deeper than the height of Deodunga, the highest peak in the world, in lat. 38° 3′ N., long. 67° 14′ W.; and 'no bottom' at 6,600 fathoms (39,600 feet), lat. 32° 55′ N., long. 47° 58′ W., indicating a chasm between the coast of America and the Western Islands, which might easily engulph the whole range of the Himalayas. This space probably represents the deepest part of the North Atlantic; but there is little doubt that these depths are greatly exaggerated. The average depth of the ocean bed does not appear to be much more than 2,000 fathoms (12,000 feet), about equal to the mean height of the elevated table lands of Asia.

The thin shell of water which covers so much of the face of the earth occupies all the broad general depressions in its crust, and it is only limited and more abrupt prominences which project above its surface as masses of land with their crowning plateaux and mountain ranges. The Atlantic Ocean covers 30,000,000 of square miles and the Arctic Sea 3,000,000, and taken together they almost exactly equal the united areas of Europe, Asia, and Africa —the whole of the old world; and yet there seem to be few depressions in its bed to a greater depth than 15,000 or 20,000 feet—a little more than the height of Mont Blanc—and except in the neighbourhood of the shores there is only one very marked mass of mountains, the volcanic group of the Açores.

The central and southern parts of the Atlantic appear to be an old depression, probably at all events coæval with the deposition of the Jurassic formations of Europe, and throughout these long ages the tendency of that great body of water has no doubt been to ameliorate the outlines, softening down asperities by the disintegrating action of its waves and currents, and filling up hollows by drifting about and distributing their materials.

The first careful surveys of the Atlantic, in which great depths were determined with considerable accuracy, are the cruises of Lieut.-Commanding Lee, in the U.S. brig 'Dolphin' (1851-52), and of Lieut.-Commanding O. H. Berryman, in the same vessel in 1852-53; but the sounding voyage in which modern appliances were first employed with perfect accuracy with a practical object was that of Lieutenant Berryman in 1856, in the U.S. steamer 'Arctic,' in which twenty-four deep-sea soundings were taken with the Brooke's and Massey's sounding machines on a great circle between St. John's, Newfoundland, and Valentia in Ireland, with a view to the laying of the first cable. The same ground was gone over by Lieutenant Dayman, in H.M.S. 'Cyclops,' in June and July 1857, and thirty-four soundings were taken, the depth being estimated by Massey's sounding-machine and a modification of Brooke's machine already described. The next important sounding expedition was that of Commander Dayman, in H.M.S. 'Gorgon,' from Newfoundland to the Açores, and thence to England. The depths were taken in this case with a lead usually 188 lbs. in weight which was lost at each cast, and albacore line with a breaking strain of 420 lbs. Only on one occasion, about a third of the way from the Açores to England, a cup-lead was let go, attached to a stronger line, in 1,900 fathoms, and came up half filled with grey ooze.

Another route for a telegraph cable having been proposed, H.M.S. 'Bull-dog' started in July 1860, under the command of Captain Sir Leopold M'Clintock, and took depths between the Færoe Islands and Iceland, and thence to Greenland and Labrador. The soundings were taken first by cod-line and an iron sinker of about 1 cwt., the line and sinker being cut off at each operation; and the sounding was then usually repeated with the 'Bull-dog' sounding-machine, with which large samples of the bottom were procured. A diary of this voyage was kept by Dr. Wallich, Naturalist to the Expedition, and was afterwards published by him as part of the extremely important memoir on the North Atlantic sea-bed, to which I have already referred. Some further questions having arisen as to the best line to be taken by an Atlantic telegraph cable, Captain Hoskyn, R.N., was despatched in the 'Porcupine' to examine the curious dip from 550 to 1,750 fathoms, described by Captain Dayman in 1857 as occurring about 170 miles west of Valentia. One important result of this cruise was the discovery of the 'Porcupine' Bank, about 120 miles west from Galway Bay, with a minimum depth of 82 fathoms.

Towards the latter part of the year 1868 H.M.S. 'Gannet,' Commander W. Chimmo, R.N., was ordered by the Admiralty to define during her homeward voyage from the West India Station the northern limits of the Gulf Stream, and to take deep soundings and temperatures. Thirteen soundings were taken with the Brooke's machine over an area of upwards of 10,000 square miles from Sable Island (lat. 43° 20′ N., long. 60° W.), at depths varying from 80 to 2,700 fathoms.

For many years past the American Government

have been prosecuting a most careful and elaborate survey of their coast-line; and latterly the Coast Survey, under the late Professor Bache and the present energetic head of the Bureau, Professor Pierce, has pushed its operations into deep water, particularly in the Gulf-stream region north-westwards of the Strait of Florida. Dredging operations have been conducted most successfully under Count Pourtales, and it will be seen hereafter that his results are a valuable complement and corroboration of our own. The Swedish Government has twice executed careful soundings in the sea between Spitzbergen and Greenland and to the south-west of Spitzbergen; in 1860 under the direction of Otto Thorell, and in 1868 through the Swedish Arctic Exploring Expedition under Captain Count von Otter of the Royal Swedish steamer 'Sophia.' In 1869 the Swedish corvette 'Josephine' sounded and dredged in the North Atlantic, taking soundings to the depth of upwards of 3,000 fathoms, and discovered the 'Josephine Bank,' with a minimum depth of 102 fathoms, in lat. 36° 45′ N., long. 14° 10′ W. to the north-west of the Strait of Gibraltar. The North-German Polar expeditions greatly increased our knowledge of the Spitzbergen and the Greenland Seas; and finally, on December 20th, 1870, the American nautical school-ship 'Mercury,' Captain P. Giraud, crossed the Tropical Atlantic to Sierra Leone, which she reached on the 14th of February, 1871. She left Sierra Leone on February 21st, and soundings and other observations were continued till she reached Havannah on the 13th of April. The object of this expedition and the character of the observers are singular and instructive. It seems that the 'Mercury' is a vessel belonging to the Commissioners in charge of the hospitals and prisons of New York, and it is employed for the purpose of training boys, committed by the magistrates for vagrancy and slight misdemeanours, to become thorough seamen. One important part of the training in this ship is that she makes long cruises, and the boys are thus fitted quickly to enter into the service of the navy or the mercantile marine. In the present cruise, the Commissioners, desiring to promote the education of the lads and to advance the interests of science as much as lay in their power, instructed the captain to obtain a series of soundings on the line of or near the equator from the coast of Africa to the mouth of the Amazon, and to observe the set of the surface currents and the temperature of the water at various depths.

The Commissioners report most favourably of this mode of training, which is now being so generally adopted in this country. For such boys the adventurous life has a special charm, and, "instead of growing up to be a curse to the community, they are made into valuable men." Two hundred and fifty scapegraces were sent out on this voyage, and on the return of the ship, in the opinion of the captain 100 of these were capable of discharging the duties of ordinary seamen.

Brooke's detaching sounding apparatus was used in the 'Mercury,' and in the report of the scientific results of the voyage, which was drawn out by Professor Henry Draper of New York, a diagram of the bed of the Atlantic at the twelfth parallel is introduced, based on fifteen soundings. It shows that, "parting from the African coast, the bed of the ocean sinks very rapidly. A couple of degrees west of the longitude of Cape Verde the soundings are 2,900 fathoms. From this point the mean depth across the ocean may be estimated at about 2,400 fathoms, but from this there are two striking departures—first, a depression, the depth of which is 3,100 fathoms; and, second, an elevation, at which the soundings are only 1,900, the general result of this being a deep trough on the African side and a narrower and shallower trough on the American."[1]

Referring to the chart (Pl. VII.), in which the greater depths are indicated by the deeper shades of blue, a shade to every 1,000 fathoms; in the Arctic Sea there is deep water ranging to 1,500 fathoms to the west and south-west of Spitzbergen. Extending from the coast of Norway and including Iceland, the Færoe Islands, Shetland and Orkney, Great Britain and Ireland, and the bed of the North Sea to the coast of France, there is a wide plateau on which the depth rarely reaches 500 fathoms, but to the west of Iceland and communicating doubtless with the deep water in the Spitzbergen Sea a trough 500 miles wide and in some places nearly 2,000 fathoms deep, curves along the east coast of Greenland. This is the path of one of the great Arctic return currents.

[1] Cruise of the School-ship 'Mercury' in the Tropical Atlantic, with a Report to the Commissioners of Public Charities and Correction of the City of New York on the Chemical and Physical Facts collected from the Deep-sea Researches made during the Voyage of the Nautical School-ship 'Mercury,' undertaken in the Tropical Atlantic and Caribbean Sea, 1870-71. By Henry Draper, M.D., Professor of Analytical Chemistry and Physiology in the University of New York. Abstracted in *Nature*, vol. v. p. 324.

After sloping gradually to a depth of 500 fathoms to the westward of the coast of Ireland in lat. 52° N., the bottom suddenly dips to 1,700 fathoms at the rate of about fifteen to nineteen feet in the 100; and from this point to within about 200 miles of the coast of Newfoundland when it begins to shoal again, there is a vast undulating submarine plain, averaging about 2,000 fathoms in depth below the surface—the 'telegraph plateau.'

A valley about 500 miles wide, and with a mean depth of 2,500 fathoms, stretches from off the south-west coast of Ireland, along the coast of Europe dipping into the Bay of Biscay, past the Strait of Gibraltar, and along the west coast of Africa. Opposite the Cape de Verde Islands it seems to merge into a slightly deeper trough, which occupies the axis of the South Atlantic and passes into the Antarctic Sea. A nearly similar valley curves round the coast of North America, about 2,000 fathoms in depth off Newfoundland and Labrador, and becoming considerably deeper to the southward; where it follows the outline of the coast of the States and the Bahamas and Windward Islands, and finally joins the central trough of the South Atlantic off the coast of Brazil, with a depth of 2,500 fathoms. A wide nearly level elevated tract with a mean depth below the surface of 1,500 fathoms, nearly equal in area to the continent of Africa, extends southwards from Iceland as far as the 20th parallel of north latitude. This plateau culminates at the parallel of 40° north latitude in the volcanic group of the Açores. Pico, the highest point of the Açores, is 7,613 feet (1,201 fathoms) above the level of the sea, which gives from the level of the plateau a height of 16,206 feet (2,701 fathoms), a little more than the height of Mont Blanc above the sea-level.

Accurate soundings are as yet much too distant to justify anything like a detailed contour map of the bed of the Atlantic, and such a sketch as the one here given can only be regarded as a first rough draft. Nothing, however, can give a more erroneous or exaggerated conception of its outline than the ideal section in Captain Maury's 'Physical Geography of the Sea,' although it is in a certain sense correct.

According to our present information, we must regard the Atlantic Ocean as covering a vast region of wide shallow valleys and undulating plains, with a few groups of volcanic mountains, insignificant both in height and extent, when we consider the enormous area of the ocean bed.

NOLSÖ, FROM THE HILLS ABOVE THORSHAVN.

CHAPTER VI.

DEEP-SEA DREDGING.

The Naturalist's Dredge.—O. F. Müller.—Ball's Dredge.—Dredging at moderate Depths.—The Dredge-rope.—Dredging in Deep Water.—The 'Hempen tangles.'—Dredging on board the 'Porcupine.'—The Sieves.—The Dredger's Note-book.—The Dredging Committee of the British Association.—Dredging on the Coast of Britain.—Dredging abroad.—History of the Progress of Knowledge of the Abyssal Fauna.

APPENDIX A.—One of the Dredging Papers issued by the British Association Committee, filled up by Mr. MacAndrew.

UP to the middle of last century the little that was known of the inhabitants of the bottom of the sea beyond low-water mark, seems to have been gathered almost entirely from the few objects found thrown upon the beach from time to time after storms, and from chance captures on lead-lines, and by fishermen on their long lines and in trawls and oyster and clam dredges. Even these precarious sources of information could not be used to the utmost, for it was next to impossible to induce fishermen to bring ashore anything except the regular objects of their industry. Even now the schoolmaster has scarcely made way enough to eradicate old prejudices. Fishermen are often so absolutely ignorant of the nature of these extraneous animals, that it is conceivable to them that they may be devils of some kind which may have the power in some occult way of influencing them and the results of their fishing. I believe, however, that with the progress of education this notion is dying out in most places, and that now fewer rarities and novelties are lost because it is 'unlucky' to keep them in the boat.

The naturalist's dredge does not appear to have been systematically used for investigating the fauna of the bottom of the sea, until it was employed by Otho Frederick Müller in the researches which afforded material for the publication in 1779 of his admirable "Descriptions and History of the rarer and less known Animals of Denmark and Norway." In the preface to the first volume Müller gives a quaint account of his machinery and mode of working which it is pleasant to read.

The first paragraph quoted gives a description of a dredge not very unlike that used by Ball and Forbes (Fig. 44), only the mouth of the dredge seems to have been square, a modification of the ordinary form which we find useful for some purposes still, but in most cases it gives fatal facilities for 'washing out' in the process of hauling in.

"Praecipuum instrumentum, quo fundi maris et sinuum incolas extrahere conabar, erat *Sacculus* reticularis, ex funiculis cannabinis concinnatus, margine aperturae alligatus laminis quatuor ferreis ora exteriori acutis, vlnam longis, quatuor vncias latis, et in quadratum dispositis. Angulis laminarum exsurgebant quatuor bacilli ferrei, altera extremitate in annulum liberum iuncti. Huic annectitur funis ducentarum et plurium orgyarum longitudine. Saccus mari immissus pondere ferrei apparatus fundum plerumque petit, interdum diuersorum et contrariorum saepe fluminum maris inferiorum aduersa actione moleque ipsius funis plurium orgyarum in via retineri, nec fundum attingere creditur."

The figure of this first 'naturalist's dredge' is taken from an ornamental scroll on the title-page of Müller's book.

"Fundo iniacens ope remorum aut venti modici trahitur, donec tractum quendam quaeuis obuia excipiendo confecerit. In cymbam denique retrahitur spe et labore, at opera et oleum saepe perditur, nubesque pro Iunone captatur, vel enim totus argilla fumante aut limo foetente, aut meris silicibus, aut testaceorum et coralliorum emortuorum quisquiliis impletur, vel saxis praeruptis et latebrosis cautibus implicitus horarum interuallo vel in perpetuum omnia experientis retrahendi inuenta frustrat; interdum quidem vnum et alterum *molluscum*, *helminthicum*, aut *testaceum* minus notum in dulce laborum lenimen reportat." Müller graphically describes the difficulties which he encountered in carrying on his work. The paucity of animal life on the Scandinavian coasts; the wild and variable climate, "aëris intemperies, marisque in sinubus et oris maritimis Norvegiae inconstantia adeo praepropera et praepostera, vt aër calidissimus vix minutorum interuallo in frigidum, tempestas serena in horridam, malacia infida in aestu ferventem pelagum haud raro mutetur." Still nothing can quell the energy of the enthusiastic old naturalist, who looks upon all his hardships as part of the day's work: "Hanc mutationem saepius cum vitae periculo et sanitatis dispendio expertus sum, nec tamen, membra licet fractus, animum demisi, nec ab incepto desistere potui. Discant dehinc historiae naturalis scituli, rariora naturae absque indefesso labore nec comparari, nec iuste nosci."[1] It does not appear, however, that Otho Frederick Müller dredged much beyond thirty fathoms, and in his day the knowledge of marine animals was not sufficiently advanced to warrant any generalization as to their bathymetrical distribution.

FIG. 44.—Otho Frederick Müller's Dredge. A.D. 1750.

The instrument usually employed in this and other northern countries for dredging oysters and clams is a light frame of iron about five feet long by a foot or so in width at the mouth, with a scraper like a narrow hoe on one side, and a suspending apparatus of thin iron bars which meet in an iron ring for the attachment of the dredge rope on the other. From the frame is suspended a bag about two feet in depth, of iron chain netting, or of wide-meshed hempen cord netting, or of a mixture of both. Naturalist dredgers at first used the oyster dredge, and all the different dredges now in use are modifications of it in one direction or in another; for in its simplicity it is not

[1] Zoologia Danica. Sev Animalivm Daniae et Norvegiae rariorum ac minvs notorvm Descriptiones et Historia. Avctore Othone Friderico Müller. Havniae, 1788.

suitable for scientific purposes. The oyster dredge has a scraper only on one side. In the skilled hands of the fishermen this is no disadvantage, for it is always sent down in such a way that it falls face foremost, but philosophers using it in deep water very generally found that whether from clumsiness or from want of sufficient practice, they had got the dredge down on its back, and of course it came up empty. Again, oyster dredgers are only allowed to take oysters of a certain size, and the meshing of the commercial dredge is so contrived as to allow all bodies under a certain considerable size to pass through. This defeats the object of the naturalist; for some of the prizes to which he attaches the highest value are mites of things scarcely visible to the unaided eye.

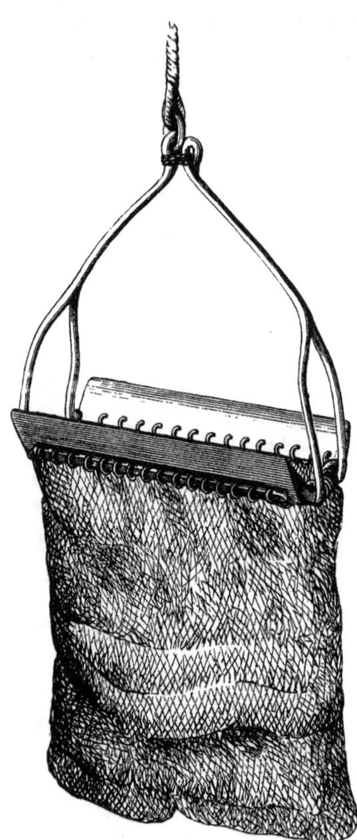

FIG. 45.—'Ball's Dredge.'

The remedy for these defects is to have a scraper on each side, with the arms attached in such a way that one or other of the scrapers must reach the ground in whatever position the dredge may fall; and to have the bag deeper in proportion to the size of the frame, and of a material which is only sufficiently open to allow the water to pass freely through, with the openings so distributed as to leave a part of the bag close enough to bring up the finest mud.

The late Dr. Robert Ball of Dublin devised the modification which has since been used almost universally by naturalists in this country and abroad under the name of 'Ball's Dredge' (Fig. 45). The dredges on this pattern used in Britain for ten years after their first introduction about the year 1838, were usually small and rather heavy—not more than from twelve to fifteen inches in length by four or four and a half inches in width at the mouth. There were two scrapers the length of the dredge-frame and an inch and a half or two inches wide, set at an angle of about 110° to the plane of the dredge's mouth, so that when the dredge was gently hauled along it took hold of the ground and secured anything loose on its surface. I have seen Dr. Ball scatter pence on the drawing-room floor and pick them up quite dexterously with the dredge drawn along in the ordinary dredging position.

Latterly we have used Ball's dredges of considerably larger size. Perhaps the most convenient form and size for dredging from a row-boat or a yawl at depths under a hundred fathoms is that represented by Fig. 45. The frame is eighteen inches long, and its width is five inches. The scrapers are three inches wide, and they are so set that the distance across between their scraping edges is seven inches and a half. The ends of the frame connecting the scrapers are round bars of iron five-eighths of an inch in diameter, and from these two curved arms of round iron of the same thickness, dividing beneath into two branches which are attached to the ends of the cross-bars by eyes allowing the arms to fold down over the dredge-mouth, meet in two heavy eyes at a point eighteen inches above the centre of the frame. The total weight of the dredge-frame and arms is twenty pounds. It ought to be of the best Lowmoor on Swedish wrought-iron. I have seen a stout dredge-frame of Lowmoor iron twisted like a bit of wax in extricating it from a jam between two stones, and, singularly enough, the dredge which came up in that condition contained the unique example of an echinoderm never found before or since.

The thick inner edges of the scrapers are perforated by round holes at distances of about an inch, and through these, strong iron rings about an inch in diameter are passed, and two or three like rings run on the short rods which form the ends of the dredge-frame. A light iron rod bent to the form of the dredge opening usually runs through these rings, and to this rod and to the rings the mouth of the dredge-bag is securely attached by stout cord or strong copper wire.

In the dredge now before me, which has worked well and seen good service, the bag is two feet in depth, and is of hand-made net of very strong twine, the meshes half an inch to the side. So open a network would let many of the smaller things through, and to avoid this the bottom of the bag, to the height of about nine inches, is lined with 'bread-bag,' a light open kind of canvas.

Many other materials have been used for dredge-bags. Raw buffalo- and cow-hides are very strong, but they are apt to become offensive. When these are used it is necessary to punch holes here and there to let the water through or to leave the seams which are sewed with thongs a little open. Another bag which I have used frequently is made of sail-cloth, with a window of strong brass wire gauze let in on either side. Nothing, however, seems to me so good as strong cord netting. The water passes easily through and carries with it a large part of the fine mud, while enough mud is retained by the bread-bag lining in the bottom to give a fair sample of its contents. It may be said that many small valuable objects may be washed through the meshes of the upper part of the dredge along with the mud, and thus lost; but, on the other hand, if the bag be very close it is apt to get filled up with mud at once, and to collect nothing more.

It is always well when dredging, at whatever depth, to ascertain the approximate depth with the lead before casting the dredge; and the lead ought always to be accompanied by a protected thermometer, for the subsequent haul of the dredge will gain greatly in value as an observation in geographical distribution if it be accompanied by an accurate note of the bottom temperature. For depths under 100 fathoms the amount of rope paid out should be at least double the depth. Under thirty fathoms, where one generally works more rapidly, it should be more nearly three times. This gives a good deal of slack before the dredge if the boat be moving very slowly, and keeps the lip of the dredge well down; and if the boat be moving too quickly through the water, by far the most common error in amateur dredging, from the low angle at which the line is lying in the water the dredge has its best chance of getting an occasional scrape. It is bad economy to use too light a rope. For a dredge such as that described, and for work round the coasts of Europe at depths attainable from a row-boat or yawl, I would recommend bolt-rope of the best Russian hemp, not less than one and a half inch in circumference, which should contain from eighteen to twenty yarns in three strands. Each yarn should bear nearly a hundredweight, so that the breaking strain of such a rope ought to be upwards of a ton. Of course it is never voluntarily exposed to such a strain, but in shallow water the dredge is often caught among rocks or coral, and the rope ought to be strong enough in such a case to bring up the boat, even if there were some little way on.

Dredging in sand or mud, the dredge-rope may simply be passed through the double eye formed by the extremities of the two arms of the dredge; but in rocky or unknown ground it is better to fasten the rope to the eye of one of the arms only, and to tie the two eyes together with about three or four turns of rope yarn. This breaks much more readily than the dredge rope, so that if the dredge get caught it is the first thing to give way under a strain, and in doing so it very often so alters the position and form of the dredge as to allow of its extrication.

The dredge is slipped gently over the side, either from the bow or from the stern—in a small boat more usually the latter—while there is a little way on, and the direction which the rope takes indicates roughly whether the dredge is going down properly. When it reaches the ground and begins to scrape, an experienced hand upon the rope can usually at once detect a tremor given to the dredge by the scraper passing over the irregularities of the bottom. The due amount of rope is then paid out, and the rope hitched to a bench or rollock-pin.

When there is anything of a current, from whatever cause, it is usually convenient to attach a weight varying from fourteen pounds to half a hundred-weight, to the rope three or four fathoms in front of the dredge. This prevents in some degree the lifting of the mouth of the dredge. If the weight be attached nearer the dredge, it is apt to injure delicate objects passing in.

The boat should move very slowly, probably not faster than a mile an hour. In still water, or with a very slight current, the dredge of course anchors the boat, and oars or sails are necessary; but if the boat be moving at all it is all that is required. I like best to dredge with a close-reefed sail before a light wind, with weights, against a very slight tide or current; but these are conditions which cannot always be commanded. The dredge may remain down from a quarter of an hour to twenty minutes, by which time, if things go well, it ought to be fairly filled.

In dredging from a small boat the simplest plan is for two or three men to haul in hand over hand and coil in the bottom of the boat. For a large yawl or yacht, and for depths beyond fifty fathoms, a winch is a great assistance. The rope takes a couple of turns round the winch, which is worked by two men, while a third takes it from the winch and coils it.

Dredging in deep water—that is, at depths beyond 200 fathoms—is a matter of some difficulty, and can scarcely be compassed with the ordinary machinery at the disposal of amateurs. Deep-sea dredging can no doubt be carried on from a good-sized steam yacht, but the appliances are so numerous and so bulky, and the work is so really hard, that it is scarcely compatible with pleasure-seeking.

I do not know that much improvement can be made upon the apparatus and method employed in the 'Porcupine' in 1869 and 1870. I will therefore describe her dredging gear and the dredging operation carried on from her at the greatest depths in the Bay of Biscay, that which tested our resources most fully, somewhat in detail.

The 'Porcupine' is a 382-ton gun-boat, fitted up for the surveying service, in which she has been employed for some years past among the Hebrides, and latterly on the east coast of England. She was assigned for our special work in 1869, with all her ordinary surveying fittings; and certain very important additions were made; among others the double-cylinder donkey engine, which worked up to about twelve horse-power, with surging drums of different sizes, large drums for bringing up light weights rapidly, and smaller drums for heavy work. This engine was set up amidships, so that lines could be led to the drums either from fore or aft. The donkey-engine proved a most serviceable little machine. We almost always used the large drum, both in dredging and sounding; and except on one or two occasions when an enormous load, once nearly a ton, came up in the dredge-bag, it delivered the rope steadily, at a uniform rate of more than a foot per second, for the whole summer.

A powerful derrick projected over the port bow. A large block was suspended at the end of the derrick by a rope which, as in the case of the sounding-line, was not directly attached to the spar but passed through an eye, and was attached to a 'bitt' on deck. On a bight of this rope was lashed a powerful accumulator, the machine already described (p. 222) as of so much use in the management of the sounding-line. In dredging from a large vessel the 'accumulator' is invaluable. From the great strength of the springs the dredge is usually drawn along without stretching them to any great degree; they become tense and taut, and yield, with a kind of slight pulsation, to the rise and fall of the vessel. Whenever they run out it is a sure indication that either the dredge has caught or the weight in it is becoming too great, and that the dredge-rope ought to be relieved by a turn of the paddle-wheel or screw. Care should be taken not to have the bight of the rope to which the accumulator is attached more than about twice the length of the unstretched springs. Springs in good order ought to stretch to much more than double their length; but it is unsafe to try them too far, as a lash from one, if it were to give way, would be most serious. When a great strain comes upon the rope, it acts first upon the accumulator, pulling down the block and stretching the elastic bands; and a graduated scale on the derrick, against which the accumulator plays, gives in

FIG. 40.– The Stern Derrick of the 'Porcupine,' showing the 'accumulator,' the dredge, and the mode of stowing the rope.

cwts. an approximation at all events to the strain on the rope.

A second derrick, nearly equally strong, was rigged over the stern, and we dredged sometimes from one and sometimes from the other. The stern derrick was, however, principally used for sounding; the letting-go board, &c., being fitted up in connection with it. We had an excellent arrangement for stowing the dredge-rope in the 'Porcupine;' an arrangement which made its manipulation singularly easy, notwithstanding its great weight—about 5,500 lbs. A row of about twenty great iron pins, about two and a half feet in length, projected over one side of the quarter-deck, rising obliquely from the top of the bulwark. Each of these held a coil of from two to three hundred fathoms, and the rope was coiled continuously along the whole row (Fig. 46). When the dredge was going down, the rope was taken rapidly by the men from these pins—'Aunt Sallies' we called them, from their ending over the deck in smooth white balls—in succession, beginning with the one nearest the dredging derrick; and in hauling up, a relay of men carried the rope along from the surging drum of the donkey-engine and laid it in coils on the pins in inverse order. Thus, in letting go, the rope passed to the block of the derrick directly from the 'Aunt Sallies;' in hauling up, it passed from the block to the surging drum of the donkey-engine, from which it was taken by the men and coiled on the 'Aunt Sallies.'

The length of the dredge-rope was 3,000 fathoms, nearly three and a half statute miles. Of this, 2,000 fathoms were 'hawser-laid,' of the best Russian hemp, $2\frac{1}{2}$ inches in circumference, with a breaking strain of $2\frac{1}{4}$ tons. The 1,000 fathoms next the dredge were 'hawser-laid,' 2 inches in circumference. A Russian hemp rope appears to be the most suitable. A manilla rope is considerably stronger for a steady pull, but the fibre is more brittle and liable to go at a 'kink.' I have never seen a wire-rope used, but I should think it would be liable to the same objection. The 'Challenger' is to be supplied with 'whale-line' for her great expedition. The frame of one of the dredges which we used in the Bay of Biscay is represented at Figs. 47 and 48. The length of

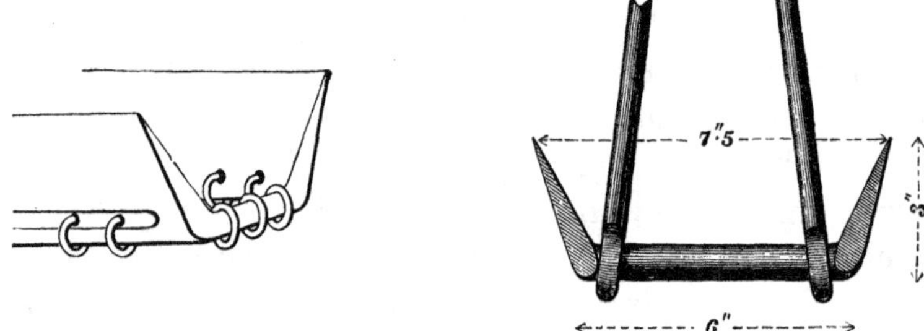

FIG. 47.—The End of the Dredge frame.

the dredge-frame is 4 ft. 6 in., and it is 6 inches wide at the throat or narrowest part. The dredge used in the deepest haul was somewhat different. About half of each arm next the eye to which the rope was attached, was of heavy chain. I doubt greatly, however, if this is an advantage. The chain drags along in front of the dredge, and may possibly obstruct the entrance of objects and injure them more than a pair of rigid arms would do. On one side the chain was attached to the arm of the dredge by a stop of five turns of spun-yarn, so that in case of the dredge becoming entangled or wedged among rocks or stones, a strain less than sufficient to break the dredge rope would break the stop, alter the position of the dredge, and probably enable it to free itself;

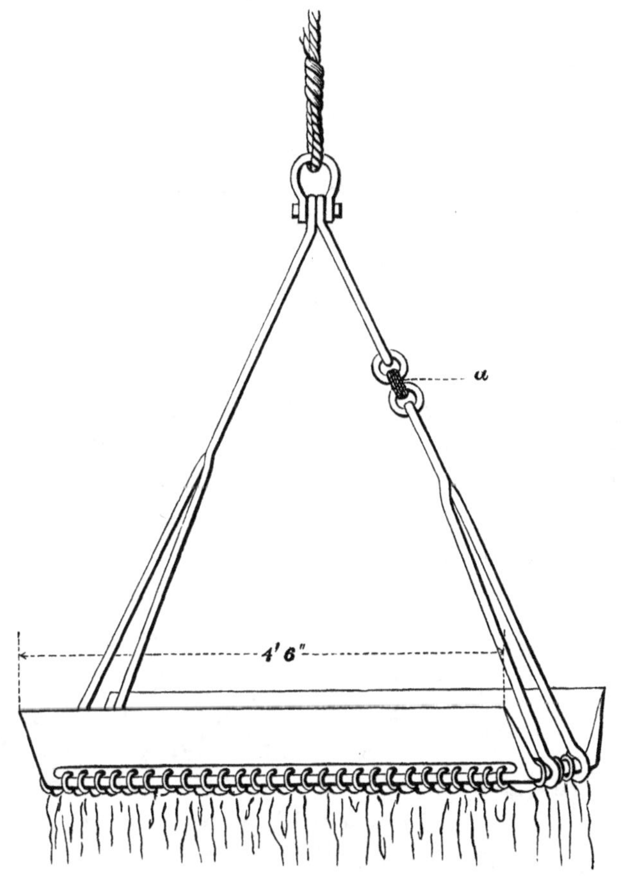

FIG. 48.—Dredge-frame showing the mode of attachment of the Bag. *a*. Spunyarn Stop.

and in case of its taking in a greater load of mud than the rope could bring up, the stop would likewise give way and allow the dredge to fall into such a position that a large part of its contents would slip out. The weight of the frame of this dredge, the largest we ever used, was 225 lbs.; it was forged by Messrs. Harland and Wolff of Belfast of the best Lowmoor iron. The dredge-bag was double—the outer of strong twine netting, the inner of bread-bag. Three sinkers—one of 1 cwt., the other two of 56 lbs. each—were attached to the dredge-rope at 500 fathoms from the dredge.

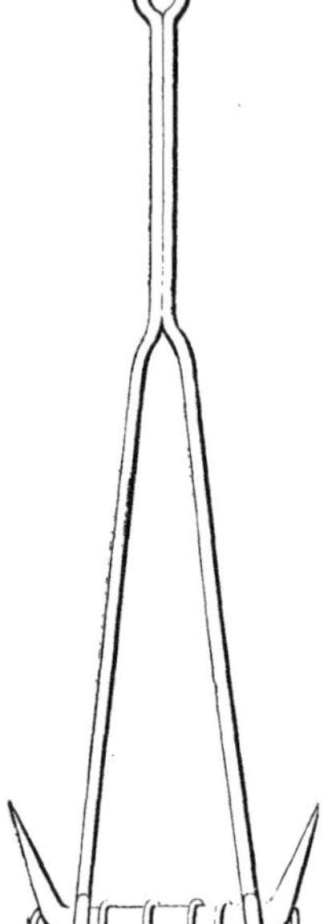

FIG. 49.—The End of the Dredge-frame, showing the mode of attachment of the Bag.

The operation of sounding at a depth of 2,435 fathoms in the Bay of Biscay on the 22nd of July, 1869, has already been described in detail. When the depth had been accurately ascertained, about 4.45 P.M. the dredge was let go, the vessel drifting slowly before a moderate breeze (force = 4) from the N.W. The 3,000 fathoms of rope were all out at 5.50 P.M. The diagram (Fig. 50) will give an idea of the various relative positions of the dredge and the vessel according to the plan of dredging adopted by Captain Calver, which worked admirably, and which appears, in fact, to be the only mode which would answer for great depths.

A represents the position of the vessel when the dredge is let go, and the dotted line A B the line of descent of the dredge, rendered oblique by the tension of the rope. While the dredge is going down the vessel drifts gradually to leeward; and when the whole (say) 3,000 fathoms of rope are out, C, W, and D might represent respectively the relative posi-

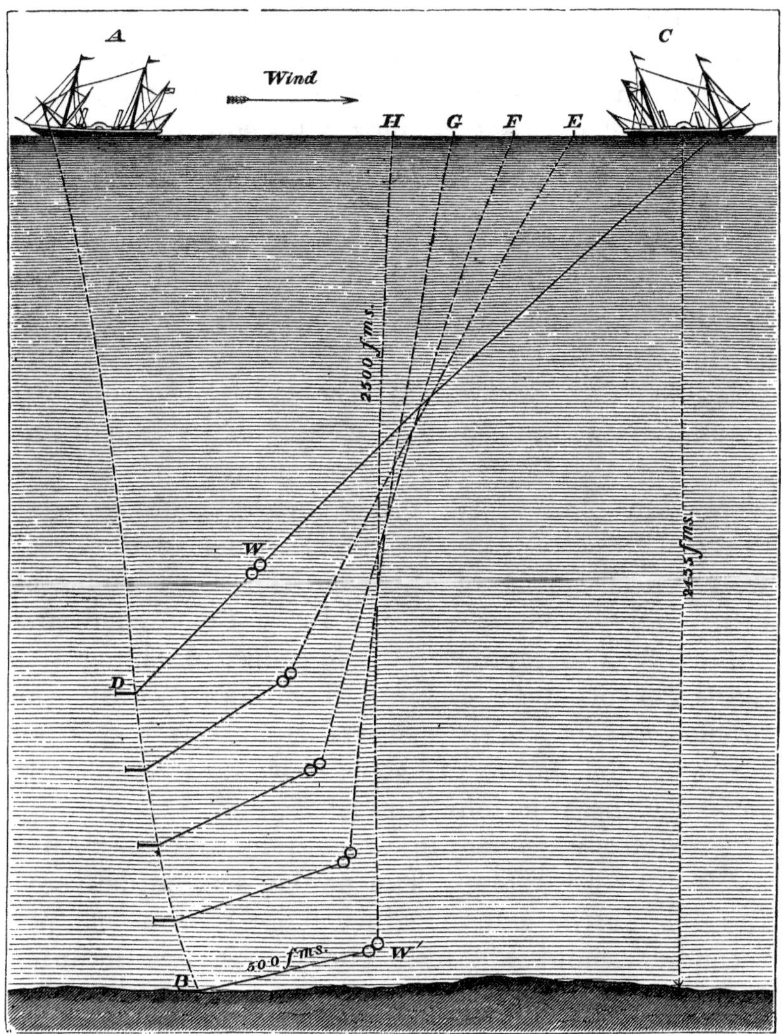

FIG. 50.—Diagram of the relative position of the Vessel, the Weights, and the Dredge, in dredging in deep water.

tions of the vessel, the weight attached 500 fathoms

from the dredge, and the dredge itself. The vessel now steams slowly to windward, occupying successively the positions E, F, G, and H. The weight, to which the water offers but little resistance, sinks from W to W′, and the dredge and bag more slowly from D to B. The vessel is now allowed to drift back before the wind from H towards C. The tension of the motion of the vessel, instead of acting immediately on the dredge, now drags forward the weight W′, so that the dredging is carried on from the weight and not directly from the vessel. The dredge is thus quietly pulled along with its lip scraping the bottom in the attitude which it assumes from the centre of weight of its iron frame and arms. If, on the other hand, the weights were hung close to the dredge, and the dredge were dragged directly from the vessel, owing to the great weight and spring of the rope the arms would be continually lifted up and the lip of the dredge prevented from scraping. In very deep dredging this operation of steaming up to windward until the dredge-rope is nearly perpendicular, after drifting for half an hour or so to leeward, is usually repeated three or four times.

At 8.50 P.M. we began to haul in, and the 'Aunt Sallies' to fill again. The donkey-engine delivered the rope at the rate of rather more than a foot per second, without a single check. A few minutes before 1 A.M. the weights appeared, and a little after one in the morning, eight hours after it was cast over, the dredge was safely hauled on deck, having in the interval accomplished a journey of upwards of eight statute miles. The dredge contained 1½ cwt.

of very characteristic pale grey Atlantic ooze. The total weight brought up by the engine was—

2,000 fathoms, 2½-inch rope	4,000 lbs.
1,000 fathoms, 2-inch rope	1,500 „
	5,500 lbs.

Weight of rope reduced to one-fourth in water =	1,375 lbs.
Dredge and bag	275 „
Ooze brought up	168 „
Weight attached	224 „
	2,042 lbs.

Much more experience will yet be necessary before we can assure ourselves that we have devised the dredge of the best form and weight for work in the deep sea. I rather think that the dredges, 150 to 225 lbs., which we have been in the habit of using, are too heavy. In many instances we have had evidence that the dredge, instead of falling gently upon the surface and then gliding along and gathering the loose things in its path, has fallen upon its mouth and dug into the tenacious mud, thereby clogging itself, so as to admit but little more. I mean to try the experiment of heavier weights and lighter dredge-frames in the 'Challenger,' and I believe it will be an improvement.

In many of our dredgings at all depths we found that, while few objects of interest were brought up within the dredge, many echinoderms, corals, and sponges came to the surface sticking to the outside of the dredge-bag, and even to the first few fathoms of the dredge-rope.

This suggested many expedients, and finally

Captain Calver sent down half-a-dozen of the 'swabs' used for washing the decks attached to the dredge. The result was marvellous. The tangled hemp brought up everything rough and moveable which came in its way, and swept the bottom as it might have swept the deck. Captain Calver's invention initiated a new era in deep-sea dredging. After various experiments we came to the conclusion that the best plan was to attach a long iron transverse bar to the bottom of the dredge-bag, and to fasten large bunches of teazed-out hemp to the free ends of the bar (Fig. 51). We now regard the 'hempen tangles' as an essential adjunct to the dredge nearly as important as the dredge itself, and usually much more conspicuous in its results. Sometimes, when the ground is too rough for ordinary dredging, we use the tangles alone. There is some danger, however, in their use. The dredge employed under the most favourable circumstances may be supposed or hoped to pass over the surface of the floor of the sea for a certain distance, picking up the objects in its path which are perfectly free, and small enough to enter the dredge mouth. If they chance to be attached in any way, the dredge rides over them. If they exceed in the least the width of the dredge-opening, at the particular angle at which the dredge may present itself at the moment, they are shoved aside and lost.

The Mollusca have by far the best chance of being fully represented in investigations carried on by the dredge alone. Their shells are comparatively small solid bodies mixed with the stones on the bottom, and they enter the dredge along with these. Echinoderms, corals, and sponges, on the contrary, are bulky objects, and are frequently partially buried in the

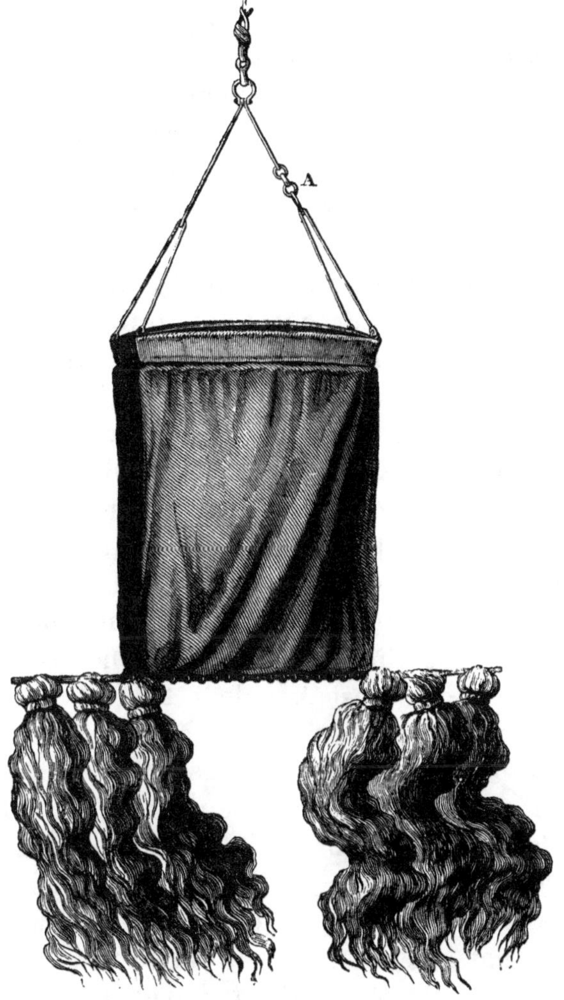

FIG. 51.—Dredge with 'hempen tangles.'

mud or more or less firmly attached, so that the dredge generally misses them. With the tangles it is the reverse. The smooth heavy shells are rarely brought up, while frequently the tangles loaded with the spiny spheres of *Cidaris*, great white-bearded *Holteniæ*, glistening coils of *Hyalonema*, relieved by the crimson stars of *Astropecten* and *Brisinga*, present as remarkable an appearance as can well be imagined. On one occasion, to which I have already referred, I am sure not fewer than 20,000 examples of *Echinus norvegicus* came up on the tangles at one haul. They were warped through and through the hempen fibres, and actually filled the tangles so that we could not get them out, and they hung for days round the bulwarks like nets of pickling onions in a greengrocer's shop. The use of the tangles, which seem so singularly well adapted to their capture, gives therefore a totally unfair advantage to the radiate groups and the sponges, and this must always be taken into account in estimating their proportion in the fauna of a particular area.

The tangles certainly make a sad mess of the specimens; and the first feeling is one of woe, as we undertake the almost hopeless task of clipping out with a pair of short nail-scissors the mangled remains of sea-pens, the legs of rare crabs, and the dismembered disks and separated arms of delicate crinoids and ophiurids. We must console ourselves with the comparatively few things which come up entire, sticking to the outer fibres; and with the reflection that had we not used this somewhat ruthless means of capture the mutilated specimens would have remained unknown to us at the bottom of the sea.

The dredge comes up variously freighted according to the locality. Usually, if dexterously managed, the bag is about half full. If, from a great depth, beyond the reach of currents, where there is only so slow a movement of the mass of water that the finest sediment is not carried away, it contains usually fine calcareous or aluminous mud alone, with the animals forming the fauna of the locality distributed through it. In shallower water we may have sand or gravel, or stones of various sizes mixed with mud and sand.

The next step is to examine the contents of the dredge carefully, and to store the objects of search for future use. The dredge is hauled on deck, and there are two ways of emptying it. We may either turn it up and pour out its contents by the mouth, or we may have a contrivance by which the bottom of the bag may be made to unlace. The first plan is the simplest and the one most usually adopted. The second has the advantage of letting the mass out more smoothly and easily, but the lacing introduces rather a damaging complication, as it is apt to loosen or give way. In a regularly organized dredging expedition, a frame is often arranged with a ledge round it to receive the contents of the dredge, but it does very well to capsize it on an old piece of tarpauling. Any objects visible on the surface of the heap are now carefully removed and placed for identification in jars or tubs of sea-water, of which there should be a number standing ready. The heap should not be much disturbed, for the delicate objects contained in it have already been unavoidably subjected to a good deal of rough usage, and the less friction among the stones the better.

Close to the place where the dredge is emptied

there ought to be one or two tubs about two feet in diameter and twenty inches deep, and each tub should be provided with a set of sieves so arranged that the lowest sieve fits freely within the bottom of the tub, and the three succeeding sieves fit freely within one another (Fig. 52). Each sieve is provided with a pair of iron handles through which the hand can pass easily, and the handles of the largest sieve are made long, so that the whole nest can be lifted without stooping and putting the arms

FIG. 52.—Set of Dredging Sieves.

into the water. The upper smallest sieve is usually deeper than the others; it is made of a strong open net of brass wire, the meshes a half inch to a side. The second sieve is a good deal finer, the meshes a quarter inch to a side. The third is finer still, and the fourth so close as only to allow the passage of mud or fine sand. The sieves are put into the tub, and the tub filled up to the middle of the top sieve with sea-water. The top sieve is then half filled with the contents of the dredge, and the set of sieves are gently moved up and down in the water. It is of great importance not to give any rotatory motion to the sieves in this part of the process, for such is very ruinous to fragile organisms. The sieves should be gently churned up and down, whether singly or together. The result, of course, is that the rougher stones and gravel and the larger organisms are washed and retained in the upper sieve. The fine mud or sand passes through the whole of the sieves and subsides into the bottom of the tub, while the three remaining sieves contain, in graduated series, the objects of intermediate size. The sieves are examined carefully in succession, and the organisms which they contain gently removed with a pair of brass or bone forceps into the jars of sea-water, or placed at once in bottles of weak spirit of wine.

The scientific value of a dredging operation depends mainly upon two things,—the care with which the objects procured are preserved and labelled for future identification and reference, and the accuracy with which all the circumstances of the dredging, position, depth, nature of ground, bottom temperature, date, &c., are recorded. With regard to the preservation of the animals, I cannot here go into detail. There are many ways of preserving, special to the different invertebrate groups; and 'taxidermy' is in itself a complicated art. I will merely mention one or two general points. A specimen in almost every group is of infinitely greater scientific value if it be preserved entire with its soft parts. For this purpose the most usual plan is to place it at once in spirit of wine diluted to about proof. Care must be taken not to put too many specimens together in one jar, or they will very shortly become discoloured; and the jars ought to be looked to carefully and the spirit tested, and if necessary renewed after they have been set aside for a day or two, as sea animals contain a large quantity of water. In hot weather, and if the specimens be bulky, it is often better to use strong spirit. The ordinary methylated spirit of commerce answers sufficiently well for ordinary purposes, though if a specimen be reserved for minute dissection, I prefer using pure, or even absolute alcohol.

For very delicate transparent objects,—such as salpæ, siphonophora, polycystina, &c.,—Goadby's solution seems to be preferable: but do what we may, a preserved specimen of one of these lovely objects is a mere *caput mortuum*, a melancholy suggestion of its former beauty; good only for the demonstration of anatomical structure.

In preserving marine animals dry, as much of the soft parts should be removed as possible, and replaced by tow or cotton, and the object to be dried should be steeped in several changes of fresh water to get rid of the whole of the salt, and then dried very thoroughly and not too quickly. Every specimen, whether dry or in spirit, should be labelled *at once*, with the number under which this particular dredging is entered in the dredger's note-book. It is wonderful how soon things get into confusion if this be not rigorously attended to. The small paper tickets with a fancy margin and gummed on the back, which haberdashers use for ticketing their goods, are to be had of all wholesale stationers at nominal prices, and they are very convenient. Their great disadvantage is that if the bottles on which they are fixed get wet they are apt to come off.

Pencils are sold by seed-merchants for writing on tallies which are to be exposed to rain. Perhaps the safest plan is to mark the number and date with such a pencil on a shred of parchment or parchment paper, and put it *into* the bottle. This may seem a trifling detail, but so great inconvenience constantly arises from carelessness in this matter, that I feel sure of the sympathy of all who are interested in the scientific aspect of dredging when I insist upon the value of accurate labelling.

It is of even greater importance that certain circumstances relating to every individual haul of the dredge should be systematically noted, either in the dredger's diary, or on a special form prepared for the purpose. The precise position of the station ought to be defined in shore dredging by giving the distance from shore and the bearings of some fixed objects; in ocean dredging by noting accurately the latitude and longitude. In the 'Lightning,' in 1868, we dredged at a station about 100 miles to the north of the Butt of the Lews, and came upon a singular assemblage of interesting animal forms. Next year, in the 'Porcupine,' we were anxious to try again the same spot to procure some additional specimens of a sponge which we were studying. The position had been accurately given in the log of the 'Lightning,' and the first haul at a depth of upwards of half a mile gave us the very same group of forms which we had taken the year before. On our return Captain Calver again dropped the dredge upon the same spot, with like success. The depth in fathoms should be carefully noted, as a most important element in determining the conditions of life and distribution of species; and the nature of the bottom—whether mud, sand, or gravel; and if the latter, it is well to state the nature and composition of the pebbles, and if possible the source from which they may probably have been derived. Now that we have in the Miller-Casella thermometer a reliable instrument for this purpose, the bottom temperature ought always to be noted. This is important whether in shallow or in deep water. In shallow water it gives a datum for determining the range of annual variation of temperature which can be endured by certain species; and at great depths it is even more important, as we are now aware that, owing to the movement of masses of water at different temperatures in various directions, totally different conditions of climate may exist in deep water within a few miles of one another, and the limits of these conditions can only be determined by direct experiment. It is important when determining the bottom temperature to note also the temperature of the surface of the sea, the temperature of the air, the direction and force of the wind, and the general atmospheric conditions. If the dredger be purely a zoologist, having no particular interest in special physical problems, it will still be well worth his while to make all the observations indicated and to publish the results. These then pass into the hands of physical geographers, to whom all trustworthy additions to the myriad of data which are required to arrive at a true generalization of the phenomena of the distribution of temperature are most acceptable.

At the Birmingham Meeting of the British Association in 1839 an important committee was appointed "for researches with the dredge, with a view to the investigation of the marine zoology of Great Britain, the illustration of the geographical distribution of marine animals, and the more accurate determination of the fossils of the pliocene period: under the superintendence of Mr. Gray, Mr. Forbes, Mr. Goodsir, Mr. Patterson, Mr. Thompson of Belfast, Mr. Ball of Dublin, Dr. George Johnston, Mr. Smith of Jordan Hill, and Mr. A. Strickland." The appointment of this committee may be regarded as the initiation of the systematic employment of this method of research. Edward Forbes was the ruling spirit, and under the genial influence of his contagious enthusiasm great progress was made during the next decade in the knowledge of the fauna of the British seas, and many wonderfully pleasant days were spent by the original committee and by many others who, from year to year, were 'added to their number.' Every annual report of the British Association contained communications from the English, the Scottish, or the Irish branches of the committee, and in 1850 Edward Forbes submitted its first general report on British marine zoology. This report, as might have been anticipated from the eminent qualifications of the reporter, was of the highest value; and taken along with his remarkable memoirs previously published, "on the distribution of the Mollusca and Radiata of the Ægean Sea," and "on the geological relations of the existing Fauna and Flora of the British Isles," may be said to mark an era in the progress of human thought.

After enumerating various additions to our knowledge of the distribution of marine invertebrata within the British area which were still to be desired, Forbes concludes his report with the following sentence: "And lastly, though I fear the consummation, however devoutly wished for, is not likely soon to be effected, a series of dredgings between the Zetland and the Færoe Isles, where the greatest depth is under 700 fathoms, would throw more light on the natural history of the North Atlantic and on marine zoology generally than any investigation that has yet been undertaken."

To Forbes's general report succeeded many reports from the different sections into which from year to year the committee divided itself. Among these I may mention particularly the very excellent work done by the Belfast dredging committee, communicated to several meetings of the Association by the late Mr. George C. Hyndman; the reports of the Dublin committee by the late Professor Kinahan and Professor E. Perceval Wright; the important lists of the fauna of the East Coast of England reported on behalf of the Natural History Society of Northumberland, Durham, and Newcastle-upon-Tyne, and of the Tyne-side Naturalists' Field Club, by Mr. Henry T. Mennell and Mr. G. S. Brady; and lastly the invaluable reports on the marine fauna of the Hebrides and Shetland, compiled at an extraordinary expense of labour, discomfort, and privation—doubtless with an immediate guerdon of infinite enjoyment

—through many years, by Mr. Gwyn Jeffreys, Mr. Barlee, the Rev. A. Merle Norman, and Mr. Edward Waller, and communicated to the Transactions of the Association from 1863 to 1868. The dredging committees of the British Association, combining the pursuit of knowledge with the recreation of their summer holidays, may be said to have worked out the fauna of the British area down to the 100-fathom line, for the dredger is now rarely rewarded by a conspicuous novelty, and must be contented that the greater number of his additions to the British list are confined to the more obscure groups.

Meanwhile some members of the dredging committee and their friends who had time and means at their disposal pushed their operations farther a-field, and did good service on foreign shores. In 1850, Mr. MacAndrew published many valuable notes on the lusitanian and mediterranean faunæ; and in 1856, at the request of the biological section of the British Association, he submitted to the Cheltenham meeting a general "report on the marine testaceous mollusca of the North-east Atlantic and neighbouring seas, and the physical conditions affecting their development." The field of these arduous labours extended from the Canary Islands to the North Cape, over about 43 degrees of latitude, and many species are recorded by him as having been dredged at depths between 160 and 200 fathoms off the coast of Norway. Subsequently, Mr. Gwyn Jeffreys went over some of the same ground, and made many additions to the lists of his predecessors.

Nor were our neighbours idle. In Scandinavia a brilliant triumvirate—Lovén of Stockholm, Steenstrup of Copenhagen, and Michael Sars of Christiania—were making perpetual advances in the knowledge of marine zoology. Milne-Edwards was illustrating the fauna of the coast of France, and Philippi, Grube, Oscar Schmidt, and others were continuing in the Mediterranean and the Adriatic the work so well begun by Donati, Olivi, Risso, Delle Chiage, Poli, and Cantraine; while Deshayes and Lacaze Duthiers illustrated the fauna of the coast of Algeria. So much progress had already been made at home and abroad, that in the year 1854 Edward Forbes considered that the time had arrived for giving to the public, at all events a preliminary sketch of the fauna of the European seas—a work which he commenced, but did not live to finish.

I need scarcely say that these operations of the British Association dredging committees were carried on generally under the idea that at the 100-fathom line, by which amateur work was practically limited, they approached the zero of animal life—a notion which was destined to be gradually undermined and finally completely overthrown. From time to time, however, there were not wanting men of great skill and experience to maintain, with Sir James Clark Ross, that "from however great a depth we may be enabled to bring up the mud and stones of the bed of the ocean, we shall find them teeming with animal life." From the very general prevalence of the negative view there was little to stimulate to the investigation of the bottom at great depths, and data gathered very slowly.

I have already referred (p. 18 *et infra*) to the

observations of Sir John Ross in 1818, of Sir James Ross in 1840, and of Mr. Harry Goodsir in 1845. In the year 1844 Professor Lovén contributed a paper, "on the bathymetrical distribution of submarine life on the northern shores of Scandinavia," to the British Association. He says, "With us the region of deep-sea corals is characterized in the south by *Oculina ramea* and *Terebratula*, and in the north by *Astrophyton, Cidaris, Spatangus purpureus* of an immense size, all living; besides *Gorgoniæ* and the gigantic *Alcyonium arboreum*, which continues as far down as any fisherman's line can be sunk. As to the point where animal life ceases, it must be somewhere, but with us it is unknown." [1]

In 1863 the same naturalist, referring to the result of the Swedish Spitzbergen expedition of 1861, when mollusca, crustacea, and hydrozoa were brought up from a depth of 1,400 fathoms, expresses the remarkable opinion, which later investigations appear generally to support, that at great depths, wherever the bottom is suitable, "a fauna of the same general character extends from pole to pole through all degrees of latitude, some of the species of the fauna being very widely distributed." [2]

In 1846 Keferstein mentions having seen in Stockholm a whole collection of invertebrate animals—crustacea, phascolosoma, annelids, spatangus, myriotrochus, sponges, bryozoa, rhizopoda, &c.—taken at a depth of 1,400 fathoms during O. Torell's Spitz-

[1] Report of the Fourteenth Meeting of the British Association, held at York in September 1844. (Transactions of the Sections, p. 50.)

[2] Forh. ved de Skand. Naturforskeres Möde i Stockholm, 1863, p 384.

bergen expedition in the 'Maclean nets,' and in the same year O. Torell alludes to one of the crustaceans from that depth being of a bright colour.[1]

In 1846 Captain Spratt, R.N., dredged at a depth of 310 fathoms forty miles east of Malta a number of mollusca which have been subsequently examined by Mr. Gwyn Jeffreys and found to be identical with species dredged at considerable depths in the northern seas during the 'Porcupine' expedition. The list includes *Leda pellucida*, PHILIPPI; *Leda acuminata*, JEFFREYS; *Dentalium agile*, SARS; *Hela tenella*, JEFFREYS; *Eulima stenostoma*, JEFFREYS; *Trophon barvicensis*, JOHNSTON; *Pleurotoma carinatum*, BIVONA; and *Philine quadrata*, S. V. WOOD. Captain Spratt observes that he "believed animal life to exist much lower, although the general character of the Ægean is to limit it to 300 fathoms."[2]

In 1850 Michael Sars, in an account of a zoological excursion in Finland and Loffoten, expressed his conviction that there is a full development of animal life at considerable depths off the Norwegian coast. He enumerated nineteen species taken by himself at depths beyond 300 fathoms, and pointed out that two of these were the largest species known of their respective genera.[3]

[1] Nachrichten der Königl. Gesellsch. der Wissensch. zu Göttingen. Marz 1846.

[2] On the Influence of Temperature upon the Distribution of the Fauna in the Ægean Sea. Report of the Eighteenth Meeting of the British Association, 1848.

[3] Beretning om en i Sommeren, 1849, foretagen zoologisk Reise i Lofoten og Finmarken. Christiania, 1850.

I have referred likewise (p. 26) to Professor Fleeming Jenkin's notes on the living animals attached to the Mediterranean cable at a depth of 1,200 fathoms, and to the results of Dr. Wallich's special investigations on board H.M.S. 'Bull-dog.'

In a general review of the progress of knowledge as to the conditions of life at great depths, these investigations deserve special notice, as, even if they must still be regarded as somewhat unsatisfactory, they distinctly mark a stage in advance. Although, from the imperfection of the means at his disposal, Dr. Wallich could not bring home evidence sufficient absolutely to satisfy others, he was convinced in his own mind from what he saw, that living beings high in the scale of organization might exist at any depth in the ocean; he expounded clearly and forcibly the train of reasoning which led him to this belief, and subsequent events have amply justified his conclusion. The space at my disposal will not allow me to quote and discuss Dr. Wallich's arguments, in some of which I thoroughly concur, while from others I am compelled to dissent. The facts were most important, and their significance increases now that they are fully confirmed and illustrated by operations on a large scale. In lat. 59° 27′ N., long. 26° 41′ W., a depth of 1,260 fathoms having been previously ascertained, "a new kind of deep-sea dredge was lowered; but in consequence of its partial failure, a second apparatus (namely, the conical cup) was employed, fifty fathoms of line in excess of the recorded depth being paid out in order to ensure the unchecked descent and impact of the instrument at the bottom. The dredge had already brought up a small quantity of unusually fine globigerina deposit and some small stones. The second instrument came up quite full of the deposit; but it was neither so free from amorphous matter, nor did it contain any of the small stones. Adhering, however, to the last fifty fathoms of line, which had rested on the ground for several moments, were thirteen ophiocomæ, varying in diameter across the arms from two to five inches." The misfortune of these star-fishes was that they did not go into the dredge; had they done so, they would at once have achieved immortality. *Now*, of course, we have no doubt that they came from the bottom, but their irregular mode of appearance left, in the condition of knowledge and prejudice at the time, a loophole for scepticism.

In three soundings, including that in which the star-fishes were obtained, at 1,260, 1,913, and 1,268 fathoms respectively, "minute cylindrical tubes occurred, varying from one-eighth to half an inch in length, and from one-fiftieth to one-twentieth of an inch in diameter. These were built up almost exclusively of very small globigerina shells, and still more minute calcareous *débris* cemented together." . . . . "The shells forming the outer layer of the tubes were colourless, and freed of all sarcodic matter; but the internal surface of the tubular cylinder was lined with a delicate yet distinct layer of reddish chitine." Dr. Wallich is satisfied that these tubes contained some species of annelid. "In a sounding taken in lat. 63° 31′ N., long. 13° 45′ W., in 682 fathoms, a portion of a *serpula*-tube five-twelfths of an inch in length, and about three-sixteenths of an inch in diameter, belonging to a known species, came up in such a condition as to leave no room for doubt that it had been broken off the rock or stone to which it was adherent by the sounding-machine, and that the animal was living; whilst a smaller *Serpula* and a cluster of apparently living polyzoa were adherent to its external surface. A minute *Spirorbis* also occurred in this sounding. Lastly, from a depth of 445 fathoms, within a short distance of the south coast of Iceland, a couple of living amphipod crustaceans were obtained, and a filamentous annelid about three-quarters of an inch in length." Basing his opinion principally upon these facts, Dr. Wallich, in conclusion, submits several propositions, the two most important of which may be said to anticipate the more remarkable results of our subsequent work. As the others are merely founded upon what I conceive to be a mistaken determination of the animal species captured, I need not now quote them.[1]

"1. The conditions prevailing at great depths, although differing materially from those which prevail at the surface of the ocean, are not incompatible with the maintenance of animal life.

* * * * * * *

"5. The discovery of even a single species, living normally at great depths, warrants the inference that the deep sea has its own special fauna, and that it has always had it in ages past; and hence that many fossiliferous strata heretofore regarded as having been

[1] And see Professor Sars' "Bemærkninger over det dyriske Livs Udbredning i Havets Dybder, med sœrligt Hensyn til et af Dr. Wallich i London nylig udkommet Skrift, 'The North Atlantic Seabed.'" (Vid.-Selsk. Forhandlinger for 1864.)

deposited in comparatively shallow water, have been deposited at great depths."[1]

In 1864, Professor Sars made a great addition to his list of species from depths of from 200 to 300 fathoms off the coast of Norway. He remarks :—"The species of animals named are not certainly very numerous (92), yet when we consider that most of them were taken accidentally, attached to the lines of the fishermen, and that only in a few instances the dredge was used at these great depths, it will be seen that there is a very interesting field here for the Naturalist furnished with the proper instruments."

In 1868 Professor Sars made a still further addition to the deep-sea fauna of the Norwegian Seas; an addition so important, that he remarks "that it is so great as to give a tolerably complete idea of the general fauna of these coasts." This increase of knowledge, Professor Sars states, is almost entirely due to the indefatigable labours of his son, G. O. Sars, an Inspector of Fisheries under the Swedish Government, who took advantage of the opportunities given by his occupation to dredge down to 450 fathoms on some parts of the coast, and among the Loffoten Islands. Sars likewise acknowledges many contributions from his old fellow-labourers, Danielssen and Koren. The number of species from depths between 250 and 450 fathoms on the coast of Norway now reaches 427, thus distributed :—

		Species.	
Protozoa	Rhizopoda	68	
	Porifera	5	
		—	73

[1] North Atlantic Sea bed, p. 154.

		Species.	
Cœlenterata	Hydrozoa	2	
	Anthozoa	20	
		—	22
Echinodermata . . .	Crinoidea	2	
	Asteridea, including Ophiuridea .	21	
	Echinoidea.	5	
	Holothuridea	8	
		—	36
Vermes	Gephyrea	6	
	Annelida	51	
		—	57
Mollusca	Polyzoa.	35	
	Tunicata	4	
	Brachiopoda	4	
	Conchifera	37	
	Cephalophora	53	
		—	133
Arthropoda	Arachnida	1	
	Crustacea	105	
		—	106

Of these 24 protozoa, 3 echinoderms, and 13 mollusca are from a depth of 450 fathoms. Professor Sars adds: "We may say, according to our present information, that the true deep-water belt commences at about 100 fathoms. The greater number of deep-sea species begin to appear then, though sparingly, and they increase in number of individuals as we descend to 300 fathoms, or in some cases to 450, when investigations have been carried so far. To what depth this belt extends, or whether there is another below it of a different character, is not yet known."[1]

In the year 1864, M. Barboza du Bocage, Director

[1] Fortsatte Bemærkninger over det dyrske Livs Udbredning i Havets Dybder, af M. Sars. (Vidensk.-Selsk. Forhandlinger for 1868.)

of the Natural History Museum of Lisbon, greatly surprised the zoological world by a notice of the occurrence on the coast of Portugal of whisps of silicious spicules resembling those of the *Hyalonema* of Japan.[1] They were brought up by the Setubal shark-fishers, who, it seemed—an equally singular circumstance—plied their vocation at a depth of 500 fathoms. Professor Perceval Wright, anxious to ascertain the full history of the case and to get *Hyalonema* in a fresh state, went to Lisbon in the autumn of 1868, and with the assistance of Professor du Bocage and some of his friends procured at Setubal an open boat and a crew of eight men, with "600 fathoms of rope, the dredge, lots of hooks and bait, and provisions for a couple of days. Leaving the port of Setubal a little before five o'clock in the evening, we, after a fair night's sailing, reached what the fishermen signed to me to be the edge of the deep-sea valley, where they were in the habit of fishing for sharks, and there, while thus engaged, they had found the *Hyalonema.* It was now about five o'clock in the morning; and the men, having had their breakfast, put the boat up to the wind, and let down the dredge; before it reached the bottom, about 480 fathoms of rope were run out, some thirty more were allowed for slack, and then we gently drew it—by hoisting a small foresail—for the distance of about a mile along the bottom. It required the united efforts of six men, hauling the line hand over hand, with the assistance of a double pulley-block, to pull in the dredge: the time thus occupied was just an

[1] Proceedings of the Zoological Society of London for the Year 1864, p. 265.

hour. The dredge was nearly full of a tenacious yellowish mud, through which sparkled innumerable long spicules of the *Hyalonema;* indeed, if you drew your fingers slowly through the mud, you would thereby gather a handful of these spicules. One specimen of *Hyalonema,* with the long spicules inserted into the mud and crowned with its expanded sponge-like portions, rewarded my first attempt at dredging at such a depth."[1] This dredging is of especial interest, for it shows that although difficult and laborious, and attended with a certain amount of risk, it is not impossible in an open boat and with a crew of alien fishermen, to test the nature of the bottom and the character of the fauna, even to the great depth of 500 fathoms.

In the year 1868, Count L. F. de Pourtales, one of the officers employed in the United States Coast Survey under Professor Pierce, commenced a series of deep dredgings across the gulf-stream off the coast of Florida; which were continued in the following year, and were productive of most valuable results. Many important memoirs at the hands of Count Pourtales, Mr. Alexander Agassiz, Mr. Theodore Lyman and others, have since enriched the pages of the Bulletin of the Museum of Comparative Zoology, and have greatly extended our knowledge of the deep-sea gulf-stream fauna; and much information has been gained as to the nature of the bottom in those regions, and the changes which are there taking place. Unfortunately a large part of the collections were in Chicago in the

[1] Notes on Deep-sea Dredging, by Edward Perceval Wright, M.D., F.L.S., from the Annals and Magazine of Natural History for December 1868.

hands of Dr. Stimpson for description at the time of the terrible catastrophe which laid a great part of that city in ashes, and were destroyed; but, by a singularly fortunate accident, our colleague Mr. Gwyn Jeffreys happened to be in Chicago shortly before the fire, and Dr. Stimpson gave him a series of duplicates of the mollusca for comparison with the species dredged in the 'Porcupine,' and a valuable remnant was thus saved. M. de Pourtales, writing to one of the editors of Silliman's Journal on the 20th of September, 1868, says: "The dredgings were made outside the Florida reef, at the same time as the deep-sea soundings, in lines extending from the reef to a depth of about 400 to 500 fathoms, so as to develop the figure of the bottom, its formation and fauna. Six such lines were sounded out and dredged over in the space comprised between Sandy Bay and Coffin's Patches. All of them agree nearly in the following particulars: from the reef to about the 100-fathom line, four or five miles off, the bottom consists chiefly of broken shells and very few corals, and is rather barren of life. A second region extends from the neighbourhood of the 100-fathom line to about 300 fathoms; the slope is very gradual, particularly between 100 and 200 fathoms; the bottom is rocky, and is inhabited by quite a rich fauna. The breadth of this band varies from ten to twenty miles. The third region begins between 250 and 300 fathoms, and is the great bed of foraminifera so widely extended over the bottom of the ocean. . . . .

"From the third region the dredges brought up fewer though not less interesting specimens, the chief of which was a new crinoid belonging to the genus *Bourguetticrinus* of D'Orbigny; it may even be the species named by him *B. hotessieri*, which occurs fossil in a recent formation in Guadaloupe, but of which only small pieces of the stem are known. I obtained half-a-dozen specimens between 230 and 300 fathoms, unfortunately more or less injured by the dredge. The deepest cast made was in 517 fathoms; it gave a very handsome *Mopsea* and some annelids."[1]

The results of the 'Lightning' cruise in 1868, in which dredging was successfully carried down to 650 fathoms, have already been recorded.

In the summer of 1870, Mr. Marshall Hall, F.G.S., with an interest in science which is unfortunately rare among yachtsmen, devoted his yacht 'Norna' to deep-sea dredging work during a cruise along the coast of Portugal and Spain. If we may judge by several preliminary sketches which have from time to time appeared at the hands of Mr. Saville Kent, the collections made during this expedition must have been extensive and valuable.[2]

The last researches in order of time are those conducted on board H.M.S. 'Porcupine' in 1869 and 1870. With the use of a Government surveying ship well found in all necessary appliances everything was in our favour, and, as has been already told, dredging was carried down to 2,435 fathoms;

[1] American Journal of Science, vol. xcvi. p. 413.

[2] Zoological Results of the 1870 Dredging Expedition of the Yacht 'Norna' off the coast of Spain and Portugal, communicated to the Biological Section of the British Association, Edinburgh, August 8, 1871. *Nature*, vol. iv. p. 456.

and the fact that there is an abundant and characteristic invertebrate fauna at all depths was placed beyond further question. As yet, little more can be said. A grand new field of inquiry has been opened up, but its culture is terribly laborious. Every haul of the dredge brings to light new and unfamiliar forms—forms which link themselves strangely with the inhabitants of past periods in the earth's history; but as yet we have not the data for generalizing the deep-sea fauna, and speculating on its geological and biological relations; for notwithstanding all our strength and will, the area of the bottom of the deep sea which has been fairly dredged may still be reckoned by the square yard.

FUGLO "FROM THE EASTERN SHORE OF VIDERO."

APPENDIX A.

One of the Dredging Papers issued by the British Association Committee, filled up by Mr. MacAndrew.

DREDGING PAPER No. 5.

Date.—7th of June, 1849.
Locality.—Off Malta.
Depth.—40 fathoms.
Distance from Shore.—1 to 2 miles.
Ground.—Sand and stones.
Region.—

Species obtained.	No. of living specimens.	No. of dead specimens.	Observations.
Dentalium dentalis	Numerous.		
,, rubescens, or fissura	. .	1	
,, tarentinum, var. (?)	. . .	1	Striated with an undulated appearance.
Cæcum trachea	. . .	2	
Ditrupa coarctata, or strangulata	Several.		
,, ,, ,, ,, ,,	. . .	2	With a notched apex.
Corbula nucleus	Several.		
Neæra cuspidata	. . .	1 and valves.	
,, costulata	1	2 and valves.	
Pandora obtusa	2		
Psammobia ferroensis . . .	. . .	Valves.	
Tellina distorta	. . .	1 and valves.	
,, balaustina	3		
,, serrata	. . .	1 and valves.	
,, depressa	. . .	1 valve.	
Syndosmya tenuis? (prismatica?)	. . .	Valves.	
Venus ovata	1	Valves.	

Species obtained.	No. of living specimens.	No. of dead specimens.	Observations.
Astarte incrassata?	8	...	Sulcated to the margin, some of them radiated.
Cardium papillosum	1		
,, minimum	1		
,, lævigatum	...	Valve.	
Cardita squamosa	5		
Lucina spinifera	5		
Diplodonta rotundata	...	1 valve.	
Modiola barbata	1		
Nucula nucleus	Several.		
Leda emarginata	3		
,, striata	4		
Arca tetragona	8		
,, antiquata	...	1 valve.	
Pectunculus glycimeris	...	1 and valves.	
Lima subauriculata	...	Valves.	
Pecten jacobæus	...	Valves.	
,, gibbus	...	Valves.	
,, polymorphus	...	Valves.	
,, testæ	1		
,, similis	...	Valves.	
,, sulcatus	...	1 and ? valves.	
Anomia patelliformis	1		
Pileopsis hungaricus	...	1	
Bulla lignaria	...	1	
,, cranchii	...	2	
,, hydatis	...	4	
,, striatula	...	1	
Rissoa bruguieri	...	3	
,, carinata (costata)	...	2	
,, acuta, var.	...	5	Longer, destitute of ribs, one very large.
,, desmarestii	...	3	
,, ,,	...	4	Like cimex, but minute.
Natica macilenta	2		
Eulima polita	...	1	
,, distorta	...	1	
Chemnitzia varicosa	...	4	Imperfect.
,, elegantissima	...	4	
,, indistincta (?)	...	2	
,, ,,		3	
Eulimella acicula	1		
Trochus tenuis, or dubius	...	1	
,, magus	Several.		
,, montagui	...	1	

Species obtained.	No. of living specimens.	No. of dead specimens.	Observations.
Trochus montagui	...	Several.	
„ „	...	Several.	
Turritella terebra	Few.	...	Small.
„ tricostalis	1		
Cerithum vulgatum, var. . .	...	1	
„ retrenlatum . . .	...	Several.	
„ „ . . .	...	2	White.
Fusus muricatus	1		
„ „	1	...	This species at Gibraltar.
Pleurotoma nanum	1		
„ secalinum . . .	1		
Murex tetrapterus	...	2	
Chenopus pes-pelecani . . .	1		
Buccinum ?	1		
Mitra ebenea	...	1	
„ „	1	...	Bright orange colour, banded, small, striated
Ringicula auriculata	...	2	
Marginella secalina	3	4	
„ clandestina . . .	Several.	Several.	
Cypræa pulex	...	2	
Cidaris histrix	3		
Zoophytes			
Algæ			

CHAPTER VII.

DEEP-SEA TEMPERATURES.

Ocean Currents and their general Effects on Climate.—Determination of Surface Temperatures.—Deep-sea Thermometers.—The ordinary Self-registering Thermometer on Six's principle.—The Miller-Casella modification.—The Temperature Observations taken during the Three Cruises of H.M.S. 'Porcupine' in the year 1869, etc.

APPENDIX A.—Surface Temperatures observed on board H.M.S. 'Porcupine' during the Summers of 1869 and 1870.

APPENDIX B.—Temperature of the Sea at different Depths near the Eastern Margin of the North Atlantic Basin, as ascertained by Serial and by Bottom Soundings.

APPENDIX C.—Comparative Rates of Reduction of Temperature with Increase of Depth at Three Stations in different Latitudes, all of them on the Eastern Margin of the Atlantic Basin.

APPENDIX D.—Temperature of the Sea at different Depths in the Warm and Cold Areas lying between the North of Scotland, the Shetland Islands, and the Færoe Islands; as ascertained by Serial and by Bottom Soundings.

APPENDIX E.—Intermediate Bottom Temperatures showing the Intermixture of Warm and Cold Currents on the Borders of the Warm and Cold Areas.

IF the surface of this world of ours were one uniform shell of dry land, other circumstances of its central heat, its relation in position to the sun, and to its investing atmospheric envelope, remaining the same, some zones would present certain peculiarities in temperature, owing to the mixture of hot and cold currents of air; but in the main, isothermal lines, that is to say, lines drawn through places having the same mean temperature, would coincide with parallels of latitude. A glance at any isothermal chart, whether for the whole year, for summer, for winter, or for a single month, will show that this is far from being the case. The lines of equal temperature deviate everywhere, and often most widely, from their normal parallelism with the parallels of latitude and with each other. A glance at the same chart will also show, that while there is an attempt, as it were, on the part of the isothermal lines to maintain their normal direction through the centre of great continents, the most marked curves, indicating the widest extensions of uniform conditions of temperature, are where there is a wide stretch of open sea extending through many degrees of latitude, and consequently including very different climatal conditions.

The lands bordering upon the ocean partake in this general diffusion of heat and amelioration of climate, and hence we have the difference between continental and insular climates—the former giving extremes of summer heat and winter cold, and the latter a much more uniform temperature, somewhat below the normal temperature within the tropics, and usually greatly above it beyond their limits.

The islands of Ireland and Great Britain and the west coast of the Scandinavian peninsula are involved in the most extreme system of abnormal curves which we have in any of the ocean basins; and to this peculiarity in the distribution of temperature in the North Atlantic we are indebted for the singular mildness of our winter climate. The chart Pl. VII., the general result reduced from many hundreds of thousands of individual observations, gives the distribution of the lines of equal mean temperature for the surface of the North Atlantic for the month of July; and it will be seen that the isotherms, instead of passing directly across the ocean, form a series of loops widening and flattening northwards, all participating in certain secondary deflections which give them a scalloped appearance, but all of them primarily referred to some common cause of the distribution of heat, having its origin somewhere in the region of the Straits of Florida.

These peculiarities in the distribution of temperature on the surface of the sea may usually be very immediately traced to the movement of bodies of water to and from regions where the water is exposed to different climatal conditions;—to warm or cold ocean currents, which make themselves manifest likewise by their transporting power, their effect in speeding or retarding vessels, or diverting them from their courses. Frequently, however, the current, although possibly involving the movement of a vast mass of water, and exerting a powerful influence upon climate, is so slow as to be imperceptible; its steady onward progress being continually masked by local or variable currents, or by the drift of the prevailing winds.

The Gulf-stream, the vast 'warm river' of the North Atlantic, which produces the most remarkable and valuable deviations of the isothermal lines which we meet with in any part of the world, is in this way imperceptible by any direct effect upon navigation beyond the 45th parallel of north latitude, a peculiarity which has produced and still produces great misconceptions as to its real character.

The mode of determining the surface temperature of the ocean is sufficiently simple. A bucket is let down from the deck of the vessel, dashed about for a little in the water to equalize the temperature, and filled from a depth of a foot or so below the surface. The temperature of the water in the bucket is then taken by an ordinary thermometer, whose error is known. A common thermometer of the Kew Observatory pattern graduated to Fahrenheit degrees can be read with a little practice to a quarter of a degree, and a good-sized centigrade thermometer to a tenth. Observations of surface-temperature are usually made every two hours, the temperature of the air being taken with each observation, and the latitude and longitude noted at noon, or more frequently by dead reckoning if required.

Every observation of the surface-temperature of the sea taken accurately and accompanied by an equally exact note of the date, the geographical position, and the temperature of the air, is of value. The surface observations taken from H.M.S. 'Porcupine' during her dredging cruise, in the summer of 1869, are given in Appendix A.

The surface-temperature of the North Atlantic has been the subject of almost an infinite number of such observations, more or less accurate. Dr. Petermann, in a valuable paper on the northern extension of the Gulf-stream, reduces the means of more than a hundred thousand of these, and deduces the scheme of curves which has been used with some slight modification in the construction of this chart.

Until very recently little or nothing has been known with any certainty about the temperature of the sea at depths below the surface. This is, however, a field of inquiry of very great importance in Physical Geography, as an accurate determination of the temperature at different depths is certainly the best, frequently the only available means of determining the depth, width, direction, and generally the path of the warm ocean currents, which are the chief agents in the diffusion of equatorial heat; and more especially of those deeper indraughts of frigid water which return to supply their place and to complete the general cycle of oceanic circulation. The main cause of this want of accurate knowledge of deep-sea temperatures is undoubtedly the defectiveness of the instruments which have been hitherto employed.

The thermometer which has been almost universally used for this purpose is the ordinary self-registering thermometer on Six's construction, enclosed in a strong copper case, with valves or apertures below and above to allow a free current of water to pass through the case and over the surface of the instrument. Six's registering thermometer (Fig. 53) consists of a glass tube bent in the form of a V, one limb terminating in a large cylindrical bulb, entirely filled with a mixture of creosote and water. The bend of the tube contains a column of mercury, and the other limb ends in a small bulb partially filled with creosote and water, but with a large space empty, or rather containing the vapour of the liquid and slightly compressed air. A small steel index, with a hair tied round it to act as a spring and maintain the index in any position which it may assume, lies free in the tube among the creosote at either end of the column of mercury. This thermometer gives its indications solely by the contraction and expansion of the liquid in the large full bulb, and is consequently liable to some slight error from the effect of variations of temperature upon the liquids in other parts of the tube. When the liquid in the large bulb expands, the column of mercury is driven upwards towards the half-empty bulb, and the limb of the tube in which it rises is graduated from below upwards for increasing heat. When the liquid contracts in the bulb, the column of mercury falls in this limb, but rises in the limb terminating in the full bulb, which is graduated from above downwards. When the thermometer is going to be used the steel indices are drawn down in each limb of the tube by a strong magnet, till they rest on each side on the surface of the mercury. When the thermometer is brought up, the height at which the lower end of the index stands in each tube indicates the limit to which the index has been driven by the mercury, the extreme of heat or cold to which the instrument has been exposed.

Unfortunately, the accuracy of the ordinary Six's thermometer cannot be depended upon beyond a very limited depth, for the glass of the bulb which contains the expanding fluid yields to the pressure of the water, and, compressing the contained fluid, gives an indication higher than is due to temperature alone. This cause of error is not constant in its action, as the amount to which the bulb is compressed depends upon its form and upon the thickness and quality of the glass; thus the error of good thermometers of the Hydrographic Office pattern varies from 7° C. to 10°·5 C. at a pressure of 6·817 lbs. on the square inch, representing a depth of 2,500 fathoms. In thoroughly well-constructed thermometers, however, such as those made by Casella and Pastorelli for the English Admiralty, the pressure error is tolerably constant; and Captain Davis, R.N., who has lately conducted important experiments on this point, expresses his opinion that by an extended series of observations a scale might be obtained to correct the thermometers hitherto in use to a close approximation to the truth, and thus utilize to some extent observations which have been already made with our ordinary instruments.

In the 'Lightning' expedition in 1868 we used the ordinary Hydrographic Office pattern, and a large number by different makers were sent with us for testing and comparison. The depths not being very great, the general temperature results came out well, and were among the most singular phenomena which we had to record. Many of the instruments were very wild at a few hundred fathoms, and several gave way under the pressure. On our return in April 1869, Dr. W. A. Miller, V.P.R.S., attended a meeting of the Deep-Sea Committee of the Royal Society at the Hydrographic Office, and proposed encasing the full bulb in an outer covering of glass containing air, in order to permit the air to be compressed by the pressure of the water on the outer shell, and thus protecting the bulb within.

Mr. Casella was directed to construct some thermometers on this plan, only instead of being filled with air, the outer shell was nearly filled with alcohol warmed to expel a portion of the remaining air, and the chamber was then hermetically sealed, leaving a bell of air and vapour of alcohol to yield to the pressure and relieve the bulb within. The 'Miller-Casella' thermometer proved so nearly perfection that it was decided to adopt it in future, and to use it as a standard in a series of experiments which were undertaken to test the ordinary Six's thermometers of the Hydrographic Office pattern. We depended upon this thermometer alone in our subsequent cruises in the 'Porcupine,' and we found it most satisfactory. During the summer of 1869 temperature observations were taken at upwards of ninety stations, at depths varying from 10 to 2,435 fathoms. Two thermometers, numbered 100 and 103 respectively were sent down at every station, and in no instance did they give the least reason to doubt their accuracy. Every observation was taken by Captain Calver himself, the lead with the thermometers attached being in every single instance let down by his own hand,

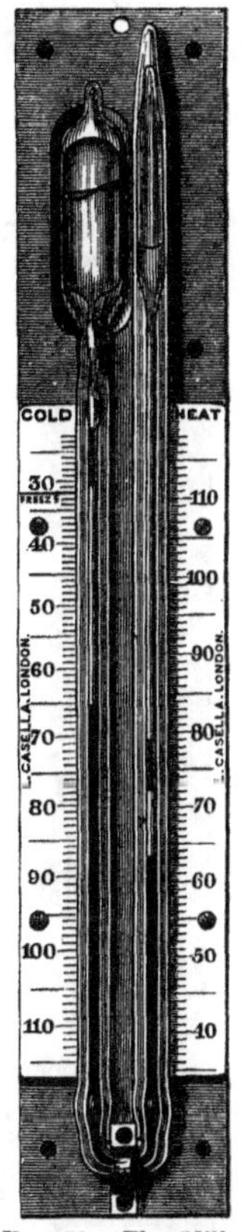

FIG. 53.—The Miller-Casella modification of Six's self-registering thermometer. The large bulb is double, with a layer of liquid and a bell of vapour between the shells, to relieve pressure.

and I have always regarded it as a remarkable evidence of my friend's care and skill that he landed those two precious instruments at the end of the year safe back at Woolwich.

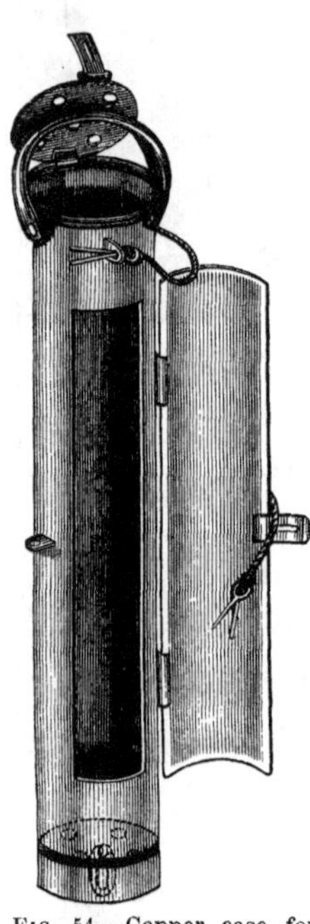

FIG. 54.—Copper case for protecting the Miller-Casella thermometer. The ends of the case above and below are perforated to allow a current of water to pass freely through.

Fig. 53 represents the latest improvements on the Miller-Casella modification of Six's self-registering thermometer. The instrument is of small size, to reduce as far as possible the friction in passing through the water. The tube is mounted in ebonite, to avoid the expansion of a wooden mounting in the water, by which the instrument is liable to get jammed in the case. The scale is of white porcelain, graduated to Fahrenheit degrees; the large bulb is enclosed in an outer shell three-fourths filled with alcohol and hermetically sealed. It is right to mention that I am informed by Sir Edward Sabine that the thermometers used by Sir John Ross in his Arctic voyage in 1818 were protected somewhat on the same principle, and that a thermometer for resisting pressure was constructed under the directions of the late Admiral Fitzroy, at the suggestion of Mr. Glaisher, which differed from the Miller-Casella pattern in little else than the outer shell being partially filled with mercury instead of alcohol, and in being somewhat less compact and more fragile than the latter instrument.[1] A modification of Phillip's maximum thermometer devised by Sir William Thomson, in which the thermometer is entirely encased in an outer shell of glass partly filled with alcohol, appears to have the smallest error of all.

A neat modification of Breguet's metallic thermometer was designed by Joseph Saxton, Esq., of the U.S. Office of Weights and Measures, for the use of the U.S. Coast Survey. A riband of platinum and one of silver are soldered with silver solder to an intermediate plate of gold, and the compound riband is coiled round a central axis of brass, with the silver within. Silver is the most expansible of the metals under the influence of heat, and platinum nearly the least. Gold holds an intermediate place, and its intervention between the platinum and silver moderates the strain, and prevents the coil from cracking. The lower end of the coil is fixed to the brazen axis, while the upper

[1] In Messrs. Negretti and Zambra's list of meteorological instruments published in 1864, a deep-sea thermometer on this plan is mentioned (p. 90): "The thermometers constructed for this purpose do not differ materially from those usually made under the denomination of Six's thermometers, except in the following most important particulars:—The usual Six's thermometers have a central reservoir or cylinder containing alcohol; this reservoir, which is the only portion of the instrument likely to be affected by pressure, has been, in Negretti and Zambra's new instrument, superseded by a strong outer cylinder of glass, containing mercury and rarefied air. By this means the portion of the instrument susceptible of compression has been so strengthened, that no amount of pressure can possibly make the instrument vary." Some obscurity is introduced into this passage by the use of the word 'superseded;' but I am assured by Messrs. Negretti and Zambra that in principle this instrument was exactly the same as that devised by Professor Miller and constructed by Mr. Casella.

end is attached to the base of a short cylinder. Any variation of temperature causes the coil to wind or unwind, and its motion acts to rotate the axial stem. This motion is magnified by multiplying wheels, and is registered upon the dial of the instrument by an index which pushes before it a registering hand, moving with sufficient friction merely to retain its place when thrust forward by the index hand of the thermometer. The instrument is graduated by trial. The brass and silver portions are thickly gilt by the electrotype process to prevent the action of sea-water upon them. The box which covers the coil and indicatory part of the thermometer is merely to protect it from accidental injury, and is open so as to permit the free passage of the sea-water. This instrument appears to answer tolerably well for moderate depths, its error up to 600 fathoms not greatly exceeding 0°·5 C.; at 1,500 fathoms, however, the error rises to 5° C., quite as great as that of the unprotected Six's thermometers, and the error is not so constant. It is evident that under great pressure little confidence can be placed upon instruments which give their indications through metal machinery.

Before H.M.S. 'Porcupine' started on her summer cruise in 1869, a valuable series of experiments were made upon the effect of pressure on various registering thermometers at Woolwich, under the superintendence of the Hydrographer and of the Deep-Sea Committee of the Royal Society. The object was to subject all the forms of deep-sea thermometers in use to pressures in a hydraulic press, equivalent to the pressures which they would encounter at different depths in the ocean, to determine the amount and sources of error, to ascertain which was the most satisfactory instrument, and if possible to construct a scale by which the observations hitherto taken with ordinary instruments might be roughly corrected, so as to be made available. As there was some difficulty in getting the use of a suitable press, Mr. Casella undertook to have a testing apparatus constructed at his own place in Hatton Garden, capable of producing a pressure of three tons on the square inch.

The results were very interesting.[1] The first experiment went to test the value of the various instruments. A Miller-Casella thermometer was placed in the cylinder with No. 57, a good thermometer by Casella, of the ordinary Hydrographic Office pattern, and they were subjected together to a pressure of 4,032 lbs., equal to 1,480 fathoms, with the following result :—

Thermometer.	Minimum.		Maximum.		Difference of Maximum.
	Before.	After.	Before.	After.	
2	8°· 6 C.	8°· 6 C.	8°· 6 C.	8°· 85 C.	0°· 25 C.
57	8 · 6	8 · 6	8 · 6	12 · 75	4 · 15

That is to say, the temperature remaining the same, the pressure forced up No. 57 to 12°·75 C., and left its index there.

1 On Deep Sea Thermometers, by Captain J. E. Davis, R.N. *Nature*, vol. iii. p. 124. Abridged from a Paper read before the Meteorological Society, April 19th, 1871.

This experiment at once proved the advantage of the encased bulb. It was repeated with other thermometers with the same pressure and for the same period of time, and it was found that while the mean difference of the encased bulbs was only 0°·95, that of the ordinary deep-sea thermometers was, as in No. 57, 7°·25. It follows, also, from these experiments, that very nearly all the difference or error is due to pressure on the full bulb, and that by encasing that bulb we have a nearly perfect instrument.

The next series of experiments was made to establish a scale by which observations by the ordinary instruments might be approximately corrected for pressure. The following table gives the errors of six thermometers at different pressures. The 'standard' is an encased Miller-Casella, the last a registering minimum thermometer by Casella enclosed in a hermetically sealed glass tube on Sir William Thomson's plan.

Pressure in Fathoms.	Standard.	No. 54.	No. 56.	No. 76.	No. 73.	Thomson.
250	0°· 4 C.	0°· 8 C.	1°· 0 C.	0°· 7 C.	0°· 8 C.	0°· 0 C.
500	0 · 4	1 · 7	1 · 5	1 · 4	1 · 7	0 · 05
750	0 · 7	2 · 2	2 · 2	2 · 3	2 · 5	0 · 0
1,000	0 · 8	2 · 9	2 · 9	2 · 7	2 · 7	0 · 2
1,250	0 · 9	3 · 5	3 · 5	3 · 5	4 · 1	0 · 05
1,500	0 · 8	4 · 3	4 · 3	4 · 0	4 · 3	0 · 3
1,750	0 · 95	4 · 6	4 · 9	4 · 7	5 · 7	0 · 2
2,000	1 · 1	5 · 4	5 · 5	5 · 3	6 · 4	0 · 3
2,250	1 · 1	6 · 2	6 · 0	6 · 0	6 · 8	0 · 4
2,500	1 · 2	7 2	6 · 7	6 · 5	7 · 6	0 · 2

The mean difference for each 250 fathoms in each thermometer is as follows :—

Thermometer.	Difference.
Standard	+ 0°· 12 C.
54	+ 0 · 72
56	+ 0 · 67
76	+ 0 · 65
73	+ 0 · 76
Thomson	+ 0 · 03

During these experiments the water in the cylinder was of course maintained as far as possible at the same—or at a known temperature; a certain amount of calorific effect must, however, be produced by the sudden compression of the water, and the next series of experiments was performed in order to determine the amount of that effect. Three of Phillips's encased maximum thermometers (Sir William Thomson's design), being entirely protected from any effect from compression, were employed for this purpose, with the following result :—

Pressure, 6,817 lbs. = 2,500 fathoms.

Thermometer.	Difference.
11,424	+ 0°· 05 C.
9,649	+ 0 · 22
9,645	+ 0 · 11

So that this source of error is absolutely trifling.

The true error of the Miller-Casella thermometer, as deduced from these observations, is—

For 250 fathoms 0°·079 C.
For 2,500 fathoms 0°·79 C.

This, therefore, may be regarded as a perfect instrument for all ordinary purposes.

A number of the instruments which had been previously tested in the press were sent out in the 'Porcupine' on her summer cruise in 1869, and on her return the results of Captain Calver's observations at different depths in the ocean were carefully compared with the effects of equivalent pressures applied to the thermometers in Mr. Casella's 'Bramah's press.' The result in the ocean, contrary to that in the hydraulic press, proves that the elasticity is not regular or in a ratio to the pressure, but that after continuing regular up to a pressure of 1,000 fathoms, it decreases in a compound ratio to a pressure of 2,000 fathoms, when its elasticity nearly ceases.

The following table gives an abstract of the behaviour of Casella's ordinary Hydrographic Office thermometers in the ocean and in the press:—

Pressure.	Error.		Per 250 Fathoms.	
	Press.	Ocean.	Press.	Ocean.
Fathoms.				
250	0°· 726 C.	0°· 738 C.	0°· 726 C.	0°· 738 C.
500	1 · 548	1 · 564	0 · 774	0 · 782
750	2 · 123	2 · 223	0 · 708	0 · 741
1,000	2 · 474	3 · 015	0 · 674	0 · 754
1,250	3 · 255	3 · 492	0 · 651	0 · 698
1,500	4 · 107	3 · 921	0 · 684	0 · 653
1,750	4 · 555	4 · 056	0 · 650	0 · 579
2,000	5 · 354	4 · 284	0 · 669	0 · 536
2,250	6 · 021	—	0 · 669	—
2,500	6 · 817	—	0 · 682	—

For taking bottom temperatures at great depths two or more of the Miller-Casella thermometers are lashed to the sounding-line at a little distance from one another, a few feet above the attaching ring of a 'detaching' sounding instrument. The lead is run down rapidly, and, after the weight has been disengaged by contact with the ground, an interval of five or ten minutes is allowed to elapse before hauling in. The shorter of these periods seems to be quite sufficient to insure the instrument acquiring the true temperature. In taking serial temperature soundings—that is to say, in determining the temperature at certain intervals of depth in deep water—the thermometers are attached above an ordinary deep-sea lead, the required quantity of line for each observation of the series run out, and the thermometers and lead are hove in each time. This is a very tedious process; one serial sounding in the Bay of Biscay, where the depth was 850 fathoms and the temperature was taken at every fifty fathoms, occupied a whole day.

I ought to mention that in taking the bottom temperature with the Six's thermometer the instrument simply indicates the lowest temperature to which it has been subjected; so that if the bottom water were warmer than any other stratum through which the thermometer had passed, the observation would be erroneous. This is only to be tested by serial soundings, but in every locality where the temperature was observed during the 'Porcupine' expeditions the temperature gradually sank, sometimes very steadily, sometimes irregularly, from the surface to the bottom, the bottom water having been constantly the coldest. It is probable that under certain conditions in the Polar seas, where the surface is sometimes subjected to intense cold, warmer water may be found below, until the balance is restored by convection. This I believe, however, to be entirely exceptional; and it may certainly be taken as the rule for all latitudes that if we disregard the film which is affected by diurnal alterations, the temperature sinks from the surface to the bottom.

The first important series of deep-water temperature observations was made during the Arctic voyage under Sir John Ross in the year 1818. On Sept. the 1st, lat. 73° 37′ N., long. 77° 25′ W., the temperature at the surface being 1°·3 C., the registering thermometer gave at eighty fathoms 0° C., and at 250 fathoms −1°·4 C. On the 6th of September, lat. 72° 23′ N., long. 73° 07′ W., the first serial sounding on record was taken, the thermometer having been let down to 500, 600, 700, 800, and 1,000 fathoms in succession, the thermometer showing each time a lower temperature and indicating at the greatest depth named a temperature of −3°·6 C. On the 19th of September, in lat. 66° 50′ N., long. 60° 30′ W., another serial sounding was taken, the temperature being registered at 100 fathoms −0°·9 C., at 200 −1°·7 C., at 400 −2°·2 C., and at 660 fathoms −3°·6 C. On the 4th of October, lat. 61° 41′ N., long. 62° 16′ W., Sir John Ross sounded, but found no ground in 950 fathoms; at the same time the self-registering thermometer was sent down, and the temperature of the sea at that depth was found to be 2° C., while at the surface it was 4° C., and the air at 2°·7 C. I am informed by General Sir Edward Sabine, who accompanied Sir John Ross's expedition, that these observations were made with registering thermometers guarded somewhat in the same way as those which we employed in the 'Porcupine.' There is almost sufficient internal evidence that the mode of protecting these thermometers must have been satisfactory, for the temperatures at the greatest depths are such as might have been expected from Miller-Casella thermometers. Unguarded instruments would certainly have given higher indications.

The last of the observations quoted, a considerable way up Davis' Strait, is of great interest. The temperature of the surface of the sea was nearly a degree and a half Centigrade above that of the air, and the temperature of the water was altogether unusually high. It is now well known that at certain seasons of the year a very marked extension of the Gulf-stream passes into the mouth of the Strait. The isotherms for September and July are shown on the chart from data kindly procured for me by Mr. Keith Johnston.

Sir Edward Sabine, in an extract from his private Journal of Sir John Ross's voyage quoted by Dr. Carpenter,[1] gives a lower temperature than any hitherto recorded. He says: "Having sounded on September 19th, 1818, in 750 fathoms, the registering thermometer was sent down to 680 fathoms, and on coming up the index of greatest cold was at 25°·75 Fahrenheit (−3°·5 C.), never having known it lower than 28° (−2°·2 C.) in former instances, even at a depth of 1,000 fathoms; and at other times

[1] Dr. Carpenter's Preliminary Report on Deep-Sea Dredgings. Proceedings of the Royal Society of London, vol. xvii. p. 186.

when close to the bottom, I was very careful in examining the thermometer, but could discover no other reason for it than the actual coldness of the water."

Notwithstanding these observations and several others telling in the same direction,—such as those of Lieutenant Lee of the U.S. Coast Survey, who in August 1847 found a temperature of 2°·7 C. below the Gulf-stream, at the depth of 1,000 fathoms, in lat. 35° 26′ N., and long. 73° 12′ W.; and of Lieutenant Dayman, who found the temperature at 1,000 fathoms, in lat. 51° N. and long. 40° W. to be 0°·4 C., the surface temperature being 12°·5 C., the impression seems to have prevailed among physicists and physical geographers that salt water followed the same law as fresh water, attaining its greatest density at a temperature of 4° C. The necessary result of this condition, were it to exist, is thus stated by Sir John Herschel: "In very deep water all over the globe a uniform temperature of 39° Fahrenheit (4° C.) is found to prevail; while above the level where that temperature is first reached, the ocean may be considered as divided into three great regions or zones—an equatorial and two polar. In the former of these warmer, and in the latter colder water is found on the surface. The lines of demarkation are of course the two isotherms of 39° mean annual temperature." Dr. Wallich gives an excellent *résumé* of this curious fallacy. He says: "But whilst the temperature of the atmosphere beyond the line of perpetual congelation goes on gradually increasing, that of the water below the isothermal line remains constant to the bottom.

Were it not for the operation of the law on which the latter phenomenon depends, the entire ocean would long since have become solidified, and both sea and land rendered unfit for the habitation of living organisms. Unlike other bodies which expand and become lighter with every rise in temperature, water attains its maximum density, not under the lowest degree of cold, but at 39°·5 Fahrenheit; and consequently so soon as the superficial layer of sea is cooled down to this degree, it descends, and allows a fresh portion to ascend and be in turn cooled. This process is continued until the whole upper stratum is reduced in temperature to 39°·5, when, instead of contracting further, it begins to expand and get lighter than the water beneath, floats on it, becomes further cooled down, and at 28°·5 is converted into ice. . . . Thus under the operation of an apparently exceptional law, the equilibrium of the oceanic circulation is maintained; for whilst at the equator the mean temperature of the surface layer of water, which is 82°, gradually decreases, until at a depth of 1,200 fathoms it becomes stationary at 39°·5, and retains that temperature to the bottom, within the Polar regions and extending to lat. 56° 25′ in either hemisphere, the temperature increases from the surface downwards to the isothermal line, beyond which it remains uniform as in the former case. Hence in lat. 56° 25′ the temperature is uniform the whole way from the surface to the bottom; and as has been found by observation about lat. 70°, the isothermal line occurs at 750 fathoms below the surface."[1]

[1] Dr. Wallich: North Atlantic Sea-bed, p. 99.

There can be no doubt that this view, which of late years has received almost universal acceptance, is entirely erroneous. It has been shown by M. Despretz,[1] as the result of a series of carefully conducted experiments which have since been frequently repeated and verified, that sea-water, as a saline solution, contracts and increases steadily in density down to its freezing-point, which is, when kept perfectly still, about $-3°\cdot67$ C. ($25°\cdot4$ F.), and when agitated $-2°\cdot55$ C.

The temperature observations of Sir James Clarke Ross during his Antarctic voyage in 1840–41, seemed to give support to the theory of a constant temperature of $4°\cdot5$ C. for deep water, but these observations have as evidently been made with unguarded instruments, as those of Sir John Ross in 1818 with instruments defended from pressure; and although I believe they must be taken as proving that in high southern latitudes the surface temperature is sometimes lower than the temperature of the water at a considerable depth beneath, still the amount of correction for pressure is uncertain, depending upon the construction of the thermometers used, and in any case it must reduce the difference considerably.

A large number of thermometers of the ordinary Hydrographic Office pattern were sent out with us, as I have already mentioned, in the 'Lightning,' and these were of course the instruments used by Staff-Commander May for his temperature observations. There was an opportunity of testing these thermometers, however, on the return of the vessel,

[1] Recherches sur le Maximum de Densité des Dissolutions aqueuses. Loc. cit.

so that we are tolerably certain by actual experiment of the amount of their error. In speaking of the 'Lightning' temperatures, I mean, therefore, the actual temperatures taken by the ordinary thermometers, corrected approximately to the standard of the Miller-Casella thermometers, afterwards used in the 'Porcupine.'

Leaving Stornoway in the 'Lightning,' on the 11th of August, 1868, and directing our course towards the Færoe banks, we sounded in 500 fathoms about 60 miles to the north-west of the Butt of the Lews, and took a bottom temperature of 9°·4 Cent. with the ordinary Six's thermometer—the only form of the instrument in use at the time. This, when corrected for pressure, gives about 7°·8 C. We were surprised to find the temperature so high, and we were at the time inclined to think that the observation, which was taken in a breeze of wind, was scarcely to be depended upon. Subsequent observations, however, in the same locality, confirmed its accuracy. On the Færoe Banks, at a depth under 100 fathoms, the bottom temperature averaged 9° C., while that of the surface was about 12° C.; temperature indications on this bank were, however, of little value, as the water is no doubt affected to some extent through its entire depth by direct solar radiation. The next observation was in lat. 60° 45′ N. and long. 4° 49′ W., at a depth of 510 fathoms, with a bottom temperature of −0°·5 C., about 140 miles nearly directly north of Cape Wrath. Then followed a series of soundings, Nos. 7, 8, 10, and 11 of the chart (Plate I.), taken while traversing the northern portion of the channel between Scotland and the Færoe plateau; and giving, respectively, the temperatures of −1°·1, −1°·2, −0°·7, and −0°·5 C. No. 9, with a depth of 170 fathoms and a temperature of 5° C., is exceptional; it is apparently the top of a circumscribed ridge or bank. We dredged at this station and got large numbers of the rare and beautiful *Terebratula cranium;* but when we tried for the same spot in the following year in the 'Porcupine,' we could not find it. On the 6th of September we sounded and took temperatures in lat. 59° 36′ N., long. 7° 20′ W., in 530 fathoms, when the mean of three thermometers, which only differed from one another by about ·3 of a degree, gave a bottom temperature of 6°·4 C. A temperature sounding, at the moderate depth of 189 fathoms, was taken on the morning of the 7th September in lat. 59° 5′ N., long. 7° 29′ W., and gave a bottom temperature of 9°·6 C. The three soundings, Nos. 13, 14, and 17, at the depths 650, 570, and 620 fathoms, extending into the North Atlantic as far westward as long. 12° 36′ W., gave a bottom temperature of 5°·8, 6°·4, and 6°·6 C., respectively.

The general result of these observations we could not but regard as very remarkable. The region which we had somewhat imperfectly examined included, in the first place, the channel about a couple of hundred miles in width, with an extreme depth of rather under 600 fathoms, extending between the northern boundary-line of the British plateau and the shoal which culminates in the Færoe Islands and their extensive banks; and secondly, a small portion of the North Atlantic extending westwards and northwards of the western entrance of the channel. We found that in these two areas, freely communicating with one another and in immediate proximity, two totally different conditions of climate existed at all depths below the immediate surface, where they differed but slightly. In the Færoe channel, at a depth of 500 fathoms, the bottom temperature averaged $-1^{\circ}\cdot0$ C., while at a like depth in the Atlantic the minimum index stood at $+6^{\circ}$ C., a difference of 7 degrees Centigrade, nearly 13 degrees Fahrenheit.

The conclusion at which we speedily arrived as the only feasible explanation of these phenomena was that an arctic stream of frigid water crept from the north-eastward into the Færoe channel lying in the deeper part of the trough, owing to its higher specific gravity; while a body of water warmed even above the normal temperature of the latitude, and therefore coming from some southern source, was passing northwards across its western entrance and occupying the whole depth of that comparatively shallow portion of the Atlantic from the surface to the bottom.

Several important facts of very general application in Physical Geography had been placed beyond doubt by these observations. It had been shown that in nature, as in the experiments of M. Despretz, sea-water does not share in the peculiarities of fresh water, which, as has been long known, attains its maximum density at 4° C.; but, like most other liquids, increases in density to its freezing-point: and it had also been shown that, owing to the movement of great bodies of water at different temperatures in different directions, we may have in close proximity two ocean areas with totally different bottom climates—a fact which, taken along with the discovery of abundant animal life at all depths, has most important bearings upon the distribution of marine life, and upon the interpretation of palæontological data.

The conditions during the 'Lightning' cruise were so unfavourable to careful observation, that we determined to take the earliest opportunity of going over this region again, and determining the limits of these warm and cold areas, and investigating their conditions more in detail. Accordingly, in the following year, when we had H.M.S. 'Porcupine' at our disposal, Dr. Carpenter and I once more left Stornoway on the 15th of August, 1869. On this occasion we had everything in our favour; the weather was beautiful, the vessel suitable, and we were provided with Miller-Casella thermometers on whose accuracy we could depend. A table of Captain Calver's valuable thermometrical observations during this cruise is given in Appendix A to this chapter.

We proceeded to very nearly the same spot where we had taken our first sounding on the former year, and took a warm area temperature of 7°·7 C. Station No. 46 (Plate IV.). We then moved on slowly towards the Færoe fishing banks, finding in succession at Stations 47, 49, and 50, – 6°·5, 7°·6, and 7°·9 C. At Station 51, about 40 miles south of the bank, there was a decided fall of temperature—the thermometer indicating 5°·6 C. at a depth of 440 fathoms; and about 20 miles directly northwards a sounding at Station 52, lat. 60° 25′ N., long. 8° 10′ W., at a depth of only 380 fathoms, gave a minimum temperature of $-0^{\circ}\!\cdot\!8$ C., showing that we had passed the boundary, and were in the 'cold area.'

At this point we requested Captain Calver to take a serial sounding, ascertaining the temperature at depths progressively increasing by 50 fathoms, which was done with the following result:—

Surface	11° · 8 C.
50 fathoms	9 · 2
100 ,, ...	8 · 4
150 ,, ...	8 · 0
200 ,, ...	7 · 5
250 ,, ...	3 · 5
300 ,, ...	0 · 6
384 (Bottom)	0 · 8

We thus ascertained that the minimum temperature was at the bottom; and this we have found to be universally the case over the whole of the area which we have examined, whatever the bottom temperature might be. And we also ascertained that the decrease in heat from the surface downwards was by no means uniform, but that while after passing the surface layer it was tolerably regular for the first 200 fathoms, there was an extraordinary fall amounting to upwards of 7° C. from 200 to 300 fathoms, at which latter depth the minimum is nearly gained.

The next few observations, Stations 53 to 59, were all within the limits of the cold area, the bottom temperature at depths ranging from 360 to 630 fathoms, nowhere reaching the freezing-point of fresh water; and at one point, Station 59, lat. 60° 21′ N., long. 5° 41′ W., at a depth of 580 fathoms, the index standing so low as $-1^{\circ}\!\cdot\!3$ C. On Saturday the 21st we took a sounding in 187 fathoms, on the edge of the Færoe plateau, and about twenty miles north of the previous station, with a temperature of 6°·9 C., and so found that we had passed the limits of the cold basin.

Our first two soundings after leaving Thorshavn (Stations 61 and 62) were in shallow water on the Færoe Bank, 114 and 125 fathoms, with a temperature of 7°·2 and 7°·0 C. respectively; but the next Station, No. 63, after a run of eighty miles, gave 317 fathoms and 0°·9 C., showing that we were once more in the cold region. From that point, passing in a south-easterly direction across the channel towards the northern point of Shetland, we traversed the cold area in its most characteristic form, finding at Station 64, lat. 61° 21′ N., long. 3° 44′ W., a depth of 640 fathoms, with a bottom temperature of −1°·2 C. Here we took another serial sounding, and its results corresponded generally with those of No. 52. The surface temperature was lower, and the temperature down to 200 fathoms somewhat lower; at 350 fathoms it was a little higher:—

Surface	9°·8 C.
50 fathoms	7·5
100 „	7·2
150 „	6·3
200 „	4·1
250 „	1·3
300 „	0·2
350 „	0·3
400 „	0·5
450 „	0·8
500 „	−1·0
550 „	−1·0
600 „	−1·1
640 „	−1·2

At this point, therefore, the ice-cold water of the Arctic current filling up the bottom of the trough is nearly 2,000 feet deep, while the temperate water above has nearly an equal depth. The lower half of the latter, however, has its temperature considerably reduced by intermixture and diffusion. Fig. 55 represents diagrammatically the general result of temperature observations in the cold area. The depth at the next Station, No. 65, was 354 fathoms, showing that the channel had begun to shoal towards Shetland; the temperature was, however, still low, almost exactly 0° C. The next Station, No. 66, eighteen miles further on towards the Shetland banks, gave a depth of 267 fathoms, with a bottom temperature of 7°·6 C., the temperature at the surface being 11°·3 C. We had therefore got beyond the edge of the trough filled by the cold stream, and passed into lesser depths occupied from the surface to the bottom by the warm southern stratum.

The next series of soundings, Nos. 67 to 75, are either in shallow water round Shetland, or in water on the shelving edge of the plateau, not deep enough to reach the frigid stream. It is of some interest that the two soundings, Nos. 68 and 69, in 75 and 67 fathoms respectively, to the east of Shetland, show a bottom temperature of 6°·6 C., while a serial sounding in the warm area at the western entrance of the Færoe Channel gives for the same depth a temperature of about 8°·8 C. This circumstance, along with others to be mentioned hereafter, would seem to show that a considerable indraught of cold water spreads over the bottom of the shallow north sea.

At Stations 76 to 86, which are along the southern

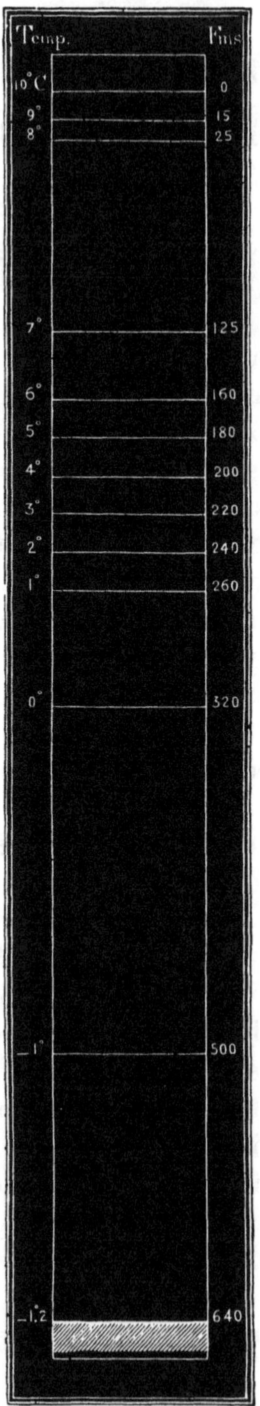

Fig. 55.—Serial sounding, Station 64.

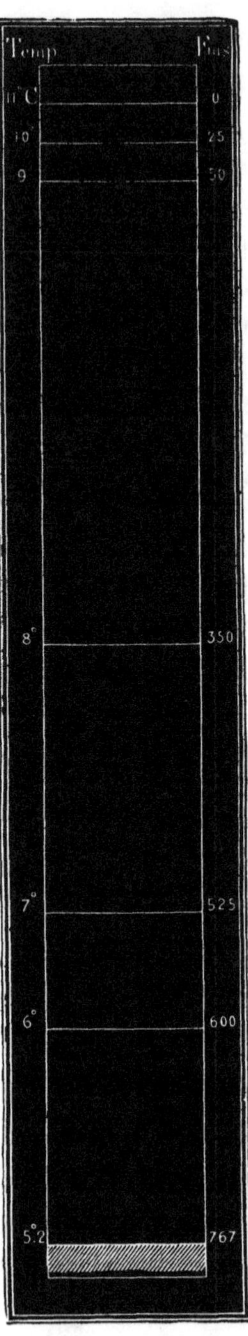

Fig. 56.—Serial sounding, Station 87

border of the cold area, temperature soundings were taken mainly with a view to define its southern limit, and they are sometimes on one side and sometimes on the other. The general result is indicated on Plate IV. by the southern border of the shaded space. Nos. 87 to 90 are once more in the warm area, the water reaching a depth of upwards of 700 fathoms, but maintaining, after the first 300 fathoms, a temperature of from 6° to 7° C. above that of corresponding depths in the cold area. At Station 87, lat. 59° 35′ N., long. 9° 11′ W., with a depth of 767 fathoms, a serial sounding was taken, which contrasts remarkably with the series at Station 64. The general result of this sounding is represented diagrammatically by Fig 56. The temperature was taken at every 100 fathoms after the first 200.

Surface	11°·4 C.
50 fathoms	9·0
100 „	8·5
150 „	8·3
200 „	8·2
300 „	8·1
400 „	7·8
500 „	7·3
600 „	6·1
767 „	5·1

It will be seen by reference to the chart that two nearly parallel series of soundings were taken, extending from the shallow water on the Scottish side to the edge of the Færoe Bank close to the western opening of the Færoe Channel, and that one of these chains, including Stations 52, 53, 54, and 86, are in the cold area, while the other chain of Stations, 48,

47, 90, 49, 50, and 51, are in the warm area. There is no great difference in depth between the two series of soundings; and there is no indication of a ridge separating them. The only possible explanation of these two so widely different submarine climates, existing apparently under the same circumstances and in close proximity to one another, is that the Arctic indraught which passes into the deeper part of the Færoe Channel is banked in at its entrance, by the warm southern stream slowly passing northwards. There is a slight but very constant depression of the isothermal lines of surface temperature in the shallow water along the west coast of Britain. This, I believe, indicates that a portion of the cold Færoe stream makes its escape, and, still banked in close to the land by the warm water, gradually makes its way southwards, so mixed and diluted as only to be perceptible by its slight effect on the lines of mean temperature. Diagrams 55 and 56 illustrate the distribution of temperature in the cold and warm areas respectively; and in Fig. 57, the results of the serial soundings Nos. 52, 64, and 87, are reduced to curves. From these diagrams, taken together, it will be seen that in the first 50 fathoms there is a rapid fall of nearly 3° C. Station No. 64 is a good deal farther north than the other two, and the surface temperature is lower, so that the fall, which is nearly to the same amount, starts from a lower point. The surface temperature is doubtless due to the direct heat of the sun, and the first rapid fall is due to the rapid decrease of this direct effect. From 50 to 200 fathoms the temperature in all three cases falls but little, remaining considerably above the normal temperature

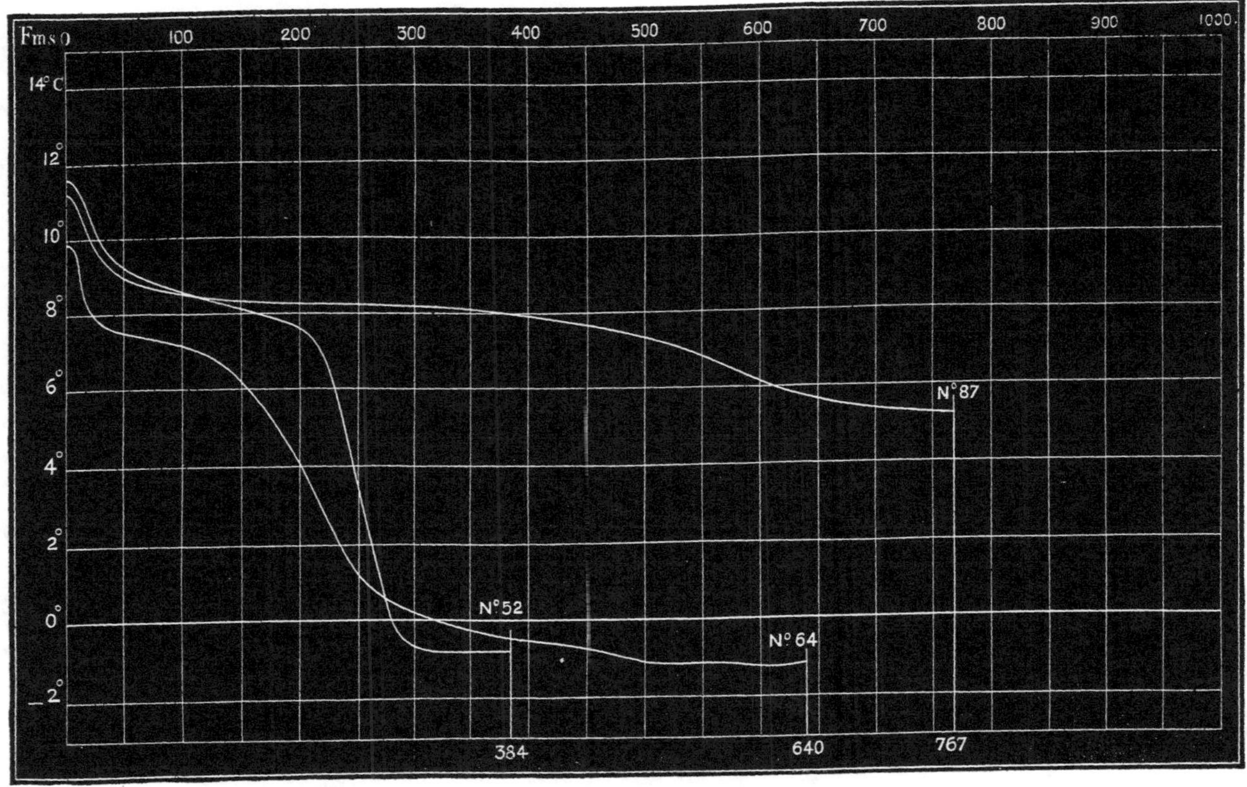

Fig. 57.—Curves constructed from serial soundings in the 'warm-' and 'cold-areas' in the channel between Scotland and Färoe.

of the ocean for the parallel of latitude. At a depth of 200 fathoms, however, the divergence between the curves of the warm and cold areas is most remarkable. The curve of the warm area, No. 87, shows a fall of scarcely half a degree at 500 fathoms, and less than one degree more at 767 fathoms at the bottom. Between 200 and 300 fathoms the cold area curves run down from 8° C. to 0° C., leaving only one degree more of gradual descent for the next 300 fathoms. The temperature of the 'hump' on the curves of the 'cold area' between 50 and 200 fathoms corresponds so nearly with that of the long gradual sinking of the curve of the warm area from the surface nearly to the bottom, that it seems natural to trace it to the same source. We therefore conclude that a shallow layer of Gulf-stream water drifting slowly northwards overlies in the cold area an indraught of cold water represented by the sudden and great depression of the curves, while in the warm area this cold indraught is absent, the Gulf-stream water reaching to the bottom.

Tracing the 'warm area' southwards from the mouth of the Færoe Channel along the coast of Scotland, we find that the area between Færoe, the Lews, and Rockall, is a kind of plateau with a depth of from 700 to 800 fathoms; and we may be certain from analogy, although this region has not yet been actually examined, with a bottom temperature not lower than 4°·5 C. Commencing opposite Rockall, and extending between the great shoal which culminates in the Rockall fishing banks and the singular isolated rock, and the west coast of Ireland, there is a wide trough deepening gradually southwards, and at length continuous with the general basin of the North Atlantic.

The temperature of this ocean valley was investigated with great care during the first and second cruises of the 'Porcupine' in 1869, and the results were so very uniform throughout the area that it will be needless to describe in detail the slight differences in different localities. These differences, in fact, only affected the surface layer of the water, and depended merely upon differences of latitude. The temperatures in deep water may be said to have been practically the same everywhere. The first chain of soundings, taken by Captain Calver during the first cruise under the scientific direction of Mr. Gwyn Jeffreys, was between Lough Swilly and Rockall. The greatest depth, 1,380 fathoms, is in the middle of the channel, and a sounding at that depth, lat. 56° 24′ N., long. 11° 49′ W., gave a bottom temperature of 2°·8 C. A depth of 630 fathoms, No. 23, a little to the south of Rockall, gave a temperature of 6°·4 C., almost exactly the same as the temperature of a like depth in the warm area off the entrance of the Færoe Channel; and a temperature at 500 fathoms, one of a series taken at Station 21 with a bottom temperature at 1,476 fathoms of 2°·7 C., was 8°·5 C., rather less than a degree higher than the temperature at a corresponding depth at Station 87. At Station 21 the temperature was taken at every 250 fathoms.

Surface	13°·5 C.
250 fathoms	9·0
500 ,, ...	8·5
750 ,, ...	5·8

1,000 fathoms	3°·5 C.
1,250 "	3·3
1,476 "	2·7

We have here on a large scale, as Dr. Carpenter has pointed out, conditions very analogous to those which exist in comparatively shallow water, and on a small scale in the cold area in the Færoe Channel. There is a surface layer of about 50 fathoms, superheated in August by direct solar radiation, and, as we see by the variations of surface isothermals, varying greatly with the seasons of the year. Next, we have a band extending here to a depth of nearly 800 fathoms, in which the thermometer sinks slowly through a range of about 5° C. Then a zone of intermixture of about 200 fathoms, where the temperature falls rapidly, and finally a mass of cold water from a depth of 1,000 fathoms to the bottom, through which, whatever be its depth, the thermometer falls almost imperceptibly, the water never reaching the dead cold of the Arctic undercurrent in the Færoe Channel, and the lowest temperature being universally at the bottom (Fig. 58).

The area investigated during the second cruise of the 'Porcupine' at the mouth of the Bay of Biscay, about a couple of hundred miles west of Ushant, may be regarded as simply a continuation southwards of the tract between Scotland and Ireland and the Rockall ridge. As, however, the depths were greater than any attained on any former occasion—were so great, indeed, as probably to represent the average depth of the great ocean basins—it may be well to describe the methods of observation and the conditions of temperature somewhat in detail.

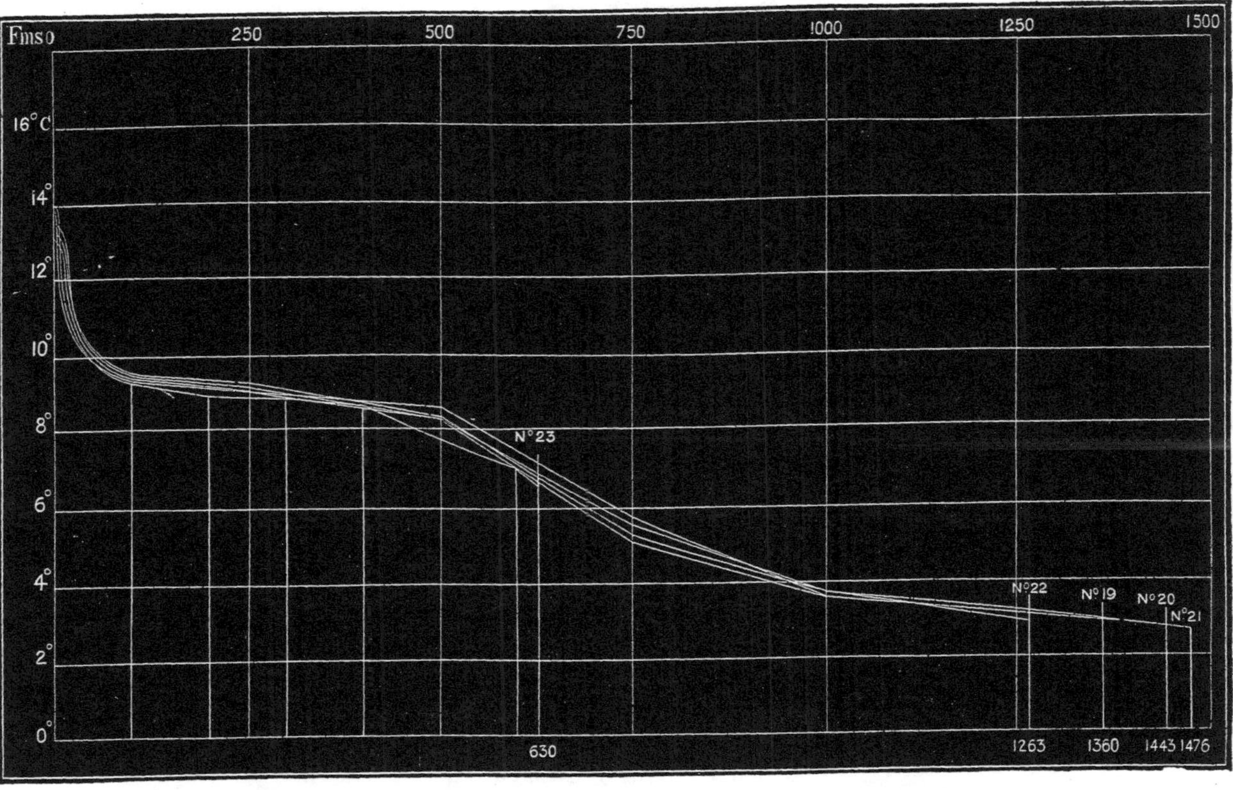

Fig. 58.—Curves constructed from serial and bottom soundings in the channel between Scotland and Rockall.

The sounding at Station No. 37, at a depth of 2,435 fathoms, has already been fully described as an example of the most recent method of determining extreme depths with accuracy. Two Miller-Casella thermometers, numbered 100 and 103 respectively, were lashed to the sounding-line in their copper cases, one a little above the other, about a fathom and a fathom and a half above the 'Hydra' sounding-machine. These two instruments had been prepared and tested with extreme care, and had been employed throughout the first cruise; their freezing-points had been again verified at Belfast in case the enormous pressure to which they had been subjected might have affected the glass, and we had absolute confidence in their indications. The indices were set before the instruments were let down at the temperature of the surface, 21°·1 C., and 21°·15 C. They were allowed to remain at the bottom for ten minutes, and on their return to the surface in upwards of two hours and a half, they were unanimous in recording a minimum of 1°·65 C., the slight differences between the two instruments, which gave the almost inappreciable error for one of them of 0°·05 C. at 21° C., being imperceptible at the lower temperature.

It had a strange interest to see these two little instruments, upon whose construction so much skilled labour and consideration had been lavished, consigned to their long and hazardous journey; and their return eagerly watched for by a knot of thoughtful men, standing, note-book in hand, ready to register this first message, which should throw so much light upon the physical conditions of a hitherto unknown world.

A series of temperature soundings, at depths increasing progressively by 250 fathoms, was taken to a depth of 2,090 fathoms, on the 24th of July, lat. 47° 39′ N., long. 11° 33′ W.

Surface . .	17°· 08 C.		
250 fathoms .	10 · 28	less than Surface . .	7°· 5 C.
500 „ .	8 · 8	„ 250 fathoms .	1 · 5
750 „ .	5 · 17	„ 500 „ .	3 · 6
1,000 „ .	3 · 5	„ 750 „ .	1 · 7
1,250 „ .	3 · 17	„ 1,000 „ .	0 · 3
1,500 „ .	2 · 9	„ 1,250 „ .	0 · 3
1,750 „ .	2 · 61	„ 1,500 „ .	0 · 3
2,090 „ .	2 · 4	„ 1,750 „ .	0 · 2

The same two Miller-Casella thermometers were employed as in the previous observation.

Another serial sounding was taken a few days late. in water 862 fathoms deep, somewhat nearer the coast of Ireland. In this case the temperature was taken at intervals of 10 fathoms from the surface to a depth of 50 fathoms, and thence at intervals of 50 fathoms to the bottom. This was done to determine exactly the rate of diminution of temperature, and the exact position of the most marked irregularities.

Surface . .	17°· 22 C.		
10 fathoms .	16 · 72	less than surface . . .	0°· 5 C.
20 „ .	15 · 22	less than 10 fathoms .	1 · 5
30 „ .	13 · 33	„ 20 „ .	1 · 9
40 „ .	12 · 44	„ 30 „ .	0 · 9
50 „ .	11 · 8	„ 40 „ .	0 · 64
100 „ .	10 · 6	„ 50 „ .	1 · 2
150 „ .	10 · 5	„ 100 „ .	0 · 1
200 „ .	10 · 3	„ 150 „ .	0 · 2
250 „ .	10 . 11	„ 200 „ .	0 · 2
300 „ .	9 · 8	„ 250 „ .	0 · 3

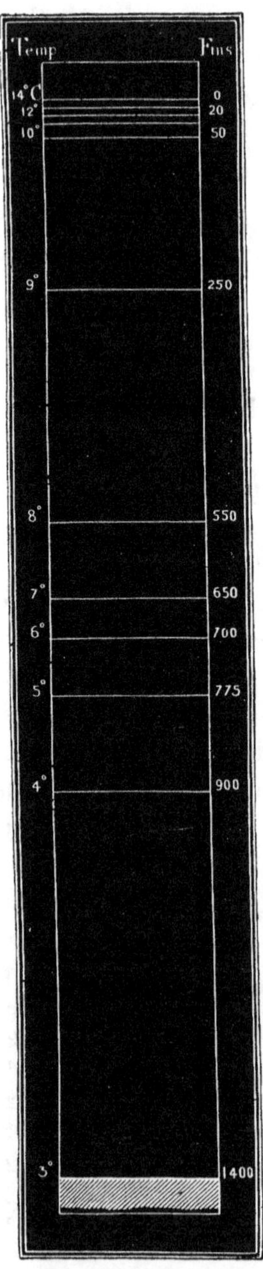

Fig. 59.—Diagram representing the relation between depth and temperature off Rockall.

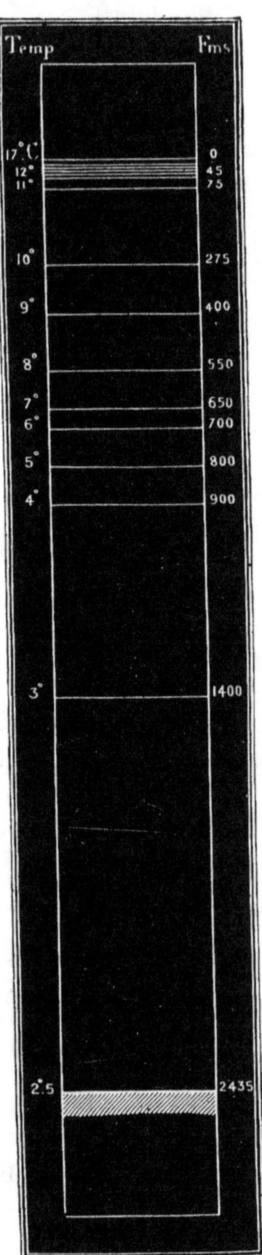

Fig. 60.—Diagram representing the relation between depth and temperature in the Atlantic basin.

Plate VI.—*Diagram of the 'Porcupine' soundings in the Atlantic and in the Færoe Channel, showing the relation between temperature and depth,—the serial soundings reduced to curves. The numbers refer to the stations on the Charts, Plates II., III., and IV.*

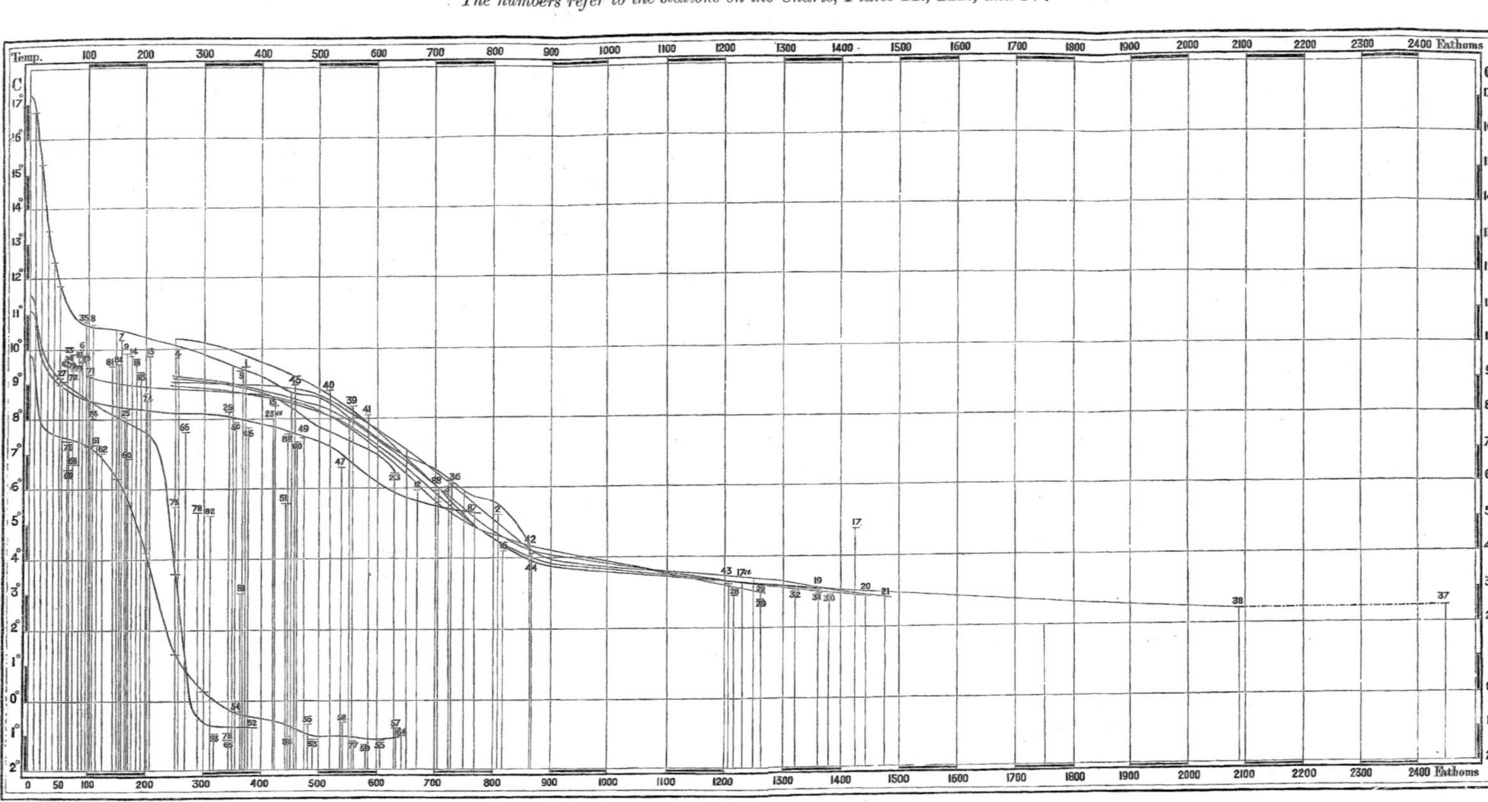

350 fathoms	9°·5 C.	less than	300 fathoms .	0°·3 C.
400 „ .	9·17	„	350 „ .	0·3
450 „ .	8·7	„	400 „ .	0·5
500 „ .	8·55	„	450 „ .	0·15
550 „ .	8·0	„	500 „ .	0·55
600 „ .	7·4	„	550 „ .	0·5
650 „ .	6·83	„	600 „ .	0·6
700 „ .	6·44	„	650 „ .	0·4
750 „ .	5·83	„	700 „ .	0·6
800 „ .	5·55	„	750 „ .	0·3
862 (Bottom)	4·3	„	800 „ .	1·25

The general result of these two series of soundings is very important. The high temperature reduced by 7°·5 C. in the first series at 250 fathoms is undoubtedly due to superheating by direct solar radiation. This is shown still more clearly in the second series, where nearly 4° C. are seen to be lost between the surface and 30 fathoms, and somewhat above 2° C. more between 30 and 100 fathoms. From 100 to 500 fathoms the temperature is still high and tolerably uniform, and it falls rapidly between 500 and 1,000 fathoms. A reference to the second series shows that this rapid fall is between 650 and 850 fathoms, in which interval there is a loss of more than 3° C. This second stage of elevated temperature from 250 to 700 fathoms, which is represented graphically by the singular 'hump' on the temperature curves in Fig. 61 and Plate VI. would seem to be caused by the north-easterly reflux under peculiar conditions, which will be referred to in next chapter, of the great equatorial current. From 1,000 fathoms downwards, the loss of temperature goes on uniformly at the rate of about 0°·3 C. for every 250 fathoms. The most singular feature in this decrease of tem-

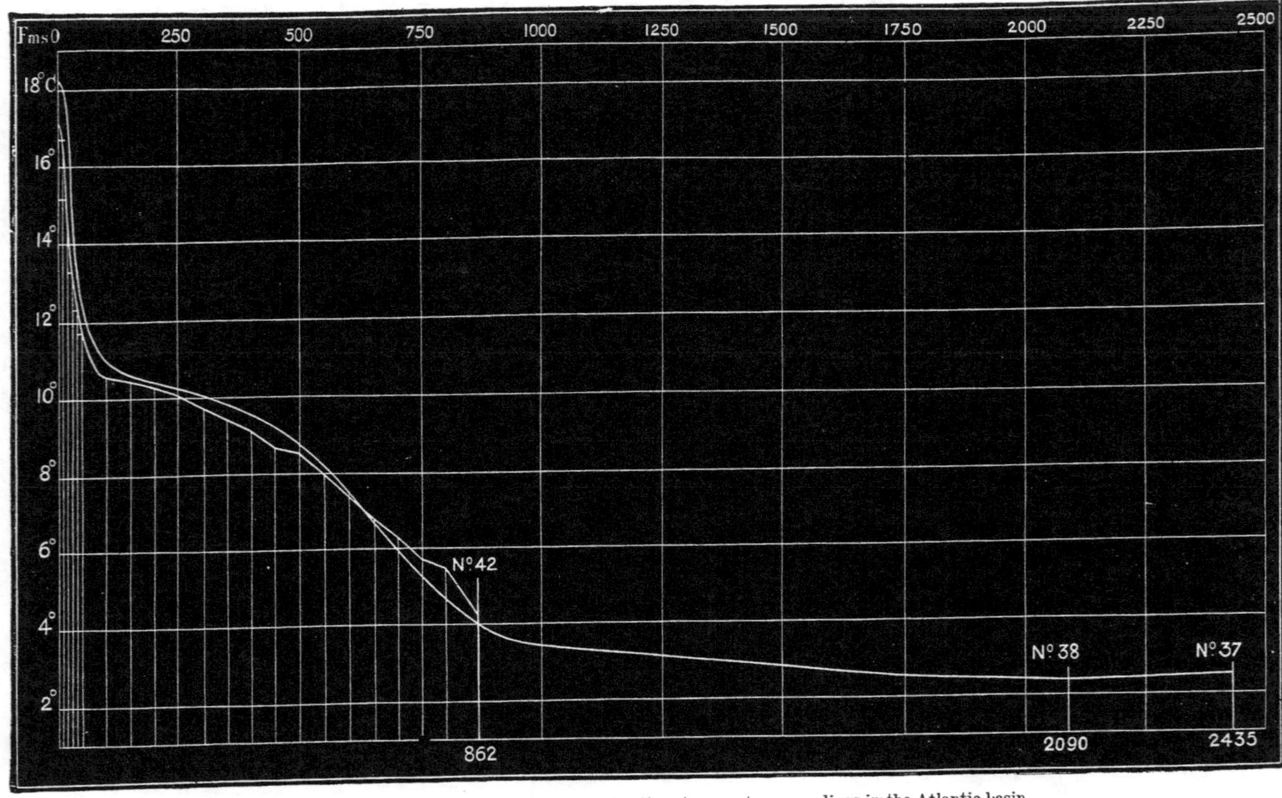

Fig. 61.—Curves constructed from serial and bottom temperature soundings in the Atlantic basin.

perature for the last mile and three-quarters is its absolute uniformity, which appears to be inconsistent with the idea of anything like a current in the ordinary sense, and rather to point to a slow and general indraught of cold water, falling in chiefly by gravitation from the coldest and deepest sources available, to supply the place of the warm water constantly moving to the northward.

In 1870, Mr. Gwyn Jeffreys took his first temperature observations at the mouth of the Channel, and found them to correspond very closely with those of the previous year; on the 9th of July the bottom temperature at 358 fathoms, Station 6 Pl. V., was 10°·0 C., against 9°·8 C., at about the same depth in a serial sounding in 1869, in the immediate neighbourhood. The next few soundings, Stations 10 to 13, are in comparatively shallow water, off the coast of Portugal, while the next four Stations, a little north of Lisbon, may serve as an example of the temperatures to a considerable depth in that latitude. Station 14, 469 fathoms, with a surface temperature of 18°·3 C., has a bottom temperature of 10°·7 C.; Station 15, at 722 fathoms, a temperature of 9°·7 C.; Station 16, at 994 fathoms, 4°·4 C.; and Station 17, at 1,095 fathoms, 4°·3 C. This result is very similar to that which we met with in 1869 off Ushant. With certain differences, which seem to depend mainly upon the differences of latitude, we have the same phenomena—a thin surface-layer, superheated by the direct rays of the sun; a layer of warm water through which the temperature descends very slowly down to 800 fathoms; a zone of intermixture and rapid descent of the thermometer of nearly 200 fathoms in thickness; and finally the deep cold layer into which these soundings do not penetrate very far, through which the temperature sinks almost imperceptibly from 4° C. The difference between these soundings and those of the year before at the mouth of the Bay of Biscay is that the temperatures at all depths are somewhat higher.

I refrain for the present from going into any detail with regard to the distribution of temperature in the Mediterranean, further than to give a mere outline of the remarkable conditions which were observed there by Dr. Carpenter.

Dr. Carpenter's observations were principally confined to the western basin of the Mediterranean, and during the months of August and September the surface temperature averaged between 23° C. and 26° C. On two occasions only the surface temperature fell considerably lower, and the fall was attributed in both cases to the influence of the colder surface current passing from the Atlantic through the Straits of Gibraltar. The following table of the series taken at Station 53 gives about the average rate of fall of temperature for the first 100 fathoms:—

Surface	25°·0 C.
5 fathoms	24·5
10 "	21·6
20 "	16·4
30 "	15·5
40 "	14·1
50 "	13·6
100 "	13·0

and Dr. Carpenter made the remarkable observation that "whatever the temperature was at 100

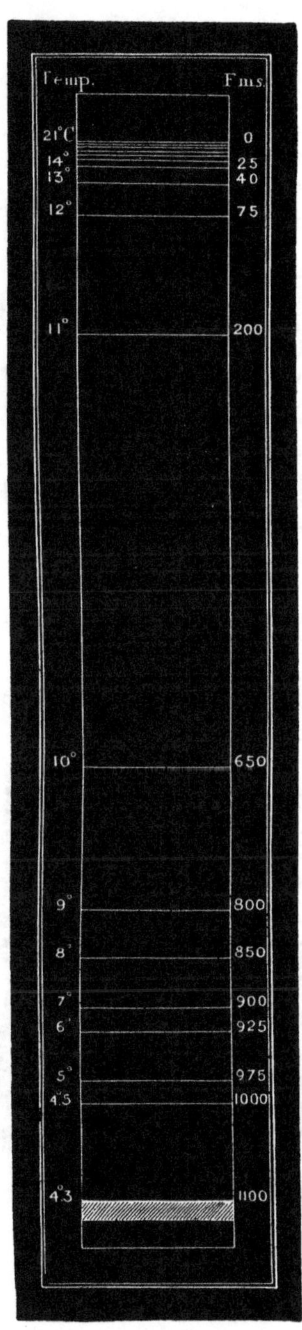

FIG. 62.—Diagram representing the relation between depth and temperature, from the temperature observations taken between Cape Finisterre and Cape St. Vincent, August 1870.

fathoms, that was the temperature of the whole mass of water beneath, down to the greatest depth explored." The temperature at 100 fathoms varies very little from 13° C. (55·5° Fahrenheit), and the Mediterranean attains in many places a depth of upwards of 1,500 fathoms, so that here we have the strange phenomenon of an underlying mass of water, 1,400 fathoms deep, of a uniform moderate temperature; a state of things singularly different from that which obtains at like depths in the Atlantic. Dr. Carpenter's ingenious speculations as to the cause of this difference will be considered later.

VAAŸ CHURCH IN SUDERÖ.

APPENDIX A.

Surface Temperatures observed on board H.M.S. 'Porcupine' during the Summers of 1869 and 1870.

I. Temperatures observed in 1869.

Date and Position.	Hour.	Temperature of Air.	Temperature of Sea-Surface.	Date and Position.	Hour.	Temperature of Air.	Temperature of Sea-Surface.
		Deg. Cent.	Deg. Cent.			Deg. Cent.	Deg. Cent.
May 28th . .	2	10·0	9·4	May 30th . .	4	10·0	9·4
	4	10·0	10·2		6	10·8	10·8
	6				8	12·2	11·1
	8				10	15·0	11·1
	10	10·0	10·5	In Valentia . .	Noon.	15·0	12·7
Off the Great Skelligs . .	Noon.	9·4	10·8		2	12·8	12·2
					4	12·5	11·4
	2		11·9		6	11·4	11·1
	4	11·6	11·1		8		
	6		11·4		10	10·0	11·1
	8				Midn.	9·4	11·1
	10	11·6	10·2	May 31st . . .	2	9·4	10·8
	Midn.	10·0	10·5		4	10·0	11·1
May 29th . .	2				6	11·1	11·1
	4	7·2			8	13·3	11·1
	6	11·6	10·2		10	13·3	11·1
	8	11·1	10·8	Lat. 51° 52′ N. Long. 11° 34′ W.	Noon.	13·9	11·6
	10	13·3	12·7				
In Dingle Bay .	Noon.	13·9	11·6		2	13·9	11·4
	2	13·9	11·4		4	12·7	
	4	12·7	11·4		6	12·2	11·9
	6		10·5		8	12·2	11·6
	8	10·0	10·5		10	11·6	11·6
	10	11·6			Midn.	11·9	11·9
	Midn.	11·1		June 1st . . .	2	12·2	12·2
May 30th . .	2	11·6			4	12·2	12·2

Date and Position.	Hour.	Temperature of Air.	Temperature of Sea-Surface.
		Deg. Cent.	Deg. Cent.
June 1st . . .	6	12·2	11·9
	8	13·0	11·9
	10	13·9	11·9
Lat. 51° 22′ N. Long. 12° 26′ W.	Noon.	14·4	11·9
	2	14·4	12·2
	4	12·2	11·6
	6	13·3	11·9
	8	12·2	11·9
	10	11·9	12·2
	Midn.	11·6	11·9
June 2nd . . .	2	11·9	11·9
	4	11·1	11·9
	6	10·5	11·9
	8	11·6	
	10	12·2	12·2
Lat. 52° 8′ N. Long. 12° 50′ W.	Noon.	15·0	12·2
	2	14·4	12·2
	4	15·0	12·2
	6	13·9	12·2
	8	11·1	11·9
	10	11·4	11·9
	Midn.	11·1	11·9
June 3rd . . .	2	11·1	11·6
	4	10·8	11·6
	6	11·1	11·9
	8	12·7	11·6
	10	15·0	11·9
Lat. 52° 26′ N. Long. 11° 41′ W.	Noon.	13·3	11·6
	2	14·7	11·9
	4	13·0	12·2
	6	11·6	12·2
	8	11·1	11·8
	10	11·1	11·6
	Midn.	10·8	11·6
June 4th . . .	2	11·1	11·6
	4	11·1	11·6
	6	11·1	11·6
	8	10·8	11·6
	10	10·5	11·6
Lat. 52° 14′ N. Long. 11° 45′ W.	Noon.	10·5	11·1

Date and Position.	Hour.	Temperature of Air.	Temperature of Sea-Surface.
		Deg. Cent.	Deg. Cent.
June 4th . . .	2	13·3	11·6
	4	13·3	11·6
	6	12·8	11·9
	8	12·8	12·2
	10	12·2	11·4
	Midn.	11·9	11·9
June 5th . . .	2	11·9	11·9
	4	11·6	11·6
	6	12·7	11·1
	8	12·7	11·1
	10	12·7	11·6
In Galway Dock	Noon.	16·1	13·3
	2	15·5	15·0
	4	13·9	
	6	15·5	
	8	13·3	
	10	13·3	
	Midn.	13·9	
June 6th . . .	2	13·3	
	4	12·7	
	6		
	8		
	10	14·4	
In Galway Dock	Noon.	12·2	
	2	17·2	
	4	19·4	
	6	19·4	
	8		
	10	13·9	
	Midn.	13·3	
June 7th . . .	2	13·3	
	4	12·7	
	6		
	8		
	10	16·1	
In Galway Dock	Noon.	18·3	
	2	17·7	
	4	17·7	
	6	17·2	
	8	15·0	
	10	13·9	
	Midn.	12·2	
June 8th . . .	2	11·1	
	4	10·0	

Date and Position.	Hour.	Temperature of Air.	Temperature of Sea-Surface.
		Deg. Cent.	Deg. Cent.
June 8th . . .	6	10·0	
	8		
	10	17·2	
In Galway Dock	Noon.	21·1	
	2	20·5	
	4	20·5	17·7
	6	20·0	
	8	16·6	15·0
	10	11·6	12·7
	Midn.	11·1	12·5
June 9th . . .	2	7·2	12·2
	4	7·7	11·6
	6	10·5	12·2
	8	12·7	12·5
	10	16·1	13·3
In Galway Dock	Noon.	19·4	13·9
	2	17·4	13·9
	4	17·2	13·6
	6	15·0	12·5
	8	11·4	12·7
	10	10·5	12·5
	Midn.	10·5	12·5
June 10th . .	2	10·0	11·6
	4	10·5	11·6
	6	10·2	12·2
	8	12·2	12·5
	10	11·6	12·5
Lat. 53° 16′ N. Long. 11° 52′ W.	Noon.	12·7	12·5
	2	13·3	12·7
	4	12·2	12·2
	6	11·6	12·7
	8	10·5	12·3
	10	10·0	12·3
	Midn.	10·0	12·3
June 11th . .	2	10·0	12·2
	4	10·0	12·2
	6	11·1	12·5
	8	11·1	12·5
	10	12·5	12·5
Lat. 53° 22′ N. Long 13° 23′ W.	Noon.	15·0	12·2
	2	13·9	12·7
	4	14·4	12·7

Date and Position.	Hour.	Temperature of Air.	Temperature of Sea-Surface.
		Deg. Cent.	Deg. Cent.
June 11th . .	6	11·9	12·7
	8	10·5	12·7
	10	11·1	12·2
	Midn.	10·0	12·2
June 12th . .	2	10·0	12·2
	4	10·2	12·3
	6	11·1	12·9
	8	11·4	13·0
	10	12·2	12·7
Lat. 53° 24′ N. Long. 15° 24′ W.	Noon.	12·2	12·7
	2	11·1	12·7
	4	12·2	12·7
	6	10·8	13·0
	8	11·1	12·9
	10	11·1	12·5
	Midn.	10·5	12·3
June 13th . .	2	10·5	11·9
	4	10·0	12·2
	6	9·1	12·2
	8	9·7	11·9
	10	9·4	12·0
Lat. 53° 28′ N. Long. 15° 08′ W.	Noon.	10·8	12 2
	2	10·5	12·5
	4	11·4	12·2
	6	11·1	12·2
	8	10·7	12·3
	10	11·1	12·2
	Midn.	11·1	12·2
June 14th . .	2	11·1	12·2
	4	11·4	12·2
	6	11·4	11·9
	8	11·9	12·5
	10	11·1	12·2
Lat. 53° 43′ N. Long. 13° 48′ W.	Noon.	13·3	12·2
	2	11·7	12·2
	4	13·0	12·2
	6	12·7	12·2
	8	11·1	11·8
	10	11·1	11·1
	Midn.	11·1	11·4
June 15th . .	2	10·8	11·1

Date and Position.	Hour.	Temperature of Air.	Temperature of Sea Surface.
		Deg. Cent.	Deg. Cent.
June 15th . .	4	10·8	11·6
	6	11·1	11·6
	8	14·4	11·6
	10	12·2	11·6
Lat. 53° 47′ N. Long. 13° 14′ W.	Noon.	12·7	10·6
	2	13·6	11·6
	4	13·0	11·6
	6	13·9	11·8
	8	10·8	11·8
	10	10·8	11·6
	Midn.	10·5	11·1
June 16th . .	2	10·0	11·7
	4	10·2	11·4
	6	12·7	11·5
	8	12·0	11·5
	10	13·9	11·6
Lat. 54° 2′ N. Long. 12° 14′ W.	Noon.	15·0	11·6
	2	13·9	11·9
	4	13·3	12·1
	6	12·2	11·6
	8	10·2	11·1
	10	11·1	11·4
	Midn.	11·4	11·4
June 17th . .	2	11·6	11·6
	4	11·6	11·6
	6	11·9	11·8
	8	13·6	11·6
	10	12·5	11·6
Lat. 54° 27′ N. Long. 11° 43′ W.	Noon.	13·9	11·8
	2	13·3	11·9
	4	13·3	11·9
	6	12·2	11·9
	8	12·2	11·6
	10	11·9	11·6
	Midn.	12·2	11·6
June 18th . .	2	11·6	11·6
	4	11·6	12·0
	6	12·2	12·0
	8	12·2	12·1
	10	12·2	12·2

Date and Position.	Hour.	Temperature of Air.	Temperature of Sea-Surface.
		Deg. Cent.	Deg Cent
Lat. 54° 10′ N. Long. 10° 59′ W.	Noon.	12·5	12·2
	2	12·9	12·2
	4	12·7	12·4
	6	12·7	11·8
	8	11·9	11·8
	10	11·4	11·6
	Midn.	11·4	11·4
June 19th . .	2	11·1	11·6
	4	11·1	11·1
	6	11·6	11·8
	8	11·6	12·2
	10	13·9	11·8
At Killibegs . .	Noon.	13·9	11·9
	2	13·3	12·2
	4	12·2	12·2
	6	11·6	12·3
	8	13·0	12·7
	10	11·1	12·2
	Midn.	10·5	12·2
June 20th . .	2	10·5	11·9
	4	11·1	11·6
	6	11·6	11·6
	8	12·7	12·2
	10	13·0	11·9
At Killibegs . .	Noon.	13·9	12·2
	2	15·0	12·2
	4	14·4	12·5
	6	14·4	12·5
	8	12·2	12·5
	10	10·0	12·2
	Midn.	10·8	12·5
June 21st . .	2	11·1	12·2
	4	11·1	12·2
	6	11·8	12·2
	8	12·2	12·2
	10	13·0	12·2
At Killibegs . .	Noon.	15·0	12·5
	2	15·3	12·2
	4	14·4	12·5
	6	13·0	12·2
	8	11·6	12·3
	10	11·1	11·6

Date and Position.	Hour.	Temperature of Air.	Temperature of Sea-Surface.	Date and Position.	Hour.	Temperature of Air.	Temperature of Sea-Surface.
		Deg. Cent.	Deg. Cent.			Deg. Cent.	Deg. Cent.
June 21st . .	Midn.	10·5	12·2	June 25th . .	4	15·0	15·0
June 22nd . .	2	11·1	11·8		6	16·1	13·9
	4	11·1	11·9		8	15·0	14·1
	6	11·1	11·6		10	15·5	15·5
	8	11·6	12·0		Midn.	14·4	15·5
	10	13·3	12·2	June 26th . .	2	14·1	15·8
At Killibegs . .	Noon.	13·3	12·2		4	13·9	15·0
	2	13·9	12·3		6	13·9	13·3
	4	13·3	12·2		8	15·3	13·6
	6	12·2	12·2		10	18·0	14·4
	8			In Donegal Bay	Noon.	19·1	13·9
	10	11·1	12·5		2	22·2	15·3
	Midn.	11·1	11·9		4	19·4	16·1
June 23rd . .	2	10·8	12·2		6	16·6	15·5
	4	11·1	12·2		8	15·5	15·5
	6	12·4	12·2		10	12·7	15·3
	8	13·9	12·2		Midn.	12·5	15·0
	10	15·5	12·5	June 27th . .	2	11·1	14·4
At Killibegs . .	Noon.	16·6	12·5		4	11·4	14·4
	2	15·5	12·5		6	12·7	13·9
	4	17·7	12·7		8	13·6	13·9
	6	16·6	13·3		10	15·5	14·4
	8	13·3	13·0	At Killibegs . .	Noon.	16·6	14·4
	10	13·6	13·3		2	20·0	15·0
	Midn.	12·7	13·0		4	17·2	14·4
June 24th . .	2	12·7	13·3		6	13·3	13·3
	4	13·3	13·3		8	13·3	13·3
	6	14·4	13·5		10	13·3	13·3
	8	15·3	13·3		Midn.	13·3	13·3
	10	16·6	13·5	June 28th . .	2	12·7	13·3
At Killibegs . .	Noon.	17·5	13·5		4	12·7	12·9
	2	17·7	13·9		6	12·7	12·7
	4	17·7	14·1		8	13·3	13·0
	6	17·2	15·0		10	13·9	13·3
	8	16·1	14·1	Lat. 54° 54′ N. Long. 10° 59′ W.	Noon.	14·7	13·3
	10	14·7	15·0				
	Midn.	14·7	15·3		2	14·7	13·3
June 25th . .	2	14·4	14·4		4	13·9	13·3
	4	14·1	14·4		6	13·0	13·9
	6	13·9	13·6		8	13·6	13·0
	8	18·3	14·4		10	12·7	13·3
	10	20·0	13·9		Midn.	12·9	13·6
At Bundoran .	Noon.	20·5	16·6	June 29th . .	2	12·7	13·3
	2	23·9	16·6		4	12·2	13·3

Date and Position.	Hour.	Temperature of Air.	Temperature of Sea-Surface.
		D g. Cent.	Deg. Cent.
June 29th . .	6	13·6	13·3
	8	14·4	13·3
	10	16·6	13·9
Lat. 55° 11′ N. Long. 11° 31′ W.	Noon.	16·6	14·4
	2	16·1	15·0
	4	15·5	14·4
	6	15·5	14·4
	8	15·0	14·4
	10	13·6	13·9
	Midn.	13·3	13·9
June 30th . .	2	13·0	14·1
	4	13·3	14·0
	6	16·6	13·9
	8	18·0	13·9
	10	16·1	14·4
Lat. 55° 44′ N. Long. 12° 53′ W.	Noon.	16·4	14·4
	2	17·7	14·5
	4	17·7	14·4
	6	15·8	15·0
	8	15·0	15·0
	10	14·4	15·3
	Midn.	13·6	14·4
July 1st . . .	2	12·7	13·9
	4	13·3	13·9
	6	15·5	14·4
	8	16·3	14·4
	10	17·3	14·7
	Noon.	17·2	14·8
	2	17·2	15·5
	4	16·6	15·0
	6	15·0	14·4
	8	14·4	14·4
	10	14·1	14·1
	Midn.	14·1	14·1
July 2nd . . .	2	14·1	13·9
	4	14·1	14·0
	6	15·0	14·1
	8	15·5	14·1
	10	15·5	14·4
Lat. 56° 9′ N. Long. 14° 10′ W.	Noon.	17·7	14·4
	2	17·4	14·7

Date and Position.	Hour.	Temperature of Air.	Temperature of Sea-Surface.
		Deg. Cent.	Deg. Cent.
July 2nd . . .	4	16·2	14·2
	6	15·5	14·5
	8	14·7	14·4
	10	15·0	14·6
	Midn.	14·4	13·9
July 3rd . . .	2	13·9	13·9
	4	13·3	13·9
	6	14·9	14·1
	8	15·5	14·1
	10	16·1	14·0
Lat. 56° 58′ N. Long. 13° 17′ W.	Noon.	15·3	13·9
	2	16·9	14·4
	4	16·1	13·9
	6	14·7	13·6
	8	13·9	12·5
	10	13·3	12·5
	Midn.	12·7	12·2
July 4th . . .	2	13·4	13·6
	4	13·9	13·9
	6	13·6	14·0
	8	14·1	13·6
	10	14·7	14·7
Lat. 56° 47′ N. Long. 12° 49′ W.	Noon.	15·0	13·9
	2	14·4	14·7
	4	14·4	14·8
	6	13·9	14·8
	8	13·9	14·9
	10	13·9	15·0
	Midn.	13·3	14·7
July 5th . . .	2	12·7	15·0
	4	13·3	15·0
	6	13·9	14·7
	8	13·9	14·7
	10	14·4	14·7
Lat. 56° 41′ N Long. 12° 56′ W.	Noon.	13·9	14·7
	2	14·4	15·0
	4	13·3	15·0
	6	12·7	14·4
	8	12·2	14·1
	10	12·5	14·4
	Midn.	12·5	14·4

Date and Position.	Hour.	Temperature of Air.	Temperature of Sea-Surface.
		Deg. Cent.	Deg Cent.
July 6th . . .	2	12·2	13·9
	4	12·7	13·9
	6	12·4	13·8
	8	13·9	14·1
	10	14·1	13·9
Lat. 56° 22′ N. Long. 11° 37′ W.	Noon.		13·9
	2	15·0	
	4	15·3	14·1
	6	13·9	14·4
	8	13·3	14·4
	10	12·0	13·9
	Midn.	11·1	13·3
July 7th . . .	2	12·7	13·3
	4	14·1	13·3
	6	14·7	13·3
	8	14·7	13·3
	10	15·0	13·4
Lat. 55° 55′ N. Long. 10° 17′ W.	Noon.	15·0	13·3
	2	15·0	13·9
	4	15·0	13·6
	6	15·0	13·9
	8	15·0	13·9
	10	14·4	13·3
	Midn.	14·4	13·3
July 8th . . .	2	14·4	13·9
	4	14·4	13·6
	6	15·5	13·9
	8	15·5	13·9
	10	15·0	13·9
Lat. 56° 6′ N. Long. 9° 36′ W.	Noon.	15·0	13·3
	2	14·7	13·6
	4	15·0	13·6
	6	13·3	13·9
	8	13·3	13·6
	10	13·3	13·9
	Midn.	12·7	12·7
July 9th . . .	2	12·2	13·9
	4	12·2	12·7
	6		
	8	14·1	13·3
	10	15·5	13·3

Date and Position.	Hour.	Temperature of Air.	Temperature of Sea-Surface.
		Deg. Cent.	Deg. Cent.
In Lough Swilly	Noon.	15·8	13·3
	2	16·1	13·3
	4	15·5	13·0
	6	15·3	13·3
	8	13·9	13·3
	10	12·2	13·3
	Midn.	11·6	12·7
July 10th . .	2	11·6	13·6
	4	12·2	13·6
	6	14·1	13·0
	8	16·1	13·4
	10	16·1	13·4
In Lough Foyle	Noon.	17·7	14·4
	2	17·7	15·0
	4	18·3	14·7
	6	16·1	14·4
	8	14·4	13·9
	10	13·9	13·3
	Midn.	14·4	13·9
July 11th . .	2	15·0	14·4
	4	13·9	14·4
	6	14·7	13·9
	8	16·3	13·9
	10	16·6	13·6
At Moville, Lough Foyle	Noon.	18·9	14·4
	2	20·5	15·5
	4	21·1	15·0
	6	18·9	14·4
	8	18·0	14·4
	10	15·8	13·9
	Midn.	15·8	14·4
July 12th . .	2	15·3	15·0
	4	13·0	14·7
	6	13·9	11·4
	8	15·5	11·1
	10	16·1	10·5
Off Belfast Lough . . .	Noon.	15·5	11·1
	2	16·1	11·1
	4	13·9	14·4
	6	14·4	14·4
	8	14·4	14·1
	10	12·7	12·2

Date and Position.	Hour.	Temperature of Air.	Temperature of Sea-Surface.	Date and Position.	Hour.	Temperature of Air.	Temperature of Sea-Surface.
		Deg. Cent.	Deg. Cent.			Deg. Cent.	Deg. Cent.
July 12th . .	Midn.	12·2	11·6	July 16th . .	4	16·1	19·4
July 13th . .	2	10·5	13·3		6	16·1	18·9
	4	11·1	13·3		8	17·7	18·9
	6	12·2	13·3		10	17·2	18·9
	8	13·3	13·6		Midn.	14·7	18·9
	10	13·3	14·1	July 17th . .	2	12·7	18·3
At Belfast . .	Noon.	15·5	15·5		4	12·2	17·2
	2	17·2	17·2		6	16·4	18·3
	4	16·6	17·2		8	17·7	18·3
	6	17·7	17·2		10	19·4	18·9
	8	15·5	17·2	At Belfast . .	Noon.	26·1	19·7
	10	12·2	16·6		2	18·9	13·9
	Midn.	11·6	16·6		4	15·3	11·6
July 14th . .	2	13·3	16·6		6	14·7	11·6
	4	13·3	16·6		8	15·0	12·7
	6	14·1	16·3		10	15·0	13·9
	8	15·8	16·6		Midn.	16·6	15·5
	10	17·5	16·6	July 18th . .	2	16·1	
At Belfast . .	Noon.	17·8	16·6		4	15·5	
	2	18·3	16·6		6	16·1	
	4	17·8			8	15·5	
	6				10	16·9	
	8			Off Tuskar L. H.	Noon.	16·6	
	10	16·1			2	18·9	
	Midn.	16·1	16·6		4	19·4	
July 15th . .	2	15·5	16·1		6	17·9	
	4	15·0	16·6		8	19·4	
	6	16·6	16·1		10	18·0	
	8	18·3	16·4		Midn.	17·7	
	10	20·5	17·7	July 19th . .	2	16·1	
At Belfast . .	Noon.	21·4			4	15·5	
	2	21·1			6	16·3	
	4	21·1			8	19·7	
	6	20·5	17·2		10	21·6	
	8	19·4	17·7	At Haulbowline	Noon.	22·8	
	10	19·4	17·2		2	20·0	
	Midn.	17·7	17·2		4		
July 16th . .	2	17·2	17·2		6	20·0	
	4	16·6	17·2		8	17·2	17·4
	6	17·5	17·2		10	16·6	16·6
	8	18·9	17·2		Midn.	16·6	16·6
	10	22·5	17·7	July 20th . .	2	16·9	17·7
At Belfast . .	Noon.	22·5	18·9		4	16·6	18·0
	2	17·2	18·9		6	17·6	18·3

Date and Position.	Hour.	Temperature of Air.	Temperature of Sea-Surface.
		Deg. Cent.	Deg. Cent.
July 20th . .	8	20·5	18·3
	10	21·1	18·9
Lat. 50° 28′ N. Long. 9° 37′ W.	Noon.	22·2	18·9
	2	20·8	19·7
	4	20·0	19·4
	6	20·0	18·9
	8	18·6	18·3
	10	17·7	18·3
	Midn.	17·2	18·0
July 21st . . .	2	17·7	17·7
	4	17·2	16·9
	6	17·7	17·5
	8	17·7	17·5
	10	18·9	17·5
Lat. 48° 51′ N. Long. 11° 8′ W.	Noon.	19·4	17·5
	2	20·8	17·2
	4	18·3	17·2
	6	18·3	17·2
	8	18·0	17·7
	10	17·7	17·7
	Midn.	17·7	17·7
July 22nd . .	2	17·7	16·9
	4	17·7	17·7
	6	18·3	18·3
	8	18·9	18·0
	10	17·2	17·7
Lat. 47° 38′ N. Long. 12° 11′ W.	Noon.	19·4	18·3
	2	19·4	18·3
	4	20·0	18·3
	6	18·9	18·3
	8	17·5	18·3
	10	17·5	18·3
	Midn.	17·2	18·0
July 23rd . .	2	17·2	18·0
	4	16·6	18·3
	6	17·7	17·7
	8	19·4	18·0
	10	19·1	18·0
Lat. 47° 39′ N. Long. 11° 52′ W.	Noon.	20·0	18·0
	2	20·0	18·3

Date and Position.	Hour.	Temperature of Air.	Temperature of Sea-Surface.
		Deg. Cent.	Deg. Cent.
July 23rd . .	4	17·2	18·3
	6	18·9	18·3
	8	17·5	18·3
	10	17·2	18·3
	Midn.	16·6	18·3
July 24th . .	2	17·2	18·3
	4	17·2	18·3
	6	17·5	
	8	18·6	18·0
	10	18·9	18·3
Lat. 47° 40′ N. Long. 11° 34′ W.	Noon.	18·3	18·3
	2	19·4	18·3
	4	18·9	18·3
	6	18·0	17·7
	8	18·0	18·0
	10	18·3	18·3
	Midn.	17·7	18·3
July 25th . .	2	17·2	18·0
	4	16·9	18·3
	6	16·6	17·7
	8	17·7	17·7
	10	18·0	17·7
Lat. 49° 1′ N. Long. 12° 22′ W.	Noon.	18·9	17·7
	2	18·3	17·7
	4	18·3	17·7
	6	18·3	17·7
	8	19·4	18·3
	10	18·3	17·7
	Midn.	18·9	17·5
July 26th . .	2	16·1	17·2
	4	16·1	17·2
	6	17·2	17·4
	8	16·1	17·5
	10	18·9	17·7
Lat. 49° 0′ N. Long. 11° 58′ W.	Noon.	18·9	17·7
	2	17·2	17·7
	4	16·9	17·7
	6	16·9	17·7
	8	16·4	17·7
	10	16·1	17·7
	Midn.	15·8	17·7

Date and Position.	Hour.	Temperature of Air.	Temperature of Sea-Surface.
		Deg. Cent.	Deg. Cent.
July 27th . .	2	15·5	17·7
	4	15·0	17·2
	6	17·2 ?	17·5
	8	14·6	17·5
	10	18·9	17·5
Lat. 49° 10′ N. Long. 12° 45′ W.	Noon.	18·0	17·5
	2	17·7	17·5
	4	18·9	17·7
	6	18·3	17·7
	8	16·1	17·7
	10	16·1	17·7
	Midn.	15·8	17·7
July 28th . .	2	15·3	17·5
	4	15·0	16·6
	6	15·5	16·9
	8	18·6	16·6
	10	17·7	16·6
Lat. 49° 59′ N. Long. 12° 22′ W.	Noon.	19·4	16·6
	2	19·7	16·9
	4	18·3	17·1
	6	16·6	16·9
	8	15·5	16·9
	10	15·8	15·5
	Midn.	16·1	16·6
July 29th . .	2	16·1	17·2
	4	15·5	17·7
	6	15·8	16·9
	8	16·4	16·9
	10	16·6	16·6
Lat. 50° 24′ N. Long. 11° 42′ W.	Noon.	17·2	16·3
	2	16·1	16·3
	4	17·7	16·3
	6	17·7	16·6
	8	16·3	17·2
	10	16·1	16·6
	Midn.	16·1	17·2
July 30th . .	2	16·1	15·8
	4	16·1	15·8
	6	17·2	15·8
	8	17·2	15·8
	10	17·2	15·5
Lat. 51° 5′ N. Long. 11° 22′ W.	Noon.	17·7	15·8
	2	17·7	
	4	17·5	16·1
	6	17·2	16·6
	8	16·6	16·6
	10	16·6	15·5
	Midn.	16·6	15·8
July 31st. . .	2	16·3	15·5
	4	15·5	15·5
	6	15·3	14·7
	8	17·2	14·7
	10	18·9	12·5
Near Cork Harbour . . .	Noon.	16·6	12·2
	2		
	4	18·3	16·1
	6	16·1	15·8
	8	14·4	14·4
	10	12·7	11·6
	Midn.	12·7	11·1
August 1st . .	2	12·2	
	4	12·2	
	6	13·9	
	8	16·6	
	10	17·5	14·7
At Queenstown.	Noon.	19·1	14·7
	2	18·9	15·3
	4	18·9	15·8
	6		
	8	13·9	15·8
	10	12·2	15·0
	Midn.	12·5	14·7
August 2nd . .	2	12·2	14·4
	4	11·9	15·0
	6	12·7	15·5
	8	15·0	15·3
	10	14·7	
At Queenstown.	Noon.	15·5	
	2	15·5	
	4	16·4	15·0
	6	15·3	15·5
	8	13·9	15·0
	10	13·9	15·0

Date and Position.	Hour.	Temperature of Air.	Temperature of Sea-Surface.
		Deg. Cent.	Deg. Cent.
August 2nd . .	Midn.	13·9	13·9
August 3rd . .	2	15·3	14·4
	4	15·5	14·1
	6	15·0	13·9
	8	15·5	13·9
	10	15·5	14·1
Lat. 52° 22′ N. Blackwater, Lat. N. 11 miles.	Noon.	16·1	13·6
	2	16·2	13·9
	4	18·3	14·1
	6	17·2	14·7
	8	15·5	13·3
	10	14·4	13·3
	Midn.	14·4	13·3
August 4th . .	2	13·9	13·9
	4	13·3	13·9
	6	13·3	12·7
	8	11·9	12·5
	10	13·9	12·2
At Copeland Island . . .	Noon.	14·4	12·5
	2	15·0	13·9
	4	16·1	16·1
	6	16·6	15·8
	8	13·3	
	10	13·3	15·0
	Midn.	11·1	13·9
August 5th . .	2	11·1	14·1
	4	10·5	14·4
	6	12·7	14·6
	8	15·3	14·7
	10	18·3	15·0
At Belfast . .	Noon.	16·9	15·5
	2	17·4	
	4	17·7	16·4
	6	12·8	15·5
	8		
	10	11·1	15·0
	Midn.	10·0	15·0
August 6th . .	2	10·5	14·7
	4	10·0	14·4
	6	12·5	14·1
	8	16·6	14·4

Date and Position.	Hour.	Temperature of Air.	Temperature of Sea-Surface.
		Deg. Cent.	Deg. Cent.
August 6th . .	10	17·7	14·7
At Belfast . .	Noon.	18·3	15·5
	2		
	4	18·9	17·2
	6	15·0	
	8	13·0	16·6
	10	11·1	16·1
	Midn.	10·0	15·0
August 7th . .	2	10·8	15·5
	4	11·1	15·5
	6	12·7	15·5
	8	14·4	15·5
	10	15·3	15·5
At Belfast . .	Noon.	15·0	15·0
	2	15·3	15·5
	4	15·0	15·5
	6	15·5	
	8		
	10	14·7	15·5
	Midn.	15·0	14·7
August 8th . .	2	13·9	15·0
	4	13·9	15·0
	6		
	8	15·0	15·0
	10	15·5	15·3
At Belfast . .	Noon.	17·2	15·8
	2	20·8	16·1
	4	16·6	15·8
	6	13·9	15·5
	8	14·4	15·8
	10	13·6	15·8
	Midn.	13·9	15·5
August 9th . .	2	13·3	15·5
	4	13·3	15·5
	6	13·3	15·3
	8	13·3	
	10	14·4	15·5
At Belfast . .	Noon.	15·0	15·5
	2	16·1	15·5
	4	16·6	15·5
	6	14·4	15·8
	8	11·4	15·5
	10	10·5	15·0
	Midn.	10·0	14·4

Date and Position.	Hour.	Temperature of Air.	Temperature of Sea-Surface.
		Deg. Cent.	Deg. Cent.
August 10th. .	2	11·1	13·9
	4	10·5	14·7
	6	10·5	14·4
	8	11·4	14·4
	10	13·9	
At Belfast . .	Noon.	15·5	15·0
	2	15·0	
	4	14·7	
	6	12·7	
	8	11·9	15·0
	10	11·6	14·4
	Midn.	11·6	13·9
August 11th. .	2	10·5	13·9
	4	11·7	13·3
	6	12·2	13·6
	8	13·3	13·9
	10	14·4	
In Belfast Lough	Noon.	14·4	14·4
	2	15·3	12·2
	4	15·0	13·0
	6	13·9	12·2
	8	12·2	12·2
	10	11·7	11·7
	Midn.	12·0	11·7
August 12th. .	2	12·2	12·2
	4	11·1	11·7
	6	11·4	12·0
	8	13·3	12·5
	10	17·2	12·7
Coll Island, North, 3 miles	Noon.	18·3	12·5
	2	15·3	13·3
	4	14·4	12·2
	6	12·7	12·2
	8	12·2	12·0
	10	11·7	12·2
	Midn.	12·0	12·2
August 13th. .	2	12·7	11·6
	4	12·5	11·6
	6	12·7	12·0
	8	12·5	12·0
	10	14·7	11·6
Shiant Islands, N. N. W. 6 miles	Noon.	13·3	11·6

Date and Position.	Hour.	Temperature of Air.	Temperature of Sea-Surface.
		Deg. Cent.	Deg. Cent.
August 13th. .	2	12·5	11·6
	4	12·7	12·2
	6	13·3	11·6
	8	12·0	12·7
	10	11·4	11·6
	Midn.	11·1	12·2
August 14th. .	2	11·6	12·0
	4	11·4	11·4
	6	11·4	12·2
	8	13·3	12·0
	10	12·7	
At Stornoway .	Noon.	15·5	12·2
	2	16·1	12·5
	4	15·0	12·7
	6	14·7	
	8	13·3	12·2
	10	13·3	12·5
	Midn.	12·7	12·2
August 15th. .	2	13·3	12·2
	4	13·3	12·2
	6	13·3	12·2
	8	13·9	12·2
	10	13·9	12·2
At Stornoway .	Noon.	14·4	12·2
	2	15·8	12·5
	4	16·1	12·5
	6	15·5	12·5
	8	13·3	12·5
	10	12·7	12·7
	Midn.	13·0	12·2
August 16th. .	2	12·7	12·2
	4	12·7	12·2
	6	13·3	12·2
	8	13·3	12·2
	10	13·6	12·2
Lat. 59° 21′ N. Long. 6° 58′ W.	Noon.	13·3	12·0
	2	13·0	12·2
	4	13·3	12·2
	6	13·3	12·2
	8	12·7	12·2
	10	12·5	12·2
	Midn.	12·2	12·2
August 17th. .	2	11·1	11·6

Date and Position.	Hour.	Temperature of Air.	Temperature of Sea-Surface.
		Deg. Cent.	Deg. Cent.
August 17th . .	4	12·2	11·9
	6	12·2	11·9
	8	12·2	
	10	13·9	12·2
Lat. 59° 36′ N. Long. 7° 12′ W.	Noon.	13·9	12·2
	2	13·6	11·9
	4	14·1	11·9
	6	13·0	11·9
	8	12·5	11·4
	10	12·7	11·1
	Midn.	12·2	11·1
August 18th . .	2	12·2	10·5
	4	12·2	11·1
	6	12·7	11·1
	8	13·9	11·4
	10	13·6	10·8
Lat. 60° 25′ N. Long. 8° 9′ W.	Noon.	13·6	11·4
	2	12·7	11·1
	4	12·5	10·8
	6	12·2	11·1
	8	12·2	11·1
	10	12·2	11·1
	Midn.	12·2	11·1
August 19th . .	2	12·2	11·1
	4	12·2	11·1
	6	12·7	11·4
	8	12·7	11·4
	10	13·3	11·4
Lat. 60° 13′ N. Long. 6° 41′ W.	Noon.	12·7	11·1
	2	13·3	11·1
	4	13·9	
	6	12·7	11·1
	8	12·7	11·1
	10	12·7	11·1
	Midn.	12·2	10·5
August 20th . .	2	12·2	10·5
	4	12·0	10·0
	6	12·2	10·8
	8	12·5	10·5
	10	12·5	10·3

Date and Position.	Hour.	Temperature of Air.	Temperature of Sea-Surface.
		Deg. Cent.	Deg. Cent.
Lat. 60° 35′ N. Long. 6° 41′ W.	Noon.	13·3	11·4
	2	12·7	11·4
	4	12·2	11·6
	6	9·4	11·4
	8	9·4	10·5
	10	9·7	10·0
	Midn.	10·0	9·4
August 21st . .	2	10·0	9·4
	4	9·4	9·4
	6	10·0	9·4
	8	10·0	10·0
	10	13·6	9·7
Off Sandö in Færoe Islands	Noon.	13·3	9·1
	2	11·4	8·8
	4	11·7	9·1
	6	11·4	9·1
	8	10·5	9·1
	10	10·8	9·4
	Midn.	10·5	9·4
August 22nd .	2	10·5	9·1
	4	10·8	9·4
	6	11·1	9·1
	8	11·6	9·4
	10	12·7	9·4
At Thorshavn .	Noon.	14·4	9·4
	2	13·3	9·7
	4	12·2	10·0
	6	13·3	9·7
	8	10·5	9·4
	10	10·0	9·4
	Midn.	10·0	9·4
August 23rd .	2	9·4	9·4
	4		
	6	10·8	9·4
	8	10·5	9·4
	10	12·7	9·7
At Thorshavn .	Noon.	12·7	9·7
	2	12·7	9·4
	4	12·7	9·4
	6	12·2	9·4
	8	11·6	9·1

Date and Position.	Hour.	Temperature of Air.	Temperature of Sea Surface.	Date and Position.	Hour.	Temperature of Air.	Temperature of Sea-Surface.
		Deg. Cent.	Deg. Cent.			Deg. Cent.	Deg. Cent.
August 23rd .	10	11·1	9·4	August 27th. .	8	11·1	11·4
	Midn.	11·1	9·1		10	11·6	11·6
August 24th. .	2	11·1	9·1	Lat. 60° 26′ N. Long. 0° 15′ E.	Noon.	12·5	11·6
	4	11·1	9·4				
	6	11·1	9·4		2	13·3	12·2
	8	11·4	9·1		4	12·2	11·9
	10	11·6	9·1		6	11·1	11·9
About 10 miles East of Haalsö	Noon.	15·5	9·1		8	11·1	12·2
					10	10·0	12·2
	2	12·0	9·7		Midn.	9·4	11·1
	4	13·3	10·0	August 28th. .	2	10·5	11·6
	6	11·1	9·4		4	12·2	11·6
	8	11·1	9·4		6	11·9	11·9
	10	10·5	9·4		8	10·0	11·1
	Midn.	11·1	9·4		10	10·0	11·1
August 25th. .	2	11·6	9·7	At Lerwick . .	Noon.	9·4	11·1
	4	11·6	9·7		2	10·5	11·1
	6	12·5	9·4		4	11·1	11·1
	8	12·5	9·7		6	9·7	11·1
	10	12·5	9·4		8	8·8	11·1
Lat. 61° 36′ N. Long. 3° 45′ W.	Noon.	12·2	9·4		10	7·5	11·1
					Midn.	7·2	11·1
	2	12·2	9·7	August 29th. .	2	7·2	11·1
	4	11·6	9·4		4	7·7	10·3
	6	11·6	9·4		6	7·7	11·4
	8	11·4	9·7		8	9·4	11·1
	10	11·4	9·1		10	9·7	11·1
	Midn.	12·0	10·5	At Lerwick . .	Noon.	9·4	11·1
August 26th. .	2	12·0	11·1		2	9·4	11·1
	4	12·0	11·1		4	9·4	11·1
	6	12·0	11·1		6	9·1	11·1
	8	12·0	11·4		8	7·7	11·1
	10	12·2	11·6		10	7·7	10·8
Lat. 61° 14 N. Long. 1° 58′ W.	Noon.	12·7	11·4		Midn.	8·9	10·8
				August 30th. .	2	8·3	11·1
	2	12·7	11·4		4	7·7	
	4	11·6	11·4		6	8·3	10·8
	6	11·1	11·4		8	10·3	11·1
	8	11·6	11·4		10	11·1	11·1
	10	11·6	11·1	At Lerwick . .	Noon.	11·6	11·1
	Midn.	11·4	11·1		2	12·7	11·4
August 27th. .	2	11·1	11·1		4	12·2	11·1
	4	11·1	11·1		6		
	6	11·1	11·1		8	7·7	11·1

Date and Position.	Hour.	Temperature of Air.	Temperature of Sea-Surface.
		Deg. Cent.	Deg. Cent.
August 30th. .	10	7·2	11·1
	Midn.	6·6	11·1
August 31st. .	2	7·2	10·5
	4	7·7	10·5
	6	10·0	11·1
	8	10·0	11·1
	10	11·6	10·8
At Lerwick . .	Noon.	12·2	11·1
	2	13·6	11·1
	4	11·1	11·1
	6	10·5	11·1
	8	11·1	11·1
	10	10·8	10·8
	Midn.	10·5	11·1
September 1st .	2	11·1	11·1
	4	11·1	11·6
	6	11·6	11·6
	8	11·6	11·6
	10	11·1	11·4
Lat. 60° 27′ N. Long. 3° 11′ W.	Noon.	11·1	11·6
	2	12·2	11·6
	4	13·3	11·4
	6	11·6	11·1
	8	11·4	11·1
	10	11·1	11·6
	Midn.	11·1	11·6
September 2nd .	2	10·8	10·8
	4	10·8	10·5
	6	11·1	10·3
	8	11·1	10·3
	10	11·1	10·3
Lat. 60° 29′ N. Long. 4° 38′ W.	Noon.	11·4	10·0
	2	11·4	10·3
	4	11·6	10·5
	6	11·6	11·1
	8	11·1	11·1
	10	11·6	11·4
	Midn.	11·1	11·6
September 3rd .	2	11·6	11·1
	4	11·1	11·1
	6	11·1	11·6
	8	11·6	11·6

Date and Position.	Hour.	Temperature of Air.	Temperature of Sea-Surface.
		Deg. Cent.	Deg. Cent.
September 3rd .	10	13·0	11·6
Lat. 60° 3′ N. Long. 5° 10′ W.	Noon.	12·7	11·6
	2	12·5	11·6
	4	12·2	11·6
	6	12·2	11·4
	8	12·5	11·4
	10	12·7	11·6
	Midn.	12·7	12·2
September 4th .	2	12·7	12·2
	4	13·3	12·2
	6	13·9	12·5
	8	13·9	12·5
	10	14·4	12·2
Lat. 59° 43′ N. Long. 6° 35′ W.	Noon.	13·3	12·2
	2	13·3	12·2
	4	13·0	12·2
	6	12·7	12·2
	8	12·7	11·6
	10	12·2	11·6
	Midn.	12·5	12·0
September 5th .	2	12·2	12·0
	4	12·5	11·6
	6	12·7	11·6
	8	12·7	11·6
	10	13·3	12·0
Lat. 59° 38′ N. Long. 8° 25′ W.	Noon.	14·4	12·2
	2	13·6	11·6
	4	12·0	11·6
	6	11·1	11·6
	8	11·1	11·6
	10	10·8	11·4
	Midn.	11·1	11·4
September 6th .	2	11·1	11·4
	4	11·1	11·4
	6	12·2	11·6
	8	13·0	11·6
	10	12·7	12·0
Lat. 59° 37′ N. Long. 9° 4′ W.	Noon.	12·7	12·2
	2	13·0	
	4	12·7	12·2

Date and Position.	Hour.	Temperature of Air.	Temperature of Sea-Surface.
		Deg. Cent.	Deg. Cent.
September 6th .	6	12·2	12·0
	8	12·2	12·2
	10	12·2	12·2
	Midn.	11·6	11·6
September 7th .	2	11·4	11·6
	4	10·5	11·6
	6	10·5	11·9
	8	12·2	11·6
	10	14·7	11·9
Lat. 59° 41′ N. Long. 7° 32′ W.	Noon.	15·5	12·2
	2	13·9	12·2
	4	13·3	12·2
	6	12·7	12·2
	8	12·5	12·5
	10	12·7	12·2
	Midn.	12·2	12·2
September 8th .	2	12·2	11·6
	4	12·7	11·9
	6	12·7	11·9
	8	13·6	12·2
	10	15·0	12·7
Lat. 59° 7′ N. Long. 6° 35′ W.	Noon.	14·4	12·7
	2	15·3	12·7
	4	15·5	12·7
	6	13·3	12·5
	8	13·3	12·5
	10	13·3	13·0
	Midn.	12·7	13·0
September 9th .	2	13·3	12·7
	4	13·3	12·7
	6	13·3	12·7
	8	13·0	12·7
	10	13·3	12·7
At Stornoway .	Noon.	13·9	12·7
	2		
	4	14·4	12·7
	6	15·3	12·7
	8	15·5	12·7
	10	15·5	13·3
	Midn.	15·5	12·7
September 10th	2	13·9	12·7
	4	14·4	12·7
September 10th	6	14·4	12·7
	8	15·0	12·7
	10	13·9	12·7
At Stornoway .	Noon.	16·3	13·3
	2	16·3	13·9
	4	15·0	13·6
	6	13·9	13·3
	8	12·7	13·3
	10	12·2	13·0
	Midn.	11·6	12·7
September 11th	2	11·1	12·7
	4	11·1	12·7
	6	11·1	12·7
	8	11·1	12·7
	10	13·9	12·7
At Stornoway .	Noon.	15·3	12·7
	2	13·3	12·2
	4	11·6	12·7
	6	11·4	12·7
	8	10·8	12·7
	10	9·7	12·2
	Midn.	9·4	12·2
September 12th	2	9·1	12·2
	4	8·9	12·2
	6	9·4	12·2
	8	11·4	12·2
	10	12·5	12·2
At Stornoway .	Noon.	12·7	12·2
	2	12·7	12·5
	4	12·7	12·5
	6	11·1	12·2
	8	10·5	12·2
	10	10·0	12·2
	Midn.	11·1	12·0
September 13th	2	10·0	11·6
	4	9·1	11·1
	6	11·1	11·6
	8	11·1	11·6
	10	13·0	12·2
In Loch Sheildag	Noon.	12·2	12·0
	2	14·1	12·2
	4	14·4	12·2
	6	13·9	12·2

Date and Position.	Hour.	Temperature of Air.	Temperature of Sea-Surface.	Date and Position.	Hour.	Temperature of Air.	Temperature of Sea-Surface.
		Deg. Cent.	Deg. Cent.			Deg. Cent.	Deg. Cent.
September 13th	8	13·0	12·2	Abreast of Mull	Noon.	12·7	13·0
	10	12·2	12·2		2	14·4	13·3
	Midn.	12·2	12·2		4	14·4	13·3
September 14th	2	11·6	12·5		6	13·6	12·7
	4	12·2	12·2		8	13·0	13·3
	6	12·5	12·2		10	12·5	13·0
	8	12·2	12·7		Midn.	12·0	13·0
	10	11·6	12·7				

II. SURFACE TEMPERATURES OBSERVED DURING THE SUMMER OF 1870.

Date and Position.	Hour.	Temperature of Air.	Temperature of Sea-Surface.	Date and Position.	Hour.	Temperature of Air.	Temperature of Sea-Surface.
		Deg. Cent.	Deg. Cent.			Deg. Cent.	Deg. Cent.
July 6th . . .	2	13·9	12·2	July 7th . . .	6	19·4	16·4
	4	14·4	12·7		8	17·2	16·1
	6	13·9	12·5		10	16·9	16·4
	8	14·7	14·7		Midn.	16·6	16·4
	10	15·3	13·6	July 8th . . .	2	16·6	16·1
Off Scilly Islands	Noon.	18·6	18·3		4	16·1	16·1
	2	19·7	17·4		6	16·9	16·1
	4	19·4	18·3		8	19·1	16·2
	6	18·9	18·3		10	20·8	16·1
	8	17·4	17·7	Lat. 48° 31′ N. Long. 10° 6′ W.	Noon.	19·6	17·2
	10	16·6	17·2				
	Midn.	16·1	17·2		2	20·0	17·5
July 7th . . .	2	16·6	16·6		4	18·6	17·5
	4	16·6	16·6		6	19·1	17·5
	6	16·6	16·6		8	17·7	17·2
	8	16·9	16·9		10	16·9	17·2
	10	17·7	16·4		Midn.	16·6	16·9
Lat. 48° 49′ N. Long. 9° 35′ W.	Noon.	18·3	16·4	July 9th . . .	2	16·1	16·9
					4	16·6	16·6
	2	19·4	16·4		6	16·1	16·6
	4	18·9	17·2		8	16·1	16·6

Date and Position.	Hour.	Temperature of Air. Deg. Cent.	Temperature of Sea-Surface. Deg. Cent.
July 9th . . .	10	17·5	16·6
Lat. 48° 26′ N. Long. 9° 43′ W.	Noon.	17·5	16·6
	2	16·4	16·6
	4	17·2	16·6
	6	16·4	16·6
	8	16·4	16·1
	10	16·6	16·6
	Midn.	16·1	16·4
July 10th . .	2	16·1	16·6
	4	16·4	16·4
	6	16·6	16·4
	8	16·4	16·4
	10	17·3	16·6
Lat. 48° 28′ N. Long. 9° 42′ W.	Noon.	16·1	16·6
	2	17·7	16·9
	4	19·4	16·9
	6	19·6	16·6
	8	16·2	16·6
	10	16·1	16·1
	Midn.	16·1	16·1
July 11th . .	2	16·1	16·6
	4	16·4	16·4
	6	16·4	16·1
	8	18·3	16·1
	10	18·6	16·6
Lat. 48° 8′ N. Long. 9° 18′ W.	Noon.	18·6	16·9
	2	18·4	17·2
	4	19·1	17·3
	6	17·3	17·4
	8	16·6	16·6
	10	17·2	17·2
	Midn.	17·2	17·7
July 12th . .	2	17·2	17·7
	4	17·7	17·7
	6	17·4	18·0
	8	17·7	18·3
	10	18·6	18·0
Lat. 46° 26′ N. Long. 9° 31′ W.	Noon.	19·1	18·2
	2	19·4	18·0
	4	17·7	18·0

Date and Position.	Hour.	Temperature of Air. Deg. Cent.	Temperature of Sea-Surface. Deg. Cent.
July 12th . .	6	17·9	18·0
	8	16·6	18·0
	10	16·6	17·2
	Midn.	16·6	17·7
July 13th . .	2	17·2	17·7
	4	17·5	18·3
	6	17·7	17·7
	8	18·6	17·5
	10	18·9	17·7
Lat. 44° 59′ N. Long. 9° 33′ W.	Noon.	19·7	18·2
	2	21·1	18·9
	4	22·5	18·9
	6	21·1	18·3
	8	17·5	18·3
	10	17·5	18·0
	Midn.	17·2	18·0
July 14th . .	2	17·7	17·9
	4	17·2	17·2
	6	16·9	16·1
	8	18·3	16·1
	10	18·6	15·5
Cape Finisterre, E. N. N. 10 miles . .	Noon.	18·6	15 8
	2	18·6	15·8
	4	19·1	15·8
	6	17·5	15·8
	8	16·6	15·5
	10	16·6	15·8
	Midn.	16·6	16·1
July 15th . .	2	16·6	16·1
	4	16·6	16·6
	6	17·5	16·4
	8	18·3	16·9
	10	18·9	17·2
Lat. 42° 11′ N. Long. 9° 13′ W.	Noon.	20·0	16·4
	2	22·3	17·5
	4	21·2	17·9
	6	19·0	18·9
	8	17·9	18·9
	10	17·7	18·9
	Midn.	18·9	19·3

Date and Position.	Hour.	Temperature of Air.	Temperature of Sea-Surface.
		Deg. Cent.	Deg. Cent.
July 16th . .	2	15·5	19·0
	4	17·2	18·9
	6	18·3	17·9
	8	20·1	19·4
	10	23·2	17·9
At Vigo . . .	Noon.	23·6	17·8
	2	23·6	17·9
	4	23·4	18·0
	6	21·6	17·2
	8	18·4	16·1
	10	17·7	16·6
	Midn.	17·2	16·9
July 17th . .	2	17·7	16·1
	4	17·5	16·5
	6	17·7	16·6
	8	19·7	16·4
	10	22·2	16·1
At Vigo . . .	Noon.	32·2	16·4
	2	26·6	16·9
	4	25·8	15·8
	6	22·5	16·4
	8	20·8	16·4
	10	20·0	16·5
	Midn.	18·6	16·2
July 18th . .	2	18·3	16·4
	4	17·7	
	6	18·9	16·1
	8	19·4	16·6
	10	18·9	
Lat. 41° 55′ N. Long. 9° 30′ W.	Noon.	19·1	16·2
	2	18·6	16·3
	4	18·9	16·3
	6	18·9	16·4
	8	18·3	16·6
	10	18·3	16·6
	Midn.	17·7	16·4
July 19th . .	2	17·7	16·9
	4	17·7	16·9
	6	19·4	16 9
	8	20·8	17·5
	10	20·1	17·7
Lat. 40° 16′ N. Long. 9° 33′ W.	Noon.	20·3	17·9
July 19th . .	2	20·3	18·0
	4	20·3	18·0
	6	19·5	17·9
	8	19·4	18·3
	10	18·9	18·4
	Midn.	18·6	18·4
July 20th . .	2	18·3	18·3
	4	18·3	18·3
	6	19·4	18·4
	8	24·4	18·9
	10	23·3	20·5
Lat. 40° 0′ N. Long. 9° 49′ W.	Noon.	24·4	21·1
	2	25·5	21·1
	4	26·3	21·8
	6	23·3	21·8
	8	21·6	19·7
	10	21·3	20·8
	Midn.	21·3	20·5
July 21st. . .	2	21·1	20·5
	4	21·5	19·7
	6	23·3	18·9
	8	22·7	19·4
	10	24·5	19·4
Lat. 39° 39′ N. Long. 9° 36′ W.	Noon.	25·5	19·4
	2	25·0	19·4
	4	23·9	19·7
	6	21·8	19·4
	8	20·1	19·4
	10	19·6	19·4
	Midn.	19·5	19·1
July 22nd . .	2	19·4	18·9
	4	18·9	18·9
	6	20·0	18·2
	8	21·2	18·3
	10	25·0	19·4
The Farilhoes, S.S.E. 5 miles	Noon.	25·0	18·9
	2	23·9	19·1
	4	23·3	20·5
	6	23·9	19·4
	8	20·0	19·4
	10	18·9	18·3

Date and Position.	Hour.	Temperature of Air.	Temperature of Sea-Surface.	Date and Position.	Hour.	Temperature of Air.	Temperature of Sea-Surface.
		Deg. Cent.	Deg. Cent.			Deg. Cent.	Deg. Cent.
July 22nd . .	Midn.	19·1	18·0	Lat. 38° 17′ N. Long. 9° 23′ W.	Noon.	20·0	18·9
July 23rd . .	2	18·9	18·5				
	4	19·3	19·4		2	20·0	19·1
	6	20·5	18·3		4	20·0	19·1
	8	23·3	20·5		6	20·0	19·4
	10	24·7	22·0		8	19·4	19·1
At Lisbon . .	Noon.	22·5	21·1		10	20·0	19·1
	2	23·6	19·1		Midn.	20·0	19·0
	4	21·6	20·0	July 27th . .	2	19·4	19·1
	6	23·0	21·6		4	19·4	19·1
	8	20·5	20·3		6	19·4	19·1
	10	19·5	19·1		8	20·0	19·0
	Midn.	20·1	19·5		10	21·3	20·0
July 24th . .	2	19·4	18·6	Lat. 37° 18′ N. Long. 9° 12′ W.	Noon.	21·1	20·3
	4	19·4	20·5				
	6	20·1	21·6		2	23·3	20·5
	8	20·8	20·8		4	21·1	20·6
	10	21·2	20·1		6	20·0	20·7
At Lisbon . .	Noon.	24·1	19·4		8	20·0	20·5
	2	23·0	20·5		10	19·4	20·5
	4	22·1	20·1		Midn.	19·5	20·8
	6	22·2	21·2	July 28th . .	2	19·4	20·3
	8	20·5	21·4		4	19·4	20·5
	10	20·0	20·0		6	19·1	20·0
	Midn.	19·4	19·7		8	21·1	21·1
July 25th . .	2	19·1	20·0		10	21·1	21·2
	4	19·0	20·0	Lat. 36° 55′ N. Long. 8° 44′ W.	Noon.	21·8	21·3
	6	20·3	19·1				
	8	20·4	19·4		2	21·6	21·6
	10	20·8	19·1		4	21·6	22·0
Lat. 38° 10′ N. Long. 9° 29′ W.	Noon.	21·8	19·4		6	20·5	20·5
					8	18·9	20·0
	2	21·1	19·4		10	18·9	19·4
	4	20·8	19·4		Midn.	18·6	19·1
	6	21·6	19·4	July 29th . .	2	18·3	19·7
	8	20·0	18·0		4	18·3	19·7
	10	18·6	17·7		6	21·1	21·6
	Midn.	18·0	17·7		8	22·1	22·4
July 26th . .	2	18·3	17·4		10	23·0	22·2
	4	18·3	17·7	Lat. 36° 45′ N. Long. 8° 8′ W.	Noon.	23·3	22·5
	6	19·1	19·1				
	8	19·4	19·1		2	23·3	22·3
	10	20·3	19·3		4	24·8	23·1

Date and Position.	Hour.	Temperature of Air.	Temperature of Sea-Surface.	Date and Position.	Hour.	Temperature of Air.	Temperature of Sea-Surface.
		Deg. Cent.	Deg. Cent.			Deg. Cent.	Deg. Cent.
July 29th . .	6	22·2	22·5	August 2nd . .	8	21·7	23·2
	8	21·1	22·3		10	22·8	24·4
	10	21·1	21·6	Lat. 36° 18′ N. Long. 6° 45′ W.	Noon.	22·8	23·0
	Midn.	20·5	21·6				
July 30th . .	2	20·3	21·9		2	22·5	23·0
	4	20·5	22·2		4	22·7	23·0
	6	20·5	22·8		6	21·8	22·8
	8	22·4	22·5		8	21·2	22·2
	10	23·3	22·9		10	21·3	22·5
Lat. 36° 27′ N. Long 6° 39′ W.	Noon.	23·9	23·1		Midn.	21·1	22·2
				August 3rd . .	2	20·5	22·0
	2	25·3	24·1		4	20·5	22·0
	4	22·5	24·1		6	21·8	22·8
	6	22·8	24·2		8	23·7	22·2
	8	21·6	24·1		10	23·3	21·8
	10	21·6	24·3	Lat. 35° 39′ N. Long. 7° 4′ W.	Noon.	21·6	22·0
	Midn.	21·5	24·3				
July 31st . . .	2	21·1	22·8		2	22·6	22·2
	4	21·9	23·3		4	24·1	22·2
	6	21·9	23·6		6	23·2	22·2
	8	22·5	24·1		8	21·8	22·2
	10	24·5	23·9		10	21·8	22·0
At Cadiz . . .	Noon.	25·2	24·0		Midn.	22·5	22·0
	2	25·1	24·1	August 4th . .	2	22·2	22·2
	4	24·0	24·3		4	22·2	22·2
	6	24·0	24·4		6	23·2	22·2
	8	23·4	24·4		8	23·9	22·2
	10	22·7	24·1		10	24·4	23·3
	Midn.	22·5	24·1	Lat. 35° 35′ N. Long. 6° 24′ W.	Noon.	25·0	23·3
August 1st . .	2	22·3	23·9				
	4	21·6	22·8		2	27·2	23·4
	6	22·5	23·9		4	25·6	23·3
	8	24·4	24·1		6	24·4	23·3
	10	24·1	24·4		8	22·2	21·8
At Cadiz . . .	Noon.	23·9	24·7		10	22·2	22·0
	2	23·6	24·4		Midn.	22·2	22·2
	4	23·6	24·4	October 1st . .	2	17·4	18·9
	6	21·6	23·3		4	17·8	18·9
	8	21·6	23·6		6	18·0	18·0
	10	21·6	23·9		8	19·4	17·9
	Midn.	21·8	23·9		10	22·1	21·5
August 2nd . .	2	21·9	23·3	In Strait of Gibraltar . .	Noon.	23·3	22·2
	4	21·3	23·0				
	6	21·6	23·3		2	24·1	23·4

Date and Position.	Hour.	Temperature of Air.	Temperature of Sea-Surface.
		Deg. Cent.	Deg. Cent.
October 1st . .	4	22·5	22·8
	6	22·0	22·6
	8	21·1	22·5
	10	21·5	22·2
	Midn.	20·8	22·6
October 2nd . .	2	21·1	22·8
	4	22·3	23·3
	6	22·6	22·9
	8	24·7	23·2
	10	24·7	23·3
Lat. 36° 27′ N. Long. 8° 31′ W.	Noon.	21·1	23·3
	2	22·6	23·4
	4	23·7	23·0
	6	20·5	22·5
	8	20·5	20·5
	10	20·5	20·8
	Midn.	20·5	21·6
October 3rd . .	2	20·0	21·1
	4	19·4	18·3
	6	19·1	20·5
	8	18·3	20·8
	10	18·6	20·5
Lat. 38° 39′ N. Long. 9° 30′ W.	Noon.	22·2	20·3
	2	21·6	20·5
	4	21·1	21·1
	6	20·5	20·6
	8	20·0	19·8
	10	20·6	20·3
	Midn.	20·5	20·5
October 4th . .	2	20·8	21·1
	4	20·6	21·1
	6	21·1	21·1
	8	21·6	21·5
	10	22·2	21·0
Lat. 40° 57′ N. Long. 9° 29′ W.	Noon.	22·2	21·9
	2	22·9	21·1
	4	22·2	21·0
	6	20·0	20·5
	8	20·3	20·4
	10	18·9	19·4
	Midn.	19·3	19·4

Date and Position	Hour.	Temperature of Air.	Temperature of Sea-Surface.
		Deg. Cent.	Deg. Cent.
October 5th . .	2	18·3	18·9
	4	18·6	19·4
	6	17·5	18·3
	8	17·2	17·2
	10	19·8	18·3
Lat. 43° 33′ N. Long. 9° 3′ W.	Noon.	20·0	17·7
	2	20·5	19·1
	4	19·8	19·3
	6	18·3	19·4
	8	17·9	18·6
	10	18·5	19·4
	Midn.	18·3	18·9
October 6th . .	2	18·1	19·4
	4	18·3	19·1
	6	18·3	18·9
	8	18·9	18·8
	10	20·1	18·6
Lat. 46° 12′ N. Long. 8° 8′ W.	Noon.	20·0	18·4
	2	19·5	18·6
	4	19·3	18·4
	6	18·3	18·0
	8	18·3	18·3
	10	17·9	18·3
	Midn.	18·3	17·7
October 7th . .	2	18·2	16·6
	4	17·6	16·6
	6	16·7	16·6
	8	16·6	17·2
	10	17·5	17·2
Lat. 48° 51′ N. Long. 5° 54′ W.	Noon.	17·5	17·0
	2	17·7	16·9
	4	17·7	13·6
	6	15·3	13·6
	8	14·7	14·1
	10	15·3	14·4
	Midn.	16·1	15·5
October 8th . .	2	15·5	15·5
	4	15·0	15·8
	6	15·6	16·0
	8	16·1	16·1
	10	16·6	16·4

Date and Position.	Hour.	Temperature of Air.	Temperature of Sea-Surface.	Date and Position.	Hour.	Temperature of Air.	Temperature of Sea-Surface.
		Deg. Cent.	Deg. Cent.			Deg. Cent.	Deg. Cent.
St. Alban's Hd., English Channel	Noon.	18·6	16·2	October 8th . .	6	15·0	15·8
					8	14·7	15·7
					10	15·5	15·6
	2	19·5	16·0	At Cowes . .	Midn.	15·3	15·5
	4	16·6	15·8				

APPENDIX B.

Temperature of the Sea at different Depths near the Eastern Margin of the North Atlantic Basin, as ascertained by Serial and by Bottom Soundings.

SERIAL SOUNDINGS.								BOTTOM SOUNDINGS.			
Depth.	Temperature. Ser. 23.	Temperature. Ser. 42.	Temperature Ser. 22.	Temperature. Ser. 19.	Temperature. Ser. 20	Temperature. Ser. 21.	Temperature. Ser. 38.	Station. No.	Depth.	Surface Temperature.	Bottom Temperature.
Fms.	Deg. Cent.	Deg. Cent.	Deg. Cent.	Deg. Cent.	Deg. Cent.	Deg. Cent.	Deg. Cent.		Fms.	Deg. Cent.	Deg. Cent.
0	14·0	17·0	13·8	12·6	13·0	13·4	17·7				
50	...	11·8						27	54	13·1	9·0
								34	75	18·9	9·8
								6	90	12·2	10·0
								35	96	17·4	10·7
100	9·1	10·6						8	106	12·3	10·6
								24	109	14·3	8·0
150	...	10·5						7	159	11·8	10·2
								14	173	11 8	9·7
								18	183	11·8	9·6
200	8·9	10·2						13	208	12·0	9·7
250	...	10·1	9·1	8·9	9·1	9·0	10·2	4	251	12·0	9·7
300	8·7	9·7						26	345	14·1	8·1
350	...	9·5						1	370	12·2	9·4
400	8·6	9·1						15	422	11·2	8·3
450	...	8·6						45	458	15·9	8·9
500	7·7	8·5	8·1	8·1	8·3	8·6	8·8	40	517	17·4	8·7
550	...	8·0						39	557	17·2	8·3
600	6·9	7·5						41	584	17·4	8·0
630	6·3										
650		6·8						23b	664	14·1	5·3
700	...	6·4						12	670	11·2	5·9
								3	723	12·5	6·1
								36	725	17·7	6·6
750	...	5·8	5·5	5·1	5·3	5·7	5·2				
800	...	5·5						2	808	12·3	5·2
								16	816	11·6	4·1
862	...	4·3						44	865	16·2	4·1
1000	...	...	3·7	3·6	3·7	3·6	3·5	43	1207	16·5	3·1
								28	1215	14·2	2·8
								17	1230	11·8	3·2
1250	...	...	...	...	3·1	3·2	3·1	29	1264	13·8	2·7
1300								32	1320	13·3	3·0
1360	...	...	...	3·0				30	1380	13·3	2·8
1400											
1443	...	...	...	...	2·7						
1476	...	...	...	...	...	2·7					
1500	...	...	...	...	...	...	2·9				
1750	...	...	...	...	...	...	2·6				
2090	...	...	...	...	...	...	2·4				
								37	2435	18·6	2·5

APPENDIX C.

Comparative Rates of Reduction of Temperature with Increase of Depth at Three Stations in different Latitudes, all of them on the Eastern Margin of the Atlantic Basin.

Depth.	Station 42. Lat. 49° 12′.		Station 23. Lat. 56° 13′.		Station 87. Lat. 59° 35′.	
	Temperature.	Difference	Temperature.	Difference.	Temperature.	Difference.
Fathoms.						
Surface.	17°· 0 C.		14°· 0 C.		11°· 4 C.	
		6°· 4 C.		4°· 9 C.		2°· 9 C.
100	10 · 6		9 · 1		8 · 5	
		0 · 4		0 · 2		0 · 3
200	10 · 2		8 · 9		8 · 2	
		0 · 5		0 · 2		0 · 1
300	9 · 7		8 · 7		8 · 1	
		0 · 6		0 · 1		0 · 3
400	9 · 1		8 · 6		7 · 8	
		1 · 0		1 · 0		0 · 5
500	8 · 1		7 · 6		7 · 3	
		0 · 6		0 · 7		1 · 2
600	7 · 5		6 · 9		6 · 1	
		1 · 7				
750	5 · 8					
						0 · 9
767					5 · 2	

APPENDIX D.

Temperature of the Sea at different Depths in the Warm and Cold Areas lying between the North of Scotland, the Shetland Islands, and the Fœroe Islands; as ascertained by Serial and by Bottom Soundings.

N.B.—The Roman numerals indicate the 'Lightning' Temperature Soundings, corrected for pressure.

Warm Area.					Cold Area.						
s 87.	Sta-tion. No.	Depth.	Surface Tempe-rature.	Bottom Tempe-rature.	Series 64.		Ser. 52.	Sta-tion. No.	Depth.	Surface Tempe-rature.	Bottom Tempe-rature.
Tempe-rature.					Depth.	Tempe-rature	Tempe-rature.				
Deg. Cent.		Fms.	Deg. Cent.	Deg. Cent.	Fms.	Deg. Cent	Deg. Cent.		Fms.	Deg. Cent.	Deg. Cent.
11·4					0	9·8	11·1				
8·9	73	84	11·5	9·3	50	7·5	9·1	70	66	11·9	7·3
	80	92	11·8	9·6				69	67	11·9	6·5
8·5					100	7·2	8·5	68	75	11·4	6·6
	71	103	11·6	9·2				61	114	10·2	7·2
	81	142	11·8	9·5				62	125	9·7	7·0
8·3	84	155	12·3	9·5	150	6·2	8·0	60	167	9·7	6·8
	85	190	12·1	9 2				IX.	170	11·1	5 0
8·2					200	4·2	7·5				
	74	203	11·4	8·7							
					250	1·2	3·5				
8·1					300	0·2	--0·7				
								63	317	9·4	−1·0
								65	345	11·1	−1·2
								76	344	10·2	−1·3
	50	355	11·4	7·9	350	−0·3		54	363	11·4	−0·3
	46	374	12·1	7·7	384		−0·8				
7·8					400.	−0·6		86	445	12·0	−1·1
	89	445	11·7	7·5	450	−0·8					
	90	458	11·7	7·3				56	480	11·4	−0·7
	49	475	12·0	7·4				53	490	11·2	−1·1
7·2					500	−1·1		X.	500	10·5	−0·7
	XII.	530	11·4	7·1				58	540	10·8	−0·7
	47	542	12·2	6·5				VIII.	550	11·6	−1·3
	XV.	570	11·1	6·3	550	−1·1		77	560	10·5	−1·3
								59	580	11·5	−1·3
6·1					600	−1·2					
	XVII.	620	11·1	6·3				55	605	11·4	−1·3
	XIV.	650	11·6	5·8				57	632	11·1	−0·8
					640	−1·4					
	88	705	11·9	5·9							
5·2											

APPENDIX E.

Intermediate Bottom Temperatures, showing the Intermixture of Warm and Cold Currents on the Borders of the Warm and Cold Areas.

Station. No.	Depth.	Surface Temperature.	Bottom Temperature.	Station. No.	Depth.	Surface Temperature.	Bottom Temperature.
	Fathoms.	Deg. Cent.	Deg. Cent.		Fathoms.	Deg. Cent.	Deg. Cent.
72	76	11·3	9·3	75	250	10·8	5·5
79	76	11·2	9·3	78	290	11·2	5·3
73	84	11·5	9·3	82	312	11·3	5·1
71	103	11·6	9·2	83	362	11·8	3·0
74	203	11·4	8·7				
66	267	11·4	7·6	15	440	10·9	5·6

CHAPTER VIII.

THE GULF-STREAM.

The Range of the 'Porcupine' Temperature Observations.—Low Temperatures universal at great Depths.—The Difficulty of investigating Ocean Currents.—The Doctrine of a general Oceanic Circulation advocated by Captain Maury and by Dr. Carpenter.—Opinion expressed by Sir John Herschel.—The Origin and Extension of the Gulf-stream.—The Views of Captain Maury; of Professor Buff; of Dr. Carpenter.—The Gulf-stream off the Coast of North America.—Professor Bache's 'Sections.'—The Gulf-stream traced by the Surface Temperatures of the North Atlantic.—Mr. Findlay's Views.—Dr. Petermann's Temperature Charts.—Sources of the underlying Cold Water.—The Arctic Return Currents.—Antarctic Indraught.—Vertical Distribution of Temperature in the North Atlantic Basin.

All the temperature investigations carried on in H.M.S.S. 'Lightning' and 'Porcupine' during the years 1868–69 and 1870, with the exception of a series of observations already referred to taken in the Mediterranean under Dr. Carpenter's direction in the summer of 1870, were included within an area nearly 2,000 English miles in length by 250 in width, extending from a little beyond the Færoe Islands, lat. 62° 30′ N., to the Strait of Gibraltar, lat. 36° N.

The greater part of this belt may be described as

the eastern border of the North Atlantic fringing Western Europe. A small but very interesting portion of it forms the channel between the Færoe Islands and the North of Scotland, one of the channels of communication between the North Atlantic and the North Sea; and a few soundings in shallow water to the east of Shetland are in the shallow North Sea basin. It is evident, therefore, that the greater part if not the whole of this belt must participate in the general scheme of distribution of temperature in the North Atlantic, and must owe any peculiarities which its thermal conditions may present to some very general cause.

All our temperature observations, except the few taken in the 'Lightning' in 1868, were made with thermometers protected from pressure on Professor Miller's plan, and the thermometers were individually tested by Captain Davis at pressures rising to about three tons to the square inch before they were furnished to the vessel; they were also more than once reduced to the freezing-point during the voyage to ascertain that the glass had been in no way distorted. The results may therefore be received with absolute reliance within the limits of error of observation, which were reduced to a minimum by the care of Captain Calver.

A large number of scattered observations, most of which have unfortunately been made with instruments which cannot thoroughly be depended upon for accuracy of detail,—the error, however, being probably in the direction of excess of heat,—established the singular fact that although the temperature of the surface of the sea in equatorial regions may reach 30° C., at the greatest depths both in the Atlantic and in the Pacific the temperature is not higher than from 2° to 4° C., sometimes falling at great depths to 0° C. I quote from Mr. Prestwich's able presidential address to the Geological Society for the year 1871, a table of the most important of these earlier observations in the Atlantic and the Pacific :[1]—

TEMPERATURES OF THE ATLANTIC.

Latitude.	Longitude.	Depth in Faths.	Temperature.		Observer and Date.
			Surface.	Bottom.	
42° 0′ N.	34° 40′ W.	780	16·7° C.	6·6° C.	Chevalier. . 1837
29 0	34 50	1400	24·4	6·1	" . . 1837
7 21	20 40	505	26·6	2·2	Lenz . . . 1832
4 25	26 6	1006	27·0	3·2	Tessan . . 1841
15 3 S.	23 14	1200	25·0	4·1	" . . 1841
25 10	7 59 E.	886	19·6	3·0	" . . 1841
29 33	10 57	1051	19·1	2·0	" . . 1841
32 20	43 50	1074	21·6	2·4	Lenz . . . 1832
38 12	54 80 W.	333	16·8	3·0	Tessan . . 1841

TEMPERATURES OF THE PACIFIC.

Latitude.	Longitude.	Depth in Faths.	Temperature.		Observer and Date.
			Surface.	Bottom.	
51° 34′ N.	161° 41′ E.	957	11·8° C.	2·5° C.	Tessan . . 1832
28 52	173 9	600	25·5	5·0	Beechey . . 1828
18 5	174 10	710	24·7	4·8	" . . 1836
4 32	134 24 W.	2045	27·2	1·7	The 'Bonite' 1837
Equator.	179 34	1000	30·0	2·5	Kotzebue . 1824
21 14 S.	196 1	916	27·2	2·2	Lenz . . . 1834
32 57	176 42 E.	782	16·4	5·4	" . . . 1834
43 47	80 6 W.	1066	13·0	2·3	Tessan . . 1841

[1] Address delivered at the Anniversary Meeting of the Geological Society of London on the 17th of February, 1871, by Joseph Prestwich, F.R.S. Pp. 36, 37.

To these may be added the observations of Lieutenant S. P. Lee, of the United States Coast Survey, who, in August 1847, recorded a temperature of 2°·7 C. below the Gulf-stream at a depth of 1,000 fathoms, lat. 35° 26′ N., long. 73° 12′ W.; and of Lieutenant Dayman, who found the temperature at 1,000 fathoms in lat. 51° N. and long. 40° W. to be – 0°·4 C., the surface temperature being 12°·5 C. These results are fully borne out by the recent determinations of Captain Shortland, R.N., who observed a temperature of 2°·5 C. in deep water in the Arabian Sea between Aden and Bombay,[1] by those of Commander Chimmo, R.N., and Lieutenant Johnson, R.N., who found at various points in the Atlantic a temperature of about 3°·9 C. at 1,000 fathoms, and a slow decrease from that point to 2,270 fathoms, where the temperature registered by unprotected thermometers was 6°·6 C., reduced by the necessary correction for pressure to about 1°·6 C.,[2] and finally by the temperature determinations of the 'Porcupine' expeditions, carefully conducted with protected instruments, but not carried nearer the tropics than the latitude of the Strait of Gibraltar; and they appear to go far to establish a nearly uniform temperature for abyssal depths, not far from the freezing-point of fresh water.

As it was evident that the low temperature for deep water in tropical regions could not be acquired

[1] Sounding Voyage of H.M.S. 'Hydra,' Captain P. F. Shortland. London: 1869.

[2] Soundings and Temperatures in the Gulf-stream. By Commander W. Chimmo, R.N. (Proceedings of the Royal Geographical Society, vol. xiii.)

by contact with the surface of the crust of the earth, the inevitable conclusion seems to have been early arrived at that, if such temperatures existed, they must be due to a general oceanic circulation,—to surface currents of warm water passing towards the poles, and compensating counter-currents of cold water from the poles towards the equator. Humboldt states that he showed, in 1812, "that the low temperature of the tropical seas at great depths could only be owing to currents from the poles to the equator."[1]

D'Aubuisson, in 1819, also attributed the low temperature of the sea at great depths at or near the equator to the flow of currents from the poles.[2]

But although the fact of the existence of currents lowering the temperature of deep water in equatorial regions was admitted by various authorities in physical geography, little light was thrown upon the causes of this circulation. Latterly, the whole subject became obscured by the very general adoption of the doctrine already referred to of a permanent temperature of 4° C. all over the world beyond a certain depth; and it was not until the publication of Captain Maury's fascinating book on the 'Physical Geography of the Sea' had given an extraordinary stimulus to the study of this department of science, that the question was again raised.

It was natural from its geographical position, and from the much greater opportunity which it offered for the accumulation of the almost infinite number

[1] Fragments de Géol. et de Climatol. Asiat., 1831.

[2] Traité de Géognosie.—Quoted in the Anniversary Address to the Geological Society of London, 1871.

of data required for the consideration of such subjects, that the basin of the North Atlantic should be selected for investigation, more particularly as peculiarities of climate seemed there to be limited in space, and well defined and even extreme in character.

It seems at first somewhat singular that there should be any room for question as to the causes, the sources, and the directions of the ocean currents which traverse the ocean in our immediate neighbourhood, and exercise a most important influence on our economy and well-being. The investigation is, however, one of singular difficulty. Some currents are palpable enough, going at a rate and with a force which make it easy to detect them, and even comparatively easy to gauge their volume and define their path; but it seems that the great movements of the water of the ocean, those which produce the most important results in the transfer of temperature and the modification of climate, are not of this character. These move so slowly that their surface movement is constantly masked by the drift of variable winds, and they thus produce no sensible effect upon navigation.

The path and limits of such bodies of moving water can only be determined by the use of the thermometer. The equalizing of the temperature of bodies of water in contact with one another and differently heated, by conduction, diffusion, and mixture, is however so slow, that we usually have but little difficulty in distinguishing currents from different sources.

Up to the present time little had been done in determining the depth and mass of currents by the thermometer, and under-currents were practically unknown; but the limits of surface currents had been traced with considerable precision by observations of the temperature of the surface of the sea, even when the movement was so slow as not to be otherwise perceptible. The amount of heat received directly from the sun may be taken approximately to depend upon latitude only, and this heat is in addition to the heat of the surface water derived from other sources, whatever these may be. Observations of surface temperature accordingly give us the heat derived directly from the sun in the region, and the heat derived from the same source during the passage of the water to the region, in addition to the original heat of the water; if, therefore, the water of any region be derived from—that is to say, form part of—a movement of water from a polar source, and if the surface water of another area on the same parallel of latitude form part of an equatorial current, although in that particular latitude they receive in both cases the same amount of heat from the sun, there will be a marked difference in their temperature. To take an extreme case; the mean temperature of the sea in the month of July off the Hebrides, in lat. 58° N., in the path of the Gulf-stream, is 13° C.; while in the same latitude off the coast of Labrador, in the course of the Labrador current, it is 4°·5 C.

The distribution of surface temperature in the North Atlantic is certainly very exceptional. A glance at the chart Pl. VII., representing the general distribution of heat for the month of July, shows that the isothermal lines for that month, instead of tending in the least to coincide with the parallels of latitude, run up into a series of long loops, some of them continued into the Arctic Sea.

The temperature of the bordering land is not affected to any perceptible degree by direct radiation from the sea; but it is greatly affected by the temperature of the prevailing winds. Setting aside the still more important point of the equalization of summer and winter temperature, the mean annual temperature of Bergen, lat. 60° 24′ N., subject to the ameliorating influence of the prevailing south-west wind blowing over the temperate water of the North Atlantic, is 6°·7 C.; while that of Tobolsk, lat. 58° 13′ N., is – 2°·4 C.

But the temperature of the North Atlantic and its bordering lands is not only raised above that of places on the same parallel of latitude having a 'continental' climate, but it is greatly higher than that of places apparently similarly circumstanced to itself in the southern hemisphere. Thus the mean annual temperature of the Færoe Islands, lat. 62° 2′ N., is 7°·1 C., nearly equal to that of the Falkland Islands, lat. 52° S., which is 8°·2 C.; and the temperature of Dublin, lat. 53° 21′ N., is 9°·6 C., while that of Port Famine, lat. 53° 8′ S., is 5°·3 C. Again, the high temperature of the North Atlantic is not equally distributed, but is very marked in its determination to the north-east coast. Thus the mean annual temperature of Halifax (Nova Scotia), lat. 44° 39′ N., is 6°·2 C., while that of Dublin, lat. 53° 21′ N., is 9°·6 C.; and the temperature of Boston (Mass.), lat. 42° 21′ N., is exactly the same as that of Dublin.

This remarkable diversion of the isothermal lines from their normal direction is admittedly caused by ocean currents affecting the temperature of the surface while conveying the warm tropical water towards the polar regions, whence there is a constant counterflow of cold water beneath to supply its place.

We thus arrive at the well-known result that the temperature of the sea bathing the north-eastern shores of the North Atlantic is raised greatly above its normal point by currents involving an interchange of tropical and polar water; and that the lands bordering on the North Atlantic participate in this amelioration of climate by the heat imparted by the water to their prevailing winds.

This phenomenon is not confined to the North Atlantic, although from its peculiar configuration and relation to the land that ocean presents the most marked example. A corresponding series of loops, not so well defined, passes southwards along the east coast of South America, and a very marked series occupies the north-eastern angle of the Pacific off the Aleutian Islands and the coast of California.

Two principal views have been held as to the causes of the currents in the North Atlantic. One of these, which appears to have been first advanced in a definite form by Captain Maury, and which has received some vague support from Professor Buff, is that the great currents and counter-currents of warm and cold water are due to a circulation in the watery shell of the globe, comparable to the circulation of the atmosphere,—that is to say, caused by tropical heat and evaporation, and arctic cold.

It is not easy to understand Captain Maury's view. He traces all ocean currents to differences in specific gravity. He says: "If we except the tides, and the partial currents of the sea, such as those that may be created by the wind, we may lay it down as a rule that all the currents of the ocean owe their origin to the differences of specific gravity between sea-water at one place and sea-water at another; for wherever there is such a difference, whether it be owing to difference of temperature or to difference of saltness, &c., it is a difference that disturbs equilibrium, and currents are the consequence."[1] These differences in specific gravity he attributes to two principal causes; differences in temperature, and excess of salts produced by evaporation. Captain Maury explains his views as to the first of these causes by an illustration. "Let us now suppose that all the water within the tropics to the depth of one hundred fathoms suddenly becomes oil. The aqueous equilibrium of the planet would thereby be disturbed, and a general system of currents and counter-currents would be immediately commenced, the oil in an unbroken sheet on the surface running towards the poles, and the water as an under-current towards the equator. The oil is supposed, as it reaches the polar basin, to be reconverted into water, and the water to become oil as it crosses Cancer and Capricorn, rising to the surface in intertropical regions, and returning as before." "Now, do not the cold water of the north, and the warm water of the gulf made specifically lighter by tropical heat, and which we see actually presenting

[1] The Physical Geography of the Sea, and its Meteorology. By M. T. Maury, LL.D.

such a system of counter-currents, hold at least, in some degree, the relation of the supposed water and oil."[1]

"There can be no doubt that Maury concludes that the waters in intertropical regions are expanded by heat, and those in polar regions are contracted by cold, and that this tends to produce a surface-current from the equator to the poles, and an under-current from the poles to the equator."[2]

With regard to increased specific gravity produced by excess of salt, Captain Maury says,—

"The brine of the ocean is the ley of the earth. From it the sea derives dynamical power, and its currents their main strength."[3] "One of the purposes which in the grand design it was probably intended to accomplish by leaving the sea salt and not fresh, was to impart to its waters the forces and powers necessary to make their circulation complete."[4] "In the present state of our knowledge concerning this wonderful phenomenon (for the Gulf-stream is one of the most marvellous things in the ocean), we can do little more than conjecture. But we have the causes in operation, which we may safely assume are among those concerned in producing the Gulf-stream. One of these is the increased saltness of its water after the trade-winds have been supplied with vapour from it, be it much or little; and the other is the diminished quantum of salt which the

[1] Captain Maury, op. cit.

[2] On Ocean Currents. Part III. On the Physical Cause of Ocean Currents. By James Croll, of the Geological Survey of Scotland. (Philosophical Magazine, October 1870.)

[3] Captain Maury, op. cit. [4] Ibid.

Baltic and the northern seas contain."[1] "Now, here we have on one side the Caribbean Sea and Gulf of Mexico with their waters of brine; on the other, the great Polar Basin, the Baltic, and the North Sea, the two latter with waters that are but little more than brackish. In one set of these sea-basins the water is heavy, in the other it is light. Between them the ocean intervenes; but water is bound to seek and to maintain its level; and here, therefore, we unmask one of the agents concerned in causing the Gulf-stream."[2]

As Mr. James Croll has very clearly pointed out, Captain Maury's two causes tend to neutralize each other.

"Now it is perfectly obvious that if difference in saltness is to co-operate with difference in temperature in the production of ocean currents, the saltest waters, and consequently the densest, must be in the polar regions; and the waters least salt, and consequently lightest, must be in equatorial and intertropical regions. Were the saltest water at the equator and the freshest at the poles, it would tend to neutralize the effect due to heat, and, instead of producing a current, would simply tend to prevent the existence of the currents which otherwise would result from difference of temperature." "According to both theories it is the differences of density between the equatorial and polar waters that gives rise to currents; but according to the one theory, the equatorial waters are *lighter* than the polar, whilst according to the other theory they are *heavier* than the polar. Either the one theory or the other may

[1] Captain Maury, op. cit. [2] Ibid.

be true, or neither; but it is logically impossible that both of these can, for the simple reason that the waters of the equator cannot at the same time be both lighter and heavier than the water at the poles." "So long as the two causes continue in action, no current can arise unless the energy of the one cause should happen to exceed that of the other, and even then a current will only exist to the extent by which the strength of the one exceeds that of the other."[1]

It seems scarcely necessary to enter further into detail in reference to Captain Maury's theory of ocean currents, which is really chiefly remarkable for its ambiguity, and for the pleasant popular style in which it is advocated; since my friend and colleague Dr. Carpenter has latterly brought into great prominence what appears to be a modification of the same view, put in a more definite form.

Professor Buff, in his excellent little volume on the Physics of the Earth, speaking of the layer of cold water derived from the Arctic seas which underlies the tropical ocean, and its method of transport, says: "The following well-known experiment clearly illustrates the manner of the movement. A glass vessel is to be filled with water with which some powder has been mixed, and is then to be heated at bottom. You will soon see, from the motion of the particles of powder, that currents are set up in opposite directions through the water. Warm water rises from the bottom, up through the middle of the vessel, and spreads over the surface; while the colder, and therefore heavier liquid, falls down at the sides of the

[1] James Croll, op. cit.

glass. Currents like these must arise in all water-basins, and even in the oceans if different parts of their surface are unequally heated."[1]

This is of course a common class-experiment illustrating convection. It is evidently impossible that movements of ocean water can be produced in this way, for it is well known that everywhere, except under certain exceptional circumstances in the polar basin, the temperature of the sea decreases from the surface to a minimum at the bottom, and tropical heat is applied at the surface only. It is singular that this irrelevant illustration should have been introduced by Professor Buff; for his account of the origin and extension of the Gulf-stream, which may be taken as the type and exponent of ocean currents, is quite consistent with the commonly received opinions.

On working up the temperature results of the 'Porcupine' expedition of 1869, Dr. Carpenter satisfied himself that the mass of comparatively warm water, 800 fathoms deep, which we had established as existing, and probably moving in a north-easterly direction, along the west coasts of Britain and the Lusitanian peninsula, could not be an extension of the Gulf-stream, but must be due to a general circulation of the waters of the ocean comparable with the circulation of the atmosphere.

"The influence of the Gulf-stream proper (meaning

[1] Familiar Letters on the Physics of the Earth; treating of the chief Movements of the Land, the Water, and the Air, and the Forces that give rise to them. By Henry Buff, Professor of Physics in the University of Giessen. Edited by A. W. Hofmann, Ph.D., F.R.S. London: 1851.

by this the body of superheated water which issues through the 'narrows' from the Gulf of Mexico), if it reaches this locality at all—which is very doubtful—could only affect the most superficial stratum; and the same may be said of the surface-drift caused by the prevalence of south-westerly winds, to which some have attributed the phenomena usually accounted for by the extension of the Gulf-stream to these regions. And the presence of the body of water which lies between 100 and 600 fathoms depth, and the range of whose temperature is from 48° (8°·85 C.) to 42° (5°·5 C.), can scarcely be accounted for on any other hypothesis than that of a great general movement of equatorial water towards the polar area, of which movement the Gulf-stream constitutes a peculiar case, modified by local conditions. In like manner the arctic stream which underlies the warm superficial strata in our cold area, constitutes a peculiar case, modified by the local conditions, to be presently explained, of a great general movement of polar water towards the equatorial area, which depresses the temperature of the deepest parts of the great oceanic basins nearly to the freezing-point." [1]

At first Dr. Carpenter appears to have regarded this oceanic circulation as a case of simple convection. "To what, then, is the north-east movement of the warm upper stratum of the North Atlantic attributable? I have attempted to show that it is part of a general interchange between polar and equatorial waters, which is quite independent of any such

[1] A Lecture delivered at the Royal Institution, abstracted with the Author's signature in *Nature*, vol. i. p. 488 (March 10th, 1870).

local accidents as those which produce the Gulf-stream proper, and which gives movement to a much larger and deeper body of water than the latter can affect. The evidence of such an interchange is two-fold—that of physical theory, and that of actual observation. Such a movement *must* take place, as was long since pointed out by Professor Buff, whenever an extended body of water is heated at one part and cooled at another; it is made use of in the warming of buildings by the hot-water apparatus, and it was admirably displayed at the Royal Institution a few months since in the following experiment kindly prepared for me by Dr. Odling." Dr. Carpenter then repeats Professor Buff's convection experiment, the heat being applied by a steam jet introduced vertically at one end of a narrow glass trough while a block of ice was wedged into the other end. "Thus a circulation was shown to be maintained in the trough by the application of heat at one of its extremities and of cold at the other, the *heated* water flowing along the *surface* from the warm to the cold end, and the *cooled* water flowing along the *bottom* from the cold to the warm end; just as it has been maintained that equatorial water streams on the surface towards the poles, and that polar water returns along the bottom towards the equator, if the movement be not interfered with by interposed obstacles, or prevented by antagonistic currents arising from local peculiarities."[1]

That such a movement *cannot* take place on this hypothesis has been already shown; and Dr. Car-

[1] The Gulf-stream. A letter from Dr. Carpenter to the Editor of *Nature*, dated Gibraltar, August 11th, 1870. (*Nature*, vol. ii. p. 334.)

penter in a lecture to the Royal Geographical Society, in an illustration drawn from two supposed basins, one under equatorial conditions and the other under polar, connected by a strait,[1] says: "The effect of surface-*heat* upon the water of the tropical basin will be for the most part limited to its uppermost stratum, and may here be practically disregarded. But the effect of surface-cold upon the water of the polar basin will be to reduce the temperature of its whole mass below the freezing-point of fresh water, the surface stratum sinking as it is cooled, by virtue of its diminished bulk and increased density, and being replaced by water not yet cooled to the same degree. The warmer water will not come up from below, but will be drawn into the basin from the surface of the surrounding area; and since what is thus drawn away must be supplied from a yet greater distance, the continual cooling of the surface stratum in the polar basin will cause a 'set' of water towards it to be propagated backwards through the whole intervening ocean in connection with it, until it reaches the tropical area." And further on in the same address: "It is seen that the application of *cold at the surface* is precisely equivalent as a moving power to that application of *heat at the bottom* by which the circulation of water is sustained in every heating apparatus that makes use of it." No doubt the application of cold to the surface of a mass of water previously at the same temperature throughout, would

[1] On the Gibraltar Current, the Gulf-stream, and the general Oceanic Circulation. By Dr. W. B. Carpenter, F.R.S. Reprinted from the Proceedings of the Royal Geographical Society of London, 1870.

have the same effect as the application of heat to the bottom, and in either case we should have an instance of simple convection, the warmer under-water rising through a colder upper layer; but that is not what we have in the polar sea; for the temperature of the arctic sea gradually sinks from a few fathoms beneath the surface to a minimum temperature, and consequent maximum density, at the bottom. Therefore in this case the application of cold at the surface is not equivalent to the application of heat to the bottom in a hot-water heating apparatus, and Dr. Carpenter has shown that he is aware of this by requiring the backward propagation of a *surface*-current.

That a certain effect in increase of specific gravity must be produced by the cooling of the surface film of the arctic ocean there seems to be little doubt; but the area of maximum effect is very limited, and during the long arctic winter the greater part of that area is protected by a thick layer of ice, one of the worst possible conductors.

It certainly appears to me that this cause is totally inadequate to induce a powerful current of great depth, six thousand miles long and several thousand miles in width, the effect which Dr. Carpenter attributes to it.

During the summer of 1870, and afterwards in 1871, Dr. Carpenter made a series of observations on the current in the Strait of Gibraltar. The existence of an under-current out of the Mediterranean was considered to be established by these observations, and the conclusions arrived at as to its cause did not differ materially from those already very generally accepted. Dr. Carpenter believes, however, that the conditions in the Strait of Gibraltar and in the Baltic Sound aptly illustrate the general circulation in the ocean, and confirm his views.

I quote from the general summary of Dr. Carpenter's address to the Geographical Society:—

"The application of the foregoing principles to the particular cases discussed in the paper is as follows:—

"VIII.—A vertical circulation is maintained in the Strait of Gibraltar by the excess of evaporation in the Mediterranean over the amount of fresh water returned into its basin, which at the same time *lowers its level* and *increases its density;* so that the surface inflow of salt water which restores its level (exceeding by the weight of salt contained in it the weight of fresh water which has passed off by evaporation) disturbs the equilibrium and produces a *deep outflow,* which in its turn lowers the level. The same may be assumed to be the case in the Strait of Babelmandeb.

"IX.—A vertical circulation is maintained in the Baltic Sound by an excess in the influx of fresh water into the Baltic; which at the same time raises its level and diminishes its density, so as to produce a *surface outflow,* leaving the Baltic column the lighter of the two, so that a *deep inflow* must take place to restore the equilibrium. The same may be assumed to be the case in the Bosphorus and Dardanelles.

"X.—A vertical circulation must, on the same principles, be maintained between polar and equatorial waters by the difference of their temperatures:

the level of the polar water being reduced, and its density increased by the surface-*cold* to which it is subjected, whilst a downward motion is also imparted to each stratum successively exposed to it; and the level of equatorial water being raised and its density diminished by the surface-*heat* to which it is exposed. (The first of these agencies is by far the more effective, since it extends to the whole depth of the water, whilst the second only affects, in any considerable degree, the superficial stratum.) Thus a movement will be imparted to the upper stratum of oceanic water from the equator towards the poles, whilst a movement will be imparted to the deeper stratum from the poles towards the equator."

It seems to me that the doctrine here propounded by my distinguished colleague, if I understand it aright, is open to the objection to which I have already referred in connection with the speculations of Captain Maury.

If the currents flow in the direction and with the permanence accepted by Dr. Carpenter in the Strait of Gibraltar and in the Baltic Sound, if their flow and its direction be due to the causes to which Dr. Carpenter attributes them, and if there be any analogy whatever between the conditions of equilibrium of these inland seas and that of the outer ocean,—none of which propositions appear to me at all satisfactorily proved,—I should think that the vast equatorial region, the path of the trade-winds and the belt of vertical solar radiation, must, so far as evaporation is concerned, resemble, or rather greatly exaggerate, the conditions of the Mediterranean. The consequent accumulation of salt,—through the whole depth of course, the brine sinking downwards,—must greatly outweigh (I give this as what Petermann would call a gratuitous speculation) the slight expansion caused by the heating of the surface layer. The more restricted arctic basin on the other hand, as was long ago pointed out by Capt. Maury, participates to a certain extent in the characteristics of the Baltic; and I am greatly mistaken if the low specific gravity of the polar sea, the result of the condensation and precipitation of vapour evaporated from the intertropical area, do not fully counterbalance the contraction of the superficial film by arctic cold.

The North Atlantic ocean bears a proportion in depth to the mass of the earth considerably less than that of the paper covering an eighteen-inch globe to that of the globe it covers, while the film heated by direct solar radiation may be represented by its surface coating of varnish, and is not actually thicker than the height of St. Paul's. Physicists seem to find a difficulty in giving us the amount of palpable effect in producing currents in this shell of water, six thousand miles in length by three thousand in width and two miles in thickness, which may be due to causes such as those relied upon by Dr. Carpenter, acting under the peculiar circumstances and to the amount in which we find them in nature; and probably we are not yet in a position to give them sufficient data to enable them to do so. Mr. Croll, a good authority in such matters, has attempted to make some calcutions, and comes to the conclusion that none of them are sufficient to overcome the friction of water and to produce any current whatever;[1] but in this view he does not certainly receive universal support. I am myself inclined to believe that in a great body of salt water at different temperatures, with unequal amounts of evaporation, under varying barometric pressures, and subject to the drift of variable winds, currents of all kinds, great and small, variable and more or less permanent, must be set up;[2] but the probable result appears to be reduced to a minimum when we find that causes, themselves of doubtful efficiency, actually antagonize one another; and that we are obliged to trust for the final effect to the amount by which the least feeble of these exceeds the others in strength. Speaking in the total absence of all reliable data, it is my general impression that, if we were to set aside all other agencies, and to trust for an oceanic circulation to those conditions only which are relied upon by Dr. Carpenter, if there were any general circulation at all, which seems very problematical, the odds are rather in favour of a warm under-current travelling northwards by virtue of its excess of salt, balanced by a surface return-current of fresher though colder arctic water.

With regard, then, to this question of a general circulation caused by difference in specific gravity, for the present I cordially endorse the opinion expressed by the late Sir John Herschel in a cautious

[1] James Croll, op. cit.

[2] On the Distribution of Temperatures in the North Atlantic. An Address delivered to the Meteorological Society of Scotland at the General Meeting of the Society July 5th, 1871, by Professor Wyville Thomson.

and excellent letter addressed to Dr. Carpenter—a letter which there is no impropriety in my quoting in full as it is already in print, and which has a special interest as being probably one of the last written by Sir John Herschel on scientific subjects:—

"COLLINGWOOD, *April 9th*, 1871.

"MY DEAR SIR,—Many thanks for your paper on the Gibraltar current and the Gulf-stream. Assuredly, after well considering all you say, as well as the common sense of the matter, and the experience of our hot-water circulation pipes in our greenhouses, &c., there is no refusing to admit that an oceanic circulation of some sort must arise from mere heat, cold, and evaporation, as *veræ causæ*, and you have brought forward with singular emphasis the more powerful action of the polar cold, or rather the more intense action, as its maximum effect is limited to a much smaller area than that of the maximum of equatorial heat.

"The action of the trade and counter-trade winds, in like manner, cannot be ignored; and henceforward the question of ocean currents will have to be studied under a twofold point of view. The wind-currents, however, are of easier investigation: all the causes lie on the surface; none of the agencies escape our notice; the configuration of coasts, which mainly determines their direction, is patent to sight. It is otherwise with the other class of movements. They take place in the depths of the ocean; and their movements and directions and channels of concentration are limited to the configuration of the sea-bottom, which has to be studied over its entire surface by the very imperfect method of sounding.

"I am glad you succeeded in getting specimens of Mediterranean water near the place of the presumed salt spring of Smyth and Wollaston, making it clear that the whole affair must have arisen from some accidental substitution of one bottle for another, or from evaporation. I never put any hearty faith in it.

"So, after all, there is an under-current setting outwards in the Straits of Gibraltar.

"Repeating my thanks for this interesting memoir, believe me, dear Sir,

"Yours very truly,

"J. F. W. HERSCHEL.

"*Dr. W. B. Carpenter.*"[1]

The second view, supported by Dr. Petermann of Gotha, and by most of the leading authorities in physical geography in Germany and Northern Europe, and strongly urged by the late Sir John Herschel in his 'Outlines of Physical Geography' published in the year 1846, attributes nearly the whole of the sensible phenomena of heat-distribution in the North Atlantic to the Gulf-stream, and to the arctic return-currents which are induced by the removal of tropical water towards the polar regions by the Gulf-stream. If we for a moment admit that to the Gulf-stream is due almost exclusively the singular advantage in climate which the eastern borders of the North Atlantic possess over the western, the origin of this great current, its extent and direction, and the nature and amount of its influence, become questions of surpassing interest. Before considering these, however, it will be well to define what is here meant by the term 'Gulf-stream,' for even on this point there has been a good deal of misconception.

I mean by the Gulf-stream that mass of heated water which pours from the Strait of Florida across the North Atlantic, and likewise a wider but less definite warm current, evidently forming part of the same great movement of water, which curves north-

[1] *Nature*, vol. iv. p. 71.

wards to the eastward of the West Indian Islands. I am myself inclined, without hesitation, to regard this stream as simply the reflux of the equatorial current, added to no doubt during its north-easterly course, by the surface-drift of the anti-trades which follows in the main the same direction.

The scope and limit of the Gulf-stream will be better understood if we inquire in the first place into its origin and cause. As is well known,—in two bands, one to the north and the other to the south of the equator,—the north-east and south-east trade-winds, reduced to meridional directions by the eastward frictional impulse of the earth's rotation, drive before them a magnificent surface current of hot water 4,000 miles long by 450 miles broad at an average rate of thirty miles a day. Off the coast of Africa near its starting-point to the south of the Islands of St. Thomas and Anna Bon, this 'Equatorial Current' has a speed of forty miles in the twenty-four hours, and a temperature of 23° C.

Increasing quickly in bulk, and spreading out more and more on both sides of the equator, it flows rapidly due west towards the coast of South America. At the eastern point of South America, Cape St. Roque, the equatorial current splits into two, and one portion trends southwards to deflect the isotherms of 21°, 15°·5, 10°, and 4°·5 C. into loops upon our maps, thus carrying a scrap of comfort to the Falkland Islands and Cape Hoorn; while the northern portion follows the north-east coast of South America, gaining continually in temperature under the influence of the tropical sun. Its speed has now increased to sixty-eight miles in twenty-four hours, and by the union with it of the waters of the river Amazon, it rises to one hundred miles (6·5 feet in a second), but it soon falls off again when it gets into the Caribbean sea. Flowing slowly through the whole length of this sea, it reaches the Gulf of Mexico through the Strait of Yucatan, when a part of it sweeps immediately round Cuba; but the main stream "having made the circuit of the Gulf of Mexico, passes through the Strait of Florida; thence it issues as the 'Gulf-stream' in a majestic current upwards of thirty miles broad, two thousand two hundred feet deep, with an average velocity of four miles an hour, and a temperature of 86° Fahr. (30° C)."[1] The hot water pours from the strait with a decided though slight north-easterly impulse on account of its great initial velocity. Mr. Croll calculates the Gulf-stream as equal to a stream of water fifty miles broad and a thousand feet deep flowing at a rate of four miles an hour; consequently conveying 5,575,680,000,000 cubic feet of water per hour, or 133,816,320,000,000 cubic feet per day. This mass of water has a mean temperature of 18° C. as it passes out of the gulf, and on its northern journey it is cooled down to 4°·5, thus losing heat to the amount of 13°·5 C. The total quantity of heat therefore transferred from the equatorial regions per day amounts to something like 154,959,300,000,000,000,000 foot-pounds.[2]

This is nearly equal to the whole of the heat

[1] Physical Geography. From the 'Encyclopædia Britannica.' By Sir John F. W. Herschel, Bart., K.H.P. Edinburgh, 1861, p. 49.

[2] On Ocean Currents. By James Croll, of the Geological Survey of Scotland. Part I. Ocean Currents in relation to the Distribution of Heat over the Globe (Philosophical Magazine. February 1870.)

received from the sun by the Arctic regions, and, reduced by a half to avoid all possibility of exaggeration, it is still equal to one-fifth of the whole amount received from the sun by the entire area of the North Atlantic. The Gulf-stream, as it issues from the Strait of Florida and expands into the ocean on its northward course, is probably the most glorious natural phenomenon on the face of the earth. The water is of a clear crystalline transparency and an intense blue, and long after it has passed into the open sea it keeps itself apart, easily distinguished by its warmth, its colour, and its clearness; and with its edges so sharply defined that a ship may have her stem in the clear blue stream while her stern is still in the common water of the ocean.

"The dynamics of the Gulf-stream have of late, in the work of Lieutenant Maury already mentioned, been made the subject of much (we cannot but think misplaced) wonder, as if there could be any possible ground for doubting that it owes its origin entirely to the trade-winds."[1] Setting aside the wider question of the possibility of a general oceanic circulation arising from heat, cold, and evaporation, I believe that Captain Maury and Dr. Carpenter are the only authorities who of late years have disputed this source of the current which we see, and can gauge and measure as it passes out of the Strait of Florida; for it is scarcely necessary to refer to the earlier speculations that it is caused by the Mississippi river, or that it flows downwards by gravitation from a 'head' of water produced by the trade-winds in the Caribbean sea.

[1] Herschel, op. cit. p. 51.

Captain Maury writes[1] that "the dynamical force that calls forth the Gulf-stream is to be found in the difference as to specific gravity of intertropical and polar waters." "The dynamical forces which are expressed by the Gulf-stream may with as much propriety be said to reside in those northern waters as in the West India seas: for on one side we have the Caribbean sea and Gulf of Mexico with their waters of brine; on the other the great polar basin, the Baltic, and the North Sea, the two latter with waters which are little more than brackish. In one set of these sea-basins the water is heavy; in the other it is light. Between them the ocean intervenes; but water is bound to seek and to maintain its level; and here, therefore, we unmask one of those agents concerned in causing the Gulf-stream. What is the power of this agent? Is it greater than that of other agents? and how much? We cannot say how much; we only know it is one of the chief agents concerned. Moreover, speculate as we may as to all the agencies concerned in collecting these waters, that have supplied the trade-winds with vapour, into the Caribbean Sea, and then in driving them across the Atlantic, we are forced to conclude that the salt which the trade-wind vapour leaves behind it in the tropics has to be conveyed away from the trade-wind region, to be mixed up again in due proportion with the other water of the sea—the Baltic Sea and the Arctic Ocean included —and that these are some of the waters, at least, which we see running off through the Gulf-stream. To convey them away is doubtless one of the offices which in the economy of the ocean has been assigned

[1] Maury's Physical Geography of the Sea, op. cit.

to it. But as for the seat of the forces which put and keep the Gulf-stream in motion, theorists may place them exclusively on one side of the ocean with as much philosophical propriety as on the other. Its waters find their way into the North Sea and Arctic Ocean by virtue of their specific gravity, while water thence, to take their place, is, by virtue of its specific gravity and by counter-currents, carried back into the gulf. The dynamical force which causes the Gulf-stream may therefore be said to reside both in the polar and in the intertropical waters of the Atlantic."

According to this view, the tropical water finds its way on account of its greater weight towards the poles, while the polar water, owing to its less weight, moves southwards to replace it. The general result would be of course a system of warm under- and cold surface-currents, and these we do not find. I merely quote the passage as a curious illustration of the adage that on most questions a good deal can be said on both sides.

We have already considered the doctrine of a general oceanic circulation, which has been so strongly advocated of late by Dr. Carpenter, and I have merely to advert in this place to the bearing which that doctrine has upon our views as to the origin of the Gulf-stream; its bearings on the extension and distribution of the current will be discussed hereafter. As already stated, Dr. Carpenter attributes all the great movements of ocean water to a general convective circulation, and of this general circulation he regards the Gulf-stream as a peculiarly modified case. In the passage already quoted (p. 370) of his address to the Royal Institution, Dr. Carpenter states, that "the Gulf-stream constitutes a peculiar case, modified by local conditions," of "a great general movement of equatorial water towards the polar area." I confess I feel myself compelled to take a totally different view. It seems to me that the Gulf-stream is the one natural physical phenomenon on the surface of the earth whose origin and principal cause, the drift of the trade-winds, can be most clearly and easily traced.

The further progress and extension of the Gulf-stream through the North Atlantic in relation to influence upon climate has been, however, a fruitful source of controversy. The first part of its course, after leaving the strait, is sufficiently evident, for its water long remains conspicuously different in colour and temperature from that of the ocean, and a current having a marked effect on navigation is long perceptible in the peculiar Gulf-stream water. "Narrow at first, it flows round the peninsula of Florida, and, with a speed of about 70 or 80 miles, follows the coast at first in a due north, afterwards in a north-east direction. At the latitude of Washington it leaves the North American coast altogether, keeping its north-eastward course; and to the south of the St. George's and Newfoundland Banks it spreads its waters more and more over the Atlantic Ocean, as far as the Açores. At these islands a part of it turns southwards again towards the African coast. The Gulf-stream has, so long as its waters are kept together along the American coast, a temperature of 26°·6 C.; but, even under north latitude 36°, Sabine found that

23°·3 C. at the beginning of December, while the sea-water beyond the stream showed only 16°·9 C. Under north latitude 40—41° the water is, according to Humboldt, at 22°·5 C. within, and 17°·5 C. without the stream."[1]

The Gulf-stream off the coast of North America has been most carefully examined by the officers of the United States Coast Survey, at first under the superintendence of Professor Bache, and latterly under the direction of the present able head of the bureau, Professor Pierce. In 1860 Professor Bache published an account of the general result.[2] Fourteen sections through the Gulf-stream had been carefully surveyed at intervals of about 100 miles along the coast—the first almost within the Gulf of Mexico, from Fortingas to Havana, and the last off Cape Cod, lat. 41° N., where the stream loses all parallelism with the American coast and trends to the eastward. These sections fully illustrate the leading phenomena during this earlier part of its course of this wonderful current, which Professor Bache well characterizes as "the great hydrographic feature of the United States."

Opposite Fortingas, passing along the Cuban coast, the stream is unbroken and the current feeble; the temperature at the surface is about 26°·7 C. Issuing from the Strait of Bemini the current is turned nearly directly northwards by the form of the land;

[1] Professor Buff, op. cit. p. 199.

[2] Lecture on the Gulf-stream, prepared at the request of the American Association for the Advancement of Science, by A. D. Bache, Superintendent U.S. Coast Survey. From the *American Journal of Science and Arts,* vol. xxx. November 1860.

a little to the north of the strait, the rate is from three to five miles an hour. The depth is only 325 fathoms, and the bottom, which in the Strait of Florida was a simple slope and counter-slope, is now corrugated. The surface temperature is about 26°·5 C., while the bottom temperature is 4°·5; so that in the moderate depth of 325 fathoms the equatorial current above and the polar counter-current beneath have room to pass one another, the current from the north being evidently tempered considerably by mixture. North of Mosquito inlet the stream trends to the eastward of north, and off St. Augustine it has a decided set to the eastward Between St. Augustine and Cape Hatteras the set of the stream and the trend of the coast differ but little, making 5° of easting in 5° of northing. At Hatteras it curves to the northward, and then runs easterly. In the latitude of Cape Charles it turns quite to the eastward, having a velocity of from a mile to a mile and a half in the hour.

A brief account of one of the sections will best explain the general phenomena of the stream off the coast of America. I will take the section following a line at right angles to the coast off Sandy Hook. From the shore out, for a distance of about 250 miles, the surface temperature gradually rises from 21° to 24° C.; at 10 fathoms it rises from 19° to 22° C.; and at 20 fathoms it maintains, with a few irregularities, a temperature of 19° C. throughout the whole space; while at 100, 200, 300, and 400 fathoms it maintains in like manner the respective temperatures of 8°·8, 5°·7, 4°·5, and 2°·5 C. This space is therefore occupied by cold water, and observation has sufficiently proved that the low temperature is due to a branch of the Labrador current creeping down along the coast in a direction opposite to that of the Gulf-stream. In the Strait of Florida this cold stream divides—one portion of it passing under the hot Gulf-stream water into the Gulf of Mexico, while the remainder courses round the western end of Cuba. 240 miles from the shore the whole mass of water takes a sudden rise of about 10° C. within 25 miles, a rise affecting nearly equally the water at all depths, and thus producing the singular phenomenon of two masses of water in contact—one passing slowly southwards, and the other more rapidly northwards, at widely different temperatures at the same levels. This abutting of the side of the cold current against that of the Gulf-stream is so abrupt that it has been aptly called by Lieutenant George M. Bache the 'Cold wall.' Passing the cold wall we reach the Gulf-stream, presenting all its special characters of colour and transparency and of temperature. In the section which we have chosen as an example, upwards of three hundred miles in length, the surface temperature is about 26°·5 C., but the heat is not uniform across the stream, for we find that throughout its entire length, as far south as the Cape Canaveral section, the stream is broken up into longitudinal alternating bands of warmer and cooler water. Off Sandy Hook, beyond the cold wall, the stream rises to a maximum of 27°·8 C., and this warm band extends for about 60 miles. The temperature then falls to a minimum of 26°·5 C., which it retains for about 30 miles, when a second maximum of 27°·4 succeeds, which includes the axis of the Gulf-stream, and is about 170 miles wide. This is followed by a second minimum of 25°·5 C., and this by a third maximum, when the bands become indistinct. It is singular that the minimum bands correspond with valley-like depressions in the bottom, which follow in succession the outline of the coast and lodge deep southward extensions of the polar indraught.

The last section of the Gulf-stream surveyed by the American Hydrographers extends in a south-easterly direction from Cape Cod, lat. 41° N., and traces the Gulf-stream, still broken up by its bands of unequal temperature, spreading directly eastward across the Atlantic; its velocity has, however, now become inconsiderable, and its limits are best traced by the thermometer.

The course of the Gulf-stream beyond this point has given rise to much discussion. I again quote Professor Buff for what may be regarded as the view most generally received among Physical Geographers :—

"A great part of the warm water is carried partly by its own motion, but chiefly by the prevailing west and north-west winds, towards the coasts of Europe and even beyond Spitzbergen and Nova Zembla; and thus a part of the heat of the south reaches far into the Arctic Ocean. Hence, on the north coast of the old Continent, we always find driftwood from the southern regions, and on this side the Arctic Ocean remains free from ice during a great part of the year, even as far up as 80° north latitude; while on the opposite coast (of Greenland) the ice is not quite thawed even in summer." The two forces invoked by Professor Buff to perform the work are thus the *vis a tergo* of the trade-wind drift, and the direct driving power of the anti-trades, producing what has been called the anti-trade drift. This is quite in accordance with the views here advocated. The proportion in which these two forces act, it is undoubtedly impossible in the present state of our knowledge to determine.

Mr. A. G. Findlay, a high authority on all hydrographic matters, read a paper on the Gulf-stream before the Royal Geographical Society, reported in the 13th volume of the Proceedings of the Society. Mr. Findlay, while admitting that the temperature of north-eastern Europe is abnormally ameliorated by a surface-current of the warm water of the Atlantic which reaches it, contends that the Gulf-stream proper, that is to say the water injected, as it were, into the Atlantic through the Strait of Florida by the impulse of the trade-winds, becomes entirely thinned out, dissipated, and lost, opposite the Newfoundland banks about lat. 45° N. The warm water of the southern portion of the North Atlantic basin is still carried northwards; but Mr. Findlay attributes this movement solely to the anti-trades—the south-west winds—which by their prevalence keep up a balance of progress in a north-easterly direction in the surface layer of the water.

Dr. Carpenter entertains a very strong opinion that the dispersion of the Gulf-stream may be affirmed to be complete in about lat. 45° N. and long. 35° W. Dr. Carpenter admits the accuracy of the projection of the isotherms on the maps of Berghaus, Dové Petermann, and Keith Johnston, and he admits likewise the conclusion that the abnormal mildness of the climate on the north-western coast of Europe is due to a movement of equatorial water in a north-easterly direction. "What I question is the correctness of the doctrine that the north-east flow is an extension or prolongation of the Gulf-stream, still driven on by the *vis a tergo* of the trade-winds—a doctrine which (greatly to my surprise) has been adopted and defended by my colleague Professor Wyville Thomson. But while these authorities attribute the whole or nearly the whole of this flow to the true Gulf-stream, *I* regard a large part, if not the whole, of that which takes place along our own western coast, and passes north and north-east between Iceland and Norway towards Spitzbergen, as quite independent of that agency; so that it would continue if the North and South American continents were so completely disunited that the equatorial currents would be driven straight onwards by the trade-winds into the Pacific Ocean, instead of being embayed in the Gulf of Mexico and driven out in a north-east direction through the 'narrows' off Cape Florida."[1] Dr. Carpenter does not mean by this to endorse Mr. Findlay's opinion that the movement beyond the 45th parallel of latitude is due solely to the drift of the anti-trades; he says, "On the view I advocate, the north-easterly flow is regarded as due to the *vis a fronte* originating in the action of cold upon the water of the polar area, whereby its level is always tending to depression."[2] The amelioration of the climate of north-western Europe is thus

[1] Dr. Carpenter: Proceedings of the Royal Geographical Society for 1870, op. cit.

[2] Op. cit.

caused by a 'modified case' of the general oceanic circulation, and neither by the Gulf-stream nor by the anti-trade drift.

Although there are, up to the present time, very few trustworthy observations of deep-sea temperatures, the surface temperature of the North Atlantic has been investigated with considerable care. The general character of the isothermal lines with their singular loop-like northern deflections, has long been familiar through the temperature charts of the geographers already quoted, and of late years a prodigious amount of data have been accumulated both abroad and by our own Admiralty and Meteorological Department.

In 1870, Dr. Petermann, of Gotha, published[1] an extremely valuable series of temperature charts, embodying the results of the reduction of upwards of 100,000 observations, derived chiefly from the following sources:—

1. From the wind and current charts of Lieutenant Maury, embodying about 30,000 distinct temperature observations.

2. From 50,000 observations made by Dutch sea-captains, and published by the Government of the Netherlands.

3. From the journal of the Cunard steamers between Liverpool and New York, and of the steamers of the Montreal Company between Glasgow and Belleisle.

4. From the data collected by the secretary of the

[1] Der Golf-Strom und Standpunkt der thermometrischen Kenntniss des Nord-Atlantischen Oceans und Landgebietes im Jahre 1870. Justus Perthe's 'Geographische Mittheilungen,' Band 16. Gotha, 1870.

Scottish Meteorological Society, Mr. Buchan, with regard to the temperature of the sea on the coasts of Scotland.

5. From the publications of the Norwegian Institute on sea-temperatures between Norway, Scotland, and Iceland.

6. From the data furnished by the Danish Rear-Admiral Irminger on sea-temperature between Denmark and the Danish settlements in Greenland.

7. From the observations made by Earl Dufferin on board his yacht 'Foam' between Scotland, Iceland, Spitzbergen, and Norway.

And finally, from the recent observations collected by the English, Swedish, German, and Russian expeditions to the arctic regions and towards the North Pole.

Dr. Petermann has devoted the special attention of a great part of his life to the distribution of heat on the surface of the ocean, and the accuracy and conscientiousness of his work in every detail are beyond the shadow of a doubt. Plate VII. is in the main copied from his charts, with a few modifications and additions derived from additional data. The remarkable diversion of the isothermal lines from their normal course is undoubtedly caused by surface ocean-currents conveying warm tropical water towards the polar regions. This is no matter of speculation, for the current is in many places perceptible through its effect on navigation, and the path of the warm water may be traced by dipping the thermometer into it and noting its temperature.

In the North Atlantic every curve of equal temperature, whether for the summer, for the winter, for a single month, or for the whole year, instantly declares itself as one of a system of curves which are referred to the Strait of Florida as a source of heat, and the flow of warm water may be traced in a continuous stream, indicated when its movement can no longer be observed by its form,—fanning out from the neighbourhood of the Strait across the Atlantic, skirting the coasts of France, Britain, and Scandinavia, rounding the North Cape and passing the White Sea and the Sea of Kari, bathing the western shores of Novaja Semla and Spitzbergen, and finally coursing round the coast of Siberia, a trace of it still remaining to find its way through the narrow and shallow Behring's Strait into the North Pacific (see Plate VII.).

Now, it seems to me that if we had only these curves upon the chart, deduced from an almost infinite number of observations which are themselves merely laboriously multiplied corroborations of many previous ones, without having any clue to their rationale, we should be compelled to admit that whatever might be the amount and distribution of heat derived from a general oceanic circulation,—whether produced by the prevailing winds of the region, by convection, by unequal barometric pressure, by tropical heat, or by arctic cold,—the Gulf-stream, the majestic stream of warm water whose course is indicated by the deflections of the isothermal lines, is sufficiently powerful to mask all the rest, and, broadly speaking, to produce of itself all the abnormal thermal phenomena.

The deep-sea temperatures taken in the 'Porcupine' have an important bearing upon this question, since they give us the depth and volume of the mass of water which is heated above its normal temperature, and which we must regard as the softener of the winds blowing on the coasts of Europe. Referring to Fig. 60, in the Bay of Biscay, after passing through a shallow band superheated by direct radiation, a zone of warm water extends to the depth of 800 fathoms, succeeded by cold water to a depth of nearly two miles. In the Rockall channel (Fig. 59) the warm layer has nearly the same thickness, and the cold underlying water is 500 fathoms deep. Off the Butt of the Lews (Fig. 56) the bottom temperature is 5°·2 C. at 767 fathoms, so that there the warm layer evidently reaches to the bottom. In the Færoe channel (Fig. 55) the warm water forms a surface layer, and the cold water underlies it, commencing at a depth of 200 fathoms,—567 fathoms above the level of the bottom of the warm water off the Butt of the Lews. The cold water abuts against the warm—there is no barrier between them. Part of the warm water flows over the cold indraught, and forms the upper layer in the Færoe channel. What prevents the cold water from slipping, by virtue of its greater weight, under the warm water off the Butt of the Lews? It is quite evident that there must be some force at work keeping the warm water in that particular position, or, if it be moving, compelling it to follow that particular course. The comparatively high temperature from 100 fathoms to 900 fathoms I have always attributed to the northern accumulation of the water of the Gulf-stream. The amount of heat derived directly from the sun by the water as it passes through any particular region, must be regarded, as I have already said, as depending almost entirely upon latitude. Taking this into account, the surface temperatures in what we were in the habit of calling the 'warm area' coincided precisely with Petermann's curves indicating the northward path of the Gulf-stream.

I extract the following from a letter dated 23rd September, 1872, from Professor H. Mohn, director of the Norwegian Meteorological Institute at Christiania, to Mr. Buchan, the excellent secretary of the Scottish Meteorological Society:—"I have this summer got some deep-sea temperatures which may be of general interest for our climate. In the Throndhjems-fjord I found 16°·5 C. on the surface, and from 50 fathoms to the bottom (200 fathoms) a very uniform temperature of 6°·5 C. in one place, and 6° C. in another place further in. In the Sœguefjord I found 16° C. on the surface, and 6°·5 C. constantly from 10 to 700 fathoms. Between Iceland and Færoe, Lieutenant Müller, commander of the Bergen and Iceland steamer, has found this summer 8° C. at the bottom in 300 fathoms. This proves that the Gulf-stream water fills the whole of the channel, contrary to what is the case in the Færoe-Shetland channel, where there is ice-cold water in a depth of 300 fathoms." The facts here mentioned are very important, and entirely confirm our results; but my chief object in giving the quotation is to show the unhesitating way in which the explanation which attributes the high temperature of the sea on the Scandinavian coast to the Gulf-stream is adopted by those best qualified to form an opinion.

The North Atlantic and Arctic seas form together a *cul de sac* closed to the northward, for there is practically no passage for a body of water through Behring's Strait. While, therefore, a large portion of the water, finding no free outlet towards the north-east, turns southward at the Açores, the remainder, instead of thinning off, has rather a tendency to accumulate against the coasts bounding the northern portions of the trough. We accordingly find that it has a depth off the west coast of Iceland of at least 4,800 feet, with an unknown lateral extension. Dr. Carpenter, discussing this opinion, says: "It is to me physically inconceivable that this surface film of *lighter* (because warmer) water should collect itself together again—even supposing it still to retain any excess of temperature—and should burrow downwards into the 'trough,' *displacing colder and heavier water*, to a depth much greater than that which it possesses at the point of its greatest 'glory'—its passage through the Florida Narrows. The upholders of this hypothesis have to explain how such a re-collection and dipping-down of the Gulf-stream water is to be accounted for on physical principles."[1] I believe that as a rule, experimental imitations on a small scale are of little use in the illustration of natural phenomena; a very simple experiment will, however, show that such a process is possible. If we put a tablespoonful of cochineal into a can of hot water, so as to give it a red tint, and then run it through a piece of india-rubber tube with a considerable impulse along the surface of a quantity of cold water in a bath, we see

[1] Dr. Carpenter's Address to Geographical Society, op. cit.

the red stream widening out and becoming paler over the general surface of the water till it reaches the opposite edge, and very shortly the rapidly heightening colour of a band along the opposite wall indicates an accumulation of the coloured water where its current is arrested. If we now dip the hand into the water of the centre of the bath, a warm bracelet merely encircles the wrist; while at the end of the bath opposite the warm influx, the hot water, though considerably mixed, envelopes the whole hand.

The North Atlantic forms a basin closed to the northward. Into the corner of this basin, as into a bath,—with a north-easterly direction given to it by its initial velocity, as if the supply pipe of the bath were turned so as to give the hot water a definite impulse,—this enormous flood is poured, day and night, winter and summer. When the basin is full —and not till then—overcoming its northern impulse, the surplus water turns southwards in a southern eddy, so that there is a certain tendency for the hot water to accumulate in the northern basin, to 'bank down'[1] along the north-eastern coasts.

It is scarcely necessary to say that for every unit of water which enters the basin of the North Atlantic, and which is not evaporated, an equivalent must return. As cold water can gravitate into the deeper parts of the ocean from all directions, it is only under peculiar circumstances that any movement having the character of a current is induced;

[1] Ocean Currents. An Address delivered to the Royal United Service Institution June 15th, 1871. By J. K. Laughton, M.A., Naval Instructor at the Royal Naval College. (From the Journal of the Institution, vol. xv.)

these circumstances occur, however, in the confined and contracted communication between the North Atlantic and the Arctic Sea. Between Cape Farewell and North Cape there are only two channels of any considerable depth, the one very narrow along the east coast of Iceland, and the other along the east coast of Greenland. The shallow part of the sea is entirely occupied, at all events during summer, by the warm water of the Gulf-stream, except at one point, where a rapid current of cold water, very restricted and very shallow, sweeps round the south of Spitzbergen and then dips under the Gulf-stream water at the northern entrance of the German Ocean.

This cold flow, at first a current, finally a mere indraught, affects greatly the temperature of the German Ocean; but it is entirely lost, for the slight current which is again produced by the great contraction at the Strait of Dover, has a summer temperature of 7°·5 C. The path of the cold indraught from Spitzbergen may be readily traced on the map by the depressions in the surface isothermal lines, and in dredging by the abundance of gigantic amphipodous and isopodous crustaceans, and other well-known Arctic animal forms.

From its low initial velocity the Arctic return current, or indraught, must doubtless tend slightly in a westerly direction, and the higher specific gravity of the cold water may probably even more powerfully lead it into the deepest channels; or possibly the two causes may combine, and in the course of ages the currents may hollow out deep south-westerly grooves. At all events, the main Arctic return currents are very visible on the chart taking this direction, indicated by marked deflections of the isothermal lines. The most marked is the Labrador current, which passes down inside the Gulf-stream along the coasts of Carolina and New Jersey, meeting it in the strange abrupt 'cold wall,' dipping under it as it issues from the Gulf, coming to the surface again on the other side, and a portion of it actually passing, under the Gulf-stream, as a cold counter-current into the Gulf of Mexico.

Fifty or sixty miles out from the west coast of Scotland, I believe the Gulf-stream forms another, though a very mitigated, 'cold wall.' In 1868, after our first investigation of the very remarkable cold indraught into the channel between Shetland and Færoe, I stated my belief that the current was entirely banked up in the Færoe Channel by the Gulf-stream passing its gorge. Since that time I have been led to suspect that a part of the Arctic water oozes down the Scottish coast, much mixed, and sufficiently shallow to be affected throughout by solar radiation. About sixty or seventy miles from shore the isothermal lines have a slight but uniform deflection. Within that line types characteristic of the Scandinavian fauna are numerous in shallow water, and in the course of many years' use of the towing net I have never met with any of the Gulf-stream pteropods, or of the lovely Polycystina and Acanthometrina which absolutely swarm beyond that limit. The difference in mean temperature between the east and west coasts of Scotland, amounting to about 1° C., is also somewhat less than might be expected if the Gulf-stream came close to the western shore.

While the communication between the North Atlantic, and the Arctic Sea—itself a second *cul de sac*—is thus restricted, limiting the interchange of warm and cold water in the normal direction of the flow of the Gulf-stream, and causing the diversion of a large part of the stream to the southwards, the communication with the Antarctic basin is as open as the day;—a continuous and wide valley upwards of 2,000 fathoms in depth stretching northwards along the western coasts of Africa and Europe.

That the southern water wells up into this valley there could be little doubt from the form of the ground; but here again we have curious corroborative evidence on the map in the remarkable reversal of the curves of the isotherms. The temperature of the bottom water at 1,230 fathoms off Rockall is 3°·22 C., exactly the same as that of water at the same depth in the serial sounding, lat. 47° 38′ N., long. 12° 08′ W. in the Bay of Biscay, which affords a strong presumption that the water in both cases is derived from the same source; and the bottom water off Rockall is warmer than the bottom water in the Bay of Biscay (2°·5 C.), while a cordon of temperature soundings drawn from the north-west of Scotland to a point on the Iceland shallow gives no temperature lower than 6°·5 C. This makes it very improbable that the low temperature of the Bay of Biscay is due to any considerable portion of the Spitzbergen current passing down the west coast of Scotland; and as the cold current to the east of Iceland passes southwards considerably to the westward, as indicated on the map by the successive depressions in the surface isotherms, the balance of probability seems to be in favour of the view that the conditions of temperature and the slow movement of this vast mass of moderately cold water, nearly two statute miles in depth, are to be referred to an Antarctic rather than to an Arctic origin.

The North Atlantic Ocean seems to consist first of a great sheet of warm water, the general northerly reflux of the equatorial current. Of this the greater part passes through the Strait of Florida, and its north-easterly flow is aided and maintained by the anti-trades, the whole being generally called the Gulf-stream. This layer is of varying depths, apparently from the observations of Captain Chimmo and others, thinning to a hundred fathoms or so in the mid-Atlantic, but attaining a depth of 700 to 800 fathoms off the west coasts of Ireland and Spain. Secondly of a 'stratum of intermixture' which extends to about 200 fathoms in the Bay of Biscay, through which the temperature falls rather rapidly; and thirdly, of an underlying mass of cold water, in the Bay of Biscay 1,500 fathoms deep, derived as an indraught falling in by gravitation from the deepest available source, whether Arctic or Antarctic. It seems at first sight a startling suggestion, that the cold water filling deep ocean valleys in the northern hemisphere may be partly derived from the southern; but this difficulty, I believe, arises from the idea that there is a kind of diaphragm at the equator between the northern and southern ocean basins, one of the many misconceptions which follow in the train of a notion of a convective circulation in the sea similar to that in the atmosphere. There is undoubtedly a gradual elevation of an intertropical belt of the underlying cold water, which is being raised by the subsiding of still colder water into its bed to supply the place of the water removed by the equatorial current and by excessive evaporation; but such a movement must be widely and irregularly diffused and excessively slow, not in any sense comparable with the diaphragm produced in the atmosphere by the rushing upwards of the north-east and south-east trade-winds in the zone of calms. Perhaps one of the most conclusive proofs of the extreme slowness of the movement of the deep indraught is the nature of the bottom. Over a great part of the floor of the Atlantic a deposit is being formed of microscopic shells. These with their living inhabitants differ little in specific weight from the water itself, and form a creamy flocculent layer, which must be at once removed wherever there is a perceptible movement. In water of moderate depth, in the course of any of the currents, this deposit is entirely absent, and is replaced by coarser or finer gravel.

It is only on the surface of the sea that a line is drawn between the two hemispheres by the equatorial current, whose effect in shedding a vast intertropical drift of water on either side as it breaks against the eastern shores of equatorial land may be seen at a glance on the most elementary physical chart.

The Gulf-stream loses an enormous amount of heat in its northern tour. At a point 200 miles west of Ushant, where observations at the greatest depths were made on board the 'Porcupine,' a section of the water of the Atlantic shows three surfaces at which interchange of temperature is taking place.

First, the surface of the sea—that is to say, the upper surface of the Gulf-stream layer—is losing heat rapidly by radiation, by contact with a layer of air which is in constant motion and being perpetually cooled by convection, and by the conversion of water into vapour.[1] As this cooling of the Gulf-stream layer takes place principally at the surface, the temperature of the mass is kept pretty uniform by convection. Secondly, the band of contact of the lower surface of the Gulf-stream water with the upper surface of the cold indraught. Here the interchange of temperature must be very slow, though that it does take place is shown by the slight depression of the surface isotherms over the principal paths of the indraught. But there is a good deal of intermixture extending through a considerable layer. The cold water being beneath, convection in the ordinary sense cannot occur, and interchange of temperature must depend mainly upon conduction and diffusion, causes which in the case of masses of water must be almost secular in their action, and probably to a much greater extent upon mixture produced by local currents and by the tides. The third surface is that of contact between the cold indraught and the bottom of the sea. The temperature of the crust of the earth has been variously calculated at from 4° to 11° C., but it must be completely cooled down by anything like a movement and constant renewal of cold water.

[1] On Deep-sea Climates. The Substance of a Lecture delivered to the Natural Science Class in Queen's College, Belfast, at the close of the Summer Session 1870, by Professor Wyville Thomson. (*Nature*, July 28th, 1870.)

All we can say, therefore, is that contact with the bottom can never be a source of depression of temperature. As a general result the Gulf-stream water is nearly uniform in temperature throughout the greater part of its depth; there is a marked zone of intermixture at the junction between the warm water and the cold, and the water of the cold indraught is regularly stratified by gravitation; so that in deep water the contour lines of the sea-bottom are, speaking generally, lines of equal temperature. Keeping in view the enormous influence which ocean currents exercise in the distribution of climates at the present time, I think it is scarcely going too far to suppose that such currents—movements communicated to the water by constant winds—existed at all geological periods as the great means, I had almost said the sole means, of producing a general oceanic circulation, and thus distributing heat in the ocean. They must have existed, in fact, wherever equatorial land interrupted the path of the drift of the trade-winds. Wherever a warm current was deflected to north or south from the equatorial belt a polar indraught crept in beneath to supply its place; and the ocean consequently consisted, as in the Atlantic and doubtless in the Pacific at the present day, of an upper warm stratum, and a lower layer of cold water becoming gradually colder with increasing depth.

I fear, then, that in opposition to the views of my distinguished colleague, I must repeat that I have seen as yet no reason to modify the opinion which I have consistently held from the first, that the remarkable conditions of climate on the coasts of Northern Europe are due in a broad sense solely to the Gulf-stream. That is to say, that although movements, some of them possibly of considerable importance, must be produced by differences of specific gravity, yet the influence of the great current which we call the Gulf-stream, the reflux of the great equatorial current, is so paramount as to reduce all other causes to utter insignificance.

THE GIANT AND THE HAG.

CHAPTER IX.

THE DEEP-SEA FAUNA.

The Protozoa of the Deep-sea.—*Bathybius.*—'Coccoliths,' and 'Coccospheres.'—The Foraminifera of the Warm and Cold Areas.—Deep-sea Sponges.—The Hexactinellidæ.—*Rossella.*—*Hyalonema.*—Deep-sea Corals.—The Stalked Crinoids.—*Pentacrinus.*—*Rhizocrinus.*—*Bathycrinus.*—The Star-fishes of the Deep-sea.—The general Distribution and Relations of Deep-sea Urchins.—The Crustacea, the Mollusca, and the Fishes of the 'Porcupine' Expeditions.

THE time has not yet arrived for giving anything like a detailed account of the deep-sea fauna; even if it were possible to do so in a popular sketch of the general results of a wide investigation. I must therefore confine myself at present to a brief outline of the distribution of the forms of animal life which were met with in the belt partially examined during the 'Porcupine' dredgings, a belt which carries the British zoological area about a hundred miles further out to seaward along the northern and western coasts of the British Isles, and into depths extending from 200 fathoms, the previous limit of accurate knowledge, to 800 and 1,000 fathoms, and in one or two instances to the extreme depth of upwards of 2,000 fathoms.

The remarkable general result that even to these great depths the fauna is varied and rich in all the marine invertebrate groups, has inundated us with new material which in several of the larger departments it will take years of the labour of specialists to work up. While referring very briefly to those orders which it has been found impossible as yet to overtake, I will enter a little more fully into the history of certain restricted groups which more particularly illustrate the conditions of the abyssal region, and the relations of its special fauna to the faunæ of other zoological provinces, or to those of earlier times. And very prominent among these special groups we find the first and simplest of the invertebrate sub-kingdoms, the Protozoa, represented by three of its classes,—the monera, the rhizopoda, and the sponges.

The monera have been lately defined as a distinct class by Professor Ernst Haeckel,[1] for a vast assemblage of almost formless beings, apparently absolutely devoid of internal structure, and consisting simply of living and moving expansions of jelly-like protoplasm; and although the special character on which Haeckel separates them from the remainder of the protozoa,—that they are propagated by no form of sexual reproduction, but simply by spontaneous division,—may probably prove deceptive as our knowledge increases, still their number, their general resemblance to one another, presenting obviously different and recognizable kinds although with very indefinable characters, and the important part which

[1] Biologische Studien. Von Dr. Ernst Haeckel, Professor an der Universität Jena. Leipzig, 1870.

they play in the economy of nature, would seem to entitle them to a systematic position of more than ordinal value. The German naturalists of the new school, in their enthusiastic adoption of the Darwinian theory of evolution, naturally welcome in these 'moners' the essential attribute of the 'Urschleim,' an infinite capacity for improvement in every conceivable direction; and to more prosaic physiologists they are of the deepest interest, as presenting the essential phenomena of life, nutrition and irritability, existing apparently simply as the properties of a homogeneous chemical compound, and independent of organization.

The monera pass into the rhizopoda, which give a slight indication of advance, in the definite form of the graceful calcareous shell-like structures which most of them secrete, and the two groups may be taken together.

The dredging at 2,435 fathoms at the mouth of the Bay of Biscay gave a very fair idea of the condition of the bottom of the sea over an enormous area, as we know from many observations which have now been made, with the various sounding instruments contrived to bring up a sample of the bottom. On that occasion the dredge brought up about 1½ cwt. of calcareous mud. There could be little doubt, from the appearance of the contents of the dredge, that the heavy dredge-frame had gone down with a plunge, and partly buried itself in the soft, yielding bottom. The throat of the dredge thus became partly choked, and the free entrance of the organisms on the sea-floor had been thus prevented. The matter contained in the dredge consisted mainly of a compact 'mortar,' of a bluish colour, passing into a thin—evidently superficial—layer, much softer and more creamy in consistence, and of a yellowish colour. Under the microscope the surface-layer was found to consist chiefly of entire shells of *Globigerina bulloides* (Fig. 2, p. 22), large and small, and fragments of such shells mixed with a quantity of amorphous calcareous matter in fine particles, a little fine sand, and many spicules, portions of spicules, and shells of Radiolaria, a few spicules of sponges, and a few frustules of diatoms. Below the surface-layer the sediment becomes gradually more compact, and a slight grey colour, due probably to the decomposing organic matter, becomes more pronounced, while perfect shells of globigerina almost entirely disappear, fragments become smaller, and calcareous mud, structureless and in a fine state of division, is in greatly preponderating proportion. One can have no doubt, on examining this sediment, that it is formed in the main by the accumulation and disintegration of the shells of globigerina—the shells fresh, whole, and living in the surface-layer of the deposit, and in the lower layers dead, and gradually crumbling down by the decomposition of their organic cement, and by the pressure of the layers above—an animal formation in fact being formed very much in the same way as in the accumulation of vegetable matter in a peat bog, by life and growth above, and death, retarded decomposition, and compression beneath.

In this dredging, as in most others in the bed of the Atlantic, there was evidence of a considerable quantity of soft gelatinous organic matter, enough to give a slight viscosity to the mud of the surface layer. If the mud be shaken with weak spirit of wine, fine flakes separate like coagulated mucus; and if a little of the mud in which this viscid condition is most marked be placed in a drop of sea-water under the microscope, we can usually see, after a time, an irregular network of matter resembling white of egg, distinguishable by its maintaining its outline and not mixing with the water. This network may be seen gradually altering in form, and entangled granules and foreign bodies change their relative positions. The gelatinous matter is therefore capable of a certain amount of movement, and there can be no doubt that it manifests the phenomena of a very simple form of life.

To this organism, if a being can be so called which shows no trace of differentiation of organs, consisting apparently of an amorphous sheet of a protein compound, irritable to a low degree and capable of assimilating food, Professor Huxley has given the name of *Bathybius haeckelii* (Fig. 63). If this have a claim to be recognized as a distinct living entity, exhibiting its mature and final form, it must be referred to the simplest division of the shell-less rhizopoda, or if we adopt the class proposed by Professor Haeckel, to the monera. The circumstance which gives its special interest to Bathybius is its enormous extent: whether it be continuous in one vast sheet, or broken up into circumscribed individual particles, it appears to extend over a large part of the bed of the ocean; and as no living thing, however slowly it may live, is ever perfectly at rest, but is continually acting and reacting with its surroundings, the bottom of the sea becomes like the surface of the sea and of the land,—a theatre of change, performing its part in maintaining the 'balance of organic nature.'

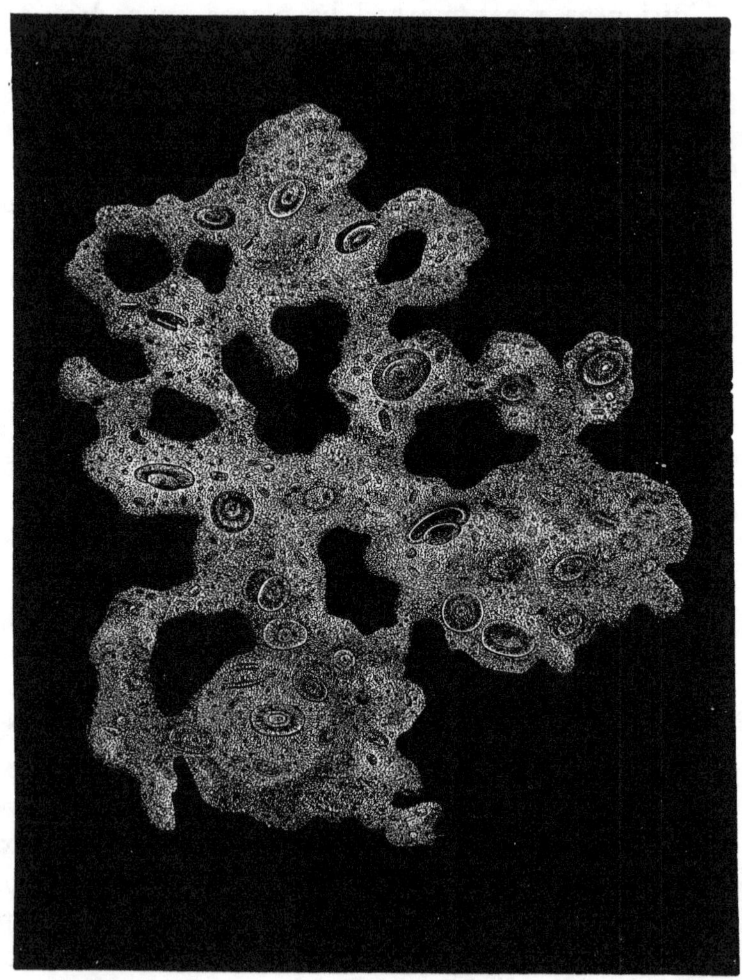

FIG. 63.—"Eine grössere Cytode von Bathybius mit eingebetteten Coccolithen. Das Protoplasma, welches viele Discolithen und Cyatholithen enthält, bildet ein Netzwerk mit breiten Strängen.' (x. 700.)[1]

[1] Biologische Studien. Von Dr. Ernst Haeckel, Professor an der Universität Jena. Leipzig, 1870.

Entangled and borne along in the viscid streams of Bathybius, we so constantly find a multitude of minute calcareous bodies of a peculiar shape, that the two were for long supposed to have some mutual relation to one another. These small bodies, which have been carefully studied by Huxley,[1] Sorby,[2] Haeckel,[3] Carter,[4] Gümbel,[5] and others, are in shape somewhat like oval shirt-studs. There is first a little oval disk about 0·01 mm. in length, with an oblong rudely facetted elevation in the centre, and round that, in fresh specimens, what seems to be a kind of frill of organic matter, then a short neck, and lastly a second smaller flat disk, like the disk at the back of a stud. To these bodies, which are met with in all stages of development, Professor Huxley has given the name of 'coccoliths.' Sometimes they are found aggregated on the surface of small transparent membranous balls, and these which seemed at first to have something to do with the production of the 'coccoliths' Dr. Wallich has called 'coccospheres' (Fig. 64). Professor Ernst Haeckel has lately described a very elegant organism belonging to the radiolaria and apparently allied to *Thalassicolla,—Myxobrachia rhopalum,*—and at the ends of some curious diverging appendages of this creature he has detected accumulations of bodies closely resembling, if not identical with, the coccoliths and coccospheres of the sea-bottom. These

[1] Quarterly Journal of Microscopical Science, 1868, p. 203.

[2] Proceedings of the Sheffield Literary and Philosophical Society, October 1860.

[3] Op. cit.

[4] Ann. and Mag. Nat. Hist. 1871, p. 184.

[5] Jahrbuch Münch. 1870, p. 753.

bodies seem to have been taken in to the *Myxobrachia* as food, the hard parts accumulating in cavities in the animal's body after all the available nourishment had been absorbed. It is undoubted that a large number of the organisms whose skeletons are mixed with the ooze of the bottom of the sea live on the surface, the delicate silicious or calcareous shields or spines falling gradually through

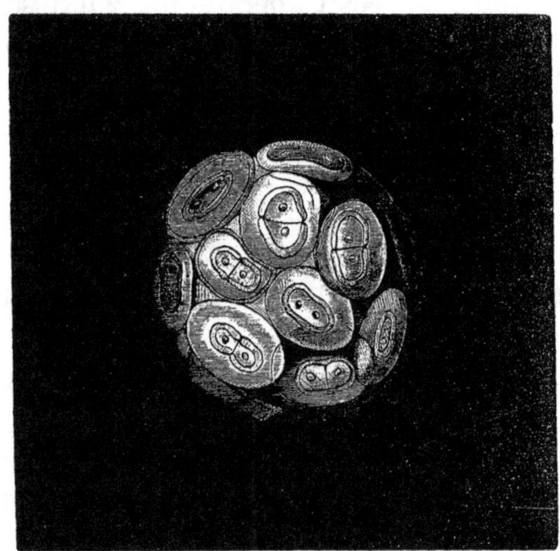

FIG. 64.—'Coccosphere.' (x. 1000.)

the water and finally reaching the bottom, whatever be the depth. I think that now the balance of opinion is in favour of the view that the coccoliths are joints of a minute unicellular alga living on the sea-surface and sinking down and mixing with the sarcode of *Bathybius*, very probably taken into it with a purpose, for the sake of the vegetable matter they may contain, and which may afford food for the animal jelly. What the coccospheres are, and what relation, if any, they have to the coccoliths, we do not know.

Living upon and among this *Bathybius*, we find a multitude of other protozoa,—foraminifera and other rhizopods, radiolarians, and sponges; and we as yet know very little of the life-history of these groups. There can be no doubt that when their development has been fully traced many of them will be found to be di- or poly-morphic, and that when we are acquainted with their mode of multiplication we shall meet with many cases of pleomorphism and wide differences between the organs and products involved in propagation and in reproduction. I feel by no means satisfied that *Bathybius* is the permanent form of any distinct living being. It has seemed to me that different samples have been different in appearance and consistence; and although there is nothing at all improbable in the abundance of a very simple shell-less 'moner' at the bottom of the sea, I think it not impossible that a great deal of the 'bathybius,' that is to say the diffused formless protoplasm which we find at great depths, may be a kind of mycelium—a formless condition connected either with the growth and multiplication or with the decay—of many different things.

Many foraminifera of different groups inhabit the deep water, lying upon or mixed in the upper layer of the globigerina ooze, or fixed to some foreign body, such as a sponge, coral, or stone; and all of these are remarkable for their large size. In the 'warm area,' and wherever the bottom is covered with ooze, calcareous forms predominate, and large sandy cristellarians, with their sand-grains bound together by calcareous cement, so that the sand-grains show out, dark and conspicuous, scattered on the surface of the white shell. Miliolines are abundant, and the specimens of *Cornuspira* and *Biloculina* are greatly larger than anything which has been hitherto met with in temperate regions, recalling the tropical forms which abound among the Pacific Islands.

In the cold area, and in the paths of cold currents, foraminifera with sandy tests are more numerous; some of those of the genera *Astrorhiza*, *Lituola*, and *Botellina* are gigantic—large examples 30 mm. long by 8 mm. in diameter.

The few hauls of the dredge which we have already had in deep water have been enough to teach us that our knowledge of sponges is in its infancy,—that those which we have collected from shallow water along our shores, and even those few which have been brought up from deep water on fishing lines, and have surprised us by the beauty of their forms and the delicacy of their lustre, are the mere margin and remnant of a wonderfully diversified sponge-fauna which appears to extend in endless variety over the whole of the bottom of the sea. I cannot attempt here more than a mere outline of the general character of the additions which have been made to our knowledge of this group. The sponges of the 'Porcupine' Expedition are now in the hands of Mr. Henry Carter, F.R.S., for description; and an excellent sketch of the sponge-fauna of the deep Atlantic, bringing information on certain groups up to a late date, has been published by the best authority we have on sponges, Professor Oscar Schmidt of Gratz.

As I have already said, the most remarkable new forms are referable to the group which seems to be, in a sense special to deep water, the Hexactinellidæ. I have already (p. 70) briefly described one of the most abundant and singular forms belonging to this order, *Holtenia carpenteri;* and all the others, though running through most remarkable variations in form and general appearance, agree with *Holtenia* in essential structure. In the Hexactinellidæ all the spicules, so far as we know, are formed on the hexradiate plan; that is to say, there is a primary axis, which may be long or short, and at one point four secondary rays cross this central shaft at right angles. Very often one-half of the central shaft is absent or is represented by a slight rounded boss, and in that case we have a spicule with a cross-shaped head, a very favourite form in the manufacture, defence, and ornament of the surface layer of these sponges; and often the secondary rays are undeveloped: but if that be so,—as in the long fibres of the whisp of *Hyalonema,*—in young spicules and in others which are slightly abnormal, four little elevations near the middle of the spicule, which contain four secondary branches of the central canal, maintain the permanence of the type. In many of the Hexactinellidæ the spicules are all distinct, and combined, as in *Holtenia,* by a small quantity of nearly transparent sarcode; but in others, as in 'Venus's flower-basket,' and the nearly equally beautiful genera *Iphiteon, Aphrocallistes,* and *Farrea,* the spicules run together and make a continuous silicious network. When this is the case the sponge may be boiled in nitric acid, and all the organic matter and other impurities thus removed, when the skeleton comes out a lovely lacy structure of the clearest glass. The six-rayed form of the spicules gives the network which is the result of their fusion great flexibility of design, with a characteristic tendency, however, to square meshes.

On the 30th of August, 1870, Mr. Gwyn Jeffreys dredged in 651 fathoms in the Atlantic off the mouth of the Strait of Gibraltar an exquisite sponge, resembling *Holtenia* in its general appearance, but differing from it in the singular and beautiful character of having a delicate outer veil about a centimetre from the surface of the sponge, formed by the interlacing of the four secondary rays of large five-rayed spicules, which send their long shafts from that point vertically into the sponge body (Fig. 65). The surface of the sponge is formed of a network of large five-radiate spicules, arranged very much as in *Holtenia;* but the spicules of the sarcode—the small spicules which are imbedded in the living sponge-jelly—are of a totally different form. A single large 'osculum' opens, as in *Holtenia*, at the top of the sponge, but instead of forming a cup uniformly lined with a netted membrane, the oscular cavity divides at the bottom into a number of branching passages as in *Pheronema annæ*, described by Dr. Leidy. I was inclined at first to place this species in the genus *Pheronema*, but Dr. Leidy's description and figure are by no means satisfactory, and may refer to some other form of the *Holtenia* group. The spicules of the 'beard' are more rigid and thicker than those of *Holtenia*, and scattered among them are some very large four-barbed grappling hooks.

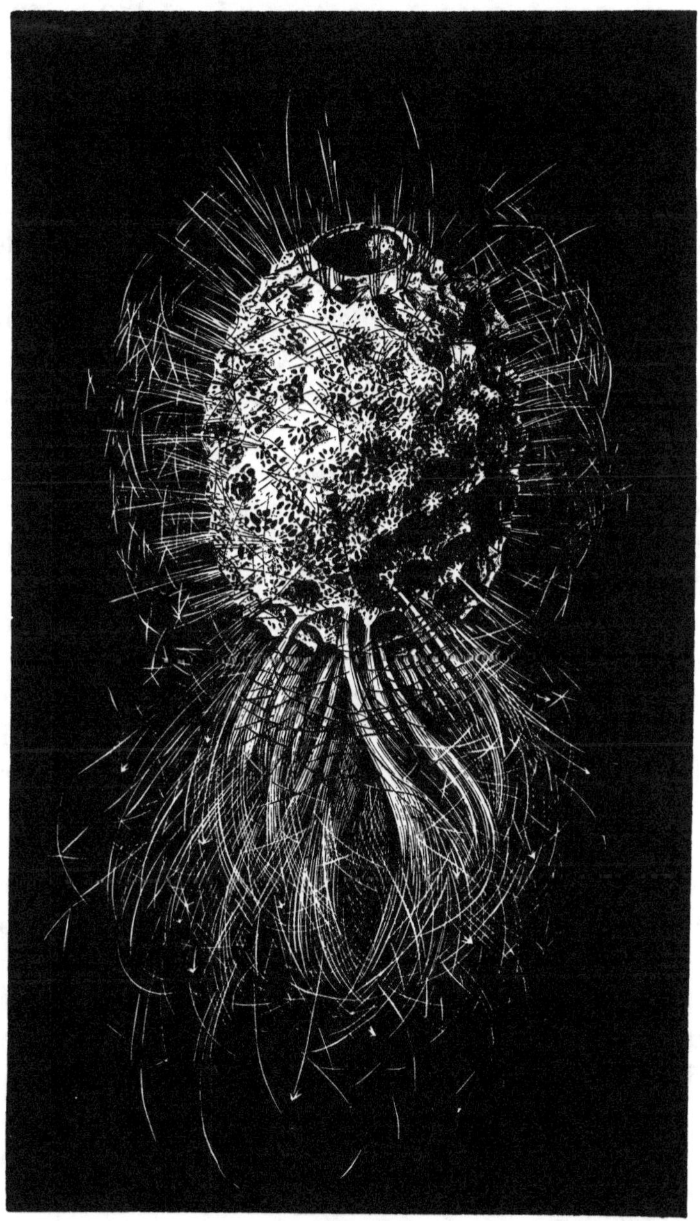

FIG. 65.—*Rossella velata*, WYVILLE THOMSON. Natural size. (No. 82, 1870.)

Off the Butt of the Lews, in water of 450 to 500 fathoms, we met on two occasions with full-grown specimens of a species of the remarkable genus *Hyalonema* (Fig. 66), with the coils in the larger examples upwards of 40 centimetres in length. *Hyalonema* is certainly a very striking object; and although our specimens belong apparently to the same species, *H. lusitanicum*, which has already been recorded by Professor Barboza du Bocage from the coast of Portugal, it is one of the most interesting additions made to the British fauna during our cruise.

A bundle of from 200 to 300 threads of transparent silica, glistening with a silky lustre, like the most brilliant spun-glass,—each thread from 30 to 40 centimetres long, in the middle the thickness of a knitting needle, and gradually tapering towards either end to a fine point; the whole bundle coiled like a strand of rope into a lengthened spiral, the threads of the middle and upper portions remaining compactly coiled by a permanent twist of the individual threads; the lower part of the coil, which, when the sponge is living, is imbedded in the mud, frayed out so that the glassy threads stand separate from one another, like the bristles of a glittering brush; the upper portion of the coil close and compact, imbedded perpendicularly in a conical or cylindrical sponge; and usually part of the upper portion of the silicious coil, and part of the sponge-substance, covered with a brownish leathery coating, whose surface is studded with the polyps of an alcyonarian zoophyte:—such is the general effect of a complete specimen of *Hyalonema*.

Fig. 66.—*Hyalonema lusitanicum*, Barboza du Bocage. Half the natural size. (No. 90, 1869.

The genus was first known in Europe by specimens brought from Japan by the celebrated naturalist and traveller, Von Siebold; and Japanese examples of *Hyalonema sieboldi*, GRAY, may now be found more or less perfect in most of the European museums. When the first specimen of *Hyalonema* was brought home, the other vitreous sponges which approach it so closely in all essential points of structure were unknown, and the history of opinion as to its relations is curious.

The being consisted of three very distinct parts: first, and greatly the most remarkable, the coil of silicious needles; then the sponge, and for long it was supposed that this was the base of the structure,—from which the glossy brush projected, spreading out above it in the water; and thirdly, the apparently constant encrusting zoophyte.

This complicated association suggested many possibilities. Was *Hyalonema* a natural production at all? Was it complete? Were all the three parts essentially connected together? And if not, were all the three independent, or did two of three parts belong to the same thing? and if so, which two?

Hyalonema was first described and named in 1835 by Dr. John Edward Gray, who has since, in one or two notices in the 'Annals of Natural History' and elsewhere, vigorously defended the essential part of his original position. Dr. Gray associated the silicious whisp with the zoophyte, and regarded the sponge as a separate organism. He looked upon the silicious coil as the representative of the horny axis of the sea-fans (*Gorgoniæ*), and the leather-like coat he regarded as its fleshy rind. He supposed that between this zoophyte and the sponge at its base, there subsisted a relation of guest and host, the zoophyte being constantly associated with the sponge; and in accordance with this view he proposed for the reception of the zoophyte a new group of alcyonarians under the name of 'Spongicolæ,' as distinguished from the 'Sabulicolæ' (*Pennatulæ*) and the 'Rupicolæ' (*Gorgoniæ*).

Dr. Gray's view seemed in many respects a natural one, and it was adopted in the main by Dr. Brandt of St. Petersburg, who in 1859 published a long memoir, describing a number of specimens brought from Japan to Russia. Dr. Brandt referred what he believed to be a zoophyte consisting of the coil and the crust, to a special group of sclerobasic zoanthcarians with a silicious axis.

One consideration militated strongly against this hypothesis of Dr. Gray and Professor Brandt. No known zoophyte had a purely silicious axis; and such an axis made up of loose separate spicules seemed strangely inconsistent with the harmony of the class. On the other hand, silicious spicules of all forms and sizes were conceivable in sponges; and in 1857 Professor Milne-Edwards, on the authority of Valenciennes, who was thoroughly versed in the structure of the *Gorgoniæ*, combined the sponge with the silicious rope, and degraded the zoophyte to the rank of an encrusting parasite.

Anything very strange coming from Japan is to be regarded with some distrust. The Japanese are wonderfully ingenious, and one favourite aim of their misdirected industry is the fabrication of impossible monsters by the curious combination of the parts of different animals. It was therefore quite possible that the whole thing might be an imposition: that some beautiful spicules separated from an unknown organism had been twisted into a whisp by the Japanese, and then manipulated so as to have their fibres naturally bound together by the sponges and zoophytes which are doubtless rapidly developed in the Mongolian rock-pools. Ehrenberg, when he examined *Hyalonema*, took this view. He at once recognized the silicious strands as the spicules of a sponge quite independent of the zoophyte with which they were encrusted; but he suggested that these might have been artificially combined into the spiral coil and placed under artificial circumstances favourable to the growth of a sponge of a different species round their base. The condition in which many specimens reach Europe is certainly calculated to throw some doubt on their genuineness. It seems that the bundles of spicules made up in various ways, are largely sold as ornaments in China and Japan. The coils of spicules are often stuck upright with their upper ends in circular holes in stones. Mr. Huxley exhibited a few years ago at the Linnæan Society a beautiful specimen of this kind now in the British Museum:—a stone has been bored, probably by a colony of boring molluscs, and a whole colony of *Hyalonemas*, old and young, are apparently growing out of the burrows, the larger individuals more than a foot in length, and the young ones down to an inch or so, like tiny camel's-hair pencils. All these are encrusted by the usual zoophyte, which also extends here and there over the stone (glued on probably), but there is no trace of the sponge. Such an association is undoubtedly artificial.

Dr. Bowerbank, another great sponge authority, takes yet another view. He maintains "that the silicious axis, its envelopment, and the basal sponge are all parts of the same animal." The polyps he regards as 'oscula,' forming with the coil a 'columnar cloacal system.'

Professor Max Schultze, of Bonn, examined with great care several perfect and imperfect specimens of *Hyalonema* in the Museum of Leyden, and in 1860 published an elaborate description of its structure. According to Schultze, the conical sponge is the body-mass of *Hyalonema*, a sponge allied in every respect to *Euplectella*; and the siliceous coil is an appendage of the sponge formed of modified spicules. The zoophyte is of course a distinct animal altogether, and its only connection with the sponge is one of 'commensalism.' It 'chums' with the sponge for some purpose of its own,—certainly getting support from the coil, probably sharing the oxygen and organic matters carried in by the ciliary system of the sponge passages. This style of association is very common. We have another example of the same thing in *Palythoa axinellæ*, SCHMIDT, a constant 'commensal' with *Axinella cinnamomea* and *A. verrucosa*, two Adriatic sponges.

In 1864 Professor Barboza du Bocage, director of the Museum of Natural History in Lisbon, communicated to the Zoological Society of London the unexpected news that a species of *Hyalonema* had been discovered off the coast of Portugal; and in 1865 he published, in the Proceedings of the same Society, an additional note on the habitat of *Hyalonema lusitanicum.* It appears that the fishermen of Setubal frequently bring up on their lines, from a considerable depth, coils of silicious threads closely resembling those of the Japanese species, which they even surpass in size, sometimes attaining a length of about 50 centimetres. The fishermen seem to be very familiar with them. They call them 'sea-whips,' but with the characteristic superstition of their class they regard all these extraneous matters as 'unlucky,' and usually tear them in pieces and throw them into the water. Judging from some specimens in the British Museum, and from Senhor du Bocage's figure, the 'glass-rope' of the Portuguese form is not so thick as that of *H. sieboldi.* There is also some slight difference in the sculpture of the long needles, but the structure of the sponge and the very characteristic forms of the small spicules are identical in the two. I doubt if there be more than varietal distinctions between the two forms; and if that be so, it adds another to the list of species common to our seas and the seas of Japan.

Perhaps the most singular circumstance connected with this discussion was that all this time we had been looking at the sponge upside down, and that it had never occurred to anyone to reverse it. We had probably taken this notion from the specimens stuck in stones, brought from Japan, and the sponge certainly looked very like the base of the edifice. Whenever the sponges were dredged on the coasts of Europe and compared with allied things, it became evident that the whisp was an organ of support passing out of the lower part of the sponge, and that the flat, or slightly-cupped disk, with a papilla in the centre receiving the upper end of the coil, with large oscular openings, and a fringe of delicate radiating spicules round the edge, was the top of the sponge, spreading out probably level with the surface of the ooze.

In essential structure *Hyalonema* very closely resembles *Holtenia*, and the more characteristic forms of the Hexactinellidæ. The surface of the sponge is supported by a square network, formed by the symmetrical arrangement of the four secondary rays of five-rayed spicules, and the sarcode which binds these branches together is full of minute feathered five-rayed spicules, which project from the branches like a delicate fringe. The oscula are chiefly on the upper disk, and lead into a number of irregular passages which traverse the body of the sponge in all directions. When we trace its development, the coil loses its mystery. On one of the *Holteniæ* from the Butt of the Lews, there was a little accumulation of greenish granular matter among the fibres. On placing this under the microscope it turned out to be a number of very young sponges, scarcely out of their germ state. They were all at first sight very much alike, minute pear-shaped bodies, with a long delicate pencil of silky spicules taking the place of the pear-stalk. On closer examination, however, these little germs proved to belong to different species, each showing unmistakeably the characteristic forms of its special spicules. Most of them were the young of *Tisiphonia*, but among them were several *Holteniæ*, and one or two were at once referred to *Hyalonema*. In two or three hauls in the same locality we got them in every subsequent stage—beautiful little pear-shaped things, a centimetre long, with a single osculum at the top, and the whisp like a small brush. At this stage the *Palythoa* is usually absent, but when the body of the sponge has attained 15 mm. or so in length very generally a little pink tubercle may be detected at the point of junction between the sponge body and the coil, the germ of the first polyp.

Hyalonema lusitanicum, BARBOZA DU BOCAGE, the species met with in the British seas and along the coast of western Europe, appears to be local, but very abundant at the stations where it occurs. I am still in doubt whether we are to regard it as identical with the Japanese species, *H. sieboldi*, GRAY.

During Mr. Gwyn Jeffreys' cruise in 1870, two specimens of a wonderful sponge belonging also to the Hexactinellidæ were dredged in 374 fathoms in rocky ground off Cape St. Vincent. The larger of these forms a complete vase of a very elegant form, nearly ninety centimetres in diameter at the top and about sixty in height (Fig. 67). The sponge came up folded together, and had much the appearance of a piece of coarse, greyish-coloured blanket. Its minute structure is, however, very beautiful. It consists, like *Holtenia*, of two netted layers, an outer and an inner, formed by the symmetrical interlacing of the four cross branches of five-rayed spicules; and, as in *Holtenia* and *Rossella*, the sarcode is full of extremely minute five and six-rayed spicules, which, however, have a thoroughly distinct character of their own, with here and there a very beautiful rosette-like spicule, another singular modification of the hexradiate type characteristic of this group. Between the two netted surfaces the sponge substance is formed of loose curving meshes of loosely aggregated bundles of long simple fibres, sparsely mixed with spicules of other forms. This sponge seems to live fixed to a stone. There are no anchoring spicules, and the bottom of the vase,

FIG. 67.—*Askonema setubalense*, KENT. One-eighth the natural size. (No. 25, 1870.)

which in our two specimens is a good deal contracted and has a square shape something like an old Irish 'mether,' has apparently been torn from some attachment. This fine species was named *Askonema setubalense*, and very briefly described from a specimen in the Lisbon Museum by Mr. Saville Kent, in a paper in which he noticed some of the sponges dredged from Mr. Marshall Hall's yacht.[1]

Sponges belonging to other groups from the deep water were nearly equally interesting. I have already alluded, p. 188, to the handsome branching sponges belonging to the Esperadiæ, which abound off the coasts of Scotland and Portugal. Near the mouth of the Strait of Gibraltar a number of species were taken in considerable quantity, belonging to a group which were at first confused with the Hexactinellidæ, on account of their frequently forming a similar and equally beautiful continuous network of silica, so as to assume the same resemblance to delicate lace when boiled in nitric acid. The Coralliospongiæ differ, however, from the Hexactinellidæ in one very fundamental character. While in the latter the spicule is hexradiate, in the former it consists of a shaft with three diverging rays at one end. These frequently spread in one plane, and they often re-divide, and frequently the spaces between them are filled up with a secondary expanse of silica, variously frilled and netted on the edge, so as to give the spicule the appearance of an ornamental flat-headed tack. These three-rayed stars or disks, in combination, support the outer membrane of sponges of this order; and spicules of the same type, fused together according to various plans, form the sponge skeleton.

This group of sponges are as yet imperfectly known. They seem to pass into such forms as *Geodia* and *Tethya;* and the typical example with which we are most familiar is the genus *Dactylocalyx*, represented by the cup-shaped pumice-like

[1] Monthly Microscopic Journal, November 1, 1870.

masses which are thrown ashore from time to time on the West Indian Islands.

Professor P. Martin Duncan has already published an account of the stony corals (the Madreporaria) of the cruise of the 'Porcupine' in 1869, and he has now in hand those procured off the coast of Portugal in 1870, some of which are of even greater interest from their close resemblance to certain cretaceous forms. Twelve species of stony corals were dredged in 1869.

Caryophyllia borealis, FLEMING (Fig. 4, p. 27), is very abundant at moderate depths, particularly along the west coast of Ireland, where many varieties are found. The greatest depth at which this species was dredged is 705 fathoms. It is found fossil in the miocene and pliocene beds of Sicily.

Ceratocyathus ornatus, SEGUENZA.—Of this pretty coral only a single specimen was taken in 705 fathoms, off the Butt of the Lews. It had not previously been known as a recent species, and was described by Seguenza from the Sicilian miocene tertiaries. *Flabellum laciniatum*, EDWARDS and HAIME, was frequent in water from 100 to 400 fathoms, from Færoe to Cape Clear. From the extreme thinness of the outer crust, this coral is excessively brittle; and although many hundreds came up in the dredge, scarcely half-a-dozen examples were entire. Another fine species of the same genus, *Flabellum distinctum* (Fig. 68), was dredged on several occasions off the Portuguese coast in 1870. The special interest attaching to this species, is that it appears to be identical with a form living in the seas of Japan.

Lophohelia prolifera, PALLAS (Fig. 30, p. 169).—Many varieties; abundant at depths from 150 to 500 fathoms all along the west coasts of Scotland and Ireland, at temperatures varying from 0° to 10° C. In some places,—as, for example, at Station 54, between Scotland and Færoe, and Station 15, between the west coast of Ireland and the Porcupine Bank,—there seem to be regular banks of it, the dredge coming up loaded with fragments, living and dead.

Five allied species of the genus *Amphihelia* occurred more sparingly.

FIG. 68.—*Flabellum distinctum* Twice the natural size. (No. 28, 1870.)

Allopora oculina, EHRENBERG, a very beautiful form, of which a few specimens were procured in the 'cold area,' at depths a little over 300 fathoms.

Thecopsammia socialis, POURTALES (Fig. 69), a form closely allied to Balanophyllia, and resembling some crag species. It had been previously dredged by Count Pourtales in the Gulf of Florida. *Thecopsammia* is tolerably common in deep water in the 'cold area,' growing in patches, five or six examples sometimes coming up on one stone.

I have already adverted to the danger we run in estimating the relative proportions in which any special groups may enter into the sum of the abyssal fauna, by the proportion in which they are recovered by any single method of capture. From their considerable size, the length and rigidity of their straggling rays, and their habit of clinging to fixed objects, the Echinodermata are not very readily taken

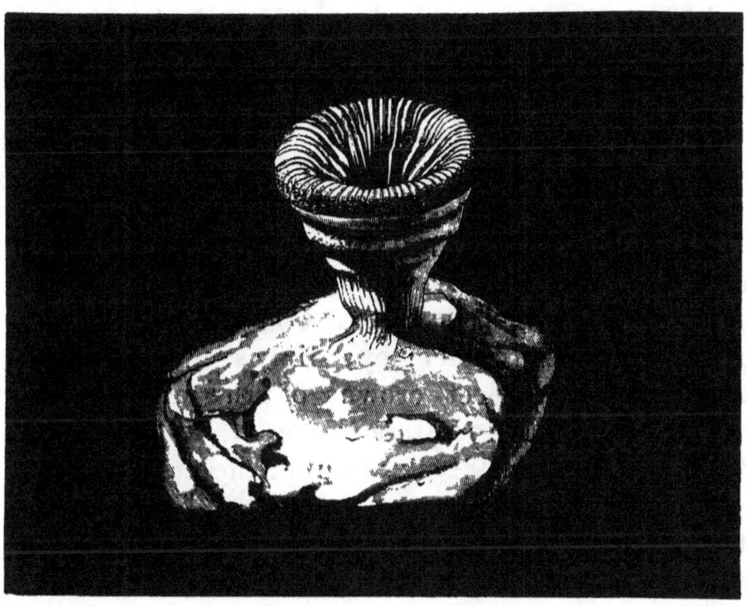

FIG. 69.—*Thecopsammia socialis*, POURTALES. Once and a half the natural size. (No. 57 1869.)

by the dredge, but they fall an easy prey to the 'hempen tangles.' It is possible that this circumstance may to a certain extent exaggerate their apparent abundance at great depths, but we have direct evidence in the actual numbers which are brought up, that in some places they must be wonderfully numerous; and we frequently dredge sponges and corals actually covered with them in the attitudes in which they lived, nestling among their fibres and in the angles of their branches. I have counted seventy-three examples of *Amphiura abyssicola*, small and large, sticking to one *Holtenia*.

Both on account of their beauty and extreme rarity, and of the important part they have borne in the fauna of some of the past periods of the earth's history, the first order of the Echinoderms, the Crinoidea, has always had a special interest to naturalists; and, on the watch as we were for missing links which might connect the present with the past, we eagerly welcomed any indication of their presence. Crinoids were very abundant in the seas of the Silurian period; deep beds of carboniferous limestone are often formed by the accumulation of little else than their skeletons, the stem joints and cups cemented together by limy sediment; and dozens of the perfect crowns of the elegant lily-encrinite are often scattered over the surface of slabs of the muschelkalk. But during the lapse of ages the whole order seems to have been worsted in the 'struggle for life.' They become scarce in the newer mezozoic beds, still scarcer in the tertiaries, and up to within the last few years only two living stalked crinoids were known in the seas of the present period, and these appeared to be confined to deep water in the seas of the Antilles, whence fishermen from time to time bring up mutilated specimens on their lines. Their existence has been known for more than a century; but although many eyes have been watching for them, until very lately not more than twenty specimens had reached Europe, and of these only two showed all the joints and plates of the skeleton, and the soft parts were lost in all.

These two species belong to the genus *Pentacrinus*, which is well represented in the beds of the lias and oolite, and sparingly in the white chalk; and are named respectively *Pentacrinus asteria*, L., and *P. mülleri*, OERSTED. Fig. 70 represents the first of these. This species has been known in Europe since the year 1755, when a specimen was brought to Paris from the island of Martinique, and described by Guettard in the Memoirs of the Royal Academy of Sciences. For the next hundred years an example turned up now and then from the Antilles. Ellis described one, now in the Hunterian Museum in Glasgow University, in the Philosophical Transactions for 1761. One or two found their way into the museums of Copenhagen, Bristol, and Paris; two into the British Museum; and one fortunately fell into the hands of the late Professor Johannes Müller of Berlin, who published an elaborate account of it in the Transactions of the Royal Berlin Academy for 1843. Within the last few years, Mr. Damon of Weymouth, a well-known collector of natural history objects, has procured several very good specimens, which are now lodged in the museums of Moscow, Melbourne, Liverpool, and London.

Pentacrinus asteria may be taken as the type of its order; I will therefore describe it briefly. The animal consists of two well-marked portions, a stem and a head. The stem, which is often from 40 to 60 centimetres in length, consists of a series of

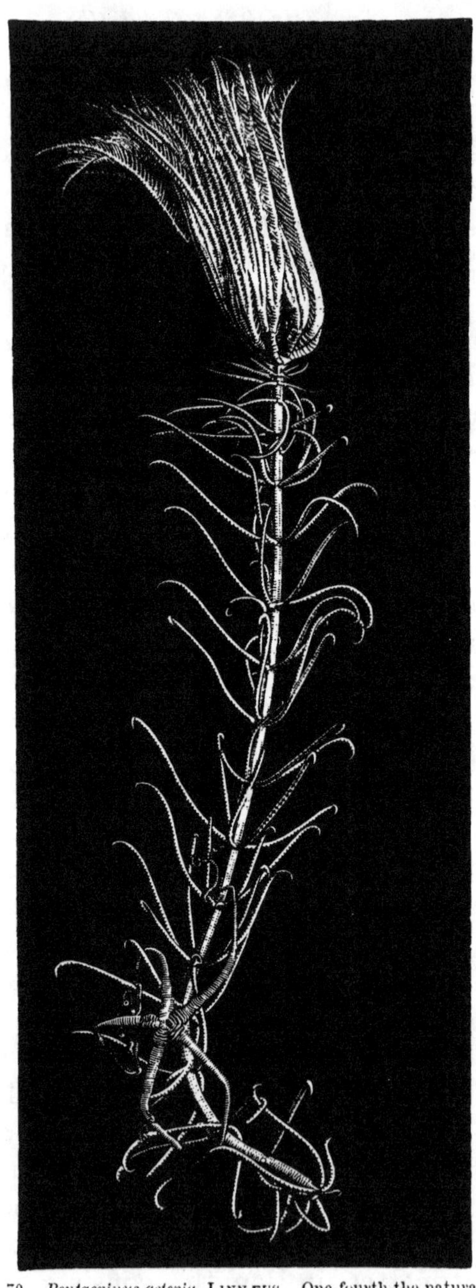

Fig. 70.—*Pentacrinus asteria*, Linnæus. One-fourth the natural size.

flattened calcareous joints; it may be snapped over at the point of junction between any two of these joints, and by slipping the point of a pen-knife into the next suture a single joint may be removed entire. The joint has a hole in the centre, through which one might pass a fine needle. This hole forms part of a canal filled during life with a gelatinous nutrient matter which runs through the whole length of the stem, branches in a complicated way through the plates of the cup, and finally passes through the axis of each of the joints of the arms, and of the ultimate pinnules which fringe them. On the upper and lower surfaces of the stem-joint there is a very graceful and characteristic figure of five radiating oval leaf-like spaces, each space surrounded by a border of minute alternate ridges and grooves. The ridges of the upper surface of a joint fit into the grooves of the lower surface of the joint above it; so that, though from being made up of man joints the stem admits of a certain amount of motion, that motion is very limited.

As the border of each star-like figure exactly fits the border of the star above and below, the five leaflets within the border are likewise placed directly one above the other. Within these leaflets the limy matter which makes up the great bulk of the joint is more loosely arranged than it is outside, and five oval bands of strong fibres pass in the interspaces right through the joints, from joint to joint, from one end of the stem to the other. These fibrous bands give the column great strength. It is by no means easily broken even when dead and dry. They also, by their elasticity, admit a certain amount of passive motion. There are no muscles between the joints of the stem, so that the animal does not appear to be able to move its stalk at will. It is probably only gently waved by the tides and currents, and by the movements of its own arms.

In *Pentacrinus asteria* about every seventeenth joint of the lower mature part of the stem, is a little deeper or thicker than the others, and bears a whorl of five long tendrils or cirri. The stem is, even near the base, slightly pentagonal in section, and it becomes more markedly so towards the head. The cirri start from shallow grooves between the projecting angles of the pentagon, so that they are ranged in five straight rows up and down the stem. The cirri are made up of about thirty-six to thirty-seven short joints; they start straight out from the stem rigid and stiff, but at the end they usually curve downwards, and the last joint is sharp and clawlike. These tendrils have no true muscles; they have, however, some power of contracting round resisting objects which they touch, and there are often star-fishes and other sea animals entangled among them. The specimen figured has thus become the temporary abode of a very elegant species of *Asteroporpa*.

Near the head the cirri become shorter and smaller, and their whorls closer. The reason of this is that the stem grows immediately below the head, and the cirrus-bearing joints are formed in this position, the intermediate joints being produced afterwards below and above each cirrated joint,—which they gradually separate from the one on either side of it, till the number of seventeen or eighteen intermediate joints is complete. At the top of the stem five little calcareous lumps like buttons stand out from the projecting ridges, and upon these and upon the upper part of the stem the cup which holds the viscera of the animal is placed. These buttons are of but little moment in this form, but they represent joints which are often developed into large, highly-ornamented plates in the various tribes of its fossil ancestors. They are called the 'basal' plates of the cup. Next, in an upper tier, alternating with the last, we have a row of five oblong plates opposite the grooves of the stem, and all cemented into a ring. These plates are separate when the animal is young; they are called the 'first radial' plates. They are the first of long chains of joints which are continued to the ends of the arms. Immediately above these plates, and resting upon them, there is a second row of plates nearly of the same size and shape, only they remain separate from one another, never uniting into a ring. These are the 'second radials,' and immediately upon these rest a third series of five, very like the plates of the other two rows, only their upper surfaces rise into a cross ridge in the centre, and they have the two sides bevelled off like the eaves of a gable, to admit of two joints being seated upon each of them instead of one. This last ring of joints are the 'radial axillaries,' and above these we have the first bifurcation of the arms. These three rings of radial joints form the true cup. In the modern species they are very small, but in many fossils they acquire a large size, and enclose, frequently with the aid of various rows of intermediate or inter-radial plates and a row of basals, a large body-cavity. The two upper joints of each ray are separated from those of the ray next it by a prolongation downwards of the plated skin which covers the upper surface or 'disk' of the body. Seated upon the bevelled sides of each radial-axillary joint, there is a series of five joints, the last of the five bevelled again like the radial axillaries for the insertion of two joints. These five joints form the first series of 'brachials,' and from the base of this series the arms become free.

The first of the brachial joints, that is to say, the joint immediately above the radial axillary, is, as it were, split in two by a peculiar kind of joint, called, by Müller, a 'syzygy.' All the ordinary joints of the arms are provided with muscles producing various motions, and binding the joints firmly together. The syzygies are not so provided, and the arms are consequently easily snapped across where these occur. This is a beautiful provision for the safety of an animal which has so wide and complicated a crown of appendages. If one of the arms get entangled, or fall into the jaws or claws of an enemy, by a jerk the star-fish can at once get rid of the embarrassed arm; and as all this group have a wonderful power of reproducing lost parts, the arm is soon restored.

When the animal is dying, it generally breaks off its arms at these syzygies; so that almost all the specimens which have been brought to Europe have arrived with the arms separate from the body.

About six arm-joints or so above the first on either branch there is a second brachial accessory and another bifurcation, and seven or eight joints farther on another, and so on, but more irregularly the farther from the centre, till each of the five primary rays has divided into from twenty to thirty ultimate branches, producing a rich crown of more than a hundred arms. The upper surface of each arm-joint is deeply grooved, the lower arched; and from one side of each, alternately on either side of the arm, there springs a series of flattened ossicles. These form the ultimate branchlets, or 'pinnules,' which fringe the arms as the barbs fringe the shaft of a feather. Unfortunately, most of the examples of *Pentacrinus asteria* hitherto procured have had the soft parts destroyed and the disk more or less injured. One specimen, however, in my possession is quite perfect. The body is covered above by a membrane closely tesselated with irregularly-formed flat plates; this membrane, after covering the disk, dips into the spaces between the series of radial joints, and with the joints of the cup completes the body-wall. The mouth is a rounded opening of considerable size in the centre of the disk, and opens into a stomach passing into a short curved intestine which ends in a long excretory tube,—the so-called 'proboscis' of the fossil crinoids,—which rises from the surface of the disk near the mouth. From the mouth five deep grooves, bordered on either side by small square plates, run out to the edge of the disk, and are continuous with the grooves on the upper surface of the arms and pinnules, while in the angles between them five thickened masses of the mailing of the disk surround the mouth like valves. These were at first supposed to answer the purpose of teeth. The crinoids, however, are not predatory animals. Their nutrition is effected in a very gentle manner. The grooves of the pinnules and arms are richly ciliated. The crinoid expands its arms like the petals of a full-blown flower, and a current of sea-water bearing organic matter in solution and suspension is carried by the cilia along the brachial and radial grooves to the mouth. In the stomach and intestine the water is exhausted of assimilable matter, and the length and direction of the excretory proboscis prevent the exhausted water from returning at once into the ciliated passages.

The other West Indian *Pentacrinus*—*P. Mülleri*—seems to be more common off the Danish Islands than *P. asteria*. The animal is more delicate in form. The stem attains nearly the same height, but is more slender. The rings of cirri occur about every twelfth joint, and at each whorl two stem-joints are modified. The upper joint bears the facet for the insertion of the cirrus, and the second is grooved to receive its thick basal portion, which bends downwards for a little way closely adpressed to the stem, before becoming free. The syzygy is between the two modified joints, and in all the complete specimens which I have seen the stem is broken through at one of these stem syzygies, and the terminal stem-joint is worn and absorbed, showing that the animal must have been for long free from any attachment to the ground.

On the 21st of July, 1870, Mr. Gwyn Jeffreys, dredging from the 'Porcupine' at a depth of 1,095 fathoms, lat. 39° 42′ N., long. 9° 43′ W., with a bottom temperature of 4°·3 C. and a bottom of soft

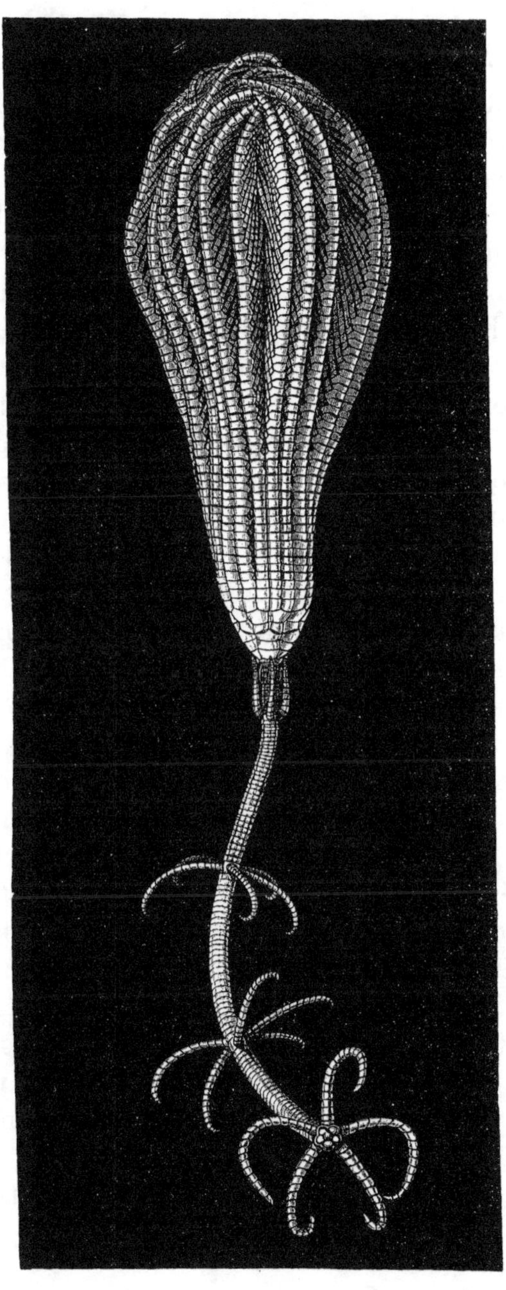

Fig. 71.—*Pentacrinus wyville-thomsoni*, Jeffreys. Natural size. (No. 17, 1870.)

mud, took about twenty specimens of a handsome *Pentacrinus* involved in the 'hempen tangles;' and this splendid addition to the fauna of the European seas my friend has done me the honour to associate with my name.

Pentacrinus wyville-thomsoni, JEFFREYS (Fig. 71), is intermediate in some of its characters between *P. asteria* and *P. mülleri;* it approaches the latter species, however, the more nearly. In a mature specimen the stem is about 120 mm. in length, and consists of five or six internodes. The whorls of cirri towards the lower part of the stem are 40 mm. apart, and the internodes contain from thirty to thirty-five joints. The cirri are rather short and stand straight out from the nodal joint, or curve sharply downwards, as in *P. asteria.* The nodal joint is single, and the syzygy separates it from the joint immediately beneath it, which does not differ materially from the ordinary internodal stem-joint. All the stems of mature examples of this species end uniformly in a nodal joint, surrounded with its whorl of cirri, which curve downwards into a kind of grappling root. The lower surface of the terminal joint is in all smoothed and rounded, evidently by absorption, showing that the animal had for long been free. This character I have remarked as occurring in some specimens of *P. mülleri.* I have no doubt that it is constant in the present species, and that the animal lives loosely rooted in the soft mud, and can change its place at pleasure by swimming with its pinnated arms; that it is in fact intermediate in this respect between the free genus *Antedon* and the permanently fixed crinoids.

A young specimen of *P. wyville-thomsoni* gives the mode in which this freedom is acquired. The total length of this specimen is 95 mm., of which the head occupies 35 mm. The stem is broken off in the middle of the eighth internode from the head. The lowest complete internode consists of 14 joints, the next of 18, the next of 20, and the next of 26 joints. There are 8 joints in the cirri of the lowest whorl, 10 in those of the second, 12 in those of the third, and 14 in those of the fourth. This is the reverse of the condition in adult specimens, in all of which the numbers of joints in the internodes, and of joints in the cirri, decrease regularly from below upwards. The broken internode in the young example, and the three internodes above it, are atrophied and undeveloped, and suddenly at the third node from the head the stem increases in thickness, and looks as if it were fully nourished. There can be no doubt that in early life the crinoid is attached, and that it becomes disengaged by the withering of the lower part of the stem.

The structure of the cup is the same as in *P. asteria* and *P. mülleri.* The basals appear in the form of shield-like projections crowning the salient angles of the stem. Alternating with these we have well-developed first radials, forming a closed ring and articulating to free second radials by muscular joints. The second radials are united by a syzygy to the radial axillaries, which as usual give off each two first brachials from their bevelled sides. A second brachial is united by syzygy to the first, and normally this second brachial is an axillary, and gives off two simple arms; sometimes, however, the radial axillary originates a simple arm only from one or both of its sides, thus reducing the total number of the arms; and sometimes one of the four arms given off from the brachial axillaries again divides, in which case the total number of arms is increased. The structure of the disk is much the same as in the species of the genus previously known.

Two other fixed crinoids were dredged from the 'Porcupine,' and these must be referred to the Apiocrinidæ, which differ from all other sections of the order in the structure of the upper part of the stem. At a certain point, considerably below the crown of arms, the joints of the stem widen by the greater development of the calcareous ring, the central tube only increasing very slightly in width. The widening of the stem joints increases upwards until a pear-shaped body is produced, usually very elegant in form, which, looking from the outside, one would take for the calyx. It is, however, nothing more than a symmetrical thickening of the stem, and the body-cavity occupies a shallow depression in the top of it included within the plates of the cup—the basals and radials—which are thicker and more solid than in other crinoids, but otherwise normally arranged. The stem is usually long and simple until near the base, where it forms some means of attachment, either as in the celebrated pear-encrinites of the forest marble, a complicated arrangement of concentric layers of calcareous cement which fix it firmly to some foreign body, or, as in the chalk *Bourguetticrinus* and in the recent *Rhizocrinus*, an irregular series of jointed branching cirri.

The Apiocrinidæ attained their maximum during

the Jurassic period, when they were represented by many fine species of the genera *Apiocrinus* and *Millericrinus*. The chalk genus *Bourguetticrinus* shows many symptoms of degeneracy. The head is small, and the arms are small and short. The arm-joints are so minute that it is scarcely possible to make up a series from the fragments scattered through the chalk in the neighbourhood of a cluster of heads. The stem, on the other hand, is disproportionately large and long, and one is led to suspect that the animal was nourished chiefly by the general surface absorption of organic matter, and that the head and special assimilative organs were principally concerned in the function of reproduction. *Rhizocrinus loffotensis*, M. SARS (Fig. 72), was discovered in the year 1864, at a depth of about 300 fathoms, off the Loffoten islands, by G. O. Sars, a son of the celebrated Professor of Natural History in the University of Christiania by whom it was described in the year 1868. It is obviously a form of the Apiocrinidæ still more degraded than *Bourguetticrinus*, which it closely resembles. The stem is long and of considerable thickness in proportion to the size of the head. The joints of the stem are individually long and dice-box shaped, and between the joints spaces are left on either side of the stem alternately, as in *Bourguetticrinus* and in the pentacrinoid of *Antedon*, for the insertion of fascicles of contractile fibres. Towards the base of the stem branches spring from the upper part of the joints; and these, each composed of a succession of gradually diminishing joints, divide and re-divide into a bunch of fibres, which frequently expand at the ends into thin calcareous laminæ, clinging to small pieces of shell, grains of sand—anything which may improve the anchorage of the crinoid in the soft mud which is nearly universal at great depths.

In *Rhizocrinus* the basal series of plates of the cup are not distinguishable. They are masked in a closed ring at the top of the stem; and whether the ring be composed of the fused basals alone, or of an upper stem-joint with the basals within it forming a 'rosette,' as in the calyx of *Antedon*, is a question which can only be solved by a careful tracing of successive stages of development. The first radials are likewise fused, and form the upper wider portion of the funnel-shaped calyx. The first radials are deeply excavated above for the insertion of the muscles and ligaments which unite them to the second radials by a true (or moveable) joint. One of the most remarkable points in connection with this species is, that the first radials—the first joints of the arm—are variable in number, some examples having four rays, some five, some six, and a very small number seven, in the following proportions. Out of seventy-five specimens examined by Sars, there were—

15	with	4	arms.
43	,,	5	,,
15	,,	6	,,
2	,,	7	,,

This variability in so important a character, particularly when associated with so great a preponderance in bulk of the vegetative over the more specially animal parts of the organism, must undoubtedly be accepted as indicating a deterioration from the symmetry and compactness of the Apiocrinidæ of the Jurassic period.

The anchylosed ring of first radials is succeeded by a tier of free second radials, which are united by a straight syzygial suture to the next series—the radial axillaries. The surface of the funnel-shaped dilatation of the stem, headed by the ring of first radials, is smooth and uniform, and the second radials and radial axillaries present a smooth, regularly-arched outer surface. The radial axillaries differ from the corresponding joints in most other known crinoids in contracting slightly above, presenting only one articulating facet, and giving origin to a single arm. The arms, which in the larger specimens are from 10 to 12 mm. in length, consist of a series of from about twenty-eight to thirty-four joints, uniformly transversely arched externally, and deeply grooved within to receive the soft parts. Each alternate joint bears a pinnule, the pinnules alternating on either side of the axis of the arm, and the joint which does not bear a pinnule is united to the pinnule-bearing joint above it by a syzygy: thus joints with muscular connections and syzygies alternate throughout the whole length of the arm.

The pinnules, twelve to fourteen in number, consist of a uniform series of minute joints, united by muscular connections. The grooves of the arms and of the pinnules are bordered by a double series of delicate round fenestrated calcareous plates, which, when the animal is contracted and at rest, form a closely imbricated covering to the nerve, and the radial vessel with its delicate cæcal tentacles. The mouth is placed in the centre of the disk, and radial canals, equal in number to the number of arms, pass across the disk, and are continuous with the arm-grooves. The mouth is surrounded by a row of flexible cirri, arranged nearly as in the pentacrinoid of *Antedon*, and is provided with five oval calcareous valve-like plates occupying the interradial angles, and closing over the mouth at will. A low papilla in one of the interradial spaces indicates the position of the minute excretory orifice.

Rhizocrinus loffotensis is a very interesting addition to the British fauna. We met with it in the Færoe Channel in the year 1869—three examples, greatly mutilated, at a depth of 530 fathoms, with a bottom temperature of 6°·4 C., Station 12 (1868). Several occurred attached to the beards of the *Holteniæ*, off the Butt of the Lews, and specimens of considerable size were dredged in 862 fathoms off Cape Clear. The range of this species is evidently very wide. It has been dredged by G. O. Sars off the north of Norway; by Count Pourtales in the Gulf-stream off the coast of Florida; by the Naturalists on board the 'Josephine,' on the 'Josephine Bank,' near the entrance of the Strait of Gibraltar; and by ourselves between Shetland and Færoe, and off Ushant and Cape Clear.

The genus *Bathycrinus* must also be referred to the Apiocrinidæ, since the lower portion of the head consists of a gradually expanding funnel-shaped piece, which seems to be composed of coalesced upper stem-joints.

The stem of *Bathycrinus gracilis* (Fig. 73) is long and delicate; in one example of a stem alone, which came up in the same haul with the one nearly perfect speci-

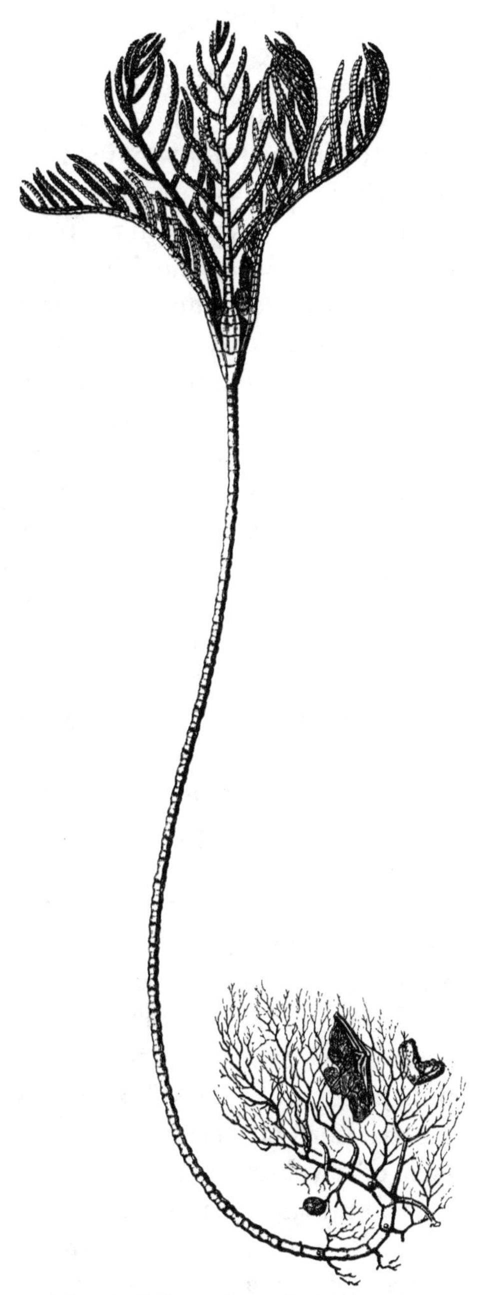

Fig. 72.—*Rhizocrinus loffotensis*, M. Sars. Once and a half the natural size. (No. 43, 1869.)

men which was procured, it was 90 mm. in length. The joints are dice-box shaped, as in *Rhizocrinus*, long and delicate towards the lower part of the stem, 3·0 mm. in length by 0·5 in width in the centre of the joint, the ends expanding to a width of 1·0 mm. As in *Rhizocrinus*, the joints of the stem diminish in length towards the head, and additions are made in the form of calcareous laminæ beneath the coalesced joints which form the base of the cup.

The first radials are five in number. They are closely apposed, but they do not seem to be fused as in *Rhizocrinus*, since the sutures show quite distinctly. The centre of each of these first radials rises into a sharp keel, while the sides are slightly depressed towards the suture, which gives the calyx a fluted appearance, like a folded filter-paper. The second radials are long, and free from one another, joining the radial axillaries by a straight syzygial union. They are most peculiar in form. A strong plate-like keel runs down the centre of the outer surfaces, and the joint is deeply excavated on either side, rising again slightly towards the edges. The radial axillary shows a continuation of the same keel through its lower half, and midway up the joint the keel bifurcates, leaving a very characteristic diamond-shaped space in the centre, towards the top of the joint; two facets are thus formed for the insertion of two first radials; the number of arms is therefore ten. The arms are perfectly simple, and in our single specimen consist of twelve joints each. There is no trace of pinnules, and the arms resemble in character the pinnules of *Rhizocrinus*. The first brachial is united to the second by a syzygial joint, but after

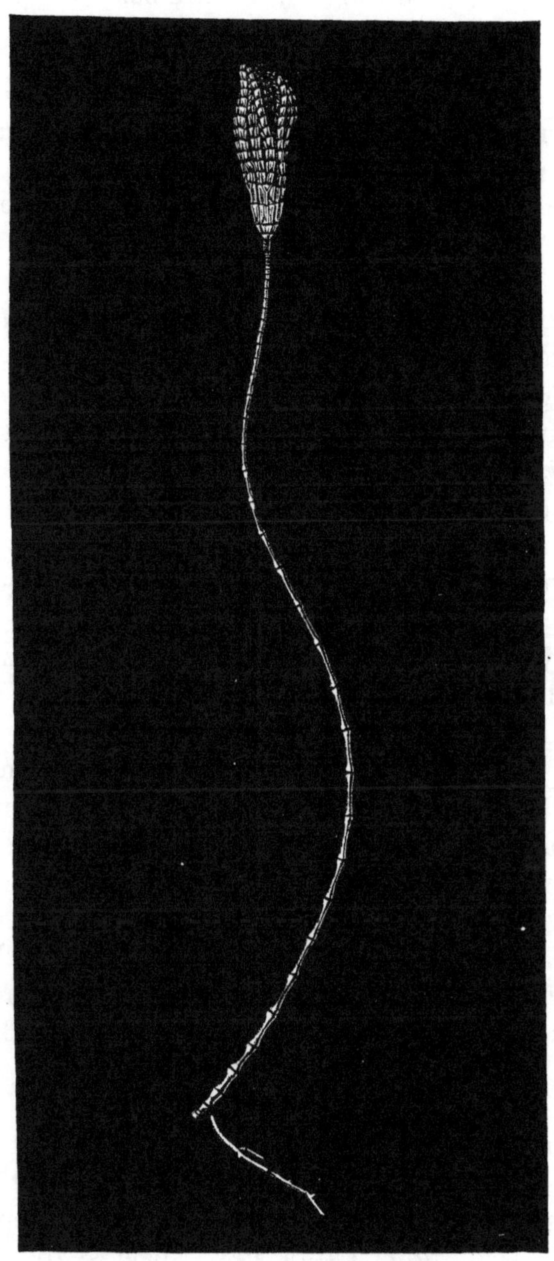

Fig. 73.—*Bathycrinus gracilis*, Wyville Thomson. Twice the natural size. (No. 37, 1869.)

that the syzygies are not repeated, so that there is only one of these peculiar junctions in each arm. The arm-grooves are bordered by circular fenestrated plates, as in *Rhizocrinus.*

Certain marked resemblances in the structure of the stem, in the structure of the base of the cup, and in the form and arrangement of the ultimate parts of the arms, evidently associate *Bathycrinus* with *Rhizocrinus*, but the differences are very wide. Five free keeled and sculptured first radials replace the uniform smooth ring formed by these plates in *Rhizocrinus.* The radial axillaries give off each two arms, thus recurring to the more usual arrangement in the order, and the alternate syzygies on the arms, which form so remarkable a character in *Rhizocrinus,* are absent.

Only one nearly complete specimen and a detached stem of this very remarkable species were met with, and they were both brought up from the very greatest depth which has as yet been reached with the dredge, 2,435 fathoms, at the mouth of the Bay of Biscay, 200 miles south of Cape Clear.

It would seem, in our present state of knowledge, that the stalked crinoids are members of the deep-sea fauna. A second specimen of another very remarkable form, *Holopus rangi,* D'ORBIGNY, has lately been procured from deep water off Barbadoes, and that species, with those already noted, makes up the tale of living forms belonging to the order which are known at the present time. It is unwise to prophesy; but when we consider that the first few scrapes of the dredge at great depths have added two remarkable new species to the living representatives of this group, until now supposed to be on the verge of extinction, and that all the known species are from depths beyond the limit of ordinary dredging, we are led to anticipate that crinoids may probably form rather an important element in the abyssal fauna.

FIG. 74.—*Archaster bifrons*, WYVILLE THOMSON. Oral aspect. Three-fourths the natural size. (No. 57, 1869.)

The general distribution of the deep-sea Asteridea has already been referred to. Perhaps the most obvious peculiarity which they present is the great preponderance of the genera *Astrogonium*, *Archaster*, *Astropecten*, and their allies. Genera belonging to other groups do not apparently become less numerous, for species of *Asteracanthion, Cribrella, Asteriscus*, and *Ophidiaster* are as abundant as they are at lesser depths; but as we go down new species with tesselated mailing on the disk and massive marginal plates seem to be perpetually added. In our own seas some few very characteristic forms, such as *Astrogonium phrygianum* and *Archaster andromeda* and *parellii*, are on the verge of the deep water, and are now and then taken at the outer limit of shore dredging, or on fishing-lines; while in the deep water all along the north and west of Scotland *Astrogonium granulare, Archaster tenuispinus*, and *Astropecten arcticus* abound, and the dredge is enriched from time to time with examples of such forms as *Archaster bifrons* (Fig. 74), *A. vexillifer*, and *Astrogonium longimanum*, MOBIUS. Many additions have been made to the singular little group of which *Pteraster* may be taken as a type, but I am inclined to think that these are to be referred along with most of the characteristic Ophiuridans rather to a fauna inhabiting median depths, and coming within range of the naturalist's dredge on the coast of Scandinavia, than to the abyssal fauna; and the same may be said of a few other forms, such as *Solaster furcifer* (Fig. 75), and *Pedicellaster typicus* which, although beyond the 200-fathom line on the coast of Britain, do not appear to have a great range of depth.

FIG. 75.—*Solaster furcifer*, VON DUBEN and KOREN. Oral aspect. Natural size. (No. 55, 1869.)

Twenty-six Echinideans were observed during the 'Lightning' and 'Porcupine' cruises off the coasts of Britain and Portugal at depths ranging from 100 to 2,435 fathoms, at which latter depth the group was represented by a small variety of *Echinus norvegicus*, and a young example of *Brissopsis lyrifera*.

Among the Cidaridæ, *Cidaris papillata*, LESKE, occurs in enormous numbers over hard ground, at depths from 100 to 400 fathoms. This species has a very wide range, inhabiting an apparently unbroken belt from the North Cape to the Strait of Gibraltar, and then passing into the Mediterranean. This is a variable form, within narrow limits of variation. The southern specimens gradually pass into the form,—it can scarcely be called a variety,—which is the type of Lamarck's species, *C. hystrix*. *Cidaris affinis*, PHILIPPI, is very common in the Mediterranean, especially along the African coast. I think this pretty little form must for the present be considered distinct. The body spines are bright scarlet, and the long spines, in marked specimens, are brown banded with red or rose, so that it is a singularly pretty object.

The genus *Porocidaris* and the three species of the family Echinothuridæ, and their interesting relations to fossil forms, have already been considered; but even these are scarcely more suggestive of early times than two genera of irregular urchins, one dredged off the coast of Scotland, and the other at the mouth of the English Channel.

The first of these is *Pourtalesia*, one species of which, *P. jeffreysi*, has already been figured and described (p. 108). According to the classification of

Desor, which makes the disjunct arrangement of the ambulacra at the apex the test character of the Dysasteridæ, this genus should be referred to that group, for the apical disk is truly decomposed as in *Dysaster* and *Collyrites*, and not merely drawn out as in *Ananchytes*. From the arrangement and form of the pore areas, however, and the general appearance and habit of the animal, I am inclined to think with Alexander Agassiz, that its affinities are more with such forms as *Infulaster*. *Pourtalesia* must be aberrant in whatever group it may be placed.

The other genus *Neolampas*, A. AG., associates itself with the Cassidulidæ in virtue of the nearly central pentagonal mouth with a tolerably distinct flocelle, the anal opening at the bottom of a deep posterior groove excavated in a projecting rostellum, the narrow ambulacral areas, and the small compact group of apical plates; but it differs from all known genera of the family, living or extinct, in having no trace of a petaloid arrangement of the ambulacra, which are reduced on the apical surface of the test to a single pore passing through each ambulacral plate, and thus forming a double row of alternating simple pores for each ambulacral area. I think I am right in identifying a single specimen, nearly 20 mm. in length, which we dredged in 800 fathoms water at the mouth of the Channel, with the species dredged by Count Pourtales at depths from 100 to 150 fathoms, in the Strait of Florida, and described by Alexander Agassiz under the name of *Neolampas rostellatus*.

Of the twenty-six Echinoderms dredged from the 'Porcupine,' six—*Echinus flemingii*, *Echinus esculen-*

tus, *Psammechinus miliaris*, *Echinocyamus angulatus*, *Amphidetus cordatus*, and *Spatangus purpureus*—may be regarded as denizens of moderate depths in the 'Celtic province,' recent observations having merely shown that they have a somewhat greater range in depth than was previously supposed. Probably *Spatangus raschi* may be an essentially deep-water form having its head-quarters in the same region. Seven species—*Cidaris papillata*, *Echinus elegans*, *E. norvegicus*, *E. rarispina*, *E. microstoma*, *Brissopsis lyrifera*, and *Tripylus fragilis*—are members of a fauna of intermediate depth; and all, with the doubtful example of *Echinus microstoma*, have been observed in comparatively shallow water off the coasts of Scandinavia. Five species—*Cidaris affinis*, *Echinus melo*, *Toxopneustes brevispinosus*, *Psammechinus microtuberculatus*, and *Schizaster canaliferus*—are recognized members of the Lusitanian and Mediterranean faunæ; and seven—*Porocidaris purpurata*, *Phormosoma placenta*, *Calveria hystrix*, *C. fenestrata*, *Neolampas rostellatus*, *Pourtalesia jeffreysi*, and *P. phiale*—are forms which have been for the first time brought to light during the late deep-sea dredging operations, whether on this or on the other side of the Atlantic. There seems little doubt that these must be referred to the abyssal fauna, upon whose confines we are now only beginning to encroach. Three of the most remarkable generic forms—*Calveria*, *Neolampas*, and *Pourtalesia*—have been found by Alexander Agassiz among the results of the deep dredging operations of Count Pourtales in the Strait of Florida, showing a wide lateral distribution, while even a deeper interest attaches to the fact that while one family type, the *Echinothuridæ*, has been hitherto only known in a fossil state, the entire group find nearer allies in the extinct faunæ of the chalk or of the earlier tertiaries than in that of the present period.

As I have already said, the mollusca procured during the three years' dredging are in the hands of Mr. Gwyn Jeffreys for identification and description. From the large number of new species, and from the complicated relations which many of the forms from deep water bear to species now widely separated from them in space, or belonging to past geological periods, the task will be a difficult one, and we cannot expect its completion for some time to come. In the meanwhile, Mr. Gwyn Jeffreys has published several preliminary sketches which are full of promise that his complete results will be of the highest interest.

Mr. Gwyn Jeffreys believes that the deep-water mollusca which were dredged throughout the whole of the area examined from the Færoe Islands to the coast of Spain, are almost all of northern origin. Most of the species which have been already described were previously known from the Scandinavian seas, and many of the undescribed species belong to northern genera. He points out that the molluscan fauna of the Arctic Sea is as yet almost unknown; but he reasons from the large collections made at Spitzbergen by Professor Torell, and from the fact that fragments of mollusca have been brought up in many deep-sea soundings within the Arctic circle, that the fauna is probably varied and rich. He instances soundings taken in 1868 by the Swedish

Arctic Expedition, which reached 2,600 fathoms, when a *Cuma* and a fragment of an *Astarte* came up in the 'Bulldog' machine. He adds, "It is evident that the majority, if not the whole of our submarine (as contradistinguished from littoral or phytophagous), mollusca originated in the North, whence they have in the course of time been transported southwards by the great Arctic currents. Many of them appear to have found their way into the Mediterranean, or to have left their remains in the tertiary or quaternary formations of the south of Italy; some have even migrated into the Gulf of Mexico."

I have great hesitation in questioning any of the conclusions of my friend Mr. Gwyn Jeffreys on a subject in which he is so excellent an authority, but I confess I do not quite see the cogency of his reasoning on this point. It would seem rather that the last change in the molluscan fauna of the British area, at moderate depths, consisted in the retirement of northern species at the close of the glacial period and the immigration of southern forms. The quaternary beds of the Clyde district contain a rich assemblage of mollusca; those of the neighbourhood of Rothesay especially representing the deeper part of the Laminarian and the Coralline zone. The broad characteristic of the fauna of this bed is that many of the most numerous species—for example, *Pecten islandicus, Tellina calcarea,* and *Natica clausa*—are now extinct in the seas of Britain, but are still met with in abundance in the seas of Scandinavia and Labrador; while many forms now extremely common in the British seas and having a southern extension are entirely absent.

We found some of the glacial shells of the Clyde beds living on the northern outskirts of our region, —*Tellina calcarea*, for instance, was very common in some of the Fjords in Færoe. It seems evident that this fauna quietly retreated northwards in the face of slowly altering circumstances. Such an instance of change of fauna, which we are able in a great degree to trace step by step, has an interesting bearing upon the great question of the contemporaneity of beds containing generally the same fauna at distant localities. We can well imagine that a block of perfectly recent silt might be brought from a locality on the verge of the Arctic circle, imbedding precisely the same species of mollusca as those contained in a block of the Clyde glacial clay, and the mineral character of the matrix in the two cases might correspond most closely; applying the ordinary geological rule, those two blocks agreeing in their palæontological characters ought to be contemporaneous,—but we know that while the northern silt belongs to the present period, the British glacial clays are overlain by a deep series of modern deposits, representing the lapse of a period of time considerable even in a geological sense, and containing a fauna of a very different character. This is no doubt a comparatively trifling case, involving beds of no great depth or importance, but it is a case in which two beds correspond palæontologically, and yet we *know* that they are not contemporaneous from one of them being overlain by a considerable thickness of newer strata, while the other is now forming, and thus furnishes a date, a rare and valuable thing in geology.

I have already pointed out that in reasoning upon the ground of identity of deep-sea forms with species hitherto found in Scandinavia, we must remember that the conditions of temperature of our southern seas at great depths—the conditions which appear to have the greatest influence upon the distribution of species—correspond very closely with those of much shallower water in the Scandinavian seas; and that consequently the corresponding fauna in the northern regions was much earlier, and is still much better known. Mr. Gwyn Jeffreys lays great stress upon the greater numbers and the greater development in size and in prominent characters of sculpture and other ornament, of the Arctic examples of species common to our deep water. This is no doubt often the case, but we must admit that in many groups, and particularly among the mollusca, there is a tendency to dwarfing in deep water, and I should think it very possible that a species may attain a greater size and development in that region where its zone of special temperature conditions comes nearest the surface,—most under the influence of air and light.

Many of the mollusca from the deep water have hitherto been found only in the northern portions of the area examined, and are generally allied to northern forms. As examples of this group I may mention two interesting additions to the already famous Shetland fauna, *Buccinopsis striata*, JEFFREYS (Fig. 76), a form somewhat allied to *Buccinopsis dalei*, which has long been one of the prizes of the Shetland seas, and *Latirus albus*, JEFFREYS (Fig. 77), known also from the coast of Norway. *Cerithium granosum*, S.

V. Wood, also common to Norway and Shetland, is found fossil in the coralline and red crag, and *Fusus sarsi*, Jeffreys, common to Shetland and Norway, is found fossil at Bridlington.

Several species have hitherto been known only from the south, and Mr. Jeffreys finds a difficulty in accounting for their presence. Thus, *Tellina compressa*, Brocchi, is known from the Canary Islands and the Mediterranean, and is fossil in the newer Italian tertiaries. *Verticordia acuticostata*, Philippi,

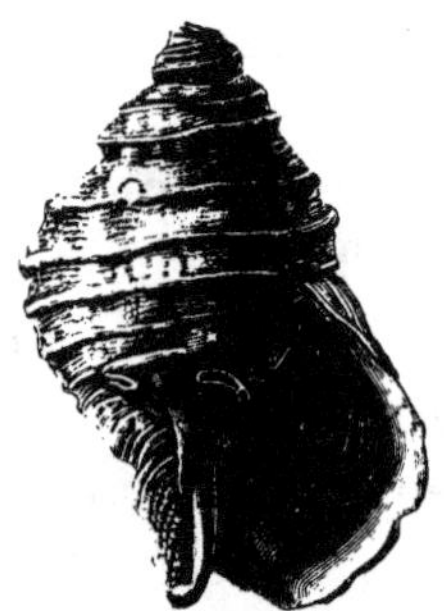

Fig. 76.—*Buccinopsis striata*, Jeffreys. Færoe Channel.

Fig. 77.—*Latirus albus*, Jeffreys. Twice the natural size. Færoe Channel.

I have already referred to as being found on the coasts of Portugal and of Japan. It is a common fossil in the coralline crag of Calabria. The mollusca which are of the most special interest, however, are those which we must refer to the abyssal fauna. About this group we know as yet very little. Like the Echinoderms, they seem to be special, and to have a wide lateral extension. *Pleuronectia lucida*, Jeffreys (Fig. 78), a pretty little clam belonging to the *Pecten pleuronectes* set, is figured both from the North Atlantic and from the Gulf of

Mexico. The abyssal mollusca are by no means devoid of colour, though, as a rule, they are paler than those from shallow water. *Dacrydium vitreum*—a curious little mytiloid shell-fish which makes and inhabits a delicate flask-shaped tube of foraminifera,

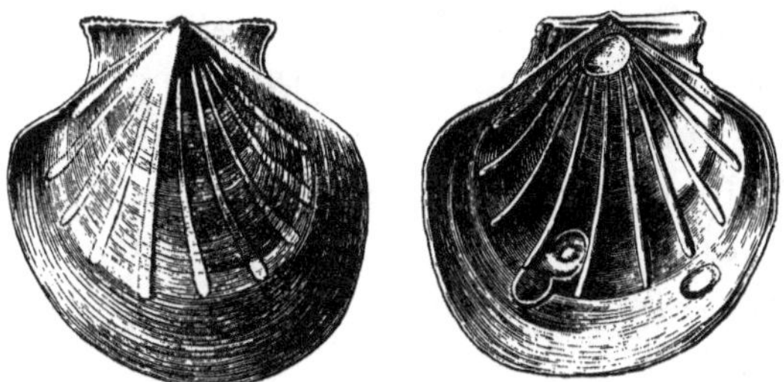

FIG. 78.—*Pleuronectia lucida*, JEFFREYS. Twice the natural size. *a*, from the Eastern Atlantic; *b*, from the Gulf of Mexico.

sponge spicules, coccoliths, and other foreign bodies, cemented together by organic matter and lined by a delicate membrane—is of a fine reddish brown colour dashed with green, from 2,435 fathoms; and the

FIG. 79.—*Pecten hoskynsi*, FORBES. Twice the natural size.

animals of one or two species of *Lima* from extreme depths are of the usual vivid orange scarlet. Neither are the abyssal mollusca universally destitute of eyes. A new species of *Pleurotoma* from 2,090 fathoms had a pair of well-developed eyes on short footstalks; and a *Fusus* from 1,207 fathoms was similarly provided. The presence of organs of sight at these great depths leaves little room to doubt that light must reach even these abysses from some source. From many considerations it can scarcely be sun-light. I have already thrown out the suggestion that the whole of the light beyond a certain depth might be due to phosphorescence, which is certainly very general, particularly among the larvæ and young of deep-sea animals; but the question is one of extreme interest and difficulty, and will require careful investigation.

BORDÖ, KUNÖ, AND KALSÖ, FROM THE HAMLET OF VIDERÖ.

CHAPTER X.

THE CONTINUITY OF THE CHALK.

Points of Resemblance between the Atlantic Ooze and the White Chalk.—Differences between them.—Composition of Chalk.—The Doctrine of the Continuity of the Chalk.—Objections.—Arguments in favour of the View from Physical Geology and Geography.—Former Distribution of Sea and Land.—Palæontological Evidence.—Chalk-flints.—Modern Sponges, and Ventriculites.—Corals.—Echinoderms.—Mollusca.—Opinions of Professor Huxley and Mr. Prestwich.—The Composition of Sea-water.—Presence of Organic Matter.—Analysis of the contained Gases.—Differences of Specific Gravity.—Conclusion.

Appendix A.—Summary of the Results of the Examination of Samples of Sea-water taken at the Surface and at various Depths. By William Lant Carpenter, B.A., B.Sc.

Appendix B.—Results of the Analyses of Eight Samples of Sea-water collected during the Third Cruise of the 'Porcupine.' By Dr. Frankland, F.R.S.

Appendix C.—Notes on Specimens of the Bottom collected during the First Cruise of the 'Porcupine' in 1869. By David Forbes, F.R.S.

Appendix D.—Note on the Carbonic Acid contained in Sea-water. By John Young Buchanan, M.A., Chemist to the 'Challenger' Expedition.

Very speedily after the first samples of the bottom of the mid-Atlantic had been brought up by the sounding-line, and submitted to chemical analysis and to microscopical examination, many observers were struck with the great similarity between its composition and structure and that of the ancient chalk. I have already described the general character and the mode of origin of the great calcareous deposit which seems to occupy the greater part of the bed of the Atlantic. If we take a piece of the ordinary soft white chalk of the south of England, wash it down with a brush in water, and place a drop of the milky product on the slide of a microscope, we find that it consists, like the Atlantic ooze, of a large proportion of fine amorphous particles of lime, with here and there a portion of a *Globigerina* shell, and more rarely one of these shells entire, and a considerable proportion—in some examples coming up to nearly one-tenth of the whole—of 'coccoliths,' which are indistinguishable from those of the ooze. Altogether two slides—one of washed down white chalk, and the other of Atlantic ooze—resemble one another so clearly, that it is not always easy for even an accomplished microscopist to distinguish them. The nature of chalk can also be well shown, as has been done by Ehrenberg and Sorby, by cutting it into thin diaphanous slices, when the mode of aggregation of the different materials can be readily demonstrated.

But while successive observers have brought out more and more clearly those resemblances,—sufficiently striking to place it beyond a doubt that the chalk of the cretaceous period and the chalk-mud of the modern Atlantic are substantially the same,—a more careful investigation shows that there are very important differences between them. The white chalk is very homogeneous, more so perhaps than any other sedimentary rock, and may be said to be almost pure carbonate of lime. I quote an analysis of the white chalk of Shoreham (Sussex), by Mr. David Forbes.[1]

Calcium carbonate	98·40
Magnesium carbonate	0·08
Insoluble rock *débris*	1·10
Alumina and loss	0·42
	100·00

Even the grey chalk of Folkestone contains a very large proportion of carbonate of lime, the other substances existing merely as impurities which can scarcely be said to enter into the composition of the rock. The following is an analysis by Mr. Forbes of the base of the Folkestone grey chalk :—

Calcium carbonate	94·09
Magnesium carbonate	0·31
Insoluble rock *débris*	3·61
Phosphoric acid . . . . Alumina and loss	} a trace
Sodium chloride	1·29
Water	0·70
	100·00

The most remarkable point in this analysis is that while white chalk is almost always associated with chert and flints, the chalk itself does not contain a particle of silica.

The chalk-mud of the Atlantic on the other hand contains not more than 60 per cent. of calcium carbonate, with 20 to 30 per cent. of silica, and varying proportions of alumina, magnesia, and oxide of iron. We must remember, however, that in the English

[1] Quoted in Mr. Prestwich's Presidential Address, 1871.

cliffs we have the chalk in its very purest form, and that in various parts of the world it assumes a very different character, and contains carbonate of lime in very different proportions. Mr. Prestwich instances a bed 28 to 30 feet thick of the white chalk (Terrain Senonien) of Touraine, in which carbonate of lime is entirely absent.

There can be no doubt whatever that we have forming at the bottom of the present ocean, a vast sheet of rock which very closely resembles chalk; and there can be as little doubt that the old chalk, the cretaceous formation which in some parts of England has been subjected to enormous denudation, and which is overlaid by the beds of the tertiary series, was produced in the same manner, and under closely similar circumstances; and not the chalk only, but most probably all the great limestone formations. In almost all of these the remains of foraminifera are abundant, some of them apparently specifically identical with living forms; and in a large number of limestones of all ages Dr. Gümbel has detected the characteristic 'coccoliths.'

Long before commencing the present investigation, certain considerations had led me to regard it as highly probable that in the deeper parts of the Atlantic a deposit, differing possibly from time to time in composition but always of the same general character, might have been accumulating continuously from the cretaceous or even earlier periods to the present day. This view I suggested in my first letter to Dr. Carpenter urging the exploration of the seabed; and from the first it has had the cordial support of my colleague, whose intimate acquaintance with some of the animal groups whose remains enter most largely into the chalk both old and new, makes his opinion on such a question particularly valuable.

On our return from the 'Lightning' cruise, during which we believed that our speculation had received strong confirmation, we used the expression,—perhaps somewhat an unfortunate one since it was capable of misconstruction,—that we might be regarded in a certain sense as still living in the cretaceous period. Several very eminent geologists, among whom were Sir Roderick Murchison and Sir Charles Lyell, took exception to this statement; but it seems that their censure was directed less against the opinion than the mode in which it was expressed; and I think I may say that the doctrine of the continuity of the chalk, in the sense in which we understood it, is now very generally accepted.

I do not maintain that the phrase 'we are still living in the cretaceous epoch,' is defensible in a strictly scientific sense, chiefly because the terms 'geological epoch' and 'geological period' are thoroughly indefinite. We speak indifferently of the 'Silurian period,' and the 'Glacial period,' without consideration of their totally unequal value; and of the 'Tertiary period,' and of the 'Miocene period,' although the one includes the other. The expression is intended rather in a popular sense to meet what was certainly until very lately the general popular impression, that a geological period has, in the region where it has been studied and defined, something like a beginning and an end; that it is bounded by periods of change—elevation, denudation, or some other evidence of the lapse of unrecorded time; and that it would be inadmissible to speak of two portions of the same continuous deposit, however distant the times of their deposition might be, and however distinct their imbedded faunæ, as belonging to different 'Geological periods.'

It was certainly in this sense that in an address to a popular audience in April 1869 I ventured to state my belief that it is not only chalk which is being formed in the Atlantic, "but *the* chalk, the chalk of the cretaceous period." Sir Charles Lyell says, in summing up his objections to this view,[1] "The reader will at once perceive that the present Atlantic, Pacific, and Indian oceans, are geographical terms which must be wholly without meaning when applied to the eocene, and still more to the cretaceous period, so that to talk of the chalk having been uninterruptedly formed in the Atlantic is as inadmissible in a geographical as in a geological sense." I confess I do not see the geographical difficulty; the "Atlantic ocean" is, undoubtedly, a geographical term, but the depression under discussion occupies the area at present expressed by that term, and to use it seems to be the simplest way of indicating its position. We believe that the balance of probability is greatly in favour of the chalk having been uninterruptedly forming over some parts of the area in question, and our belief is founded upon many considerations, physical and palæontological.

All the principal axes of elevation in the north of Europe and in North America have a date long anterior to the deposition of the tertiary, or even of the

[1] The Student's Elements of Geology. By Sir Charles Lyell, Bart., F.R.S. London, 1871. P. 265.

newer secondary beds, although some of them, such as the Alps and the Pyrenees, have received great accessions to their height in later times. All these newer beds have therefore been deposited with a certain relation in position to certain main features of contour which are maintained to the present day. Many oscillations have doubtless taken place since, and every spot on the European plateau may have probably alternated many times between sea and land; but it is difficult to show that these oscillations have occurred in the north of Europe to a greater extent than from 4,000 to 5,000 feet, the extreme vertical distance between the base of the tertiaries and the highest point at which tertiary or post-tertiary shells are found on the slopes and ridges of mountains. A subsidence of even 1,000 feet would, however, be sufficient to produce over most of the northern land a sea 100 fathoms deep, deeper than the German Ocean; and an elevation to a like amount would connect the Shetland and Orkney Islands and Great Britain and Ireland with Denmark and Holland, leaving only a long deep Fjord separating a British peninsula from Scandinavia. When we bear in mind the abundant evidence which we have that these minor oscillations, with a maximum range of 4,000 to 5,000 feet, have occurred again and again all over the world within comparatively recent periods, alternately uniting lands and separating them by shallow seas, the position of the deep water remaining throughout the same, the importance of an accurate determination of the depth of intervening sea in all speculations as to geographical distribution and the origin of special faunæ becomes most apparent.

From a glance at the map (Pl. VIII.), and remembering that nearly the same arrangement exists in regard to the newer rocks of North America, it would seem that the sum of these minor elevations and subsidences has produced a general elevation of the edges, and a general contraction,—of a basin the long axis of which coincides roughly with the long axis of the Atlantic. The Jurassic beds crop out along the outer edge of the basin, the cretaceous beds form a middle band, while the tertiaries occupy the troughs and valleys. All of these, however, maintain a certain parallelism determined by the contour of the earlier land and the direction of the older mountain ridges, to one another, and to the shores of the present sea.

From the parallel of 55° north latitude, at all events to the equator, we have on either side of the Atlantic a depression 600 or 700 miles in width, averaging 15,000 feet in depth. These two valleys are separated by the modern volcanic plateau of the Açores. It does not seem to us to be at all probable that any general oscillations have taken place in the northern hemisphere sufficient either to form these immense abysses, or, once formed, to convert them into dry land.

Reasoning partly upon physical and partly upon palæontological grounds, Mr. Prestwich thinks it probable that the ancient chalk ocean which formed a great transverse belt entirely across southern and eastern Europe and central Asia on the one hand, and across the Isthmus of Panama and southern North America on the other, was cut off by a land barrier from the Arctic Sea, and on that account possessed a much higher and more equable temperature to the bottom; and there is every reason to believe that such a land barrier did exist to the north of the great Atlantic basin, and continuous with the belt of northern land on which there is no deposition of cretaceous rocks. He says that "if such a land barrier existed at the period of the chalk, and that barrier was submerged during the earlier part of the tertiary period, it would, taken in conjunction with the very different conditions of depth under which the chalk and lower tertiaries were found, go far to account for the great break in the fauna of the two periods."

From the information we have as to the depths in the South Atlantic and the North Pacific, there seems to be no reason, however, to suppose that a barrier has recently existed shutting off the polar sea of the southern hemisphere; and I confess I cannot quite see how the result suggested by Mr. Prestwich could follow, without taking into account another condition of whose existence we seem to have evidence. A band of cretaceous rocks has been shown to extend round the world a little to the north of the equator wherever we have dry land; and it has likewise been shown, from considerations of depth, that this chalk band probably extended also across our great ocean basins. At that time, then, it seems that no continent ranging from north to south interrupted the drift of the equatorial current, deflecting the heated equatorial water to north and south and inducing a return indraught of polar water. This would undoubtedly remove one great cause, if not the sole cause, of the present low temperature of deep water between the tropics.

According to this view, the reduction of the temperature, the cause of the break in the fauna, would depend more upon the elevation of Central America and the Isthmus of Panama and the intertropical eastern coast of the continent of Asia, than even upon the depression of the northern barrier and the throwing open of the Arctic basin.

"If at any former period the climate of the globe was much warmer or colder than it is now, it would have a tendency to retain that higher or lower temperature for a succession of geological epochs. . . . The slowness of climatical change here alluded to would arise from the great depth of the sea as compared with the height of the land, and the consequent lapse of time required to alter the position of continents and great oceanic basins. . . . The mean height of the land is only 1,000 feet, the depth of the sea 15,000 feet. The effect, therefore, of vertical movements equally 1,000 feet in both directions, upwards and downwards, is to cause a vast transposition of land and sea in those areas which are now continental, and adjoining to which there is much sea not exceeding 1,000 feet in depth. But movements of equal amount would have no tendency to produce a sensible alteration in the Atlantic or Pacific oceans, or to cause the oceanic or continental areas to change places. Depressions of 1,000 feet would submerge large areas of existing land; but fifteen times as much movement would be required to convert such land into an ocean of average depth, or to cause an ocean three miles deep to replace any one of the existing continents."[1]

[1] Lyell, Principles of Geology, 1867. Pp. 265-6.

The wide extent of Tertiaries in Europe and the north of Africa sufficiently proves that much dry land has been gained in tertiary and post-tertiary times, and the great mountain-masses of Southern Europe give evidence of great local disturbance. But although the Alps and the Pyrenees are of sufficient magnitude to make a deep impression upon the senses of men, taking them together, these mountains would if spread out only cover the surface of the North Atlantic to the depth of six feet, and it would take at least two thousand times as much to fill up its bed. It would seem by no means improbable, that while the edges of what we call the great Atlantic depression have been gradually raised, the central portion may have acquired an equivalent increase in depth; but it seems most unlikely that while the main features of the contour of the northern hemisphere remain the same, an area of so vast extent should have been depressed by more than the height of Mont Blanc. On these physical grounds alone we are inclined to believe that a considerable portion of this area has been continually under water, and that consequently a deposit has been forming there uninterruptedly, from the period of the chalk to our own.

I will now turn to the palæontological bearings of the question. Long ago Mr. Lonsdale showed that the white chalk was mainly made up of the *débris* of foraminifera, and Dr. Mantell estimates the number of these shells at more than a million to a cubic inch. In 1848 Dr. Mantell, speaking of the chalk, says that it "forms such an assemblage of sedimentary deposits as would probably be presented to observation if a mass of the bed of the Atlantic, 2,000 feet in thickness, were elevated above the waters and became dry land; the only essential difference would be in the generic and specific characters of the imbedded animal and vegetable remains."[1] In 1858 Professor Huxley spoke of the Atlantic mud as "modern chalk."[2] Very early the identity of some of the chalk foraminifera with species now living was observed. Mr. Prestwich, in his able *résumé* of this question, so often quoted, gives a table drawn up by Professor Rupert Jones of 19 species of foraminifera out of 110 from the Atlantic mud identical with chalk forms, viz.:—

Species of Foraminifera found in both the Atlantic Mud and the Chalk of England and Europe.	Other older Formations in which they are also found.				
	Upper Jurassic.	Lower Jurassic.	Rhætic and Trias.	Permian.	Carboniferous.
Glandulina lævigata, D'ORBIGNY	×	—	×	—	—
Nodosaria radicula, LINN.	×	×	×	—	—
„ *raphanus*, LINN.	—	×	×	—	—
Dentalina communis, D'ORBIGNY	×	×	×	×	×
Cristellaria cultrata, MONT.	×	×	×	—	—
„ *rotulata*, LAM.	×	×	×	—	—
„ *crepidula*, F. and M.	—	×	—	—	—
Lagena sulcata, W. and J.	—	—	—	—	—
„ *globosa*, MONTAGU	—	—	—	—	—
Polymorphina lactea, W. and J.	×	—	—	—	—
„ *communis*, D'ORBIGNY.	—	—	—	—	—
„ *compressa*, D'ORBIGNY.	×	×	×	—	—
„ *orbignii*, EHR.	—	—	—	—	—
Globigerina bulloides, D'ORBIGNY	—	—	—	—	—
Planorbulina lobatula, W. and J.	—	—	—	—	—
Pulvinulina micheliana, D'ORBIGNY	—	—	—	—	—
Spiroplecta biformis, P. and J.	—	—	—	—	—
Verneuilina triquetra, VON M.	—	—	—	—	—
„ *polystropha*, REUSS	—	—	—	—	—

[1] Wonders of Geology, 6th edition, 1848. Vol. i. p. 305.

[2] Saturday Review.

And the following table, showing the number of foraminifera common to the Atlantic mud and various geological formations in England:—

Total in the deep Atlantic.	Common to the following Formations.							
	Crag.	London clay.	Chalk.	Upper Jurassic.	Lower Jurassic.	Rhætic and Upper Trias.	Permian.	Carboniferous.
110	53	28	19	7	7	7	1	1

The morphology of the foraminifera has been studied with great care, and the differences between closely allied so-called species are so slight that it is possible that in many cases they should only be regarded as varieties; but this careful criticism and appreciation of minute differences renders it all the more likely that the determinations are correct, and that animal forms which are substantially identical have persisted in the depths of the sea during a considerable lapse of geological time.

In the late deep-sea dredgings by M. de Pourtales off the American coast, and by H.M. ships 'Lightning' and 'Porcupine,' and Mr. Marshall Hall's yacht 'Norna' off the west coast of Europe, no animal forms have been discovered belonging to any of the higher groups, so far as we are as yet aware, specifically identical with chalk fossils; and I do not think that we have any right to expect that such will be found. To a depth of 5,000 feet or so a large portion of the North Atlantic is at present heated very considerably above its normal temperature, while the Arctic and Antarctic indraught depresses the bottom temperature in deep water to a like extreme degree. These abnormal temperatures are dependent upon the present distribution of sea and land; and I have already shown that we have evidence of many oscillations, in modern times geologically speaking, which must have produced totally different conditions of temperature over the same area. Accepting, as I believe we are now bound to do in some form, the gradual alteration of species through natural causes, we must be prepared to expect a total absence of forms identical with those found in the old chalk, belonging to groups in which there is sufficient structural differentiation to require or to admit of marked variation under altering circumstances. The utmost which can be expected is the persistence of some of the old generic types, and such a resemblance between the two faunæ as to justify the opinion that, making due allowance for emigration, immigration, and extermination, the later fauna bears to the earlier the relation of descent with extreme modification.

I have already mentioned that one of the most remarkable differences between the recent Atlantic chalk-mud and the ancient white chalk is the total absence in the latter of free silica. It would seem, from the analysis of chalk, that silicious organisms were entirely wanting in the ancient cretaceous seas. In the chalk mud, on the other hand, silica is found in abundance, in most specimens to the amount of from 30 to 40 per cent. A considerable portion of this is inorganic silica—sand; and its presence is doubtless due to the circumstance that our dredgings have hitherto been carried on in the neighbourhood of land and in the path of slight currents, whilst the extreme purity of the white chalk of Sussex would seem to indicate that it had been laid down in deep still water far from land. A considerable proportion of the silica of the chalk-mud, however, consists of the spicules of sponges, of the spicules and shields of radiolarians, and of the frustules of diatoms; and this organic silica is uniformly distributed through the whole mass. Taken in connection with the absence of diffused silica in the white chalk, we have the singular fact of the presence of regular layers of flinty masses of nearly pure silica, presenting frequently the external form of more or less regularly-shaped sponges, and frequently filling up the cavities of sea-urchins or bivalve shells. If we take the simple instance of pure grey flint filling up entirely the cavity of an urchin, such as *Galerites albo-galerus*, or *Ananchytes ovatus*, and showing at the oral opening of the shell a little projecting knob, like a bullet-mould filled with lead, we have no escape from the conclusion that after the death of the urchin the silica has percolated into the shell in solution or in a gelatinous condition, and the silica must have previously existed in some other form, either in the chalk or elsewhere. In the chalk which contains not a trace of silica we often find the moulds and outlines of organisms which we know to have been silicious, from which the whole of the silica has been removed; and I have more than once seen cases in which a portion of the delicate tracery of a silicious sponge has been preserved entire in a flint, while the remainder of the vase which projected beyond the outline of the flint appeared in the chalk as a trelliswork of spaces, vacant, or loosely filled with peroxide or carbonate of iron. It therefore seems certain that by some means or other the organic silica, distributed in the shape of sponge spicules and other silicious organisms in the chalk, has been dissolved or reduced to a colloid state, and accumulated in moulds formed by the shells or outer walls of imbedded animals of various classes. How the solution of the silica is effected we do not precisely know. Once reduced to a colloid condition, it is easy enough to imagine that it may be sifted from the water by a process of endosmose, the chalk matrix acting as a porous medium, and accumulated in any convenient cavities.

In various localities in the chalk and green-sand of the North of England the peculiar bodies which are called Ventriculites are excessively abundant,—elegant vases and cups with branching root-like bases, or groups of regularly or irregularly spreading tubes, delicately fretted on the surface with an impressed network like the finest lace. In the year 1840 the late Mr. Toulmin Smith published the result of many years' careful study of these bodies, and gave a minute and most accurate description of their structure. He found them to consist of tubes of extreme tenuity, delicately meshed, and having between them interspaces usually with very regular cubial or octohedral forms. These tubes in the Ventriculites found in chalk were empty, or contained a little red ochreous matter; but when a ventriculite or a portion of one happened to be entangled in a flint, it was either incorporated with the flint or replaced by silica. Mr. Toulmin Smith supposed that the skeleton of the ventriculite had been originally calcareous, and he referred the group to the Polyzoa. When Mr. Toulmin Smith studied the Ventriculites, the Hexactinellidæ—the sponges with six-rayed meshes or spicules—were practically unknown, though there

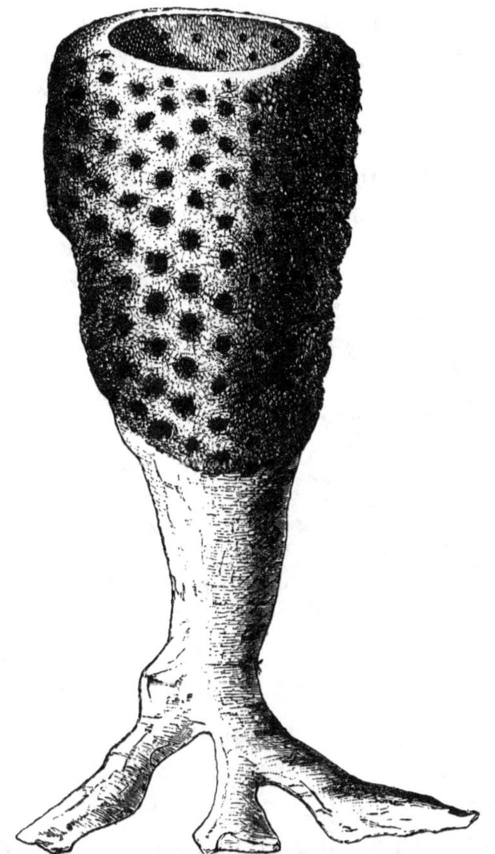

FIG. 80.—*Ventriculites simplex*, TOULMIN SMITH. Once and a half the natural size.

were already a few examples in museums. One of the first results of deep-sea dredging was the discovery that the chalk-mud of the deep sea is in many places literally crowded with these; and when we compare such recent forms as *Aphrocallistes, Iphiteon, Holtenia,* and *Askonema* with certain series of the chalk Ventriculites, there cannot be the slightest doubt that they belong to the same family—in some cases to very nearly allied genera. Fig. 80 represents a very beautiful specimen of *Ventriculites simplex* preserved in flint, for which I am indebted to Mr. Sanderson of Edinburgh. Looking at this in the light of our knowledge of *Euplectella* or *Aphrocallistes beatrix,* we have no difficulty in working out its structure, even to the most minute microscopic detail.

Other sponges, belonging chiefly to the Lithistidæ and the Corticatæ, reproduce with wonderful accuracy the more irregular sponge-forms of the chalk and greensand; and a group, as yet undescribed, but apparently an aberrant family of the Esperiadæ, send out long delicate tubes, which contract slightly, but in a most characteristic way, at the point of their insertion into the sponge body, recalling very forcibly the peculiar manner in which the tube-like root processes join the sponge in such genera as the vaguely defined *Choanites.*

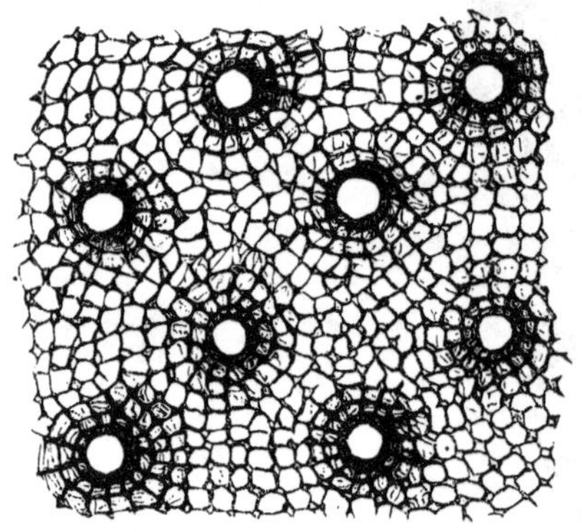

FIG. 81.—*Ventriculites simplex,* TOULMIN SMITH. Outer surface; four times the natural size.

One sponge belonging to the group is represented at Fig. 83. A sphere 15 to 20 mm. in diameter consists of a smooth glossy external rind, composed of closely meshed pin-headed spicules, with two kinds of 'spicules of the sarcode,' one large, C-shaped, the other much more minute, answering to Bowerbank's 'tridentate equianchorate' type; every now and then

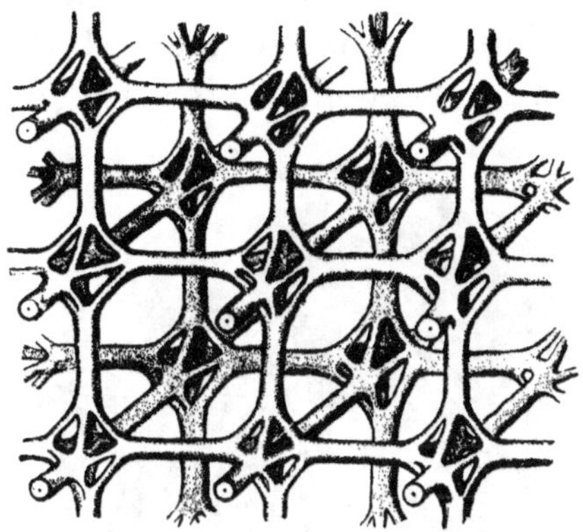

FIG. 82.—*Ventriculites simplex*, TOULMIN SMITH. Section of the outer wall, showing the structure of the silicious network. (x. 50.)

the rind thus formed coming to the margin of a small pore. The interior of the sphere is filled with soft semi-fluid sarcode, supported by the loosest possible

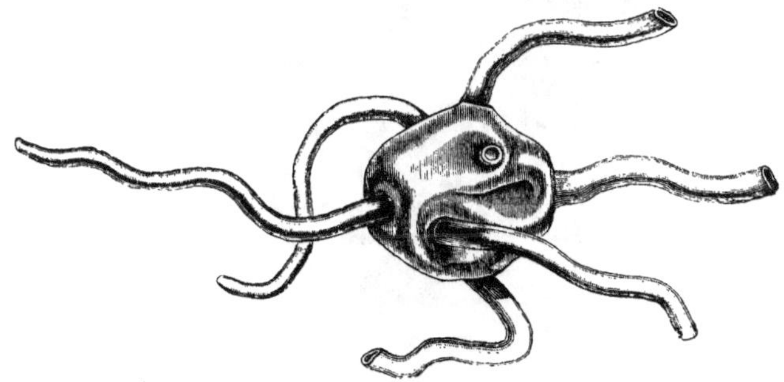

FIG. 83.—*Cœlosphæra tubifex*, WYVILLE THOMSON. Slightly enlarged. Off the coast of Portugal.

mesh-work of granular horny matter and pin-headed spicules. From points apparently irregularly placed on the surface of the sponge, tubes about 3 mm. in diameter run out in all directions; the walls of the tubes are thin and delicate, being more so towards the distant ends, where the tubes contract slightly to an open orifice. At the proximal end, at the junction between the tube and the sponge body, there is also a contraction, and a slight pit-like involution of the surface of the sponge. There is something very characteristic in this pecu-

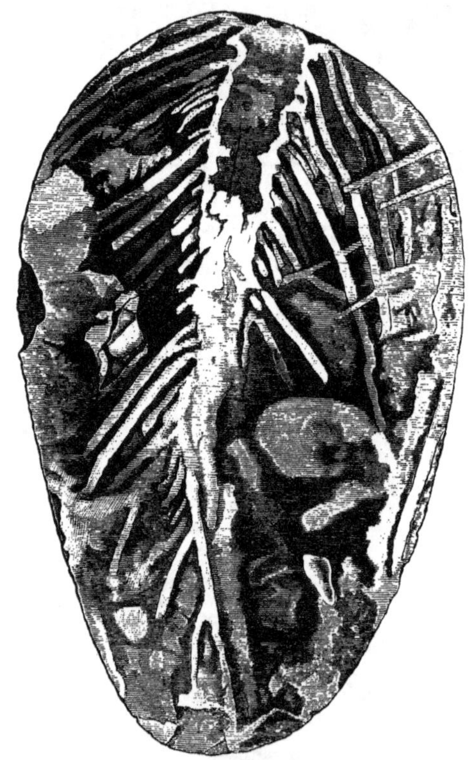

FIG. 84.—'*Choanites.*' In a flint from the white chalk.

liar form of junction which it is not easy to define, but which almost forces the conviction that there is the closest relation between these recent forms and tube-bearing fossil sponges such as *Choanites*.

Professor Martin Duncan mentions several corals

from the coast of Portugal more nearly allied to chalk forms than to any others, but it is in the Echinodermata that the peculiar relation between the ancient and the modern faunæ becomes most apparent. To review briefly the chief points bearing upon this question. The Apiocrinidæ, the group of fixed crinoids which I have already described, are abundant throughout the whole range of the Jurassic rocks, their remains being frequently very abundant in the thick cream-coloured limestone beds of the oolites. Towards the close of the Jurassic period, the typical genera disappear, and in the chalk we find the group represented by an evidently degenerate form, *Bourguetticrinus*. In some tertiary-beds fragments of the stems of a small *Bourguetticrinus* have been found, and such were likewise discovered in the recent lime breccia of Guadaloupe, which contained the well-known human skeleton now in the British Museum. There can be little doubt that these tertiary and post-tertiary fragments are to be referred rather to the genus *Rhizocrinus*, which we now know to be so widely distributed, living, in deep water. Now in this series of Apiocrinidæ, extending from the Forest marble to the present time, although there is a succession of constantly changing species, yet the gradual degradation in development in the same direction throughout the series seems to point unmistakeably to some form of continuity, to a type gradually succumbing to conditions slowly altering in an unfavourable direction.

The other family of the stalked crinoids, the Pentacrinidæ, are in a different position. They are abundant in the Lias; very abundant in the lower oolite, where slabs are often found almost made up of them, with a characteristic deep-water association of *Cidaris*, *Astrogonium*, and *Astropecten;* and although not abundant in the English chalk, several species are found, and these show no tendency to degeneracy. As might be expected, such remains are rare in the shallow-water tertiaries. With regard to their distribution in modern seas, from the apparent abundance of *P. asteria* and *P. mülleri* in deep water in the West Indies, and of *P. wyville-thomsoni* off the coast of Portugal, it is very possible, as I have already said, that they may occupy a much more important place in the abyssal fauna than we at present imagine.

Nearly all the additions from the deep water to the list of the Asteridea fall into the genera *Archaster* and *Astropecten*, or into the various subdivisions of the old genus *Goniaster*. From their breaking up into a multitude of undistinguishable ossicles by the decomposition of their soft organic matter immediately after death, the fossil remains of star-fishes are comparatively rare, and are scarcely met with except in fine calcareous formations, such as the Wenlock limestone,—and in later times in the fine yellow limestones of the oolites, and in the white chalk. In the latter formation, deposited apparently very much under the same circumstances as the Atlantic chalk-mud, the general character of the group of imbedded star-fishes is almost the same as in the modern fauna of the deep Atlantic.

The Echinidea are a more typical order. From the compactness of their tests they are more readily preserved entire, and from the earliest periods their characteristic and harmoniously varying series are of considerable value in the discrimination of the different formations. In the soft white chalk of the south of England their remains are extremely abundant. Perhaps the most abundant and characteristic fossils in the chalk are the Cidaridæ, and these more than any other chalk fossils illustrate the peculiar conditions under which the chalk has been laid down. The great spines of *Cidaris* are attached to the plates of the shell by a central ligament which passes from the cup on the spine to a perforation in the ball on the plate, and by a membrane which rises from the plate and passes over the base of the spine. The spines are, however, so disproportionately large, and the soft matter softens and decomposes so rapidly after death, that it is difficult to keep the spines attached to a specimen prepared even with considerable care. In the chalk, tests of *Cidaris* are frequently preserved absolutely entire, with all the spines in position; so that by carefully working out the chalk with a penknife, we can here have the whole animal perfect. It is difficult to see precisely how this result can have been produced. The urchin must have sunk into the soft chalk-mud and been covered up by a sufficient quantity to support its spines and test, and allow the whole to become gradually compacted into a solid mass. One of the new deep-sea Cidarites belongs to a genus which had previously been supposed to be extinct, but the chalk-mud forms generally do not show any special approach to any particular chalk species. Still the general character of the group is the same. The Echinothuridæ were previously known only as chalk fossils, so that their presence apparently in abundance in the recent chalk-mud is a clear instance of the preservation of one of the old types hitherto supposed to be extinct. The same may be said of *Pourtalesia*, which must associate itself either with *Ananchytes* or with *Dysaster*, both of which are types of groups likewise supposed to have been lost. We thus find that, while no Echinoderm hitherto discovered in the deep water is specifically identical with any chalk form, not only does the abyssal fauna with its abundance of the Cidaridæ, Echinothuridæ, and irregular urchins, and the disproportionate numbers of the genera *Astropecten*, *Astrogonium*, and *Stellaster*, and their allies among starfishes, singularly resemble the chalk in general facies; but several genera approach chalk forms more closely than they do any hitherto known in a living state —approach them so closely as almost to force upon us the conviction that their relation is one of descent, accompanied by change of conditions and consequent modification, though not to any extreme degree.

As I have already stated, the whole of the mollusca from the deep water which had been previously described as fossils were known from tertiary and post-tertiary beds; with the very doubtful exception of our common *Terebratulina caput-serpentis*, which certainly approaches very closely *Terebratula* striata from the chalk.

It is not surprising that this should be the case. It is a marked character of the European Tertiaries that with the exception of some of the older beds in the south of Europe, all of them have been deposited in shallow water; so that the tertiary beds represent the mineral accumulations and the fauna of the margin of some sea. We may say that they have been deposited in the shallow water of tertiary seas whose deep-sea fauna is unknown, and this mode of expression is most in accordance with previous ideas; but if the view here advocated be correct, we must regard the tertiaries as the deposits formed and exposed by depressions and upheavals of the borders of the cretaceous sea; of a sea which, with many changes of condition produced by the same oscillations which alternately exposed and submerged the tertiaries, existed continuously, depositing conformable beds of chalk-mud from the period of the ancient chalk.

Mollusca are chiefly shallow-water forms, although some of them are special to deep water, and others have a great vertical range. As I have already said, considering the many changes in the conditions which most affect animal life which have occurred during later geological times, we cannot expect to find any animals of the higher groups specifically identical with chalk fossils; the difficulty in the case seems rather to be to account for the identity of many living deep-water species with species found in the Tertiaries. I think, however, that we can find a clue. Most of the species common to the modern Atlantic and to tertiary beds are now found in the Atlantic at much greater depths than those at which they were imbedded in the tertiary seas. This we know by the species from shallower water which are associated with them in the Tertiaries. They are, therefore, species which had a considerable vertical range; and probably while many of the shallower water forms were exterminated by elevations or other change affecting the first one or two hundred fathoms, they were enabled to survive, the deeper part of their habitat having suffered but little alteration.

Sir Charles Lyell says: "The reader should be reminded that in geology we have been in the habit of founding our great chronological divisions, not on foraminifera and sponges, nor even on echinoderms or corals, but on the remains of the most highly organized beings available to us, such as mollusca. . . . In dealing with the mollusca, it is those of the highest or most specialized organizations which afford us the best characters in proportion as their vertical range is the most limited. Thus the cephalopoda are the most valuable, as having a more restricted range in time than the gasteropoda, and these again are more characteristic of the particular stratigraphical subdivisions than the lamellibranchiate bivalves, while these last again are more serviceable in classification than the brachiopoda, a still lower class of shell-fish, which are the most enduring of all." With great deference to Sir Charles Lyell, I cannot regard the most highly specialized animal groups as those most fitted to gauge the limits of great chronological divisions, though I admit their infinite value in determining the minor subdivisions.

The culmination of such animal groups, such as we find in the marvellous abundance and variety of both orders of cephalopods at the end of the Jurassic and the commencement of the cretaceous period, undoubtedly brings into high relief, and admirably illustrates to the student, the broad distinctive characters of the mezozoic fauna; but speaking very generally, the more highly a mollusc is specialized the shallower is the water which it inhabits. The cephalopods are chiefly pelagic and surface things, and their remains are consequently found in deposits from all depths. To this general pelagic distribution of cephalopods there seem to be two remarkable exceptions, and these the two members of their class which are by far the most interesting in their geological relations. *Nautilus pompilius* inhabits the deep water of the Pacific, while the habitat of *Spirula australis* is unknown. The shell of *Spirula* is thin and light, and, probably after the death of the animal and by the decomposition of organic matter, it becomes filled with air, and the emptied shell floats, and is drifted along on the surface of the sea. Tropical shores are strewn with the pearly little coil, which attracts attention by the elegance of its form. It is abundant on all shores in the path of the Gulf-stream. Sysselmann Müller gave me, a few years ago, a quantity which had been drifted on the south-western shores of different islands of the Færoe group. Still the structure of the animal of *Spirula* may be said to be unknown. One specimen only, which was described by Professor Owen, was found nearly perfect on the coast of New Zealand by Mr. Percy Noel. I suppose there can be little doubt that this is a deep-water form, and I hope that with our deep-sea dredging we shall soon clear up its economy; but in the meantime the evident abundance of the animal and our ignorance of its history are very suggestive. In the London clay one or two examples of a fossil have been found, nearly allied to *Spirula*, but differing in this respect—that a solid conical rostrum projects backwards, its half-calcified, half-horny substance enclosing the greater part of the curved spiral shell. Now if the recent *Spirula* had been weighted with such a rostrum it would probably have remained up to the present time utterly unknown to us. It is unwise to prophesy, but I certainly look upon some form allied to *Spirulirostris* as one of the most likely spoils of the deep sea. From the Tertiaries we pass to the Cretaceous forms, and find in *Belemnitella* the chambered shell straightened and reduced, and the 'guard' greatly increased in size. If Belemnites were deep-sea animals, as seems very probable, and if any of them still exist,—from the form and weight of their shells it is scarcely possible that they should ever be thrown up on the shore, and without deep-sea dredging they might remain for ever unknown. I merely mention this to show that it is by no means safe to base even what little argument might rest upon it, upon the absence at the present time of all representatives of the cretaceous cephalopodous fauna.

The gasteropods, with comparatively few exceptions, range from the shore to a depth of 100 to 200 fathoms, and lamellibranchs become scarcer at a slightly greater depth; while some orders of brachiopods, crustacea, echinoderms, sponges, and foraminifera, descend in scarcely diminished numbers to a depth of 10,000 feet. In fact, the bathymetrical range of the various groups in modern seas corresponds remarkably with their vertical range in ancient strata.

A change in the distribution of sea and land involving a mere change in the course of an ocean-current might modify the conditions of an area for most cephalopods and all pteropods, heteropods, and other surface living animals of high type, even to their extinction. By oscillations of 500 feet up or down, the great mass of gasteropods, and all reef-building corals, would be forced to emigrate, would become modified, or would be destroyed,—and another hundred fathoms would exterminate the greater number of bivalves; while elevations and depressions to ten times that amount might only slightly affect the region of brachiopods, echinoderms, and sponges.

After a careful consideration of the results of recent investigations, we are strengthened in our confidence in the truth of the opinion which we previously held, that the various groups of fossils characterizing the tertiary beds of Europe and North America represent the constantly altering fauna of the shallower portions of an ocean whose depths are still occupied by a deposit which has been accumulating continuously from the period of the pre-tertiary chalk, and which perpetuates with much modification the pre-tertiary chalk fauna. I do not see that this view militates in the least against the "reasoning and classification" of that geology which we have learned from Sir Charles Lyell; our dredgings only show that these abysses of the ocean—abysses which Sir Charles Lyell admits in the passage quoted above, to have outlasted on account of their depth a succession of geological epochs—are inhabited by a special deep-sea fauna, possibly as persistent in its general features as the abysses themselves. I have said at the beginning of this chapter, that I believe the doctrine of the 'continuity of the chalk,' as understood by those who first suggested it, now meets with very general acceptance; and in evidence of this I will quote two passages in two consecutive anniversary addresses by Presidents of the Geological Society, and we may have every confidence that the statements of men of so great weight, made under such circumstances, indicate the tendency of sound and judicious thought. Professor Huxley, in the anniversary address for the year 1870, says :—"Many years ago[1] I ventured to speak of the Atlantic mud as 'modern chalk,' and I know of no fact inconsistent with the view which Professor Wyville Thomson has advocated, that the modern chalk is not only the lineal descendant, so to speak, of the ancient chalk, but that it remains, so to speak, in possession of the ancestral estate ; and that from the cretaceous period (if not much earlier) to the present day, the deep sea has covered a large part of what is now the area of the Atlantic. But if *Globigerina* and *Terebratula caput-serpentis* and *Beryx*, not to mention other forms of animals and of plants, thus bridge over the interval between the present and the mezozoic periods, is it possible that the majority of other living things underwent a sea-change into something new and strange all at once ?"

And Mr. Prestwich, in the presidential address for 1871, says :—"Therefore, although I think it highly probable that some considerable portion of the deep sea-bed of the mid-Atlantic has continued submerged since the period of our chalk, and although the more adaptable forms of life may have been transmitted in unbroken succession through this channel, the immigrations of other and more recent faunas may have so modified the old population, that the original

[1] Saturday Review, 1858 : "Chalk, Ancient and Modern."

chalk element is of no more importance than is the original British element in our own English people."

Mr. Prestwich thus fully admits the high probability of the 'continuity' for which we contend. The last question which he raises in the sentence quoted is one of enormous difficulty, which we have as yet no data to solve. It is perhaps not very much harder, however, after all, than the problem in ethnology which he has selected as an illustration.

Several other very important questions bearing upon the conditions of the ocean at great depths, occupied the attention of the naturalists in scientific charge of the dredging cruises of the 'Lightning' and 'Porcupine.' An assistant versed in the methods of chemical and physical research accompanied the vessel on each occasion. A son of Dr. Carpenter, Mr. William Lant Carpenter, B.A., B.Sc., went on the first cruise with Mr. Jeffreys. Mr. John Hunter, F.C.S., a promising young chemist, since deceased, accompanied me to the Bay of Biscay, and Mr. Herbert Carpenter, a younger son of my colleague, was our companion during the third long cruise in the Færoe channel.

The specific gravity of the water was taken at each station, and in the serial soundings the water-bottle was let down to the intermediate depths and the water carefully tested. The differences observed were very slight, but they were as a rule confirmatory of Professor Forschammer's opinion that Arctic water contains less salt than the sea-water of temperate and intertropical regions.

As I have already mentioned (page 46), organic matter in appreciable quantity was detected by the permanganate test everywhere, and at all depths. The gas contained in the water was carefully analysed, and it was found, as a general result, that the amount of free carbon dioxide increased and the proportion of oxygen diminished with increased depth. There seemed to be reason to believe, however, that the quantity of carbon dioxide depended to a great degree upon the abundance of the higher forms of life. Mr. Lant Carpenter used always to predict a bad haul for the zoologists when he found the proportion of carbon dioxide to the oxygen and nitrogen unusually low. The great increase in the quantity of carbon dioxide was just above the bottom. The general average of thirty analyses of surface-water gives the following as the proportions of the contained gases present:—Oxygen 25·1, nitrogen 54·2, carbon dioxide 20·7; this proportion was subject, however, to great variations. Intermediate water gave an average percentage of oxygen 22·0, nitrogen 52·8, and carbon dioxide 26·2; while bottom waters gave—oxygen 19·5, nitrogen 52·6, and carbon dioxide 27·9. But bottom water, at a comparatively small depth, often contained as much carbon dioxide as intermediate water at much greater depths. In one of the serial soundings, in which the water was taken at every 50 fathoms, three analyses gave the following singular result:—

	750 Fathoms.	800 Fathoms.	Bottom, 862 Faths.
Oxygen	18·8	17·8	17·2
Nitrogen	49·3	48·5	34·5
Carbon dioxide . .	31·9	33·7	48·3

The greatly increased percentage of carbon dioxide in the stratum of sea-water immediately overlying the sea-bed, was here accompanied by a great abundance of animal life.

I can scarcely regret that the space at my disposal will not allow me to enter at present into the many very important bearings of these physical investigations, for I am compelled to admit that I do not place thorough confidence in our results. The observations and analyses were undoubtedly conducted with great care and skill, but the difference between different samples—in specific gravity, and more especially in chemical composition and the relative proportion of the ingredients—is so very slight, that more exact methods than those which have been hitherto employed will be required to insure accurate results.

In such investigations everything depends upon the perfection of the means of bringing up water from any given depth; and the principle of the construction of the water-bottle used in the 'Porcupine' was faulty. It consists of a strong tube of brass about two feet in length and two inches in internal diameter, containing rather more than a litre and a half, and closed at each end by a brass disk. In the centre of each of these disks there is a round aperture closed by a well-ground conical valve, both valves opening upwards when the instrument is in position for being let down.

In passing down through the water, a continuous current is supposed to raise the valves and run through the bottle, thus keeping it constantly filled with the water of the layer through which it is passing. On reversing the motion in hauling up, the valves fall into their places, and the contents of the tube at the greatest depth are brought to the surface. This bottle appeared to answer fairly, and we often had evidence, from its turbidity, that bottom-water came up; but subsequent experiments have shown that it cannot be depended upon, and some of the reasons are sufficiently obvious. The instrument will not work at all unless the descending motion be sufficiently steady and rapid to maintain a current capable of keeping two heavy brass valves open to their full extent; if there be the slightest reversal, or jerk, or irregularity in hauling up, the water is—at all events partially—changed; the two valves, even when thoroughly open, are directly in the path of the ingress and egress of the water—and there is reason to believe that the water is not so rapidly and thoroughly changed as we at first imagined. A perfectly satisfactory water-bottle is still a desideratum, but I believe that one which was used by Dr. Mayer and Dr. Jacobsen in the German North Sea expedition of the past summer, goes far to remedy most of these defects. I hope we may be in a better position to give an opinion a year hence.

I give, in the appendix to this chapter, an abstract of the general results of the chemical investigations carried on during the 'Porcupine' cruises of 1869; and I add a note, for which I am indebted to my friend Mr. J. Y. Buchanan, who accompanies me as chemist to the 'Challenger' expedition, which will show how much has yet to be done before we can hope to come to any really satisfactory conclusion as to the amount and condition of the gases contained in sea-water. Neither, I regret to say, can we place much reliance on the determination of organic matter in sea-water by the permanganate method, although there is every probability that the general result at which we arrived—that organic matter is contained in the water of the ocean in all localities and at all depths—is substantially true. The application of the exact methods of modern science to this line of inquiry is new, and it will require long and patient work to bring it to perfection. The one real advance which has been made in this direction is the addition to the appliances for the investigation of the physics of the deep sea; of a correct and trustworthy instrument by which ocean temperatures can be ascertained to any depth with what may be regarded as absolute accuracy for all practical purposes.

KUNÖ, FROM VAAŸ IN BORDÖ.

APPENDIX A.

Summary of the Results of the Examination of Samples of Sea-water taken at the Surface and at various Depths. By WM. LANT CARPENTER, B.A., B.Sc.

Surface-waters.—Care was taken to obtain these samples as pure as possible, and free from any contamination caused by matters derived from the vessel, by dipping them up in clean vessels at a few inches below the surface at or near the bow of the ship. In two instances, however, the samples were taken from abaft the paddles.

Waters taken at depths below the surface.—It was found desirable to coat the brass Water-Bottles internally with sealing-wax varnish, owing to the corrosive action of the sea-water. The apparatus was then found to work perfectly satisfactorily in all cases in which there was sufficient weight on the sounding-line to which they were attached to keep the bottles perpendicular, or nearly so. When, from the smallness of the attached weight, or the roughness of the sea, the sounding-line was at an acute angle with the general level of the sea-surface while it was being drawn up, the results of the examination of water thus obtained rendered it highly probable that some water at or near the surface had found its way into the bottle, and that its contents were not to be relied on as coming from the lowest depths.

When bottom-water was obtained from depths beyond 500 fathoms, it was almost invariably charged with a quantity of very fine mud in suspension, rendering it quite turbid. Many hours' standing was necessary for the deposit of this; but it was readily removed by filtration. In no instance was there any evidence of water from great depths being much more highly charged with dissolved gases than surface-waters; a considerable elevation of temperature being in *all* cases necessary for the evolution of any dissolved gas.

Mode of examining Samples.—The samples of water thus taken were examined with as little delay as possible, with a view to determine:—

(1) The specific gravity of the water.

(2) The total quantity of dissolved gases contained in them, and the relative proportions of oxygen, nitrogen, and carbonic acid.

(3) The quantity of oxygen necessary to oxidize the organic matter contained in the water; distinguishing between
a, the decomposed organic matter, and
b, the easily decomposable organic matter.

(1) The specific gravity determinations were made at a temperature as near 60° Fahr. as possible, with delicate glass hydrometers, so graduated that the specific gravity could be read off directly to the fourth decimal place with ease.

(2) The apparatus for the analysis of the gases dissolved in the sea-water was essentially that described by Prof. Miller in the second volume of his 'Elements of Chemistry.' It was found necessary to make several modifications in it, to adapt it to the motion of the vessel. These consisted chiefly in suspending much of it from the cabin-ceiling, instead of supporting it from beneath, and in rendering all the parts less rigid by a free use of caoutchouc tubing, &c., the utmost care being taken to keep all joints tight.

It was found possible to make correct analyses, even when the vessel was rolling sufficiently to upset chairs and cabin-furniture.

The method of analysis may be thus summarized:—From 700 to 800 cubic centimetres of the sample to be examined were boiled for about thirty minutes, in such a way that the steam and mixed gases evolved were collected over mercury in a small graduated Bunsen's gas-holder, all access of air being carefully guarded against. The mixed gases were then transferred to two graduated tubes in a mercurial trough, where the carbonic acid was first absorbed by a strong solution of caustic potash; and subsequently the oxygen was absorbed by the addition of pyrogallic acid, the remaining gas being assumed to be nitrogen.

The results of the analyses were always corrected to the standard temperature of 0° Cent., and to 760 millimetres' barometric pressure, for comparison among themselves and with others. In nearly every case the duplicate analyses from the same gaseous mixture agreed closely, if they were not identical.

(3) The examination of the sea-water for organic matter was made according to the method detailed by Prof. Miller in the Journal of the Chemical Society for May 1865, with an addition suggested by Dr. Angus Smith. Each sample of water was divided into two; to one of these a little free acid was added, and to both an excess of a standard solution of permanganate of potash. At the end of three hours the reaction was stopped by the addition of iodide of potassium and starch, and the excess of permanganate estimated by a standard solution of hyposulphide of soda. The portion to which free acid was added gave the oxygen required to oxidize the decomposed and easily decomposable organic matter; the second portion gave the oxygen required by the decomposed organic matter alone, which was usually from about one-half to one-third of the whole.

The following is a summary of the total number of observations, analyses, &c., made during the three cruises respectively:—

	First Cruise.	Second Cruise.	Third Cruise.	Total.
Specific-gravity determinations .	72	27	26	125
Duplicate gas-analyses	45	23	21	89
Organic-matter tests	137	26	32	195

Specific Gravity.—The specific gravity of surface-water was found to diminish slightly as land was approached; but the average of thirty-two observations upon water at a sufficient distance from land to be unaffected by local disturbances was 1·02779, the maximum being 1·0284 and the minimum 1·0270.

It was almost always noticed that, during a high wind, the specific gravity of surface-water was *above* the average.

The average of thirty observations upon the specific gravity of intermediate water was 1·0275, the maximum being 1·0281 and the minimum 1·0272.

The specific gravity of bottom-waters at depths varying from 77 to 2,090 fathoms, deduced from an average of forty-three observations, was 1·0277, the maximum being 1·0283 and the minimum 1·0267.

It will be noticed that the average specific gravity of bottom-water is slightly less than that of surface-water. In several instances the specific gravities of surface- and of bottom-waters taken at the same place having been compared, that of the bottom-water was found to be appreciably less than that of the surface-water. Thus—

At 1425 fathoms' depth (Station 17) it was . .	1·0269
Surface at the same	1·0280

And

At 664 fathoms' depth (Station 26 *b*) it was . .	1·0272
Surface at the same	1·0280

According, however, to a series of observations made at the same spot (Station 42) at intervals of fifty fathoms, from 50 to 800, the specific gravity increased with the depth from 1·0272 at 50 fathoms to 1·0277 at 800 fathoms.

Several series of specific-gravity observations were made near the mouths of rivers and streams; showing the gradual mixture of fresh and salt water, and the floating of lighter portions above the denser sea-water, as well as the reverse effect produced by the influence of tidal currents. Thus outside Belfast Lough a rapid stream of water of specific gravity 1·0270 was found above water which, at a depth of seventy-three fathoms, had a specific gravity of 1·0265.

Gases of Sea-water.—The analyses of the gaseous constituents of sea-water may be divided into two groups: (1) Analyses of surface-waters. (2) Analyses of waters below the surface; and these last may be again subdivided into (*a*) intermediate, and (*b*) bottom-waters.

The total quantity of dissolved gases in sea-water, whether at the surface or below it, was found to average about 2·8 volumes in 100 volumes of water.

The average of thirty analyses of surface-waters made during the expedition gave the following proportions:—

	Percentage.	Proportion.
Oxygen	25·046	100
Nitrogen . . .	54·211	216
Carbonic acid . . .	20·743	80
	100·000	

These were thus distributed over the three cruises, and the maxima and minima of each constituent are thus shown:—

	Number of analyses.	Average per-centage.			Average proportion.			Oxygen.		Nitrogen.		Carbonic Acid.	
		Oxy-gen.	Nitro-gen.	Car-bonic Acid.	O.	N.	CO_2	Max. per cent.	Min per cent.	Max. per cent.	Min. per cent.	Max. per cent.	Min. per cent.
First Cruise .	19	24·47	52·95	22·58	100	216	92	28·78	19·60	62·95	46·35	32·0	12·72
Second Cruise.	2	31·33	54·85	13·82	100	175	44	37·10	25·56	59·63	50·07	24·37	3·27
Third Cruise .	9	24·86	56·73	18·41	100	228	74	45·28	13·98	68·67	41·42	27·14	5·64

It is interesting to remark that surface-water contains a greater quantity of oxygen and a less quantity of carbonic acid during the prevalence of strong wind. The following is an average of five analyses made under such conditions:—

		Per cent.	Proportion.	General average.	
5	Oxygen	29·10	100	25·046	100
	Nitrogen . . .	52·87	182	54·211	216
	Carbonic acid . .	18·03	62	20·743	83

In the two cases which presented the remarkable small *minima* of carbonic acid with a great excess of oxygen, the water had been accidentally taken from immediately abaft the paddles, where it had been subject to violent agitation in contact with air.

Of water at various depths beneath the surface, fifty-nine analyses were made. Those in the first cruise, twenty-six in number, were chiefly from bottom-water at depths from 25 to 1,476 fathoms. In the second cruise the twenty-one analyses chiefly belonged to two series,—the first of samples taken at intervals of 250 fathoms, from 2,090 to 250 fathoms inclusive; and the second of samples taken at intervals of fifty fathoms from 862 to 400 fathoms inclusive. In the third cruise twelve analyses were made,—eight of bottom-water, of which one-half were in the "cold area," and four at intermediate depths.

The general average of the fifty-nine analyses of water taken below the surface gives:—

	Percentage.	Proportion.
Oxygen	20·568	100
Nitrogen	52·240	254
Carbonic acid	27·192	132
	100·000	

It will be seen from this that while the quantity of nitrogen is only 1·97 per cent. less than in surface-water, the quantity of oxygen is diminished by 4·48 per cent., and the quantity of carbonic acid increased by 6·45 per cent. This difference is greater if bottom-waters only are compared with surface-waters.

	30 Surface.		24 Intermediate.		35 Bottom.	
	Per cent.	Proportion.	Per cent.	Proportion.	Per cent.	Proportion.
Oxygen . . .	25·05	100	22·03	100	19·53	100
Nitrogen . . .	54·21	216	51·82	235	52·60	261
Carbonic acid .	20·74	83	26·15	119	27·87	143
	100·00		100·00		100·00	

The two series of analyses, before referred to, performed during the second cruise upon intermediate waters at successive depths over the same spot, both show a regular increase of the carbonic acid and diminution of the oxygen, as the depth increases, the percentage of nitrogen varying but slightly.

These general results appear to show that the oxygen diminishes and the carbonic acid increases with the depth until the bottom is reached; but that *at* the bottom, whatever the depth from the surface, the proportions of carbonic acid and of oxygen do not conform to this law, bottom-water at a comparatively small depth often containing as much carbonic acid and as little oxygen as intermediate water at a greater depth. No instance occurred during the first two cruises in which (where samples of surface and intermediate or bottom-waters were taken at the same place) the quantity of carbonic acid was less and of oxygen greater than at the surface; the only exception occurred in the third cruise, at a place where, it is believed, currents of water were meeting.

It was frequently noticed that a large percentage of carbonic acid in bottom-water was accompanied by an abundance of animal life, as shown by the dredge; and that where the dredge-results were barren, the quantity of carbonic acid was much smaller. The greatest percentage of carbonic acid ever found was accompanied by an abundance of life; while at a short distance (62 fathoms) above the bottom, the proportion of carbonic acid was conformable to the law of variation with depth before referred to:—

	Bottom, 862 fms.	800 fms.	750 fms.
Oxygen	17·22	17·79	18·76
Nitrogen	34·50	48·46	49·32
Carbonic acid . . .	48·28	33·75	31·92
	100·00	100·00	100·00

The lowest percentage of carbonic acid (7·93) ever found in bottom-water, occurring at a depth of 362 fathoms, was accompanied by a "very bad haul."

In crossing the wide channel from the north-west of Ireland towards Rockall, where the water for some distance is over 1,000 fathoms depth, so that the other circumstances varied very little, if at all, the proportion of carbonic acid appeared to vary with the dredge-results; so that the analyst ventured to predict whether the collection would be good or not before the dredge came to the surface—drawing his inference from the results of his analyses of the gases of the bottom-water. In each case his prediction was justified by the result.

	STATION 17. 1,425 fms.	STATION 19. 1,360 fms.	STATION 20. 1,443 fms.	STATION 21. 1,476 fms.
Oxygen	16·14	17·92	21·34	16·68
Nitrogen	48·78	45·88	47·51	43·46
Carbonic acid . .	35·07	36·20	31·15	39·86
	100·00	100·00	100·00	100·00
	Good haul.	Good haul.	Bad haul.	Good haul.

In the analyses made of the water in the cold area, and generally in the third cruise, there appears, as might be expected from the various currents, &c., a greater variation in the results than in the other series. In the bottom and intermediate waters the nitrogen appears to be rather in excess of the average, and the carbonic acid has a large range of variation—from 7·58 per cent. at Station 47 (540 fathoms, temp. 43°·8) to 45·79 per cent. at Station 52 (384 fathoms, 30°·6 Fahr.). The average of the surface-waters is much the same as in the other parts of the cruise.

It may be worth notice that in localities where the greatest depth did not exceed 150 fathoms, the results of the gas-analysis of bottom- and surface-water were frequently so nearly the same, whatever the amount of animal life on the bottom, as to lead to the supposition that there might be at that limit a sufficient circulation, either of the particles of the water itself or of the gases dissolved in it, to keep the gaseous constitution alike throughout. The coincidence of this depth with the extreme depth at which fish are usually found to exist in these seas is suggestive.

Organic matter.—With a view to test the method of analysis by permanganate of potash, two or three series of analyses were made where fresh and salt water mixed together, as in Killibegs Harbour, Donegal Bay, &c.; and the results in all cases justified the expectation formed, that the amount of permanganate was an index of the comparative purity of the water, both as regards the "decomposed" and the "decomposable" organic matter.

Disregarding the above series, a total of 134 experiments were made upon sea-water, which may be thus divided:—

56 upon surface-water,
18 " intermediate water,
60 " bottom-water,

134

during the first and third cruises.

The results are given in the quantity of oxygen in fractions of a gramme required to oxidize the organic matter in a litre of water.

Average of 56 analyses of surface-water:—

No.			
28.	Decomposed . . .	0·00025	Total 0·00095.
28.	Decomposable . .	0·00070	

	Maximum.	Minimum.	
Decomposed . . .	0·00094	0·00000	4 cases.
Decomposable . .	0·00100	0·00000	1 case.
Total . . .	0·00194	0·00000	1 case.

Average of 18 analyses of intermediate water:—

No.			
9.	Decomposed . . .	0·00005	Total 0·00039.
9.	Decomposable. . .	0·00034	

In 7 out of 9 there was no "decomposed" organic matter; and in 3 out of 9 there was no organic matter at all, as indicated by this test.

In this series the analyses of the observations made during the second cruise are not included, as the calculations have been differently made.

Average of 60 analyses of bottom-water:—

No.			
26.	Decomposed . . .	0·00047	Total 0·00088
34.	Decomposable. . .	0·00041	

	Maximum.	Minimum.	
Decomposed . .	0·00105	0·00000	2 cases.
Decomposable . .	0·00148	0·00000	1 case.
Total . .	0·00253	0·00000	1 case.

These figures appear to show (1) that intermediate waters are more free from organic contamination than either surface- or bottom-waters, as might be expected from the comparative absence of animal life in these waters; (2) that the total absence of organic matter is least frequent in bottom-waters, and most frequent in intermediate waters, surface-waters occupying a middle place in this respect; and (3) that there is not much difference between bottom- and surface-waters, either in the total quantity of organic contamination or in the relative proportions of the "decomposed" and "easily decomposable" organic matter.

It may be worth notice that when the bottom-water from great depths was muddy, tests made before and after filtration showed that some of the organic matter was removed by this operation.

APPENDIX B.

Results of the Analyses of Eight Samples of Sea-Water collected during the Third Cruise of the 'Porcupine.' By Dr. FRANKLAND, F.R.S.

ROYAL COLLEGE OF CHEMISTRY,
November 15*th*, 1869.

DEAR DR. CARPENTER,—Herewith I enclose results of analyses of the samples of sea-water collected during your recent cruise in the 'Porcupine.'

I shall not attempt to draw any general conclusions from these results; your own intimate knowledge of the circumstances under which the different samples were collected will enable you to do this much better than I.

There is, however, one point which is highly remarkable, and to which I would draw your attention; it is the large amount of very highly nitrogenized organic matter contained in most of the samples, as shown of the determinations of organic carbon and organic nitrogen, and the proportion of organic carbon to organic nitrogen. For the purposes of comparison, I have appended the results of analyses of Thames-water and of the water of Loch Katrine, the former representing probably about a fair average of the proportion of organic nitrogen reaching the sea in the rivers of this country, but being presumably considerably greater than that contributed by rivers in other parts of the world. If this be so, it follows either that soluble nitrogenous organic matter is being generated from inorganic materials in the sea, or that this matter is undergoing concentration by the evaporation of the ocean,—the rivers and streams continually furnishing additional quantities whilst the water evaporated takes none away.

The amounts of carbonate of lime given in the table are obtained by adding the number three (representing the solubility of carbonate of lime in pure water) to the temporary hardness which denotes the carbonate of lime thrown down on boiling. As the determination of temporary hardness in water containing so much saline matter is not very accurate, the numbers in the columns headed 'Temporary Hardness' and 'Carbonate of Lime' must only be regarded as rough approximations to the truth; moreover, a small proportion of carbonate of magnesia is mixed with the carbonate of lime and estimated with it.

In all their peculiar features these analytical results agree with those which I have previously obtained from numerous samples of sea-water collected by myself off Worthing and Hastings.

Yours very truly,

E. FRANKLAND.

RESULTS OF ANALYSIS expressed in Grammes per 100,000 Cubic Centimetres of Water.

Number of Sample.	Description.	Sp. Gravity at 15°·5 C.	Total Solid Matter in solution.	Organic Carbon.	Organic Nitrogen.	Proportion of organic N. to organic C.	Ammonia.	Nitrogen as Nitrates and Nitrites.	Total combined Nitrogen.	Silica.	Chlorine.	Hardness. Temporary.	Hardness. Permanent.	Hardness. Total.	Carbonate of Lime, approximate.
47	Surface, temp. 54°	1·0268	4074	·647	·134	1:4·83	·022	·030	·182	·90	2028·1	70·7	818·3	889·0	73·7
47	Bottom, 542 fathoms, temp. 43°·8	1·0268	4070	·331	·163	1:2·03	·022	·032	·213	—	2034·4	42·4	832·4	874·8	45·4
87	Surface, temp. 52°·6	1·0269	4036	·321	·098	1:3·38	·017	·056	·168	2·10	1987·5	98·9	804·2	903·1	101·9
87	Bottom, 767 fathoms, temp. 41°·4	1·0268	4132	·313	·096	1:3·26	·020	·061	·173	1·10	2026·9	84·8	818·3	903·1	87·8
54	Surface, temp. 52°·5	1·0266	4110	·281	·169	1:1·61	·007	·025	·200	·75	2017·5	42·4	818·3	860·7	45·4
54	Bottom, 363 fathoms, temp. 31°·4	1·0268	4030	·136	·161	1: ·84	·004	·041	·205	·10	2014·4	56·5	860·7	917·2	59·5
64	Surface, temp. 49°·7	1·0265	4116	·170	·217	1: ·78	·005	·043	·264	·30	1996·2	56·5	860·7	917·2	59·5
64	Bottom, 640 fathoms, temp. 29°·6	1·0262	3920	·217	·252	1: ·86	·008	·039	·298	·10	1988·1	56·5	846·6	903·1	59·5
	Thames, mid-stream at low water, London Bridge, April 27th, 1869	...	30·35	·455	·075	1:6·07	·032	·181	·282	...	1·95	...	..	22·7	
	Water of Loch Katrine . . .	...	3·00	·161	·011	1:14 64	·001	·000	·012	...	·905	...	...	·3	

APPENDIX C.

Notes on Specimens of the Bottom collected during the First Cruise of the 'Porcupine' in 1869. By DAVID FORBES, F.R.S.

ATLANTIC MUD contained in a small bottle marked 'Soundings No. 20, 1,443 fathoms.'

A complete analysis of this sample shows its chemical composition to be as follows:—

Carbonate of lime	50·12
Alumina[1] ('soluble in acids')	1·33
Sesquioxide of iron ('soluble in acids') . . .	2·17
Silica (in a soluble condition)	5·04
Fine insoluble gritty sand (rock *débris*) . . .	26·77
Water	2·90
Organic matter	4·19
Chloride of sodium and other soluble salts . .	7·48
	100·00

If we compare the chemical composition as above with that of ordinary chalk, which consists all but entirely of carbonate of lime, and seldom contains more than from 2 to 4 per cent. of foreign matter (clay, silica, &c.), it will be seen that it differs chiefly in containing so very large an amount of rock-matter in a fine state of division. If we subtract the water, organic matter, and marine salts, which would probably in greatest part be removed before such mud could in process of ages be converted into solid rock, even then the amount of carbonate of lime or pure chalk would not be more than at highest some 60 per cent. of the mass.

As such deposits must naturally be expected to vary greatly in mechanical character and chemical composition, it would be

[1] With phosphoric acid.

premature to generalize as to the actual nature of the deposits now in course of formation in the depths of the Atlantic, before a careful examination had been made of a series of such specimens from different localities. The soluble silica is principally from silicious organisms.

As regards the probable origin of the pebbles and gravel found in the various dredgings, it will be at once seen, from the description, that they consist principally of fragments of volcanic rocks and crystalline schists. The former of these have in all probability come from Iceland or Jan Mayen; whilst the latter, associated as they are with small fragments of grey and somewhat altered calcareous rock, would appear to have proceeded from the north-west coast of Ireland, where the rocks are quite identical in mineral character. The north of Scotland and its islands also contain similar rocks; but, without being at all positive on this head, I am rather inclined to the opinion that they have been derived from Ireland, and not necessarily connected with any glacial phenomena, believing that their presence may be accounted for by the ordinary action of marine currents.

PEBBLES FROM 1,215 FATHOMS (STATION 28).

The stones were all subangular, the edges being all more or less worn or altogether rounded off. The specimens were thirty-eight in number, and upon examination were found to consist of—

5 Horblende schist; the largest of these (which also was the largest in size of the entire series) weighed 421 grains ($\frac{7}{8}$ of an ounce), was extremely compact, and was composed of black hornblende, dirty-coloured quartz, and some garnet.

2 Mica schist; quartz with mica, the largest weighing 20 grains.

5 Grey pretty compact limestone, the largest being 7 grains in weight.

2 Fragments (showing the cleavage faces rounded off on edges) of orthoclase (potash felspar), evidently derived

from granite; the largest of the two fragments weighed 15 grains.

5 Quartz, milky in colour or colourless; the largest of these weighed $90\frac{3}{4}$ grains, and showed evidence of having been derived from the quartz-veins so common in clay-slate.

19—38 Fragments of true volcanic lava, most of which were very light and scoriaceous (vesicular), although some small ones were compact and crystalline; and in these the minerals augite, olivine, and glassy felspar (Sanadine) could be distinctly recognized. Among these were fragments of trachytic, trachydoleritic, and pyroxenic (basaltic) lavas, quite similar to those of Iceland or Jan Mayen of the present period, from which they had probably been derived.

GRAVEL FROM 1,443 FATHOMS (STATION 20).

This sample of gravel consisted of 718 subangular fragments, in general not above from $\frac{1}{4}$ to $\frac{1}{2}$ grain in weight, with occasionally some of a little greater size; but the most considerable of all (a fragment of mica schist) only weighed 3 grains. They consisted of:—

3 Fragments of orthoclase felspar.

4 Bituminous or carbonaceous shale (? if not accidental).

5 Fragments of shell (undistinguishable species).

4 Granite, containing quartz, orthoclase, and muscovite.

15 Grey compact limestone.

69 Quartzose mica schist.

317 Hornblende schist; sometimes containing garnets.

273 Quartzite fragments, with a very few fragments of clear quartz. The majority of the pieces being of a dirty colour, often cemented together, were evidently the *débris* of quartzite rocks or beds of indurated sandstone, and not from granite.

28 Black compact rock, containing augite, most probably a volcanic basalt.

——

718

FROM 1,263 FATHOMS (STATION 22).

A single rounded pebble, weighing 18 grains, chiefly quartz, with a little of a black mineral hornblende or tourmaline, probably from a metamorphic schist.

GRAVEL FROM 1,366 FATHOMS (STATION 19*a*).

Consisted of 51 small subangular pieces of rock, all less than ½ grain in weight, excepting only one fragment (angular) of quartz, which weighed 2 grains; they consisted of—

19 Fragments of quartz, all of which appeared to have proceeded from the disintegration of crystalline schists, and not from granite.
9 Hornblende schist.
8 Mica schist.
7 Loose, dirty-white tufaceous limestone.
3 Small fragments of augite or tourmaline (? which).
1 Fragment of quartz, with tourmaline.
4 Fragments of indistinct and uncertain character.
—
51

GRAVEL FROM 1,476 FATHOMS (STATION 21).

Six small subangular fragments, the largest of which did not exceed two grains in weight; they were respectively—

1 Yellow quartz.
1 Quartzose chlorite schist.
3 Mica schist.
1 Small fragment, apparently of volcanic lava.
—
6

The specimen from Rockall is not a fragment of any normal rock, but is only a brecciaform aggregate, principally consisting of quartz, felspar, and crystals of green hornblende, held together by a silicious cement. It has evidently been broken from the projecting edge of a fault or vein-fissure; and although it cannot settle the matter definitely as to what rocks this islet may really be composed of, it would indicate that it most probably is a mass of hornblendic gneiss or schist, and certainly not of true volcanic origin. I may mention that it does not at all resemble any of the fragments found in the deep-sea dredgings which I have as yet examined.

APPENDIX D.

Note on the Carbonic Acid contained in Sea-water. *By* JOHN YOUNG BUCHANAN, M.A., Chemist to the 'Challenger' Expedition.

At a meeting[1] of the Chemical Society last summer, Dr. Himly mentioned that Dr. Jacobsen, of Kiel, had found that carbonic acid is only very imperfectly separated from sea-water by boiling *in vacuo.* This was confirmed by Dr. Jacobsen himself in a letter to *Nature* of August 8, 1872. Almost at the very same time the German North Sea Expedition arrived in Leith, when I had the privilege of hearing the confirmation of it from his own mouth, as well as his conjecture that it was probably owing to the presence of salts with water of hal-hydration, such as sulphate of magnesia, that the carbonic acid was retained with such vigour.

Having assured myself by experiment that, as a matter of fact, carbonic acid *is* retained by sea-water with considerable energy, the last traces of it having scarcely disappeared before the contents of the retort were reduced to dryness, I set on foot a series of analytical experiments, so as to determine which of the salts it was, whose presence was the cause of the anomaly in question. The result of these experiments was shortly this: Distilled water, solution of chloride of sodium and solution of chloride of magnesium, each saturated with carbonic acid, behaved on distillation alike, giving off the whole of their carbonic acid in the first eighth of the distillate. Solutions, however, of sulphate of magnesia and of sulphate of lime behaved like

[1] Chemical Society Journal, 1872, p. 455.

the others at first, giving off the surplus carbonic acid dissolved in the first eighth of the distillate. The amount of carbonic acid coming off then fell very low, gradually increasing, however, until a half had been distilled over, when the amount coming off again reached a maximum, the quantity then diminishing, but rarely entirely disappearing as the contents of the retort approached dryness. It is clear, then, that in the sulphates of magnesia and lime we have an agent capable of retaining carbonic acid in the way in which we see it in sea-water; whether there may be other agents present, capable of doing the same work, will be brought to light when the subject has been more fully investigated. An independent set of experiments were made on the variation with pressure of the coefficient of absorption for carbonic acid of a solution containing 1·23 per cent. of crystallized sulphate of magnesia, kept at a constant temperature of 11° C. The result was, that at 610 mm. pressure the sulphate of magnesia solution dissolved sensibly the same quantity of carbonic acid as the same volume of water would have done; in other words, their coefficients of absorption were identical. Below 610 mm. that of the saline solution was the greater; above 610 mm. the reverse was the case. The curve, however, is not a straight line, and it appears to cut that of water again at a pressure of about 800 mm.

The facts above related naturally suggest to the chemist the question, what is the body formed when sulphate of magnesia and carbonic acid meet each other in solution?

It is clear that, besides the carbonic acid dissolved, there is some retained by a stronger bond, and which is only liberated when the concentration has proceeded a certain distance. Is the decomposition caused by the loss of water, or by the rise of boiling-point? The difference between the boiling-points of the solution, when it has just ceased to give off the merely dissolved carbonic acid, and when the retained gas is being given off in greatest quantity, does not exceed 1° C.; and it is difficult to believe that the compound should remain practically intact at 101° and decompose rapidly at 102°. Again, if the compound is decomposed by the water alone, we should expect, that the more dilute the solution, the easier would be the decomposition. Adopting Erlenmeyer's view of the position of the halhydration water in sulphate of magnesia ($HO - Mg - O - SO_2 - OH$), we might suppose the carbonic acid simply to replace the molecule of water, thus—$Mg \langle {}^{O - SO_2}_{O - CO} \rangle O$; but it would be contrary to all analogy for such a body to be more stable in dilute than in moderately concentrated solutions of the same temperature. If, on the other hand, we suppose the CO_2 to interpose itself between the Mg and the basic HO, we have a body of this form: $HO - CO - O - Mg - O - SO_2 - OH$. It is conceivable that such a body would in the process of concentration become dehydrated, when the anhydrous salt $Mg \langle {}^{O - SO_2}_{O - CO} \rangle O$ would be formed, which would then split up into CO_2 and $MgSO_4$. Assuming now that the body formed has this constitution, it is evident that, for a given mixture of sulphate of magnesia, water and carbonic acid, the amount of the above body formed will be a function of the temperature, the pressure and the duration of their action upon one another. Now, at great depths in the sea, where atmospheric influences are insensible, these conditions are most completely fulfilled. The temperature is low, the pressure high, and the time practically unlimited. Sea-water contains on an average about two grammes of crystallized sulphate of magnesia in the litre; and if the reaction were complete, the two grammes of sulphate of magnesia, or one litre of sea-water, would absorb 181·4 cubic centimetres of carbonic acid. Supposing only one-fifth part of the sulphate of magnesia to be thus saturated with carbonic acid, we have provision in one litre of sea-water for the removal of over 36 cubic centimetres of carbonic acid. We have thus in the sulphates (for the lime-salt appears to act even more energetically) an agent which in the ocean depths performs one of the two important functions of plants in shallow waters and in the air, namely, the removal of the carbonic acid eliminated by the animals; the task of replenishing the oxygen supply is accomplished by the system of ocean circulation. Moreover, it would be difficult to conceive circumstances more favourable to the formation of this body than those which exist at the bottom of the ocean. The temperature is generally little over that of melting ice; the pressure often exceeds several hundred atmospheres; whilst the carbonic acid, being produced gradually, and coming *in statu nascendis* in contact with the saline solution, is in the condition most favourable for easily entering into chemical combination.

The amount of this salt formed depending on the pressure, it is evident that, on bringing up a sample of water from a great depth, a part of the carbonic acid, which was bound before, will become free under the atmospheric pressure; and, moreover, as the amount decomposed varies with the time, it is evident that the amount of free carbonic acid, obtained by boiling *in vacuo,* will vary with the depths from which the sample was obtained, with the time it stands before boiling, with the temperature to which it is exposed during boiling, and with the duration of that operation. Hence it is easy to see how, assuming the body above mentioned to have been formed, Dr. Jacobsen found that the quantity of carbonic acid obtained by boiling *in vacuo* was no measure of the amount actually present, and that even portions of the same sample gave discordant results.

It will be seen from the above remarks that solutions of carbonic acid in sea-water and in blood resemble each other in almost every particular; only in the latter the retaining body is phosphate of soda, whilst in the former it is sulphate of magnesia, both of which contain constitutional water. The physical conditions, under which carbonic acid is eliminated from the blood and from sea-water, are also very similar.

In the investigation of the behaviour of carbonic acid and of other gases to saline solutions, there is a practically unlimited field for useful research. The determination of the absorption coefficients of sulphate of magnesia solution for carbonic acid alone, under varying conditions of temperature, pressure, concentration, and duration of action, would afford interesting and profitable occupation for more than one chemist.

INDEX.

A.

Acanthometrina, 98.
Ægu nasuta, 127.
Ægean Sea, Mollusca and Radiata of, 5.
Agassiz, Alexander, Echinoderm Fauna on the two sides of the Isthmus of Panama, 13; on *Echinocyamus*, 117, 277.
Allman, Professor, F.R.S., list of animal forms found at great depths, 27.
Allopora oculina, 169, 170, 432.
Amathia carpenteri, 175.
Amphidetus cordatus, 459.
Amphihelia profunda—A. oculata—A. miocenica—A. atlantica—A. ornata, 169.
Amphiura abyssicola, 123.
Antedon celticus, 76; *A. escrichtii—A. sarsii*, 124.
Aphrocallistes bocagei, 95.
Archaster bifrons, 122; *A. vexillifer*, 150; *A. andromeda*, 150; *A. parelii*, 456; *A. tenuispinus*, 456.
Arcturus baffini, 127, 128.
Askonema setubalense, 429.
Asterophyton linkii, 19.
Astrorhiza limicola, 75.
Atavism, 9.
Atretia gnomon, 90.

B.

Bache, Professor A. D., Superintendent U.S. Coast Survey, on the Gulf-stream, 386.
Bathybius haeckelii, 412.
Bathycrinus gracilis, 450, 453.
Bathyptilum carpenteri, 77.
Berryman, Lieutenant, U.S.N., deep-sea soundings in the U.S. brig 'Dolphin,' 227–229.
Bocage, Professor Barboza du, Director of the Nat. Hist. Museum, Lisbon, 275; on *Hyalonema*, 425.
Bowerbank, Dr., F.R.S., on *Hyalonema*, 425.
Brandt, Dr., on *Hyalonema*, 423.
Brisinga coronata, 67, 118; *B. endecacnemos*, 66, 99, 118; description of, by Absjörnsen, P. Chr., 68.
Brissopsis lyrifera, 118, 457, 459.
Brooke, J. M., U.S.N., sounding apparatus, 21, 211, 213.
Browning, Lieutenant, 83.
Buccinopsis striata, 464.
Buchanan, John Young, M.A., on the Carbonic Acid contained in Sea-water, 518, 521.
Buff, Professor Henry, on ocean currents, 368; on the Gulf-stream, 389.

C.

Calver, Captain, skill in conducting dredging operations, 83; serial soundings, 309.
Calveria hystrix, 156, 459; *C. fenestrata*, 159, 182, 459.
Caprella spinosissima, 126.
Carpenter, Dr. William B., F.R.S., 3; Preliminary Report of the Dredging Operations in the 'Lightning,' 133; Temperature Observations in the Mediterranean, 326; Theory of Ocean Currents, 368, 369; Observations on the currents in the Strait of Gibraltar, 373; on the Gulf-stream, 390.
Carpenter, W. Lant, B.A., B.Sc., 85; Analysis of Sea-water, 498, 502–511.
Caryophyllia borealis, 27, 431.
Ceratocyathus ornatus, 431.
Cerithium granosum, 463.
Chalk, 409; analysis of, 469.
Chimmo, W., Commander R.N., 230; temperatures of the Atlantic, 359.
Choanites, 494.
Chondrocladia virgata, 187.
Cidaris papillata, 76; *C. hystrix*, 116, 193, 459; *C. affinis*, 193, 457, 459.
Cladorhiza abyssicola, 112.
Coccoliths, 413.
Coccospheres, 414.
Cœlosphæra tubifex, 485.

Coralline Zone, 16.
Crinoidea, 434.
Croll, James, on ocean currents, 376, 381.

D.

Dacrydium vitreum, 465.
Darwin, Charles, M.A., F.R.S., 'Origin of Species,' 8.
D'Aubuisson, on deep-sea temperatures, 360.
Davis, Captain, R.N., testing thermometers, 290, 295.
Dayman, Joseph, Commander R.N., 23, 229, 302; temperatures of the Atlantic, 359.
Deep-sea Sounding, 205; cup-lead, 210; Brooke's deep-sea sounding apparatus, 211, 213; the 'Bulldog' sounding-machine, 215; the 'Fitzgerald' sounding machine, 217; the 'Hydra' sounding-machine, 218; donkey-engine, 221; derricks, 221; the 'accumulator,' 222; observed rate of descent of the sounding instrument, 223; Massey's sounding-machine, 225.
Deep-sea Temperature, doctrine of, 35; distribution of heat in the sea, 36; cold wall, 37; minimum temperature of the sea, 38; proximity of warm and cold areas, 131; great uniformity of temperature at all depths in the Mediterranean, 191, 285; serial soundings for temperature, 309–325.
Depth of the Sea, 1; first successful dredgings at great depths, 3; animal forms found at depths of from 70 to 1,200 fathoms, 27; animal life abundant at the bottom of the sea, 31; average depth of the sea, 31; absolute stillness at great depths, 37; penetration of light, 45; abundance of the genera *Astropecten* and *Archaster*, 121.
Despretz, M., researches on the maximum density of saline solutions, 35; temperature of greatest density of sea-water, 307.
Dorynchus thomsoni, 174.
Dredging Apparatus: Müller's dredge, 239; Ball's dredge, 240; deep-sea dredges, 246; derrick, 247; accumulator, 247; Aunt Sallies, 249; dredge-rope, 249; dredging in shallow water, 244, 245; dredging in deep water, 253; hempen tangles, 256, 257; emptying the dredge, 259; dredging-sieves, 260.
Dredging Committee, members of, 265; Belfast Dredging Committee, 266.
Dredging Operations, on the coast of Ireland, 266; of England, 266; of Shetland and the Hebrides, 266; of Portugal and the Mediterranean, 267; of the North-east Atlantic, 267; of Norway, Sweden, and Denmark, 268; of the Adriatic, 268; of Algeria, 268; Spitzbergen, 269; Malta, 270; Finland and Loffoten Islands, 270; United States, 277.
Dredging Paper, 281.
Duncan, Professor P. Martin, F.R.S., on deep-sea corals, 431.

E.

Echinocucumis typica, 125, 175; *Echinocyamus angulatus*, 117, 459; Echinothuridæ, wide distribution of, 171; *Echinus elegans*, 76, 459; *E. esculentus*, 458; *E. flemingii*, 116, 458; *E. melo*, 459; *E. microstoma*, 171, 459; *E. norvegicus*, 76, 116, 459; *E. rarispina*, 459; *E. rarituberculatus*, 116.
Ethusa granulata, 176.
Euplectella, 73.
Eusirus cuspidatus, 125, 126.
Evolution, doctrine of, 9.

F.

Findlay, A. G., on the Gulf-stream, 390.
Fishes, new species of, 130.
Flabellum distinctum, 432.
Florida, fauna of the Strait of, 171.
Foraminifera, 115, 166, 415, 478.
Forbes, David, F.R.S., analysis of the white chalk of Shoreham, 469; of the Folkestone grey chalk, 469; on specimens of Atlantic mud, 514–518.
Forbes, Edward, F.R.S., 4; on the distribution of marine forms, 6; on the immutability of species, 6; specific centres of distribution, 7; the law of representation, 8, 13; zones of depth, 15; representative forms, 17; inverted analogy between the distribution of the fauna and flora of the land and of the sea, 44; on dredging, 266.
Fossil Echinidæ, 162.
Frankland, Dr., F.R.S., analysis of sea-water, 511–513.
Fusus sarsi, 464.

G.

Geryon tridens, 88.
Globigerina bulloides, 22, 416.
Gonoplax rhomboides, 87.
Goodsir, Henry, deep dredging in Davis' Strait, 21.
Gray, Dr. John Edward, F.R.S., on *Hyalonema*, 422.
Gulf-stream, 286, 356; description of, 379; progress and extension of, through the North Atlantic, 385.

H.

Haeckel, Professor Ernst, 9; biological studies, 408.
Halichondridæ, 74.

Hall, Marshall, F.G.S., cruise of the 'Norna,' 279.
Herschel, Sir John F. W., the doctrine of a constant temperature of 4° C. at great depths, 35; letter to Dr. Carpenter, 378; description of the Gulf-stream, 381.
Hexactinellidæ, 70, 416.
Holothuria ecalcarea, 125.
Holtenia carpenteri, 71; wide distribution of, 75, 101, 167, 417, 427.
Humboldt, Baron von, on deep-sea temperatures, 360.
Hunter, John, M.A., F.C.S., 85; analysis of sea-water, 497.
Huxley, Professor T. H., Sec R.S., on life at great depths, 23; on the chalk-mud of the Atlantic, 496.
Hyalonema, 73, 101, 167, 276, 417, 422, 428; *H. lusitanicum*, 420, 421; *H. sieboldi*, 422.
Hymenaster pellucidus, 120.

I.

Inskip, Staff-Commander, 83.
Isthmus of Panama, Echinoderm Fauna on the two sides of, 13.

J.

Jeffreys, J. Gwyn, F.R.S., distribution of marine mollusca, 40; first cruise of the 'Porcupine,' 84; dredging off the south coast of Ireland, 121; fourth cruise of the 'Porcupine,' 178, 267, 278, 418, 428; temperature observations, 325.
Jenkin, Professor Fleeming, C.E., F.R.S., cable between Sardinia and Bona, 26; first absolute proof of the existence of highly-organized animals at depths of upwards of 1,000 fathoms, 30.

K.

Kent, W. Saville, F.L.S., the 'Norna' expedition, 75, 279; on *Askonema setubalense*, 429.
Kophobelemmon mülleri, 75.
Korethraster hispidus, 119.

L.

Laminarian Zone, 15.
Latirus albus, 464.
Laughton, J. K., M.A., on ocean currents, 398.
Lee, Lieutenant, U.S.N., deep-sea soundings, 229, 392.
'Lightning,' cruise of the, 57; the Færoe Banks, 60; the Færoe Islands, 61; Thorshavn, 61; first attempt at dredging in deep water, 64; the 'cold area, 69; the 'warm area,' 70; Stornoway, 76; general results of the cruise, 78.
Littoral Zone, 15.
Lituola, 115, 194.
Lophohelia prolifera, 76, 169, 432.
Lovén, Professor, additions to the knowledge of marine zoology, 267; on bathymetrical distribution of submarine life, 269.
Lyell, Sir Charles, Bart., F.R.S., on the cretaceous period, 472; on the continuity of the chalk, 476, 491.
Lyman, Theodore, memoirs in the 'Bulletin of the Museum of Comparative Zoology,' 277.

M.

M'Clintock, Admiral Sir Leopold, voyage of the 'Bulldog,' 24.
Maury, M. F., LL.D., Captain U.S.N., 23; theory of ocean currents, 368; on the Gulf-stream, 383.
May, Staff-Commander, cruise of the 'Lightning,' 57, 304.
Mean annual temperatures: Hebrides, 362; Labrador, 362; Bergen, 363; Tobolsk, 363; Færoe Islands, 363; Falkland Islands, 363; Dublin, 363; Port Famine, 363; Halifax, 363; Boston, 363.
'Mercury,' cruise of the, 233.
Milne-Edwards, Alphonse, list of the animals found on the Mediterranean cable from the depth of 1,100 fathoms, 28, 268.
Mohn, Professor H., on surface and deep-sea temperatures on the west coast of Norway, 396.
Müller, Otho Frederick, 237; his dredge, 239.
Munida, 76, 161.

N.

Neolampas, 358; *N. rostellatus*, 459.
Norman, Rev. A. Merle, addition to the Shetland fauna, 124; preliminary notice of the crustacea of the 'Porcupine' Expedition, 176; Shetland dredgings, 267.
Nutrition of animals at great depths, 45.
Nymphon abyssorum, 129.

O.

Oceanic circulation, 79, 284; Dr. Carpenter's theory of, 372.
Ophiacantha spinulosa, 76, 148, 172.
Ophiocten sericeum, 76, 123.
Ophiomusium lymani, 172.
Ophiopeltis securigera, 124.
Ophioscolex purpurea, 123; *O. glacialis*, 123.

Ophiothrix lütkeni, 100.
Orbitolites tenuissimus, 91, 194.
Orbulina universa, 23.

P.

Pecten hoskynsi, 465.
Pedicellaster typicus, 456.
Pentacrinus wyville-thomsoni, 186, 443; *P. asteria*, 436; *P. P. Mülleri*, 442.
Petermann, Dr., on the Gulf-stream, 287, 379, 392.
Pheronema annæ, 418.
Phormosoma placenta, 171, 459.
Phosphorescence, 98, 148.
Pierce, Professor, on the Gulf-stream, 386.
Platydia anomioides, 146.
Pleuronectia lucida, 464, 465.
Polycystina, 98.
'Porcupine,' first cruise of the, 82; equipment of the vessel, 83; results of the first dredging, 86; first trial of the Miller-Casella thermometers, 88; Porcupine Bank, 88; trip to Rockall, 89; second cruise, 93; dredging at the depth of 2,435 fathoms, 95; return to Belfast, 100; third cruise, 101; *Holtenia* ground, 104; the hempen tangles, 105; Thorshavn, 106; discovery of Arctic stream, 110; Shetland plateau, 111; predominance of the Arctic fauna, 131; fauna of the warm area off the north coast of Scotland, 177; return to Belfast, 178; fourth cruise of the 'Porcupine,' 179; cruise in the Mediterranean, 190; fauna near the African coast, 192; Adventure Bank, 192; Malta, 194; temperature soundings near Stromboli, 195; return to Cowes, 196.
Porocidaris purpurata, 102, 459.
Pourtales, Count L. F. de, deep-sea dredgings across the Gulf-stream off the coast of Florida, 277.
Pourtalesia jeffreysi, 103, 457, 459, 489; *P. phiale*, 90, 459.
Predominance of protozoa, 47.
Preservation of specimens, 261.
Pressure, conditions of, at great depths, 32; methods of testing the actual pressure, 34; effect of pressure on the thermometer, 294.
Prestwich, Joseph, F.R.S., President of the Geological Society: Temperatures of the Atlantic, 358; on the continuity of the chalk, 496.
Psammechinus microtuberculatus, 457; *P. miliaris*, 459.
Psolus squamatus, 125.
Pteraster militaris, 171.

R.

Rhabdammina abyssorum, 75.
Rhizocrinus loffotensis, 76, 124, 447, 451.
Richards, Rear-Admiral, C.B., F.R.S., Hydrographer to the Navy, 3.
Ross, Sir James Clark, R.N., deep dredgings in the Antarctic Sea, 20; temperature observations, 304.
Ross, Sir John, voyage of discovery in Baffin's Bay, 18; machine for taking up soundings from great depths, 209; temperature observations during the Arctic voyage, 300.
Rossella velata, 419.
Royal Society, letter to, from Dr. Carpenter, recommending a systematic course of deep-sea dredging, 53; letter from the Secretary of, to the Secretary of the Admiralty, 55; reply from the Admiralty, 56: (see also 133–141.)

S.

Sabine, General Sir Edward, K.C.B., extracts from private journal, 18, 300.
Sars, Professor Michael, list of animals of all the invertebrate groups living at a depth of 300 to 400 fathoms, 33, 268, 270, 274.
Schizaster canaliferus, 459.
Schmidt, Professor Oscar, on Hexactinellidæ, 70; Cometella, 114, 268, 416.
Schultze, Professor Max, on *Hyalonema*, 425.
Serpula, 273.
Sharks at great depths, 34.
Shortland, Captain, R.N., temperatures of deep water in the Arabian Sea, 359.
Smith, Toulmin J., on Ventriculites, 482.
Solaster furcifer, 119, 456; *S. papposus*, 118.
Spatangus raschi, 118; *S. purpureus*, 459.
Spirorbis, 273.
Spratt, Captain, R.N., dredging in the Mediterranean, 270,
Steenstrup, Professor, additions to the knowledge of marine zoology, 268.
Stylocordyla borealis, 114.
Surface-temperature, mode of determining the, 287; distribution of, in the North Atlantic, 362.

T.

Tanks for the transportation of living fish, 59.
Tellina calcarea, 462; *T. compressa*, 464.
Temperature of the crust of the earth, 404.
Terebratula septata, 130.
Thecophora semisuberites, 147; *T. ibla*, 148.
Thecopsammia socialis, 433.
Thermometer, Six's, 288; Miller-Casella,

291 ; Breguet's metallic thermometer, 293 ; Negretti and Zambra's thermometer, 293.
Thomson, Sir William, F.R.S., thermometer in a sealed glass tube, 296.
Tisiphonia agariciformis, 74, 167.
Toxopneustes brevispinosus, 459.
Tripylus fragilis, 118, 459.

V.

Variation, 9.
Ventriculites simplex, 483 ; outer surface, 484 ; section of the outer wall, 485.
Verticordia acuticostata, 464.

W.

Wallace, Alfred Russel, on natural selection, 8.
Waller, Edward, dredging off the South coast of Ireland, Hebrides, and Shetland Islands, 121 ; on the fauna of the Hebrides, 267.
Wallich, G. C., M.D., F.L.S., the North Atlantic Sea-bed, 24, 271, 302.
Wright, Professor Perceval, deep dredging off the coast of Portugal, 276.

Z.

Zone of deep-sea corals, 16.
Zoroaster fulgens, 153.

THE END.

LONDON :
R. CLAY, SONS, AND TAYLOR, PRINTERS,
BREAD STREET HILL.

BEDFORD STREET, COVENT GARDEN, LONDON,
January 1873.

MACMILLAN & CO.'S CATALOGUE of WORKS in MATHEMATICS and PHYSICAL SCIENCE; ncluding PURE and APPLIED MATHEMATICS; PHYSICS, ASTRONOMY, GEOLOGY, CHEMISTRY, ZOOLOGY, BOTANY; PHYSIOLOGY ANATOMY and MEDICAL WORKS generally; and of WORKS in MENTAL and MORAL PHILOSOPHY and Allied Subjects.

MATHEMATICS.

Airy.—Works by Sir G. B. AIRY, K.C.B., Astronomer Royal:—

ELEMENTARY TREATISE ON PARTIAL DIFFERENTIAL EQUATIONS. Designed for the Use of Students in the Universities. With Diagrams. Crown 8vo. cloth. 5*s*. 6*d*.

It is hoped that the methods of solution here explained, and the instances exhibited, will be found sufficient for application to nearly all the important problems of Physical Science, which require for their complete investigation the aid of Partial Differential Equations.

ON THE ALGEBRAICAL AND NUMERICAL THEORY OF ERRORS OF OBSERVATIONS AND THE COMBINATION OF OBSERVATIONS. Crown 8vo. cloth. 6*s*. 6*d*.

In order to spare astronomers and observers in natural philosophy the confusion and loss of time which are produced by referring to the ordinary treatises embracing both *branches of probabilities (the first*

Airy (G. B.)—*continued.*

relating to chances which can be altered only by the changes of entire units or integral multiples of units in the fundamental conditions of the problem; the other concerning those chances which have respect to insensible gradations in the value of the element measured), this volume has been drawn up. It relates only to errors of observation, and to the rules, derivable from the consideration of these errors, for the combination of the results of observations.

UNDULATORY THEORY OF OPTICS. Designed for the Use of Students in the University. New Edition. Crown 8vo. cloth. 6*s*. 6*d*.

The undulatory theory of optics is presented to the reader as having the same claims to his attention as the theory of gravitation,—namely, that it is certainly true, and that, by mathematical operations of general elegance, it leads to results of great interest. This theory explains with accuracy a vast variety of phenomena of the most complicated kind. The plan of this tract has been to include those phenomena only which admit of calculation, and the investigations are applied only to phenomena which actually have been observed.

ON SOUND AND ATMOSPHERIC VIBRATIONS. With the Mathematical Elements of Music. Designed for the Use of Students of the University. Second Edition, revised and enlarged. Crown 8vo. 9*s*.

This volume consists of sections, which again are divided into numbered articles, on the following topics:—General recognition of the air as the medium which conveys sound; Properties of the air on which the formation and transmission of sound depend; Theory of undulations as applied to sound, etc.; Investigation of the motion of a wave of air through the atmosphere; Transmission of waves of soniferous vibrations through different gases, solids, and fluids; Experiments on the velocity of sound, etc.; On musical sounds, and the manner of producing them; On the elements of musical harmony and melody, and of simple musical composition; On instrumental music; On the human organs of speech and hearing.

A TREATISE ON MAGNETISM. Designed for the Use of Students in the University. Crown 8vo. 9*s*. 6*d*.

As the laws of Magnetic Force have been experimentally examined, with philosophical accuracy, only in its connection with iron and steel, and in the influence excited by the earth as a whole, the accurate portions of this work are confined to the investigations connected with these metals and the earth. The latter part of the work, however, treats in a more general way of the laws of the connection between Magnetism on the one hand and Galvanism and Thermo-Electricity on the other. The work is divided into Twelve Sections, and each section into numbered articles, each of which states concisely and clearly the subject of the following paragraphs.

Ball (R. S., A.M.)—EXPERIMENTAL MECHANICS. A Course of Lectures delivered at the Royal College of Science for Ireland. By ROBERT STAWELL BALL, A.M., Professor of Applied Mathematics and Mechanics in the Royal College of Science for Ireland (Science and Art Department). Royal 8vo. 16*s*.

The author's aim in these twenty Lectures has been to create in the mind of the student physical ideas corresponding to theoretical laws, and thus to produce a work which may be regarded either as a supplement or an introduction to manuals of theoretic mechanics. To realize this design, the copious use of experimental illustrations was necessary. The apparatus used in the Lectures and figured in the volume has been principally built up from Professor Willis's most admirable system. In the selection of the subjects, the question of practical utility has in many cases been regarded as the one of paramount importance, and it is believed that the mode of treatment which is adopted is more or less original. This is especially the case in the Lectures relating to friction, to the mechanical powers, to the strength of timber and structures, to the laws of motion, and to the pendulum. The illustrations, drawn from the apparatus, are nearly all original and are beautifully executed. "In our reading we have not met with any book of the sort in English."—Mechanics' Magazine.

Bayma.—THE ELEMENTS OF MOLECULAR MECHANICS. By JOSEPH BAYMA, S.J., Professor of Philosophy Stonyhurst College. Demy 8vo. cloth. 10*s*. 6*d*.

Of the twelve Books into which this treatise is divided, the first and second give the demonstration of the principles which bear directly on the constitution and the properties of matter. The next three books contain a series of theorems and of problems on the laws of motion of elementary substances. In the sixth and seventh, the mechanical constitution of molecules is investigated and determined: and by it the general properties of bodies are explained. The eighth book treats of luminiferous ether. The ninth explains some special properties of bodies. The tenth and eleventh contain a radical and lengthy investigation of chemical principles and relations, which may lead to practical results of high importance. The twelfth and last book treats of molecular masses, distances, and powers.

Boole.—Works by G. BOOLE, D.C.L, F.R.S., Professor of Mathematics in the Queen's University, Ireland :—

A TREATISE ON DIFFERENTIAL EQUATIONS. Third Edition. Edited by I. TODHUNTER. Crown 8vo. cloth. 14*s.*

Professor Boole has endeavoured in this treatise to convey as complete an account of the present state of knowledge on the subject of Differential Equations, as was consistent with the idea of a work intended, primarily, for elementary instruction. The earlier sections of each chapter contain that kind of matter which has usually been thought suitable for the beginner, while the latter ones are devoted either to an account of recent discovery, or the discussion of such deeper questions of principle as are likely to present themselves to the reflective student in connection with the methods and processes of his previous course. "A treatise incomparably superior to any other elementary book on the subject with which we are acquainted."— Philosophical Magazine.

A TREATISE ON DIFFERENTIAL EQUATIONS. Supplementary Volume. Edited by I. TODHUNTER. Crown 8vo. cloth. 8*s.* 6*d.*

This volume contains all that Professor Boole wrote for the purpose of enlarging his treatise on Differential Equations.

THE CALCULUS OF FINITE DIFFERENCES. Crown 8vo. cloth. 10*s.* 6*d.* New Edition revised.

In this exposition of the Calculus of Finite Differences, particular attention has been paid to the connection of its methods with those of the Differential Calculus—a connection which in some instances involves far more than a merely formal analogy. The work is in some measure designed as a sequel to Professor Boole's Treatise on Differential Equations.

Brook-Smith (J).—ARITHMETIC IN THEORY AND PRACTICE. By J. BROOK-SMITH, M.A., LL.B., St. John's College, Cambridge; Barrister-at-Law; one of the Masters of Cheltenham College. Crown 8vo. 4*s*. 6*d*.

Writers on Arithmetic at the present day feel the necessity of explaining the principles on which the rules of the subject are based, but few as yet feel the necessity of making these explanations strict and complete; or, failing that, of distinctly pointing out their defective character. If the science of Arithmetic is to be made an effective instrument in developing and strengthening the mental powers, it ought to be worked out rationally and conclusively; and in this work the author has endeavoured to reason out in a clear and accurate manner the leading propositions of the science, and to illustrate and apply those propositions in practice. In the practical part of the subject he has advanced somewhat beyond the majority of preceding writers; particularly in Division, in Greatest Common Measure, in Cube Root, in the chapters on Decimal Money and the Metric System, and more especially in the application of Decimals to Percentages and cognate subjects. Copious examples, original and selected, are given.

Cambridge Senate-House Problems and Riders, WITH SOLUTIONS:—

1848–1851.—PROBLEMS. By FERRERS and JACKSON. 8vo. cloth. 15*s*. 6*d*.

1848–1851.—RIDERS. By JACKSON. 8vo. cloth. 7*s*. 6*d*.

1854.—PROBLEMS AND RIDERS. By WALTON and MACKENZIE. 8vo. cloth. 10*s*. 6*d*.

1857.—PROBLEMS AND RIDERS. By CAMPION and WALTON. 8vo. cloth. 8*s*. 6*d*.

1860.—PROBLEMS AND RIDERS. By WATSON and ROUTH. Crown 8vo. cloth. 7*s*. 6*d*.

1864.—PROBLEMS AND RIDERS. By WALTON and WILKINSON. 8vo. cloth. 10*s*. 6*d*.

These volumes will be found of great value to Teachers and Students, as indicating the style and range of mathematical study in the University of Cambridge.

Cambridge and Dublin Mathematical Journal. The Complete Work, in Nine Vols. 8vo. cloth. 10*l*. 10*s*.

Only a few copies remain on hand. Among contributors to this work will be found Sir W. Thomson, Stokes, Adams, Boole, Sir W. R. Hamilton, De Morgan, Cayley, Sylvester, Jellet, and other distinguished mathematicians.

Cheyne.—Works by C. H. H. CHEYNE, M.A., F.R.A.S.:—

AN ELEMENTARY TREATISE ON THE PLANETARY THEORY. With a Collection of Problems. Second Edition. Crown 8vo. cloth. 6*s*. 6*d*.

In this volume, an attempt has been made to produce a treatise on the Planetary theory, which, being elementary in character, should be so far complete as to contain all that is usually required by students in the University of Cambridge. This Edition has been carefully revised. The stability of the Planetary System has been more fully treated, and an elegant geometrical explanation of the formulæ for the secular variation of the node and inclination has been introduced.

THE EARTH'S MOTION OF ROTATION. Crown 8vo. 3*s*. 6*d*.

The first part of this work consists of an application of the method of the variation of elements to the general problem of rotation. In the second part the general rotation formulæ are applied to the particular case of the earth.

Childe.—THE SINGULAR PROPERTIES OF THE ELLIPSOID AND ASSOCIATED SURFACES OF THE NTH DEGREE. By the Rev. G. F. CHILDE, M.A., Author of "Ray Surfaces," "Related Caustics," &c. 8vo. 10*s*. 6*d*.

The object of this volume is to develop peculiarities in the Ellipsoid; and, further, to establish analogous properties in the unlimited congeneric series of which this remarkable surface is a constituent.

Dodgson.—AN ELEMENTARY TREATISE ON DETERMINANTS, with their Application to Simultaneous Linear Equations and Algebraical Geometry. By CHARLES L. DODGSON, M.A., Student and Mathematical Lecturer of Christ Church, Oxford. Small 4to. cloth. 10*s*. 6*d*.

The object of the author is to present the subject as a continuous chain of argument, separated from all accessories of explanation of illustration. All such explanation and illustration as seemed necessary for a beginner are introduced either in the form of foot-notes, or, where that would have occupied too much room, of Appendices.

Earnshaw (S., M.A.)—PARTIAL DIFFERENTIAL EQUATIONS. An Essay towards an entirely New Method of Integrating them. By S. EARNSHAW, M.A., of St. John's College, Cambridge. Crown 8vo. 5*s.*

The peculiarity of the system expounded in this work is, that in every equation, whatever be the number of original independent variables, the work of integration is at once reduced to the use of one independent variable only. The author's object is merely to render his method thoroughly intelligible. The various steps of the investigation are all obedient to one general principle: and though in some degree novel, are not really difficult, but on the contrary, easy when the eye has become accustomed to the novelties of the notation. Many of the results of the integrations are far more general than they were in the shape in which they appeared in former Treatises, and many Equations will be found in this Essay integrated with ease in finite terms, which were never so integrated before.

Ferrers.—AN ELEMENTARY TREATISE ON TRILINEAR CO-ORDINATES, the Method of Reciprocal Polars, and the Theory of Projectors. By the Rev. N. M. FERRERS, M.A., Fellow and Tutor of Gonville and Caius College, Cambridge. Second Edition. Crown 8vo. 6*s.* 6*d.*

The object of the author in writing on this subject has mainly been to place it on a basis altogether independent of the ordinary Cartesian system, instead of regarding it as only a special form of Abridged Notation. A short chapter on Determinants has been introduced.

Frost.—Works by PERCIVAL FROST, M.A., late Fellow of St. John's College, Mathematical Lecturer of King's College, Cambridge:—

THE FIRST THREE SECTIONS OF NEWTON'S PRINCIPIA. With Notes and Illustrations. Also a Collection of Problems, principally intended as Examples of Newton's Methods. Second Edition. 8vo. cloth. 10*s.* 6*d.*

Frost—*continued.*

The author's principal intention is to explain difficulties which may be encountered by the student on first reading the Principia, *and to illustrate the advantages of a careful study of the methods employed by Newton, by showing the extent to which they may be applied in the solution of problems; he has also endeavoured to give assistance to the student who is engaged in the study of the higher branches of mathematics, by representing in a geometrical form several of the processes employed in the Differential and Integral Calculus, and in the analytical investigations of Dynamics.*

AN ELEMENTARY TREATISE ON CURVE TRACING. 8vo. 12*s.*

The author has written this book under the conviction that the skill and power of the young mathematical student, in order to be thoroughly available afterwards, ought to be developed in all possible directions. The subject which he has chosen presents so many faces, pointing in directions towards which the mind of the intended mathematician has to radiate, that it would be difficult to find another which, with a very limited extent of reading, combines, to the same extent, so many valuable hints of methods of calculations to be employed hereafter, with so much pleasure in its present use. In order to understand the work it is not necessary to have much knowledge of what is called Higher Algebra, nor of Algebraical Geometry of a higher kind than that which simply relates to the Conic Sections. From the study of a work like this, it is believed that the student will derive many advantages. Especially he will become skilled in making correct approximations to the values of quantities, which cannot be found exactly, to any degree of accuracy which may be required.

Frost and Wolstenholme.—A TREATISE ON SOLID GEOMETRY. By PERCIVAL FROST, M.A., and the Rev. J. WOLSTENHOLME, M.A., Fellow and Assistant Tutor of Christ's College. 8vo. cloth. 18*s.*

Intending to make the subject accessible, at least in the earlier portions to all classes of students, the authors have endeavoured to explain completely all the processes which are most useful in dealing with ordinary theorems and problems, thus directing the student to the selection of methods which are best adapted to the exigencies of each problem. In the more difficult portions of the subject, they have considered themselves to be addressing a higher class of students;

and they have there tried to lay a good foundation on which to build, if any reader should wish to pursue the science beyond the limits to which the work extends.

Godfray.—Works by HUGH GODFRAY, M.A., Mathematical Lecturer at Pembroke College, Cambridge:—

A TREATISE ON ASTRONOMY, for the Use of Colleges and Schools. 8vo. cloth. 12*s.* 6*d.*

This book embraces all those branches of Astronomy which have, from time to time, been recommended by the Cambridge Board of Mathematical Studies: but by far the larger and easier portion, adapted to the first three days of the Examination for Honours, may be read by the more advanced pupils in many of our schools. The author's aim has been to convey clear and distinct ideas of the celestial phenomena. "It is a working book," says the Guardian, *"taking Astronomy in its proper place in the Mathematical Sciences. . . . It is a book which is not likely to be got up unintelligently."*

AN ELEMENTARY TREATISE ON THE LUNAR THEORY, with a Brief Sketch of the Problem up to the time of Newton. Second Edition, revised. Crown 8vo. cloth. 5*s.* 6*d.*

These pages will, it is hoped, form an introduction to more recondite works. Difficulties have been discussed at considerable length. The selection of the method followed with regard to analytical solutions, which is the same as that of Airy, Herschel, etc., was made on account of its simplicity; it is, moreover, the method which has obtained in the University of Cambridge. "As an elementary treatise and introduction to the subject, we think it may justly claim to supersede all former ones."—London, Edinburgh, and Dublin Phil. Magazine.

Green (George).—MATHEMATICAL PAPERS OF THE LATE GEORGE GREEN, Fellow of Gonville and Caius College, Cambridge. Edited by N. M. FERRERS, M.A., Fellow and Tutor of Gonville and Caius College. 8vo. 15*s.*

The publication of this book may be opportune at present, as several of the subjects with which they are directly or indirectly concerned have recently been introduced into the course of mathematical study at Cambridge. They have also an interest as being the work of an almost entirely self-taught mathematical genius. The Papers comprise the following:—An Essay on the application of Mathematical Analysis to the Theories of Electricity and Magnetism—On the Laws of the Equilibrium of Fluids analogous to the Electric Fluid—On the Determination of the Attractions of Ellipsoids of variable Densities—On the Motion of Waves in a variable Canal of small depth and width—On the Reflection and Refraction of Sound—On the Reflection and Refraction of Light at the Common Surface of two Non-Crystallized Media—On the Propagation of Light in Crystallized Media—Researches on the Vibrations of Pendulums in Fluid Media. "It has been for some time recognized that Green's writings are amongst the most valuable mathematical productions we possess."—Athenæum.

Hemming.—AN ELEMENTARY TREATISE ON THE DIFFERENTIAL AND INTEGRAL CALCULUS. For the Use of Colleges and Schools. By G. W. HEMMING, M.A., Fellow of St. John's College, Cambridge. Second Edition, with Corrections and Additions. 8vo. cloth. 9*s*.

"*There is no book in common use from which so clear and exact a knowledge of the principles of the Calculus can be so readily obtained.*"—Literary Gazette.

Jackson.—GEOMETRICAL CONIC SECTIONS. An Elementary Treatise in which the Conic Sections are defined as the Plane Sections of a Cone, and treated by the Method of Projections. By J. STUART JACKSON, M.A , late Fellow of Gonville and Caius College. Crown 8vo. 4*s*. 6*d*.

This work has been written with a view to give the student the benefit of the Method of Projections as applied to the Ellipse and Hyperbola. When this method is admitted into the treatment of Conic Sections there are many reasons why they should be defined, not with reference to the focus and directrix, but according to the original definition from which they have their name, as Plane Sections of a Cone. This method is calculated to produce a material simplification in the treatment of these curves and to make the proof of their properties more easily understood in the first instance and more easily remembered. It is also a powerful instrument in the solution of a large class of problems relating to these curves.

Morgan.—A COLLECTION OF PROBLEMS AND EXAMPLES IN MATHEMATICS. With Answers. By H. A. MORGAN, M.A., Sadlerian and Mathematical Lecturer of Jesus College, Cambridge. Crown 8vo. cloth. 6*s.* 6*d.*

This book contains a number of problems, chiefly elementary, in the Mathematical subjects usually read at Cambridge. They have been selected from the Papers set during late years at Jesus College. Very few of them are to be met with in other collections, and by far the larger number are due to some of the most distinguished Mathematicians in the University.

Newton's Principia.—4to. cloth. 31*s.* 6*d.*

It is a sufficient guarantee of the reliability of this complete edition of Newton's Principia *that it has been printed for and under the care of Professor Sir William Thomson and Professor Blackburn, of Glasgow University. The following notice is prefixed:—"Finding that all the editions of the* Principia *are now out of print, we have been induced to reprint Newton's last edition [of* 1726] *without note or comment, only introducing the 'Corrigenda' of the old copy and correcting typographical errors." The book is of a handsome size, with large type, fine thick paper, and cleanly-cut figures, and is the only recent edition containing the whole of Newton's great work.*

Parkinson.—Works by S. PARKINSON, D.D., F.R.S., Fellow and Tutor of St. John's College, Cambridge:—

AN ELEMENTARY TREATISE ON MECHANICS. For the Use of the Junior Classes at the University and the Higher Classes in Schools. With a Collection of Examples. Fourth Edition, revised. Crown 8vo. cloth. 9*s.* 6*d.*

In preparing a fourth edition of this work the author has kept the same object in view as he had in the former editions—namely, to include in it such portions of Theoretical Mechanics as can be conveniently investigated without the use of the Differential Calculus, and so render it suitable as a manual for the junior classes in the University and the higher classes in Schools. With one or two short exceptions, the student is not presumed to require a knowledge of any

Parkinson—*continued.*

branches of Mathematics beyond the elements of Algebra, Geometry, and Trigonometry. Several additional propositions have been incorporated in the work for the purpose of rendering it more complete, and the collection of Examples and Problems has been largely increased.

A TREATISE ON OPTICS. Third Edition, revised and enlarged. Crown 8vo. cloth. 10*s*. 6*d*.

A collection of Examples and Problems has been appended to this work, which are sufficiently numerous and varied in character to afford useful exercise for the student. For the greater part of them, recourse has been had to the Examination Papers set in the University and the several Colleges during the last twenty years.

Phear.—ELEMENTARY HYDROSTATICS. With Numerous Examples. By J. B. PHEAR, M.A., Fellow and late Assistant Tutor of Clare College, Cambridge. Fourth Edition. Crown 8vo. cloth. 5*s*. 6*d*.

This edition has been carefully revised throughout, and many new Illustrations and Examples added, which it is hoped will increase its usefulness to students at the Universities and in Schools. In accordance with suggestions from many engaged in tuition, answers to all the Examples have been given at the end of the book.

Pratt.—A TREATISE ON ATTRACTIONS, LAPLACE'S FUNCTIONS, AND THE FIGURE OF THE EARTH. By JOHN H. PRATT, M.A., Archdeacon of Calcutta, Author of "The Mathematical Principles of Mechanical Philosophy." Fourth Edition. Crown 8vo. cloth. 6*s*. 6*d*.

The author's chief design in this treatise is to give an answer to the question, "Has the Earth acquired its present form from being originally in a fluid state?" This edition is a complete revision of the former ones.

Puckle.—AN ELEMENTARY TREATISE ON CONIC SECTIONS AND ALGEBRAIC GEOMETRY. With numerous Examples and Hints for their Solution; especially designed for the Use of Beginners. By G. H. PUCKLE, M.A., Head Master of Windermere College. New Edition, revised and enlarged. Crown 8vo. cloth. 7*s*. 6*d*.

This work is recommended by the Syndicate of the Cambridge Local Examinations, and is the text-book in Harvard University, U.S. The Athenæum *says the author "displays an intimate acquaintance with the difficulties likely to be felt, together with a singular aptitude in removing them."*

Routh.—AN ELEMENTARY TREATISE ON THE DYNAMICS OF THE SYSTEM OF RIGID BODIES. With numerous Examples. By EDWARD JOHN ROUTH, M.A., late Fellow and Assistant Tutor of St. Peter's College, Cambridge; Examiner in the University of London. Second Edition, enlarged. Crown 8vo. cloth. 14*s.*

In this edition the author has made several additions to each chapter: he has tried, even at the risk of some little repetition, to make each chapter, as far as possible, complete in itself, so that all that relates to any one part of the subject may be found in the same place. This arrangement will enable every student to select his own order in which to read the subject. The Examples which will be found at the end of each chapter have been chiefly selected from the Examination Papers which have been set in the University and the Colleges in the last few years.

Smith's (Barnard) Works.—See EDUCATIONAL CATALOGUE.

Snowball.—THE ELEMENTS OF PLANE AND SPHERICAL TRIGONOMETRY; with the Construction and Use of Tables of Logarithms. By J. C. SNOWBALL, M.A. Tenth Edition. Crown 8vo. cloth. 7*s.* 6*d.*

In preparing the present edition for the press, the text has been subjected to a careful revision; the proofs of some of the more important propositions have been rendered more strict and general; and a considerable addition of more than two hundred examples, taken principally from the questions set of late years in the public examinations of the University and of individual Colleges, has been made to the collection of Examples and Problems for practice.

Tait and Steele.—DYNAMICS OF A PARTICLE. With numerous Examples. By Professor TAIT and Mr. STEELE. New Edition. Crown 8vo. cloth. 10*s*. 6*d*.

In this treatise will be found all the ordinary propositions, connected with the Dynamics of Particles, which can be conveniently deduced without the use of D'Alembert's Principle. Throughout the book will be found a number of illustrative examples introduced in the text, and for the most part completely worked out; others with occasional solutions or hints to assist the student are appended to each chapter. For by far the greater portion of these, the Cambridge Senate-House and College Examination Papers have been applied to.

Taylor.—GEOMETRICAL CONICS; including Anharmonic Ratio and Projection, with numerous Examples. By C. TAYLOR, B.A., Scholar of St. John's College, Cambridge. Crown 8vo. cloth. 7*s*. 6*d*.

This work contains elementary proofs of the principal properties of Conic Sections, together with chapters on Projection and Anharmonic Ratio.

Todhunter.—Works by I. TODHUNTER, M.A., F.R.S., of St. John's College, Cambridge:—

"*Perspicuous language, vigorous investigations, scrutiny of difficulties, and methodical treatment, characterize Mr. Todhunter's works.*"—Civil Engineer.

THE ELEMENTS OF EUCLID; MENSURATION FOR BEGINNERS; ALGEBRA FOR BEGINNERS; TRIGONOMETRY FOR BEGINNERS; MECHANICS FOR BEGINNERS.—See EDUCATIONAL CATALOGUE.

ALGEBRA. For the Use of Colleges and Schools. Fifth Edition. Crown 8vo. cloth. 7*s*. 6*d*.

This work contains all the propositions which are usually included in elementary treatises on Algebra, and a large number of Examples for Exercise. *The author has sought to render the work easily intelligible to students, without impairing the accuracy of the demonstrations, or contracting the limits of the subject. The Examples, about* Sixteen hundred and fifty *in number, have been selected with*

Todhunter (I.)—*continued.*

a view to illustrate every part of the subject. The work will be found peculiarly adapted to the wants of students who are without the aid of a teacher. The Answers to the Examples, with hints for the solution of some in which assistance may be needed, are given at the end of the book. In the present edition two New Chapters and Three hundred *miscellaneous Examples have been added.* "*It has merits which unquestionably place it first in the class to which it belongs.*"—Educator.

KEY TO ALGEBRA FOR THE USE OF COLLEGES AND SCHOOLS. Crown 8vo. 10*s*. 6*d*.

AN ELEMENTARY TREATISE ON THE THEORY OF EQUATIONS. Second Edition, revised. Crown 8vo. cloth. 7*s*. 6*d*.

This treatise contains all the propositions which are usually included in elementary treatises on the theory of Equations, together with Examples for exercise. These have been selected from the College and University Examination Papers, and the results have been given when it appeared necessary. In order to exhibit a comprehensive view of the subject, the treatise includes investigations which are not found in all the preceding elementary treatises, and also some investigations which are not to be found in any of them. For the second edition the work has been revised and some additions have been made, the most important being an account of the Researches of Professor Sylvester respecting Newton's Rule. "*A thoroughly trustworthy, complete, and yet not too elaborate treatise.*" —Philosophical Magazine.

PLANE TRIGONOMETRY. For Schools and Colleges. Fourth Edition. Crown 8vo. cloth. 5*s*.

The design of this work has been to render the subject intelligible to beginners, and at the same time to afford the student the opportunity of obtaining all the information which he will require on this branch of Mathematics. Each chapter is followed by a set of Examples: those which are entitled Miscellaneous Examples, *together with a few in some of the other sets, may be advantageously reserved by the student for exercise after he has made some progress in the subject. In the Second Edition the hints for the solution of the Examples have been considerably increased.*

Todhunter (I.)—*continued.*

A TREATISE ON SPHERICAL TRIGONOMETRY. Third Edition, enlarged. Crown 8vo. cloth. 4*s.* 6*d.*

The present work is constructed on the same plan as the treatise on Plane Trigonometry, to which it is intended as a sequel. In the account of Napier's Rules of circular parts, an explanation has been given of a method of proof devised by Napier, which seems to have been overlooked by most modern writers on the subject. Considerable labour has been bestowed on the text in order to render it comprehensive and accurate, and the Examples (selected chiefly from College Examination Papers) have all been carefully verified. "For educational purposes this work seems to be superior to any others on the subject."—Critic.

PLANE CO-ORDINATE GEOMETRY, as applied to the Straight Line and the Conic Sections. With numerous Examples. Fourth Edition, revised and enlarged. Crown 8vo. cloth. 7*s.* 6*d.*

The author has here endeavoured to exhibit the subject in a simple manner for the benefit of beginners, and at the same time to include in one volume all that students usually require. In addition, therefore, to the propositions which have always appeared in such treatises, he has introduced the methods of abridged notation, *which are of more recent origin: these methods, which are of a less elementary character than the rest of the work, are placed in separate chapters, and may be omitted by the student at first.*

A TREATISE ON THE DIFFERENTIAL CALCULUS. With numerous Examples. Fifth Edition. Crown 8vo. cloth. 10*s.* 6*d.*

The author has endeavoured in the present work to exhibit a comprehensive view of the Differential Calculus on the method of limits. In the more elementary portions he has entered into considerable detail in the explanations, with the hope that a reader who is without the assistance of a tutor may be enabled to acquire a competent acquaintance with the subject. The method adopted is that of Differential Coefficients. To the different chapters are appended Examples sufficiently numerous to render another book unnecessary; these Examples being mostly selected from College Examination Papers. This and the following work have been translated into

Todhunter (I.)—*continued.*

Italian by Professor Battaglini, who in his Preface speaks thus:—"In publishing this translation of the Differential and Integral Calculus of Mr. Todhunter, we have had no other object than to add to the books which are in the hands of the students of our Universities, a work remarkable for the clearness of the exposition, the rigour of the demonstrations, the just proportion in the parts, and the rich store of examples which offer a large field for useful exercise."

A TREATISE ON THE INTEGRAL CALCULUS AND ITS APPLICATIONS. With numerous Examples. Third Edition, revised and enlarged. Crown 8vo. cloth. 10*s*. 6*d*.

This is designed as a work at once elementary and complete, adapted for the use of beginners, and sufficient for the wants of advanced students. In the selection of the propositions, and in the mode of establishing them, it has been sought to exhibit the principles clearly, and to illustrate all their most important results. The process of summation has been repeatedly brought forward, with the view of securing the attention of the student to the notions which form the true foundation of the Calculus itself, as well as of its most valuable applications. Every attempt has been made to explain those difficulties which usually perplex beginners, especially with reference to the limits *of integrations. A new method has been adopted in regard to the transformation of multiple integrals. The last chapter deals with the Calculus of Variations. A large collection of Exercises, selected from College Examination Papers, has been appended to the several chapters.*

EXAMPLES OF ANALYTICAL GEOMETRY OF THREE DIMENSIONS. Third Edition, revised. Crown 8vo. cloth. 4*s*.

A TREATISE ON ANALYTICAL STATICS. With numerous Examples. Third Edition, revised and enlarged. Crown 8vo. cloth. 10*s*. 6*d*.

In this work on Statics (treating of the laws of the equilibrium of bodies) will be found all the propositions which usually appear in treatises on Theoretical Statics. To the different chapters Examples are appended, which have been principally selected from University Examination Papers. In the Third Edition many additions have been made, in order to illustrate the application of the principles of the subject to the solution of problems.

Todhunter (I.)—*continued.*

A HISTORY OF THE MATHEMATICAL THEORY OF PROBABILITY, from the Time of Pascal to that of Laplace. 8vo. 18*s.*

The subject of this work has high claims to consideration on account of the subtle problems which it involves, the valuable contributions to analysis which it has produced, its important practical applications, and the eminence of those who have cultivated it; nearly every great mathematician within the range of a century and a half comes under consideration in the course of the history. The author has endeavoured to be quite accurate in his statements, and to reproduce the essential elements of the original works which he has analysed. Besides being a history, the work may claim the title of a comprehensive treatise on the Theory of Probability, for it assumes in the reader only so much knowledge as can be gained from an elementary book on Algebra, and introduces him to almost every process and every special problem which the literature of the subject can furnish.

RESEARCHES IN THE CALCULUS OF VARIATIONS, Principally on the Theory of Discontinuous Solutions: An Essay to which the Adams' Prize was awarded in the University of Cambridge in 1871. 8vo. 6*s.*

The subject of this Essay was prescribed in the following terms by the Examiners:—"A determination of the circumstances under which discontinuity of any kind presents itself in the solution of a problem of maximum or minimum in the Calculus of Variations, and applications to particular instances. It is expected that the discussion of the instances should be exemplified as far as possible geometrically, and that attention be especially directed to cases of real or supposed failure of the Calculus." While the Essay is thus mainly devoted to the consideration of discontinuous solutions, various other questions in the Calculus of Variations are examined and elucidated; and the author hopes he has definitely contributed to the extension and improvement of our knowledge of this refined department of analysis.

Wilson (W. P.)—A TREATISE ON DYNAMICS. By W. P. WILSON, M.A., Fellow of St. John's College, Cambridge, and Professor of Mathematics in Queen's College, Belfast. 8vo. 9*s.* 6*d.*

Wolstenholme.—A BOOK OF MATHEMATICAL PROBLEMS, on Subjects included in the Cambridge Course. By JOSEPH WOLSTENHOLME, Fellow of Christ's College, some time Fellow of St. John's College, and lately Lecturer in Mathematics at Christ's College. Crown 8vo. cloth. 8*s.* 6*d.*

CONTENTS :—*Geometry (Euclid)—Algebra—Plane Trigonometry—Geometrical Conic Sections—Analytical Conic Sections—Theory of Equations—Differential Calculus—Integral Calculus—Solid Geometry—Statics—Elementary Dynamics—Newton—Dynamics of a Point—Dynamics of a Rigid Body—Hydrostatics—Geometrical Optics—Spherical Trigonometry and Plane Astronomy. In some cases the author has prefixed to certain classes of problems fragmentary notes on the mathematical subjects to which they relate.*

"*Judicious, symmetrical, and well arranged.*"—Guardian.

PHYSICAL SCIENCE.

Airy (G. B.)—POPULAR ASTRONOMY. With Illustrations By Sir G. B. AIRY, K.C.B., Astronomer Royal. Seventh and cheaper Edition. 18mo. cloth. 4*s.* 6*d.*

This work consists of Six Lectures, which are intended "to explain to intelligent persons the principles on which the instruments of an Observatory are constructed (omitting all details, so far as they are merely subsidiary), and the principles on which the observations made with these instruments are treated for deduction of the distances and weights of the bodies of the Solar System, and of a few stars, omitting all minutiæ of formulæ, and all troublesome details of calculation." The speciality of this volume is the direct reference of every step to the Observatory, and the full description of the methods and instruments of observation.

Bastian.—Works by H. CHARLTON BASTIAN, M.D., F.R.S., Professor of Pathological Anatomy in University College, London, etc. :—

THE MODES OF ORIGIN OF LOWEST ORGANISMS: Including a Discussion of the Experiments of M. Pasteur, and a Reply to some Statements by Professors Huxley and Tyndall. Crown 8vo. 4*s.* 6*d.*

The present volume contains a fragment of the evidence which will be embodied in a much larger work—now almost completed—relating to the nature and origin of living matter, and in favour of what is termed the Physical Doctrine of Life. "It is a work worthy of the highest respect, and places its author in the very first class of scientific physicians. . . . It would be difficult to name an instance in which skill, knowledge, perseverance, and great reasoning power have been more happily applied to the investigation of a complex biological problem."—British Medical Journal.

Bastian (H. C.)—*continued.*

THE BEGINNINGS OF LIFE: Being some Account of the Nature, Modes of Origin, and Transformations of Lower Organisms. In Two Volumes. With upwards of 100 Illustrations. Crown 8vo. 28*s.*

The subject of this work is one of the highest interest not only to scientific men, but to intelligent men of all kinds. Dr. Bastian's labours in this direction are already well known and highly valued, even by those who differ from his conclusions. These volumes contain the results of several years' investigation on the Origin of Life, and it was only atfer the author had proceeded some length with his observations and experiments that he was compelled to change the opinions he started with for those announced in the present work —the most important of which is that in favour of "spontaneous generation"—the theory that life has never ceased to be actually originated. The First Part of the ork is intended to show the general reader, more especially, that the logical consequences of the now commonly accepted doctrines concerning the "Conservation of Energy" and the "Correlation of the Vital and Physical Forces" are wholly favourable to the possibility of the independent origin of "living" matter. It also contains a view of the "Cellular Theory of Organisation." In the Second Part of the work, under the head "Archebiosis," the question as to the present occurrence or non-occurrence of "spontaneous generation" is fully considered. "He has made a notable contribution to the literature of scientific research and exposition."—Daily News. "*It is a book that cannot be ignored, and must inevitably ad to renewed discussions and repeated observations, and through these to the establishment of truth.*"—A. R. WALLACE *in* Nature.

Birks (T. R.)—ON MATTER AND ETHER; or, The Secret Laws of Physical Change. By THOMAS RAWSON BIRKS, M.A., Professor of Moral Philosophy in the University of Cambridge. Crown 8vo. 5*s.* 6*d.*

The author believes that the hypothesis of the existence of, besides matter, a luminous ether, of immense elastic force, supplies the true and sufficient key to the remaining secrets of inorganic matter, of the phenomena of light, electricity, etc. In this treatise the author endeavours first to form a clear and definite conception with regard to the real nature both of matter and ether, and the laws of mutual action which must be supposed to exist between them. He then endeavours to trace out the main consequences of the fundamental hypothesis, and their correspondence with the known phenomena of physical change.

Blanford (W. T.)—GEOLOGY AND ZOOLOGY OF ABYSSINIA. By W. T. BLANFORD. 8vo. 21*s.*

This work contains an account of the Geological and Zoological Observations made by the author in Abyssinia, when accompanying the British Army on its march to Magdala and back in 1868, *and during a short journey in Northern Abyssinia, after the departure of the troops. Part I. Personal Narrative; Part II. Geology; Part III. Zoology. With Coloured Illustrations and Geological Map. "The result of his labours," the* Academy *says, "is an important contribution to the natural history of the country."*

Cooke (Josiah P., Jun.)—FIRST PRINCIPLES OF CHEMICAL PHILOSOPHY. By JOSIAH P. COOKE, Jun., Ervine Professor of Chemistry and Mineralogy in Harvard College. Crown 8vo. 12*s.*

The object of the author in this book is to present the philosophy of Chemistry in such a form that it can be made with profit the subject of College recitations, and furnish the teacher with the means of testing the student's faithfulness and ability. With this view the subject has been developed in a logical order, and the principles of the science are taught independently of the experimental evidence on which they rest.

Cooke (M. C.)—HANDBOOK OF BRITISH FUNGI, with full descriptions of all the Species, and Illustrations of the Genera. By M. C. COOKE, M.A. Two vols. crown 8vo. 24*s.*

During the thirty-five years that have elapsed since the appearance of the last complete Mycologic Flora no attempt has been made to revise it, to incorporate species since discovered, and to bring it up to the standard of modern science. No apology, therefore, is necessary for the present effort, since all will admit that the want of such a manual has long been felt, and this work makes its appearance under the advantage that it seeks to occupy a place which has long been vacant. No effort has been spared to make the work worthy of confidence, and, by the publication of an occasional supplement, it is hoped to maintain it for many years as the "*Handbook for every student of British Fungi. Appended is a complete alphabetical Index of all the divisions and subdivisions of the Fungi noticed in the text. The book contains* 400 *figures.* "*Will maintain its place as the standard English book, on the subject of which it treats, for many years to come.*"—Standard.

Dawson (J. W.)—ACADIAN GEOLOGY. The Geologic Structure, Organic Remains, and Mineral Resources of Nova Scotia, New Brunswick, and Prince Edward Island. By JOHN WILLIAM DAWSON, M.A., LL.D., F.R.S., F.G.S., Principal and Vice-Chancellor of M'Gill College and University, Montreal, &c. Second Edition, revised and enlarged. With a Geological Map and numerous Illustrations. 8vo. 18*s.*

The object of the first edition of this work was to place within the reach of the people of the districts to which it relates, a popular account of the more recent discoveries in the geology and mineral resources of their country, and at the same time to give to geologists in other countries a connected view of the structure of a very interesting portion of the American Continent, in its relation to general and theoretical Geology. In the present edition, it is hoped this design is still more completely fulfilled, with reference to the present more advanced condition of knowledge. The author has endeavoured to convey a knowledge of the structure and fossils of the region in such a manner as to be intelligible to ordinary readers, and has devoted much attention to all questions relating to the nature and present or prospective value of deposits of useful minerals. Besides a large coloured Geological Map of the district, the work is illustrated by upwards of 260 *cuts of sections, fossils, animals, etc.* "*The book will doubtless find a place in the library, not only of the scientific geologist, but also of all who are desirous of the industrial progress and commercial prosperity of the Acadian provinces.*"—Mining Journal. "*A style at once popular and scientific. . . . A valuable addition to our store of geological knowledge.*"—Guardian.

Flower (W. H.)—AN INTRODUCTION TO THE OSTEOLOGY OF THE MAMMALIA. Being the substance of the Course of Lectures delivered at the Royal College of. Surgeons of England in 1870. By W. H. FLOWER, F.R.S., F.R.C.S., Hunterian Professor of Comparative Anatomy and Physiology. With numerous Illustrations. Globe 8vo. 7*s*. 6*d*.

Although the present work contains the substance of a Course of Lectures, the form has been changed, so as the better to adapt it as a handbook for students. Theoretical views have been almost entirely excluded: and while it is impossible in a scientific treatise to avoid the employment of technical terms, it has been the author's endeavour to use no more than absolutely necessary, and to exercise due care in selecting only those that seem most appropriate, or which have received the sanction of general adoption. With a very few exceptions the illustrations have been drawn expressly for this work from specimens in the Museum of the Royal College of Surgeons.

Galton.—Works by FRANCIS GALTON, F.R.S. :—

METEOROGRAPHICA, or Methods of Mapping the Weather. Illustrated by upwards of 600 Printed Lithographic Diagrams. 4to. 9*s*.

As Mr. Galton entertains strong views on the necessity of Meteorological Charts and Maps, he determined, as a practical proof of what could be done, to chart the entire area of Europe, so far as meteorological stations extend, during one month, viz. the month of December, 1861. Mr. Galton got his data from authorities in every part of Britain and the Continent, and on the basis of these has here drawn up nearly a hundred different Maps and Charts, showing the state of the weather all over Europe during the above period. "If the various Governments and scientific bodies would perform for the whole world for two or three years what, at a great cost and labour, Mr. Galton has done for a part of Europe for one month, Meteorology would soon cease to be made a joke of."—Spectator.

HEREDITARY GENIUS: An Inquiry into its Laws and Consequences. Demy 8vo. 12*s*.

"*I propose,*" *the author says,* "*to show in this book that a man's natural abilities are derived by inheritance, under exactly the same limitations as are the form and physical features of the whole organic world. I shall show that social agencies of an ordinary character, whose influences are little suspected, are at this moment working towards the degradation of human nature, and that others are working towards its improvement. The general plan of my argument is to show that high reputation is a pretty accurate test of high ability; next, to discuss the relationships of a large body of fairly eminent men, and to obtain from these a general survey of the laws of heredity in respect of genius. Then will follow a short chapter, by way of comparison, on the hereditary transmission of physical gifts, as deduced from the relationships of certain classes of oarsmen and wrestlers. Lastly, I shall collate my results and draw conclusions." The* Times *calls it "a most able and most interesting book;" and* Mr. Darwin, *in his "Descent of Man" (vol.* i. *p.* 111*), says, "We know, through the admirable labours of Mr. Galton, that Genius tends to be inherited."*

Geikie (A.)—SCENERY OF SCOTLAND, Viewed in Connection with its Physical Geography. With Illustrations and a new Geological Map. By ARCHIBALD GEIKIE, Professor of Geology in the University of Edinburgh. Crown 8vo. 10*s*. 6*d*.

"*We can confidently recommend Mr. Geikie's work to those who wish to look below the surface and read the physical history of the Scenery of Scotland by the light of modern science.*"—Saturday Review.

"*Amusing, picturesque, and instructive.*"—Times.

Guillemin.—THE FORCES OF NATURE: A Popular Introduction to the Study of Physical Phenomena. By AMÉDÉE GUILLEMIN. Translated from the French by MRS. NORMAN LOCKYER; and Edited, with Additions and Notes, by J. NORMAN LOCKYER, F.R.S. Illustrated by 11 Coloured Plates and 455 Woodcuts. Imperial 8vo. cloth, extra gilt. 31*s*. 6*d*.

M. Guillemin is already well known in this country as a most successful populariser of the results of accurate scientific research, his works, while eloquent, intelligible, and interesting to the general reader, being thoroughly trustworthy and up to date. The present work consists of Seven Books, each divided into a number of Chapters, the Books treating respectively of Gravity, Sound, Light, Heat, Magnetism, Electricity, and Atmospheric Meteors.

The programme of the work has not been confined to a simple explanation of the facts: but an attempt has been made to grasp their relative bearings, or, in other words, their laws, and that too without taking for granted that the reader is acquainted with mathematics. The author's aim has been to smooth the way for those who desire to extend their studies, and likewise to present to general readers a sufficiently exact and just idea of this branch of science. The numerous coloured illustrations and woodcuts are not brought into the text merely for show, but each one is really illustrative of the subject. The name of the translator and editor is a sufficient guarantee both that the work is of genuine scientific value and that the translation is accurate and executed with intelligence. "This book is a luxurious introduction to the study of the Physical Sciences. M. Guillemin *has found an excellent translator in* Mrs. Norman Lockyer, *while the editorship of* Mr. Norman Lockyer, *with his notes and additions, are guarantees not only of scientific accuracy, but of the completeness and lateness of the information."* —Daily News.

Hooker (Dr.)—THE STUDENT'S FLORA OF THE BRITISH ISLANDS. By J. D. HOOKER, C.B., F.R.S., M.D., D.C.L., Director of the Royal Gardens, Kew. Globe 8vo. 10*s.* 6*d.*

The object of this work is to supply students and field-botanists with a fuller account of the Plants of the British Islands than the manuals hitherto in use aim at giving. The Ordinal, Generic, and Specific characters have been re-written, and are to a great extent original, and drawn from living or dried specimens, or both. "Cannot fail to perfectly fulfil the purpose for which it is intended."—Land and Water. "*Containing the fullest and most accurate manual of the kind that has yet appeared.*"—Pall Mall Gazette.

Huxley (Professor).—LAY SERMONS, ADDRESSES, AND REVIEWS. By T. H. HUXLEY, LL.D., F.R.S. New and Cheaper Edition. Crown 8vo. 7*s.* 6*d.*

Fourteen Discourses on the following subjects:—(1) *On the Advisableness of Improving Natural Knowledge:*—(2) *Emancipation—Black and White:*—(3) *A Liberal Education, and where to find it:*—(4) *Scientific Education:*—(5) *On the Educational Value of*

Huxley (Professor).—*continued.*

the Natural History Sciences:—(6) *On the Study of Zoology:*—(7) *On the Physical Basis of Life:*—(8) *The Scientific Aspects of Positivism:*—(9) *On a Piece of Chalk:*—(10) *Geological Contemporaneity and Persistent Types of Life:*—(11) *Geological Reform:*—(12) *The Origin of Species:*—(13) *Criticisms on the "Origin of Species:"*—(14) *On Descartes' "Discourse touching the Method of using One's Reason rightly and of seeking Scientific Truth." The momentous influence exercised by Mr. Huxley's writings on physical, mental, and social science is universally acknowledged; his works must be studied by all who would comprehend the various drifts of modern thought.*

ESSAYS SELECTED FROM LAY SERMONS, ADDRESSES, AND REVIEWS. Crown 8vo. 1*s.*

This volume includes Numbers 1, 3, 4, 7, 8, *and* 14, *of the above.*

LESSONS IN ELEMENTARY PHYSIOLOGY. With numerous Illustrations. Sixth Edition. 18mo. cloth. 4*s.* 6*d.*

This book describes and explains, in a series of graduated lessons, the principles of Human Physiology, or the Structure and Functions of the Human Body. The first lesson supplies a general view of the subject. This is followed by sections on the Vascular or Venous System, and the Circulation; the Blood and the Lymph; Respiration: Sources of Loss and of Gain to the Blood; the Function of Alimentation; Motion and Locomotion; Sensations and Sensory Organs; the Organ of Sight; the Coalescence of Sensations with one another and with other States of Consciousness; the Nervous System and Innervation; Histology, or the Minute Structure of the Tissues. A Table of Anatomical and Physiological Constants is appended. The lessons are fully illustrated by numerous engravings. The new edition has been thoroughly revised, and a considerable number of new illuslrations added: several of these have been taken from the Rabbit, the Sheep, the Dog, and the Frog, in order to aid those who attempt to make their knowledge real, by acquiring some practical acquaintance with the facts of Anatomy and Physiology. "Pure gold throughout."—Guardian. "*Unquestionably the clearest and most complete elementary treatise on this subject that we possess in any language.*"—Westminster Review.

Jellet (John H., B.D.)—A TREATISE ON THE THEORY OF FRICTION. By JOHN H. JELLET, B.D., Senior Fellow of Trinity College, Dublin; President of the Royal Irish Academy. 8vo. 8*s*. 6*d*.

The Theory of Friction, considered as a part of Rational Mechanics has not, the author thinks, received the attention which it deserves. On this account many students have been probably led to regard the discussion of this force as scarcely belonging to Rational Mechanics at all; whereas the theory of friction is as truly a part of that subject as the theory of gravitation. The force with which this theory is concerned is subject to laws as definite, and as fully susceptible of mathematical expression, as the force of gravity. This book is taken up with a special investigation of the laws of friction; and some of the principles contained in it are believed to be here enunciated for the first time. The work consists of eight Chapters as follows:—I. Definitions and Principles. II. Equilibrium with Frictions. III. Extreme Positions of Equilibrium. IV. Movement of a Particle or System of Particles. V. Motion of a Solid Body. VI. Necessary and Possible Equilibrium. VII. Determination of the Actual Value of the Acting Force of Friction. VIII. Miscellaneous Problems—1. *Problem of the Top.* 2. *Friction Wheels and Locomotives.* 3. *Questions for Exercise.* "*The book supplies a want which has hitherto existed in the science of pure mechanics.*"—Engineer.

Kirchhoff (G.)—RESEARCHES ON THE SOLAR SPECTRUM, and the Spectra of the Chemical Elements. By. G. KIRCHHOFF, Professor of Physics in the University of Heidelberg. Second Part. Translated, with the Author's Sanction, from the Transactions of the Berlin Academy for 1862, by HENRY R. ROSCOE, B.A., Ph.D., F.R.S., Professor of Chemistry in Owens College, Manchester. Part II. 4to. 5*s*.

"*It is to Kirchhoff we are indebted for by far the best and most accurate observations of these phenomena.*"—Edin. Review. "*This memoir seems almost indispensable to every Spectrum observer.*"—Philosophical Magazine.

Lockyer (J. N.)—ELEMENTARY LESSONS IN ASTRONOMY. With numerous Illustrations. By J. NORMAN LOCKYER, F.R.S. Ninth Thousand. 18mo. 5*s*. 6*d*.

The author has here aimed to give a connected view of the whole subject, and to supply facts, and ideas founded on the facts, to serve as a basis for subsequent study and discussion. The chapters treat of the Stars and Nebulæ; the Sun; the Solar System; Apparent Movements of the Heavenly Bodies; the Measurement of Time; Light; the Telescope and Spectroscope; Apparent Places of the Heavenly Bodies; the Real Distances and Dimensions; Universal Gravitation. The most recent Astronomical Discoveries are incorporated. Mr. Lockyer's work supplements that of the Astronomer Royal. "The book is full, clear, sound, and worthy of attention, not only as a popular exposition, but as a scientific 'Index.'—Athenæum. "*The most fascinating of elementary books on the Sciences.*"—Nonconformist.

Macmillan (Rev. Hugh).—For other Works by the same Author, see THEOLOGICAL CATALOGUE.

HOLIDAYS ON HIGH LANDS; or, Rambles and Incidents in search of Alpine Plants. Crown 8vo. cloth. 6*s.*

The aim of this book is to impart a general idea of the origin, character, and distribution of those rare and beautiful Alpine plants which occur on the British hills, and which are found almost everywhere on the lofty mountain chains of Europe, Asia, Africa, and America. In the first three chapters the peculiar vegetation of the Highland mountains is fully described; while in the remaining chapters this vegetation is traced to its northern cradle in the mountains of Norway, and to its southern European termination in the Alps of Switzerland. The information the author has to give is conveyed in a setting of personal adventure. "One of the most charming books of its kind ever written."—Literary Churchman. "*Mr. M.'s glowing pictures of Scandinavian scenery.*"—Saturday Review.

FOOT-NOTES FROM THE PAGE OF NATURE. With numerous Illustrations. Fcap. 8vo. 5*s.*

"*Those who have derived pleasure and profit from the study of flowers and ferns—subjects, it is pleasing to find, now everywhere popular—by descending lower into the arcana of the vegetable kingdom, will find a still more interesting and delightful field of research in the objects brought under review in the following pages.*"—Preface. "*The naturalist and the botanist will delight in this volume, and those who understand little of the scientific parts of the work will linger over the mysterious page of nature here unfolded to their view.*"—John Bull.

Mansfield (C. B.)—A THEORY OF SALTS. A Treatise on the Constitution of Bipolar (two-membered) Chemical Compounds. By the late CHARLES BLACHFORD MANSFIELD. Crown 8vo. 14*s*.

"*Mansfield,*" *says the editor,* "*wrote this book to defend the principle that the fact of voltaic decomposition afforded the true indication, if properly interpreted, of the nature of the saline structure, and of the atomicity of the elements that built it up. No chemist will peruse this book without feeling that he is in the presence of an original thinker, whose pages are continually suggestive, even though their general argument may not be entirely concurrent in direction with that of modern chemical thought.*"

Mivart (St. George).—ON THE GENESIS OF SPECIES. By ST. GEORGE MIVART, F.R.S. Crown 8vo. Second Edition, to which notes have been added in reference and reply to Darwin's "Descent of Man." With numerous Illustrations. pp. xv. 296. 9*s*.

The aim of the author is to support the doctrine that the various species have been evolved by ordinary natural laws (for the most part unknown) controlled by the subordinate action of "natural selection," and at the same time to remind some that there is and can be absolutely nothing in physical science which forbids them to regard those natural laws as acting with the Divine concurrence, and in obedience to a creative fiat originally imposed on the primeval cosmos, "in the beginning," by its Creator, its Upholder, and its Lord. Nearly fifty woodcuts illustrate the letter-press, and a complete index makes all references extremely easy. Canon Kingsley, in his address to the "Devonshire Association," says, "Let me recommend earnestly to you, as a specimen of what can be said on the other side, the 'Genesis of Species,' by Mr. St. George Mivart, F.R.S., a book which I am happy to say has been received elsewhere as it has deserved, and, I trust, will be received so among you." "In no work in the English language has this great controversy been treated at once with the same broad and vigorous grasp of facts, and the same liberal and candid temper."—Saturday Review.

Nature.—A WEEKLY ILLUSTRATED JOURNAL OF SCIENCE. Published every Thursday. Price 4*d.* Monthly Parts, 1*s.* 4*d.* and 1*s.* 8*d.*; Half-yearly Volumes, 10*s.* 6*d.* Cases for binding Vols. 1*s.* 6*d.*

"*Backed by many of the best names among English philosophers, and by a few equally valuable supporters in America and on the Continent of Europe.*"—Saturday Review. "*This able and well-edited Journal, which posts up the science of the day promptly, and promises to be of signal service to students and savants.*"—British Quarterly Review.

Oliver.—Works by DANIEL OLIVER, F.R.S., F.L.S., Professor of Botany in University College, London, and Keeper of the Herbarium and Library of the Royal Gardens, Kew :—

LESSONS IN ELEMENTARY BOTANY. With nearly Two Hundred Illustrations. Twelfth Thousand. 18mo cloth. 4*s.* 6*d.*

This book is designed to teach the elements of Botany on Professor Henslow's plan of selected Types and by the use of Schedules. The earlier chapters, embracing the elements of Structural and Physiological Botany, introduce us to the methodical study of the Ordinal Types. The concluding chapters are entitled, "How to Dry Plants" and "How to Describe Plants." A valuable Glossary is appended to the volume. In the preparation of this work free use has been made of the manuscript materials of the late Professor Henslow.

FIRST BOOK OF INDIAN BOTANY. With numerous Illustrations. Extra fcap. 8vo. 6*s.* 6*d.*

This manual is, in substance, the author's "Lessons in Elementary Botany," adapted for use in India. In preparing it he has had in view the want, often felt, of some handy résumé *of Indian Botany, which might be serviceable not only to residents of India, but also to any one about to proceed thither, desirous of getting some preliminary idea of the botany of the country. It contains a well-digested summary of all essential knowledge pertaining to Indian Botany, wrought out in accordance with the best principles of scientific arrangement.*"—Allen's Indian Mail.

Penrose (F. C.)—ON A METHOD OF PREDICTING BY GRAPHICAL CONSTRUCTION, OCCULTATIONS OF STARS BY THE MOON, AND SOLAR ECLIPSES FOR ANY GIVEN PLACE. Together with more rigorous methods for the Accurate Calculation of Longitude. By F. C. PENROSE, F.R.A.S. With Charts, Tables, etc. 4to. 12*s.*

The author believes that if, by a graphic method, the prediction of occultations can be rendered more inviting, as well as more expeditious, than by the method of calculation, it may prove acceptable to the nautical profession as well as to scientific travellers or amateurs. The author has endeavoured to make the whole process as intelligible as possible, so that the beginner, instead of merely having to follow directions imperfectly understood, may readily comprehend the meaning of each step, and be able to illustrate the practice by the theory. Besides all necessary charts and tables, the work contains a large number of skeleton forms for working out cases in practice.

Roscoe.—Works by HENRY E. ROSCOE, F.R.S., Professor of Chemistry in Owens College, Manchester :—

LESSONS IN ELEMENTARY CHEMISTRY, INORGANIC AND ORGANIC. With numerous Illustrations and Chromo-litho of the Solar Spectrum, and of the Alkalies and Alkaline Earths. New Edition. Thirty-first Thousand. 18mo. cloth. 4*s.* 6*d.*

It has been the endeavour of the author to arrange the most important facts and principles of Modern Chemistry in a plain but concise and scientific form, suited to the present requirements of elementary instruction. For the purpose of facilitating the attainment of exactitude in the knowledge of the subject, a series of exercises and questions upon the lessons have been added. The metric system of weights and measures, and the centigrade thermometric scale, are used throughout this work. The new edition, besides new woodcuts, contains many additions and improvements, and includes the most important of the latest discoveries. "We unhesitatingly pronounce it the best of all our elementary treatises on Chemistry."—Medical Times.

SPECTRUM ANALYSIS. Six Lectures, with Appendices, Engravings, Maps, and Chromolithographs. Royal 8vo. 21*s.*

A Third Edition of these popular Lectures, containing all the most recent discoveries and several additional illustrations. "In six lectures he has given the history of the discovery and set forth the facts relating to the analysis of light in such a way that any reader of ordinary intelligence and information will be able to understand what 'Spectrum Analysis' is, and what are its claims to rank among the most signal triumphs of science."—Nonconformist. *"The lectures themselves furnish a most admirable elementary treatise on the subject, whilst by the insertion in appendices to each lecture of extracts from the most important published memoirs, the author has rendered it equally valuable as a text-book for advanced students."*—Westminster Review.

Roscoe and Jones.—THE OWENS COLLEGE JUNIOR COURSE OF PRACTICAL CHEMISTRY. By Professor ROSCOE and FRANCIS JONES, Chemical Master in the Grammar School, Manchester. 18mo. with Illustrations. 2*s*. 6*d*.

Stewart (B.)—LESSONS IN ELEMENTARY PHYSICS. By BALFOUR STEWART, F.R.S., Professor of Natural Philosophy in Owens College, Manchester. With numerous Illustrations and Chromolithos of the Spectra of the Sun, Stars, and Nebulæ. New Edition. 18mo. 4*s*. 6*d*.

A description, in an elementary manner, of the most important of those laws which regulate the phenomena of nature. The active agents, heat, light, electricity, etc., are regarded as varieties of energy, and the work is so arranged that their relation to one another, looked at in this light, and the paramount importance of the laws of energy, are clearly brought out. The volume contains all the necessary illustrations. The Educational Times *calls this "the beau-ideal of a scientific text-book, clear, accurate, and thorough."*

Thudichum and Dupré.—A TREATISE ON THE ORIGIN, NATURE, AND VARIETIES OF WINE. Being a Complete Manual of Viticulture and Œnology. By. J. L. W. THUDICHUM, M.D., and AUGUST DUPRÉ, Ph.D., Lecturer on Chemistry at Westminster Hospital. Medium 8vo. cloth gilt. 25*s*.

In this elaborate work the subject of the manufacture of wine is treated scientifically in minute detail, from every point of view. A chapter is devoted to the Origin and Physiology of Vines, two to the

Principles of Viticulture; while other chapters treat of Vintage and Vinification, the Chemistry of Alcohol, the Acids, Ether, Sugars. and other matters occurring in wine. This introductory matter occupies the first nine chapters, the remaining seventeen chapters being occupied with a detailed account of the Viticulture and the Wines of the various countries of Europe, of the Atlantic Islands, of Asia, of Africa, of America, and of Australia. Besides a number of Analytical and Statistical Tables, the work is enriched with eighty-five illustrative woodcuts. "A treatise almost unique for its usefulness either to the wine-grower, the vendor, or the consumer of wine. The analyses of wine are the most complete we have yet seen, exhibiting at a glance the constituent principles of nearly all the wines known in this country."—Wine Trade Review.

Wallace (A. R.)—CONTRIBUTIONS TO THE THEORY OF NATURAL SELECTION. A Series of Essays. By ALFRED RUSSEL WALLACE, Author of "The Malay Archipelago," etc. Second Edition, with Corrections and Additions. Crown 8vo. 8*s*. 6*d*. (For other Works by the same Author, see CATALOGUE OF HISTORY AND TRAVELS.)

Mr. Wallace has good claims to be considered as an independent originator of the theory of natural selection. Dr. Hooker, in his address to the British Association, spoke thus of the author: "Of Mr. Wallace and his many contributions to philosophical biology it is not easy to speak without enthusiasm; for, putting aside their great merits, he, throughout his writings, with a modesty as rare as I believe it to be unconscious, forgets his own unquestioned claim to the honour of having originated independently of Mr. Darwin, the theories which he so ably defends." The Saturday Review *says: "He has combined an abundance of fresh and original facts with a liveliness and sagacity of reasoning which are not often displayed so effectively on so small a scale." The Essays in this volume are:—I. "On the Law which has regulated the introduction of New Species." II. "On the Tendencies of Varieties to depart indefinitely from the Original Type." III. "Mimicry, and other Protective Resemblances among Animals." IV. "The Malayan Papilionidæ, as illustrative of the Theory of Natural Selection." V. "On Instinct in Man and Animals." VI. "The Philosophy of Birds' Nests." VII. "A Theory of Birds' Nests." VIII. "Creation by Law." IX. "The Development of Human Races under the Law of Natural Selection." X. "The Limits of Natural Selection as applied to Man."*

Warington.—THE WEEK OF CREATION; OR, THE COSMOGONY OF GENESIS CONSIDERED IN ITS RELATION TO MODERN SCIENCE. By GEORGE WARINGTON, Author of "The Historic Character of the Pentateuch Vindicated." Crown 8vo. 4*s*. 6*d*.

The greater part of this work it taken up with the teaching of the Cosmogony. Its purpose is also investigated, and a chapter is devoted to the consideration of the passage in which the difficulties occur. "A very able vindication of the Mosaic Cosmogony, by a writer who unites the advantages of a critical knowledge of the Hebrew text and of distinguished scientific attainments."—Spectator.

Wilson.—Works by the late GEORGE WILSON, M.D., F.R.S.E., Regius Professor of Technology in the University of Edinburgh:—

RELIGIO CHEMICI. With a Vignette beautifully engraved after a design by Sir NOEL PATON. Crown 8vo. 8*s*. 6*d*.

"George Wilson," says the Preface to this volume, "had it in his heart for many years to write a book corresponding to the Religio Medici *of Sir Thomas Browne, with the title* Religio Chemici. *Several of the Essays in this volume were intended to form chapters of it. These fragments being in most cases like finished gems waiting to be set, some of them are now given in a collected form to his friends and the public. In living remembrance of his purpose, the name chosen by himself has been adopted, although the original design can be but very faintly represented." The Contents of the volume are:—"Chemistry and Natural Theology." "The Chemistry of the Stars; an Argument touching the Stars and their Inhabitants." "Chemical Final Causes; as illustrated by the presence of Phosphorus, Nitrogen, and Iron in the Higher Sentient Organisms." "Robert Boyle." "Wollaston." "Life and Discoveries of Dalton." "Thoughts on the Resurrection; an Address to Medical Students." "A more fascinating volume," the* Spectator *says, "has seldom fallen into our hands." The* Freeman *says: "These papers are all valuable and deeply interesting. The production of a profound thinker, a suggestive and eloquent writer, and a man whose piety and genius went hand in hand."*

Wilson—*continued.*

THE PROGRESS OF THE TELEGRAPH. Fcap. 8vo. 1*s.*

"*While a complete view of the progress of the greatest of human inventions is obtained, all its suggestions are brought out with a rare thoughtfulness, a genial humour, and an exceeding beauty of utterance.*"—Nonconformist.

Winslow.—FORCE AND NATURE: ATTRACTION AND REPULSION. The Radical Principles of Energy graphically discussed in their Relations to Physical and Morphological Development. By C. F. WINSLOW, M.D. 8vo. 14*s.*

The author having for long investigated Nature in many directions, has ever felt unsatisfied with the physical foundations upon which some branches of science have been so long compelled to rest. The question, he believes, must have occurred to many astronomers and physicists whether some subtle principle antagonistic to attraction does not also exist as an all-pervading element in nature, and so operate as in some way to disturb the action of what is generally considered by the scientific world a unique *force. The aim of the present work is to set forth this subject in its broadest aspects, and in such a manner as to invite thereto the attention of the learned. The subjects of the eleven chapters are:—I. "Space." II. "Matter." III. "Inertia, Force, and Mind." IV. "Molecules." V. "Molecular Force." VI. "Union and Inseparability of Matter and Force." VII. and VIII. "Nature and Action of Force—Attraction—Repulsion." IX. "Cosmical Repulsion. X. "Mechanical Force." XI. "Central Forces and Celestial Physics."* "*Deserves thoughtful and conscientious study.*"—Saturday Review.

Wurtz.—A HISTORY OF CHEMICAL THEORY, from the Age of Lavoisier down to the present time. By AD. WURTZ. Translated by HENRY WATTS, F.R.S. Crown 8vo. 6*s.*

"*The discourse, as a* résumé *of chemical theory and research, unites singular luminousness and grasp. A few judicious notes are added by the translator.*"—Pall Mall Gazette. "*The treatment of the subject is admirable, and the translator has evidently done his duty most efficiently.*"—Westminster Review.

WORKS IN PHYSIOLOGY, ANATOMY, AND MEDICAL WORKS GENERALLY.

Allbutt (T. C.)—ON THE USE OF THE OPHTHALMOSCOPE in Diseases of the Nervous System and of the Kidneys; also in certain other General Disorders. By THOMAS CLIFFORD ALLBUTT, M.A., M.D. Cantab., Physician to the Leeds General Infirmary, Lecturer on Practical Medicine, etc. etc. 8vo. 15*s*.

The Ophthalmoscope has been found of the highest value in the investigation of nervous diseases. But it is not easy for physicians who have left the schools, and are engaged in practice, to take up a new instrument which requires much skill in using; it is therefore hoped that by such the present volume, containing the results of the author's extensive use of the instrument in diseases of the nervous system, will be found of high value; and that to all students it may prove a useful hand-book. After four introductory chapters on the history and value of the Ophthalmoscope, and the manner of investigating the states of the optic nerve and retina, the author treats of the various diseases with which optic changes are associated, and describes the way in which such associations take place. Besides the cases referred to throughout the volume, the Appendix contains details of 123 *cases illustrative of the subjects discussed in the text, and a series of tabulated cases to show the Ophthalmoscopic appearances of the eye in Insanity, Mania, Dementia, Melancholia and Monomania, Idiotcy, and General Paralysis. The volume is illustrated with two valuable coloured plates of morbid appearances of the eye under the Ophthalmoscope. "By its aid men will no longer be compelled to work for years in the dark; they will have a definite standpoint whence to proceed on their course of investigation."* —Medical Times.

THE EFFECTS OF OVERWORK AND STRAIN ON THE HEART AND GREAT BLOOD-VESSELS. (Reprinted from St. George's Hospital Reports.) 2*s*. 6*d*.

Anderson.—ON THE TREATMENT OF DISEASES OF THE SKIN; with an Analysis of Eleven Thousand Consecutive Cases. By Dr. McCall Anderson, Professor of Practice of Medicine in Anderson's University, Physician to the Dispensary for Skin Diseases, etc., Glasgow. Crown 8vo. cloth. 5*s.*

The first part of this work, which it is believed will be found of the greatest value to all medical men, as well as to all who are interested in its subject, consists of a carefully tabulated and critical analysis of 11,000 *cases of skin disease,* 1,000 *of these having occurred in the author's private practice, and the rest in his hospital practice. These cases are all classified under certain distinct heads, according to the nature and cause of the disease, while a number of the more interesting cases are alluded to in detail. The second part of the work treats of the Therapeutics of Diseases of the Skin, and will be found to contain many valuable hints, the results of a long and extensive experience, as to the most successful method of treating their multitudinous forms.*

Anstie (F. E.)—NEURALGIA, AND DISEASES WHICH RESEMBLE IT. By Francis E. Anstie, M.D., M.R.C.P., Senior Assistant Physician to Westminster Hospital. 8vo. 10*s.* 6*d.*

Dr. Anstie is well known as one of the greatest living authorities on Neuralgia. The present treatise is the result of many years' careful independent scientific investigation into the nature and proper treatment of this most painful disease. The author has had abundant means of studying the subject both in his own person and in the hundreds of patients that have resorted to him for treatment. He has gone into the whole subject indicated in the title ab initio, *and the publishers believe it will be found that he has presented it in an entirely original light, and done much to rob this excruciating and hitherto refractory disease of many of its terrors. The Introduction treats briefly of Pain in General, and contains some striking and even original ideas as to its nature and in reference to sensation generally.*

Barwell.—THE CAUSES AND TREATMENT OF LATERAL CURVATURE OF THE SPINE. Enlarged from Lectures published in the *Lancet.* By Richard Barwell, F.R.C.S., Surgeon to and Lecturer on Anatomy at the Charing Cross Hospital. Second Edition. Crown 8vo. 4*s.* 6*d.*

Having failed to find in books a satisfactory theory of those conditions which produce lateral curvature, Mr. Barwell resolved to investigate the subject for himself ab initio. *The present work is the result of long and patient study of Spines, normal and abnormal. He believes the views which he has been led to form account for those essential characteristics which have hitherto been left unexplained; and the treatment which he advocates is certainly less irksome, and will be found more efficacious than that which has hitherto been pursued. Indeed, the mode in which the first edition has been received by the profession is a gratifying sign that Mr. Barwell's principles have made their value and their weight felt. Many pages and a number of woodcuts have been added to the Second Edition.*

Corfield (Professor W. H.)—A DIGEST OF FACTS RELATING TO THE TREATMENT AND UTILIZATION OF SEWAGE. By W. H. CORFIELD, M.A., B.A., Professor of Hygiene and Public Health at University College, London. 8vo. 10*s*. 6*d*. Second Edition, corrected and enlarged.

The author in the Second Edition has revised and corrected the entire work, and made many important additions. The headings of the eleven chapters are as follow:—I. "Early Systems: Midden-Heaps and Cesspools." II. "Filth and Disease—Cause and Effect." III. "Improved Midden-Pits and Cesspools; Midden-Closets, Pail-Closets, etc." IV. "The Dry-Closet Systems. V. "Water-Closets." VI. "Sewerage." VII. "Sanitary Aspects of the Water-Carrying System." VIII. "Value of Sewage; Injury to Rivers." IX. "Town Sewage; Attempts at Utilization." X. "Filtration and Irrigation." XI. "Influence of Sewage Farming on the Public Health." An abridged account of the more recently published researches on the subject will be found in the Appendices, while the Summary contains a concise statement of the views which the author himself has been led to adopt: references have been inserted throughout to show from what sources the numerous quotations have been derived, and an Index has been added. "Mr. Corfield's work is entitled to rank as a standard authority, no less than a convenient handbook, in all matters relating to sewage."—Athenæum.

Elam (C.)—A PHYSICIAN'S PROBLEMS. By CHARLES ELAM, M.D., M.R.C.P. Crown 8vo. 9*s*.

CONTENTS :—"*Natural Heritage.*" "*On Degeneration in Man.*" "*On Moral and Criminal Epidemics.*" "*Body* v. *Mind.*" "*Illusions and Hallucinations.*" "*On Somnambulism.*" "*Reverie and Abstraction.*" *These Essays are intended as a contribution to the Natural History of those outlying regions of Thought and Action whose domain is the debateable ground of Brain, Nerve, and Mind. They are designed also to indicate the origin and mode of perpetuation of those varieties of organization, intelligence, and general tendencies towards vice or virtue, which seem to be so capriciously developed among mankind. They also point to causes for the infinitely varied forms of disorder of nerve and brain—organic and functional—far deeper and more recondite than those generally believed in.* "*The book is one which all statesmen, magistrates, clergymen, medical men, and parents should study and inwardly digest.*"—Examiner.

Fox.—Works by WILSON FOX, M.D. Lond., F.R.C.P., Holme Professor of Clinical Medicine, University College, London, Physician Extraordinary to her Majesty the Queen, etc. :—

DISEASES OF THE STOMACH: being a new and revised Edition of "THE DIAGNOSIS AND TREATMENT OF THE VARIETIES OF DYSPEPSIA." 8vo. 8*s.* 6*d.*

ON THE ARTIFICIAL PRODUCTION OF TUBERCLE IN THE LOWER ANIMALS. With Coloured Plates. 4to. 5*s.* 6*d.*

In this Lecture Dr. Fox describes in minute detail a large number of experiments made by him on guinea-pigs and rabbits for the purpose of inquiring into the origin of Tubercle by the agency of direct irritation or by septic matters. This method of inquiry he believes to be one of the most important advances which have been recently made in the pathology of the disease. The work is illustrated by three plates, each containing a number of carefully coloured illustrations from nature.

ON THE TREATMENT OF HYPERPYREXIA, as Illustrated in Acute Articular Rheumatism by means of the External Application of Cold. 8vo. 2*s.* 6*d.*

The object of this work is to show that the class of cases included under the title, and which have hitherto been invariably fatal, may, by a judicious use of the cold bath and without venesection, be brought to a favourable termination. Minute details are given of the successful treatment by this method of two patients by the author, followed by a Commentary on the cases, in which the merits of the mode of treatment are discussed and compared with those of methods followed by other eminent practitioners. Appended are tables of the observations made on the temperature during the treatment; a table showing the effect of the immersion of the patients in the baths employed, in order to exhibit the rate at which the temperature was lowered in each case; a table of the chief details of twenty-two cases of this class recently published, and which are referred to in various parts of the Commentary. Two Charts are also introduced, giving a connected view of the progress of the two successful cases, and a series of sphygmographic tracings of the pulses of the two patients. "A clinical study of rare value. Should be read by everyone."—Medical Press and Circular.

Galton (D.)—AN ADDRESS ON THE GENERAL PRINCIPLES WHICH SHOULD BE OBSERVED IN THE CONSTRUCTION OF HOSPITALS. Delivered to the British Medical Association at Leeds, July 1869. By DOUGLAS GALTON, C.B., F.R.S. Crown 8vo. 3*s*. 6*d*.

In this Address the author endeavours to enunciate what are those principles which seem to him to form the starting-point from which all architects should proceed in the construction of hospitals. Besides Mr. Galton's paper the book contains the opinions expressed in the subsequent discussion by several eminent medical men, such as Dr. Kennedy, Sir James Y. Simpson, Dr. Hughes Bennet, and others. The work is illustrated by a number of plans, sections, and other cuts. "An admirable exposition of those conditions of structure which most conduce to cleanliness, economy, and convenience."—Times.

Harley (J.)—THE OLD VEGETABLE NEUROTICS, Hemlock, Opium, Belladonna, and Henbane; their Physiological Action and Therapeutical Use, alone and in combination. Being the Gulstonian Lectures of 1868 extended, and including a Complete Examination of the Active Constituents of Opium. By JOHN HARLEY, M.D. Lond., F.R.C.P., F.L.S., etc. 8vo. 12*s*.

The author's object throughout the investigations and experiments on which this volume is founded has been to ascertain, clearly and definitely, the action of the drugs employed on the healthy body in medicinal doses, from the smallest to the largest; to deduce simple practical conclusions from the facts observed; and then to apply the drug to the relief of the particular conditions to which its action appeared suited. Many experiments have been made by the author both on men and the lower animals; and the author's endeavour has been to present to the mind, as far as words may do, impressions of the actual condition of the individual subjected to the drug. "Those who are interested generally in the progress of medical science will find much to repay a careful perusal."—Athenæum.

Hood (Wharton).—ON BONE-SETTING (so called), and its Relation to the Treatment of Joints Crippled by Injury, Rheumatism, Inflammation, etc. etc. By WHARTON P. HOOD, M.D., M.R.C.S. Crown 8vo. 4*s.* 6*d.*

The author for a period attended the London practice of the late Mr. Hutton, the famous and successful bone-setter, by whom he was initiated into the mystery of the art and practice. Thus the author is amply qualified to write on the subject from the practical point of view, while his professional education enables him to consider it in its scientific and surgical bearings. In the present work he gives a brief account of the salient features of a bone-setter's method of procedure in the treatment of damaged joints, of the results of that treatment, and of the class of cases in which he has seen it prove successful. The author's aim is to give the rationale of the bone-setter's practice, to reduce it to something like a scientific method, to show when force should be resorted to and when it should not, and to initiate surgeons into the secret of Mr. Hutton's successful manipulation. Throughout the work a great number of authentic instances of successful treatment are given, with the details of the method of cure; and the Chapters on Manipulations and Affections of the Spine are illustrated by a number of appropriate and well-executed cuts. "Dr. Hood's book is full of instruction, and should be read by all surgeons."—Medical Times.

Humphry.—Works by G. M. HUMPHRY, M.D., F.R.S., Professor of Anatomy in the University of Cambridge, and Honorary Fellow of Downing College:—

THE HUMAN SKELETON (including the Joints). With 260 Illustrations, drawn from nature. Medium 8vo. 28*s.*

Humphry (G. M.)—*continued.*

In lecturing on the Skeleton it has been the author's practice, instead of giving a detailed account of the several parts, to request his students to get up the descriptive anatomy of certain bones, with the aid of some work on osteology. He afterwards tested their acquirements by examination, endeavouring to supply deficiencies and correct errors, adding also such information—physical, physiological, pathological, and practical—as he had gathered from his own observation and researches, and which was likely to be useful and excite an interest in the subject. This additional information forms, in great part, the material of this volume, which is intended to be supplementary to existing works on anatomy. Considerable space has been devoted to the description of the joints, because it is less fully given in other works, and because an accurate knowledge of the structure and peculiar form of the joints is essential to a correct knowledge of their movements. The numerous illustrations were all drawn upon stone from nature; and in most instances, from specimens prepared for the purpose by the author himself. "Bearing at once the stamp of the accomplished scholar, and evidences of the skilful anatomist. We express our admiration of the drawings."—Medical Times and Gazette.

OBSERVATIONS IN MYOLOGY. 8vo. 6*s.*

Professor Humphry's previous works have gained for him a very high position as an original anatomist, and the present it is believed will fully sustain that reputation, as well as prove valuable to al who take an interest in the higher problems of anatomy. The work includes the Myology of Cryptobranch, Lepidosiren, Dog-Fish, Ceratodus, and Pseudopus Pallasii, with the Nerves of Cryptobranch and Lepidosiren and the Disposition of Muscles in Vertebrate Animals. The volume abounds in carefully executed illustrations.

Huxley's Physiology.—See p. 27, preceding.

Journal of Anatomy and Physiology.

Conducted by Professors HUMPHRY and NEWTON, and Mr. CLARK of Cambridge, Professor TURNER of Edinburgh, and Dr. WRIGHT of Dublin. Published twice a year. Old Series, Parts I. and II., price 7*s.* 6*d.* each. Vol. I. containing Parts I. and II., Royal 8vo., 16*s.* New Series, Parts I. to IX. 6*s.* each, or yearly Vols. 12*s.* 6*d.* each.

Lankester.—COMPARATIVE LONGEVITY IN MAN AND THE LOWER ANIMALS. By E. RAY LANKESTER, B.A. Crown 8vo. 4*s.* 6*d.*

This Essay gained the prize offered by the University of Oxford for the best Paper on the subject of which it treats. This interesting subject is here treated in a thorough manner, both scientifically and statistically.

Maclaren.—TRAINING, IN THEORY AND PRACTICE. By ARCHIBALD MACLAREN, the Gymnasium, Oxford. 8vo. Handsomely bound in cloth, 7*s.* 6*d.*

The ordinary agents of health are Exercise, Diet, Sleep, Air, Bathing, and Clothing. In this work the author examines each of these agents in detail, and from two different points of view. First, as to the manner in which it is, or should be, administered under ordinary circumstances: and secondly, in what manner and to what extent this mode of administration is, or should be, altered for purposes of training; the object of "training," according to the author, being "to put the body, with extreme and exceptional care, under the influence of all the agents which promote its health and strength, in order to enable it to meet extreme and exceptional demands upon its energies." Appended are various diagrams and tables relating to boat-racing, and tables connected with diet and training. "The philosophy of human health has seldom received so apt an exposition."—Globe. *"After all the nonsense that has been written about training, it is a comfort to get hold of a thoroughly sensible book at last."*—John Bull.

Macpherson.—Works by JOHN MACPHERSON, M.D. :—

THE BATHS AND WELLS OF EUROPE; Their Action and Uses. With Hints on Change of Air and Diet Cures. With a Map. Extra fcap. 8vo. 6*s.* 6*d.*

This work is intended to supply information which will afford aid in the selection of such Spas as are suited for particular cases. It exhibits a sketch of the present condition of our knowledge on the subject of the operation of mineral waters, gathered from the author's personal observation, and from every other available source of information. It is divided into four books, and each

Macpherson (J.)—*continued.*

book into several chapters:—Book I. Elements of Treatment, in which, among other matters, the external and internal uses of water are treated of. II. Bathing, treating of the various kinds of baths. III. Wells, treating of the various kinds of mineral waters. IV. Diet Cures, in which various vegetable, milk, and other "cures" are discussed. Appended is an Index of Diseases noticed, and one of places named. Prefixed is a sketch map of the principal baths and places of health-resort in Europe. "Dr. Macpherson has given the kind of information which every medical practitioner ought to possess."—The Lancet. "*Whoever wants to know the real character of any health-resort must read Dr. Macpherson's book.*"—Medical Times.

OUR BATHS AND WELLS: The Mineral Waters of the British Islands, with a List of Sea-bathing Places. Extra fcap. 8vo. pp. xv. 205. 3*s.* 6*d.*

Dr. Macpherson has divided his work into five parts. He begins by a few introductory observations on bath life, its circumstances, uses, and pleasures; he then explains in detail the composition of the various mineral waters, and points out the special curative properties of each class. A chapter on "The History of British Wells" from the earliest period to the present time forms the natural transition to the second part of this volume, which treats of the different kinds of mineral waters in England, whether pure, thermal and earthy, saline, chalybeate, or sulphur. Wales, Scotland, and Ireland supply the materials for distinct sections. An Index of mineral waters, one of sea-bathing places, and a third of wells of pure or nearly pure water, terminate the book. "This little volume forms a very available handbook for a large class of invalids."—Nonconformist.

Maudsley.—Works by HENRY MAUDSLEY, M.D., Professor of Medical Jurisprudence in University College, London:—

BODY AND MIND: An Inquiry into their Connection and Mutual Influence, specially in reference to Mental Disorders; being the Gulstonian Lectures for 1870. Delivered before the Royal College of Physicians. Crown 8vo. 5*s.*

The volume consists of three Lectures and two long Appendices, the general plan of the whole being to bring Man, both in his physical

Maudsley (H.)—*continued.*

and mental relations, as much as possible under the scope of scientific inquiry. The first Lecture is devoted to an exposition of the physical conditions of mental function in health. In the second Lecture are sketched the features of some forms of degeneracy of mind, as exhibited in morbid varieties of the human kind, with the purpose of bringing prominently into notice the operation of physical causes from generation to generation, and the relationship of mental to other diseases of the nervous system. In the third Lecture are displayed the relations of morbid states of the body and disordered mental function. Appendix I. is a criticism of the Archbishop of York's address on "The Limits of Philosophical Inquiry." Appendix II. deals with the "Theory of Vitality," in which the author endeavours to set forth the reflections which facts seem to warrant. "It distinctly marks a step in the progress of scientific psychology." —The Practitioner.

THE PHYSIOLOGY AND PATHOLOGY OF MIND. Second Edition, Revised. 8vo. 16*s.*

This work is the result of an endeavour on the author's part to arrive at some definite conviction with regard to the physical conditions of mental function, and the relation of the phenomena of sound and unsound mind. The author's aim throughout has been twofold: I. To treat of mental phenomena from a physiological rather than from a metaphysical point of view. II. To bring the manifold instructive instances presented by the unsound mind to bear upon the interpretation of the obscure problems of mental science. In the first part, the author pursues his independent inquiry into the science of Mind in the same direction as that followed by Bain, Spencer, Laycock, and Carpenter; and in the second, he studies the subject in a light which, in this country at least, is almost entirely novel. "Dr. Maudsley's work, which has already become standard, we most urgently recommend to the careful study of all those who are interested in the physiology and pathology of the brain."—Anthropological Review.

Practitioner (The).—A Monthly Journal of Therapeutics. Edited by FRANCIS E. ANSTIE, M.D. 8vo. Price 1*s.* 6*d* Vols. I to IX., 8vo. cloth. 10*s.* 6*d.* each.

Radcliffe.—DYNAMICS OF NERVE AND MUSCLE. By CHARLES BLAND RADCLIFFE, M.D., F.R.C.P., Physician to the Westminster Hospital, and to the National Hospital for the Paralysed and Epileptic. Crown 8vo. 8*s.* 6*d.*

This work contains the result of the author's long investigations into the Dynamics of Nerve and Muscle, as connected with Animal Electricity. The author endeavours to show from these researches that the state of action in nerve and muscle, instead of being a manifestation of vitality, must be brought under the domain of physical law in order to be intelligible, and that a different meaning, also based upon pure physics, must be attached to the state of rest. "The practitioner will find in Dr. Radcliffe a 'guide, philosopher, and friend,' from whose teaching he cannot fail to reap a plentiful harvest of new and valuable ideas."—Scotsman.

Reynolds (J. R.)—A SYSTEM OF MEDICINE. Vol. I. Edited by J. RUSSELL REYNOLDS, M.D., F.R.C.P. London. Second Edition. 8vo. 25*s.*

"*It is the best Cyclopædia of medicine of the time.*"—Medical Press.

Part I. General Diseases, or Affections of the Whole System. § I.—Those determined by agents operating from without, such as the exanthemata, malarial diseases, and their allies. § II.—Those determined by conditions existing within the body, such as Gout, Rheumatism, Rickets, etc. Part II. Local Diseases, or Affections of particular Systems. § I.—Diseases of the Skin.

A SYSTEM OF MEDICINE. Vol. II. Second Edition. 8vo. 25*s.*

Part II. Local Diseases (continued). § I.—Diseases of the Nervous System. A. General Nervous Diseases. B. Partial Diseases of the Nervous System. 1. *Diseases of the Head.* 2. *Diseases of the Spinal Column.* 3. *Diseases of the Nerves. § II.—Diseases of the Digestive System. A. Diseases of the Stomach.*

A SYSTEM OF MEDICINE. Vol. III. 8vo. 25*s.*

Part II. Local Diseases (continued). § II. Diseases of the Digestive System (continued). B. Diseases of the Mouth. C. Diseases of the Fauces, Pharynx, and Œsophagus. D. Diseases of the Intestines. E. Diseases of the Peritoneum. F. Diseases of the

Liver. G. Diseases of the Pancreas. § III.—Diseases of the Respiratory System. A. Diseases of the Larynx. B. Diseases of the Thoracic Organs. "One of the best and most comprehensive treatises on Medicine which have yet been attempted in any country." —Indian Medical Journal. *"Contains some of the best essays that have lately appeared, and is a complete library in itself."*—Medical Press.

Reynolds (O.)—SEWER GAS, AND HOW TO KEEP IT OUT OF HOUSES. A Handbook on House Drainage. By OSBORNE REYNOLDS, M.A., Professor of Engineering at Owens College, Manchester, Fellow of Queen's College, Cambridge. Second Edition. Crown 8vo. cloth. 1*s*. 6*d*.

The author's chief object in writing on this subject is to suggest a plan for preventing the evil which has been causing so much alarm since the recent illness of the Prince of Wales—viz. the back-flow of gas into our houses. Of the plan he here suggests, he has now had four years' experience, and has, without exception, found it to answer perfectly. He applied it to his own house, a house of the ordinary type drained into a foul sewer, at a cost of about fifty shillings. Before the introduction of the new plan it was never free from smells; while since, there has been no annoyance of the kind, nor have the drains required any attention whatever. The plan is very simple and can be applied to any house without requiring the inside drains to be disturbed. Besides fully explaining the plan and showing its application by means of illustrations, the author throws out suggestions with regard to drainage generally which many will find to be very valuable. "Professor Reynolds' admirable pamphlet will a thousand times over repay its cost and the reader's most attentive perusal."—Mechanics' Magazine.

Seaton.—A HANDBOOK OF VACCINATION. By EDWARD C. SEATON, M.D., Medical Inspector to the Privy Council. Extra fcap. 8vo. 8*s*. 6*d*.

The author's object in putting forth this work is twofold: First, to provide a text-book on the science and practice of Vaccination for the use of younger practitioners and of medical students; secondly, to give what assistance he could to those engaged in the administration of the system of Public Vaccination established in England.

For many years past, from the nature of his office, Dr. Seaton has had constant intercourse in reference to the subject of Vaccination, with medical men who are interested in it, and especially with that large part of the profession who are engaged as Public Vaccinators. All the varieties of pocks, both in men and the lower animals, are treated of in detail, and much valuable information given on all points connected with lymph, and minute instructions as to the niceties and cautions which so greatly influence success in Vaccination. The administrative sections of the work will be of interest and value, not only to medical practitioners, but to many others to whom a right understanding of the principles on which a system of Public Vaccination should be based is indispensable. "Henceforth the indispensable handbook of Public Vaccination, and the standard authority on this great subiect."—British Medical Journal.

Symonds (J. A., M.D.)—MISCELLANIES. By JOHN ADDINGTON SYMONDS, M.D. Selected and Edited, with an Introductory Memoir, by his Son. 8vo. 7*s.* 6*d.*

The late Dr. Symonds of Bristol was a man of a singularly versatile and elegant as well as powerful and scientific intellect. In order to make this selection from his many works generally interesting, the editor has confined himself to works of pure literature, and to such scientific studies as had a general philosophical or social interest. Among the general subjects are articles on "the Principles of Beauty," on "Knowledge," and a "Life of Dr. Prichard;" among the Scientific Studies are papers on "Sleep and Dreams," "Apparitions," "the Relations between Mind and Muscle," "Habit," etc.; there are several papers on "the Social and Political Aspects of Medicine;" and a few Poems and Translations selected from a great number of equal merit. "A collection of graceful essays on general and scientific subjects, by a very accomplished physician."—Graphic.

WORKS ON MENTAL AND MORAL PHILOSOPHY, AND ALLIED SUBJECTS.

Aristotle.—AN INTRODUCTION TO ARISTOTLE'S RHETORIC. With Analysis, Notes, and Appendices. By E. M. COPE, Trinity College, Cambridge. 8vo. 14*s.*

This work is introductory to an edition of the Greek Text of Aristotle's Rhetoric, which is in course of preparation. Its object is to render that treatise thoroughly intelligible. The author has aimed to illustrate, as preparatory to the detailed explanation of the work, the general bearings and relations of the Art of Rhetoric in itself, as well as the special mode of treating it adopted by Aristotle in his peculiar system. The evidence upon obscure or doubtful questions connected with the subject is examined; and the relations which Rhetoric bears, in Aristotle's view, to the kindred art of Logic are fully considered. A connected Analysis of the work is given, and a few important matters are separately discussed in Appendices. There is added, as a general Appendix, by way of specimen of the antagonistic system of Isocrates and others, a complete analysis of the treatise called Ῥητορικὴ πρὸς Ἀλέξανδρον, *with a discussion of its authorship and of the probable results of its teaching.*

ARISTOTLE ON FALLACIES; OR, THE SOPHISTICI ELENCHI. With a Translation and Notes by EDWARD POSTE, M.A., Fellow of Oriel College, Oxford. 8vo. 8*s.* 6*d.*

Besides the doctrine of Fallacies, Aristotle offers, either in this treatise or in other passages quoted in the Commentary, various glances over the world of science and opinion, various suggestions or problems which are still agitated, and a vivid picture of the ancient system of dialectics, which it is hoped may be found both interesting and instructive. "*It will be an assistance to genuine students of Aristotle.*"—Guardian. "*It is indeed a work of great skill.*"—Saturday Review.

Boole. — AN INVESTIGATION OF THE LAWS OF THOUGHT, ON WHICH ARE FOUNDED THE MATHEMATICAL THEORIES OF LOGIC AND PROBABILITIES. By GEORGE BOOLE, LL.D. Professor of Mathematics in the Queen's University, Ireland, &c. 8vo. 14*s.*

The design of this treatise is to investigate the fundamental laws of those operations of the mind by which reasoning is performed; to give expression to them in the symbolical language of a Calculus, and upon this foundation to establish the science of Logic and construct its method; to make that method itself the basis of a general method for the application of the mathematical doctrine of Probabilities; and, finally, to collect from the various elements of truth brought to view in the course of these inquiries some probable intimations concerning the nature and construction of the human mind. The problem is one of the highest interest, and no one is better able than Professor Boole to treat of this side of it at any rate.

Butler (W. A.), Late Professor of Moral Philosophy in the University of Dublin :—

LECTURES ON THE HISTORY OF ANCIENT PHILOSOPHY. Edited from the Author's MSS., with Notes, by WILLIAM HEPWORTH THOMPSON, M.A., Master of Trinity College, and Regius Professor of Greek in the University of Cambridge. Two Volumes. 8vo. 1*l.* 5*s.*

These Lectures consist of an Introductory Series on the Science of Mind generally, and five other Series on Ancient Philosophy, the greater part of which treat of Plato and the Platonists, the Fifth Series being an unfinished course on the Psychology of Aristotle, containing an able Analysis of the well known though by no means well understood Treatise, περὶ ψυχῆς. *These Lectures are the result of patient and conscientious examination of the original documents, and may be considered as a perfectly independent contribution to our knowledge of the great master of Grecian wisdom. The author's intimate familiarity with the metaphysical writings of the last century, and especially with the English and Scotch School of*

Butler (W. A.)—*continued.*

Psychologists, has enabled him to illustrate the subtle speculations of which he treats in a manner calculated to render them more intelligible to the English mind than they can be by writers trained solely in the technicalities of modern German schools. The editor has verified all the references, and added valuable Notes, in which he points out sources of more complete information. The Lectures constitute a History of the Platonic Philosophy—its seed-time, maturity, and decay.

SERMONS AND LETTERS ON ROMANISM.—See THEOLOGICAL CATALOGUE.

Calderwood.—Works by the Rev. HENRY CALDERWOOD, M.A., LL.D., Professor of Moral Philosophy in the University of Edinburgh :—

PHILOSOPHY OF THE INFINITE: A Treatise on Man's Knowledge of the Infinite Being, in answer to Sir W. Hamilton and Dr. Mansel. Cheaper Edition. 8vo. 7*s.* 6*d.*

The purpose of this volume is, by a careful analysis of consciousness, to prove, in opposition to Sir W. Hamilton and Mr. Mansel, that man possesses a notion of an Infinite Being, and to ascertain the peculiar nature of the conception and the particular relations in which it is found to arise. The province of Faith as related to that of Knowledge, and the characteristics of Knowledge and Thought as bearing on this subject, are examined; and separate chapters are devoted to the consideration of our knowledge of the Infinite as First Cause, as Moral Governor, and as the Object of Worship. "A book of great ability . . . . written in a clear style, and may be easily understood by even those who are not versed in such discussions."—British Quarterly Review.

A HANDBOOK OF MORAL PHILOSOPHY. Crown 8vo. 6*s.*

It is, we feel convinced, the best handbook on the subject, intellectually and morally, and does infinite credit to its author.—Standard.

Elam.—A PHYSICIAN'S PROBLEMS.—See MEDICAL CATALOGUE, preceding.

Galton (Francis).—HEREDITARY GENIUS: An Inquiry into its Laws and Consequences. See PHYSICAL SCIENCE CATALOGUE, preceding.

Green (J. H.)—SPIRITUAL PHILOSOPHY: Founded on the Teaching of the late SAMUEL TAYLOR COLERIDGE. By the late JOSEPH HENRY GREEN, F.R.S., D.C.L. Edited, with a Memoir of the Author's Life, by JOHN SIMON, F.R.S., Medical Officer of Her Majesty's Privy Council, and Surgeon to St. Thomas's Hospital. Two Vols. 8vo. 25*s.*

The late Mr. Green, the eminent surgeon, was for many years the intimate friend and disciple of Coleridge, and an ardent student of philosophy. The language of Coleridge's will imposed on Mr. Green the obligation of devoting, so far as necessary, the remainder of his life to the one task of systematising, developing, and establishing the doctrines of the Coleridgian philosophy. With the assistance of Coleridge's manuscripts, but especially from the knowledge he possessed of Coleridge's doctrines, and independent study of at least the basal principles and metaphysics of the sciences and of all the phenomena of human life, he proceeded logically to work out a system of universal philosophy such as he deemed would in the main accord with his master's aspirations. After many years of preparatory labour he resolved to complete in a compendious form a work which should give in system the doctrines most distinctly Coleridgian. The result is these two volumes. The first volume is devoted to the general principles of philosophy; the second aims at vindicating à priori *(on principles for which the first volume has contended) the essential doctrines of Christianity. The work is divided into four parts: I. "On the Intellectual Faculties and processes which are concerned in the Investigation of Truth." II. "Of First Principles in Philosophy." III. "Truths of Religion." IV. "The Idea of Christianity in relation to Controversial Philosophy."*

Huxley (Professor.)—LAY SERMONS, ADDRESSES, AND REVIEWS. See PHYSICAL SCIENCE CATALOGUE, preceding.

Jevons.—Works by W. STANLEY JEVONS, M.A., Professor of Logic in Owens College, Manchester:—

THE SUBSTITUTION OF SIMILARS, the True Principle of Reasoning. Derived from a Modification of Aristotle's Dictum Fcap. 8vo. 2*s.* 6*d.*

Jevons—*continued.*

"*All acts of reasoning,*" *the author says,* "*seem to me to be different cases of one uniform process, which may perhaps be best described as the* substitution of similars. *This phrase clearly expresses that familiar mode in which we continually argue by analogy* from like to like, *and take one thing as a representative of another. The chief difficulty consists in showing that all the forms of the old logic, as well as the fundamental rules of mathematical reasoning, may be explained upon the same principle; and it is to this difficult task I have devoted the most attention. Should my notion be true, a vast mass of technicalities may be swept from our logical text-books and yet the small remaining part of logical doctrine will prove far more useful than all the learning of the Schoolmen.*" *Prefixed is a plan of a new reasoning machine, the* Logical Abacus, *the construction and working of which is fully explained in the text and Appendix.* "*Mr. Jevons' book is very clear and intelligible, and quite worth consulting.*"—Guardian.

Maccoll.—THE GREEK SCEPTICS, from Pyrrho to Sextus. An Essay which obtained the Hare Prize in the year 1868. By NORMAN MACCOLL, B.A., Scholar of Downing College, Cambridge. Crown 8vo, 3*s.* 6*d.*

This Essay consists of five parts: I. "*Introduction.*" *II.* "*Pyrrho and Timon.*" *III.* "*The New Academy.*" *IV.* "*The Later Sceptics.*" *V.* "*The Pyrrhoneans and New Academy contrasted.*"—"*Mr. Maccoll has produced a monograph which merits the gratitude of all students of philosophy. His style is clear and vigorous; he has mastered the authorities, and criticises them in a modest but independent spirit.*"—Pall Mall Gazette.

M'Cosh.—Works by JAMES M'COSH, LL.D., President of Princeton College, New Jersey, U.S.

"*He certainly shows himself skilful in that application of logic to psychology, in that inductive science of the human mind which is the fine side of English philosophy. His philosophy as a whole is worthy of attention.*"—Revue de Deux Mondes.

THE METHOD OF THE DIVINE GOVERNMENT, Physical and Moral. Tenth Edition. 8vo. 10*s.* 6*d.*

M'Cosh (J.)—*continued.*

This work is divided into four books. The first presents a general view of the Divine Government as fitted to throw light on the character of God; the second deals with the method of the Divine Government in the physical world; the third treats of the principles of the human mind through which God governs mankind; and the fourth is on Pastoral and Revealed Religion, and the Restoration of Man. An Appendix, consisting of seven articles, investigates the fundamental principles which underlie the speculations of the treatise. "This work is distinguished from other similar ones by its being based upon a thorough study of physical science, and an accurate knowledge of its present condition, and by its entering in a deeper and more unfettered manner than its predecessors upon the discussion of the appropriate psychological, ethical, and theological questions. The author keeps aloof at once from the à priori *idealism and dreaminess of German speculation since Schelling, and from the onesidedness and narrowness of the empiricism and positivism which have so prevailed in England.*"—Dr. Ulrici, in "Zeitschrift für Philosophie."

THE INTUITIONS OF THE MIND. A New Edition. 8vo. cloth. 10*s.* 6*d.*

The object of this treatise is to determine the true nature of Intuition, and to investigate its laws. It starts with a general view of intuitive convictions, their character and the method in which they are employed, and passes on to a more detailed examination of them, treating them under the various heads of "Primitive Cognitions," "Primitive Beliefs," "Primitive Judgments," and "Moral Convictions." Their relations to the various sciences, mental and physical, are then examined. Collateral criticisms are thrown into preliminary and supplementary chapters and sections. "The undertaking to adjust the claims of the sensational and intuitional philosophies, and of the à posteriori *and* à priori *methods, is accomplished in this work with a great amount of success.*"—Westminster Review. "*I value it for its large acquaintance with English Philosophy, which has not led him to neglect the great German works. I admire the moderation and clearness, as well as comprehensiveness, of the author's views.*"—Dr. Dörner, of Berlin.

AN EXAMINATION OF MR. J. S. MILL'S PHILOSOPHY: Being a Defence of Fundamental Truth. Crown 8vo. 7*s.* 6*d.*

M'Cosh (J.)—*continued.*

This volume is not put forth by its author as a special reply to Mr. Mill's "Examination of Sir William Hamilton's Philosophy." In that work Mr. Mill has furnished the means of thoroughly estimating his theory of mind, of which he had only given hints and glimpses in his logical treatise. It is this theory which Dr. M'Cosh professes to examine in this volume; his aim is simply to defend a portion of primary truth which has been assailed by an acute thinker who has extensive influence in England. "In such points as Mr. Mill's notions of intuitions and necessity, he will have the voice of mankind with him."—Athenæum. *"Such a work greatly needed to be done, and the author was the man to do it. This volume is important, not merely in reference to the views of Mr. Mill, but of the whole school of writers, past and present, British and Continental, he so ably represents."*—Princeton Review.

THE LAWS OF DISCURSIVE THOUGHT: Being a Text-book of Formal Logic. Crown 8vo. 5*s.*

The main feature of this Logical Treatise is to be found in the more thorough investigation of the nature of the notion, in regard to which the views of the school of Locke and Whately are regarded by the author as very defective, and the views of the school of Kant and Hamilton altogether erroneous. The author believes that errors spring far more frequently from obscure, inadequate, indistinct, and confused Notions, and from not placing the Notions in their proper relation in judgment, than from Ratiocination. In this treatise, therefore, the Notion (with the term, and the Relation of Thought to Language) will be found to occupy a larger relative place than in any logical work written since the time of the famous Art of Thinking. *"The amount of summarized information which it contains is very great; and it is the only work on the very important subject with which it deals. Never was such a work so much needed as in the present day."*—London Quarterly Review.

CHRISTIANITY AND POSITIVISM: A Series of Lectures to the Times on Natural Theology and Apologetics. Crown 8vo. 7*s.* 6*d.*

These Lectures were delivered in New York, by appointment, in the beginning of 1871, *as the second course on the foundation of the Union Theological Seminary. There are ten Lectures in all, divided into three series:—I. "Christianity and Physical Science" (three lectures). II. "Christianity and Mental Science" (four lectures). III. "Christianity and Historical Investigation" (three lectures). The Appendix contains articles on "Gaps in the Theory of Development;" "Darwin's Descent of Man." "Principles of Herbert Spencer's Philosophy." In the course of the Lectures Dr. M'Cosh discusses all the most important scientific problems which are supposed to affect Christianity.*

Masson.—RECENT BRITISH PHILOSOPHY: A Review, with Criticisms; including some Comments on Mr. Mill's Answer to Sir William Hamilton. By DAVID MASSON, M.A., Professor of Rhetoric and English Literature in the University of Edinburgh. Crown 8vo. 6*s.*

The author, in his usual graphic and forcible manner, reviews in considerable detail, and points out the drifts of the philosophical speculations of the previous thirty years, bringing under notice the work of all the principal philosophers who have been at work during that period on the highest problems which concern humanity. The four chapters are thus titled:—I. "A Survey of Thirty Years." II. "The Traditional Differences: how repeated in Carlyle, Hamilton, and Mill." III. "Effects of Recent Scientific Conceptions on Philosophy." IV. "Latest Drifts and Groupings." The last seventy-six pages are devoted to a Review of Mr. Mill's criticism of Sir William Hamilton's Philosophy. "We can nowhere point to a work which gives so clear an exposition of the course of philosophical speculation in Britain during the past century, or which indicates so instructively the mutual influences of philosophic and scientific thought."—Fortnightly Review.

BRITISH NOVELISTS.—See BELLES LETTRES CATALOGUE.

LIFE OF MILTON.—See BIOGRAPHICAL CATALOGUE.

Maudsley.—Works by HENRY MAUDSLEY, M.D., Professor of Medical Jurisprudence in University College, London:—

BODY AND MIND: An Inquiry into their Connection and Mutual Influence, specially in reference to Mental Diseases. See MEDICAL CATALOGUE, preceding.

Maudsley (H.)—*continued.*

THE PHYSIOLOGY AND PATHOLOGY OF MIND. See MEDICAL CATALOGUE, preceding.

Maurice.—Works by the Rev. FREDERICK DENISON MAURICE, M.A., Professor of Moral Philosophy in the University of Cambridge. (For other Works by the same Author, see THEOLOGICAL CATALOGUE.)

SOCIAL MORALITY. Twenty-one Lectures delivered in the University of Cambridge. New and Cheaper Edition. Cr. 8vo. 10*s.* 6*d.*

In this series of Lectures, Professor Maurice considers, historically and critically, Social Morality in its three main aspects: I. "The Relations which spring from the Family—Domestic Morality." II. "The Relations which subsist among the various constituents of a Nation—National Morality." III. "As it concerns Universal Humanity—Universal Morality." Appended to each series is a chapter on "Worship:" first, "Family Worship;" second, "National Worship;" third, "Universal Worship." "Whilst reading it we are charmed by the freedom from exclusiveness and prejudice, the large charity, the loftiness of thought, the eagerness to recognize and appreciate whatever there is of real worth extant in the world, which animates it from one end to the other. We gain new thoughts and new ways of viewing things, even more, perhaps, from being brought for a time under the influence of so noble and spiritual a mind."—Athenæum.

THE CONSCIENCE: Lectures on Casuistry, delivered in the University of Cambridge. New and Cheaper Edition. Crown 8vo. 5*s.*

In this series of nine Lectures, Professor Maurice, with his wonted force and breadth and freshness, endeavours to settle what is meant by the word "Conscience," and discusses the most important questions immediately connected with the subject. Taking "Casuistry" in its old sense as being the "study of cases of Conscience," he endeavours to show in what way it may be brought to bear at the present day upon the acts and thoughts of our ordinary existence. He shows that Conscience asks for laws, not rules;

Maurice (F. D.)—*continued.*

for freedom, not chains; for education, not suppression. He has abstained from the use of philosophical terms, and has touched on philosophical systems only when he fancied "they were interfering with the rights and duties of wayfarers." The Saturday Review *says: "We rise from them with detestation of all that is selfish and mean, and with a living impression that there is such a thing as goodness after all."*

MORAL AND METAPHYSICAL PHILOSOPHY. New Edition and Preface. Vol. I. Ancient Philosophy and the First to the Thirteenth Centuries; Vol. II. the Fourteenth Century and the French Revolution, with a glimpse into the Nineteenth Century. 2 Vols. 8vo. 25*s.*

This is an Edition in two volumes of Professor Maurice's History of Philosophy from the earliest period to the present time. It was formerly scattered throughout a number of separate volumes, and it is believed that all admirers of the author and all students of philosophy will welcome this compact Edition. The subject is one of the highest importance, and it is treated here with fulness and candour, and in a clear and interesting manner. In a long introduction to this Edition, in the form of a dialogue, Professor Maurice justifies some of his own peculiar views, and touches upon some of the most important topics of the time.

Murphy.—HABIT AND INTELLIGENCE, in Connection with the Laws of Matter and Force: A Series of Scientific Essays. By JOSEPH JOHN MURPHY. Two Vols. 8vo. 16*s.*

The author's chief purpose in this work has been to state and to discuss what he regards as the special and characteristic principles of life. The most important part of the work treats of those vital principles which belong to the inner domain of life itself, as distinguished from the principles which belong to the border-land where life comes into contact with inorganic matter and force. In the inner domain of life we find two principles, which are, the author believes, coextensive with life and peculiar to it: these are Habit and Intelligence. He has made as full a statement as possible of the laws under which habits form, disappear, alter under altered circumstances, and vary spontaneously. He discusses that most important of all questions, whether intelligence is an ultimate fact, incapable of being resolved into any other, or only a resultant from the laws of habit. The latter part of the first volume is occupied with the discussion of the question of the Origin of Species. The first part of the second volume is occupied with an inquiry into the process of mental growth and development, and the nature of mental intelligence. In the chapter that follows, the author discusses the science of history, and the three concluding chapters contain some ideas on the classification, the history, and the logic, of the sciences. The author's aim has been to make the subjects treated of intelligible to any ordinary intelligent man. "We are pleased to listen," says the Saturday Review, *"to a writer who has so firm a foothold upon the ground within the scope of his immediate survey, and who can enunciate with so much clearness and force propositions which come within his grasp."*

Thring (E., M.A.)—THOUGHTS ON LIFE-SCIENCE. By EDWARD THRING, M.A. (Benjamin Place), Head Master of Uppingham School. New Edition, enlarged and revised. Crown 8vo. 7*s.* 6*d.*

In this volume are discussed in a familiar manner some of the most interesting problems between Science and Religion, Reason and Feeling. "Learning and Science," says the author, "are claiming the right of building up and pulling down everything, especially the latter. It has seemed to me no useless task to look steadily at what has happened, to take stock as it were of men's gains, and to endeavour amidst new circumstances to arrive at some rational estimate of the bearings of things, so that the limits of what is possible at all events may be clearly marked out for ordinary readers. . . . . This book is an endeavour to bring out some of the main facts of the world."

Venn.—THE LOGIC OF CHANCE: An Essay on the Foundations and Province of the Theory of Probability, with especial reference to its application to Moral and Social Science. By JOHN VENN, M.A., Fellow of Gonville and Caius College, Cambridge. Fcap. 8vo. 7*s.* 6*d.*

This Essay is in no sense mathematical. Probability, the author thinks, may be considered to be a portion of the province of Logic regarded from the material point of view. The principal objects of this Essay are to ascertain how great a portion it comprises, where we are to draw the boundary between it and the contiguous branches of the general science of evidence, what are the ultimate foundations upon which its rules rest, what the nature of the evidence they are capable of affording, and to what class of subjects they may most fitly be applied. The general design of the Essay, as a special treatise on Probability, is quite original, the author believing that erroneous notions as to the real nature of the subject are disastrously prevalent. "Exceedingly well thought and well written," says the Westminster Review. *The* Nonconformist *calls it a "masterly book."*

LONDON: R. CLAY, SONS, AND TAYLOR, PRINTERS, BREAD STREET HILL